THE COMPLETE GUIDE
TO THE
Soviet Union

CONTENTS

LIST OF ILLUSTRATIONS

All the pictures are by permission of Novosti Press Agency unless otherwise stated

AUTHOR'S NOTE

Our publishers deserve our most grateful thanks for their advice and enthusiastic encouragement as we worked together with a great distance between us. The very varied quality of the map material caused our cartographer considerable headaches, none of which he found insurmountable. Our editor Caroline Dawnay cheered us particularly by making a special trip to Leningrad, inspired, she told us, by her interest in the country brought about through her enjoyment of working on the book.

EDITOR'S NOTE

Republics are to be found in the alphabetical guide (Part II) under the names of their capital towns. They are listed in the index in capital letters. Towns for which maps have been provided are marked *map* in the index, and M on the endpaper, where it is also possible to see which towns are capitals of republics, and which republic other listed towns come under.

All the information in the Guide is as up to date as possible. Readers will appreciate, however, that the Soviet Union consists of a very large area, and it has not always been easy to double check details. Some map originals seemed to be inadequate but alternatives were hard to come by. The publishers would be grateful for notice of any corrections for subsequent editions of the Guide.

INTRODUCTION

This is our second guidebook. Our first was *A Motorist's Guide to the Soviet Union*. We have greatly expanded the scope of this second volume and completely revised it, bringing it right up to date.

The purpose of this Guide to the Soviet Union is to cover all those parts of the country which are open to foreigners. There are already a number of books written by those who have some experience of travelling in the country and have used their knowledge in general and usually subjective descriptions of the Soviet Union. At the other end of the scale are the guidebooks put out by each town and city and by each museum and picture gallery. We have tried to find the golden mean between these two, keeping our personal feelings from intruding but attempting to provide practical advice and interesting information on the widely differing areas within the competence of this book.

Omitted are the detailed descriptions which will be given by the local guides concerning factory production, farm statistics or information about places of specific interest such as research institutes, universities, etc.

The towns and cities are listed alphabetically, with out-of-town places of interest within easy driving distance entered under the name of the relevant city. The description of each town falls roughly into three sections: (a) *facts*—general description, history, geographical location, population, etc.; (b) *places of interest*—churches, museums, theatres, parks, etc.; and (c) *information*—hotels, restaurants, shops, etc. Several motor trips are described with all the places of interest included as they occur along the route. They include the Caucasian Coastal Road, the Crimean Circular Route and the Georgian Military Highway.

We would strongly recommend that you keep a firm hold on this book while you are touring the Soviet Union; very often it will prove to be the only source of information at all. The guidebooks which appear in different cities from time to time are in very limited editions and soon disappear from the bookstalls. In Leningrad and Moscow, on the other hand, there will be additional material printed in foreign languages, particularly French, English and German, concerning the museums.

HOW TO GET THERE

The Soviet Union can be reached by all the usual means of transport and there are also many opportunities for including a part of the Soviet Union in your itinerary if your route lies in Europe, Asia or the Far East. Your travel agent will be glad to help you.

Many of the larger international airlines fly directly to Moscow but there are other ports of entry including Leningrad and Kiev which are connected with direct routes to Europe. Erevan is linked with Beirut and Tashkent with Kabul, Afghanistan. You can also go by train to Persia or Turkey or by sea from the Soviet Far East to Hong Kong as well as from Leningrad to London. Other routes are from the ports of France, Italy, Greece and Turkey to Odessa, and from Vienna along the Danube to the river port of Izmail.

The Soviet Union is at the cross roads of international travelling. It seems a shame that many of those travelling to Australia or to Tokyo and back do not even consider the idea of breaking their journey in Tashkent so that they can visit Samarkand and Bukhara; just a day in each of these two cities would provide a wealth of memories. Even if these travellers are really pressed for time, surely they should spare a day for Moscow or for Leningrad. Those who stop in Copenhagen need only travel to the other end of the Baltic Sea to visit Leningrad.

Tourism in Russia has yet to reach industrial level. Soviet citizens are themselves only just discovering how exciting it is to travel; as millions of them make their first journeys about their own country, the local authorities try to do their best to cope with the increasing demands upon their facilities and services.

Each year new places are added to the list of those ready to receive foreign guests. Those which are still closed are not necessarily security risks; they simply lack proper accommodation. Tourists from abroad are still regarded as V.I.P.s here; they would never have to sleep on a park bench or in a railway station waiting room. But failure to book (booking is essential) may be the reason for some delay in the issuing of a visa. For the same reason it is often difficult to alter one's plans; it means taking someone else's accommodation.

A journey in Russia can include the hiring of a car, for Hertz are now operating with Intourist. The same principles of hire-it-here, leave-it-there are observed, insurance coverage can be obtained and credit cards are now honoured as they are elsewhere.

The foreigner is looked upon with lively curiosity, especially in the provinces. People are eager to meet him and talk just for friendship's sake—not because they might make a rouble or two out of his acquaintance. Those who offer to show one round and give their advice would be utterly surprised if their motives were to be thought mercenary. The museum guide will even be insulted if one tries to slip him a few coins; his outstretched hand at the end of the tour is only to say goodbye.

Tourists are welcome guests everywhere in the country. They are ushered to the front of the queue, given the best seats in the theatre, and served the choicest portion of meat in the restaurant. Intourist has learned, from observing its Western counterparts, to charge for every service it offers, but this does not affect the attitude of the people who look after you during your stay. The hotel staff, the waitresses, the shop assistants, the taxi-drivers—if these people smile kindly and try to help, it is not because they will receive an extra bonus; you are their guest—if, on the other hand, they are cross and rude no tip will change them. Those who go out of their way to be pleasant during their working hours will treat you just as warmly wherever you meet.

Everyone is familiar with complaints about the service and other difficulties awaiting the visitor to the Soviet Union. Often they are justifiable but again the inadequacies are not exclusive to this country. We have both travelled extensively round the world and so have a basis upon which to comment.

Certainly you will find here a great number of historical monuments under restoration, and probably just as many still in a state of dilapidation. The picture is one of both love and negligence towards the past, but the final impression will almost certainly be good.

If there are any disappointments in store for the foreign visitor to this country, certainly there will be much to see and hear and enjoy that is new. A holiday in the U.S.S.R. can be guaranteed to provide many unforgettable memories and we hope you will take the opportunity of travelling through it with us again and again.

MOSCOW   VICTOR AND JENNIFER LOUIS

PART I

General Information

HISTORY OF RUSSIA AND THE SOVIET UNION

The Soviet Union consists of 15 republics. The whole country is often referred to as Russia, but this is really the name of the largest of the republics, the Russian Federation. The Soviet Union is in most part based on the former territories of the Russian Empire, and the history of the country as a whole is mainly the history of Russia. The other 14 republics are: the Ukraine, Belorussia, Latvia, Lithuania, Estonia, Moldavia, Georgia, Armenia, Azerbaijan, Kazakhstan, Uzbekistan, Tajikistan, Turkmenistan and Kirghizia. The country, which is the largest in the world, occupies one-sixth of the world's land mass, 22,402,200 sq. km. The population numbers 251,000,000 (1975), the third largest population in the world, following China and India. Moscow Time (2 hours ahead of Central European Time) is adhered to by the western part of the Soviet Union.

800–882: The formation of the first Russian state dates from this time. In the south a Slav tribe known as the Polyane founded the Kiyevan state with its centre called Kiev after Prince Kii of the Polyane. In the north was the Novgorod State: when in 862 Norsemen, led by the Varangians Rurik, Sineus and Truvor, were invited by the Novgorod Republic to come and restore order, one of them, Rurik, became the first of the Rurikids to rule in Russia. Their reign lasted until the 17th century.

882: Oleg, Rurik's successor, conquered Kiev and this united both the states.

988: Prince Vladimir of Kiev introduced Christianity into Russia.

1169: Kiev began to decline in importance. Prince Andrei of Vladimir attacked and conquered Kiev, and proclaimed Vladimir (800 km. north-east of Kiev) the new capital.

1223: Russia's first encounter with the advance army of Genghis Khan took place in this year, and this was, in fact, the beginning of the Tatar invasions.

1237–42: The Tatars under Baty Khan conquered Russia and established in the Volga steppes the rule of the 'Golden Horde' to which all Russia became vassal and paid tribute.

1380: Dmitri Donskoi (Demetrius of the Don), the Grand-Prince of Muscovy, won a considerable battle against the Tatars. The Grand-Princedom of Muscovy had by this time obtained power over most of the older principalities by acting as tax-collector for the Tatars. Although Dmitri Donskoi's battle was not decisive, the Tatar grip on the country was greatly loosened.

1462–1505: Ivan III of Muscovy laid the foundations of the future Russian Empire when, between 1465 and 1488, he annexed the rich and strong city of Novgorod with its vast territories, defied the Tatars by refusing to pay them further taxes, and routed the Golden Horde's armies sent against him. This ended the 250-year-long Tatar oppression.

1533–84: Ivan IV (known as 'the Terrible'). In 1547 Ivan assumed the title of Tsar (the word is derived from 'Caesar') of All the Russias. To Ivan IV goes the credit of building a powerful and united Russian state; during his reign the last of the other independent principalities disappeared from the map of Russia. Ivan IV received his nickname for his severe persecution of the boyars (barons) who possessed great influence in government. Ivan the Terrible organised a special bodyguard known as the 'oprichina' which arrested prominent boyars, tried them, and usually executed them for 'treason'. In 1552 and 1557 respectively the Tatar kingdoms of

Kazan and Astrakhan were conquered. In 1582 Russia's conquest of Siberia began.

1598: Feodor I, Ivan IV's son, died; he was succeeded by his brother-in-law, Boris Godunov, and in 1610 the Interregnum began, caused by the appearance of two false Dmitris, each claiming in turn to be Dmitri, Ivan the Terrible's youngest son who had died in 1591. Both impostors were supported by the Poles. Organised government collapsed and a disastrous civil war ensued.

1612: Kosma Minin, a Russian meat merchant, with Prince Pozharsky gathered an army of volunteers and finally drove the Poles from the country. Mikhail Romanov was elected tsar, thus founding the Romanov dynasty.

1645–76: Alexei I.

1676–82: Feodor II.

1689–1725: Peter I (the Great). Peter I was one of the most outstanding statesmen and warriors in Russian history; he may rightly be called the 'enlightener of Russia', for he introduced Western customs, culture, and technical achievements into his backward country. He also extended Russian dominion to the southern shore of the Caspian sea, won access to the Baltic, reorganised the national economy, founded a new army and Russia's first large fleet. He founded St. Petersburg (now Leningrad) in 1703, and defeated the Swedish army at the Battle of Poltava in 1709. In 1721 he assumed the imperial title.

1725–7: Catherine I, widow of Peter I.

1727–30: Peter II, grandson of Peter I.

1730–40: Anna Ivanovna, daughter of Ivan, half-brother to Peter I.

1740–1: Ivan VI, great-grandson of Ivan, the half-brother of Peter I.

1741–61: Yelizaveta Petrovna, daughter of Peter I.

1761–2: Peter III, nephew of Yelizaveta and grandson of Peter I.

1762–96: Catherine II (the Great), widow of Peter III. Catherine's reign is notable for the extension of Russian territory after the three partitions of Poland, for victorious wars with Turkey, and for the cession of the Crimea and Danubian principalities. During this period Russia became a great power.

1796–1801: Paul I, son of Catherine II. Paul was unpopular with the nobility and was eventually assassinated in his palace.

1801–25: Alexander I, son of Paul I. In 1812 Napoleon invaded Russia and was defeated.

1825–55: Nicholas I, third son of Paul I. During the short interregnum caused by Alexander I's sudden death, a group of aristocratic officers made the first military attempt to overthrow the autocracy of the tsars, and to change the system of serfdom. This rebellion took place on 14 December 1825, and the rebels were accordingly known as the Decembrists. The uprising was promptly suppressed, and its leaders were hanged or sent to Siberia; but the very fact of its occurrence served as a powerful impetus for the further development of liberal thought in Russia, although its immediate effect was to produce a period of intense persecution and affirmation of the autocratic powers of Tsar Nicholas. In 1853–6 the Crimean War with England, France, and Turkey ended with Russia's defeat.

1855–81: Alexander II, son of Nicholas I. In 1861 the tsar issued a decree for the emancipation of the serfs, making possible industrial expansion. The Caucasus was conquered and in 1877–8 the war with Turkey was won, resulting in the liberation of Bulgaria.

1881–94: Alexander III, son of Alexander II.

1895–1916: Nicholas II was the last Russian tsar. The Russo-Japanese war (1904–5) ended with a Russian defeat. In 1905 the first revolution took place with the armed insurrection of the workers and the establishment of a more democratic form of constitutional monarchy. In 1914 Russia entered World War I. In February 1917 there was the bourgeois-democratic revolution, after which the provisional government was formed; and on 7 November (25 October, by the old calendar) occurred the October Socialist Revolution of workers, peasants and soldiers led by Lenin's Communist Party (the Bolsheviks) after which the Soviet State was established.

1918: The Soviet government moved from Petrograd (Leningrad) to Moscow, which once again became the capital of Russia. The country was in a critical situation and the young Republic had to contend with the opposition of the White Russians (counter-revolutionaries) and with foreign intervention.

1918–22: Civil War.

1924: Lenin died and Soviet leadership passed to Stalin.

1941–5: World War II. Russia and her allies defeated the Axis powers.

1953: Stalin died and collective leadership was instituted.

THE SOVIET GOVERNMENT

The Supreme Soviet has two chambers of equal power: the Council (soviet) of the Union and the Council of Nationalities (re-elected every four years). It is the legislative body and elects the Praesidium, consisting of a president, 15 vice-presidents (one from each Union republic), a secretary, and 16 members. The Praesidium is the highest organ of government between sessions of the Supreme Soviet. Nikolai Podgorny is the president of the Praesidium (since 1964).

The Council of Ministers coordinates the work of the Ministries. Its present chairman is Alexei Kosygin (since 1964).

THE SOVIET COMMUNIST PARTY

This is the only political party. According to the party charter, every four years its 15,000,000 members (1975) should elect a Central Committee of 175 members, and the Central Committee elects a Politburo of 15 members, with 5 candidate-members. The present General Secretary is Leonid Brezhnev (since 1964).

The Komsomol (abbreviation for the 'Young Communist League') is a youth organisation for people between the ages of 14 and 28.

PUBLIC HOLIDAYS

1 January:	New Year's Day
1–2 May:	International Labour Day, celebrated by parades and demonstrations.
9 May:	Victory Day

| 7–8 November: | October Revolution Day, so called because the revolution took place on 25 October 1917 according to the old calendar, which differs from the Gregorian calendar by 13 days. This holiday, regarded as the National Day, is also celebrated by parades and demonstrations. |
| 5 December: | Constitution Day, commemorating the adoption of the Constitution in 1936. |

The Soviet Union also marks 23 February as Soviet Army and Navy Day, 8 March as International Women's Day (commemorating the 2nd International Conference of Socialist Women which took place in Copenhagen in 1910), Lenin's birthday on 22 April, and other days for the Air Force, Tank Corps, Railwaymen, etc.

THE RUSSIAN ORTHODOX CHURCH

The Eastern Orthodox Church is the second largest body of organised Christians in the world. It consists of a number of independent and self-governing Churches, among them the Churches of Russia and Georgia and the autonomous Churches of Estonia and Latvia which are also independent except that the appointment of their chief bishops requires the sanction of their Mother Church, the Church of Russia.

When in the 11th century Russia adopted Orthodoxy, the religion had already a thousand years' experience behind it, and so the books, the doctrine, the music and paintings, the monastic system, and even the architectural style were taken over as they stood in working order. They were regarded as an integrated whole, already as perfect as may be, as the name 'Orthodox' even then conveyed, meaning 'that which guards and teaches the right belief' and admits of no alteration. The rigidity and conservatism of the Russian Church was enhanced by centuries of threat from enemies of other faiths. The only change was the translation of the Greek texts into old Slavonic, though in general language has never been a problem; as the Russian Church spread, so the Arabian and Tatar peoples had suitable translations made for them and the peoples of the north and right across Siberia were provided for in their turn.

As is to be expected, different parts of the country and different times in the history of the Soviet Union have produced variations of the form of ecclesiastical architecture, but it is still safe to say that most Russian churches are built on a rectangular plan and have five domes, with the largest in the middle. If the church is in a good state of preservation the domes may be gilded, painted silver or some bright colour, and surmounted by a Greek cross. The bell-tower, which has no clock, is generally a separate structure standing nearby.

Inside the church the sanctuary is separated from the main body of the building by the iconostasis, a screen with sacred pictures (icons) painted on it. The icons may be richly framed and decorated, and have a lamp burning before them. Slender wax candles, which are on sale in the church, are also placed before them by the faithful.

Of the three doors leading through the iconostasis, the central one, known as the Holy Door, is used by priests only. The language used during the services is Church Slavonic.

There are no seats in the church and although the services are long the congregation remains standing. The very stance is an act of worship. If, as a visitor, you get tired feet, you will not be the first to complain. In 1656 the Archdeacon of Aleppo wrote pathetically, 'As for the Muscovites, their feet must surely be of iron.' The singing, which is always unaccompanied but in which the congregation readily joins, is led by the choir, dressed in ordinary clothes and usually standing out of sight.

The head of the Church is the Patriarch of Moscow and All Russia, and the bishops of Moscow, Leningrad, Kiev, Minsk and Novosibirsk bear the title of Metropolitan.

Although the Russian Orthodox Church is quite separate from the Soviet State, a government council has been set up to maintain relations between the state and the religious bodies. This is the Council for Religious Affairs which has its headquarters in Moscow.

The following are among the more usual names of churches in Russia: 'Tserkov' or 'Khram' means Church; 'Sobor' means Cathedral.

Church of . . .

the Annunciation	Blagoveschenskaya
the Epiphany	Bogoyavlenskaya
the Ascension	Voznesenskaya
the Resurrection	Voskresenskaya
the Apparition of the Virgin	Znamenskaya
the Immaculate Conception	Zachatievskaya
the Elevation of the Cross	Krestodvizhenskaya
the Protection and Intercession of the Virgin	Pokrovskaya
the Transfiguration	Preobrazhenskaya
the Nativity of the Virgin	Rozhestvo Bogoroditsi
the Assumption	Uspenskaya
the Holy Trinity	Troitskaya

Very many churches are also dedicated to favourite saints, and those to St. Nicholas, SS. Peter and Paul, St. George, SS. Boris and Gleb, St. Vladimir, St. Dmitri, SS. Cosmo and Damian, and St. Sergei are easily recognisable from their Russian names. More difficult are St. John the Baptist (Ioann Predtecha) and the prophet Elijah (Iljya Prorok).

PASSPORTS AND OTHER FORMALITIES

In order to enter and leave the Soviet Union a foreigner must have a valid national passport and Soviet entry visa. Before a visa can be issued, the applicant must have proof that hotel accommodation has been reserved through Intourist or Sputnik. On presentation of such proof, Soviet tourist visas are issued free of charge usually within a seven-day period from the time of application to the Soviet Embassy or Consulate in the tourist's own country. (Visas for private journeys to visit relatives or friends may take much longer.)

Foreign tourists' arrivals in the Soviet Union are registered when they hand over their passports at the first Intourist service point indicated on the visa.

It is forbidden to bring the following into the Soviet Union:
- (a) arms and ammunition
- (b) printed matter, films, photographs, negatives, drawings, etc. 'which are hostile to the U.S.S.R. in political or economic respects'.

    Printed matter, plants (fruit, seeds, etc.) and animals are liable to inspection by customs authorities.

It is forbidden to take out of the Soviet Union:
- (a) arms and ammunition
- (b) precious works of art such as paintings, sculptures and rugs.

    Antiques (including furniture, icons, musical instruments, etc.) may only be taken with the permission of the Ministry of Culture and on payment of 100% duty on the value of the article.

Items of value (watches, pearls, jewellery, foreign currency) must be declared and registered on entry to the country in order that they may be taken out when you leave. A camera, cine-camera, wireless, typewriter or musical instrument may be included in one's luggage, and it is permitted to purchase an additional camera in the Soviet Union to take out of the country.

INSURANCE

Many foreign insurance companies are unwilling to insure the persons or possessions of tourists to the Soviet Union, or if they do so, their premiums are very high. Ingosstrakh (Upravlenie Inostrannovo Strakhovaniya is the full title) will probably offer more favourable terms. The address is: Moscow K–12, Kuibyshev St. 11/10 (cables: Ingosstrakh, Moscow). There are also representatives of Ingosstrakh at most of the entry points to the Soviet Union who will be glad to help if the traveller has not taken out a policy before arrival.

WHAT TO TAKE

It is worth every tourist's while to consider packing certain items which they will not find readily available in Russia: for instance, stain remover, air freshener, colour films, ballpoint refills and razor blades. Tourists should also remember any medicine to which they are accustomed, e.g. analgesics, indigestion tablets, laxatives, although of course you would be able to find a Russian substitute.

Chewing gum is not on sale in the U.S.S.R., nor are familiar brands of sweets, so if you enjoy these be sure to bring a small stock, a part of which will be gladly accepted by your new Russian friends. You may also be thankful for a jar of marmalade.

Along with the above-mentioned items, ladies should bring with them a supply of cosmetics, sanitary towels and tissues.

Children will probably ask you if you have any coins, match-boxes, stamps or badges to exchange with them.

Pipe-smokers are advised to bring a sufficient quantity of their favourite brand of tobacco with them if they do not want to switch to a Russian variety. If you use a lighter do not forget extra flints and some lighter fuel.

Voltage in Russia is 220 and 50 cycles. It is sometimes 127, but this is not usual.

CLIMATE AND CLOTHING

The climate in the European part of Russia is moderately continental, but graduates to subtropical on the southern shore of the Crimea and in parts of Transcaucasia.

Moscow's temperature averages 18·5°C. (65°F.) in July. The best weather is between May and September, but thunderstorms are likely during very hot spells. The autumn may be cold and wet, or there may be an 'Indian summer', but this is without fail the 'velvet season' in the Crimea and Caucasus. Moscow's winter begins in mid-November, and snow and frosts are likely to last until the thaw at the beginning of April. Leningrad, being on the coast, has a milder, wetter climate than Moscow, and Kiev, being further south, is generally warmer.

Other average July temperatures are as follows:

	Centigrade	Fahrenheit
Kharkov	20·6°	69°
Kiev	19·3	67
Leningrad	17·5	64
Lvov	18·7	66
Minsk	17·5	64
Odessa	22·1	72
Sochi	23·0	74
Tbilisi	24·1	75
Yalta	24·2	75
The water at the edge of the Black Sea	27–29°	81–84°

East of the Urals the climate is much more extreme. In Central Asia the summer temperature may remain at more than 40°C. for weeks, and during the Siberian winter the mercury may drop to −50°C. and freeze there.

In summer light clothing will be sufficient, but tourists should bring at least one warm outfit. A plastic mackintosh and overboots or galoshes will probably also be useful. Evening dress will not be necessary, nor any formal dress or suit for visiting restaurants or theatres in the evening. On the whole it is sensible to be conservatively dressed. Low-cut dresses, shorts and trousers for women are still unusual.

Tourists planning a winter visit are advised to bring a heavy fur or sheepskin coat, a fur hat, and warm scarf, boots and gloves. (What passes for a winter coat in England, thick tweed with a fur collar, is only regarded as an autumn coat in Moscow!) A spare sweater and woollen socks may be necessary. Those including Siberia in a winter itinerary may encounter such Arctic conditions that cameras refuse to function.

MONEY

The Russian rouble is divided into 100 kopeks. There are notes for 1, 3, 5, 10, 25, 50 and 100 roubles, copper coins for 1, 2, 3 and 5 kopeks, and nickel coins for 10, 15, 20 and 50 kopeks and 1 rouble. (2-kopeks coins are very useful to save for use in the automatic telephone kiosks.)

On entering the country tourists have to declare the amount of foreign currency they bring in. They should be careful to save the certificate they are given as it must be shown on leaving the Soviet Union.

Normal Russian shops and restaurants do not accept foreign currency. There are some special tourist shops in the larger cities, and the main Intourist hotels have kiosks where only foreign currency is accepted. Otherwise money has to be changed at the bank or in the Intourist hotels where there is a special cashier to deal with it. (They will not, however, accept the currencies of other Communist countries.) Travellers' Cheques are also accepted there. The cashier will give you a receipt for the amount of money changed and at the end of your visit the roubles you have left over will be changed back into your own currency providing you save all your bank receipts to show how much money you have changed. No roubles may be taken in or out of the country, although naturally you can take small change with you as a souvenir.

SOVIET TRAVEL SERVICES

The Government Tourist Board was inaugurated by the U.S.S.R. Council of Ministers in 1964 and soon afterwards Local Tourist Boards were set up in the principal republics of the Soviet Union. Their task has been to develop the tourist industry by opening up new centres, extending facilities, and advertising. They provide information about the U.S.S.R. and about passport, visa and customs regulations. Moscow address: Marx Prospect 16; TEL. 292–22–60, TELEX 7211.

The three Soviet travel agencies are the Tourist Council of the Trade Unions, Sputnik, and Intourist. The first organises visits made by Trade Union delegations, and Sputnik is the International Youth Tourist Bureau which specialises in young people's group tours of the Soviet Union. Sputnik's Moscow address is: Lebyazhny Pereulok 4; TEL. 223–95–12. Intourist is the largest travel agency in the Soviet Union and deals with all types of foreign travel, both that of visitors to the Soviet Union and that of Soviet citizens going abroad. In the Soviet Union the company owns hotels and restaurants and has offices or representatives in most of the larger towns visited by tourists. Their Moscow address is: Marx Prospect 16; TEL. 292–27–68; cables: Intourist, Moscow.

Intourist's offices in the West are:

Austria:	Park-Ring 10, Vienna 1010; TEL. 521501
Belgium:	119 rue Royale, Brussels 1; TEL. 170378
Berlin, West:	Olivaer Platz 8, 1 Berlin 15
Canada:	2020 Stanley St., Montreal 110
Denmark:	Vester Farimagsgade, Copenhagen; TEL. 112527
France:	7 boulevarde des Capucines, Paris 2; TEL. 7424740
Great Britain:	292 Regent St., London W.1; TEL. 01–580–4974
Holland:	Honthorstraat 42, Amsterdam Z; TEL. 798 964
Italy:	Via Bonncompagnia 14/6, Rome 00187; TEL. 482 557
Japan:	Roppongi Heights Building 1–16, 4-chome, Roppongi, Minato-ku, Tokyo
Sweden:	Sergeigatan 21, Stockholm C; TEL. 215 934
Switzerland:	Usteristrass 9, Loewenplatz, Zürich
United States:	45 East 49th St., New York City; TEL. (212) 7523030

Apart from the above, Intourist has agency contracts with many foreign travel firms throughout the world.

ACCOMMODATION

All accommodation and other services for foreign tourists visiting the Soviet Union are provided through Intourist which has a wide network of branch offices both in Russia and abroad. (See preceding section, 'Soviet Travel Services'.)

Hotels have a laundry, a barber and a hairdresser, and facilities for the repair of shoes and clothing. Charges are made according to the standard price lists; hotel residents need not queue at the hairdresser's in their own hotel. Dry cleaning services should be used with caution. Tipping is officially disapproved of in the Soviet Union, and Intourist employees will certainly not expect gratuities. 20 kopeks is sufficient for taxi drivers, doormen and cloakroom attendants. A waiter might expect 5–7% of the bill where service is not already charged. All classes of tourist can have two pieces of luggage carried free of charge; the cost for each additional piece is 20 kopeks—except at railway stations where it is 30 kopeks.

Because of the ever-increasing number of tourists coming to Russia there is still a shortage of hotel accommodation. But if you have bought a tour from Intourist, you will be provided with reservations. There will probably not be a choice of hotels, nor will you be able to change your room. In most large towns open to foreigners there is an Intourist hotel; the other hotels belong to the town, and they are often chartered by Intourist to cope with the overflow.

When you arrive the receptionist will ask for your passport. The most important place in the hotel for you is the Service Bureau (or the Administrator's Office) where you will be able to have all sorts of problems solved, from ordering your breakfast (if you do not speak Russian) to getting tickets for theatres.

The hotel staff are, almost without exception, honest, and there is rarely any complaint of theft.

Tours are usually purchased in advance and may be divided into the following categories:

1. *De Luxe Suite Class*   (available in Moscow and Leningrad only) costing 114.00 roubles per person per day. Included is a 3–5 room suite in a leading hotel, breakfast, a chauffeur-driven car, the services of a guide-interpreter, and entrance fees to museums.

2. *De Luxe Class*   (available in most of the larger towns and cities of the Soviet Union) costing 45.00 roubles per person per day. Included is an excellent room with bath in a central hotel, three meals a day within the De Luxe price limit, and the use of a car for up to 3 hours a day. The arrangements for a guide-interpreter and for museum fees are the same as for De Luxe Suite Class.

3. *First Class*   costing 28.00 roubles per person per day and including a hotel room with bath and telephone, three meals a day as per the First Class menu (but not including wines and spirits) and one half-day excursion daily by car or coach with a guide-interpreter. The full-time services of a guide-interpreter may be provided if application for such service has been made to Intourist at least two weeks before the tourist's arrival in the Soviet Union.

4. *Tourist Class*   costing 15.50 roubles per person per day but not available everywhere (e.g. not in Kiev or Tashkent, nor in Moscow or Leningrad between certain dates). Included are the same services as are provided for First Class except that the hotel rooms are smaller and without a private bath or shower, and the meals must be chosen from the Tourist Class menu.

5. *Business Tour*   costing 7.20 roubles per person per day. The services provided are the same as for First Class except that excursions are not included.

RESTAURANTS AND FOOD

Cafés usually close at 10.00 or 11.00 pm, and restaurants at 11.00 or 11.30 pm although diners are not admitted during the half-hour before closing time. The best restaurants usually accept Intourist meal coupons. 'Intourist' restaurants and a few others have their menus printed in several languages. Not all dishes have prices beside them. Those not marked are not available that particular day. Tourists are always issued with vouchers for meals.

RECOMMENDED RUSSIAN FOOD

ikra	black caviar. Remember to ask for toast (*tost*) and butter (*maslo*)
krasnaya ikra	red caviar, excellent with sour cream (*smetana*)
salat iz sverzhikh agoortsov so smetanoy	cucumber salad with sour cream
borshch	beetroot soup
shchi	cabbage soup
rasolnik	hot soup, usually of pickled vegetables
akroshka	cold soup with a 'kvass' base (very refreshing). Portions of soup are large, but one may ask for a half-portion
syomga s limonom	smoked salmon with lemon
beef Stroganov	beef stewed in smetana with fried potatoes
kutlyety po Pajarski	good chicken cutlets

kutlyeta po Kiyevski	fried rolled breast of chicken (beware of the melted butter inside which is liable to squirt)
pirozhki	savoury fried rolls with various fillings
bliny	small pancakes, eaten with caviar, fish, melted butter, smetana
aladi	crumpets, eaten with jam as well as the other things listed for bliny
pyelmeni	meat dumplings
stakan kiselya	dessert of thickened cranberry juice
gooryev skaya kasha	semolina with various dried fruits
marozhnoye	ice-cream, eaten all the year round. Try 'assorti' in a special ice-cream parlour.

WINES AND SPIRITS AND SOFT DRINKS

All alcoholic drinks must be ordered in grammes or by the bottle.

Small glass	100 g.
Large glass	200 g.
Small bottle (2/3 regular size)	500 g./·5 litre
Normal bottle	750 g./·75 litre

Vodka: If you enjoy strong drinks we may suggest you do as the Russians do, namely, ask for a special variety—Starka. There are other kinds too, including Tminaya (caraway flavour), lemon vodka, Zveroboy (animal killer), Ahotnichaya vodka (hunters' vodka), Ghorilka s pertsem (Ukrainian vodka with peppers in it), and one of the best is Yubileinaya (Jubilee).

Wine: The best wine comes from the Crimea and the Caucasus. Some names are:

Dry white	Tsinandali No. 1
Medium dry white	Tvishi No. 19 or Tetra No. 26
Dry red	Mookoozani No. 3
Medium dry red	Hvanchkara No. 20 (Stalin's favourite)
	Oosoohoolaoori No. 21 or Kinsmaraooli No. 22
Champagne:	Dry	Sookhoye
	Medium dry	Palusookhoye
	Sweet	Sladkoye
	Red (not pink) medium dry	Tsimlyanskoye

There are Russian equivalents to Port (portvein), Madeira (madera), and Vermouth (vermoot). In general there is a wide choice of wine from Eastern Europe.

Brandy and Liqueurs: The best brandy comes from Armenia (armyanskii kanyak). Most liqueurs have French names, but the resemblance to the originals may be slight.

Mineral Water: The most common mineral waters are Narzan and the slightly salty Barzhomi. Fresh water is seldom served at table, unless particularly asked for.

Fizzy fruit drinks include 'Limonad' and various others: orange, cherry, apple, and pear. There is also a Russian Coca-Cola, 'Sayani'.

Outside in the street you may buy a glass of 'kvass' (fermented bread-water), or plain soda water.

In case the salt or sugar has been left off your breakfast tray or you wish to buy some fruit in the market, here is a short list of food items with their approximate pronounciation:

Bread	hlyeb	Tea	chai
Water	vada	Coffee	kofye
Boiled water	keepatok	Apples	yabloki
Milk	malako	Pears	grooshi
Butter	masla	Grapes	veenograd
Cheese	syir	Lemon	leemon
Eggs	yaitsa	Strawberries	kloobnika
Yoghourt	kifir	Cucumbers	agoortsi
Sour cream	smetana	Tomatoes	pamidori
Salt	sol	Wine	veeno
Sugar	sakhar	Beer	peevo
Cold sausage	kolbasa	Soft fruit	yagodi
Ham	vecheena	Fruit	frookti
Sweets	kanfyeti	Chocolate	shokolad

ENTERTAINMENT

Visitors to Russia should apply to the Service Bureau of their hotel for tickets for shows, and the sooner this is done the greater is the chance of obtaining tickets. The majority of theatre performances begin at 7.00 pm, the Circus and concerts at 7.30 pm, and most performances do not end later than 11.00 pm. On Sundays there are matinées at 11.00 am. Tourists may only know whether or not they have tickets on the day of the performance.

Tickets are priced between 1 and 3 roubles. As well as from Intourist, tickets can be bought from 'theatre agents' and small booking-office kiosks just inside the Metro stations, or in the street. Tickets bought from these kiosks can be obtained a few days in advance, but it is hard to get any for something popular.

Like most tourists, you will want to see a ballet in Moscow or Leningrad, but do not be disappointed to learn that the ballet season does not include the summer months (end of May to the beginning of September). But during the summer leading dancers often perform separately throughout the country, and sometimes even at open-air shows. Synopses of the best-known operas and ballets are printed in English, and are obtainable at the Intourist Service Bureaux.

The new music and drama festivals are proving immensely popular, and we recommend that if possible you arrange your visit to coincide with one of them. 'Moscow Stars' takes place in Moscow (5–13 May), 'Russian Winter' (25 Dec–5 Jan) and 'White Nights' in Leningrad (21–29 June). Ask Intourist for a festival programme and book your tickets in advance to avoid disappointment.

Other interesting performances are given at the Puppet Theatre, the various circuses and the 'Romany' Gypsy Theatre—the only one of its kind in the world—where most of the plays include gypsy dances and songs. Symphony concerts are given all the year round, and feature world famous soloists.

Concerts and circus performances usually have one interval, while plays and operas have two or three. These last up to twenty minutes each, and most theatres have a large foyer where the audiences promenade anti-clockwise. Often theatres have an exhibition of theatrical pictures, stage models, etc., and always a buffet and a bookstall. Smoking is allowed only in specified places, and in the entrance foyer. Before curtain-up there is a series of three warning bells; the doors of the stalls are firmly shut after the last bell, but upstairs doors are left open for latecomers.

Outdoor clothing is not allowed in the auditorium. If you have a coat to leave, it is wise to pay the cloakroom attendant 30 kopeks at the same time for a pair of binoculars, no matter how close to the stage your seat. After the performance you will then be able to go to the front of the slow-moving queue to collect your possessions.

Films in Russia are, not surprisingly, practically always in Russian. Sometimes Moscow's 'Metropole' Cinema shows foreign films in the original language. You can buy your own ticket, or ask Intourist to help you. In Moscow there is a 'Classic' cinema where only old films, including silent ones, are shown. There is circorama too. Non-stop film showing does not exist in Russia, and each ticket entitles you to one film and its newsreel only; the auditorium is emptied between showings. Different films may be showing at a single cinema during the course of the day. The highest ticket price is 50 kopeks. It is strictly forbidden to smoke in the auditorium.

Clubs in the Soviet Union belong to various enterprises and organisations, and there are clubs for professionals (artists, writers, etc.). Some of these have restaurants which are not open to the public, although a Russian friend might invite you there. There are no night clubs, bars, or pubs.

Parks are open all the year round. In the winter time they are used for skiing and skating, and in the summer there are facilities for boating (30 kopeks per hour, plus a small deposit for the safe return of the boat), sports grounds, playgrounds with swings and merry-go-rounds, open air concerts, and dance areas. There are also various restaurants, cafés and ice-cream stalls. Entrance to all parks is free, and they remain open till 11.00 pm. Most large Russian cities have their own zoos and botanical gardens.

HUNTING AND FISHING

Intourist organises hunting trips for foreign visitors in the game reserves of the West and Northern Caucasus, near Krasnodar, Irkutsk, Kherson, and Kubinsk. Depending on the reserve, hunting is for deer, roe deer, boar, bear, European bison, and wild goat. The season is from mid-July until February, depending upon the choice of game. Most hunting tours last from 2 to 5 days.

Tours must be paid for in advance and included in the cost are meals and accommodation at the hotel and hunting lodge, transport to and from the hunting reserve, the services of an interpreter at the reserve, and of an Intourist representative who will meet tourists at all points of arrival and departure. Experienced huntsmen accompany the hunters, rifles and ammunition are provided if required, and the tourist receives his trophies after the hunt.

Among the fish which can be caught in the rivers of the central part of Russia are perch, pike, carp, roach, 'ruff', and 'crucian'. In the Volga, in addition to these, there are zander or 'pike-perch'. In the Black Sea, particularly in the Odessa region, bullhead, sea perch, mackerel and 'stavrida' can be found.

SHOPPING

The larger cities now have foreign currency shops just as the leading Intourist hotels have foreign currency souvenir kiosks. In Moscow and Leningrad they go under the general title of 'Beryozka' (birchtree) shops. Here one may purchase souvenirs and other items for convertible currency considerably cheaper than in the ordinary shops, where they may be difficult to find. It is definitely advisable, before paying roubles for things like furs or silverware, to check whether they are available in the foreign currency shops.

Each city has a department store called the Univermag. When in Moscow, it is worth while visiting the largest department store, GUM, pronounced 'goom', on Red Square. It is built in the form of arcades of small shops on three floors, all under one roof. Some of the larger stores have information desks and members of the sales staff who speak foreign languages.

There are no prestige shops; the prices are the same for identical articles whether they are bought in Red Square or in a Siberian village store. All the shops are state-run with fixed prices. The markets are different. Here there are co-operative stalls (usually with fixed prices) and private stalls (where bargaining is permitted, but hardly worth the trouble). The prices in the markets and those of the flower-sellers in the streets usually depend upon supply and demand. The markets close at 5 pm.

The florist's shops are state-run and in the big cities they will take orders to deliver flowers to any address at any time. Other shops will not deliver your purchases to your hotel or pack them up and post them for you.

In most of the shops it is necessary first to pay at the cash desk and then take the receipt to the sales girl to exchange it for what you have chosen. Self-service shops are also popular; they are run just the same as in the West.

With the exception of the shops where basic food items are sold, all are closed on Sundays, but on other days they usually stay open as late as 7 or 8 pm. Most of the food shops close during their lunch hour between 1 and 2, while the other shops close between 2 and 3; the largest stores, however, stay open without a break. There are specialised shops which stock particular commodities. They include 'Children's World', 'The Shoe House' and 'The House of Material'.

Western non-communist newspapers are sometimes to be found at Moscow's international airport (Sheremetievo) and on the bookstalls of the leading hotels. Communist newspapers from abroad are on sale throughout the country as are local publications in foreign languages.

Antique shops are only worth visiting in Moscow and Leningrad; in other places they only stock such things as second-hand clothing and musical instruments. New, and strictly enforced, regulations have been introduced concerning antiques. Now official permission is required to export specific items and a payment of 100% duty is levied. This is only avoidable if the item is small and could be considered part of one's personal possessions. Antiques are very often enormously overpriced, but sometimes it is possible to pick up a unique piece for a song.

The antique shops are known here as Commission Shops. The merchandise comes from individuals who use the state-run shop to sell things for them. Seven per cent is deducted by the shop for handling. People staying long enough do have the chance of bargaining with the seller through the shop. In any case the price will be reduced by the shop if there is no sale after a while, but the usual practice is to buy immediately if something attractive turns up on the shelves because the turnover is very quick. If you do not have enough money with you, a particular item will be put aside for a few hours. No cheques are accepted or used in the Soviet shops. Purchases can be returned within three days if a defect is found which was not pointed out at the time of the sale.

It is probably worth noting that no salesman will try to persuade a customer to buy something else more expensive; the opposite may even be the case. And if the salesgirl advises the customer something suits her, it is not because she is thinking about her commission. Perhaps the sight of an assistant buried in a book, and more ready to answer 'nyet' to your request than to climb the steps and look, might prove distinctly annoying, but you need never fear that anyone will breathe anxiously down your neck as they encourage you to make your choice, nor will anyone in the street attempt to steer you into a particular shop to buy.

COMPARATIVE CLOTHING SIZES (APPROXIMATE)

Shoes: Infants' and Children's

English	0	1	2	3	4	5	6	7	8	9	10	11	12	13
Continental	15	17	18	19	20	22	23	24	25	27	28	29	31	32

Shoes: Adults'

English	1	2	3	4	5	6	7	8	9	10	11	12	13
Continental	33	34	$35\frac{1}{2}$	37	38	$39\frac{1}{2}$	$40\frac{1}{2}$	42	43	$44\frac{1}{2}$	$45\frac{1}{2}$	47	48

Shirts & Collars:

English (ins.)	13	$13\frac{1}{2}$	14	$14\frac{1}{2}$	15	$15\frac{1}{2}$	16	$16\frac{1}{2}$	17	$17\frac{1}{2}$	18
Continental (Cm.)	33	34	36	37	38	39	41	42	43	44	46

Hats:

English	6	$6\frac{1}{2}$	$6\frac{3}{4}$	6	7	7	$7\frac{1}{4}$	$7\frac{1}{2}$	7
Continental	53	54	55	56	57	58	59	60	61

Stockings & Socks:

English (ins.)	5	$5\frac{1}{2}$	6	$6\frac{1}{2}$	7	$7\frac{1}{2}$	8	$8\frac{1}{2}$	9	$9\frac{1}{2}$	10	$10\frac{1}{2}$
Continental (cm.)	8	10	12	14	16	18	20	22	24	26	28	30

Dresses:

English	10	12	14	16	18	WX	OS
European	36	37	38	40	42	44	46
Russian	42	44	46	48	50	52	54

IDEAS FOR PRESENTS

Black caviar is always popular. It is sold in small, sealed jars. If you can stretch to a 2-kilo tin, the taste is very much better. You might dole it out around friends and relatives. Balalaika and instructions; electric samovar (check the voltage as both 127 v. and 220 v. are available); fur hat; embroidered skull-cap from Uzbekistan or dress-length of zig-zag patterned silk; Ukrainian hand-embroidered shirt or blouse; embroidered table linen; toys, especially glove-puppets and space-age vehicles; chess sets; gramophone records and books (comparatively inexpensive); traditional silver gilt and enamel ware (e.g. tiny fork for lemon slices or butter balls, or child's spoon with animal handle); ivory, wood, alabaster or pottery ornaments; hand-painted trays and boxes; dolls in the national dress of the fifteen republics.

Russian cameras and watches are good quality and are often priced very favourably compared with the West. Lenses and other camera equipment are worth consideration. So too are radios and razors.

WEIGHTS AND MEASURES

The Soviet Union uses the metric system of measurement. Here are some useful equivalents:

0·6 litre	1 pint
1 litre	$1\frac{3}{4}$ pints
1 kilogram	2 lb 2 oz
1 kilometre	$\frac{5}{8}$ mile
1 metre	$39\frac{1}{4}$ inches
1 hectare	$2\frac{1}{2}$ acres

Gallons	Litres	Miles	Kilometres
1	4·5	1	1·6
2	9·0	2	3·2
3	13·6	3	4·8
4	18·2	4	6·4
5	22·7	5	8·0
6	27·3	10	16·0
7	31·8	20	32·2
8	36·4	30	48·2
9	40·9	40	64·4
10	45·5	50	80·5
11	50·0	60	96·6
12	54·6	70	112·7
		80	128·7
		90	144·8
		100	160·9

Temperatures are measured in Centigrade. To convert Centigrade to Fahrenheit, multiply by 9, divide by 5, and add 32. To convert Fahrenheit to Centigrade, subtract 32, multiply by 5, and divide by 9.

Air Pressure for motor tyres is measured in kilograms per sq. cm. instead of lb per sq. inch.

14 lb = 1·00 kg	32 lb = 2·25 kg
18 lb = 1·26 kg	36 lb = 2·53 kg
22 lb = 1·54 kg	40 lb = 2·80 kg
28 lb = 1·96 kg	

PUBLIC TRANSPORT

The most popular form of transport in the largest cities is the underground *Metro*. The fare is 5 kopeks for any distance.
Tickets in Moscow for any distance cost:

> *bus*—5 kopeks
> *trolleybus*—4 kopeks
> *tram*—3 kopeks

Some other towns still work on the fare-stage system. In some large towns public transport operates without a conductor and instead there is a money-box for your fare. Public transport services stop at 1.00 am.

Taxis have a chequered pattern on their doors, and when free show a green light in the corner of the windscreen. You can catch a taxi in the street, or at a taxi rank, or call for one by telephone. It costs 10 kopeks to hire a taxi and then the charge is 10 kopeks per kilometre; waiting costs 1 rouble per hour. There are also taxi services which ply to and fro along certain routes; these are called 'marshrootnoye' taxis and the charge is 10 kopeks for any distance along the route.

Trains. Most 'soft' (i.e. first) class sleeping compartments are designed for 4 people. There are also some for 2, but not on all lines. Check whether your train has a restaurant car, otherwise expect a 20–40 min. stop at large towns when you can visit the restaurant at the station. Each carriage has a conductor who will provide glasses of hot tea and sugar from his own electric samovar.

Air. The Soviet airline, Aeroflot, has a different idea from many other airlines as to what constitutes a long flight. It is advisable to take chocolate or biscuits with you; snacks are provided on some flights, but certainly not on the two-hour journeys between Moscow and the south, nor on the one-hour Moscow-Leningrad flights. Air fares inside the Soviet Union are very reasonable, a factor worthy of note when a trip is being planned.

Sea Travel. Tourists can reach Russia by Soviet ships sailing regularly to Odessa (or other Black Sea ports) from Marseilles, Genoa, Naples, Athens, Istanbul, and Varna in Bulgaria and also from Alexandria, Beirut, and Famagusta, or to Leningrad from Montreal and London, calling in at the Scandinavian capitals *en route*. On the Caspian Sea there is a service between Baku and the Iranian port of Pahlevi and in the far east between Nakhodka, Yokohama, and Hong Kong. The Soviet Danube Steamship Co. has four vessels cruising the river from Vienna to the Soviet port of Izmail. Non-Soviet ships also operate on these lines.

It is possible to vary one's tour considerably by making use of the ships which ply between the ports of the Black Sea.

Odessa	Port (morskoi vokzal), TEL. 2–07–86 or 9–85–51
	Booking Office: Karla Marksa Sq. 1
	Administrator: TEL. 2–09–54
	Inquiry Office: TEL. 2–09–44
Yalta	'Morskoi Vokzal', Bulvarnaya St. 5 TEL. 25–35
Novorossiisk	'Morskoi Vokzal', Lenina St. 10
	TEL. 23–17 or 20–35, ext. 1–24
Sochi	'Morskoi Vokzal', Voikova St.
	TEL. 66–2–03 or 66–2–52
Sukhumi	'Morskoi Vokzal', Rustaveli Prospect 16
	TEL. 7–38

The Cost of Car Ferry Between the Ports of the Black Sea
(in roubles per ton)

Ports	Yalta	Novorossiisk	Tuapse	Sochi	Sukhumi
Odessa	12·90	17·37	18·53	19·70	20·86
Yalta	—	12·13	13·68	14·46	16·21
Novorossiisk	—	—	6·89	8·25	12·13
Tuapse	—	—	—	5·05	9·02
Sochi	—	—	—	—	7·28

Additional costs:
1 Loading and unloading charge of 1·30 roubles per ton at each port.
2 Cargo Tax of 1·44 roubles per ton.

CAR HIRE

Foreign tourists may hire self-drive Volga or Moskvich cars through Intourist. The costs of hire in roubles, including insurance, servicing and maps per 24 hours, are as follows:

Car	1–10 days	11–20 days	Over 20 days	Charge per km.
Volga	6·30	5·85	5·40	6 kopeks
Moskvich	4·50	4·05	3·60	4 kopeks

For a minimum of seven days and for use only within the city where hired, cars can be hired with unlimited mileage. Chauffeur-driven cars are also available, and include the 6-seat Chaika model. Chaikas are however only for hire in Moscow, Leningrad and Kiev and are not provided for travel between cities. Other cities where Volgas and Moskviches can be hired are: Sochi, Yalta, Brest, Minsk, Kiev, Kharkov, Odessa, Lvov, Tbilisi, Sukhumi, Kishinev, and Erevan. (Chauffeur-driven cars only are supplied in Tallinn, Vilnius, Riga, and Tashkent.) Cars

---

PLATE OPPOSITE
Autumn in the mountains of the Crimea

can be delivered from any of these cities to any other where Intourist service is available, but the tourist must pay for the empty run at the rate of 8 kopeks per km. for a Volga and 6 kopeks per km. for a Moskvich.

Petrol coupons can be purchased from Intourist offices or hotel Service Bureaux.

POST, TELEPHONE, ETC.

Any post to be forwarded to Moscow should be addressed c/o Intourist, Moscow (or any other large city), U.S.S.R. The more information on the envelope, the better; e.g. John Brown, from England, arriving Moscow 2nd July.

Intourist will keep it for you to collect. Usually post from European countries takes 3–10 days, and from the United States and Canada a week or more. The address *must* be legible.

Airmail letters abroad cost 16 kopeks and postcards 14 kopeks. Express rate is an extra 18 kopeks, and ordinary mail 6 and 4 kopeks respectively.

Telegrams and telephone calls abroad are priced as follows:

Country	Telegraph: cost per word ordinary rate†	Telephone: cost per 3 min*
	kopeks	roubles
Austria	19	3·00
Belgium	21	3·29
Denmark	20	2·88
Finland	11	1·23
France	17	4·23
Federal Germany	18	3·32
Great Britain	21	4·28
Italy	21	3·79
Netherlands	20	2·46
Norway	19	3·44
Sweden	18	2·41
U.S.A. (New York)	23	10·80
U.S.A. (other cities)	30	(8·10 on Sundays)

† Telegrams may be sent LT or ELT at half-price
* Reverse charge calls may be made, but no calls at all between midnight and 2.30 am.

Parcels involve complications. Incoming parcels are not delivered, but recipients will be notified of their arrival by post. Customs duty must be paid when they are collected (this may be inexplicably high) and also a small charge for the repacking of the parcel after customs inspection!

PLATES OPPOSITE
The simplicity of this 9th century monastery, *above*, built on the shores of Lake Sevan near Erevan in Armenia contrasts with the ornate cathedral at Alma-Ata, *below*, the second tallest wooden building in the world. Built in 1904, today it is the Central Museum of Kazakhstan.

To send a parcel out of the Soviet Union, do not pack the article at all. Buy a standard wooden box at the post office (the largest size available is approximately 45 × 25 × 25 cm). The post office assistants will pack it for you. The maximum weight, including packing, is 10 kilograms and this costs 3·05 roubles to England and 4·74 roubles to the United States. Airmail parcels of similar size and weight cost 16·40 roubles to England and 27 roubles to the United States.

Printed matter to be sent by book post will also be packed for you. The cost per kilogram, whatever the destination, is 45 kopeks.

It is forbidden to send the following out of the Soviet Union by post: caviar or any food in tins, more than 12 gramophone records in a single parcel, pre-revolutionary editions of any book, and also gold, silver or precious stones.

Local Telephones.   Most Intourist hotels have automatic telephones in each room. One should usually dial '8' before the town number needed; frequent regular buzzing means 'line engaged'. With non-automatic telephones you should ask the operator for 'gorod' and wait for a continuous buzzing sound before you dial. If you cannot manage to say room numbers in Russian, you may use English or French very slowly, number by number. In case of emergency ask the operator for 'Service Bureau' or 'administrator'.

Telephone kiosks.   Put a 2-kopek coin in the slot, lift the receiver, wait for a continuous buzzing, and then dial.

Long distance calls.   Such calls made from a hotel must be ordered through the Service Bureau; they may take an hour to come through. Otherwise one should go to a long distance telephone office ('peregovornyi punkt'); there one might be asked to pay for 3 or 5 minutes' conversation in advance.

PHOTOGRAPHY

Photographs and cine-films may be taken during your visit, but you must obtain permission from the administration of factories, railway stations and government offices before taking pictures of them, and permission is needed to photograph people in service uniform.

It is forbidden to take photographs of any military object, seaports, hydro-electric installations, bridges, scientific research institutions, radio, telephone and telegraph stations, and no photographs should be taken from planes or trains.

It is advisable to bring a supply of film with you, which (if it is not colour film) you may have developed before you leave. Photo-studio 'Intourist' is at the Metropole Hotel in Moscow. If you use Soviet colour film it would be best to have it developed before you leave.

FOREIGN EMBASSIES IN MOSCOW
(And Consulates if located at a different address)

Afghanistan	Skatertny Per. 25	TEL. 290–17–87
Algeria	Krapivinsky Per. 1–a	TEL. 223–02–98
Argentina	Lunacharskovo St. 8	TEL. 241–66–81
Consular section:	Kutuzovsky Pr. 7/4, Apt. 253	TEL. 243–13–94

Australia	Kropotkinsky Per. 13	TEL. 241–20–35
Austria	Starokonyushenny Per. 1	TEL. 202–19–41
Bangladesh	Zemledelchesky Per. 6	TEL. 246–79–00
Belgium	Stolovy Per. 7	TEL. 203–65–66
Consular section:	Khlebny Per. 15	TEL. 203–65–66
Bolivia	Lopukhinsky Per. 5	TEL. 202–25–09
Brazil	Gertsena St. 54	TEL. 290–40–22
Bulgaria	Leningradsky Prospect 20	TEL. 250–06–83
Burma	Gertsena St. 41	TEL. 291–05–34
Burundi	Uspensky Per. 7	TEL. 299–72–00
Cambodia	Serpov Per. 6	TEL. 244–78–57
Cameroon	Vorovskovo St. 40	TEL. 290–65–49
Canada	Starokonyushenny Per. 23	TEL. 241–90–34
Central Africa	Gilyarovskovo St. 20	TEL. 284–42–31
Chad	Elizarovoi St. 10	TEL. 227–88–50
China	Druzhba St. 6	TEL. 143–15–40
Colombia	Burdenko St. 20	TEL. 246–64–31
Congo	Kropotkinsky Per. 12	TEL. 246–00–76
Cuba	Mosfilmovskaya St. 40	TEL. 147–45–55
Cyprus	Gertsena St. 51	TEL. 290–21–54
Czechoslovakia	Yulius Fuchika St. 12/14	TEL. 253–75–07
Denmark	Per. Ostrovskovo 9	TEL. 202–78–66
Ecuador	Gorokhovsky Per. 12	TEL. 261–55–44
Egypt	Gertsena St. 56	TEL. 291–32–09
Ethiopia	Kropotkinskaya Naberezhnaya 35	TEL. 203–11–65
Finland	Kropotkinsky Per. 15/17	TEL. 246–45–40
France	Dimitrova St. 43	TEL. 231–85–06
Gabon	Vesnina St. 16	TEL. 241–00–80
German Democratic Republic	Stanislavskovo St. 10	TEL. 294–00–25
Consular section:	Stanislavskovo St. 20	TEL. 294–00–25
Federal Republic of Germany	Bolshaya Gruzinskaya St. 17	TEL. 255–00–13
Ghana	Skatertny Per. 14	TEL. 202–18–70
Great Britain	Naberzhnaya Morisa Toreza 14	TEL. 231–95–55
Greece	Stanislavskovo St. 4	TEL. 290–22–74
Guinea	Pomerantsev Per. 6	TEL. 202–76–52
Guinea–Bissau	26 Batinskikh–Komissarov St. Apt. 8/9	TEL. 434–46–41
Hungary	Mosfilmovskaya St. 62	TEL. 143–86–11
Iceland	Khlebny Per. 28	TEL. 290–47–42
India	Obukha St. 6–8	TEL. 297–08–20
Indonesia	Novokuznetskaya St. 12	TEL. 231–95–49
Iran	Pokrovsky Bld. 7	TEL. 297–46–19
Iraq	Pogodinskaya St. 12	TEL. 246–37–20
Italy	Vesnina St. 5	TEL. 241–15–34
Irish Republic	Grokholski Per. 5	TEL. 281–05–70
Japan	Sobinovsky Per. 5a	TEL. 291–85–00
Jordan	Sadovskikh Per. 3	TEL. 299–34–30

Kenya	Bolshaya Ordinka St. 70	TEL. 233–86–65
Korea	Stanislavskovo St. 9	TEL. 290–60–13
Kuwait	3rd Neopalimovsky Per. 13/5	TEL. 245–08–25
Laos	Kachalova St. 18	TEL. 290–12–81
Lebanon	Sadovo-Samotechnaya St. 14	TEL. 295–20–83
Liberia	Mosfilmovskaya St. 58	TEL. 147–90–06
Libya	Merzlyakovsky Per. 20	TEL. 291–11–75
Luxemburg	Khruschevsky Per. 3	TEL. 202–21–71
Malaysia	Mosfilmovskaya St. 50	TEL. 147–15–14
Mali	Novokuznetskaya St. 11	TEL. 231–22–60
Mauritania	Bolshaya Ordynka St. 66	TEL. 231–19–12
Mexico	Schukina St. 4	TEL. 202–13–56
Mongolia	Pisemskovo St. 11	TEL. 290–30–61
Consular section:	Spaso-Peskovsky Per. 7/1	TEL. 241–10–46
Morocco	Per. Ostorvskovo 8	TEL. 202–01–95
Nepal	2nd Neopalimovsky Per. 14/7	TEL. 241–94–34
Netherlands	Kalashny Per. 6	TEL. 291–29–99
New Zealand	Vorovskovo St. 44	TEL. 290–34–85
Nigeria	Kachalova St. 13	TEL. 290–37–83
Norway	Vorovskovo St. 7	TEL. 290–38–72
Pakistan	Sadovo-Kudrinskaya St. 17	TEL. 250–39–91
Peru	Smolensky Bld. 22/14, Apt. 12	TEL. 246–68–36
Poland	Mitskevicha St. 1	TEL. 290–49–11
Portugal	Grokholsky Per. 3	TEL. 280–31–47
Rumania	Mosfilmovskaya St. 64	TEL. 143–04–20
Rwanda	B. Ordynka St. 72	TEL. 233–86–29
Senegal	Donskaya St. 12	TEL. 236–85–28
Sierra Leone	Khlebny Per. 21	TEL. 203–62–00
Singapore	Per. Voyevodina 5	TEL. 241–37–02
Somali	Spasopeskovskaya Pl. 8	TEL. 241–96–24
Spanish Trade Mission	Paliashvili St. 3	TEL. 290–41–52
Sri Lanka	Shepkin St. 24	TEL. 281–91–26
Sudan	Vorovskovo St. 9	TEL. 290–39–93
Sweden	Mosfilmovskaya St. 60	TEL. 147–90–09
Switzerland	Per. Stopani 2/5	TEL. 295–53–22
Syria	Mansurovsky Per. 4	TEL. 203–15–21
Tanzania	Pyatnitskaya St. 33	TEL. 231–81–46
Thailand	Eropkinsky Pereulok 3	TEL. 202–48–74
Tunisia	Kachalova St. 28/1	TEL. 291–63–78
Turkey	Vadkovsky Per. 7/37	TEL. 289–50–92
Uganda	Per. Sadovskikh 5	TEL. 253–05–74
Upper Volta	Meschanskaya St. 17	TEL. 284–37–66
Uruguay	Pr. Mira 74, Apt. 160	TEL. 284–56–05
U.S.A.	Tchaikovskovo St. 19/23	TEL. 252–00–11
Venezuela	Ermolovoi St. 13–15	TEL. 299–95–61
Democratic Republic of Vietnam	B. Pirogovskaya St. 13	TEL. 245–10–92
South Vietnam	Karmanitsky Per. 6/8	TEL. 241–26–39

Yemen Arab Republic	Kropotkinskaya Naberezhnaya 3	TEL. 246–64–28
Yemen P.D.R.	A. Tolstoy St. 14	TEL. 203–77–38
Yugoslavia	Mosfilmovskaya St. 46	TEL. 147–41–06
Zaire	Per. Ostrovskovo 10	TEL. 202–16–65
Zambia	Prospect Mira 52–a	TEL. 281–05–66

FOREIGN TRAVEL AGENCIES IN MOSCOW

American Express Company, Hotel Metropole 384	TEL. 225–63–84
Balkantourist (Bulgaria), Hotel Metropole 2045	TEL. 221–85–75
Ibusz (Hungary), Hotel National 241	TEL. 203–51–32
Orbis (Poland), Hotel National 106	TEL. 203–74–39
Reiseburo DDR, Hotel Berlin 216–217	TEL. 294–88–93

CONSULATES OUTSIDE MOSCOW

Besides having their consulates in Moscow, some countries also have consular facilities in other Soviet cities:

Batumi:
Turkish Consulate, Oktyabrsky Prospect 8, TEL. 39–09

Kiev:
Czechoslovak Consulate, Ul. Karl Liebknecht 28, TEL. 93–04–71, 93–04–87
DDR Consulate, Ul. Chekistov 3, TEL. 93–58–22
Hungarian Consulate, Ul. Oktyabrskoy Revolutsii 8, TEL. 93–81–51
Polish Consulate, Omsky Per. 6, TEL. 33–13–13, 33–11–14
Rumanian Consulate, Bekhterevsky Per. 5, TEL. 79–02–80

Leningrad:
DDR Consulate, Admiralteyskaya Nab. 10, TEL. 11–81–58
FRG Consulate, Vasilievsky Ostrov, 3rd Liniya 12, TEL. 13–03–52
Finnish Consulate, Chaikovsky Ul.71, TEL. 73–73–21
French Consulate, Moika Naberezhnaya 15, TEL. 15–84–04
Japanese Consulate, Moika Naberezhnaya 29, TEL. 15–44–24
Polish Consulate, Ryleyeva St. 35, TEL. 73–37–37
Swedish Consulate, 10th Liniya 11, TEL. 18–35–26
United States Consulate, Grodnensky Per. 4, TEL. 73–21–04

Minsk:
DDR Consulate, Ul. Sakharov 26, TEL. 33–36–96, 33–42–17

Nakhodka:
Japanese Consulate, Ul. Lunacharskovo 9, TEL. 75–15, 75–19

Odessa:
Indian Consulate, TEL. 22–43–33

VOCABULARY

The Alphabet

Vowels

Russian	English	Pronounced
а	a	as a in 'father' (when in a stressed syllable) or as u in 'up'
я	—	as ya in 'yard'
э	e	as e in 'pet'
е	—	as ye in 'yet'
и	i	as i in 'hit'
ы	—	as e in 'me' pronounced with a strong Midland accent
о	o	as o in 'hot'
е	—	as ya in 'yacht'
у	u	as u in 'pull'
ю	—	as u in 'union'

Consonants

б	b	as b in 'box'
д	d	as d in 'dog'
ф	f	as f in 'fish'
г	g	as g in 'go'
х	kh	as ch in 'loch'
ж	zh	as s in 'pleasure'
к	k	as k in 'king'
л	l	as l in 'like'
м	m	as m in 'man'
н	n	as n in 'nimble'
п	p	as p in 'pin'
р	r	as r in 'arrow'
с	s	as s in 'miss'
т	t	as t in 'take'
в	v	as v in 'vat'
з	z	as z in 'zebra'

Double Consonants

ц	—	as ts in 'eats'
ч	—	as ch in 'chair'
ш	—	as sh in 'ship'
щ	—	as shch in 'cash cheque'

Accent Letters

ь	soft sign (in transliterated words)
ъ	hard sign
й	short i (as 'y' in 'guy')

Numbers

1	один	udeen'
2	два	dva
3	три	tree
4	четыре	chyety'rye
5	пять	pyat
6	шесть	shest
7	семь	syem
8	восемь	vo'syem
9	девять	dye'vyat
10	десять	dye'syat
11	одиннадцать	udeen'atsut
12	двенадцать	dvyenat'sut
13	тринадцать	treenat'sut
14	четырнадцать	chetyr'natsut
15	пятнадцать	pyatnat'sut
16	шестнадцать	shestnat'sut
17	семнадцать	syemnat'sut
18	восемнадцать	vosyemnat'sut
19	девятнадцать	dyevyatnat'sut
20	двадцать	dvat'sut
21	двадцать один	dvat'sut udeen
22	двадцать два	dvat'sut dva
30	тридцать	treet'sut
40	сорок	so'rok
50	пятьдесят	pyatdyesyat'
60	шестьдесят	shestdyesyat
70	семьдесят	syemdyesyat
80	восемьдесят	vo'syemdye syat
90	девяносто	dyevyano'sto
100	сто	sto
200	двести	dvye'sti
300	триста	tree'sta
400	четыреста	chety'ryesta
500	пятьсот	pyatsot
600	шестьсот	shestsot'
900	девятьсот	dyevyatsot'
1000	тысяча	ty'syacha

Telling the Time

To tell the time, one must always state the number of hours first, and then the number of minutes. (There is a second way of telling the time in Russian which is more complicated grammatically. 8.20 would be literally 'twenty minutes of the ninth'.) The simple method given here will be perfectly adequate.

In the evening, especially when giving the times of film performances, train departures, etc., Russians tend to use the 24-hour system (saying 18.45 for 6.45 pm).

What is the time?
кото́рый час?
kato'ryi chas?

It is one o'clock, two o'clock
час, два часа́.
chas, dva chasa'

It is five past three (pm)
три часа́ пять мину́т, пятна́дцать ноль пять.
tree chasa'pyat minoot'*or* pyatnat' sut nol pyat

It is twenty to five.
четы́ре часа́ со́рок мину́т, шестна́дцать со́рок.
chety'rye chasa'so'rok minoot'*or* shestnat'sut so'rok

It is twelve o'clock mid-day, midnight.
по́лдень, по́лночь.
pol'dyen, pol'noch

am	утра́	utra
pm	ве́чера	vye'chera
This morning	сего́дня у́тром	syevod'nya oot rom
This afternoon	сего́дня днём	syevod'nya dnyom
This evening } Tonight }	сего́дня ве́чером	{ syevod'nya vye'cherom
Night	ночь	noch
Tomorrow evening	за́втра ве́чером	zav'tra vye'cherom
Tomorrow morning	за́втра у́тром	zav'tra oot'rom
The day after tomorrow	послеза́втра	poslyezav'tra
Yesterday	вчера́	vchera'
The day before yesterday	позавчера́	pozavchera'
Last night	вчера́ но́чью	vchera'noch'yu
Early	ра́но	ra'no
Late	по́здно	poz'dno
How long?	как до́лго	kak dol'go?
An hour	час	chas
A minute	мину́та	minoo'ta
Half a moment	мину́точку	minoo'tochku
In a moment	сейча́с	sichas'

ASKING THE WAY
Would you please tell me . . .
скажи́те пожа́луйста . . .
skazhee'tye pazhal'sta . . .

> where there is a grocer's, baker's, market, chemist's here?
> где здесь продма́г, бу́лочная, ры́нок, апте́ка?
> gdye zdyes prodmag', boo'lochnaya, ry'nok, aptye'ka?

> where there is a restaurant, café, cafeteria here?
> где здесь рестора́н, кафе́, столо́вая?
> gdye zdyes restoran', kafay', stalo'vaya?

> cinema, theatre, park, museum, church?
> кино́, теа́тр, парк, музе́й, це́рковь?
> kino', tyea'tr, park, moozei', tser'kov?

> where there is a lavatory here?
> где здесь убо́рная?
> gdye zdyes ubor'naya?

Highway	шóссе	sho'sai	Turning	поворо́т	pavarot'
Road	доро́га	daro'ga	To the left	нале́во	nalye'va
Street	у́лица	oo'litsa	To the right	напра́во	napra'va
Square	пло́щадь	plosh'chad	Straight on	пря́мо	prya'ma
Lane	переу́лок	pyeryeoo' lok	Here	сюда́	syuda'
Dead-end	тупи́к	tupik	There	туда́	tuda'
Town	го́род	go'rod	Back	наза́д	nazad'
Village	село́	syelo	Forest	лес	lyes
Village	дере́вня	dyerev'nya	Field	по́ле	po'lye
House	дом	dom	River	река́	reka'
Sea	мо́ре	mo'rye	Lake	о́зеро	o'zyero
Black Sea	Чёрное море	chor'noye morye	Hill	гора́	gara'

Who speaks English, French, German here?
кто здесь говори́т по-англи́йски, по-францу́зски, понеме́цки?
kto zdyes gavareet' panglee'ski, pafrantsoos'ki, panimyets'ki?

May I have an interpreter?
мо́жно попроси́ть перево́дчика?
mozh'no papraseet' perevod'chika?

We are tourists from England, America, France, Germany, Italy.
Мы тури́сты из Англии, Аме́рики, фра́нции, Герма́нии, Ита́лии.
my tooris'ti iz an'glii, ame'riki, fran'tsii, germa'nii, ita'lii.

We are going to the town of . . .
Мы е́дем в горо́д...
my ye'dyem v gorod' . . .

We have come from the town of . . .
Мы е́дем из го́рода...
my ye'dem iz go'roda . . .

I do not understand Russian.
Я не понима́ю по-русски
ya ne panima'yu paroos'ki.

What is this called in Russian?
как э́то называ́ется по-ру́сски?
kak e'to nazyva'yetsa paroos'ki?

Yes	да	da
No	нет	nyet
Thank you	спаси́бо	spasi'bo
Please	пожалуйста	pazhal'sta
Hello	здра́вствуйте	zdrav'st-vuytye
Good-bye	до свида́ния	dasvidanya
Good	хорошо́	kharasho'
Bad	пло́хо	plo'kho
Much, many	мно́го	mno'go
Little, few	ма́ло	ma'la
When?	когда́	kagda?
Where?	где?	gdye?
Why?	почему́?	pachimoo'?
Quickly	бы́стро	by'stra
Slowly	ме́дленно	myed'lenna
I	я	ya
He	он	on
She	она́	ana'
We	мы	my
You	вы	vy

FIRST AID

In the Soviet Union medical care is free of charge and tourists who fall ill during their trip are also entitled to free medical care. In case you are unwell, notify an Intourist representative and a doctor will be called immediately. There is no charge for the doctor's visit, but the patient pays for any medicines according to standard prices.

There are First Aid Posts and hospitals at regular intervals along the Intourist routes, and in Moscow there is a special clinic which cares for foreign tourists. Its address is Gertsena St. 12, telephone numbers 229–73–23 and 229–03–82. Its staff includes qualified doctors and nurses, and there are X-ray, physiotherapy, dental and other departments.

VOCABULARY

I feel ill
Я плохо себя чувствую.
ya plo'kho syebya' choo'stvuyu

I have a head-, ear-, tooth-, stomach-ache, sore throat.
У меня болит голова, ухо, зуб, живот, горло.
u myenya'baleet'galava', oo'kho, zoob, zhivot', gor'lo

I have a cough, cold, influenza.
У меня кашель, насморк, грипп
u myenya' ka'shyel, na'smork, grip

I have diarrhoea, constipation.
У меня понос, запор.
u myenya' panos', zapor

I have broken my arm, my leg.
Я сломал руку, ногу.
ya slamal roo'ku, no'gu

I have burnt my hand, my leg, my finger.
Я обжёг руку, ногу, палец.
ya abzhog rooku, no'gu, pa'lyets

I have sprained my ankle.
У меня растряжение ноги.
u myenya' rastyazhe'niye naghee'

I have a blister.
Я натёр себе ногу.
ya natyor'sibye'no'gu

I have a rash, a swelling.
У меня сыпь, опухоль.
oo myenya'syp, o'pukhol

She is very tired.
она очень устала.
una o'chyen usta'la

He has a temperature.
У него температура.
oo nyevo' temperatoo'ra

What is the matter with you?
На что вы жалуетесь?
na shto vy zhaloo'yetyes?

Where is the hospital?
где здесь больни́ца?
gdye zdyes balni'tsa?

Call an ambulance.
Позови́те ско́рую по́мощь.
pazovi tye sko'ruyu po'moshch

It is necessary to call a doctor immediately.
ну́жно сро́чно позва́ть врача.
noozh na sroch na pazvat' vracha'

I have lost my appetite.
У меня пропал аппетит.
u myenya' propal' apeteet'.

Fainting fit	óбморок	ob'marok
Infection	инфéкция	infek'tsiya
Burn	ожóг	azhog
Inflammation	воспалéние	vospale'niye
Sprain	вывих	vy'vikh
Convulsion	сýдорога	soo'daraga
Fracture	перелóм	pyerelom
Inoculation	приви́вка	priveev'ka
Anaesthetic	наркóз	narkoz
Dressing	перевя́зка	pyerevyaz'ka
Injection	укóл	ukol'
Nurse	медсестрá	myedsyestra'
Medicines	лекáрства	lekar'stva
An aspirin	áспирин	as'pirin
First aid kit	перевя́зочные срéдства	pyerevya'zochnyye sryedstva
Castor oil	кастóрка	kastor'ka
Disinfectant	дезинфицирýющее срéдство	dizinfitseeroo'yushcheye sryed'stvo
Epsom Salts	англи́йская соль	anglee'skaya sol
Iodine	йод	yod
Ointment	мазь	maz
A pill	пилю́ля	pilyoo'lya
Quinine	хини́н	khineen'
A bandage	бинт	bint
Cotton-wool	вáта	va'ta

PART II

Alphabetical Guide to Towns

ABKHAZIA
See Sukhumi, p. 286

ABRAMTSEVO
See Moscow, p. 232

ALMA-ATA
In Kazakh: Almaty
Population—730,000 (1970). Capital of the
Kazakh Soviet Socialist Republic.

KAZAKHSTAN
Area: 1,064,000 sq. miles
Population—13,000,000 of which 43% are
Russians, 30% Kazakhs and the rest includes
Ukrainians, Tatars and Uzbeks.

Kazakhstan is situated in the middle of the Eurasian continent. It stretches west almost to the R. Volga and the Caspian Sea and eastwards to the Altai Mountains. In the south east it touches along the Chinese border. Its capital is Alma-Ata and the other major towns are Chimkent, Karaganda, Petropavlovsk, Semipalatinsk, Akmolinsk, and Uralsk.

The climate is mostly continental and dry so the country is mainly steppe and semi-desert with forests covering but 5% of the territory. There is black earth in the north, and in the south east are some places with a comparatively mild climate.

Kazakhstan is very rich in minerals including gold, coal, iron ore, copper and several other non-ferrous metals. The principal industries are coal-, iron- and copper-mining, oil extraction and processing, engineering, and chemical industries which have been developed during the last twenty years. Local agriculture is concerned with growing rice, cotton and fruit in the south while in the north cattle-breeding and wheat-growing are predominant. This country was one of the major areas to be developed during the 1953–6 virgin lands campaign.

The Kazakhs originate from the Kypchacs and other Turkic, Mongol and Iranian groups which broke away from the Golden Horde in the middle of the 16th century and migrated to present-day Kazakhstan. They formed three nomadic states here, the Senior Zhouz in the south east, the Middle Zhouz in the northern and central parts, and the Junior Zhouz in the north west. By the middle of the 18th century the Junior and Middle Zhouzes had grown fearful of the strength of the Dzhungar Kalmyks warrior state and sought Russian protection. The Senior Zhouz merged with the Russian Empire in 1846.

The Russian administration almost nullified the power of the Sultans and there were several Kazakh uprisings led by them. In 1916 a strong popular uprising broke out led by a Bolshevik called Amangeldy Imanov. Tsarist troops were diverted from suppressing this entirely because of the revolution which broke out in Petrograd in February, 1917.

In 1920 the Kirghiz Autonomous Republic was set up in the region, in 1925 the area was enlarged and renamed the Kazakh Autonomous Republic and in 1936 it became the Kazakh Soviet Socialist Republic.

Souvenirs from Kazakhstan could include pottery vases, silk chiffon scarves, and holders for tea-glasses, all decorated with traditional local designs.

A few words of Kazakh:

hello	salem
I am a tourist	men tourist
thank you	rakhmet
yes	ya
no	zhok
good	zhaksa
bad	zhaman
I don't understand	men tusinbaimen
Please fetch me an	
interpreter	magan tilmash kerek
good-bye	hosh bolingez
how do you do?	hal kalai

Alma-Ata
Until 1921 Alma-Ata was known as Verny, but it is famous for its Aport apples, which sometimes weigh 500 gm. each, and the name Alma-Ata literally means 'father of apples'.

Alma-Ata lies to the south of the Kazakh Steppe, on the foothills of the snowcapped Zailiysky Alatau range, at 2600 ft. above sea level. China is 300 km. away to the south across the mountains. On either side of Alma-Ata flow the Bolshaya Alma-Atinka and the Malaya Alma-Atinka rivers. In summer the temperature may rise to 40°C. (104°F.) and the winter extreme is −34°C. (−28·1°F.) although it is usually milder than that.

Nomads lived on this site in the centuries B.C. According to the reports of a 7th-century Chinese traveller and of Marco Polo who came this way in the 8th century, later there was a town here. In the 13th and 14th centuries it was of some commercial importance but it was laid waste by the Tatars and never recovered.

In 1854 a military fortress was built as an important strategic point where routes from Central Asia to Siberia and West China crossed. The fortress was situated where ancient settlements had been and was called Zailiiskoye. The following year it was renamed Verny, 'reliable'. Cossack and Tatar settlements sprang up beside the fortress and in 1867 Verny was made a town. During the next thirty years many Russian and Ukrainian families were encouraged to make their homes there, and by a special order of 1870 every house-owner was obliged to plant trees along his part of the street. Today Alma-Ata is known as the Garden City because of this greenery.

In 1887, all but one of the town's 1788 houses were destroyed in an earthquake. Then it was decreed that only single storey houses of wood should be built, except in the centre, where a few two-storey places were allowed. This meant that the earthquake of 1911 was not so disastrous.

In the 1890s Verny began to be used as a place to which political prisoners were exiled. They were behind some of the political demonstrations and strikes in 1905–7. It is recorded that the Town Council in 1915 turned down the proposal to install more street lamps on the grounds that 'respectable citizens stay at home after dusk'.

After the 1917 Revolution Verny was included in the Turkestan Soviet Republic, and in 1921 its name was changed to Alma-Ata. It became the capital of Kazakhstan, instead of Kzyl-Orda, in 1929, and thereafter developed rapidly, especially when the Turksib railway was finished.

Komsomolskaya St. crosses the city from east to west dividing it roughly in half. There are many educational establishments along its 10-km. length. At intersection with the main street, Kommunistichesky Prospect, is the civil and business centre. Alma-Ata's largest buildings are in the blocks nearby lining Kirova, Vinogradova, Mira and Kalinina Streets. The biggest building of all which towers above the others is *Government House*. This five-storey (40 m.) building designed by Rubanenko was recently completed and is decorated with granite and marble. The space in front is used for parades and demonstrations. Opposite stands the former Government House, which now accommodates some university faculties. It was built by Ginzburg in the 1930s in constructivist style. *The University* (founded in 1934) has nine faculties attended by about 9000 students, with a further 3000 taking correspondence courses.

The Kazakh Academy of Sciences, Shevchenko St., was founded in 1946 and supervises over twenty research institutes. The architect of its main building was Schusev.

Kommunistichesky Prospect is a 4-km. avenue which connects the railway station with the upper part of the city. Many government buildings and offices are located here and some modern buildings of concrete and glass are under construction. Nevertheless it is a general rule that new buildings are no higher than five storeys (35% of the new houses will be three-storey and 20% four-storey) and new buildings are designed so as to be proof against earthquakes.

Gorky St. (formerly Trade St.) is the main shopping street.

Alma-Ata is beautifully located with snowy peaks rising up in the hinterland and verdant greenery along the straight, wide streets with little 'ariks' (irrigation canals) flowing beside them.

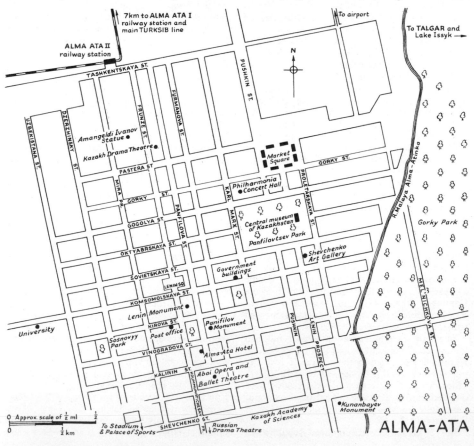

Over ten million trees have been planted here since the city was founded.

The town is laid out rather like a chessboard. 3–5 km. avenues run from north to south, and in the extreme south they begin to climb uphill, so that every block is 4 m. higher than the one before it. There are typical Siberian wooden houses, white-walled Ukrainian houses, and the mudbrick houses of Asia. People spend most of their free time out of doors. The newest parts of the city are the suburbs in the south-west and the north-west.

The city's industries include food, tobacco, engineering, textiles, leather, printing, and film making. Among the souvenirs offered for sale are attractive vases and scarves decorated with traditional national designs.

These five buildings are all open for religious services:

St. Nicholas's Cathedral, Kalinin St. 46. Built in 1914.

Church of Our Lady of Kazan, Malaya Stanitsa

Church of the Intercession, Alma-Ata, 1st district

Mosque, Pushkin St. 16

Synagogue, Proletarskaya St. 48

Other places of interest are: *The Central Museum of Kazakhstan* in Panfilovtsev Park. The museum is housed in the Ascension Cathedral, erected in 1904 by Zenkov. It is the second tallest wooden building in the world; the bell tower of six separate parts is 54·5 m. high and was built without a single nail. The museum has over 40,000 exhibits. Open 10–5; closed Tues.

Shevchenko Art Gallery, Sovietskaya St. 22. The works of Soviet and Western artists hang side by side with those of local painters. Open 10–6.30; closed on the last two days of each month.

Observatory, in Malo-Almatinskoye Uscheliye, 12 km. from Alma-Ata

Kunanbayev Monument, Abaya Prospect. Abai Kunanbayev (1845–1904) is the Kazakh poet and composer who is honoured as the creator of the Kazakh literary language.

Amangeldi Imanov Equestrian Statue, in a garden off Kommunistichesky Prospect, opposite the Kazakh Drama Theatre. Amangeldi Imanov (1873–1919) was a local hero who led the national independence campaign in 1916. He later became a Communist. The statue by Askar-Sarydzha was unveiled in 1950.

Lenin Monument, Lenin Sq. The sculptor of the 7 m. statue was Vuchetich.

Panfilov Monument, Panfilova St. Major-General Panfilov was sent with his division from Alma-Ata to help defend Moscow in 1941. Twenty-eight men withstood an attack by fifty German tanks and were justly awarded the title of Heroes of the Soviet Union.

Dzerzhinsky Monument, Dzerzhinsky St

Bust of Pavel Vinogradov, in front of the Russian Drama Theatre. Vinogradov was the head of the first Bolshevik organisation in this area.

Bust of Lugansky, Kommunistichesky Prospect, in front of the Town Hall. Sergei Lugansky was a pilot who became a national hero during World War II.

Abai Opera and Ballet Theatre, Kalinina St. 112. The company was founded in 1934. Then Prostakov, the designer, had the theatre built in 1941. It seats 1250. Local Kazakh colours and ornaments were used for the decor.

Russian Drama Theatre, at the crossing of Dzerzhinskova and Vinogradova Streets.

Kazakh Drama Theatre, Kommunistichesky Prospect. The company was founded in 1926 and the theatre built in 1962.

Youth Theatre, Kalinina St. 81

Circus, Mechnikova St., near the stadium. Performances during the summer only.

Philharmonia Concert Hall. The Kurmangazi Orchestra of National Instruments gives concerts here.

Palace of Sports, at the crossing of Lenin and Abai Prospects. This large, modern building was opened in 1970 for the Lenin centenary. In many ways it resembles the Palace of Congresses in the Moscow Kremlin. There is a hall with 3,000 seats and although it is called the Palace of Sports, it is also used for political meetings and artistic performances. It is considered the finest piece of architecture in the Kazakh capital.

Agricultural and Industrial Exhibition, Timiryazeva St. The exhibition is housed in three pavilions.

Urozhai (harvest) Stadium, Mechnikova St. This stadium seats 35,000.

Artificial Lake, near the airport. The construction of this lake was finished in 1961. Now there are 35 hectares (87 acres) of bathing beaches. Boats can be hired.

Gorky Park, Gogolya St., in the eastern part of the city on the right bank of R. Malaya Alma-Atinka. Here is the Aral restaurant. There are also cafés, and a restaurant serving Kazakh national food. Here too boats can be hired. There is a dance hall, the 'Spartak' stadium, an open air theatre and a children's railway, called the Small Turksib Rly. The park covers 7 hectares (17·5 acres), and the oldest part of it was planted as a public garden in 1866. The beautiful central avenue is over a mile long.

Zoo, Klevernaya St. 126. The zoo, which is near Gorky Park, was founded in 1937.

Children's Park, Kalinina St., in Pine Park. There is a newly-built House of Pioneers here.

Kazakhstan Hotel and Restaurant (Intourist), Kommunistichesky Prospect, 49. TEL. 9–21–26. There is a swimming pool in the courtyard.

Alma-Ata Hotel, Panfilova St. 119

Ala-Tau Hotel, Kirova St. 142

Issyk Restaurant, Panfilova St. 133

Dzhetysu Restaurant, Panfilovtsev Park

Aral Restaurant, Gorky Park

Ice-cream parlour, at the crossing of Kalinina and Baiseitova Streets

G.P.O., Kirova St. 134

Bank, Panfilova St.

Central Department Store, Kommunistichesky Prospect 52, opposite the 'Kazakhstan' Hotel

Book shop, Karl Marx St. 68

Jeweller's, Karl Marx St. 48

Souvenirs, Furmanova St. 105

Souvenir kiosk, Kirova St., in a park opposite the main building of the University.

Market, Proletarskaya St. 48. If Aport apples are not available in the restaurants, they can easily be bought here during the season.

Children's World Department Store, at the crossing of Kommunisticheskaya Prospect and Komsomolskaya St.

Taxi ranks, at the crossing of Tulebayeva and Gorky Streets, at the crossing of Kalinina and Baiseitova Streets, near the central market and the railway station.

Skating rink, 22 km. from the city, up in the mountains on the left bank of R. Malaya Alma-Atinka. This skating rink, 5380 ft. above sea level, is used for international competitions and the surrounding slopes are used for skiing in winter and for climbing in summer.

Lake Issyk

Not to be confused with Lake Issyk-Kul in Kirghizia, this is a spot worthy of visiting up in the mountains, 60 km. east of Alma-Ata. On the way up to the lake, at the 8 km. mark is an obelisk where Mikhail Kalinin as President of the U.S.S.R. gave the Kalinin Collective Farm the charter to its land in 1935. At 11 km. stands a monument to the Bolsheviks, Alexandr Berezovsky and Karp Ovcharov, who were shot here in 1917 during the Civil War. At 12 km. to the right of the road an obelisk marks the place where General Panfilov's division, known for its brave part in the defence of Moscow in 1941, was formed. At 18 km. in good weather there is a view of Talgar Peak, at 5017 m. the highest point of the Zailiyskiy Alatau. At 21 km. to the left stands a monument to the soldiers who fell in 1918 during the Civil War.

At 23 km. is the small town of *Talgar* (pop. 30,000), which was formerly the Cossack village of Sofiyskaya. Nearby are the remains of a 10th–14th century fortress which stood on the trade route to China. There is a restaurant on the main street in Talgar.

The road runs through attractive country with orchards and vineyards and excellent panoramic views. At 46 km. from Alma-Ata is the village of Issyk, formerly known as the Cossack settlement of Nadezhdinskaya, and from here a side road runs 14 km. to the lake. Up at a height of 1620 m. is the small white rotunda known as the 'Pavilion of Air'.

Lake Issyk was formed in the Tan-Shan Mountains 1780 m. above sea level about 8000 years ago when a landslide blocked R. Issyk. The area of the lake is 1 sq. km., its length 1850 m., its width 780 m. and its depth 57 m. The lowest water level is in April and it rises 15 m to its highest in August when the waterfall is at its best. The colour of the water is greenish-blue, but it may change during the course of the day from deep blue to light green. It is very cold, the maximum temperature in July being only 9°C. (48°F.). Some of the more hardy locals are courageous enough to go swimming but it is not recommended on the northern shore. At Malinovaya Bukhta (Raspberry Bay) and other places along the eastern shore where the water is a little warmer. There are no fish in the lake, a phenomenon which still puzzles scientists. In the neighbouring river, however, there are excellent trout.

Beside the lake is a hotel, restaurant, and a café. Boats can be hired out.

Dzhabayev Museum, 70 km. from Alma-Ata. The Kazakh poet, Dzhambul Dzhabayev (1846–1945), spent his last years here and his single-storey house has been opened as a museum. His mausoleum is nearby.

ALUPKA

See Crimean Circular Route, p. 89

ALUSHTA

See Crimean Circular Route, p. 83

ARKHANGELSKOYE

See Moscow, p. 232

ARMENIA

See Erevan, p. 98

ASHKHABAD

Population—253,000 (1970). Capital of the Turkmeni Soviet Socialist Republic.

TURKMENISTAN, TURKMENIA

Population—2,160,000. There are people of 70 different nationalities here, with Turkmens making up 62% of them. The rest include Russians, Kazakhs, Armenians, Baluchi, and Kurds. The Turkmens originated from Caucasian cattle-breeding tribes who lived in the steppes and from Turkic nomads of Mongolian stock who came from the east.

Turkmenia is the southernmost republic of the Soviet Union. Its borders reach down to Iran and Afghanistan. The greater part of its territory is taken up by the vast Kara-Kum (black sands) Desert and the majority of the population lives in oases stretching along the rivers and canals. Water has always been a problem in these parts, but the situation has been alleviated to a great extent by the building of the Kara-Kum Canal that already runs for 1000 km. There are wide-scale experiments in progress in distilling fresh water from the Caspian, using atomic installations, but in the meantime fresh water is still shipped across the Caspian Sea from the Caucasian coast to the Turkmeni port of Krasnovodsk and in many parts of the republic people rely on traditional methods of collecting snow and rainwater.

Present-day Turkmenistan was once the site of the powerful states of Parthia, Bactria, Khorezm, and Margiana. There were prosperous towns and cities where outstanding scholars, poets and architects lived and worked. The course of history was suddenly changed in the 13th century by the devastating invasion of Genghis-Khan.

Between the 17th and 19th centuries, Turkmenistan was fought for by Persian shahs, Khivan khans, the emirs of Bukhara, and the rulers of Afghanistan. In the late 19th century it became part of the Russian Empire. Soviet rule was proclaimed here in 1917 but in 1918 the region was occupied by British troops. Civil war lasted until 1920 and in February 1925 the Turkmeni Soviet Socialist Republic was formed.

The climate here is very hot and dry. The average temperature for July is 29°C. (84°F.) In winter the sky is usually clear but sometimes the temperature drops in the northern regions to −29°C. (−20°F.). Depending upon the geography, above-zero temperatures usually last from 193–276 days each year. The mountains encircling Turkmenia are considered young, and earthquakes are frequent. The most powerful tremors registered (force 10) were in 1895 in the Krasnovodsk area and in 1948 in the capital city of Ashkhabad when the place was completely devastated in less than a minute.

The traditional dwelling of the nomadic Turkmen tribes was the 'yurta' or 'kara-oi', a collapsible tent formed by an intricate wooden framework covered with rush mats and felt. Inside the yurta were laid gaily-coloured rugs and the walls were hung with tapestry and woven bags where clothes and household utensils were kept. Although today most people live in brick houses with a covered terrace on the shady side, the yurta is still very much in evidence. It is often set up near the house as a summer dwelling.

Following ancient tradition, the Turkmens greatly enjoy organising a festival called a 'toi' to mark a wedding, the birth of a child (formerly only the birth of a boy baby, but now girls are honoured too), harvest time, and other family and social events. The guests at a toi are given refreshments, and are entertained by horse racing, wrestling bouts and other games.

National dishes include 'kara-chorbe' (peppery meat soup) and 'fitchi' (meat pies). As in the other republics of Central Asia, 'chok-chai' (green tea) is drunk after meals, but there are also some pleasant local wines for there is a wine factory in Ashkhabad. 'Yasman-salik' is a very sweet sherry-type wine which won a gold medal in Belgrade in 1956. Among others worthy of recommendation are 'Kara-uzyum' and 'Ter-bash'.

National costumes are now giving way to European dress, but many men still wear red or crimson robes over a white shirt and have high, shaggy sheepskin hats or smaller ones of astrakhan. The women wear a long sack-dress and narrow trousers trimmed with a band of embroidery at the ankle. The head-dress is decorated with coins and pendants and their national silver jewellery is very striking, especially the heavy bracelets and brooches set with semi-precious stones.

Mosques where services are held can be found throughout the republic. The Turkmens have followed Islam since the 10th century. They belong to the Sunnite sect of Mohammedanism and are led by Iman-Khatib of the Talhatan-Baba mosque, who represents the Ecclesiastical Board of Moslems in Central Asia and Kazakhstan. Many still make the traditional pilgrimage to Mecca, to the Kaaba Temple.

Oil is Turkmenia's basic source of wealth. The republic holds third place in U.S.S.R. oil production, after the Russian Federation and Azerbaijan. But its fame comes from the rugs which are exported to over 50 countries and are admired by all visitors. Turkmeni carpet weaving involves truly artistic workmanship. It is said here, 'Spread out your rug and I will read your heart.' Often known in Europe as Bukhara rugs, the Turkmenian rugs are richly coloured, as a rule in different shades of red. The designs, which are strictly geometrical, vary from tribe to tribe. The republic is also famous for astrakhan pelts (called 'karakul' here) and for its horses. The annual output of pelts is the largest in the Soviet Union: 1,300,000. Particularly valued are the pure white ones which have a moiré effect and look pearly in the sunlight. Strange as it may seem, it is the severe desert conditions and particularly the scantiness of water and fodder that ensure the high quality of karakul. Local pelts are said to retain their qualities for as long as 50 years. Turkmenian horses have long been exported to the east and to Europe. The Argamak (Akal-Teke) strain is particularly beautiful and has great endurance. It was used to breed Arab, English and Persian horses among others.

A nomadic way of life does not leave much opportunity for schooling and it is recorded that before 1917 only seven in every thousand Turkmen were literate. Illiteracy has been almost completely overcome and, a significant sign of the progress of this Asian people, the 171,000 children now attending school include 74,000 girls. The Turkmen used to write in Arabic and then changed to Latin letters before changing again, this time to Cyrillic, in 1930; the Turkmeni alphabet includes five extra letters.

Some words of Turkmeni:

hello	se'lam
I am a tourist	men turist
please	bash uthtene
thank you	sag bol
yes	hova
no	yok
good	govi
bad	ervet
I don't understand	men dushemok
please fetch an interpreter for me	manya dilmachi chagerung
good-bye	hosh sag bolin
how do you do?	kaiplering nakhili

Ashkhabad

Between 1921 and 1924 Ashkhabad was known as Poltoratsk, and then it resumed its former name. The legend of the city's name is as follows:

Once upon a time there was a young girl by the name of Amu, meaning 'desirable', and a boy called Ashik, meaning 'love'. The ill-fated young couple made Allah angry and so he turned the girl into a river and the young man into a city, soon to be called Ashik-abad or Ashkhabad, 'city-in-love'. A desert lay between them and the lovers never had a chance to meet. Ashkhabad suffered from thirst but Amu, whose water overflowed, was powerless to help her beloved.

The story is frequently retold today now that the Kara-Kum Canal brings the waters of the R. Amu-Darya to Ashkhabad. The Turkmeni proverb says, 'Water is more precious than diamonds' and the people relate that when all the peoples of the world were awaiting the gifts of God, they themselves had an abundance of sun and fertile earth, but were unlucky with water. Throughout the centuries they have had to strive with Allah for their right to have water. The new canal runs for nearly 1,000 km. past once desolate places with names like Cursed-by-God and No-Road.

The city of Ashkhabad stands in the centre of the Akhal-Teke Oasis. On the northern side, the Kara-Kum Desert comes right in close to the city, and to the south the Kopet-Dag Mountains form an encircling amphitheatre. The climate here is of the dry, continental type, with autumn as the most pleasant season. Summer temperatures average 40–45°C. (104–113°F.) in the shade, and in the open 60–70°C. (140–158°F.) or even higher, making it the hottest place in the Soviet Union. There is no rain at all during the summer months.

Ashkhabad was founded in 1881 by the Russians on the site of a village called Askhabad. The place had been taken without a single shot by Russian General Mikhail Skobelev (1843–1882) and for many years served as a Russian military stronghold in the area. The first civilians to settle were Russian traders and retired servicemen. Other nationalities included Persians, Armenians, and Jews. It is recorded that in 1886 every second man was a member of a merchant family. The population rose rapidly with the construction of the railway, but halted for a short time in 1892 because of a cholera epidemic. Trade with Persia stimulated business and Ashkhabad stood on the crossroads of the trade routes. A considerable proportion of Soviet-Iranian trade still goes through this city which lies 40 km. from the Iranian border.

It was the railway workers who were responsible for the strikes here in 1905–7 and soon after the 1917 Revolution, in the December of that year, Soviet power was established. This was overthrown, then the city was run by Muslim nationalists and anti-Bolshevik representatives, known as the Trans-Caspian Government; the British at that time supported the anti-Bolshevik forces here in Ashkhabad. Soviet power was restored in 1919 and the city renamed Poltoratsk in honour of Commissar Pavel Poltoratsky who was

Central ASHKHABAD

shot during the revolt. The following year the city was made the centre of the Turkmenia Region, becoming the capital of Turkmenia in 1924.

The fortress in the centre became the focal point of the new town. It used to stand on the small hill behind the 'Turkmenistan' Hotel; the military barracks had to be accommodated too. Consequently radial streets fanned out to the south, the south-west and the west and also ran parallel to the railway line. The area of the city now measures nearly 6000 hectares (2,500 acres). The distance across it from north-east to south-west is about 22 km. The majority of the population lives in the hilly south-western sector while the north is mostly occupied by offices, colleges, and factories. Following the earthquake in 1929 the Institute of Anti-Seismatic Construction has played an important role in the growth of the city. Builders now use a great deal of ferro-concrete and one building incorporates springs in its foundations. A terrible nine-point earthquake with its epicentre only 25 km. south-east of the city occurred on the night of 5 October 1948, and ruined the city, especially the houses made from mud bricks and roofs. The local museum was one of the few buildings to remain standing. After the earthquake the factories were moved out to the suburbs and new houses were designed to withstand any future earthquake. The buildings sprang up along the same street plan as before because of the trees and drainage channels, which had not been disturbed. The city is now twice the size it was before the earthquake. There are fifty industrial enterprises producing food, carpets, glass, and machinery. Gorky University was founded in 1960. Together with agricultural and medical institutes and other colleges, 10,000 students are catered for. This is a considerable achievement when one realises that before the revolution of 1917 not a single Turkman had higher education. The local Academy of Sciences controls twelve research institutes. Its main building is a large block in Gogol St. In front of the Academy will stand a monument to Makhtumkuli, the 18th-century philosopher and poet who is considered the founder of Turkmeni literature.

The Communist Party Headquarters in Karl Marx St. is decorated with traditional local designs. In Karl Marx Sq. (formerly known as Skobolev Sq.) a fountain and flowerbeds are being laid out following the designs of the local carpets. The buildings around this square include the Town Hall, Aeroflot's offices, the Turkmeni Ministry of Culture, the Central Library, and the main bank. From here streets fan out to the centre of the city and to the suburbs. Gogol St. crosses the city's three main streets, First-of-May, Engels, and Svobodi Prospect. The offices of the Supreme Soviet and the Council of Ministers, decorated with national designs, stand on Gogol St. near the 'Turkmenistan' Hotel and opposite is the Khudozhestvenny Cinema.

Fine Art Museum, Svobodi Prospect 84. Open 12–7; closed Thurs. The collection was founded in 1939 and now the six thousand exhibits include paintings, sculpture, and graphics by local, Russian, and foreign artists. There are examples of local craftsmanship, perhaps the most interesting of which are the carpets. The pride of the museum is an enormous carpet of 192 sq. m. There is also a collection of Eastern works of art.

Local Museum, Babaeva St. 2. Open 12–7; closed Thurs.

Carpet Factory and Museum, Liebknecht St. 23, where it crosses Svobodi Prospect. Here about two hundred workers are trained and employed to produce what are known throughout the world as Bukhara carpets. In fact every Turkmeni tribe had its own carpet ornament and these are faithfully reproduced today. Most popular of all have always been the Tekke carpets, but the name of Bukhara was used to describe them because they were marketed there. Many of the local girls working here wear their national dress. The sharp curved knife they use for cutting the wool is called a 'kesser'. The museum is up on the first floor. Among the exhibits are reversible carpet portraits. Among the local souvenirs manufactured here are tiny carpets, carpet chair seats, handbags and other articles all woven in authentic designs.

Lenin Monument, in Lenin Garden. The bronze statue of Lenin pointing to the east by Tripolskaya was unveiled in 1927. The unusual pedestal is decorated with carpet patterns executed in majolica tiles. Beside the monument is the *Lenin Museum*.

Makhtumkuli Monument, near the theatre. Makhtumkuli (1730–1780s), also known as Fragi, was a poet and philosopher, and founder of Turkmeni classical literature. He pleaded for unity among the warring Turkmeni tribes and maintained a hostile attitude to the local religious leaders.

War Memorials, in the garden between Universitetskaya and Karl Marx Squares. One is dedicated to soldiers of World War II and the other to revolutionary fighters.

Turkmen Drama Theatre, Prospect Svobodi, at the corner of Pushkin St. The building is embellished with local designs and colours.

Makhtumkuli Opera and Ballet Theatre, Engelsa St. 9. This theatre was founded in 1941.

Pushkin Russian Drama Theatre, Pervomaiskaya St. 9a. Founded 1926.

Philharmonic Society, Engelsa St. 13. This comprises a choir, a dance ensemble, and an orchestra of national instruments.

Ashkhabad's oldest park is the one with the longest name: the Twentieth Anniversary of the Founding of the Young Communist League Park. Here there is a Summer Theatre, a restaurant providing shashliks and lyula-kebabs, an amusement arcade, a sports area, and a statue of Lenin. Its address is Svobodi Prospect 69.

Kirov Park, Svobodi Prospect

Soviet Army Officers' Park, in front of the University

Botanical Garden, Timirazeva St. This garden was founded in 1930 and now contains about a thousand different species of trees and shrubs. There are Victoria water lilies, cacti, and palms. Opposite is the Kalinin Agricultural Institute.

Republic Stadium, opposite the wine factory

Sad Keshi Botanical Garden, Pervomaiskaya St.

Turkmenistan Hotel and Restaurant, (Intourist) Gogol St. 19. TEL. 58–35

Ashkhabad Hotel and Restaurant, Krimskaya St. 72/2; TEL. 21–36

Oktyabrskaya Hotel and Restaurant, Lenin Prospect; TEL. 65–28

Kolkhozchi Hotel and Restaurant, Engelsa St.; TEL. 34–26

Gulistan Restaurant, Pervomayskaya St., at the crossing with Liebknecht St.; the restaurant is on the first floor, while the ground floor is run as a café.

Gorka Shashlik Bar, on the small hill behind the 'Turkmenistan' Hotel. This is in the open-air.

Milk Bar, at the east end of Svobodi Prospect

Shashlik Bar and Slot-machine Café, Engels St., at the corner of Kalinina St. This is also open-air.

There are tea rooms in all the markets.

Bank, Svobodi Prospect 73

Telephone and Telegraph Office, Engelsa St. 18

G.P.O., at the crossing of Karl Liebknecht St. and Mopr St. Liebknecht St. is in the centre of the main shopping area. Here are:

Department store, at the crossing with Pervomayskaya St.

Podarki Gift Shop

Jeweller's

Vostok Food Shop

Central Bookshop, Zhitnikova St. 40

Secondhand Bookshop, Engels St

Paintings and Objets d'Art, Pyervomaiskaya St. and Karl Marx St. 14

Taxi rank, in front of the Makhtumkuli Opera and Ballet Theatre.

Annau

12 km. to the west of Ashkhabad, an interesting trip out for those interested in old civilisations. The site was inhabited from the 3rd to the 1st centuries B.C. Excavations began in 1904 when an American archaeologist, Pempelli, launched an expedition. Clay pillars, the remains of ancient towns, are scattered between the mountains and the railway line. The remains of a mausoleum stand on one of the slopes; it is supposed to have been built by a great-grandson of Timur. A mosque was built there in 1455 by Khan Abdul Qasim-Babir and was destroyed by the earthquake of 1948. Excavations have revealed that one of the embankments near the mausoleum was erected in the 3rd century B.C., immediately after the decline of Alexander the Great's empire.

Water Sport Park, 15 km. out of Ashkhabad. The fine beaches here date from the completion of the third section of the Kara-Kum Canal on 12 May, 1962.

ASKANIA-NOVA

See Kherson, p. 138

ASTRAKHAN

(Formerly Khadzhi-Tarkhan). Population—411,000 (1970)

Astrakhan lies 22 m. below sea level on a huge island in the Volga delta. Although it is over 100 km. from the Caspian Sea, it still serves as both a river and a sea port. It is bounded on one side by the main stream of the Volga and on the other by a large branch known as R. Bolda. To the south numerous watercourses run from the Bolda back into the Volga, so forming the island. In addition R. Kutum divides the city into two parts which are linked by more than thirty bridges. The central part is on the left bank and the industrial section on the right. 75 km. of dykes protect the city from the Volga's floodwater, because the lowest buildings are only 4 m. above the normal water level.

The hottest time of the year here is in July and August when the temperature may be as high as 40°C.

Astrakhan was founded in the 13th century at the time when the Mongols reached this area. The first settlement was on the right bank of the Volga, but it was ruined in 1395 by Timur (Tamerlane). The town revived and served as the capital of the Astrakhan Khanate (1460–1556). When Ivan the Terrible conquered Kazan in 1552, the Russians easily took the territory along the Volga too. The last Khan of Astrakhan, Derbish-Ali, fled, and the town was taken without any resistance at all. Thus Russia gained access to the Caspian Sea and also held the whole of the Volga; Ivan the Terrible added Tsar of Astrakhan to his other titles.

Astrakhan had neither natural defences nor good fortifications, so it was decided to build a new town at Zayachi Bugor on the left bank of the river. The fortress was built in 1558 and this is the date usually given for the foundation of the city.

In the 17th century the town played an important part in trade with the Caucasus, Central Asia, Persia, and India. It was known for the way it supported the peasants' revolts, particularly that of Bolotnikov (1606–7). It was Stepan Razin's last stronghold in 1670–1. A local revolt against the reforms of Peter the Great was violently put down in 1705, and later Peter the Great used Astrakhan as his base in his Persian campaign.

In 1714 shipbuilding yards were opened for the construction of the Caspian fleet, and from here Russian influence spread, primarily by trade, to the Caucasus, Turkestan, and Persia. By the first half of the 19th century Russia had penetrated so far to the south and to the east that Astrakhan lost its importance as a trading centre with these areas, but the amount of internal trading traffic passing through the city increased immensely.

The fishing industry of Astrakhan has always been a source of its wealth; today more than half the adult population is employed in some aspect of the fishing industry. Because of the abundance of fish, the waters of Astrakhan were known as the 'golden depths' and at the beginning of this century one third of the total Russian catch was taken here. As Astrakhan grew many British, French, Swedish and other foreign companies saw fit to invest their capital in the city's economy.

There are over 60 valuable types of fish caught here and today, apart from catching fish, local industries include canning and smoking fish, preparing caviar, shipbuilding, the manufacture of building materials, and various branches of the food industry. The cannery at Avgustovskaya St. 25 is one of the largest of its kind in the U.S.S.R. There is also a marine school here, medical and pedagogical institutes, and an institute for the study of the fish industry.

Kremlin, Zayachy Hill. This white-walled fortress dates from the 16th century and the Uspensky (Assumption) Cathedral inside, in Russian Baroque style, was built in 1700. The city's old bridge with dozens of arches is over two miles long.

Spaso-Preobrazhenski (Transfiguration) Monastery, at the crossing of Trusova and Kommunisticheskaya Streets. Here stands one of the original corner towers of the monastery which was founded in 1597.

The Yacht Club, Krasnaya Naberezhnaya 2. This typical 19th-century house was formerly the Merchants' Stock Exchange.

House of Pioneers, Krasnaya Naberezhnaya 7. Another 19th-century house which belonged to a wealthy timber merchant named Gubin.

The Governor's House, Sovietskaya St. 5. This is now the local party building.

Chernishevsky House, Chernichevskova St. 4. There is a plaque on the wall commemorating the time in 1883 when the Russian philosopher, Nikolai Chernishevsky, lived here in exile.

Ulyanovs' House, Ulyanov St. 9. This two-storey house belonged to Lenin's grandfather; a plaque on the wall lists the Ulyanov family.

Local Museum, Sovietskaya St. 15. Open 11–6; closed Thurs. The museum was founded in 1897. It has a natural history section and also covers pre-revolutionary and Soviet happenings.

Kirov Museum, Trusova St. 45. Open 11–6; closed Thurs.

Kustodiev Picture Gallery, Sverdlova St. 81. Open 11–5; closed Mon. Founded in 1918. On the second floor is a collection of Old Russian art which includes some fine icons. The first floor has contemporary art from the beginning of the present century. The ground floor has more Soviet art and also two halls devoted to Oriental and Western art. The gallery was named after Boris Kustodiev (1878–1927) the artist. He was a pupil of Repin. His works are displayed in a separate room.

Monument to Seamen who fell during the Civil War, in Morskoi Sad (Marine Garden) at the end of Sovietskaya St. The monument takes the form of a lighthouse with two guns on either side. It was designed by the architect Nikolayev and unveiled in 1921. It stands over the seamen's graves.

Kirov Monument, Kirov Garden. The 3·5 m. bronze figure by Tomsky is a copy of the one in Leningrad. It was unveiled in 1939.

Trusov Monument, Trusov Garden. Alexander Trusov (1888–1919) was a revolutionary.

Monument to victims of the Civil War, Bratsky Garden. This monument was unveiled in 1918 and there is also an obelisk dedicated to the memory of those who fell in World War II.

Kirov Drama Theatre, Sovietskaya St. 28. The theatre which can seat 910 was built in 1883. The company has a history going back to 1810, almost as long as any provincial Russian theatre.

Karl Marx Summer Drama Theatre, Kalinina St. 51, in Karl Marx Park. This wooden theatre, painted in pink and green, was built 70 years ago by an unknown architect. It was originally called the Arcadia Theatre.

Youth Theatre, Burova St. 18

Philharmonia, Kirova St. 32

Karl Marx Park, Kalinina St. 51

Lenin Park, Respublikanskaya St.

Gorky Park, by the river

Trud (labour) Stadium, Strelka Boldy

Open air Swimming Pool, Dzerzhinskova St. 1

Swimming Baths, Kuibisheva St. 3

Yacht Club, Krasnaya Naberezhnaya 2

Astrakhanskaya Hotel & Volga Restaurant, Ulyanova St. 6; TEL. 26–62

Novo-Moskovskaya Hotel & Restaurant, Sovietskaya St. 4; TEL. 26–77

Leto Restaurant, Kalinina St. 51, in Marx Park

Leto Café Gorky St. 3/4

Café, Kirova St. 17

Café, Aladina St. 8

Shashlik Bar, Krasnova Znameni St. 12

G.P.O. and Telegraph Office, Kirova St. 27/10

Department Store, Kirova St. 7

Bookshop, Kirova St. 20

Taxi Rank, Oktyabrskaya Sq.

Fourteen hours downstream towards the Caspian Sea is *The Bird Sanctuary*. It was founded in 1940 and is now well populated with egrets, ibis, black herons, coots, spoonbills, and pelicans. There are lotuses and yellow water lilies flowering there in August, but at that time it is also extremely hot and humid. There is a legend about the origin of the lotus flowers:

Once there lived a khan whose lovely wife, Astra, fell ill. It was feared that she would die, but the khan heard that far away in the east there was a country where a beautiful flower grew, the fragrance of which would cure his wife. He travelled to India and brought back some lotus seeds, but his wife was already dead and so he threw the seeds into the water.

AZERBAIJAN
See Baku, p. 56

BAIKAL
See Irkutsk, p. 120

BAKHCHISERAI
See Crimean Circular Route, p. 90

BAKU

(In Azerbaijani: Baki) Population—1,261,000 (1970). Capital of the Azerbaijan Soviet Socialist Republic.

AZERBAIJAN

Area: 33,400 sq. miles. Population—5,177,000 (1970) of which 67% are Azerbaijanis, who are Turkic speaking people, 14% are Russians, and 12% are Armenians.

Azerbaijan is situated in eastern Transcaucasia. Its capital is Baku and other large towns include Kirovabad and Sumgait.

The country used to be the stronghold of the magians, or fireworshippers. They had temples here and tended perpetual flames, and from this the place got its name, for 'azer' means 'fire'.

In the 3rd century A.D. it fell under Persian domination, after 641 A.D. the Moslems invaded it, and in the 8th century it was conquered by the Arabs. From the 11th century it was under the Seljuk Turks until it was overrun by the Mongols, under Genghis-Khan in the 13th century and Timur in the 14th.

In the 15th century the area consisted of several Turkic-speaking Azerbaijan states and for the next three hundred years it was the object of rivalry between Persia and Turkey. In 1723–35 part of the country belonged to Russia, but it became part of the Russian Empire only in 1828, after the Russo-Persian War.

Soviet power was established in Azerbaijan after the Russian revolution of 1917 but was followed for a short time by a parliamentary republic which existed until 1920. Then with the help of the Red Army Soviet power was re-established and Azerbaijan joined the Transcaucasian Soviet Federative Socialist Republic until, in 1936 upon the abolition of the Federation, it became a Union Republic of the U.S.S.R.

Local dishes include 'doga', which is a soup of rice, peas, herbs, and sour milk, and 'bozartma', which is mutton stew. Attractive souvenirs are the shawls with bright designs printed on fine, woollen material.

Turkey changed its alphabet from Arabic to Latin letters in 1926, but in Azerbaijan the change was not made until 1929. The second change, to the Cyrillic alphabet, was made in 1940. At school, children have the opportunity to study Turkish, Arabic, and Persian.

Here are a few words of Azerbaijani:

hello	salaam aleihum
I am a tourist	man turistam
please	buyurun
thank you	sakh olun
yes	bali
no	khe-ish
good	yakhshi
bad	pees
I don't understand	basha dushmuram
please fetch me an interpreter	mana tardzhumachi charurun
good-bye	alvida
how do you do?	nedzhsineez

Baku

The name of the city of Baku comes from the Persian 'badkube', meaning a squall blown up by mountain winds.

Baku rises up from the seashore forming an amphitheatre on the southern coast of the Peninsula of Apsheron and the western coast of the Caspian Sea. The climate is dry, and strong northerly winds (khazri) blow frequently. The summer is hot with an average temperature in July and August of 26°C. (79°F.), and the short winter is mild with an average January temperature of 3°C. (38°F.).

Local naptha springs have been known here for many hundreds of years. Although the first written record of a town on this site dates from the 9th century, some historians consider it was in fact founded in the 5th or 6th century during the rule of the Persian Sassanid dynasty. Some say that there was a city called Gagara on this site not later than the 4th century. The area belonged first to the Arabs, secondly to the Shirvan Khans, then to the Turks from 1583–1606, next to the Persians under whom the Baku Khanate was founded in 1747, and from 1806 it became Russian. (It had in fact been subject to Russia before, between 1723 and 1735, but was returned to Persia.)

Before the revolution Baku was the scene of active revolutionary work. A series of strikes between 1903 and 1907 led to the signing of the first agreement in Russia between workers and oil industrialists. In 1914 nearly 50,000 workers went out on strike. Soviet power was established in 1917, but from 1918 to 1920 when the town was taken by the Red Army, Baku was the centre of the anti-Bolshevik Azerbaijan Republic run by the Mussavat Muslim Party (which was pan-Islamic and pro-Turkish and supported by British and Turkish troops).

The population of the city is principally Azerbaijani, Russian, and Armenian. The Azerbaijani language is very similar to Turkish but today the Cyrillic alphabet is used. Baku is expanding rapidly nowadays. A hundred years ago the population was 14,000, in 1914 it was 200,000, now it is more than a million.

Baku's present prosperity is chiefly due to the oil. The oil fields started to be exploited in the 1870s and at the beginning of this century the Apsheron Peninsula held an important place in the world's oil production. Most of the refineries and the oil trade were in foreign hands. So were the largest plants—the Nobel and the Rothschild. Since 1935 oil has been obtained from the sea bed by building artificial islands in the open sea. From Baku an oil pipeline now runs to the port of Batumi on the Black Sea coast.

Baku is itself one of the largest ports in the

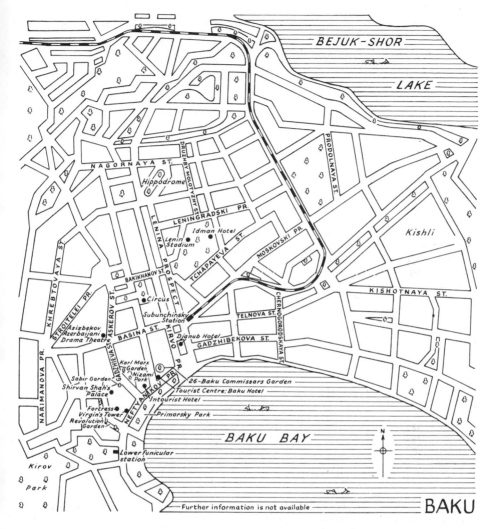

BAKU

— Further information is not available —

U.S.S.R. It is about 350 km. from the Iranian port of Pekhlevi and Soviet ships sail to and fro about four times a month, the one-way trip taking about 18 hours.

The town's industry is primarily dependent on oil; there are refineries, cracking plants and engineering works. Besides these, however, there are flourishing chemical and food industries.

Government House is an imposing twelve-storey building with one thousand rooms on the north side of the bay where there were once goods depots. It was designed by Rudnev and Munts and also houses the local ministries. The large, but strangely misnamed, *Central Square* in front of it is used for parades and festivities. The busiest places in the centre of town are in fact *Zabaidke* and *Kommunisticheskaya Streets*.

The Azerbaijani Academy of Sciences stands on Kommunisticheskaya St. Known as 'Ismailiye', it was built in 1910 at the behest of oil millionaire,

Musa Nagiev, in memory of his son. At that time it was used by a charitable society. Baku is also the location of Kirov University, 91 scientific research institutes, and a polytechnical institute with five faculties and 3000 students. 70,000 other students are studying in Baku too, although not all are engaged full time. The Akhundov Library in a new building at 26 Baku Commissars St. has three million books.

On Nizami St. stands one of Baku's largest structures, a *skyscraper block of flats*. It was built in the 1930s when a great deal of building was going on. There was more after the Second World War. Gadzhiev St. is an old street that has been completely reconstructed so that it is now double its former width. It ends in Dmitrov Sq. and it was the first street in Baku to be built according to a single architectural plan. There are many other new buildings to see, including the *Pyotr Montin Settlement*, just outside Baku.

The Town Hall, Kommunisticheskaya St., was built in 1870 as the Duma building. There is a pretty clock over the entrance and the coat-of-arms of Baku is used as a motif on the walls. The building now used as the House of Pioneers was built in the early 20th century by a rich merchant. On Neftyanikov (oilworkers) Prospect, the road which runs around the bay close to the sea, is a *chess pavilion* built in the same style as a pavilion at the World Fair in Brussels. Further along the avenue, beside the sea is a *parachute tower*, 73 m. high.

Subunchinsky Railway Station, Lenin Prospect is a structure of historical importance. It was built in the 1920s in a mixture of many styles topped by a minaret by the architect, Bayev. It was one of the first stations built for the country's new electrified railway.

Icheri Shekher (inner city), the old town, is partly surrounded by walls. About 130 years ago the whole of Baku was contained within the citadel. The walls, built between the 12th and 16th centuries, have been reconstructed several times. The last time the walls were used to defend the city was in 1826 when the Persian army was at the gates. They were restored in 1953–4. Originally they were double, and in some places they measure 15 m. on the outside while on the inside the highest point is 5 m. Part of the wall was demolished to make room for caravanserais. The Multani (known as the Indian) Caravanserai still exists at Gala St. 12 (about 50 m. from the Virgin's Tower, see below). It was built in the 17th century and on the opposite side of the street, at No. 9, is the 14th-century Bukhara Caravanserai, built around an octagonal courtyard and with the original archways now blocked to provide living accommodation.

In the southern part of the citadel and only about 50 m. from the caravanserais is *Kiz-Kalasyi* (Virgin's Tower). This massive structure (29 m. high, 16–16·5 m. in diameter and with walls 5 m. thick at the bottom and at least 4 m. thick at the top) dates from the first half of the 12th century and is believed to have been built by Sultan Masud as part of the city's early fortifications. The foundations, however, may be much older, 5th or 6th century. Once the tower consisted of eight floors and a flight of 116 steps led to the top. On the western side an ancient inscription on the stone reads, 'Kube Masud bin Daud' (the tower of Masud, son of David). On the eastern side a rectangle of wall projects. About a hundred years ago the sea came up to the foot of the tower, and for several years, until 1909, it was used as a lighthouse.

It gets its name, the Virgin's Tower, from the legend that a certain khan of Baku wished to marry his own daughter. The girl tried in vain to dissuade him, and then had the idea of asking her father first to build a tower hoping that by the time it was completed he would have changed his mind. However when the tower was ready the khan came one stormy night to claim his bride, who threw herself in desperation into the sea below.

Bakikhanov House, Gala St. 46. This is an imposing 18th-century merchant's house. Other separate buildings of interest in the citadel include the remains of the *Mirza Akhmed Mosque* (1345) at Voennaya St. 6, the disused *Gadzhi Bami Mosque* (16th-century) at Mali Krepostnoi Pereulok 8, and the *Djouma Mosque* and *Bathhouse*. The *Synikh Kala Minaret*, the oldest building in Baku, is near the Virgin's Tower and on the sea side of the Palace. Its name means 'ravaged' and it was built in 1077–8 'by the order of Seyad-ed-Din, son of Mohammed I'.

Shirvan Shah's Palace or the Palace of the Khans stands in the old part of the town at the end of Zamkovski Pereulok and surrounded by the citadel wall. The five wells on its territory were dug long before the palace was built. In the 15th century Khalil-Ulla I (1417–62), a ruler of the Derbent dynasty of Shirvan Shahs, built a mosque here as well as a family mausoleum, the palace, and a court of justice. The main building of the palace is two-storey and built of finely finished stone. The exact date of its construction is not known but originally it had fifty-two rooms, twenty-seven downstairs and twenty-five above. The shah lived upstairs while the servants' quarters and the storage rooms were below. The palace has been reconstructed several times and now there are sixteen upper rooms. It houses part of the Baku Museum.

Divan-Khane, the court of justice, is a small 15th-century, octagonal pavilion in the centre of a square courtyard, galleried on three sides, to the right as one comes out of the main building. To the left is the intricately carved main portal with hexagonal medallions inscribed in Arabic. One has the general Moslem creed and the other the Sheid version. The pavilion is surrounded on three sides by twenty columns. The inner portal to the central chamber is decorated in a pattern taken from local flora. Beside this is an Arabic inscription from the Koran which says, 'God said glory to him and blessing, and God called peace and blessing to the house and leads in the right way whomsoever he wishes. Those who do good will be good and with surplus, nor dust nor disgrace will cover their faces. They will be inhabitants of Heaven where they will dwell for ever.' Over all six doors 'Ali' is written in Arabic inside hexagonal medallions. The holes in the inside wall were for pegs from which carpets were hung.

The hole in the centre of the floor of the pavilion was supposedly used at the time of executions when the victim's head dropped through it into a channel and floated out to sea; the body was given to relatives. The chamber below is now dry. Some historians think that Divan-Khane was used as a reception hall or state council chamber. At any rate it was never completed, although other doorways were prepared for carving.

In the courtyard are relics of masonry and stone sepulchres and on the opposite side of the pavilion from the main portal a steep stone stair leads up to a small, blue-domed chamber.

Below the palace in a pleasant fountained courtyard is the *Shah's Mausoleum*, or 'turbe', built in 1435 with a beautiful arch over the entrance. Inscriptions indicate that it was constructed on the orders of Khalil-Ulla. Beside the mausoleum is the *Shah's Mosque* with two stone domes of different sizes and a minaret 22 m. high. It was built in 1441–2, also by Shah Khalil-Ulla, as proved by the inscription under the balcony. Through a gate across the courtyard are the remains of the Shah's bathhouse. The unexpected advertisements for Camel cigarettes and a certain Hotel Melenoez on the walls of houses nearby have been left over from when a film, 'The Merman', was shot here.

The Dervish Mausoleum or *Seid Yakhiya Bakuvi Mausoleum* is another octangular building on the palace territory. It was built in 1464 over the graves of the court scientist, astrologer, doctor, and mathematician. It consists of a ground floor and an underground chamber. Inside part of the ancient decor remains: black and red drawing inlaid on a surface of white stucco. The outside walls are built of alternate wide and narrow layers of limestone, giving an effect of lightness, and surmounted by an octangular pyramid. Next to the mausoleum are the foundations of the small *Kegubade Medresseh* where Seid Yakhiya Bakuvi worked and taught. The small octagonal pool on the other side of the mausoleum was constructed sometime between the 13th and the 15th centuries.

The Murad Gates, built in 1585, are the gates leading to the palace from the north-east. The attractive portal is decorated with stalactites and stone carvings, but the purpose of the construction is not clear. Possibly it was intended as the magnificent entrance to a house which was never completed. The gates are closed and one has to go around the outside of the walls to see the decorations.

The best way to the palace is via Kommunisticheskaya St. 4. Turn here along 3rd Kommunistichesky Pereulok and up the steps under the coat-of-arms on the old fortress wall. At the top keep straight ahead and then turn right along Zamkovski Pereulok. The palace complex is open 11–6; closed Fri.

Mosques are usually called after those who donated the money for their construction. Two that are still in use in Baku are: *Tazapir* ('taza' meaning 'new') *Mosque*, Akhundova St. 7. This was built in 1906 from money donated by a woman named Nabad Khanum. It has two minarets and is used by the Sheids. The second is *Azhdarbek Mosque*, Samed Vurgun St. 58. Built in 1911 with a large green dome and a minaret, this mosque is used by both the Sheids and the Sunids.

Church of the Nativity of the Virgin (Russian Orthodox), Ketskhoveli St. 205

Church of Michael the Archangel (Russian Orthodox), Ismailov St.

Church of St. Gregory the Enlightener (Armenian Gregorian), Efima Saratova St. 27. Built in 1863.

Armenian Church of Our Lady, Menzhinskova St. 11, near the Virgin Tower. Built in the 18th century.

Synagogue, Gogolya St.

There are two old houses of architectural interest in Polukhina St.

History of Azerbaijan Museum, Maligina St. 4. The building used to belong to oil millionaire Tagiyev, and the city art collection was once housed here. There are also many valuable works of art made from gold. The collection of historical exhibits dates from 1896. There is also a room showing the local fauna. This includes bears, wild pigs, and eagles. Open 10–5; closed Fri.

Lenin Museum, in a newly opened building on Neftyanikov Prospect. Open 12–5; closed Mon.

Nizami Literary Museum, Kommunisticheskaya St. 33. The museum is housed in a building specially erected for the Museum of the History of Azerbaijani Literature, and between the columns are many sculptures of outstanding Azerbaijani writers. It bears the name of Nizami of Ganjahvi (whose real name was Iliyas Usif Ogli, 1141–1203), a poet whose works are well-known in eastern literature. Many of them have been translated into European languages. He is especially famous for his five long poems forming the Khamse which has 30,000 couplets. In one of his poems he describes how Baku welcomed Alexander the Great. The museum contains manuscripts, miniatures, and carpets. Open 12–6; closed Thurs.

Kirov Museum, Khagani St. 18. This is where Sergei Kirov (1886–1934), one of the leading Bolsheviks, lived during the time of his work in Baku. Open 12–5.

Azizbekov Museum, Montina St. 105. This was the birthplace of Meshadi Azizbekov (1876–1918). He was a leading local Bolshevik and among the twenty-six commissars shot in 1918. Open 12–5.

Agricultural Museum, Neftyanikov Prospect, by the entrance to Marine Park. Not of any great interest. Open 12–4.

Zardabi Natural History Museum, Shaumyana St. 9. There is a good collection of local fauna here. Open 8–2; closed Mon.

Rustama Mustafayev Art Museum, Chkalova St. 9. This national art collection contains works from the 18th century to the present day, as well as examples of Russian and West European art (mostly copies). There are also carpets, embroidery, and china. The building was originally constructed for oil millionaire Gugasov in 1876. On the first floor is the Eastern Room decorated in red and gold and an Arabic inscription which is a quotation from the Koran. It was used as a chapel and as a guest room for eastern visitors. Open 12–6; closed Wed.

Lenin Monument, on the square side of Government House. This 12 m. sculpture by D. Karyagdi (1861–1942) was unveiled in 1954.

Kirov Monument, in Kirov Park, on the hillside near the funicular railway above the town to the west. This well-known Bolshevik, who was assassinated in Leningrad in 1934, was head of the local Communist Party organisation from 1921–5. The statue by P. Sabsai was unveiled in 1939.

Azi-Aslanov Monument, Kirov Park. Major-General Azi-Aslanov fell in World War II.

Nizami Monument, in a garden near Azizbekov St. The 6 m. bronze statue of the local 12th-century poet is by F. Abdurakhmanov and was unveiled in 1949. The granite pedestal is decorated with bronze bas-reliefs illustrating his works.

Akhundov Monument, on the former Kaganovich St. Mirze Fatali Akhundov (1812–78) was a philosopher and writer. P. Sabsai designed the monument in 1928.

Sabir Monument, in a garden on Kommunisticheskaya St., near the Academy of Sciences. Mirza Alekper Sabir (1862–1911) was a poet, and Keilikhis made the monument in 1923.

Monument to the twenty-six Commissars of Baku, in 26-Bakinskikh-Komissarov Sq. The British are usually blamed for the death of these men, shot in 1918. Tripolskaya was the sculptress and Pavlevich the architect of the monument which was unveiled in 1923. There is an eternal flame here and a red granite monument on the right, bearing the inscription: 'Here lie the brave fighters for communism, 26 Baku commissars evilly shot on 20 September 1918, by hirelings of the imperialists.' The square is further decorated with busts of the more famous of the commissars—Shaumyan, Azizbekov, Dzhaparidze, and Fioletov, created by Sabsai in 1928.

Samed Vurgun Vekilov (1906–56) is commemorated by a *large bronze statue* on a column of polished red granite in the square near the railway station. The building with three arches behind the statue is Railway House.

Narevan Statue, Zevina St., just outside the Vesna Café. Narevan was a poetess who lived from 1830–97. Her statue, the only monument to a woman in Baku, shows her seated with a pencil in her hand.

The impressive *fountain* near Intourist Hotel depicts a character from one of Nizami's stories. It is Bakhramshah who is shown killing a dragon which had prevented people from reaching a spring of fresh water.

Azizbekov Azerbaijani Drama Theatre. The company was founded in 1873 but this building is quite new.

Akhundov Opera and Ballet Theatre, Nizami St. 27

Russian Drama Theatre, Khagani St. 7

Gorki Youth Theatre, Nizami St. 32

Magomayev Philharmonic Concert Hall, Kommunisticheskaya St. 2

House of Folk Art, Myasnikova St. 3

Gadzhibekov Conservatoire, Dmitrova St. 98. The building of the conservatoire was specially constructed for the purpose in 1941.

Kirov Park, Lermontov St. 9, on the slopes above the west side of the town. Maxim Gorky

said that the view over the bay from this point was better than that of Naples, and a few years later, at the end of the 1930s, a park was opened here. The centre of the park is best reached by the funicular railway (ticket, 5 kopeks) which was opened in 1960 and which rises 100 m. over a distance of 500 m. (It operates from 7 a.m. till 11 p.m., but is closed Mon. until 3 p.m.) In the park are an open-air theatre, sports facilities, cafés, a disused tea-room, and the Druzhba Restaurant with an excellent view over the bay. There is also the statue to Kirov and a monument to Major-Gen. Azi-Aslanov.

Nizami Garden, Rabochi Prospect 57. This park was formerly known as Nobel Park and surrounded Villa Petrolea.

Dzerzhinsky Park, Chapayev St. 37

Lenin Stadium, near Dzerzhinsky Park. The stadium was built in 1953 and can seat 50,000. Near it is the Palace of Sport and the Baku Children's Railway.

Hippodrome Racecourse, 16th-Nagornaya St.

Neftyanik Swimming Pool, Rabochi Prospect 57. This is a 25 m. heated indoor pool, constructed in 1953 and used for competitions.

Botanical Garden, Lokbatanskoye Chaussee. The garden was founded in 1935 and covers a territory of 16 hectares (40 acres).

The city bathing beach is near Government House.

Zoo, Saraikina St. 2

Youzhnaya (south) Hotel and Restaurant, Shaumyana St. 31. TEL. 3–12–64

Intourist Hotel and Restaurant, Neftyanikov Prospect 63. TEL. 2–63–00

Azerbaijan Hotel and Restaurant, Bakhikhanova St. TEL. 2–31–11.

Baku Hotel and Restaurant, Maligina St. 13. TEL. 3–49–70

Public Bath-House, Shorsa St. 130

Metro Restaurant, at the crossing of Gogol and Nizami Streets

Shirvan Restaurant, Kirova Prospect 15

Vesna, or Bakhar, Café, Zevina St. 11

Nargiz Café, Karl Marx Garden, which is still locally known by the old name of Parapet, as is also all the surrounding area near Saratovtsa Yefima St.

Bank, Kirova Prospect 17

Central Department Store, Bairamova St. 5

Carpet shops, Gorky St. 1 and Zevina St. 11

Gift Shop, Nizami St. 20

Book Arcade, Yefimova St. 46

Photographic Printing and Developing, 28th-April St. 17

Commission Shops where second-hand goods including antiques are sold, 28th-April St. 42, Shmidt St. 22, and Karaiva St. 32

Camera Shop, Kommunisticheskaya St. 21

Jeweller's, Zevina St. 11 and Nizami St. 28

Paintings, Nizami St. 18

Central Market, Samed Vurgun St. 73

Taxi Ranks, Aznefti Sq., Molodyozhi Sq., and the central railway station

In the south-west part of Baku Bay, about 250 m. from the shore on a small *island* can be seen the ruins of a mediaeval fortress. Archaeologists excavated some inscribed stones which indicate it was built in 1234. There is a legend that this is the remains of the town of Sabail, now lying at the bottom of the sea.

Surakhani
About 16 km. north-east of the centre of the town in this village stands a fireworshippers' temple, founded in the 18th century, and the *Monastery of Atesh-Gede*, founded by Indians who were trading in this area. The temple itself is a square building with a cupola and four stone columns supporting the arches. Pipes were built into the columns and gas burned above the temple as well as from the central well. The fireworshippers used to burn their dead over this flame. The monastery was abandoned in 1887 though the gas is still burning and the buildings are kept up.

Sumgait
40 km. from Baku. Foreign visitors may visit Sumgait if they ask permission.

Bilgya
45 km. from Baku. There is a good bathing beach near the village of Bilgya, part of which is reserved by Intourist.

Kobystan
60 km. to the south of Baku. On one of the cliff faces of Mount Beyukdash is carved a Latin inscription of the first century A.D. which is unique in that it is the most easterly inscription in that language to have been discovered. There is, besides, a great range and variety of carvings here, the earliest dating from the Stone Age while the most recent belong to the Middle Ages. There are scenes showing hunting, harvesting, and dancing among a total of about 4000 drawings.

BAKURIANI
This winter sports resort is up in the Caucasus Mountains, about 200 km. from Tbilisi. It can be reached by both rail and road. There are limited facilities for all types of winter sports, but the skiing here is excellent.

BATUMI
Population—120,000 (1970)

Batumi is the capital of the Ajar (Atchar) Autonomous Republic; the Ajars are Muslim Georgians who were forced to adopt Islam. It lies along the shore of one of the best bays in the Black Sea and is an important resort. It has a moist, warm, subtropical climate with an average annual temperature of 14·4°C. (August 23·2°C., January 6·4°C.). The sea bathing season starts in April and lasts until November.

The place was first mentioned by Pliny (23–73 A.D.) as Bathus. The settlement was on the left bank of R. Bat (from which derives the Georgian name, Bat-om-i). The Greeks understood it as 'Badus' (deep) although the river itself is not and never has been so. It is also said that 'Batus' means stone; the river-bed is certainly very stony. Today the river is called Korolis-Tskali.

In ancient times the part of the Black Sea coast near Batumi, a land of legendary wealth, was called Colchis, Land of the Sun. The mythical Argonauts sailed here to find the Golden Fleece. As early as the 4th century B.C. the Romans came and Bathus was the site of a Roman encampment. In the 4th century A.D. a state called Lazika was formed here, but after the fall of the Western Roman Empire it was subject to Byzantium. In the 6th–7th centuries this area saw unremitting struggles between Byzantium and Persia.

From the 10th century Ajaria was part of Georgia, but from the second half of the 15th century the Turks began trying to annex this area. It was captured in 1547, when the Turks destroyed the churches, virtually eradicated Christianity, and converted the local population to Islam. The local landlords in particular had to become converts in order to protect their property. From the 17th century the majority of the Ajarians, who are a western branch of the Karveli group of Georgians, have been Moslems. They use some Turkish words in their vocabulary. Today nearly half the local population is Georgian, one third is either Russian or Ukrainian, and the rest are Armenians and Greeks.

In 1878, after the Russian victory in the Russo-Turkish War, Batumi with the adjoining area, having been dominated by the Turks for 300 years, was placed under Russian authority. At that time Batumi was a small, poor village with 2000 inhabitants. Trade was at a standstill and the port of little significance. However at the end of the 19th century Batumi grew considerably, both as a city and as a port. Between 1878 and 1886 it operated as a Free Port. Batumi gained further importance at the beginning of the 20th century when an oil pipeline from Baku was extended here, thus turning Batumi into part of the oil export trade.

In 1918 the Turks seized the city but had to abandon it almost immediately. It was under British occupation for more than a year and then in 1921 with the advent of Soviet power Batumi became the capital of the Ajarian Autonomous Republic.

There is no architectural centre of the city. Of the three main squares, Lenin Sq. is officially the central one and used for holiday demonstrations, but it is located in the suburbs. Many new houses have sprung up among the old single-storey buildings. Part of the old town can still be seen but it has lost its oriental quality. The Russians built some administrative buildings here and some mansions typical of the last century and the beginning of this, both of which are easily distinguished.

Besides the work connected with the port, local industries today include oil refining, the manufacture of machinery for the food industry, woodworking and furniture manufacture, tobacco and some food industries. There is a pedagogical institute here and a marine school.

St. Nicholas's Cathedral, Telmann St. 20. This was built at the turn of the century and services are held in both Georgian and Russian.

Mosque, Chkalov St. 6, in the old part of the city. Open for services.

Synagogue, 8th Marta St.

Local Museum, Dzhinzaradze St. 4. In the ethnographical section on the ground floor is an interesting exhibition of national costumes. Open 10–7.

Revolution Museum, Gorky St. 8. Displayed here is the equipment of an underground printing shop and the portraits and personal belongings of local revolutionaries. Open 11–6; closed Mon.

Aquarium, Ninoshvili St. 37. 50 different kinds of fish are kept here. Open 10–6; closed Mon.

Lenin Monument, Lenin Sq. Unveiled in 1955.

Chavchavadze Drama Theatre, Rustaveli St. 1. Built in 1951–2 to seat 650 people.

Summer Theatre, in Primorsky Park. This theatre was built in Georgian style in 1948.

Planetarium, Sverdlov St. 26. Housed in the disused Armenian church.

Circus, Baratashvili St.

Dynamo Stadium, near Lenin Sq. This stadium has seats for 20,000.

Yacht Club, Primorskoye Ozero

Children's Yacht Club, Engels St. 4

Primorsky Park (formerly called City Boulevard) is adjoined by a long and wide beach. There is a restaurant here and the Summer Theatre. Magnolias, palms, and other subtropical trees have been planted here.

The Young Pioneers' Park is beside a lake, and schoolchildren act as the crew of a ship that sails here. The park extends for 18 hectares (45 acres) and contains a considerable collection of local flora and fauna. The first few trees were planted here in 1881 by Alexander II and the park was called Alexandrovsky Park. At the entrance to the

park is a sculpture commemorating the first local girl pilot, Gogitidze, and a bust of a test-pilot called Dzinacharadze.

Intourist Hotel & Restaurant, Ninoshvili St. 11. TEL. 9–73–31. Built in 1939 following a design by Schuser.

1st *May Hotel and Restaurant*, Karl Marx St. 45

Restaurant, in Primorsky Park

There are various small cafés in the city where Georgian dishes can be found; recommended is 'khachapuri' (cheese pie) which is available fresh in the morning as Georgians like it for breakfast.

Bank, Lenin St. and Oktyabrsky Prospect 27

Turkish Legation, Oktyabrsky Prospect 8

Department Store, Chavchavadze St.

Market, Chavchavadze St.

The coastal area which stretches for about 35 km. between Batumi to Kobuleti is known as the resort area. There are many sanatoria and private houses here. There is a good motor road and also the local railway links them with Batumi. Beside the road, on a hill on the right near the bridge over R. Korolis Tskali, stand the ruins of a medieval tower known here as Queen Tamara's Castle.

Makhindzhauri

6 km. from Batumi. The name means 'place of the maimed' and refers to the tortures which the Turks made the Georgian Christians suffer as they forced them to accept Islam. There is a good beach here with Marine Park behind it. There are also mineral springs.

Makhindzhauri Café

Zelyoni Mys

8 km. from Batumi. The name means 'green cape' and in Georgian it is Mtsvane Kontskhi. This resort is 72 m. above sea level and is famous for its Botanical Garden which is the largest in the country. It was founded in 1912 by the botanist, Prof. Andrei Krasnov (1862–1914) as a most comprehensive collection of subtropical flora. His dream was to turn the place into a garden-exhibition, with items such as a Mexican boulevard or a Chilean town planted with date and coconut palms where Creole women in the taverns would serve tourists with liqueurs distilled from local fruit. Among other ideas, he wanted a few Negro families to settle here and pygmies from the mountains of New Guinea, and to build a Chinese house on the top of the hill.

Professor Krasnov died in 1914 but the garden continued to grow. Since 1925 it has also become an important scientific research centre, and in 1930 the XVI Party Congress ordered the subtropical region of the Caucasus to be turned into a Soviet Florida and California—meaning that it should be the most important area for the growing of citrus fruits. The garden now stretches for three miles along the coast, covers almost 300 acres, and has 1500 varieties of trees, divided into the following sections: Transcaucasian, Australian, New Zealand, Himalayan, Sino-Japanese, North American, South American, and Mediterranean.

The Japanese Courtyard is worthy of special attention.

While working here in the garden, Professor Krasnov hurt his leg and it turned gangrenous. He died at the age of 52 and was buried in the garden, on the hill overlooking the sea. In 1962, marking the centenary of his birth, a monument was set up on his grave with the inscription: 'To the Founder of this Garden—Krasnov'. The bust was made by his grand-daughter, Krasnova-Vertinskaya.

Abkhazia Restaurant

Café, by the entrance to the Botanical Garden.

A little further along the coast is Chavka where the first tea plantation was made in 1883 by a retired engineer named Solontsev, who reaped his first harvest two years later. The first commercial planting was made in 1885. Tea bushes were brought from Hankow in China and a group of Chinese tea specialists were invited to assist. The first real crop was harvested in 1894. Now 6000 people live here and over 35,000 tons of tea are produced each year. There is also an Institute of Tea and Subtropical Cultures.

Tsikhis-Dziri

Tsikhis-Dziri stands on a cape rising 70–92 m. above sea level and is 19 km. from Batumi. In 523 A.D. Byzantine Emperor Justinian ordered that a fortress be built here on the top of a high rock; it was called Petra and a Byzantine garrison was sent to man it under the leadership of the local King Tsate who was a convert to the Christian faith. The present name means 'foundations of a fortress' and the ruins are very picturesque. The place was at one time called Justinian's Town, and excavations carried out in 1962 helped to find out more about it. In some places there were 2 or 3 storeys underground and it was the centre of a system of underground tunnels. The southern side has survived best, and visitors enjoy climbing up the slopes to it, especially in the evening when they can watch the sunset. Tsikhis-Dziri was a very real stronghold, not only because of the fortress, but because of its natural position. The Russian army failed to pass through this way as they marched on Batumi during the campaigns of 1829 and 1877–8. The cape divided this part of the coastline into the north and south beaches; the southern beach is the wider and is covered with small pebbles.

Tsikhis-Dziri has some of the most important citrus plantations in the country. The orange and lemon trees growing on the terraces near the fortress were planted in 1934, and there is an enormous greenhouse where lemons are picked all year round.

The slopes of *Tsikhis-Dziri Gorge* are covered with what remains of the ancient forest of Colchis and there is a waterfall 17 m. high. Another favourite spot to walk to is *Sergeyev Kamen* (Sergei's Stone) with this name written on it.

The Nauka (Science) Sanatorium now occupies a house built on the cape in 1909 by an engineer called Skarzhinsky. He copied a castle he had seen in Naples, and palm trees from the Canary Islands were planted in the park.

Kobuleti

Kobuleti stands but 10 m. above sea level, is about 30 km. from Batumi and stretches for 10 km. along the shore. It has an excellent beach of fine, clean sand and pebbles, in places up to 100 m. wide and it dries very quickly. The water is shallow here and the place is especially good for children. The beach is backed by pine trees.

Kobuleti first became popular at the beginning of this century when many retired tsarist generals built villas here. The local inhabitants are proud of the splendid view over the valley and say that they can enjoy a combination of the French Riviera and Switzerland. There is a plantation of medical herbs nearby.

Intourist Hotel, a skyscraper building, is under construction

Restaurant

Cafés

Theatre

Park

BELORUSSIA
See Minsk, p. 193

BOGOLYUBOVO
See Vladimir, p. 329

BORODINO
See Moscow, p. 232

BRATSK
See Irkutsk, p. 121

BREST
(Formerly Brest-Litovsk). Population—122,000 (1970)

This border town stands on the right bank of the R. Mukhovets, at the point where it flows into the R. Bug.

BREST

It has been known as a fortified town since 1017. From then onwards it was frequently fought over by the Poles, Lithuanians, and Russians. In 1240 it was completely devastated by the Tatars, but was already rebuilt by 1275. It became Lithuanian in 1319, Polish in 1569, Russian in 1795, and again Polish from 1919 until 1939. In 1596 the council which established the Uniate Church met here. These Christians, also known as the Greek Catholics, acknowledged the Pope as their head but retained the Russian Orthodox Church.

When Brest became Russian in 1795, its position on the western border of the country increased its strategic and trade importance. It was decided to build a really strong fortress there, but this plan was delayed because of the Napoleonic Wars, and only in 1830 did Nicholas I approve a plan for the proposed fortress. The then existing pentagonal castle was demolished in 1831, and the town itself was transferred in 1833 to a site 5 km. to the east. Between 1838 and 1842 this whole area was under construction. The fortress and its outer defences were situated on four islands in the R. Bug. Surrounding the whole structure was an earth wall 10 m. high. The central citadel had a two-storey barrack square, 1·8 km. in circumference and with walls 2 m. thick, which could hold over 12,000 soldiers. During its history the stronghold was reinforced several times.

The peace treaty of Brest-Litovsk was signed here on 3rd March 1918. This was a separate treaty between Russia and Germany, by which Russia gave up much of her former territory, including the Baltic countries and the Ukraine, and also demobilised her army. The Soviet government withdrew from the treaty unilaterally when Germany was defeated.

The fortress withstood the German attack in 1941 for about a month, when all the surrounding area had fallen and the German front line had advanced far to the east. In 1965 the town was acclaimed a 'fortress-hero' in recognition of its valour. There is now a museum in the fortress in commemoration of this brave stand, which has since been described in many poems and in books. The Museum is open 11–4, and closed Mon.

Today Brest is a major transportation centre. Five railway lines meet there, and it is the frontier town on the Moscow-Warsaw line. It also stands on the Dnieper-Bug Canal. It has various food and light industries, and there is a pedagogical institute in the town.

Semyonovsky Church, on the main road through the town

　Museum, Lenin St. 34

　Drama Theatre, Lenin St. 21

　Bug Hotel and Restaurant, Lenin St. 2. TEL. 44–53

Byelorus Restaurant, at the crossing of Pushkinskaya St. and Sovietskaya St.

BUKHARA (Bokara)

Population—112,000 (1970)

The inhabitants of this ancient city are mainly Uzbeks, but there are many Tadzhiks, Russians and Jews and as many as sixteen other nationalities. Most of the inhabitants speak three languages, Uzbek, Tadzhik (which resembles Pharsee or Persian), and Russian.

Although archaeological excavations trace the story of Bukhara back to the 1st century A.D., it has in fact been known since the 2nd century B.C. when Chinese travellers visited it. Some of them gave its name as Poo Kho, and others called it Noo Me. This confusion lasted for hundreds of years so that the 10th-century historian, Narshakhi, wrote that Bukhara had more names than any other city at that time. It was the Chinese and the Uygurs who at that time called it Bukhar, meaning 'the temple of idols', but today some Russian scientists think that its name is derived from the Sanskrit 'bihara' meaning 'monastery'.

According to legend, Prince Seyavush of Persia came to Bukhara, married the khan's daughter, and built the fortress known as the Ark. Certainly the whole Bukhara region was under Persian rule between the 6th and 4th centuries B.C. From the time that Alexander the Great conquered Persia in 329 B.C. until the 2nd century B.C., the lands were under Greek rule.

During the first five centuries A.D. Bukhara was part of a number of different states in turn, including Kushan and the Epithalites' or White Huns' State under Attila, Scourge of God (406–53), and was one of the most important centres of both trade and culture in Central Asia. Its trade connections linked it with Persia, India and China among other countries.

In 709, after a bloody struggle, the Arabs seized Bukhara, and their rule was notable for the series of revolts against them. The movement of the Men in White led by a certain Moukanna was the longest lasting of these uprisings and legend tells that at the moment of their defeat and while surrounded by their oppressors, the rebels threw themselves into a great fire, together with their leader.

In the 9th century the Samanid family rose to power. Originally they had been the governors appointed by the Arabs, but they became a powerful land-owning family. Ismail Samani was the first of the dynasty which ruled Bukhara from 874 to 999. Under the Samanid's rule Bukhara became the capital of a vast feudal state embracing nearly the whole territory of Central Asia. In the 10th century Bukhara was famed as the centre of culture of that time. Among the enlightened citizens

---

PLATES OPPOSITE

The Kremlin at Pskov and, *below*, the Mamayev Hill in the Hero-city of Volgograd, memorial to the battle of Stalingrad in World War II.

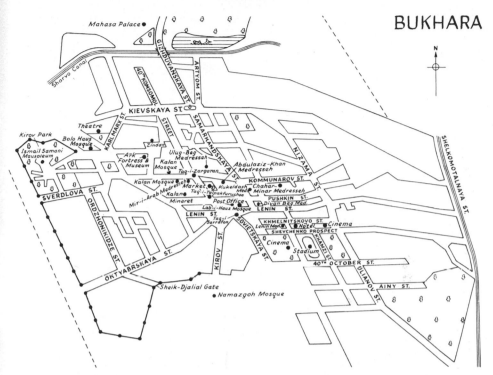

BUKHARA

of Bukhara were the poet, Abul Hassan Rudaki, and the physician and philosopher, Abu-Ali-Ibn-Sina (otherwise known as Avicenna, 980–1037). Rudaki, who died in 941, said that Bukhara was better than Baghdad. The Karakhanids ruled Bukhara from 999 till 1141 and the Kara-Kitays from 1141 till 1206. Monuments dating from the first period are the Arslan-Khan Minaret (which, with the Amir and the Mir-i- Arab Medressehs, is part of the Kalan Mosque ensemble), the Maghak-il-Attari Mosque, the Namazgoh Mosque, and the Chashma-Ayub Tomb.

After 1206 Bukhara belonged to the powerful state of Khorezm but in 1220 was over-run by the Mongols of Genghis-Khan. The city was razed to the ground and its inhabitants enslaved. By the second half of that century Bukhara had gradually recovered so that when Marco Polo visited it he called it 'the city of high grandeur'.

In 1370 Bukhara fell under the jurisdiction of Timur (also known as Tamerlane or Tamberlaine) and lost its political importance to Samarkand which Timur had chosen as his capital.

The Saybanids' dynasty began in 1506 and by the end of the 16th century Bukhara had become the capital of the state which came to be called the Khanate of Bukhara. The period brought back flourishing trade and the city acquired the appearance which it preserved until the 1919 revolution. It was surrounded by a wall about 12 km. long, 5 m. thick and 10 m. high.

In 1595 a new dynasty, the Ashtarkhanids (who were descendants of the rulers of Astrakhan) came to power, and by the end of their rule in the 18th century Bukhara had lost much of its economic and cultural importance. When in 1740 the Persian Shah Nadir captured Bukhara he appointed a local landlord, Mohammad Rahim, as his governor. The latter proclaimed himself Emir and founded Bukhara's last dynasty—the Mangids (1753–1920). Under Mangid rule Bukhara turned from the centre of local culture to the centre of religious obscurantism and political reaction. In theological Moslem literature it was called Bukhara-y-Sherif (holy Bukhara).

In the 1860s and the 1870s the tsarist government started its attempts to take over Bukhara. In 1868 the Russian General Kaufman defeated the Emir's army after a short struggle and Bukhara became a Russian protectorate. In subsequent years the slave trade was abolished, telegraph and post offices were built, and between 1877 and 1888 the first railway was laid from Krasnovodsk to Samarkand. Schools and hospitals were built near the railway stations, but life was not very bright. In Bukhara they complained, 'Only air is

PLATES OPPOSITE
Two graceful palaces in the environs of Moscow: *above*, Arkhangelskoye, and *below*, the elaborate 18th-century theatre at Ostankino Palace Museum.

untaxed.' At the beginning of the 20th century a political movement called 'Djadidizm' was formed. 'Djadid' means 'new' in Arabic and the party was similar to the liberal Young Turkey movement in Turkey at the same period.

The 1919 uprising against the Emir was led by the Communist Party who called for help and in September 1920 Red Army troops took the city after four days' fighting and Bukhara was declared a republic. It joined the Soviet Union in 1924 and became a regional centre of Uzbekistan.

More than thirty of the architectural monuments of the ancient city of Bukhara are considered to be of national importance. They belong to all periods from the 9th century up to the present day. *The Sharud Canal* running through the city roughly from east to west used to supply as many as eighty-five 'hauzes' or reservoirs which formed the water supply system of Bukhara. With the passing of the years the level of the city rose, and so the canal was constantly raised and relined; all the same it now appears to flow at the bottom of a deep rift in many places. In the past the hauzes were used for drinking water, and for washing in, and were rife with bacteria and extremely unwholesome. Now only five of the original twenty largest hauzes remain and of these five, two are empty. They are 10 m. deep and were built in 1620. The water was usually changed every two weeks.

The wall of the city is earthen, 8 m. high and 12 km. in circumference. It was first built in the 15th–16th century but was constantly being damaged and rebuilt. *The Tali-Pach Gate* is the only one of the eleven to survive. It has been restored.

New Bukhara is growing up around the old mud houses. Every year new streets are lined with prefabricated four-storey houses. Uliyanova and Khamza Streets are the central thoroughfares of the new town. A special housing complex is being built to provide new accommodation for the inhabitants of the old town.

Local industry is mainly cotton ginning, and the manufacture of silk textiles, Astrakhan fur, food products, and components for prefabricated buildings. It is interesting to pay a visit to the *Gold-Embroidering Factory*, Detsky Pereulok 4. 240 workers are employed here and one can inspect the articles they produce, gowns, shoes and 'tubeteiki' (national skull caps). These items are on sale in local shops as well as in Moscow. The factory itself is the largest of a small number of similar enterprises that exist in the Soviet Union.

The donkeys that are to be seen wandering about the streets of Bukhara in fact belong to no one in particular. They are rounded up once a week and taken out to the surrounding villages by the lorry load. The villagers use them to bring their goods to market, particularly to the busy Sunday markets, and then abandon them and return home by more modern means of transport.

The Ark is the oldest structure in Bukhara. It is the city fortress, parts of which are at least 2,000 years old. It now forms the main section of the local museum. It is situated on an artificial hill 16–20 m. high, and covers more than 6 acres. The wall surrounding it has been rebuilt several times and the existing one is believed to have been erected about two or three hundred years ago. Until the Arab invasion the Ark served as the residence of the governors of the city. Several times during the 12th–14th centuries various invaders ruined it and its present form dates from the 16th century. The ceremonial entrance is protected by two pillar-like towers connected by a gallery above which the Emir's musicians and the city guards usually lived. The big leather lash that usually hung on the wall as a symbol of the Emir's power had once, according to tradition, belonged to the Persian warrior, Rustam, the same that Matthew Arnold tells of in his poem, 'Sohrab and Rustam'.

All the buildings inside the fortress are from the 17th–20th centuries, during the time the Emirs used it as their residence, together with their ministers and members of the nobility. The entrance to the citadel is by way of a long covered gallery, flanked by rooms on both sides. Some of these were used for storing water, while others served as prison cells. *The Djouma Mosque* with a carved wooden porch was built in 1919. The narrow street leading from the mosque runs to a small cupola called *Charsu* over the entrance to Salam-Khana (court of greetings), the Emir's reception hall and the highest point of the citadel. From here doors lead on to a balcony overlooking the Registan. To the right of Charsu were the stables, and in fact Charsu is in the paved Mews' Court. It contains the 'saganah' (tomb) supposed to be that of the founder of the fortress, Prince Seyavush.

To the left of Charsu is *Kurynish-Khana*, the place where the Emirs were crowned and where they received foreign ambassadors. In Chyl Dukhtaron in the northern part of the fortress forty girls were, according to legend, tortured and thrown into a well at the command of Emir Nasroulla.

Zindan, Kolkhoznaya St. Formerly the Emir's prison, this was built in the 18th century. There are prison cells, some of which are below ground. The prisoners were given their food from above. There was a well-like pit for special offenders where the Emir kept specially bred vermin and reptiles to torture his prisoners. Stoddart and Connolly, the two British officers sent in 1843 to offer British assistance against Russian incursions, spent many months in one of the cells and also in the pit, and nearby is the place where they were beheaded. Zindan now forms part of the Bukhara Museum and there are two dummy prisoners at the bottom of the pit. Open 9–5; closed Tues.

In front of the Ark lies the square called *the Registan* (with Marx St. as its address) across which stands the *Bolo Haus (near-the-pool) Mosque*. This was usually visited on Friday by the Emirs when they came to Bukhara, and valuable carpets were laid between it and the Ark, especially for the occasion. Founded in 1712, the mosque was rebuilt at the beginning of the 18th century and enlarged in 1917. It is characterised by twenty wooden columns.

Behind the mosque, on the site of an old cemetery, is *Kirov Park* in which some of the oldest monuments of Bukhara are to be found. On the road to the park, a little to the south-west of the Registan, are two *medressehs* (Muslim theological colleges) now standing on either side of the street, but still called *Kosh (double) Medresseh* because they stand so close. The effect is very imposing. *Modari-Khan* (Khan's Mother), to the east, was built in 1566 and *Abdullah-Khan*, to the west, in 1589. The latter is the grander and more richly decorated of the two, and it is distinguished by its architectural originality. The first was built by Abdullah Khan for his mother, and the second was built for him by his own son.

In Kirov Park the *Ismail Samani Mausoleum* (built between 892 and 907) is a cube-shaped building with a hemispherical cupola resting on four archways. Four smaller cupolas around the larger one give the whole structure an appearance of lightness. It became almost completely buried and so survived the ravages of Genghis-Khan. The walls are 1·8 m. thick, which partly accounts for the fact that the mausoleum is still standing after a thousand years. Some restorations were carried out in 1934. An interesting point is that it has no main façade—all four sides are identical, each containing a lancet arch over an entrance. The gallery running around the top of the outer walls has forty window openings. The walls themselves, both inside and out, are decorated with ornamental terracotta; the decorations seem to change several times during the day, depending upon the angle at which the sun's rays strike them, and they appear most effective of all by moonlight. This feature of the building is architecturally unique.

Chronicles testify that the mausoleum was built by the founder of the Samanid dynasty, Ismail Samani, in honour of his father and that later Ismail himself was buried here. For centuries the Muslim mullahs fostered the illusion that Ismail Samani was alive and helping his people. There were two openings in the tombstone inside the mausoleum, one for questions and requests and another for answers supplied by the mullahs.

Also in Kirov Park, Lenin St., and not far from the Ismail Samani Mausoleum is the 12th-century *Mazaar Chashma-Ayub*. The four parts of the rectangular structure were all built at different times and crowned by cupolas of different design. The northern and southern sides of the monument are particularly interesting. Inside the mazaar is an ice-cold spring. Legend has it that long ago before the foundation of the city and in a year of terrible drought, Job came to these parts. The people were dying of thirst but when Job struck the earth with his staff a spring of water started to flow, hence the name Chashma-Ayub (spring of Job).

Maghak-i-Attari Mosque, Frunze Sq., opposite the open air cinema. The name of this mosque indicated that once this was the place where medicinal herbs were sold. It was founded no later than the 9th century but has been rebuilt many times, in the 12th, 16th, and 20th centuries. The building appears to have sunk down 6 m. into the earth, but in fact the ground level has risen with the passage of time as is usual in places that have been inhabited for many centuries. In the 1930s archaeological excavations revealed five layers of floors, helping to prove that this was the site of a 5th-century fire-worshippers' temple, before the arrival of Islam. At a depth of more than 10 m. were found signs of a Buddhist monastery; this helped to identify the date of the foundation of Bukhara as 1st century A.D.

The southern portal (pishtak) of the mosque is a masterpiece of oriental architecture with many different styles, including carved alabaster, turquoise tiles and polished brick. Its small finely-carved columns make it particularly beautiful.

The Kalan (great) Mosque, Kolkhoznaya St., by the market. This is the city's principal mosque and together with the Great Minaret and the Mir-i-Arab Medresseh forms an architectural ensemble sometimes called the Bukhara Forum. It was built in 1514 on the site of a 12th-century Karakhanid mosque and is one of the oldest and, after Bibi Khanum in Samarkand, the second largest mosque in Central Asia. The cupola is higher than any other structure in Bukhara except the Great Minaret and gives the mosque its second name of Kok-Gumbaz (blue dome). The mosque has seven entrances and covers an area of 9,906 sq. m. It is a so-called open mosque and the gallery of the courtyard is roofed by 288 cupolas supported by 208 pillars. It can take a congregation of 10,000 in the courtyard, under the gallery and on the roof.

The Kalan Minaret near the centre of town is linked to the Kalan Mosque by a stone arch. Kalan was also the name of one of the rulers of the Karakhanid dynasty. The minaret was built in 1127 by Arslan-Khan, and at 46·5 m. high is the tallest structure in Central Asia. It is pillar-shaped, tapering slightly at the top, and is of terracotta laid on a thick alabaster solution. Inside is a spiral staircase of 104 steps leading up to a rotunda with 16 archlike openings. The belt of light blue enamel at the top is 16th century.

In the past on Fridays four muedzins called the faithful to prayer. Their call was relayed by the muedzins of two hundred other Bukhara mosques. The minaret also served as a watch tower and as a beacon for smoke signals to guide approaching merchant caravans. When Genghis-Khan reached the centre of Bukhara, he halted his horse in front of the minaret for a long time and put his finger to his mouth in a gesture of amazement; then he ordered the city to be entirely destroyed with the exception of the minaret. The legend attached to the two marble plaques fixed to the minaret near the top is that in the 16th century two men on two different occasions managed to climb the minaret using a hammer and awl, and when they had each fixed their plaque they came safely down again.

During the period of the Mangid dynasty criminals were thrown from the top of the minaret, but the practice ceased with the abolition of slavery in 1868. In general the treatment of wrong-doers was extremely gory. As late as 1820 it is recorded that the punishment for 'murder, revolt, forgery, treason, adultery and drunkenness' was death by beating on the back of the head until the victim lost consciousness. Thereafter his throat was cut, he was hanged, taken down, beheaded and the severed head nailed up by the ears for a period of three days while the body was handed over to his relatives. At the end of the 19th and the beginning of the 20th century the minaret was called Manari-Kalan, the Tower of Death. In September 1920, the establishment of Soviet power was declared from the top of the minaret.

Many legends about its origin have arisen during the minaret's 800 years of existence. One says that the architect laid foundations based on a solution of clay, camel's milk, eggs, and bull's blood. He then disappeared, only returning after two years when the solution had considerably hardened. Another legend says that the architect asked to be buried nearby, in a place situated as far from the minaret as the height of the building itself. Tourists are still shown his grave. Recent restoration works have included cleaning the 10 m. foundation of layers of mud.

The Mir-i-Arab Medresseh (Kolkhoznaya St., near the market) stands opposite the Kalan Mosque. It was built in 1534 and takes its name from the Sheik Abdulla from Yemen whose nickname was Mir-i-Arab and who is buried here along with many of his numerous relatives. The room in which they lie is richly decorated. Mir-i-Arab's tomb is the large one in the window recess. Another interesting one is that with a wooden cover instead of a tombstone. It marks the grave of Mir-i-Arab's pupil, Obaidolla-Khan Sheibanid.

The medresseh is the only one in Central Asia to be serving its rightful purpose of a Moslem theological training college. It was closed in 1925 but was re-opened in 1946, permission for this being granted by the state as a token of gratitude to Soviet Islam for its valuable part in the war effort. The students study religion, Islamic law, and Arabic, and usually return home to preach. There are about 400 mosques still operating in the U.S.S.R. and as many as thirty students graduate from the medresseh each year. There are now seventy-five students following a nine-year course. The building consists of two storeys of arched cloisters around a central courtyard. Each archway leads into a small cell which serves either as a classroom or as accommodation for four students; traditionally the classrooms should be on the ground floor and the students' rooms above. Before the 1917 revolution the medressehs were the only schools operating in Bukhara.

Ibn-Sein Library is behind the medresseh. It was built in 1914 as the Kalan Medresseh (or the Emir Medresseh). Now it contains 150,000 books and a good collection of ancient manuscripts.

Ulug-Beg Medresseh, just up Kolkhoznaya St., under the archway. This medresseh was built in 1417. It is rectangular with a courtyard and a wide portal serving as an entrance over which there was once a library (Ketab-Khana). The medresseh was built by a Persian architect called Ismail for Ulug-Beg, the famous astronomer and administrator. It was completely rebuilt in 1583 and has been restored many times since. The decorations are of a scientific and mainly astronomical character, owing to Ulug-Beg's proclivities. A wooden plaque on the gate bears the inscription, 'It is the duty of every true Moslem, man and woman, to strive after knowledge.' The decorative tiles have been restored recently. Soviet scientists spent much time trying to find out their chemical composition and finally the secret of their production was discovered, and a small factory founded in Bukhara to produce exactly the right enamel for their restoration.

Abdulaziz-Khan Medresseh, Kolkhoznaya St., stands facing the Ulug-Beg Medresseh and forms an architectural ensemble with it. It has a summer mosque in the courtyard and the winter mosque is in the western corner of the entrance passage. Both are richly decorated with majolica, glazed tiles, brick mosaic, and carved marble. On the facings of the walls are various paintings of animals and also of Chinese motifs, bearing witness to the fact that in the 17th century there existed trade relations between China and Bukhara. The left part of the façade and the right part of the courtyard appear lacking in decoration for the reason that before the medresseh was really completed Abdulaziz-Khan was overpowered and the work, begun in 1652, ceased.

Kukeldash Medresseh, Lab-i-Hauz Sq. This is one of the largest and grandest medressehs in Central Asia. The facing has much in common with that of the Abdullah-Khan Medresseh, built ten years later. The entrance door is made of carved wooden planks fastened with wooden pegs and inside the courtyard is a fine portal of blue, green, and white brick. The building contains 160 cells (hudjras) and today houses the local record office.

Lab-i-Hauz Sq. itself is of interest to the visitor for it is still one of Bukhara's liveliest market places and one of the most attractive spots in the city. It is so called because of the large pool in the centre which has been there since 1620. 'Hauz' means 'pool' and the name of the square, 'over-the-pool'. The ensemble of buildings around the square was completed under the Ashtarkhanid dynasty. On the same side of the square as the Kukeldash Medresseh is the Yr-Nazaar-Ilchei Medresseh, which was called after the Bukharan Ambassador to Catherine the Great, and was built at her expense. On the west side of the square is the Lab-i-Hauz Mosque (1611) and the Khanigah (prayer house) of Divan Beg. Opposite is the

Divan Beg Medresseh, built in 1622 as a caravanserai and then rebuilt as a medresseh which accounts for its having no mosque. On its façade and the right wing it bears an effigy of the mythological Semurg Bird and a deer.

The Chahar-Minar Medresseh, built in 1807, belongs to a much later period than most of the other ancient monuments of Bukhara and in style it resembles an Indian mosque. Its name means 'four minarets' but in fact the four towers are not true minarets. They are nevertheless very imposing, being covered with cornflower blue and dark blue bricks and crowned with blue cupolas. The cupolas, just as those of many of the other buildings in Bukhara, are topped with special spikes to encourage storks to build their nests there. These birds have been nesting in Bukhara for a thousand years or more, but it is one of the few places in Central Asia that they favour.

In the 15th century a number of buildings connected with the commercial life of the city appeared in Bukhara. Among them were five cupolas constructed at the crossroads on Shah-Restan, the main shopping street. Inside the cupolas were little shops and the cupolas themselves were called after the trade they housed. Still in existence are the grey domes of the *Taq-i-Sarrafon* (at the crossing of Sovietskaya and Lenin Streets) where the money-changers did business, the *Taq-i-Talpakfurushon* (Pushkin and Frunze Streets) where skull caps were and are still sold, and the *Taq-i-Zargaran*, the goldsmiths' bazaar which used to be the centre of the whole trading area.

To the south of the city in Kirov St. is *Namazgoh Mosque*, its name meaning 'the place of prayer'. It was built in the 12th century on the site of an estate with a rich orchard and a zoo, as an out-of-town mosque of the type constructed for great religious holidays when the city mosques could not house all the faithful. It was redecorated in the 14th century with horizontal majolica plates bearing bright blue, navy, and white inscriptions in Arabic. The cupola-crowned gallery was added in the 16th century. The architecture of the main entrance is similar to that of the Maghak-i-Attari Mosque and the west wall is attractively decorated in terracotta and blue majolica.

In the eastern part of Bukhara, just beyond the railway station at Lenin St. 180, are two more buildings of interest. The larger, a *mausoleum and mosque* built in the 13th or 14th century, is connected with the name of Saifuddin Bukharzi, a Moslem theologian who died in 1262. It consists of two rooms, one for prayer and one with the tomb. The walls of the building and the cupola, both of which were cracking, have been reinforced with iron. Nearby is another *mausoleum* which stands over the grave of a Mongol noble, Buyan Quli Khan, a descendant of Genghis-Khan who was killed in Samarkand in 1358. It is lavishly decorated, being faced both inside and out with terracotta in bright blue, navy, violet, and white. The imposing portal on the eastern side is richly decorated so that it appears to be covered with stone lacework. The mausoleum was completely restored in 1926.

There are three mosques open in Bukhara. The best one to visit is *Hodzha-Zai-Edin Mosque,* Vodoprovodnaya St. 5.

Synagogue, Tsentralnaya St. 20. According to local tradition, the Bukharan Jews came originally from Shiraz in the time of Timur and indeed he may have brought some of them with him from Baghdad. They wear traditional costumes on feast days and have some special customs of their own. Their native language is either Tadzhik or Uzbek.

History Museum and Local Museum, in the Ark, Registan Sq. open 9–5; closed Tues. These hours apply to all museums and monuments which can be closed in Bukhara. Application should be made through Intourist for them to be open at any other time.

Lenin Monument, in front of the Intourist Hotel

Frunze Monument, in Frunze Park. General Mikhail V. Frunze was the old-time communist whose troops defeated the last emir.

Revolution Obelisk, in front of the railway station, and dedicated to those who died in 1920.

Music and Drama Theatre, near Kirov Park

Summer Branch of the Music and Drama Theatre, Lenin St. 61 opposite Lab-i-Haus.

Stadium, Shevchenko Prospect.

Intourist Hotel and *'Shark' (meaning 'eastern') Restaurant*, Lenin Sq. TEL. 22–76

'Bukhara' Restaurant, Frunze Sq.

Branch of the 'Bukhara' Restaurant, Kirov St.

Café, Lenin St. 84

Ice Cream Parlour and Tea Room, Frunze Sq.

Shashlik Bar, in a small garden near the Intourist Hotel

Bank, Lenin St. 41

Taxi ranks, Kukeldash Sq. and at the railway station.

Char-Bakir (four girls) Medresseh, 7 km. from town. This medresseh was built in the 16th–17th century. One can reach the top of the building through a side entrance, and from there is a good panoramic view. The ancient cemetery nearby was the burial place of prominent Bukharans. There are two mosques on the ground floor of the medresseh. Char-Bakir can be reached by car.

The *Setori-y-Mahi-Hasa Palace* (also known as Mahasa) lies 14 km. to the north of Bukhara. It was built in 1911–12 as a summer residence by the last of the emirs, Said-Alim-Khan, a despotic gentleman who had a hundred wives (some even say four hundred and fifty). The artificial style of the palace resulted from a mixture of the poorer features of Central Asian architecture and elements introduced by the Europeanised tastes of the last emir. European influence is felt in all the details of the construction of the single storey, L-shaped building. Interesting are the Summer Room with stained glass windows, the Ministerial Room painted in colours which were mixed with egg, and the large white Ceremonial Hall with mirrored walls.

Today the palace forms part of the Bukhara Museum and is used as a rest home. Peacocks stroll in the park and the local inhabitants like to point out the little stone pavilion from which they say the emir could watch his womenfolk bathing in the large pool below. The smaller palace nearby was built by Ahad, the last emir's father, and retains all the elements of the old national architectural style. Now it houses a lung sanatorium for children.

THE CAUCASIAN COASTAL ROAD

The Caucasian Coastal Road links a succession of seaside towns and villages, some of them large holiday resorts and some smaller and less crowded. There are bays and beaches all the way and to the left of the road rise the rocky foothills of the Caucasus Mountains, in many places lush with subtropical vegetation. There are a number of side trips which can be made to beauty spots further inland, up the valleys; particularly recommended are those to Krasnaya Polyana and to Lake Ritsa.

Our road begins at Ghelendzhik and runs south-east for about 355 km. to the resort and seaport of Sukhumi. See map, p. 73.

Ghelendzhik

The name means 'white bride', possibly because it was once a centre of the slave trade. Ghelendzhik is situated in an oval bay hemmed in by two capes, the rugged Tolstyi (thick) and the gently sloping Tonky (thin). The beach is stony except for a sandy patch known as Solntsedar, below Cape Tonky. It is a sunny place, with excellently pure and dry air, and strong winds. The average annual temperature is 13°C. (55°F.), and the average temperature in July and August is 24°C. (75°F.); the bathing season lasts from June until October.

The Greek town of Toricos was situated here in the 6th century B.C. This was succeeded by other towns—Pagri and, after a further few hundred years, Eptala. In the time of the Turkish occupation Eptala was the chief port for the export of local girls to the Turkish harems. In 1864 Kazaks were settled here, but they were used to working steppe soil and were unable to live off this forest land; and later foreigners were invited to settle in their place. Greeks and Czechs arrived in 1877 and made their homes in the surrounding region.

Now Ghelendzhik is a flourishing seaside resort with Lenin St. as its main thoroughfare. It is planned, by 1980, to provide accommodation for 1,000,000 summer visitors instead of the current 250,000 in the 100 km. of coastline on either side of the resort.

Nearby, in the valley of the R. Ashampe, is the Black Sea Oceanology Research Settlement.

Beside the bay burial mounds of the 6th and 10th centuries B.C. have been found, as well as a settlement of primitive man with implements of the Late Stone Age and the Bronze Age. 5 km.

away near the R. Aderba are some ancient barrows.

Local Museum, Lenin St. 23. Open 8–1 and 2–5; closed Mon.

Partisans' Monument, Lermontov Boulevard. This statue of a seaman, a factory worker and a peasant was erected to commemorate the partisans of the Civil War.

Lermontov Monument, on the promenade

World War II Victory Monument, on the sea shore, near the town stadium

Ghelendzhik Hotel and Restaurant

Platan (Plane tree) Restaurant

Mayak (Lighthouse) Restaurant

Café, Lenin St.

G.P.O., Lenin St.

Ghelendzhik Motel, Lunacharsky St. on the right and 5 km. from Ghelendzhik town centre. The motel has a 2-storey hotel, small bungalows, an eating house, garage, and a Service and Filling Station.

Camping Site, Lunacharsky St., opposite the Motel on the left side of the road, and even nearer to the sea. The site has a café, shop, and a hiring depot.

Ghelendzik has a boat hire station and boats take trips to Golubaya Bukhta (Blue Bay), north of Cape Tonky, and one of the prettiest places on this part of the coast.

It is 63 km. from here to Arkhipo-Osipovka.

Divnomorsk

The turning to this place is 7 km. outside Ghelendzhik. The name meaning 'marvellous sea' was given to this place in 1964. The old name of Falshivy (False) Ghelendzhik is more curious. It arose because the bay is so similar in appearance to that of Ghelendzhik that ships find it hard to know where they are.

The good beach is of sand and fine shingle; and the sea bed is sandy and slopes gently, reaching a depth of 1·5 m. 8–9 m. from the shore.

At 3 km. south of this point is the most picturesque part of the region called Dzhankhot after a local noble of the last century and meaning 'born-with-a-silver-spoon-in-the-mouth'.

Nearby is a grove of pine trees. The Russian writer Korolenko lived here at the beginning of the 20th century and called it 'a basket of greenery'.

Beyond the turning to Divnomorsk the main road runs further back from the sea, following the Novorossisk-Sukhumi Highway. Work on this road was begun in 1891 when 300,000 peasants eagerly volunteered to work on it because of the famine in parts of Russia at that time. It was accordingly known as Hungry Highway.

At the 57 km. milestone stands a large Bronze Age stone tomb.

Café, at the 689/58 km. milestone.

The road, lined with azaleas, now runs over the *Mikhailovsky Pass*, 325 m. above sea level. The highest mountain is Mount Tkachegochuk (Land of the Gods). A curative spring discovered 100 years ago can be seen on the left side of the road, on the way up the 4-km. long steep hill.

At the other side, at the bottom of the hill, there is another spring and a statue of a girl with her hair in plaits. She is kneeling down and the stream runs out of her water jar.

The orchards in the valley of the mountain river Dougab and in the surrounding area belong to one of the biggest farms in the region, the *Mikhailov Pass Farm*, with 1350 hectares (3375 acres) mostly under fruit and vines.

From the highway a side road runs down to the seaside villages of Krinitsa and Betta.

Krinitsa

At the end of the last century a group of intellectuals following Leo Tolstoy's teaching decided to take up manual labour, and founded a farm colony here. The Tolstoy Monument was erected in 1910. The beach is pebbly, and 3–4 m. from the shore the water reaches a depth of 1·5–2 m.

Betta

This village founded in the 1890s is 8 km. south of Krinitsa. It has a shingle beach and a sandy seabed.

The next part of the road is known as Pshadsky Pass (546 m. above sea level). Near the statue of a she-bear with two cubs is a sign '100 m.' indicating the way to one of the biggest tombs in the region.

Pshada

The obelisk in the main square was erected to commemorate the heroes of the Civil War.

There is an eating house here.

Arkhipo-Osipovka

This place stands on the bank of the R. Vulcan. In 1840 there was an uprising of a large army of 12,000 locals against the Russian garrison of 59 who held the fortress. The garrison fought back and finally in despair asked for a volunteer to set fire to the powder room. A certain Arkhip Osipov came forward and as he rushed to his doom with a blazing torch he shouted 'Brothers, remember Arkhip Osipov!' The explosion was so great that there was but a single survivor to tell the story afterwards. A white cross, commemorating the event, stands on a small hill near the sea. It was erected in 1876 at the order of Alexander II.

There is a fruit-preserving factory in the town.

From the suspension bridge over the R. Vulcan a paved path runs down for 1300 m. to the sea. The beach in the bay is pebbly with patches of sand; boats can be hired.

Kavkaz Restaurant, by the turning to the camping site.

Russkiye Kvass i Akroshka Snack Bar Kvass is a drink made from fermented rye bread and flavoured with raisins. It is a good thirst-quencher in summer and is also used as the base of *akroshka*, a cold, summer soup containing meat, hard-boiled egg, cucumber, radishes, spring onions, dill, and other herbs.

Volna (wave) Café, by the beach
Post and Telegraph Office
Camping Site, on the edge of the sea, among pine trees and sheltered by the hills

Further along the road, at the 141/425 km. milestone is a path with a convenient slope running down to Golden Beach; this is a sandy beach 6 km. long and 50–75 m. wide.

Dzhubga

This resort lies in the valley of the R. Dzhubga among sweet chestnut woods and large tobacco plantations. Although Dzhubga was founded as long ago as 1832, it has not grown to be a large resort. The beach is of sand and shingle; there is a boat hire station in the town, and the fishing is good.

A pre-historic tomb can be seen in the vicinity.

Druzhba Restaurant
Motel, in the village, on the right of the main road. Accommodation is in 2-storey buildings, with an eating house, and a kitchen garden.

Filling and Repair Station with Carwash, both at the Motel

On the road leading into Novo-Mikhailovskoye there is a turning which takes one down to a tourist base and to the sea.

Novo-Mikhailovskoye

This part of the coast is known as Zolotaya Dolina (Golden Valley); there is a sandy beach and the sea is shallow. *The Orlyonok (eaglet) Pioneer Camp* is situated here in grounds of 300 hectares (750 acres). There is a swimming pool, a stadium and a school here so that it can be used by children in the good weather both before and long after the summer holidays.

Primorsky (seaside) Restaurant

Tuapse

The name means 'two waters' in the Cherkess language; it was so called because the R. Tuapse and the R. Pauk flow into the sea at this point.

The climate is more moderate than it is farther south, and makes this a good fruit farming area. What used to be a small seaside town has grown into a port and a manufacturing centre. A railway line and two pipelines link it with the oil fields of the north Caucasus. Oil refining, ship repairing, engineering, and metal processing are carried on.

Karl Marx St. is the main throughfare of the town.

A small Russian fortress called Veliaminov Fort was founded here in 1838 (one of the 17 established in these parts to assist in the conquering of the Caucasus) but it was blown up by the Russians themselves in 1854; parts of the stronghold remained until 1897.

Local Museum, Politayeva St. 8. Open 10–6; closed Tues.

Lenin Monument, beside the main road
Seamen's Club, in the port, in the Palace of Seamen

Yuzhnaya (South) Hotel, Vokzalnaya St. 8. TEL. 3–12

Tuapse Restaurant, Karl Marx St. beside the main road

Café, Pirovskoy St. 2

G.P.O., Karl Marx St. 9/10

Bank, Karl Marx St. 22

Bookshop, Karl Marx St. 7/9

Filling Station, beside the main road into town

Service Station, beside the main road into town

Ashei

This is a pleasant little seaside resort.

Lazarevskoye

This resort is called after Admiral Mikhail Lazarev (1788–1851), who commanded the Black Sea Fleet between 1833 and 1850.

It stands at the mouth of the R. Psezuapsye, which has a good bathing beach of sand and shingle, where the water gets deep quickly. The bathing season lasts from June to October, but is best in the autumn when the temperature of the water has risen to 22°C. (72°F.).

The place was originally founded as a fortress in 1839. Since the beginning of the 20th century tea has been cultivated in this region, which was in fact the first place in Russia to grow it. Now there are many tea farms in the neighbourhood.

Church of the Nativity of the Virgin, built at the beginning of the 19th century

Lazarev Monument, near the ruined fortress walls and the railway station

Odoyevsky Monument Alexander Odoyevsky. (1802–39) was a poet who was sentenced to 10 years hard labour in Siberia for active participation in the 1825 St. Petersburg revolt, and who was afterwards sent here as a soldier; it was here that he died of malaria in 1839. The monument was unveiled in December 1952.

Hotel

Volna (Wave) Holiday Home. This home is for young foreign visitors.

Priboi Restaurant, at the Motel, Pobeda St. 2

Motel, Service and Filling Station, Pobeda St. 2. On the left of the main road are small bungalows, and on the right is the car park, service station, and restaurant. 150 m. from the Motel is a buffet.

Camping Site, Sochinskoye Chaussee 2a, on the right of the main road towards the sea. This turning is the first on the right after the bridge over the R. Psezuapsye, and the camping site is at the mouth of the river, near the sea. There are a buffet, shop, self-service kitchen, and other facilities.

The Mamedovo Ravine is near Lazarevskoye. There are small waterfalls here and some ancient tombs in the shape of old sea chests.

It is 79 km. from Lazerovskoye to Sochi.

At the 253/494 km. milestone is the *Tourist Café*.

Loo

(pronounced to rhyme with 'door')

1·5 km. from the main road are the ruins of an 11th–12th-century church.

Gorizont (horizon) Café

Dagomyss

There is a big tea factory here; furniture is also manufactured in the town.

Park, on the western slopes of Mount Armyanka. This park which was formerly imperial property, was founded in 1900, and many rare trees flourish in its Mediterranean climate.

Krasnodarsky Chai Tearoom

Dagomyss Hotel, towards the sea on the right side of the road. The hotel is situated in wooded grounds where nut trees, crab apples and wild pears grow, and has 2 hotel-type buildings, an eating house, sports grounds, a reading room, television, an open air cinema, a fully equipped and covered car park, and carwash. *The Filling and Service Station* are also here.

Camping Site, near the motel. Motor-boats leave for Sochi from this place.

It is 23 km. from here to Sochi.

Sochi

Population—225,000 (1970)

The name derives from that of a local tribe, the Shashe. The largest resort on the north-eastern coast of the Black Sea, Sochi stretches along the shore for 30·5 km. and lies between the R. Mamaika and the R. Kudepsta. Its climate is as fine as that of Nice, San Remo, and other popular places in Europe. The average summer temperature is 23°C. (73°F.), and the temperature of the sea rises from 18°C. (64°F.) in mid-June to 29°C. (84°F.) later in the summer and in the early autumn; the sea bathing season lasts for five months. Autumn is from October until December, and spring begins in March. The best time of the year is late summer, known in these parts as the 'velvet season'.

Compared with other places along this coast, Sochi is a young town. The fortress founded in 1838 used to be called Navagenskoye, and in 1840 it held out against a local uprising when it was besieged. The heroine of the occasion was the Commander's wife, Mme. Posipkina, who even under fire walked with her parasol along the earth wall to encourage the men. The Commander was afterwards promoted and Mme. Posipkina received a costly necklace as a personal gift from Tsaritsa Alexandra. At one time the fortress was called Alexandria after the Tsaritsa. In 1894 it was still the site of a military settlement, but received the title of town in 1896. Its curative properties were then recognised and in 1909 it became known as the Caucasian Riviera, and as a health resort it really dates from this time. The opening of the railway line in 1925 led to speedier growth, and since 1933, when it was decided to turn Sochi into a resort of national importance, millions of roubles have been spent on it and the best Soviet architects, including I. Zholtovsky and A. Shusiev, have been employed in the construction of the resort. The harbour building was completed in

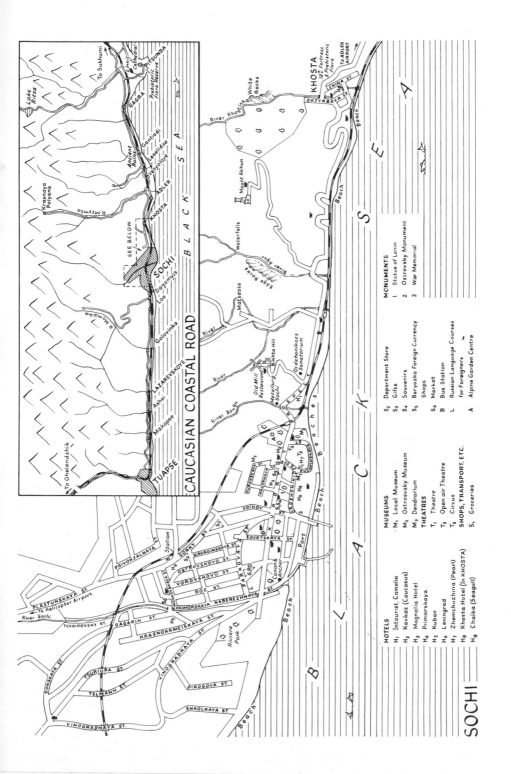

SOCHI

HOTELS
H₁ Intourist, Camelia
H₂ Kavkaz (Caucasus)
H₃ Magnolia Hotel
H₄ Primorskaya
H₅ Kuban
H₆ Leningrad
H₇ Zhemchuzhina (Pearl)
H₈ Khosta Hotel (in KHOSTA)
H₉ Chaika (Seagull)

MUSEUMS
M₁ Local Museum
M₂ Ostrovsky Museum
M₃ Dendrarium

THEATRES
T₁ Theatre
T₂ Open air Theatre
T₃ Circus

SHOPS, TRANSPORT, ETC.
S₁ Groceries
S₂ Department Store
S₃ Gifts
S₄ Souvenirs
S₅ Beryozka Foreign Currency Shops
S₆ Market
B Bus Station
L Russian Language Courses for Foreigners
A Alpine Garden Centre

MONUMENTS
1 Statue of Lenin
2 Ostrovsky Monument
3 War Memorial

CAUCASIAN COASTAL ROAD

1955; its spire is 37 m. high.

The Sochi Experimental Station of Subtropical and Southern Fruit Crops lies up the valley of the R. Bzugu. It was first organised in 1894 when it dealt chiefly with garden crops, but now tea, vines, and other fruits are studied here.

At present visitors to this area number over a million annually and there are 58 palatial sanatoria with more being built. Since 1958 the *Chaika (Seagull) Sanatorium* has accepted visitors from abroad; it has a funicular railway connecting it with the beach just as the *Lazurny Bereg* (Azure coast) and the *Ordzhonikidze Sanatoria* have. The Ordzhonikidze Sanatorium is among the largest and most splendid of all. It was built between 1935 and 1941 by Kuznetsov in Italian renaissance style, and part of the interior has been decorated by artists from the villages of Palekh and Mstera in traditional Russian style. Flights of white marble steps lead up to it. The *Metallurg (Steel worker), Sochi*, and *Rossia Sanatoria*, among others, have heated sea-water swimming pools to attract people there in the winter. The Sochi and *Dzerzhinsky Sanatoria* are linked with the beach by tall lift towers and the *Noviye Sochi Sanatorium* has a lift inside the cliff going down 35 m. It was built in 1961. From here a tunnel of 112 m. leads to the beach.

Since the spring of 1961 the territory around has been known as Greater Sochi; it includes 145 km. of coastline, running from Vesyoloye to Shapse (near Tuapse). Included in the total accommodation of Greater Sochi are 60 sanatoria, 20 holiday homes, 10 tourist bases, and over 20 Pioneer Camps for children.

Cathedral of the Archangel Michael, Mayachnaya St. 14. The cathedral was built in 1852, and is open for service.

Ruins of the Fortress of 1838, not far from the lighthouse.

Local Museum, Ordzhonikidze St. 29. Open 10–6; closed Tues. Sections on the natural history of the Caucasus and the Black Sea.

Ostrovsky Museum, Ostrovskov Lane 4. Open 10–6 daily; closed Wed. Nikolai Ostrovsky (1904–36) served in the civil war and then at the age of 20 became paralysed, blind, and bedridden. He moved to Sochi in 1924 and wrote 'How the Steel Was Tempered' and the greater part of 'Born of the Storm', now standard literature for Soviet youth. The museum is located in his house and in a new building completed in 1957; the street is called after him, as are a school and a library.

Statue of Lenin, Kurortny St.

War Memorial, Voikova St.

Cannon and Anchor, Primorskaya Naberezhnaya. On the sea shore and near the Pushkin Library is a cannon on a concrete pediment, and in front of it stands an anchor weighing 2800 kg. which was made in the Urals in 1719.

Theatre, Teatralnaya Sq. Built in 1937 to hold 1100 people, by architect K. Chernopyatov.

Open Air Theatre, Frunze Park, Chernomorskaya Sq. Built in 1937.

Circus, Pushkin Prospect. This holds 1180 people.

During the summer season many touring performers and companies come to Sochi, as do exhibitions.

Dendrarium, Kurortny Prospect 74. Open 10–6. The Dendrarium covers an area of 16 hectares (40 acres) and is divided in two by Kurortny Prospect. It contains as many as 1600 different shrubs and trees, including subtropical specimens, from all over the world and is really worth a visit. The upper part is the most decorative with a pavilion, sculptures, and fountains, while the lower part is more natural with bamboo groves and magnolias. It is planned to extend the territory to 60 hectares (150 acres).

Riviera Park covers 10 hectares (25 acres) and contains 100 different species of trees and bushes from all parts of the world; there is a subtropical section. There are a number of cafés here, a dance floor, and an open air variety stage.

There is a stadium in Sochi as well as three swimming pools, a boat hire station, tennis courts, and as many as 400 sports grounds.

Other parks include Frunze Park and those belonging to the sanatoria.

Camelia (Intourist) Hotel and Restaurant, Kurortny Prospect 91, TEL. 99–03–97. There is a Beryozka Shop in the hotel which accepts foreign currency and the hotel has its own bathing beach. The Intourist organisation also rents accommodation for foreign visitors at the Chaika, Kirov, Lazurny Bereg and Caucasians Riviera Sanatoria.

Primorskaya Hotel and Restaurant, Sokolova St. 1, TEL. 92–58–27. The hotel faces the sea.

Youzhnaya (south) Hotel, Teatralnaya St. 8, TEL. 21–69; Intourist office TEL. 28–29

Kuban Hotel, Gagarin St. 5, TEL. 2–27–78, 2–40–50

Chaika (seagull) Sanatorium, Kurortny Prospect 98

Magnolia Hotel and Restaurant, Kurortny Prospect 50, TEL. 99–56–72.

Leningrad Hotel & Restaurant, Morskoi Per. 2, TEL. 92–36–86

Zhemchuzhina (pearl) Hotel & Restaurant, Chernomorskaya St. 5

Svetlana Restaurant, Pushkinskaya St. 10

Gorka (hill) Restaurant, Voikov St. 22

Goluboye (light blue) Restaurant, Voikov St. 8

Primorye (seaside) Restaurant, Chernomorskaya St. 10

Dieticheski (dietetic) Restaurant, Voikov St. 10

Akhun Restaurant, on the slopes of Mt. Bolshoi Akhun

Noviye Sochi Restaurant, Vinogradnaya St.

G.P.O., Vorovskovo St. 35, TEL. 05

Bank, Ordzhonikidze St. 2

Sochi Information Bureau, Gorky St. 3

Beryozka Foreign Currency Shops, Kurortny Prospect 91 & Primorskaya St. 16a

Souvenirs, Kurortny Prospect 25

Gifts, Gorky St. 40

Holidaymakers' Requirements, Kooperativnaya St. 6

Bookshops, Voikov St. 5 & 16

Chemist, Kurortny Prospect 24

Art Shop, Boulevarnaya St. opposite Morskoi Vokzal

Jeweller's, Kurortny Prospect 26

Market, Kirpichnaya St. 30

Adler Airport, 36 km. out of town; TEL. 92–33–11

Sputnik International Youth Camp, at the foot of Mount Akhun

Lenin Sanatorium, 3 km. from the Rheumatics Institute. The walk leads through a wooded park and across mountain streams and gorges with good views.

Bikhta Hill (305 m.), 6·5 km. from the Voroshilov Sanatorium. There is a good view of Sochi from this hill. *Old Mill Restaurant* is here.

Ravine of the R. Agur The road begins 8 km. south of Sochi, runs through forest land, and ends in a car park. From here a path with pleasant views leads on across a small bridge over the R. Agur to a little lake. Although it is 7 m. deep, the bottom is clearly visible. The waterfall of the R. Agur (27 m. high) is nearby, and a path leads up to a second waterfall.

Mount Akhun. Near the turning to the Agur Waterfalls is another turning from which a good road leads to Mount Akhun (663 m.). It is 22 km. from the centre of Sochi to the mountain. 3 km. up this mountain road are the ruins of a 13th-century church. *'Akhun' Restaurant* is on the mountain and a look-out tower, 30 m. high, built by Vorobyev in 1936, commands a good view of the snow-covered tops of the main Caucasus range, of Sochi, and of the whole region around. From near the tower a path runs down the mountain to the Agur Ravine and waterfalls.

Matsesta

20 km. from Sochi. The name means 'firewater', and refers to the mineral springs discovered in 1837 in the valley of the R. Matsesta, the waters of which cause the skin to redden. Now new wells have been sunk to a depth of 1524 m. and the water is 38°C (100°F.). It has nearly three times the highest sulphur content ever found in a natural spring and its supplies are inexhaustible.

The water is recommended for treating circulatory, muscular, nervous, gynaecological, and skin diseases. Intourist's courses of treatment last for 26 days.

Restaurant, in the building of the salt-water baths.

Orliniye Skaly (eagle Rocks), 377 m. above sea level, walking distance from Matsesta. The path leads through the orchards of the Matsesta Valley and then climbs steeply through the woods above the town. There are pits beside the trail, remains of naturally formed limestone caves. From the top there is a fine panorama of the Bolshoi Akhun and the Caucasus Mountains and below, at the foot of the precipice, is the Agura with its first waterfall and the little lake.

At the 435/312-km. milestone is *Filling Station No. 3*. It gives round-the-clock service and its telephone no. is 56–83.

Khosta

The name comes from 'kho' meaning 'be careful' and 'sta' meaning 'river'. The legend from which the name is derived tells of an outlaw who lived in the ravine and who used to scare people passing by. On Italian maps of the 13th–15th centuries, in the place of present-day Khosta, a Genoese settlement called 'Kasto' is shown. In 1901–3 fertile plots of land were given to people on the condition that within three years they cleared the ground, where necessary, and began to build.

The little R. Khostinka runs out of a deep ravine. Khosta is surrounded by mountains on three sides, and lies on the edge of a small bay on a good beach of mixed sand and shingle, better than the beaches at Sochi. The mountains protect the resort from the north-west winds, so that it is always calm and warm here; the temperature is 1 or 2 degrees warmer than in Sochi.

Khosta is famous for its *marine park*, founded in 1930, and near this is a *box and yew park* which covers 300 hectares (750 acres) and lies 3 km. inland from the sea. In the middle of the park are the ruins of a 12th-century fortress, supposedly Genoese.

A path leads up the valley to the White Rocks (200 m.).

Khosta Restaurant, Kiparisovaya St. 5

Volna (wave) Restaurant

Adler

Adler stands at the mouth of the R. Mzymta ('fierce' in Georgian), which rises 1990 m. up in the mountains; the whole area used at one time to be a hotbed of malaria. The winter here is colder than in Sochi, and the summer hotter but with less rain. Now tea and tobacco, citrus fruits, plums, olives, and vines are grown, and fruit trees and violets begin to flower in the middle of January. There are some sandy patches on the wide shingle beach.

In the north-western suburbs of Adler there is a big tea factory, and across the bridge over the R. Mzymta is a large poultry farm which supplies all the resorts in this region. On the left bank of the R. Mzymta, south of Adler, is the Yuzhniye Kultury Horticultural Research Station. A good park with attractive ponds was laid out here in 1910. There is a rose garden, and an avenue leading down to the sea. The station covers 20 hectares (50 acres) and includes 800 kinds of subtropical plants.

As recently as 1968 a new beauty spot appeared near Adler. Huge rocks, the largest weighing about 100 tons, were dislodged by the force of wind and water and fell with tremendous crashes into the river. The local seismic station registered earth tremors of 4 degrees at the time. The rocks settled to form a natural dam and the lake that built up behind it is 2 km. long and 300 m. wide.

The water is 19 m. deep in places.

One of Adler's suburbs is being developed as a new resort for a further 5000 visitors. Adler is the southernmost point of the territory of the Russian Federation, and its airport also serves Sochi.

Fortress, by the sea. These are the remains of a fortress built here in 1837.

Russian Soldiers' Monument, on the Boulevard. This monument commemorates the Russian soldiers who fell in the Russo-Turkish War.

Bestuzhev-Marlinsky Monument, in the park. The Russian writer Bestuzhev-Marlinsky was among the Russian soldiers shot here when they landed in 1837.

Motel, Pervomaiskaya St. 41, in the centre of Adler and 10 minutes walk from the sea. This motel has shops, a café, and a fully equipped car park. The filling and service station are both open 7 am–6 pm.

Camping Site, on the road from Adler to Gagra; turn right towards the sea at the village of Vesoloye (Happy), 10 km. from Adler. The camping site is in a eucalyptus grove on the territory of the local state farm, and close to the edge of the sea.

Krasnaya Polyana

Krasnaya Polyana where the territory of the Caucasus State Reservation begins, can be reached by a very spectacular road from Adler. It was built in 1899 by engineer Konstantinov. Over the first hill and past the village of Golitsinka there are the ruins of a monastery and also some stalactite caves. Then the road runs through the Akhtsu Gorge with the R. Mzymta roaring at the bottom. In the gorge the road runs through a tunnel, and travellers used to light large candles before entering it. The road just before the tunnel is called 'Carry us through, O Lord', as is part of the Daryal Ravine in the northern Caucasus. The obelisk with a star on the top, which stands just before the tunnel, commemorates the Red Army men who died here in 1920, and the metal obelisk on the other side of the tunnel, on the river bank, is dedicated to the partisans who died here at the same time. The stream which gushes out from the rocks on the left of the road forms a waterfall known as 'Maiden's Tears'.

The road climbs on, passing mineral springs such as the Narzan, Borzhomi, and Yessentuki springs, and finally reaches Krasnaya Polyana nestling in the hills. Here there is an average annual temperature of 21°C (70°F). The reservation itself covers 100,000 hectares (250,000 acres) and has about 1400 different kinds of trees and plants, and 60 species of mammals including deer, boar, panthers, bears, and a herd of more than 60 bison.

Krasnaya Polyana has been inhabited since prehistoric times, both on account of its advantageous geographical position and because of its proximity to routes leading to passes over the mountains. Both Stone Age and Bronze Age tombs have been found here and the ruins of the fortress in the vicinity date back to the reign of

Mithradates the Great of Pontus. The natural riches of the area included furs, game, honey, wax, and precious woods and they attracted expeditions from Byzantium, Greece, Rome and Genoa.

Until the middle of the 19th century, Krasnaya Polyana was inhabited by members of various mountain tribes like the Cherkassians who, in 1864, were the last in the whole of the Caucasus to hold out against the Russians. However on 21 May 1864, a religious service was held for 25,000 soldiers and afterwards a manifesto was read out announcing the end of the war in the Caucasus. Following this, most of the local Cherkassians moved to Turkey. Their village of Kbaade was renamed Romanovsk in honour of the imperial family but the place remained desolate until in 1878 about forty Greek families moved here from Stavropol Province. It was they who first used the name Krasnaya Polyana (red glade), because of the russet-coloured ferns and bracken in the autumn. Some years later a group of Estonian peasants settled close to the village too.

In 1898 a special state commission visited Krasnaya Polyana and found it suitable for development as a mountain resort; a sign was put up on the road into the village reading 'The Town of Romanovsk', but apart from the construction of an imperial hunting lodge and the proclamation that the area was a royal hunting reserve, no further development took place.

During the civil war, Krasnaya Polyana changed hands several times and the fighting accounts for the two obelisks by the road, mentioned above.

The mountains surrounding Krasnaya Polyana are Mt. Achiskho (2365 m), Mt. Aibga (2380 m) and Mt. Shoogoos (3245 m.). It is possible to walk to Mt. Achishkho, to Lake Kardivach, and through the Kutakheku Pass to Lake Ritsa (24 km.).

Back again on the main road, as it leads out of Adler is the *Cosmos Restaurant*.

Filling Station, at the 428/319 km. milestone
Shashlik Bar, at the 419/328 km. milestone
Camping Site, at the 416/331 km. milestone

Vesyoloye
Druzhba (friendship) Restaurant

Leselidze
Camping Site

Gantiadi
The ruins of a 5th–6th-century church can be seen in this village. Motorists should turn towards the sea from the main road.

Motel, near the sea among eucalyptus trees, has an eating house and showers and a car park. There is good bathing from June to October.

Gagra
This resort is located on a narrow strip of coastland, and at this point the mountains, which are of

porous limestone, full of gorges and caves, come down very close to the sea. Some of the peaks rise to 2750 m. Gagra is the warmest place on the eastern coast of the Black Sea; roses bloom in the winter and the trees are nearly always green. From May till November the sea is between 16 and 23°C. (61–73°F.). The beach is of shingle with some sandy places. Thanks to the climate, experiments are being made with the cultivation of cacao. In the last fifteen years several hundred trees have been planted.

This spot has long been known as a fortified place. In 600 B.C. it went by the name of Triglit, and its fate was closely linked with that of Rome and Greece, and later with Genoa. Gagra was then under Turkish rule, as was most of the Black Sea coast, until it was taken by Russia in 1830. It began to develop as a resort in 1901 when Prince Alexander Oldenburgsky decided to popularise it. In a short time hotels, a quay, and other tourist facilities were constructed, and the Prince built himself a palace which can still be seen.

Today there are about 30 sanatoria, mostly located on the steep slopes of the mountains. Paths, avenues and steps join them to the *Marine Park*, which runs for 3 km. beside the sea, and covers 14 hectares (35 acres). Many of the trees and shrubs are subtropical and there are statues, fountains, and an artificial lake with black and white swans, in the park. At the eastern end of the park is a semi-circular colonnade and a car park. To the west of the park the little R. Gagripsh runs into the sea. In the grounds of the Zhoekvara Sanatorium are the remains of a 6th–7th-century church. Gagra's plantation of cork oak was transplanted from Africa in the first half of the 19th century. The trees have now reached a height of 30 m.

There are many pleasant walks in the vicinity. The *ravine of the R. Tsikherva*, at the beginning of which there is a two-storey cave, is 3 km. away. It is about 8 km. to the picturesque *ravine of the R. Zhoekvara* which is surrounded by cliffs, and has two waterfalls. By the road are the ruins of a watchtower known as the *Marlinsky Tower*. Another walk of about 10 km. leads to a grotto with a spring in the ravine of the R. Gagripsh; the path has a good view of the sea and goes through beechwoods.

Gagripsh (Beauty of Gagra) Hotel and Restaurant. It is said locally that this three-storey hotel was built without a nail.

Holodnaya Rechka Motel is 8 km. from Gagra, inland from the main road; it has a cinema, a rest room, baths, showers, a shop, a post office, and an international telephone call box. There are also an open car park, a garage, a service station, a carwash and a filling station. The motel is near the sea and has its own beach, and it is 70 km. from here to Lake Ritsa.

Repair Station, by the main road on the way out of Gagra to the south.

New Gagra is near Gagra. There are a big market, many small shops, a hotel, and a filling station in the town.

Gagra Mountain Resort, 5·5 km. inland as the crow flies, is linked to the sea shore by a cable-car railway. A 28 km. motor road is under construction.

Ritsa

The turning inland from the main road to Ritsa (39 km.) is at the 713/429 km. milestone, at a place called Bzipi. Ritsa can be visited from May to November, but in winter the valley is blocked with snow. Sheep and goats are taken up to seek pasture in Ritsa in the summer, and bees are also transported there by night in their hives and are taken down to the sea again in the autumn.

At the turning is the R. Bzipi, and the ruins of old watch towers stand at this point. There is also a factory producing prefabricated building parts for use in the growing town of Pitsunda. Near the turning is a large cave where Stone Age remains were found. Down a smooth cliff near the road there runs a little stream called 'Maiden's Tears'; a little further on is a second cliff and a stream known as 'Man's Tears'. To the left of the road are the ruins of a 10th–12th-century fortress and an 8th-century Christian church.

5 km. further is the village of Shota Rustaveli, and a little further along the road on the left stand the ruins of a 13th-century watch tower.

At the 14-km. milestone lies *Goluboye Ozero* (blue lake). The lake, supplied by underwater springs, really is blue. It is over 70 m. deep and its temperature is never higher than 7–12°C (45–54°F). After the Blue Lake, the road follows the valley of the R. Geggi; the river is yellow on one side and steel-blue on the other because the waters of the Geggi and the R. Upshara flow, hardly mixing, along a single river bed, just as the Black and White Aragvi rivers do in the southern Caucasus. The road zig-zags up through the narrow Upsharsky Ravine (25 m. wide), where the cliffs rise to over 400 m. on either side. After the last climb *Mount Atsetuk* (2455 m.) and *Mount Agepsta* (3261 m.) can be seen from the road, their summits covered with snow.

Lake Ritsa lies 925 m. above sea level. It is 2·6 km. long, 1 km. wide and 115 m. deep. The water is cold, and the temperature never rises above 15°C (59°F). The lake appeared a few hundred years ago, after a great landslide from *Mount Pshegishkha* (Table Mountain) had dammed the R. Lashipse. The story attached to its formation is as follows:

Once upon a time there were three hunter brothers who lived in the mountains beside a gentle stream. Their names were Atsetuk, Agepsta, and Pshegishkha. Every evening their lovely sister Ritsa cooked for them in the high mountain valley that they had made their home.

One day they were very late in returning, but Ritsa sang happily to herself and to the stars while she waited. Her song was heard by the bandit brothers, Geggi and Upshara, and the latter rushed away on horseback to seek the owner of the sweet voice.

On seeing her he was filled with passion, and he seized her fiercely despite her cries for help. Her plight was seen by the mountain eagle who flew off to tell her brothers. They all ran back as fast as they could, without letting Upshara know of their approach. Pshegishkha threw his shield at the intruder, but missed him and the shield blocked the stream and caused the water to rise, quickly forming a lake.

Ritsa was so filled with shame that she plunged into the lake and the waters instantly turned as clear as teardrops. In dismay her three brothers pursued Upshara, caught him, and threw him into the lake too, where he would have drowned but for the bubbling and seething of the water which cast him over the shield-dam. He rushed madly down to join his brother Geggi, tearing down trees and boulders on his way; but Ritsa's three brothers turned to stone and still watch over the sparkling waters of the lake.

Ritsa Hotel and Restaurant

Shashlik Bar, across the lake, by motor boat

Motel. The buildings of this motel are interesting, being built in the style used by the boyars (Russian aristocrats) up till the 17th century.

Eating House

Filling and Service Station

From the lake, beside which Stalin had a country house, the road runs for 16 km. along the valley of the R. Lashipse until this river joins the valley of the R. Avadhara, 1600 m. above sea level and containing mineral springs. A new spa called Avadhara is developing here.

Pitsunda

This resort is also known by the Georgian name of Bichvinta (pine grove). The turning to it is at the 706/422-km. milestone, at a village called Alahadze. The road passes eucalyptus groves, and for a few miles goes through the Monk's Avenue, planted as a penance by the monks of the local monastery.

Pitsunda is on the same latitude as Nice and has a bathing season of 4 to 5 months. The pine trees, the good harbour, and the average of 216 sunny days each year make it a very pleasant place in which to stay.

In 700 B.C. settlers from Miletus had built among other towns and settlements the 'great and rich town of Pitiunt'. A Greek colony settled in 500 B.C., and excavations are today in progress. The name comes from Pitus, the Greek for 'pine tree'; the particular pines that grow here are Pinus Pithysa, which in the past were felled for shipbuilding because they were so straight and made such strong masts. In 100 B.C. Pitiunt, with other towns near by, fell into the hands of Mithradates the Great of Pontus. It was known as one of the rich towns of Colchis; later Pitsunda came under Roman rule and was then invaded by the Persians. In A.D. 55 St. Andrew and Simon the Canaanite visited Pitsunda on their missionary travels, and

St. Andrew was buried here.

It was Justinian I who finally converted the inhabitants to Christianity in the 6th century, and who built the large cathedral dedicated to St. Sophia in 551. This cathedral played an important part in local life, and was for about 1000 years the seat of the Abkhazian patriarchs, until under the Turks in the 15th century Pitsunda lost its former glory. The church was restored in 1869, and was dedicated to the Assumption of the Virgin Mary. The surrounding wall had been built earlier, in the 17th century, from the ruins of Pitiunt. The cathedral is in Byzantine style, and local legend says that within it lies the grave of St. John the Golden-Tongued who died here during his exile in the 5th century. The acoustics of the cathedral are such that the voices of a few singers sound like a full choir. The building is now open as a museum.

Fourteen-storey hotels are being built in the town instead of the usual sanatoria. It is eventually expected to cater for 10,000 holidaymakers, and will serve as a model for the laying out of other resorts.

Near the cathedral stretches *Lake Inkit* and here begins an area of 200 hectares (500 acres) running for 7 km. and beside the sea covered by ancient flora of the tertiary period. Lake Inkit, which is the largest of the three lakes in this region, has good fishing, and nutria are successfully bred on its shores.

The poultry farm near Pitsunda has a small restaurant with good fresh products.

Pitsunda Motel, close to the sea on Pitsunda Cape. Motorists should leave the main road by an asphalted road signposted to the Cape, and running towards the sea. After 12 km., at the end of an avenue of cypresses, they will arrive at the Motel. There is a sports ground by the motel.

Filling Station, at the 384/363-km. milestone, back on the main road.

Mussera

Mussera lies 12 km. off the road towards the sea. The turning to the right is at the 727/423-km. milestone. Mussera is in one of the loveliest parts of this region, known as the Abkhazian Switzerland. The road leads through woods of beech and oak, groves of eucalyptus and palm, citrus and tea plantations. The soil here is very porous and the atmosphere in consequence unusually dry. There is an excellent park in Mussera and from here a 3-km. motor road runs down to the beach.

Café

Gudauta

This resort is also known as Palm Haven or Box Bay. It spreads out on the high shore of a small bay and the sandy beach, especially at the eastern end, is one of the wildest and best on the Abkhazian coast.

Inland on Mount Dzihra (2634 m.) there are rich deposits of silver and lead, and there are also mineral springs nearby. Wine, tobacco, maize, and fruit are produced locally and there is a tea factory in the resort.

In 1870–1, during the mass emigration of Armenians from Turkey, a large settlement was founded here, and later the Armenians were joined by the Abkhazians, Greeks, and other nationalities.

Odzhonikidze Park
Hotel
Market, Likhny, 5 km. from Gudauta. This village, also called Souk-Su (cold water), was of great historic importance for Abkhazia. It has been inhabited since 600 B.C., and until 1863 it was the seat of the Abkhazian rulers, the Shervashidzes. The ruins of their palace still exist near a sacred grove, and nearby stands an *11th-century church* built in Byzantine style as a copy of the church at Pitsunda. There were several attempts to build the palace itself, but efforts were successful only after a young couple had been buried alive under the foundations. The *Lime of Truth*, a tree which is hundreds of years old and under which the Abkhazian nobles used to dispense justice, can be seen at Likhny.

In 1866 the place was witness to a bloody uprising when a Russian civil servant was chopped into small pieces by the local inhabitants and his other assistants and some Cossacks were killed.

In the meadow in front of the palace, on the third Sunday in October, an annual harvest holiday takes place with horseback competitions that attract the best riders in the country.

The group of 40 small houses was formerly used by Stalin's guards when they protected his house nearby. Recently they have been used to put up visiting East Europeans.

Zoloti Bereg (Golden Beach), 10 km. from Gudauta. In spite of the implications of its name, the beach here is pebbly.

Novi-Afon

Novi-Afon stands near the sea on the R. Psyrtskha. The bathing season here lasts for 6 or 7 months.

The ancient Greek colony here was called Nycopsia or Anacopia. The Romans were here in A.D. 2, and the remains of their constructions can be seen on *Iverskaya Hill* (350 m.) which is a favourite walk for tourists. On the slope of the hill is a Byzantine wall with a tower, and on the hilltop are three other towers remaining from the Roman fortress, Aspar, supposedly built in the time of Emperor Trajan. In the late 6th century Anacopia became the seat of the Byzantine rulers of Abkhazia, and on the hilltop there are also the ruins of an 8th-century Christian church, restored in the 11th–12th century, which contains ancient sepulchres with Byzantine decorations.

At the end of the ravine of the R. Psyrtskha (4 km.) is the *Monk's Cave* and the remains of the *Church of Simon the Canaanite* (10th–11th century); Simon was the apostle who came here with St. Andrew. The remains of a 13th-century Genoese tower stand in the grounds of the Primorskii

Sanatorium down by the sea; another walk leads to *Armyanskaya Ravine* and to the *Spusk Hill* (800 m.) where there is a two-storey house known as the Swallow's Nest.

The name Novi-Afon means 'New Athos', for the monks of Mount Athos founded a large monastery here in 1875. The imposing *cathedral* dedicated to the Martyr Pantilemon was built in 1900. It is in Byzantine style and is designed to take a congregation of 3000. The height of the main dome is 40 m., and the cathedral's length 50 m. and its width 32 m. The frescoes decorating the interior were completed in 1914. Since 1959 the cathedral has been open to the public from 11–5 as a museum. Also in the monastery complex is the 9th-century *Church of Simon the Canaanite*, reconstructed from the ruins of a 4th-century temple; this now contains a library. Of the three other churches, the most interesting is the *Iberian Chapel*, from which there is an excellent view of the surrounding countryside.

Originally there were 720 monks here, and Novi-Afon was one of the richest monasteries in Russia, being granted 14,400 hectares (36,000 acres) at the time of its foundation. After the revolution the monastery was shut down, and in 1924 most of the monastery buildings were turned into sanatoria. The monks' orchards and gardens grew into the *Abkhazia Farm*, which possesses the largest olive grove on the coast (65 hectares/162 acres), which was also planted out by the monks.

Goluboye Ozero (blue lake) appeared after the monks had constructed Russia's first hydroelectric station in 1912. Since then the waterfall fed by the R. Psyrtskha has provided electricity for the surrounding region. The power station was reconstructed in 1935.

Novi-Afon's attractive park contains palms, magnolias, oleanders, and cypresses.

Iverskiye Caves A miniature electric railway carries tourists into the heart of the caves, long known locally as the Bottomless Pit. Stalactites, stalagmites and glassy lakes abound, but summer visitors are advised to take a jacket as the underground temperature is only about 12°C.

Psyrtskha Restaurant, in the town centre
Restaurant, near Swan Lake by the sea
Motel, at the 27-km. milestone (from Sukhumi), among cypresses and by an olive grove. At the motel are the Gemo Restaurant and a café.

Esheri

There are dolmens (ancient tombs) to be seen near the road at this point.

Eshera Restaurant, in the ravine. This is a very modern establishment, and is one of the best restaurants on the coast.

Sukhumi

See p. 286. End of the Caucasian Coastal Road

CHEKHOV

See Yasnaya Polyana, road to, p. 342

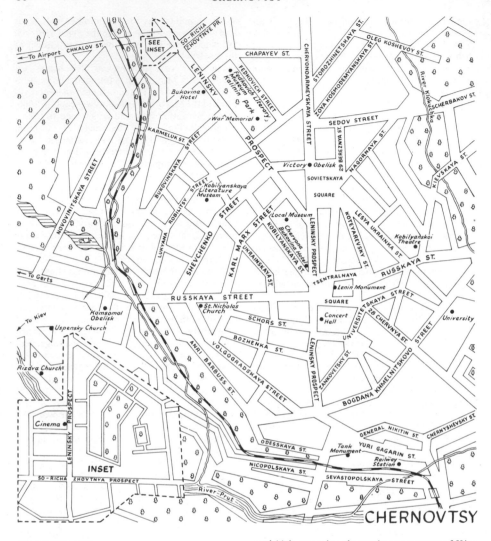

CHERNOVTSY

CHERKASSY
See Kiev, p. 148

CHERNIGOV
See Kiev, p. 148

CHERNOVTSY
Ukrainian: Chernivtsi,
Rumanian: Cernauti,
German: Czernowitz
Population—190,000 (1971)

The town stretches for 12 km. along the banks of the R. Prut. The whole territory is famous for its beech-trees (pronounced 'buk' in Russian) and from these it gets its alternative name of Bukovina.

The town's name was first recorded in 1408, and it was founded at the beginning of the 15th century near another small town, Chern, only the remains of which are to be seen today. Earlier, in the 10th

and 11th centuries, the territory was part of Kiev Rus, and in the 12th and 13th centuries part of the Volyn Princedom. In the first half of the 13th century the place was invaded by Tatars and Mongolians who stayed there for over 100 years. From the middle of the 14th century it was a part of the state of Moldavia, so that from the 16th century onwards it was indirectly under Turkish rule. After the Russian-Turkish peace treaty of 1774 the territory passed to Austria. Chernovtsy became a town in 1786 and the capital of Bukovina in 1849. The area went to Rumania in 1918 and finally to Russia in 1940, after which it was united with the Ukrainian Republic.

Many of Chernovtsy's buildings were designed by Austrian architects. Those in Tsentralnaya Sq. date mostly from the 19th century. The town's main street, Leninsky Prospect (formerly known as High St.), is one of the oldest in the town; another is Russkaya St. which runs for 6 km. from

Tsentralnaya Sq. Again, most of the buildings on the street are 19th century.

Chernovtsy has a university, founded in 1875, and a medical institute. Its main industries are connected with food, textiles, and machine building.

The population includes many Ukrainians and Jews. One can even hear Yiddish spoken on the streets—an unusual thing in large Soviet towns.

Cathedral, Leninsky Prospect

Catholic Church, Leninsky Prospect

Church of Saint Nicholas, Volgogradskaya St. Built of wood in 1607, this is the oldest church in Chernovtsy.

Rathaus, Tsentralnaya Sq. This building dates from 1843–7, and is now used by the Local Executive Committee.

Local Museum, Kobilyanskaya St. 28 Open 10–5; closed Wed.

Kobilyanskaya Literature Museum, Dmitrov St. 5. Open 10–4; closed Tues. The Ukrainian writer, Olga Kobilyanskaya (1861–1942), lived here for more than 50 years.

Fedkovich Literary Museum, Kotsubinsky St. 2. Open 10–5; closed Tues. This building in University Park in the suburbs of Chernovtsy was built in 1864–82 by the Czech architect Josef Hlavka (1831–1908), and was formerly the residence of the Bukovina Metropolitans. It is in a mixed style, showing Byzantine and Mauritanian elements. Damaged in 1944, the main part of the building is still under restoration. Yuri Fedkovich (1834–88) was a Ukrainian writer who lived here at one time. The Museum occupies five rooms of the building; some faculties of the University are also housed here. In the park there is a monument to the architect Hlavka.

Planetarium, Gorky St. 12. The Planetarium stands in the grounds of the Local Museum.

Lenin Monument, Tsentralnaya Sq. The monument was unveiled in 1951.

Victory Obelisk, Sovietskaya Sq. It is in this square that parades and mass meetings take place. The 22-m.-high granite obelisk designed by Petrashevich was unveiled in 1946 to commemorate the victory of World War II.

Tank Monument, Gagarin Sq. This tank on a stone block was the first to enter the town on the occasion of its liberation in 1944.

War Memorial, Kalinin Park. This obelisk commemorates the officers who fell here during the Second World War.

Kalinin Park, Dzerzhinsky St. 1. This park, opened in the 1830s, is the town's largest. It contains an open air theatre seating 2200, and at the entrance to the park stands a monument to Kalinin which was unveiled in 1956.

University Botanical Garden, Fedkovich St. 11, near Kalinin Park. This garden was founded in 1877 and now covers 3·7 hectares (9·25 acres).

Dynamo Stadium, Leningradskaya St. 1

Kobilyanskoi Ukrainian Music and Drama Theatre, Teatralnaya Sq. 1. This theatre was built in 1904–5 by the Viennese architects Fellner and Helmer who also designed the opera houses in Vienna and Odessa. The façade is decorated with figures from Greek mythology, and the walls with busts of Goethe, Schiller, and Beethoven, among others.

Philharmonia Concert Hall, Pobeda Sq. 10

Bukovina Intourist Hotel and Restaurant, Leninsky Prospect 141, TEL. 20–47.

Kiev Hotel and Restaurant, Leninsky Prospect 46, TEL. 39–10.

Radyanska Hotel, Universitetskaya St. 34

Chervona Bukovina Hotel and Café, Tsentralnaya Sq. 1, TEL. 40–05.

Dniester Hotel, Kobilyanskaya St.

Motel and Camping Site, Novoselitskaya St. 3·5 km. east of Chernovtsy – beach and café.

G.P.O., Pochtovaya St.

Central Department Store, Leninsky Prospect

Arts and Crafts, Tsentralnaya Sq. The town is famed for its wood carving.

Gora Tsetsino, 7 km. out of town. On the top of this mountain, which is 541 m. high, are the remains of a 14th-century fortress.

Gorecha

This is another suburb of Chernovtsy, on the high bank of the R. Prut. The remains of a monastery church built in 1767 with money donated by Catherine the Great stands here, and there are some frescoes to be seen in the church. By the river at this point there is a sandy bathing beach.

THE CRIMEAN CIRCULAR ROUTE

The Crimean peninsula is only saved from being an island by the five-mile wide Perekop Isthmus which links it to the mainland. The shallow Sea of Azov bounds it on the east and the Black Sea on

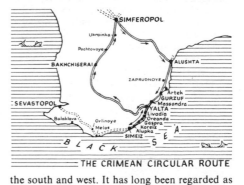

THE CRIMEAN CIRCULAR ROUTE

the south and west. It has long been regarded as the Riviera of the Soviet Union and many have written about the beauty of the precipitous cliffs and subtropical vegetation of its southern shore. Immediately behind this coast rises a range of mountains 50 km. in length. Although they drop sharply to the sea, the Crimean Mountains slope gradually to the north, running down into the steppeland which makes up three-quarters of the area of the Crimea. Although the central plain becomes very dry in summer, the mountains provide good pasture at that time.

Some visitors come to the Crimea just to enjoy the sea and sunshine of the coast, staying in Yalta or in one of the smaller resorts. Others travel there by rail or air and then hire a car to explore the region. Below are described the places of greatest interest as they occur on a route which runs from Simferopol, where the Crimea's main airport is situated, through Alushta to Yalta, and then back to Simferopol through Bakhchiserai.

The earliest recorded inhabitants of the peninsula were the Taurians of the coastal mountains and the Scythians who grew corn in the inland steppes. The capital of the Scythian kingdom was Neapolis, near modern Simferopol. In the 6th century B.C. Greek colonies began to grow up at various points along the coast, but Eastern Crimea fell into Roman hands and by the 4th century A.D. was a part of the East Roman Empire. In the 3rd century A.D. the so-called Crimean Goths settled along the southern coast, and some remains of Slav culture of a similar date have also been found there. The Greek settlements fell under Byzantine influence and were eventually destroyed by the Great Migrations.

In the 13th century Genoese colonies were founded, and at the same time Mohammedan Tatars invaded the north of the peninsula, and the Genoese possessions fell to them in 1475. The stormy period of Turkish rule ended when in 1783 Catherine the Great forced the last khan to abdicate, and converted the Crimea into a Russian Province.

During the next hundred years there were several wars with Turkey, and with each war more Tatars left the Crimea. At the end of the 18th century as many as 300,000 left, and when the hundred years were over only 60,000 remained. Soon after this most of the Christian Greeks were moved from the Crimea to the region north of the Sea of Azov, and Russian colonisation of the Crimea was speeded up by the discovery of the agreeable southern climate. At the beginning of the 19th century courtiers and nobles were already building luxurious palaces beside the sea.

Alexander Pushkin described it in verse:

Enchanting region! Full of life
Thy hills, thy woods,
    thy leaping streams,
Ambered and rubied vines
    all rife
With pleasure, spot of fairy
    dreams!
Valleys of verdure, fruits and
    flowers,
Cool waterfalls and fragrant
    bowers!
All serve the traveller's heart
    to fill
With joy . . .

Soviet power was established in 1920, marking the end of the Civil War in Russia. The Crimea had been the last refuge of the members of aristocratic families who had mansions there. Today, in

Yalta's Marine Park stands an obelisk bearing the words: 'The beautiful villas and mansions, formerly the property of wealthy landlords and capitalists, and the palaces of the former tsars and grand-dukes, shall be used as sanatoria and health centres for industrial and agricultural workers.'

This is a quotation from the decree signed by Lenin in December 1920.

Soon after the Crimea was liberated from German occupation in 1944 the last of the Tatar population was transferred to the Tatar Republic on the Volga and to the Middle Asian Republics. Russians and Ukrainians from territories badly war-damaged moved down to the Crimea. Ten years later the peninsula passed from the administration of the Russian Federation to that of the Ukraine. There are signs and notices to be seen in the Ukrainian tongue, but the principal language now used there is Russian.

The R. Dnieper has been diverted; instead of flowing into the Black Sea, to the north-west of the Crimean peninsula, it flows through the 368-km. long North Crimean Canal to Kerch on the shore of the Sea of Azov. From Dzhankoi a system of canals spreads to irrigate the dry Crimean steppe.

The Crimea is also famous for the sieges of Sevastopol (Sebastopol) lasting 349 days during the Crimean War, and 250 days during 1941–2, after which it was proclaimed a Hero Town.

Simferopol
Population—250,000 (1970)

Simferopol stands picturesquely beside the River Salgir. It is the capital of the Crimea and covers the site of the ancient Scythian town of Neapolis (3rd–4th century B.C.), where the Scythian king Skilur resided. In the 16th–17th centuries the Tatar town of Ak-Metchet (White Mosque) stood here, with the residence of Kalgar Sultan. After the annexation of the Crimea to Russia in 1783, the name of the town was changed to Simferopol, a combination of two Greek words meaning 'collective city', because it was the home of people of different nationalities.

Parts of the former Scythian capital have been excavated, and there are also settlements of primitive man, such as Chokurcha Cave, to be seen in the vicinity.

The industries here are mainly connected with food and tobacco, using the products grown in the region. One factory makes rose and lavender oil. Besides this there are machine building and electrical goods factories. There are also medical, agricultural, and teachers' training colleges in Simferopol.

Leninsky Boulevard runs for about 1 km. from the railway station to the centre of the town, and a monument to Lenin stands on it. During the summer season some of the central streets, including Pushkinskaya St. and its surrounding by-streets, are closed to traffic and used only by pedestrians.

Local Museum, Pushkinskaya St. 18. Open 10–3; closed Wed. The museum contains the Tavrica Library, called after the old name for the Crimea, which has some 50,000 books on the Crimea. The Neapolis excavations are also a part of the museum. These are to be found just off the main Alushta road, near the town; a signpost saying '1 km.' points the way. The remains of the old defence walls are there, together with some houses, a mausoleum, and tombs with frescoes.

Picture Gallery, Karl Liebknecht St. 35, open 10–4; closed Tues.

Apart from the Lenin monument already mentioned there is a Turkish obelisk at the crossing of Zhukovsky and Liebknecht Streets. This was unveiled in 1842 to commemorate the liberation of the Crimea from the Turks in 1771. On the bank of the R. Salgir is a monument to Suvorov, marking the site of the Russian military camp which was there in 1777. Another war memorial is a T-34 tank in Pioneer Garden, on Karl Marx St; this commemorates the liberation of Simferopol in 1944.

Gorky Drama Theatre, Pushkinskaya St. 15

Ukrainian Music and Drama Theatre, Mendeleyev St. 3

Puppet Theatre

Simferopol Reservoir, 3 km. along the Alushta road. There is a bathing beach and there are also boating facilities.

Ukraina Intourist Hotel and Restaurant, R Luxemburg St. 9, TEL. 94–44–72.

Yuzhnaya (South) Hotel, Karl Marx St. 7

Simferopol Hotel, Kirov St. 22

Vokzalnaya (Station) Hotel, at the station

Astoria Restaurant, Karl Marx St. 16

Airport Hotel, at the airport

Simferopol Restaurant, Karl Marx St. 2

Dorozhnyi (on-the-road) Restaurant, at the station

Otdykh (Rest) Restaurant, Kirov Garden

Chaika (Seagull) Restaurant, beside the reservoir

Café, Karl Marx St. 15

G.P.O., Karl Marx St. 17

Telegraph Office, Rosa Luxemburg St. 11.

Helicopters fly between Simferopol and Yalta, taking 25 mins., at a cost of 5 roubles. Trolleybuses run to Alushta and Yalta. There is a bus service to Yalta, and taxis are also available.

The old coast road was built over 130 years ago by Russian soldiers. The last part, leading to Yalta, was full of twists and bends; for instance, on a 4-mile stretch near the Kastel Mountain there were 220 sharp bends. In 1961 the road was largely reconstructed so that the part in question has now no more than 7 corners.

Service Station, Michurin St. 55, TEL. 1–66. Open 8 am to 4 pm.

Filling Station, Michurin St. 55 (at the same address as the service station). Diesel oil is available; round-the-clock service.

23 km. from Simferopol on the road to Alushta is the *Druzhba (Friendship) Restaurant*.

31 km. from Simferopol is the *Pereval (Pass) Motel*. It stands 766 m. above sea level, and between July and September, when it is very hot down by the sea, it is never more than 24°C (75°F) by day and 20°C (68°F) by night up here. It stands near a trolleybus route which reaches Alushta in 25–30 min; Alushta is 17 km. away. The motel has a restaurant, a car park, and a carwash.

5 km. on from the Pereval Motel is the *Kutuzov Fountain*. It was here that in 1774 the famous Russian field-marshal, as a 26-year-old colonel, fought the Turks and lost the sight of an eye. The fountain was built to his memory in the 19th century and was reconstructed in 1957.

Alushta (Pronounced 'alooshta')

This place, at the southern end of the valley of the mountain rivers Ulu-Uzen and Demergi, was originally called Aluston, meaning 'Valley of Winds'. It was founded by the Byzantine Emperor Justinian, and stood until the 13th century. Remains of the Byzantine fortifications are still to be seen. In the 14th century Aluston was rebuilt by the Genoese; it grew into a considerable town and was ruled by a council until 1475 when it passed into Turkish hands. In 1783 it was joined to Russia with the rest of the Crimea, and was proclaimed a town in 1902.

There are 15 sanatoria and rest homes in the Alushta region. The Alushta, Kastel, and Taurida State Farms grow grapes for wine, and make the wine themselves. The local vineyards were first laid out by German settlers in 1826.

The promenade is officially called after Lenin but it is generally known simply as the Naberezhnaya (Embankment). The best shops are here, and in Tavricheskaya St. The Alushta *Geophysical Station* (founded 1952) is in Partizanskaya St.

The *bathing beaches* at Alushta are among the best in the Crimea. Recommended are those opposite the Slava (glory) Sanatorium and below the Naberezhnaya, as well as the town beach.

A *stone tower* in Genueskaya St. remains from the 6th-century Aluston fortress, and the *Genoese towers* stand on the ruins of part of the old fortress.

On *Revolution Sq.* there is a monument to the members of the local government who were shot in 1918.

Golovkinsky Monument, Rabochy Ugolok, at the foot of Mount Kastel. This is a monument to the hydro-geologist who worked in the Crimea 1886–97.

Magnolia Hotel, Naberezhnaya 1

Tavrida Hotel, Lenin St. 22

Pansionat-Alushta Motel, Rabochy Ugolok (workers' corner). Parking place, repair station, and spare parts available; cabins and tents, showers, restaurant, café, shops, hairdresser, G.P.O. telephone, good bathing beaches. Workers' Corner is 3 km. from town. It was formerly known as 'Professors' Corner', being founded in 1872 when some professors built their houses there.

Volna (Wave) Restaurant, Naberezhnaya 1

Poplavok (Fishing Float) Restaurant, Naberezhnaya
G.P.O., 15-Aprelya St. 1
Podarki (Gift) Shop, Naberezhnaya 2
Market, Tavricheskaya St. 29
Special permission is necessary to visit the
Zapovednik—the 75,000-acre nature reserve
which was established in 1923 on the former im-
perial hunting territory. There are 36 species of
animals including Crimean deer, roe deer, and
wild sheep (imported in 1913 from Corsica) and
135 species of birds. Interesting plants include the
Crimean edelweiss. The Zapovednik is 18 km.
from Alushta and it is here that the Intourist
organise hunting expeditions.
Filling Station and Service Station, at the Motel,
Rabochii Ugolok, 3 km. from the centre of
Alushta.

Artek

Artek, the large holiday centre for children
belonging to the Pioneer organisation, is not far
from Gurzuf. Altogether 24,000 children come
each summer including foreign visitors. The territory stretches for 7 km. along the coast, and the
accommodation is divided into 4 camps. More
buildings are now under construction. In the
grounds are the *Pushkin Rock*, grottoes, and a
monument in memory of the poet.

Gurzuf

On an inland rock stand the remains of an ancient
Byzantine *fortress* called Gurzuvit, dating back to
the time of Justinian I (6th century). This fortress
was taken by the Genoese, and reconstructed and
reinforced by them in the 14th–15th centuries.
When the Crimea had become Russian, Catherine
the Great gave Gurzuf to her favourite, Prince
Potemkin. Today there are many sanatoria at
Gurzuf, including that of the Ministry of Defence,
and the town is a favourite haunt for artists.

To the west of the valley is a rocky bulge known
as 'Eagle's Eyrie', where white-headed griffon-
vultures nest. To the north-east is the 565-m. Ayu-
Dagh (Bear Mountain) where there are the relics
of an ancient Tauridian settlement and also of a
Genoese settlement. The legend of Ayu-Dagh is as
follows:

Once upon a time, when no one lived in the
Crimea except bears and panthers, the bears were
ruled by a very large and cunning old bear. From
time to time they would go out on forays to see
what they could steal, and one day they found a
wreck upon the shore. Wrapped in a bundle was a
tiny baby girl, the sole survivor of the shipwreck,
and they took her back to their den and cared for
her.

She grew up into a beautiful maiden with a singing voice so sweet that the bears would happily
listen to her songs from morning to night. One day
after a wild storm she was walking along the
shore. She was alone because the bears had gone
off hunting, and she found a small boat which had
been washed up by the angry waves; lying exhaus-

ted in the bottom of the boat was a handsome
young man. She helped him to a hiding place and
nursed and fed him there in secret. He explained
that he had been sold into slavery and decided to
run away, but had been caught in the storm.

The maiden grew to love him dearly and they
planned to sail away together; they made mast and
sails, and one night set out across the sea. The old
bear noticed the young girl's absence and rushed
down to the sea, waded in and began to drink and
drink; the other bears joined him and did likewise
until the strong current they made brought the
little boat back to the shore. Then the maiden sang
to them again so sweetly of her love that they
stopped drinking and let them sail away. But the
old bear stood where he was in the sea, looking out
to the horizon, and after thousands of years he can
still be seen, his body full of caves, his shaggy fur
changed to thick woods and his head a great cliff.

There is another legend of Gurzuf, this time attached to the two *Odolar Rocks* which are to be
seen in the sea near the coast. They are the rem-
nants of a cape which once existed, rising 40 m.
above the sea. The story runs thus:

Long ago when Gurzuf was no more than thick
forest there was a strong fortress on the top of
Bear Mountain. There the twin brothers Prince
George and Prince Peter lived. They loved each
other dearly, fought and played side by side, and
were never apart, for on her deathbed their
mother, the Princess Helen, had asked them to
revere the memory of their father and never to
quarrel. Their most valued servant was the green-
bearded Nimpholis; when he raised his sword in
his long arms, hundreds fell, and when he
breathed the grass was flattened and little waves
appeared on the sea.

One night he came to the brothers and said that
he had to leave them, but he gave them two presents 'not to be used for any evil purpose, nor to
gain anything by force'. When he had gone they
opened the two mother-of-pearl caskets and in
one found an ivory stick with a label: 'Raise me
and the seas will open; lower me and you will learn
the secrets of the seas'; in the second casket was a
pair of silver wings and the message, 'We will
carry you wherever you wish.'

Soon after this, news was brought to them of
twin sisters of great beauty, and the brothers
vowed to win their love. They hurried to the town
where the maidens lived, slew the inhabitants and
carried off their prizes, but instead of love they
were shown scorn. They hoped to change matters
by showing off their magic powers, but when they
all flew together amidst the clouds and lightning,
Nimpholis's voice told them to return, and the sisters laughed at their obedient cowardice. Then
they entered the sea to visit the Sea King; again
Nimpholis called to them to turn back, but the
brothers feared the sisters would jeer at them
again, and so went on until the King of the Sea
killed them all with two waves of his trident. The
bodies floated to the surface and were united to
form twin rocks as a reminder of the sad end of all

attempts to force the human heart to love.

The 40-acre *Pushkin Park* was laid out by the Duc de Richelieu. Pushkin stayed in the original chateau when he visited the Rayevsky family in 1820. Today the park contains a very large sanatorium belonging to the Ministry of Defence, and other buildings, some dating from the end of the last century and others added at different times between 1936 and 1953. The fountains here are reputedly the most beautiful in the Crimea; one called 'Night' is to be found in front of Block 2, and the others are 'Mother Love', 'Rachel', and 'Nymph'. Also in the park is *Korovin House*, built in 1911 for the Russian artist and landscape painter Konstantin Korovin; Soviet and foreign artists now come here for holidays.

In 1959 the *International Youth Tourist Centre* was opened to the west of Pushkin Park.

Restaurant, Leningradskaya St. 1

Car Park (with attendant), Zelenaya St.

G.P.O., Leningradskaya St. 12

Massandra

Today liqueurs, wines, and champagne are made in this town. Wine-making began in Massandra in 1785, and by 1850 the vineyards had been extended along the entire southern coast of the Crimea, the wines gradually taking the place of foreign wines on the Russian market, and even winning recognition at international exhibitions. It was here that, at the end of the 19th century, Prince Golitsyn, a friend of Tsar Alexander I and Minister of Education from 1816 to 1824, began to build up his collection of wines. The collection is still preserved, having been saved from invading armies on two occasions, in 1920 and 1941–3.

In 1897 a cellar was excavated in the mountain side to hold 3,500,000 litres (nearly 1,000,000 gal.) apart from storing 1,000,000 bottles of wine. Radiating from a central hall are 7 tunnels, each 150 m. long and 4–5 m. in width, and there is a constant temperature of 10–12°C (50–54°F) in the cellar.

The grounds of the *Magarach Institute* come right down to Massandra. This experimental nursery was founded 130 years ago and now possesses 700 different types of vines from all over the world, besides several thousand hybrids.

To the east of Massandra along the coast lie the *Nikitsky Botanical Gardens*, laid out in 1812 by the botanist, Christian Steven. The three parks cover over 60 acres, and there are more than 1000 species of trees and shrubs. Also of interest is the rich herbarium with over 80,000 plants.

At the entrance of the Botanical Gardens stands the *Sechenov Medical Research Institute* where the possibilities of curing tuberculosis in the Crimea are investigated.

Massandra Hotel, in Massandra Park, open in summer only.

Camping Site, in Massandra Park among the pine trees. There is an inexpensive restaurant, a café, shops, a do-it-yourself kitchen, showers, a post office, a telephone, sports grounds, a service station, and a car wash.

Restaurant, in Massandra Park. Massandra also has a good bathing beach.

Service Station, Massandra Park, near the Camping Site; TEL. 37–25. Open 8 am–4 pm.

Yalta

Population—60,000 (1971)

Yalta (the name means 'shore') was originally an ancient Greek settlement. It lies in a broad amphitheatre between two rivers, R. Vodopadnaya (waterfall) to the west, and R. Bystraya (rapid) to the east. The surrounding mountains are between 1200 m. and 1400 m. high, and in the valley the average temperature in July is 24°C. (75°F.).

All the passenger ships sailing to the Crimea and the Caucasus come to Yalta's port, and so do the local boats which ply to and fro along the Crimean coast. The quay from which the latter leave is opposite the central Polyclinic.

Yalta was first mentioned in writing at the beginning of the 12th century, by an Arabian geographer, as the Byzantine port and fishing village of Dzhalita. In the 14th century it was known as the Genoese colony of Etalita. In the 15th century it passed into Turkish hands, and remained under

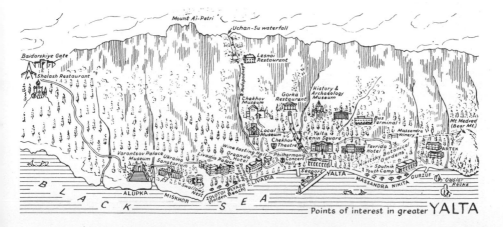

Points of interest in greater YALTA

Turkish domination until it became Russian at the end of the 18th century, when it grew in size and was surrounded by prosperous estates. In 1837 there were already many villas in the district, and it was fairly well known; then, by the order of Nicholas I who was there at the time, Yalta was proclaimed a town, and by the end of the 19th century it had become a favourite resort.

In 1854, during the Crimean War, French ships under Admiral Changarnier landed and their crews robbed the local population.

There are about 80 sanatoria in the Yalta region and perhaps as many as 20 holiday homes. Forty of the sanatoria are in Yalta itself and there are also two research institutes in the town.

Motorists' Notes: Most of the streets in Yalta are narrow and many are one-way streets; some, including the Promenade, are entirely closed to motor traffic.

Franklin D. Roosevelt St., formerly Bulvarnaya St., leads from the port to the centre of the town and is one of Yalta's oldest streets. A small bridge over the R. Bystraya links it with the Promenade, officially Lenin Promenade, but known simply as Naberezhnaya (Embankment). The resort *Polyclinic*, built in 1912 as the Villa Helen, stands here; it has 60 surgeries and supplies all kinds of medical help and advice.

The central part of the Promenade joins the Town Garden, which was laid out in the 1880s.

From the *Oreanda Hotel* the Promenade leads to *Primorskii Seaside Park* where there is a 12·5-m. monument to Gorky, unveiled in 1956. There is another *Gorky statue* and an *obelisk* bearing Lenin's decree at the entrance to the park. This has a column of 10 m. and was unveiled in 1951. There is a *monument to the writer Chekhov* (unveiled 1953) to be seen in the park, and the local film studios are there as well.

At the end of Primorsky Park, where Yalta runs into Livadia, stands the huge building of the *Rossia Sanatorium*, built in 1957. The former Rossia Hotel (1875), now the Bolshevik Sanatorium, is behind the Ukraina Restaurant.

A 12·5-m. *statue of Lenin*, which was unveiled in 1954, stands at the end of the Promenade.

The Alexander Nevsky Cathedral, Sadovaya St. 2. This cathedral was built in 1902, with an exterior in old Russian style and an interior in Byzantine style; it is open daily for visitors.

Local Museum, Pushkinskaya St. 25. Open 10–4, closed Wed. This is housed in what was formerly a Roman Catholic church, built in 1914 in late English Gothic style.

Chekhov Museum, Kirov St. 112. Open 10–4, closed Tues. This is in the house to which Chekhov moved in 1898 and where he lived until his final illness in 1904. It is in the village of Chekhovo (formerly Autka).

History and Archaeology Museum, Zagorodnaya St. 3. Open 10–5, closed Wed.

Literary Museum, Pavlenko Proyezd 10. Open 10–5 Thurs. Sat. and Sun. only.

Wine-Tasting Hall, Litkens St. 1. Open 11–8.

Lectures on Crimean wine-production, followed by sampling, are given in this hall.

Fisherman's Club, Sverdlov St. 3

Chekhov Theatre, Litkens St. 13

Philharmonia Concert Hall, Litkens St. 13

Intourist Hotel and Restaurant, Massandra Park

Oreanda (Intourist) Hotel, Restaurant, and Café, Lenin St. 35/2, TEL. 2–27–94. This hotel is 30 m. from the sea.

Ukraina Hotel and Yalta Restaurant, Botkin St. 18

Primorskii Seaside Hotel and Restaurant, Sverdlov St. 13

Yuzhnaya (South) Hotel and Restaurant, Bulvarnaya St. 10/12, TEL. 28–68.

Gnyozdishko (Little Nest) Hotel and Restaurant, Kirov St., near Chekhov Museum, TEL. 3–37–50.

Yalta Hotel, Sadovaya St. 4

Tavrida Hotel and Restaurant, Lenin St. 13, TEL. 2–32–84.

Krym Hotel and Restaurant, Kommunalnaya St. 1

Ukraina Restaurant, Promenade 34; also rooftop self-service restaurant.

Priboi (Tide) Restaurant, Primorsky Park

Leto (Summer) Restaurant, Primorsky Park

Otdykh (Rest) Restaurant. This open-air restaurant is on the roof of the main building of the sea port.

Aquarium Restaurant, Moskovskaya St. The restaurant bridges one of Yalta's small rivers.

Ukraina Café, Promenade 34

Avtomat Café, Promenade 10

Motel, Lomonosov St. 25. Beside the R. Vodopadnaya. Hotel, tents, showers, inexpensive restaurant, service station, filling station, car park, carwash. The motel is situated among cypresses, plantains, and other southern trees.

Nagornyi Park, on Darsan Hill. This park was only recently planted, and commands a good view over Yalta and the bay.

The local bathing beaches are to be found at Kommunarov St., Massandrovskaya St., Zheltyshevka St., Lechebnyi Plyazh (medical bathing), and Primorsky Boulevard. However, the best beach in the Crimea is the Zolotoi Plyazh at Miskhor, and Intourist is responsible for a section of it.

G.P.O., Lenin St. 34

Photographer's, Promenade 10 and Kalinin Garden. Open daily, 10–6.

There are two *markets*, Tsentralnyi Rynok and Pushkinsky Rynok.

Taxi Ranks, Pushkinsky Rynok; Krymsky Proyezd, near the Seaman's Franklin D. Roosevelt St., near the harbour.

Filling Stations, Ushelnoye, Kievskaya St. on the main road into Yalta, and Engels St. 1. The latter is always open.

Service Station and Car Park, Ushelnoye, Engels St. 6, TEL. 35–40.

The *Promenade*. Here the best shops are to be found, as well as the best restaurants and cafés.

South-westwards along the coast from Yalta are a whole succession of resorts which have been enjoyed since the beginning of the 19th century. The mountains here drop sharply down to the sea and some of the resorts are close to the water and some much higher up among the rocks and trees. They are all within easy reach of anyone staying in Yalta.

Livadia

At the end of the 18th century Livadia was a Greek village called Ai-Yan-Su (St. John's Spring), but in 1860 the territory was bought for the imperial family and the place was again given its original name of Livadia (meadow). The present-day buildings took the place of older palaces which were entirely demolished, with the exception of the small Byzantine-style bell-tower and the Byzantine-style Church of the Raising of the Cross. This church was built in 1866 and is decorated with frescoes by Monighetti and Professor Grimm.

The 1945 Yalta Conference was held here, but Livadia is now a sanatorium.

Livadia Palace. The large palace, known as the White Palace, was built in 1911 from designs by Krasnov as a summer residence for Nicholas II. The three-storey palace which is now Sanatorium No. 2 belonged to Baron Frederiks, the tsar's chamberlain, and the third large palace was built in New Renaissance style for the tsar's suite. Like the White Palace, these were designed by Krasnov. All three buildings were completed between April 1910 and September 1911. 2500 people helped in the construction, sometimes even working at night by the light of bonfires and torches.

The White Palace was built in the early Italian Renaissance style, the main motifs in the design being taken from Florence. The marble was carved by Italians and the marble decorations around the doors are taken from motifs by Raphael. The palace itself is built of white Inkerman granite quarried near Sevastopol. There are two inner courtyards, one in Moorish style and one a copy of the Monastery court of St. Mark's in Florence. There are altogether 60 rooms in the White Palace. The 1945 conference was held in the white hall, which is now used as the sanatorium dining hall. It was in this palace that President Roosevelt and the American delegation stayed. The windows of the palace are so planned that they each look onto a different view, and the indoor frames are designed to look like picture frames. On a balcony on the left side of the façade is a gargoyle copied from Notre Dame in Paris.

Opposite the entrance is a small marble column inscribed in Arabic, a present to the tsar from the Shah of Persia. There is also a Moorish fountain of exquisite workmanship with 'Livadia' written upon it in Arabic. It is built over a natural spring and the water still flows. On a platform in front of the palace are Roman benches of the 1st–3rd centuries A.D., and an ancient red Roman well.

From the southern corner of the third palace runs the *Tourists' Path* (formerly the Tsar's Path), a mile in length and leading to a semi-circular columned shelter overlooking Oreanda.

In the park is an *open air theatre* seating 1000 people.

Livadia State Farm Vineyards were organised here in 1922, based on the former imperial vineyards and wine cellars.

Oreanda

Oreanda stretches right down to the sea; its name is derived from a Greek word meaning 'boundary'. Nicholas I purchased the territory, and in 1852 an imperial palace was built here. This was burned down in 1882 and the remains were used in the construction of the *Church of the Pokrova Bogorodits* which the Academician Avdeyev designed in Byzanto-Georgian style. The interior mosaic decorations are by Salviazzi of Venice.

The park is magnificent, with ponds shaped like the Black and Caspian Seas and the Sea of Azov.

Oreanda is divided naturally into two parts, upper and lower. *Lower Oreanda Sanatorium*, built in 1948–58, is a most impressive building. The third block of this institution has an indoor swimming pool, 18 m. long and 2·5 m. deep, filled with warmed sea water.

Gaspra and Koreiz

The boundaries of these places are hard to define, as, like the other southern Crimean villages, they ramble over the mountainsides. Gaspra takes its name from the Greek word for 'white'.

Leo Tolstoy visited this spot in 1901 and 1902 and stayed in what is now known as the '*Yasnaya Polyana' Sanatorium*, named after his estate near Moscow, and there is a memorial plaque to Tolstoy by the front door. The writers Gorky, Korolenko, Kuprin, and Chekhov visited him here. The grey stone *palace* in Alexandro-Gothic style was built in the 1830s by Prince Golitsyn who called it his 'romantic Alexandria'. The architect was Elson (also responsible for Leningrad's St. Isaac's Cathedral) and the construction was supervised by the Englishman Henry Hunt, who had previously supervised the construction of Vorontsov's palace at Alupka.

Soon after the construction was completed Princess Golitsyna, accompanied by hundreds of attendants, moved there, taking half a year over her journey from St. Petersburg, from where she was banished. She was slightly demented, and spent her time in the Crimea preaching Christianity to the Crimean Tatars whom she tracked down with a Bible in one hand and a whip in the other. She was locally known as the 'old she-devil'.

In the park is a grotto and a pond shaped like the Black Sea.

The Yusupov Palace is a horseshoe-shaped building standing in its own park. It was designed by a local architect, Eshliman, and was completed in 1904. The Soviet delegation to the 1945 Yalta Conference stayed here, and today it is used by the

Soviet Union's foreign guests. Nearby is a pool in the shape of a fallen leaf.

The Subkhi Sanatorium, named after a Turkish Communist, has a fishpond decorated with marble capitals, brought from excavations in Greece or Italy.

The Rosa Luxemburg Sanatorium, named after the German Communist, is now a children's sanatorium. Its fine park is known as 'the Second Nikitsky Botanical Garden', and contains a marble well decorated with exotic birds and other sculptures. The well, whose steps are guarded by two ancient lions, was supposedly brought from Greece. Also of interest is the rock called the White Head or Napoleon's Head.

Cape Ai-Todor is a rock standing 26 m. high, covered with shrubby growth and crowned with a lighthouse.

Inexpensive Restaurant No. 17

G.P.O., Gaspra, Stroi Gorodok

Miskhor

Miskhor takes its name from the Greek words meaning 'middle town'. It is 12 km. from Yalta and is considered to be the warmest resort on the southern coast of the Crimea. Its park, which was laid out in 1790, is worthy of note. It contains over 300 species of trees, and stretches over level ground from the beach to Kommunari Sanatorium.

There are a great many sanatoria in Miskhor, some housed in new buildings and some in the former royal palaces.

Krasnoye Znamya (Red Banner) Sanatorium has an unusual Moorish appearance, with its battlements, silver domes, and coloured mosaics. When it was the palace of the Grand-Prince Peter Nikolayevich it was called Dulber (beautiful). It was designed by the architect Krasnov, who also planned the tsar's palace of Livadia, and was built in 1895–7. In 1938 a second sanatorium building, designed to harmonise with the original palace, was constructed nearby.

Sosnovaya Rosha (Pine Grove) Sanatorium is surrounded by 100-year-old trees. A small hunting lodge remains near it.

Ukraina Sanatorium is the largest in Miskhor. It has an indoor swimming pool and provides bathing all the year round.

The Dnieper Sanatorium stands near the Ukraina Sanatorium. It is built in the style of a Swiss chalet, and was originally the Hara Estate. In the park is an unusually-shaped Greek courtyard with 12 marble columns, a central fountain and a Spanish vase supposed to be over 2000 years old. It was brought from Greece at the beginning of the 20th century at the wish of a Greek princess who was married to one of the Romanovs. On the way to the lighthouse, on the highest point of the promontory, is a look-out place with a wide view. In 1959 a special lift, 61 m. high, was constructed from the beach to the cliff-top. A new part of the sanatorium, recently constructed, is a pier with summer sleeping accommodation.

The Zhemchuzhina (Pearl) Sanatorium belongs to the Ministry of Defence, and is situated in a valley. From it a road runs up to the *Swallow's Nest* high on the cliffs, which drop sheer from this point to the sea. The villa was built in 1912 for Baron Steingel, a German oilman, who called it his 'Castle of Love'. The engineer Sherwood designed it in Gothic style, following, it is supposed, the architectural plan of a medieval castle on the Rhine. In spite of its precarious situation, the villa survived the severe earthquake of 1927 when a piece of the cliff collapsed. It is at present under restoration.

Another vantage point for a view is *Kapitansky Mostik* (the Captain's Bridge). This look-out place is 70 m. above sea level and is reached after a climb of 315 steps. Looking down one can see the Sail Rock from which seagulls and cormorants dive for fish, and also a sculptured eagle with its wings spread.

Nearby is the *Kichkinei (tiny) Palace*, one of the palaces formerly belonging to the Romanovs. It is built in Eastern style, its towers like little minarets. The architect Tarasov designed the palace just before the outbreak of World War I, and it now houses a children's sanatorium.

Near the sanatorium is a winding path called *Kurpati*, which may be translated in many ways, among them Girl's Path. It was constructed in 1936 on territory formerly belonging to the tsar. There is a solar energy installation nearby.

Zolotoi Plyazh (Golden Beach) is the best place for bathing on the southern coast of the Crimea. It is 70 m. wide and stretches for 400 m. along the shore. This is also the site of the Intourist bathing beach. Here is the legend of the origin of the bright pebbles:

The last of the Turkish khans named Hadji-Ahmed-Aga lived in Yalta with his son Del-Balta (Mad Axe). Together they robbed the local population, but were defeated in battle by the Russians in 1771, and planned to flee across the sea to Turkey. The waves, however, refused to bear them, and the wrecked ships with the dead bodies and the rich booty of gold and silver were scattered upon the shore. Since that time it has been known as the Golden Beach.

At the west end of Miskhor there is a pavilion called the *Tourists' Shelter* which commands a fine view towards Alupka and the Vorontsov palace.

In the sea there is a statue of a mermaid (rusalka in Russian), which illustrates another Miskhor legend:

When the Crimea was still under the rule of the Turkish sultan there lived in the village of Miskhor a lovely maiden called Arza. While she was fetching water on her wedding day she was kidnapped by the wicked Ali-Baba and his pirate band, and taken to Istanbul to be sold to the sultan. A year later she escaped with her tiny baby boy and committed suicide in the Bosphorus. That very day a mermaid appeared at Miskhor. She is still supposed to return annually on the day of the kidnapping to visit the spring and drink the water there.

Altogether there are three statues—a girl fetching water beside a natural spring, an evil turbanned gentleman watching her, and a mermaid with her baby on a low rock in the sea. Bernstam was the sculptor.

Rusalka (Mermaid) Restaurant, in Miskhor Park

Miskhor Restaurant, (inexpensive) near the quayside

Inexpensive Restaurant, No. 22 by Zolotoi Plyazh

G.P.O., in Miskhor Park

Souvenir Shop, in a pavilion on the Esplanade

Photographers, Miskhor Krymskaya St. 2, Zolotoi Plyazh

Boats for Hire, Miskhor beach; also for hire: deckchairs, cameras, games, towels. Boats coming from Yalta call in at Miskhor, and for motorists there is a good car park near the beach.

Alupka

The beach here is pebbly and the high cliffs culminate in the jagged 1,400 m. Ai-Petri.

Alupka's visitors have included Gorky and Mayakovsky.

The item of greatest interest here is the *Vorontsov Palace*, situated in a 100-acre park where over 200 exotic and decorative plants and abundant rocks have been used in skilful landscaping. In the upper section of the park stand three great trees, a Mexican pine, a Lebanon cedar, and an Italian pine.

The palace was built between 1828 and 1846 by the owner of Alupka, Count (later Prince) Mikhail Vorontsov (1782–1856). The stone was quarried on the estate, and the quarry itself is now known as the 'Alupka Chaos'.

Vorontsov was brought up in England, and returned to Russia at the age of 18. He was a favourite of both Alexandra I and Nicholas I, and was appointed Governor-General of the Novorossia Region. Because he was a confirmed Anglophile his contemporaries called him 'Lord Warrensoff'—all the more so when he decided to build his palace in imitation of an English mansion. The project of the palace was drawn up by Edward Blair, from Britain, and the construction was carried out under the English architect, Henry Hunt.

Marble was brought from Italy, and masons and sculptors came from Italy to work on it. The walls are of diorite, and are so strong that they have withstood earthquakes. The architectural pattern of the palace follows in silhouette the outline of the Ai-Petri mountain behind it. The architecture itself unites in modern form elements of late English Gothic, English Elizabethan, and the eastern style of India. The northern façade is primarily of English inspiration and the southern of Indian. The south entrance bears a close resemblance to the portal of the Great Mosque in Delhi; the frieze decorating the portal has an Arabic inscription, six times repeated—a quotation from the Koran saying 'There is no happiness, but it comes from Allah'. Altogether the decorative work on the palace took almost 10 years to complete.

The three pairs of marble lions beside the steps were specially carved in Italy under the supervision of the sculptor Bonanni, and were copied from Canova's lions which decorate the tomb of Pope Clement XII in Rome.

The palace contains over 150 rooms; inside there is a museum containing some copies of famous paintings, and also a number of Dutch, French, English, Ukrainian, and Russian originals. Among them is a portrait of Vorontsov himself, and in the winter garden a bust of William Pitt the younger can be seen.

It was in this palace that Mr. Churchill and the members of the British delegation stayed during the 1945 Yalta conference.

Magnolia Hotel, Letchikov St. 23

Alupka Restaurant, Kirov St. 2

G.P.O., Voikov St. 26

There is a *car park* near the main bus stop.

Simeiz

This is the most peaceful resort of all, and lies at the end of the southern coast of the Crimea. In 1885 the village was visited by Tolstoy, and the Ukrainian writer M. Kotsubinsky lived here from 1895–7.

The local vineyards provide grapes for the Massandra Trust's wine cellars which are located on the outskirts of the village. Here Crimean Tokay, Muskat, Kagor, and other wines are made.

Simeiz is a favourite health resort for the relief and cure of pulmonary tuberculosis, and has many sanatoria.

The fine bathing beach is protected by towering rocks, the highest being Loshadinaya Golova (Horse's Head) 1325 m. The Koshka ('Cat'—from its shape) Mountain rises 259 m. above sea level. Remains of the ancient Tauri tribe have been found on the mountain top in 70 barrows hidden amidst dense juniper shrubbery. There are also ruins of Tauri houses and a small fortress. Opposite the Koshka Mountain is the Panea Rock where the remains of Byzantine walls are to be seen. Beside the sea is Swan Cliff, 85 m. high, and at its foot lie the remains of the Monk Cliff which fell during a severe storm in 1931. In the sea, closing in the Simeiz bay, is a 50-m. high rock called Diva (Maiden).

The Koshka Mountain, the Monk Cliff, and the Diva rock are all connected in the following legend of Simeiz:

Long ago there lived a wicked man who enjoyed a life of lust and pleasure. However, as he grew older he repented of this life and went to live as a hermit, eventually gaining the reputation of being the holiest monk in this part of the world. His undeserved honour made the devil and the evil spirits very angry; and so the devil came to the old man's cave in the form of a cat and sang songs of love and the joys of family life until the monk took it by the tail and flung it out of the cave. Another day an evil spirit took on the shape of a lovely girl and appeared in the monk's net while he was fishing on the shore. She embraced the old man and he remembered his past life which had so long been forgotten. The devil and the evil spirit laughed to see his real nature showing itself, but the good spirits of the place were angered at such disrespect for all that human beings hold dear and sacred. They turned all three to stone, thus creating the Maiden rock, and, standing back from that, the Monk cliff, and overlooking the whole valley, the hunchbacked Cat mountain, in the shape that the devil had chosen for himself.

Simeiz Observatory was founded in 1900, and is open to visitors on Tues. and Fri., from 12 noon to 2.0 pm. It is advisable to obtain permission from Intourist before making the visit.

The Krasnyi Mayak (Red Lighthouse) Sanatorium is situated in the centre of Simeiz. It was formerly the Villa Xenia, built in Gothic style in 1911. A little higher up there is a second building belonging to the Sanatorium. It is in Moorish style and was built in 1925. The main street of Simeiz is Leninsky Prospect.

Inexpensive Restaurant, Sovietskaya St.

Café, Leninsky Prospect

G.P.O., Sovietskaya St.

Yalta is the starting point for the return journey to Simferopol via Bakhchiserai. (Intourist permission is necessary before setting out upon this part of the road.) The total distance is 111 km.

Leaving Yalta, the main road climbs up and over the Ai-Petri Mountain and the scenery is very beautiful.

At the 16/56-km. milestone stands the *Silver Pavilion*. There is a parking place to the right of the road and a 50-m. walk leads to the Pavilion which is on a look-out point with a remarkable view of Yalta and out over the sea.

At the 22/50-km. milestone, at the summit of Ai-Petri, there is a *restaurant*, a *meteorological station*, and another lookout point. For hundreds of years people have enjoyed climbing to the top of Ai-Petri to watch the sunrise.

Bakhchiserai ('the Palace of Gardens')

Bakhchiserai lies on the R. Churyuk-Su (rotten water). It dates from 1501, when the Crimean Khans transferred the capital from Khan Mengli-Gerai. The Khans resided here until 1783. The town is divided into the old part and the new; only the main street is partly built with new houses.

Khan's Palace (Khan-Serai)· open 9–4, closed Wed. The Palace is the home of the local History and Archaeology Museum.

All silent now those spacious halls,
And courts deserted, once so gay
With feasters thronged within their walls,
Carousing after battle fray.
Even now each desolated room
And ruined garden luxury breathes,

Gold listens, shrubs exhale perfume.
The shattered casements still are there
Within which once, in days gone by,
Their beads of amber chose the fair,
And heaved the unregarded sigh.

Pushkin

The 16th–18th-century palace consists of a number of buildings, including the Harem, now inhabited by waxworks. The Fruit Room was designed by a Persian artist, Omar, in the 18th century. There is a pleasant garden, a falcon tower, and a mosque dating from the middle of the 18th century. The cemetery of Khan Gerai's dynasty is also to be seen. During its history the palace has been partly burned and robbed, but it was rebuilt for Catherine the Great's visit in 1783, and was restored again in 1837 for Nicholas I to see. This restoration, however, was not well done, and only in 1900 was restoration carried out with consideration for the past and not simply for oriental style.

In the palace is the famous *Fountain of Tears*, built in 1756, which inspired Pushkin and the Polish poet Miczkiewicz. This is its story:

The Khan Krim-Gerai was well known for his cruelty; it was he who ordered the death of all the boys of his family who stood higher than the hub of his chariot wheel, so that no one would seize power from him. People said that instead of a heart he had a lump of wool. However, when he fell in love with Delarai, a slave girl, he realised that he had indeed a living heart. Delarai could not return his love and soon died of sorrow.

Krim-Gerai grieved deeply; he asked the Persian craftsman, Omar, to 'make a stone that will continue my grief through the centuries, that will cry as only a man's heart can'. Omar thought that if the stony heart of the khan could weep, then so could a stone, and he made a marble fountain and carved flower petals with a human eye in the centre from which would fall heavy drops like human tears, day and night till the end of time. Omar carved a marble snail on the fountain too, to symbolise the khan's doubt of the use of his life to him—or of his laughter and sadness, his love and his hatred.

Hotel and Restaurant, Lenin St. 93

Restaurant, on the road to Simferopol

Inexpensive Restaurant, Lenin St. 77

G.P.O., Pochtovaya St. 18

Telegraph and Telephone, Lenin St. 75

Beside the main road, near Bakhchiserai, are a number of *round domes*. These are 15th–18th-century mausoleums in the old Tatar cemetery.

Bakhchiserai's local museum is responsible for 14 ancient cave towns in the vicinity. The following are probably of greatest interest:

Uspensky–Peshchernyi Monastery is about 2 km. from Bakhchiserai, past the village of Staroselye on the road to Chufut-Kaleh. The road is fairly good.

This is a cave monastery, no longer inhabited, located in the mountainside. In it are a Cathedral of the Assumption of the Virgin, and four churches dedicated to St. Constantine and St. Helen, St. Mark, St. George, and St. Innocent. The monastery existed before the Turks came to the Crimea, and the legend of its foundation goes thus:

Once upon a time a dragon appeared in the mountains, and devoured many of the villagers and their cattle. The rest fled down into the valley, and in despair prayed to the Virgin Mary to help them. Then a strange light appeared upon one of the heights and shone there for three or four days. The sheerness of the cliff-face made it impossible to climb up, so 84 steps were cut in the rock. At the top was found an icon of Our Lady with a lamp burning before it, and nearby the fearful dragon lay dead. The people carried the icon down to the valley in gratitude—but it returned to its former position of its own accord; after several attempts to move it was decided to found a church there on the cliff top, and so a cave was dug and dedicated to the Virgin and soon a monastery grew up around it. The icon's fame spread far and wide, and it was revered not only by the Crimean Greeks, but also by the Tatars and even the Turkish Khans.

The monastery was active until the Russians came to the Crimea, but when the Crimean Greeks were transferred to the Sea of Azov in 1778 they took the icon with them and the monastery lost much of its magnetism. It was, however, rebuilt in 1850. Visitors can climb the 84 steps cut in the cliff, and get a good view of Bakhchiserai and Jehosophat's Valley.

Chufut-Kaleh There is a lot of room to park cars at the Uspensky-Peschernyi Monastery and from there the walk to Chufut-Kaleh is a little over a mile. The path leads to a nut grove at the end of which there is a fountain, and from here a path leads up the mountain to the gate of Chufut-Kaleh.

Chufut-Kaleh, also known as the Jewish Fortress, is a dead city perched on a narrow limestone plateau. Possibly it is the most interesting of all these cave towns; it is also the easiest of access. The former inhabitants belonged to the Jewish sect called the Karaites or Qaraites. These are disciples of the letter of the Law of Moses, adhering to Judaism without accepting the Talmud and other holy Jewish books, or the traditions of the Elders. The place was inhabited from the 17th century and the last family left the town in the 1870s. The fortress, however, and the town, were known of in the 14th century.

Today Chufut-Kaleh is a town of dead streets and ruined houses. The remains of synagogues can be seen and in the centre is a *mausoleum* built in Moorish style in 1437. This was erected by a khan to his daughter who, according to legend, heard her father coming while she was in her lover's arms, and threw herself over the cliff.

Katchi-Kalen Katchi-Kalen lies about 9 km. to the south of Bakhchiserai, opposite the village of Bashtanovka.

Katchi-Kalen was a cave monastery dating from the 9th–10th centuries. The caves were hewn from the living rock. There are many of them at different levels, joined by steps and bridges.

Tepe-Kermen Tepe-Kermen is 7 km. to the east of Bakhchiserai.

The name means 'hill fortress'. There are over 200 caves, on 18 different levels, linked by streets and galleries. Inside are as many as 10,000 rooms and the ruins of several churches, including one dating from the 9th–10th century.

Mangup-Kaleh is just over 67 km. from Yalta and 20 km. south of Bakhchiserai, near the village of Tankovoye. In this village there is a house with a spire, now used as a children's home; cars may be left here. Mangup-Kaleh is 7 km. further on. From here a bad road leads to the villages of Krasnyi-Mak and Zalesnoye, and from there a path leads up the mountain to the cave town.

Mangup-Kaleh was founded in the 5th–6th century. The Basilica of St. Constantine and St. Helen, dating from the time of Justinian, was discovered in 1912–13. In the 14th century the town was the capital of the Gothic princedom and was known as Doros or Theodoros. In 1745 it was sacked by the Turks and deserted by its inhabitants.

There is a well-preserved Turkish fort to be seen, and among the ruins are the remains of a two-storey palace in the Acropolis, a *Christian church*, a *Tatar mosque*, and a *Karaite synagogue*.

Back on the main Bakhchiserai-Simferopol road, near the village of Partizanskoye, is the *Crimean Observatory*. Here, in memory of Academician Schein, the biggest telescope in Europe, with a mirror 2·6 m. in diameter has been installed. It is 18 km. from here to Simferopol, which completes the Crimean Circular Route.

DILIJAN
See Erevan, p. 106

DONETSK
Population—880,000 (1970)
Known as Yuzovka until 1924 and then as Stalino until 1961.

> None yet brought the Donbas to its knees,
> Nor will any ever bring it down.
>
> Pavel Besposhadny

Donetsk, on R. Kalmius, is the central city of the Donbas region and is often called the Miners' Capital. After Kiev and Kharkov it is the Ukraine's third largest city.

The Donbas (taking its name from its location in the basin of the R. Don) covers a total area of 1860 sq. km. and stretches 110 km. from east to west and 50 km. from north to south. There are good deposits of anthracite and steam coal in comparatively thin seams. The Russian scientist, Dmitry Mendeleyev (famous for his periodic table), spent three months in the Donbas in 1888 and wrote, 'I was struck by the inexhaustible rich-

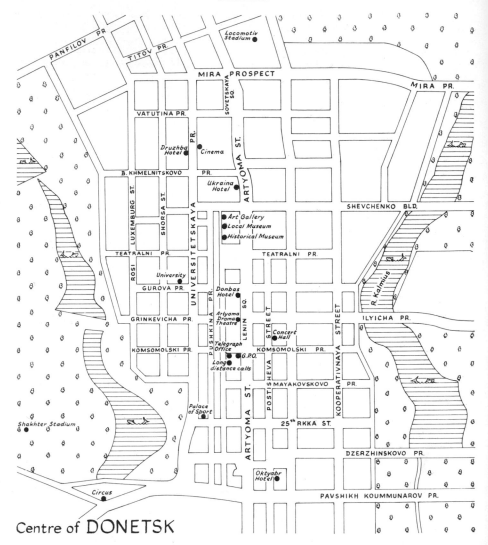

Centre of DONETSK

ness of the area, surpassing anything I have ever seen, not only in Russia but in Europe and America as well.' It has proved to be the most important coal basin in the European part of the U.S.S.R. and geologists have found coal to a depth of 1800 m. In 1957 it was estimated that there were 240,620 million tons.

In 1721 Peter the Great showed interest in the news of a clerk, Grigory Kapustin, that coal was to be found in the area, but things moved slowly. The area was taken from the Crimean Tatars in 1739 and mining began only in 1798. There were settlements on the site of Donetsk at the end of the 18th century but the first mine was not opened there until 1820 and the date of the foundation of the city is regarded as 1869.

It rapidly grew into an industrial centre after the establishment in 1872 of a metallurgical plant by the Welshman, John Hughes (1814–89), who

started his career as a blacksmith. In 1869 with a capital of £300,000 and the sanction of the Russian government he founded the New Russian Metallurgical Company in London. Subsequently, and still with no knowledge of Russia or of the Russian language, he organised a new factory in the sparsely populated country north of the Sea of Azov. The equipment shipped from Britain was put ashore at Taganrog, the nearest port, and teams of oxen were used for the final stage of the journey. Some experts and skilled workers came from England, but the majority were from the provinces of Northern Russia. *The Church of St. David and St. George* was built for the foreigners' use and even today in Leninskaya St. are some typical English houses of red brick called the three- and four-rouble houses because that was the rent charged for them.

The settlement was called Yuzovka after

Hughes. The fortunate combination of pit-coal, iron ore and manganese ensured its prosperity but the development was strange to Russian eyes. It was described as a 'town of weeping blast furnaces whose tears are molten metal' and the numerous chimneys were reminiscent of a forest after a fire, with the blackened treetops still smoking. It was also noted for the strikes which occurred repeatedly after 1874. The Bolsheviks were later to find support from the local workers. The railway connection added to Yuzovka's affluence and the expanding village grew into a town by 1917.

The town's boundaries include over forty villages where miners live. Some of them— Kalinovka, Vetka, Putilovka, Larinka, Zakop, and Standart—are linked with the centre of town, but most of them have their own clubs and social establishments. New blocks of flats, factories, and institutes have taken the place of the old huts. One of the largest regions of the town bears the name of the village of Yuzovka.

Donetsk was under enemy occupation from October 1941 to September 1943. It was heavily damaged and almost all the administrative buildings were destroyed. Nevertheless both the town and the mines were restored by 1950 and the coal output is now three times that of the whole of Russia in 1913. This one city produces more metal today than the whole country did then. It is often called the 'city of metal and coal' and indeed there are about fifty coal mines right in the city itself. The oldest of all, *Tsentralno-Zavodskaya*, is near Dzerzhinskova Sq. (Factories and mines are not described in this guide; they can only be visited by special arrangements through Intourist.)

Artyoma is the name of the main street. Its 10-km. length connects the Metallurgical Factory with the railway station. It is the busiest and the most attractive street of the city, and the administrative buildings of the town hall and the local Party committee are here, as well as the Polytechnical Institute, the best hotels, the Lokomotiv Stadium, and the best shops and cafés. The new Pushkina and Mayakovskovo Prospects, together with Universitetskaya St., are also impressive. Shevchenko Boulevard runs for 5 km. connecting the centre of the town with Cheryomushki, a new residential area which has grown rapidly since 1959. The complex of *Lenin Sq.* was only finished in 1955. The new buildings of the *House of Soviets*, the *drama theatre* and the *concert hall* stand on the site of older buildings, among them the pre-revolutionary 'English Club'. The imposing fountain in the centre of the square is illuminated after dark. Parallel to Artyoma is Universitetskaya Prospect, running from the city garden. Along it are the *University buildings, the House of Architects, the Palace of Sport*, and a new *Intourist hotel*. Donetsk's numerous parks and gardens improve the look of the city but their more practical purpose is to help freshen the smoke-laden air. This industrial town takes the greatest pride in the annual display of flowers in the city park. The first display was arranged in 1956.

The plans for future construction in Donetsk spread over twenty years. The city is to cover 400 sq. km. with offices, theatres, etc. in the centre, surrounded by the residential areas, each a separate and independent suburb. Underground springs will be used for forming lakes with beaches and boating stations within the city limits.

The suburbs of Donetsk have already met those of Makeyevka, another quickly-growing industrial centre (see below) 13 km. from Donetsk, and soon the two towns will merge.

Apart from the local coal mining and metallurgy there are important machine-building and chemical industries. Factories produce mining equipment and agricultural machinery, and there are light and food industries. Since 1959 local industry has run on natural gas piped from Stavropol in the North Caucasus. Donetsk has polytechnical, medical, and commercial institutes as well as a number of scientific research institutes. The University opened in 1964.

St. Nicholas Church, near Leninskaya St.

Local Museum, Artyoma St. 84. Open 10–6, closed Tues. Sections include the natural history of the Donbas, archaeology (including stone figures of the 8th–13th centuries), and the history of the Donbas.

Art Gallery, Pushkina Pr. 35. Open 12–6, closed Wed.

Planetarium, Artyoma St.

Nikita Khruschev's House, Kirova St. 90. The Khruschev family lived here in 1912. It was in Donetsk in the early 1920s that Khruschev began his political career.

Lenin Monument, Lenin Sq.

Flerovsky Obelisk, Flerovsky Garden. Vasili Bervi-Flerovsky (1829–1918) was a sociologist and philosopher who lived and died in Donetsk.

Dzerzhinsky Bust, Dzerzhinsky Garden

Shevchenko Monument, Shevchenko Boulevard. The monument by Vronsky and Oleinik was unveiled in 1955. The upper part of the pedestal is decorated with a bronze bas-relief depicting the heroes of the poet's work. He himself is also shown here, reading his poetry to the Russian writers, Chernyshevsky and Dobrolubov.

Fighters for Soviet Power Monument, Pogibshikh Kommunarov Garden. Unveiled in 1957.

Monument to Stratonauts, on the way to the city park. The two-metre statue of a pilot marks the burial place of four pilots (Batenko, Stobun, Ukrainskii, and Kuchumov) who died after an accident with a stratospheric balloon in 1938. The statue by Belostotski was unveiled in 1953.

Col. Franz Grinkevich Monument, in the garden beside the opera and ballet theatre. The colonel's soldiers made the monument themselves, pulling the T-34 tank up into position unaided, and cementing it there on the pedestal. Also in this garden is the grave of Lt. Gen. Kuzma Gurov (1901–43), marked by his bust.

Opera and Ballet Theatre, Artyoma St. 82

Artyoma Drama Theatre, Artyoma St.

Concert Hall, Postichera St. Here is the only Czechoslovakian organ in the Ukraine. The Hall seats 600.

Puppet Theatre, Artyoma St.

Circus, Kuibysheva St. There are seats for 2,000.

Shakhter (miner) Stadium, opened in 1949; room for 50,000

Lokomotiv Stadium, place for 50,000

Khimik Swimming Pool, Smolyanka

There are sixteen ponds within the city, but the pride of place is held by the city reservoir in the valley of R. Kalmius. There are sports grounds here and a bathing beach.

Druzhba Hotel & Restaurant, Universitetskaya St. 48, TEL. 3–40–76

Ukraina Hotel & Restaurant, Artyoma St. 88. This ten-storey building is the city's tallest. 600 rooms.

Donbas Hotel & Restaurant, Artyoma St. 80

Oktyabr (October) Hotel, Posticheva St. This was formerly the Great Britain Hotel.

Troyanda (rose) Restaurant, Artyoma St.

Kalmius Restaurant, Makeyevskoye Chaussee

Moskva Restaurant, Artyoma St. 71

Metallurg Restaurant, Artyoma St., by the garden

Sport Restaurant, Universitetskaya St.

Otdykh (rest) Cafe, Artyoma St. 108

Utro (morning) Cafe, Pavshikh Kommunarov Sq.

Sputnik Cafe, by Avtovokzal

Beryozka Café, Lenin Sq.

G.P.O. and Telegraph Office, Artyoma St. 72

Bank, Artyoma St. 38

Bookshops, Artyoma St. 79 & 125

Department Store, Artyoma St. 125

Art Salon, Artyoma St. 127

Taxi Ranks, Theatre Sq. and Central Sq.

Makeyevka

Population—400,000 (1970)

Known as Dmitriyevsk until 1930.

Founded in 1899 on R. Gruzskaya (a tributary of R. Kalmius), it is one of the major industrial centres of the area with iron and steel, coal mining, chemical industry, and heavy engineering. The settlement began growing after the organisation in Paris of the Russian Iron and Steel Plants Company, which started construction here in 1898–1900. Most of the plant existing at the time of the Second World War was severely damaged.

There is a Mining Security Institute here. The pride of Makeyevka is the *Palace of Metalworkers*, built in 1959 for 1000 people. In front of it stands a *monument to Sergei Kirov*.

DRUSKININKAI

This spa lies in the extreme south of Lithuania, 150 km. from Vilnius. 'Druska' means 'salt' and its name comes from its saline springs. It is located on the right bank of R. Nemunas, into which flows the rapid rivulet, Ratnychele. The town was founded in the 14th century when a protecting castle was built. It was declared a resort by special decree in 1794 but it really counts its days from 1837 when it was fully recognised by the public.

It was here, on 22 August 1891, that the late sculptor, Jacques Lipchitz, was born. His real name was Chaim Jacob Lipchitz and he was the son of a wealthy building contractor. After attending school in Bialystok where he began to draw and model, he went to study engineering in Vilna (Vilnius) because his father was opposed to his artistic leanings. His mother sent him to Paris in 1909 without his father's knowledge, and his artistic training began in earnest. It was interrupted in 1912 when he had to return to Russia for military service, but he had had tuberculosis and was discharged as unfit. He then left Russia, never to return. Lipchitz eventually took French citizenship, but nevertheless chose for his bride a Russian poet, Berthe Kitrosser. He left occupied France during the war and lived the rest of his life in the United States.

Now Druskininkai is one of the biggest all-year-round resorts in Lithuania. People are attracted here by the pine forest and the excellent beaches along R. Nemunas. There are modern sanatoria and mud baths. The spa is recommended for the treatment of diseases of the joints, the nervous system, the heart, and the circulatory system.

Kirov St. runs through the town from the railway station to Melnikaites St. by the entrance to the park. There are mineral water and mud bath establishments here and also a *statue of Maryte Melnikaite* by Autinis; she was a partisan during the last war, and was made a Heroine of the Soviet Union.

July 21st St. Liepos 21 is the shopping centre of the resort and has a covered market.

Chiurlionis Memorial Museum, Chiurlionis St. The Lithuanian painter and composer, Mikalojus K. Chiurlionis (1875–1911), spent his childhood here. His personal possessions and documents are on display.

Lake Druskouis is in the town and there is a boating station there.

Hotel and Turistas Café, Central Sq.

Ratnychele Restaurant

The environs of Druskininkai are very picturesque with small lakes among the dense pinewoods. The Valley of Raigardas, which inspired Chiurlionis in his paintings and music, is very beautiful. Raigardas has been made a national park because of its unique landscape, and it is also known as the site of the 'sunken town'. A local legend says that the rich town of Raigardas stood here before it disappeared under the earth.

DUSHANBE (Formerly Stalinabad)

Population—374,000 (1970)

Capital of the Tajik Soviet Socialist Republic

TAJIKISTAN

Population—2,900,000. The Tajiks account for 55% of the population and are the oldest inhabitants of the region. Other nationalities living here include Russians, Uzbeks, Tatars, and Ukrainians.

The country is almost entirely mountainous and the Soviet Union's highest peaks are to be found here, in the Pamirs—Mt. Kommunism (formerly Mt. Stalin) (7495 m.) and Mt. Lenin (7134 m.). To the south of Mt. Kommunism lies Fedchenko Glacier, 71·2 km. in length, the longest continental ice river in the world. Almost all the greatest rivers of Central Asia also flow through the republic, and Tajikistan is the region most liable to earthquakes in the U.S.S.R.

The country has three climatic belts; in the lowlands it is hot and dry, while in the cooler foothills there is more rain, and in the mountains there is little precipitation but the average temperature is below freezing. The mean temperature for January varies from −1°C. (30°F.) in the north to 3°C. (37°F.) in the south. In the month of July it is 23°C. (73°F.) and 30°C. (86°F.) respectively. The wild life is similarly varied. In the southern lowlands tigers, deer, and many kinds of waterfowl are to be found. In the higher plateaux there are antelopes and huge lizards about 1·5 m. long and in the Pamirs live bears and wild sheep.

The Tajiks are a very old people. Their ancestors lived here in the state of Sogdiana at the beginning of the 1st century B.C. The Tajiks come from Iranian stock but the name only appeared in the 8th century A.D. when the country was conquered by the Arabs. Two centuries later the Turks took it over. Part of the Tajik territory was incorporated into the Russian Empire in 1895 when an Anglo-Russian commission fixed the northern frontier of Afghanistan on the R. Pyandj and separated the Russian and Indian Empires by an Afghan corridor. Soviet power was finally established here in 1920, at the end of the civil war in Russia. In 1929 it was proclaimed an autonomous republic and received statehood within the U.S.S.R.

Tajiks differ in appearance from the other peoples of Central Asia. Dark-eyed, dark-haired and suntanned, they have European features. High in the Pamirs one meets blue-eyed and blond Tajiks who speak a slightly different language. They are descendants of the native population which escaped the Mongolian conquest in the inaccessible mountains. The Tajiks are a people of poets and sages. Their respect for the elderly is only equalled by their love for children. The republic has one of the highest birthrates in the Soviet Union. They also show a great fondness for birds as these are considered a symbol of happiness.

Unlike the rich and fertile valleys, the regions of the Pamirs are still very mysterious. Even primitive civilisation was late in reaching this out-of-the-way corner of the world, and today people still live according to the old customs and superstitions of their forebears. A local legend says that two angels lowered the sheep from heaven to help people make a living here and for a long time everything about a sheep was held sacred. A fallen sheep was even mourned like a human being. Dairy products are still the staple foods.

Pamir dwellings have very intricate wood carvings. A project is under way to resettle mountain folk in the lowlands where they can enjoy more comfort, but not all of them are willing to leave their present homes, however hard a living they may have. The Pamir roads are only open to traffic for three months of the year.

Beautiful pottery and ceramics have been made in Tajikistan since earliest times. There are all kinds of pottery for household use, decorative kinds and some that is simpler for wedding festivals (called 'toi', which used to last, with short intervals, for over a month, and attracted crowds of guests). Tajik embroidery is also famous. One only needs to look at the skull caps the men wear. It is the custom for a bride to embroider a skull cap for her groom. Women have fine embroidery on their dresses too.

Tajikistan plays an appreciable part in the Soviet economy. The finest fibre cotton is grown here, and uranium and polymetallic ores are mined. A unique power station is being built on the Vakhsh River, near the town of Nurek. The name of the river means 'turbulent' and there is a legend of a Tajik boy called Nur who fell in love with a girl but was told she would marry him only if he could tame the Vakhsh. He tried to dam it with boulders, but it only swirled and foamed the more. At last he threw an enormously big rock into the river and that only made it angrier still so he admitted defeat. However, for his brave attempt the small settlement on the banks of the Vakhsh was called Nurek after him and now it is the site of one of the world's largest hydropower stations. It has the highest concrete dam in the world—300 m.—but apart from that, erecting it in a zone of frequent earthquakes made it a particularly difficult engineering feat. Nurek is 70 km. from the capital.

A few words of Tajik:

hello	salom
I am a tourist	man turist
please	markhamat
thank you	rakhmat
yes	kha
no	nahz
bad	bad (*yes, it's true!*)
I don't understand	man namefakhmam
Please fetch me an interpreter	marhamat ba man tarjimonro taklif namyed
good-bye	haier *or* hai
how do you do?	akhvoli shumo chi tavr

Dushanbe

Tajikistan's capital is situated in the Gissar Valley, beside R. Dushabe, a tributary of the Vakhsh. 'Dushanbe' in the Tajik tongue simply means 'second night' which is the third day of the eastern week and falls on Monday. It was so called because of the big weekly market which was held on

DUSHANBE

Mondays, and the old name was revived in 1961.

The town lies on the same latitude as Spain and Portugal and is about 846 m. above sea level. The climate is continental; in summer the temperature rises to 40°C. (104°F.) and in winter it falls to −20°C. (−4°F.). For almost half the year there is no rain and there is unlikely to be any during the months of August and September which is the time of the fruit harvest. The rainy season starts at the end of October and finishes at the end of May.

The site has been inhabited since ancient times. Local archaeologists have found pottery dating from the 2nd century B.C. to the 13th century A.D. From the 16th century the area belonged to the Bukhara Khanate and the territory was known as Eastern Bukhara. First mentioned in chronicles in 1676 as a poor town with a semi-ruined mud fortress in the centre, the present town was formed from three villages (kishlak). Sari-Asiya became the northern part of the town, Shakhmansur the southern part, and Dushanbe the centre. The latter was the largest of the three; it had five hundred houses and was known for the colourful bazaar which was held there every Monday (hence the name, as explained above).

In 1920–1 Dushanbe was the residence of the Emir of Bukhara, Seid-Alim-Khan, who escaped here from Bukhara itself. The place was entirely ruined during the civil war and when it was made the centre of an autonomous republic in 1924 it had but forty-two houses, and the civil population numbered 242. At that time only four of the new capital's houses had wooden floors and the street lighting consisted of one oil-lamp on Bazaar Sq. Hyenas and jackals used to roam nearby and could be heard howling during the night.

The town grew rapidly. The population rose from 5600 in 1926 to 82,500 in 1939. In 1929 it was proclaimed the capital of the newly formed Tajik Republic, renamed Stalinabad, and linked by rail with the main railway network of the country.

There are now food and textile industries here, with silk and cotton mills. The city's educational establishments include the University (1948) and polytechnical, medical, agricultural, and pedagogical institutes. Here also is the Tajik Academy of

Sciences (1951).

The main thoroughfare, *Lenin Prospect*, is nearly 16 km. long and runs north from Privokzalnaya Sq., in front of the railway station. The most important buildings are on Lenin Prospect itself or in its vicinity; their names are mostly prefaced by the word 'new', as far as the local people are concerned. Lenin Prospect is crossed by many smaller streets and some of those parallel to it look like green tunnels as the foliage from the trees on either side meets overhead.

Aini Sq., the first through which Lenin Prospect runs from the station end, is called after the founder of Soviet Tajik literature, Sadriddin Aini (1878–1954). He was the first president of the local Academy of Sciences and there is a monument to him in the square. The new *Dushanbe Hotel* has recently been built here. A number of the institutes of the Academy stand in Aini St. which runs out of the square. Also near the square is the *Vatan (motherland) Cinema* built in national style, and further on is the three-storey building of the *University*, founded in 1948.

Rudaki Sq. is notable for its fountains. Abul-Hassan Rudaki (mid-9th century–941) was the poet who is celebrated as the founder of Tajik national literature and who held the post of court poet of the Samanids. In the square called after him is a *hotel*, a *concert hall*, and a big food store, *Gastronom*. A little further along Lenin Prospect is *Firdouse Library* with over a million books and ancient manuscripts.

In *Lenin Sq.* is a monument to Lenin which was unveiled in 1960, and the *20th Anniversary Obelisk* bearing the republic's coat-of-arms and commemorating the founding of Soviet Tajikistan. Around the square are the impressive Government House and other offices and ministries including Communications House. On both sides of Lenin Prospect, especially after Lenin Sq., are the small, twisted streets of the old town with mud houses typical of Central Asia. These are condemned as no longer habitable and each year sees more and more modern buildings taking their place.

Putovskova Sq. is surrounded by local Communist Party headquarters and the Drama Theatre, and Lenin Prospect then runs into Sari-Asiya (northern village), the one-time village that forms the northern suburbs of the town. Here is the newly planted Aini Park where there is a small rotunda resembling a mausoleum with a bust of Aini.

The buildings listed immediately below are all open for religious services:

Khadzi-Yakub Mosque, Dushanbinskaya St. 64. This was built at the end of the 19th century and is one of the four still in use.

St. Nicholas's Church (Russian Orthodox), Druzhbi Narodov Prospect 58. Built in 1946.

Baptist Chapel, Chekhov St.

Synagogue, Dekhkanskaya St. 26

Local History Museum and Bekhzoda Fine Art-Museum, Aini St. 31. Local handicrafts are included among the other exhibits here. Open 11–5; closed Tues.

Ethnographical Museum of the Academy of Sciences' Institute of History and Archaeology, Kuibyshev St. 12

Sadriddin Aini Monument, Aini Sq.

Obelisk, Lenin Sq., commemorating the 20th anniversary of the foundation of the Tajhik Republic.

It is planned to erect a *monument to Rudaki* in front of the *Vakhsh Hotel*.

Aini Opera and Ballet Theatre, Lenin Prospect 26

Lakhuti Tajik Drama Theatre, Lenin Prospect 72

Mayakovsky Russian Drama Theatre, Lenin Prospect 66

Open-air Theatre (Zelyoni Teatr), Frunze Park

Circus, Kommunisticheskaya St. 54

Komsomol Park and Lake, Putovskova St. The construction of this artificial lake began in 1939 but was suspended during the war. There is a beach, a boating station, and a restaurant in the park.

Frunze Stadium, opposite Komsomol Lake. This is the largest stadium in Dushanbe.

Dynamo Stadium, Shevchenko St. 36

Botanical Garden, Karamova St. This garden was founded in 1934.

Zoo, Komsomol Park

Shapkin Racecourse, Novi Posyelok

Lenin Park, Lenin Prospect. In the park are an amusement arcade, a dance floor, and the open-air Leto (summer) Restaurant. Here also is Sadriddin Aini's grave and a monument to those who fell during the Civil War.

Dushanbe (Intourist) Hotel and Restaurant, Lenin St. 7, TEL. 2–45–92.

Vakhsh Hotel and Restaurant (Intourist), Lenin Prospect 26/2. Intourist TEL. 45–92.

Pamir Restaurant, Kirova St. 21A

Dushanbe Restaurant, Komsomol Lake

Leto (summer) Restaurant, Lenin Prospect, in the park

Molodyozhnoe (youth) Cafe, Putovskova St.

Bakhor (spring) Ice-cream Parlour, Lenin Prospect, opposite the railway station

Penny-in-the-Slot Café, Lenin Prospect 52

Rokhat (leisure) Tea-room, Lenin Prospect 70. This tea-room is decorated in national style.

G.P.O., Lenin Prospect 52

Bank, Lenin Prospect 29

Department Store, Lenin Prospect 73

Bookshop, Lenin Prospect 75

Souvenirs, Lenin Prospect 54

Markets: Putovsky, Putovskova St.; Zelyeni, Lakhuti St.

Arts and Crafts, Lenin Prospect 70. Open 11–5, closed Mon. There is pottery on sale here and traditional tobacco horns, among other things, at prices from 3·50 roubles.

Taxi ranks, near the Vakhsh Hotel, on Lenin Prospect, by the Central Park, and by the railway station.

Varzob Ravine, 40 km. out of town. Here amid lovely scenery stands the hydropower station built in 1937 on R. Varzob. There are beaches, and boats can be hired on the reservoir.

At the 45 km. mark a little further along the same road a side road branches off to Khodzha-Obi-Garm.

Khodzha-Obi-Garm

52 km. from Dushanbe. This health resort lies between 1740 and 1960 m. above sea level and in days gone by many pilgrims were attracted here to seek cures from the mineral springs. The rivers Mazar and Kalandia provide picturesque waterfalls. There is a restaurant here too.

EREVAN

Population—767,000 (1970)
Capital of the Armenian Soviet Socialist Republic

ARMENIA

(In Armenian: Ayastan)
Area: 29,800 sq. km.
Population—2,492,000 (1970), 78% of which is Armenian and the rest Russian, Azerbaijani, and Kurd.

Armenia is one of the republics of the U.S.S.R., situated in the south of central Transcaucasia. Its principal towns are the capital, Erevan, and Leninakan.

The Armenians are one of the most ancient peoples of the world. In the 8th–7th centuries B.C. the tribes of Hayas conquered the tribes of Armens and later on other Urartu tribes, hence the two names of the country, Ayastan (as the Armenians call it) and Armenia (as is well known to the Greeks, Persians, and Romans). Sometimes the Armenians refer to it as Ayastan-Karastan, meaning Armenia 'country of stones'; this is an apt name as one third of the territory is rocky and arid.

During the country's 3000 years of history, it has known heroic ups and tragic downs. Once its might was compared to that of ancient Rome, and then it became the most backward province of Persia. Its position on the main trade route between east and west was the main reason for its being constantly conquered and reconquered, and then regaining its independence. In 519 B.C. the Armenians were conquered by Persia, and in 334 B.C. by Alexander the Great. In 189 B.C. the country regained its independence and by the middle of the 1st century B.C. it became one of the most powerful states in the near east, especially during the reign of Tigranes II (95–56 B.C.) when Armenian territory reached from the Caucasus Mountains down to the Mediterranean Sea. Tigranes was finally defeated by Pompey, and his country fell under Roman rule.

The country became Christian in A.D. 301, following the conversion of Tridates III by St. Gregory the Enlightener, but at the end of the 4th century, Armenia was divided between Persia and Byzantium. In 628 the whole country became a province of Byzantium and in 652 it was conquered by the Arabs. It was only in 886 that Armenian independence was regained, to last for another 160 years.

From the middle of the 11th century, the country was invaded and conquered successively by the Seljuk Turks, the Mongols, and Timur. In the 16th century it was a bone of contention between Persia and Turkey and was always under the rule of one or other of these.

In 1826, as a result of the Russo-Persian War, eastern Armenia became part of the Russian Empire. A revival of national feeling at the end of the 19th century was halted by the massacres of 1894–6. Then and during World War I, when the Turks were aided by the Germans, 1,500,000 Armenians (half the small country's population) lost their lives. Many only escaped by fleeing abroad. Now there is a steady trickle of Armenians returning to their country and many repatriates have settled in the suburbs of Erevan on Norka Hill.

After the Russian revolution of 1917, Armenia first became part of the Transcaucasian Federation (which soon disintegrated) and after that was ruled by the Dashnaktsutyun Party, which advocated Armenian independence, until in 1920 it became part of the Transcaucasian Federal Republic of the U.S.S.R. Soviet power was established in December 1920, and although there was a revolt in February 1921, it was never challenged after April of that year. Since 1936 Armenia has been a Union republic of the U.S.S.R.

Soviet Armenia lays claim to Turkish Armenia. This includes the holy mountain of Ararat and in spite of the fact that it is no longer theirs, the Armenians are proud to depict it on their coat-of-arms. It is said that when the Turks protested about this, saying that the mountain was on Turkish territory, the Soviet reply was that although the Turkish symbol was the crescent, surely it did not mean that they laid claim to the moon. The highest mountain in Armenia is the four-peaked Mount Aragatz (4016 m). Here in 1946 at the village of Burakan, one of the leading Soviet observatories was built.

The Armenian alphabet was composed in the 4th century A.D. by Maesrob Mashtotz and is still in use today. Armenia had its own university in the Middle Ages.

Some words and phrases of modern Armenian:

hello	voghdzuyin
I am a tourist	Yes tourist em
please	khntrem
thank you	shorhakalutyun
yes	ayi-ye
no	votch
good	lav
I don't understand	Yes chen haskanoom
good-bye	tsertesootyun
how do you do?	barev dzez

Many modern buildings in Armenia contain traditional architectural elements, and frequent use is made of the classic decorative designs carved into the stonework. Often they are built of the same pink tufa or dark grey basalt that have been used through the ages.

There are over 2500 buildings and other monuments of historical interest in Armenia, and the church architecture especially deserves attention. The earliest churches were basilical, with a nave or a nave flanked by two aisles. Gradually the central stone cupola was introduced and the ground plan changed to cruciform. The 5th–7th centuries were a golden age of ecclesiastical building and many other forms were tried too, including circular and polygonal, but typical of almost all is the stone cupola on a circular or polygonal drum surmounted by a conical top. These churches were bare to a point of austerity, the only decoration being sculpted friezes around the windows.

In the 9th–11th centuries, when the monasteries were founded, decoration gradually became more apparent. The conical roof of the cupola became corrugated, bas-reliefs and high reliefs were introduced including those featuring animals as well as purely formal designs, and in addition, the first frescoes graced the walls. Most important of all innovations was the pointed arch, first used in 1001 in the Cathedral of Ani. The churches retained their simple lines, but a large narthex, or porch, was built in front. Through the years the monastic buildings increased in number and complexity but always showed a remarkable geometric sense. They housed libraries and schools and were vital centres of learning and art until the Mongol invasions.

New ecclesiastical buildings appeared only in the 17th century when they tended to return to the basilical style with the central cupola but added an open gallery and a belfry to the western façade. At this time belfrys were also added to the older churches, not always harmoniously. The arabesques in the designs of the stonework patterns and the use of alternating red and black stone show the influence of Moslem art.

The inventiveness and skill of the Armenian stonemasons had long been known far and wide. In 806–11 Oton Matsaetsi built St. Germain-des-Pres and the belfry of Charlemagne's palace in Aachen. Armenian influence spread further when the crusades formed an important link, for the road to Jerusalem lay through Armenia, and later when the Mongols descended from the east, Armenian workers themselves emigrated westwards. They were called upon to repair the dome of St. Sophia in Constantinople and to build the church of San Satiro in Milan. In 1221 St. Trophime in Arles had its main entrance restored by an Armenian mason, and many other churches and cathedrals in France not only bear witness to the popularity of the Armenian style, but were actually carved with the special trademarks of Armenian masons. In particular one may mention St. Chapelle in Paris, where in three medallions illustrating the story of Noah's ark appears the silhouette of Zvarnots cathedral, complete in every detail.

Today the churches in the Balkan countries display ample evidence of Armenian work and it is the interesting theory of the French archaeologist, François Choisy, that the Armenian style of decoration spread along the Dniestr and the Vistula to Scandinavia and thence to Scotland, Ireland, and Normandy, where it was reflected in Romanesque ornament.

Erevan

One of the legends about the derivation of the name Erevan is that it comes from the Armenian 'ereval' (or erevangal) meaning 'it appears', and is what Noah shouted when he first saw land after the flood, before he landed on Mount Ararat. The story gives no explanation why Noah used the Armenian language to shout in. Historians have suggested that Erevan was the centre of the Eri tribe.

Erevan is the capital of Armenia and is divided into two parts by R. Razdan which flows down from Lake Sevan. The hilly plateau on the right bank of the river was completely untouched and has only recently been included in the growing city. The highest part of Erevan stands 1042 m. above sea level. Its highest temperature is 40°C. in summer and its lowest is −20°C. in winter.

Mount Ararat, which the Armenians hold sacred, can be seen from Erevan although it is on Turkish territory. It stands 5156 m. high.

Erevan's founding is lost in the darkness of history. Archaeologists have made some amazing finds just outside the city on Arinberd Hill. The name means 'bloody hill' and it has certainly seen much bitter fighting over the centuries. It is also fairly certain now that this was the site of Erebuni because stone slabs have been found in different places in the vicinity all bearing the same inscription: 'Argishti, son of Menua, founded the town of Erebuni to the glory of the land of Bianili and to instil fear into his enemies. I have settled 6600 prisoners from the land of Khatti and the land of Tsupani there.'

In the 8th century B.C. Erebuni was an important centre of the Urartu kingdom. It traded actively with Egypt, Greece, and Rome; among other items discovered here is an amulet of the Egyptian god, Bas, dragon-slayer, guardian of the sleeping and of female beauty, and also 68 large ceramic jars (about 2 m. tall) which were used to store grain and wine. Of even greater interest are the ruins of an elegant palace surrounded by a double wall for defence. The gateway has been found, and inside are the remains of a temple-tower and a hall where 30 mighty pillars of pine rose, each from a basalt pediment. Some of the timber is in such a good state of preservation that it could be used today. The archaeologists are anxious that their discoveries, particularly the paintings and bas-reliefs on the whitewashed walls, should not fall victim to wind and weather.

Further information is not available

EREVAN

It has been suggested that the site be covered with a tent-like roof slung on steel cables from a single central support.

The first written mention of Erevan in Armenian was in the 7th century. In 1387 the town was attacked by Timur's hordes and from 1500 it had military importance as a frontier town between the rivals, Persia and Turkey. The Turkish army occupied it in 1554 and in 1639 the country of Armenia was divided between Turkey and Persia. Erevan fell in the eastern section and so was under Persian rule. Later still the town changed hands

again and the Turks held it for ten years. In 1735 the Persians moved back again.

One of the principal aims of the Russo-Persian wars of 1804–13 and 1826–9 was the capture of the Erevan Khanate, but the Russian army only moved in in 1827. A special thanksgiving service was held in St. Petersburg and the keys and flags of the captured fortress were displayed in procession along the streets of the Russian capital. Erevan was the administrative centre and was also of strategic importance.

It was still a typical Asian town with labyrinthine streets and clay houses. Tsar Nicholas I who visited Erevan in 1837 called it a 'clay pot'. The first town planning and reconstruction took place in the 1850s. One of the reasons for the rebuilding given by the local authorities was that the twisty streets 'make police observation difficult'. The best buildings were those put up along Astafyevskaya St., now Abovyan St.

The most important item in the local industry became vodka and wine production. Shustov's famous Russian brandy was produced here and the production of spirits concerned 90% of Erevan's industry. The town itself grew as thousands of Armenians came there after the Turkish massacres during World War I.

In December 1918, representatives of the Entente came to Erevan and it was recorded that an order was given to move the clocks 50 minutes forward so that local time would correspond to that adhered to by the British fleet. Maj. Gen. L. C. Dunsterville, head of the British Mission to the Caucasus, also issued an order that the signs in the streets be written in English.

The city's most interesting streets are *Lenin Prospect* and *Ordzhonikidze Prospect. Abovyan St.* and *Teryan St.* are among the most fashionable with many theatres, cinemas, hotels, and shops. The centre of Erevan is *Lenin Sq.*; it was built as an architectural whole using the Armenian national style of architecture. The most impressive building is *Government House* designed by A. Tamanyan. It was Tamanyan also who planned the reconstruction of Erevan in 1924. Other buildings here are *Trade Union House*, the *central post office*, the *Armenia Hotel*, and the *Historical Museum*. The whole panorama of the square is mirrored in a large pool in front of the History Museum.

On Lenin Prospect, opposite the History of Erevan Museum, stands the largest *department store*; it is of an interesting national design devised by architects Agababyan and Arakyelyan.

On the left bank of R. Razdan, not far from Victory Bridge, are the Ararat wine cellars, designed by Israelyan. Close by is the *Ararat brandy distillery*, built in national architectural style by Markaryan in 1953. The *Victory Bridge* itself was built in 1945 by architects Ovnanyan, Mamidzanyan, and Asatryan. The new bridge over the river is 364 m. long and 58 m. high, making it much larger than Victory Bridge.

Barekamutsyan (friendship) St. is in one of the newest areas and is lined with impressive buildings such as those of the *Supreme Soviet* and the *Academy of Sciences*. Another rapidly developing part is the Nork region; this is where many immigrants have settled down, and it is linked with Kirov St. down below by a funicular railway.

St. Sarkis Church, near Victory Bridge. Built in the 19th century.

St. Oganes's Church, Konda region; also of 19th-century construction.

Mosque, Lenin Prospect. This was built in the 1660s.

Baptist Church, Nardosa St. 90

Historical Museum, Lenin Sq. This museum was founded in 1921 and includes archaeological, ethnographical, and numismatic departments. It has a good display of items discovered in excavations, the oldest of which come from the most ancient town on Soviet territory, Urartu (8th–7th century B.C.) and includes the bronze shields of the kings of Urartu. A special hall is devoted to the excavation of Dvin, the capital of Armenia from the 4th to the 10th centuries A.D., and of Ani, capital from the 10th to the 13th centuries A.D.

Among samples of local craftsmanship are 15th–17th century monastery doors of carved woodwork and a 17th-century throne of the Katolikos, head of the Armenian Church. There are also a number of other ecclesiastical items, musical instruments, and carpets. Open 10.30–4.30; closed Mon.

Revolution Museum, Lenin Sq., in the same building as the Historical Museum. This museum was opened in 1960 to commemorate the 40th anniversary of Soviet power in Armenia. It illustrates the revolutionary movement in the country before the revolution and the progress after 1920.

Geological Museum, Abovyan St. 20. Open Tues. and Fri. only from 11–3.

History of Erevan Museum, Lenin Prospect 6. Located in a 17th-century Persian mosque, this museum is divided into two departments, pre- and post-revolutionary. It contains Persian arms and flags which were captured here and also the keys to the town fortress. There are excavated items as well. Open 11–4.30; closed Mon. This building also houses *Erevan Planetarium*.

Matenadaran Library of Ancient Manuscripts, Lenin Prospect 111. This is one of the largest storage places of its kind in the world. It contains over 13,000 items, some of which are more than 1500 years old. The building was specially designed in 1959 by architect Grigoryan. Most of the manuscripts are of Armenian origin from the 6th to 8th centuries. There are works of historians, mathematicians, astronomers, and philosophers but there are also manuscripts from Persia and the Arab countries as well as Latin and Greek manuscripts. Some works of the ancient Greeks are known today only because the Armenian translations survived; one example is Xenon's 'Tractate on Nature' which is illustrated by delightful miniatures. There is a book of the gospels written on parchment in 887, and a book of sermons weighing 32 kg. which needed 607 calves' skins to complete, and which was transcribed in 1205.

The nucleus of this collection (and the library's name) came from Echmiadzin Library in 1920 but it was added to by items from other monasteries and from private collections. Here is also the oldest manuscript in Europe to be written on paper, dating from 971.

Open 9–5 Tues., Wed., and Thurs. only.

Armenian Literature and Art Museum, Spandaryan St. 1. Here are the personal archives of a number of famous Armenian writers and also an exhibition about the Armenian theatre since 53 B.C. Open 11–4.30; closed Wed.

Armenian Picture Gallery, Abovyan St. This gallery was opened in 1921 and ranks among the best in the Soviet Union, after those of Moscow and Leningrad. There are about 14,000 works of art, dating from the early Middle Ages until the present day. There is a section displaying porcelain and a special hall with 17th–19th-century east European art. There are paintings by Tintoretto, Rubens, Van Dyck, Jordaens, Courbet, Delacroix, and Fragonard. There is also a fine collection of gravures. Open 11–5; closed Wed. and Thurs. Also housed in the Gallery is a small Theatrical Museum.

Armenian Natural History Museum, Lenin Prospect 6. Open 11–5.30; closed Tues.

Khachatur Abovyan (1805–48) Museum, in his house in Kanakir. This author and ethnographer created the modern Armenian literary language. Open 11–5.30; closed Wed.

Tumanyan Museum, Moskovskaya St. 40. Ovanes Tumanyan (1869–1923) was a famous Armenian poet. The museum was built in 1953 to commemorate the 30th anniversary of his death. The wide flight of steps leading up to the museum has as many steps as there were years of his life. Open 11–5.30; closed Wed.

Avetik Isaakyan (1875–1957) Museum, Plekhanova St. 32. The museum is in the poet's house. Open 11–5.30; closed Wed.

Saryan Museum, Moskovskaya St. Martiros Saryan (1880–1972) was a well-known Armenian landscape artist who studied in Moscow between 1897 and 1903. His style was much influenced by Cézanne and other French post-impressionists. His house contains nearly 1000 of his works painted during the past 60 years and is sometimes called the Second Armenian Picture Gallery.

Statue of David of Sasun, by the railway station. This equestrian statue is of David, a legendary hero immortalised in a national epic, on his magic steed, Dzhelali. The bowl into which water is trickling is specially symbolic of the Armenian people's anger which will rise and overflow if the freedom and happiness of their country is endangered; at this point David will intervene to crush the enemy. The statue by Kochar stands 12·5 m. high on a basalt rock. It was unveiled in 1959.

Sayat-Nova Monument, in a garden in front of a music school called after him on Lenin Prospect. Arutin Sayadyan (1712–95) was the poet's real name. Arutunyan's sculpture was unveiled in 1962.

Abovyan Monument, in a small garden at the end of Abovyan St. The statue of Khachatur Abovyan is by Stepanyan and Tamanyan.

Tumanyan and Spendaryan Monuments, in front of the State Opera House. The monuments to Ovanes Tumanyan, the classical author, and to the composer, Alexander Spendaryan, are by Sarkisyan and Chubaryan.

Nalbandyan and Isaakyan Monuments, Semi-Circular Boulevard. The monument to Michael Nalbandyan (1829–66), a writer and revolutionary, is by Nikogosyan and that to Avetik Isaakyan is by Bagdasaryan.

Genocide Victims' Memorial, overlooking Tsitsernakaberd Park. The architects, Sashur Kalashyan and Artur Tarkhanyan, and the sculptor, Ovanes Khachatryan, were responsible for the three parts of this moving tribute to those who died in the slaughter of 1915 when over a million Armenians perished at the hands of the Turks. The Alley of Mourning is 110 m. long and 10 m. wide, paved with smooth basalt; along the left side is to be built a wall with illustrations in high relief of episodes in the massacre. The Alley leads to the open-air Mausoleum, where twelve stone buttresses form a circle, their sloping sides giving the whole the impression of a truncated pyramid. Between the buttresses, twelve flights of steps lead down to the sunken place, 20 m. in diameter which they encircle. In the centre burns an eternal flame and the silence is only broken by the funeral music by the Armenian composers, Komitass and Yekmalian. The interior surfaces of the buttresses will bear inscriptions in Armenian, Russian, English, French, Spanish, German, and Arabic relating the story of the massacre; visitors will be able to read about it for themselves in this quiet place rather than listen to the spoken explanation of a guide.

Beyond the Mausoleum rises a 40-m. column symbolising eternal life and brotherhood. From here there is a splendid view of Erevan etched on the grey background of Mount Ararat, sacred to all Armenians.

Shaumyan Monument, Shaumyan Sq. Stepan Shaumyan (1878–1918) was an Armenian communist and at one time chairman of the Baku Council. He was the leader of the twenty-six commissars who were shot, and the statue depicts the moment of his death. It was sculpted in pink granite by Merkurov, stands 3·5 m. high and was unveiled in 1931.

Soviet Power Monument, Akhtanak Park. This basalt monument unveiled in 1970 to commemorate the 50th anniversary of Soviet power in Armenia was designed by Sarkis Gurzadyan and Jim Torosyan. There are three terraces, the lowest serving as a platform for the Erevan-Sevan railway line, the second with a fine view over Erevan and the Ararat Valley for observation purposes, and the third crowned by a rectangular column, 50 m. high and bearing on each of its four sides the ancient Armenian symbol for eternity. Next to the column stands a block, 30 m. square, into which is to be inserted a polished stone slab with commemorative inscriptions. When the monument is completed, the Northern Cascade will sweep down from the foot of the column with a waterfall and flights of steps to the end of Tumanyan St.

Lenin Monument, Lenin Sq. This statue, also by Merkurov, is of copper with a pedestal of polished Armenian granite. Its total height is 18·5 m. and it was unveiled in 1940. Behind the monument burns an eternal flame to the memory of the heroes of the revolution.

Gukasyan Monument, near Abovyan Garden. Gukas Gukasyan was the founder of the Armenian Young Communist League. The sculpture by Sarkisyan was unveiled in 1935.

Stepanyan Monument, in Kirov Children's Park. Nelson Stepanyan is a World War II veteran, twice Hero of the Soviet Union.

Marble Hands, in Semi-Circular Boulevard. These marble hands were sent to Erevan as a token of friendship from Carrara in Italy in 1962.

Opera and Ballet Theatre, Lenin Prospect 54. This theatre has 1200 seats.

Sundukyan Drama Theatre, Shaumyan St. 2, in the park. Performances here are in Armenian.

Stanislavsky Drama Theatre, Abovyan St. 35. In this theatre the performances are in Russian.

Musical Comedy Theatre, Shaumyan St. 4

Mikoyan Youth Theatre, Moskovskaya St. 35

Large Philharmonic Hall, Lenin Prospect 46. This hall seats 1400.

Small Philharmonic Hall, Abovyan St. 2

Circus, 26–Kommisars St. 5

Racecourse, in the village of Verkhni Charbakh. Racing on Sun. at 3 pm.

Republican Stadium, Gnuni St. 65. This stadium can seat 20,000.

Zoo, Avanskoye Chaussee, 2 km. from Erevan. The zoo covers an area of 28 hectares (70 acres) and is open 8.30–7.

Botanical Garden, Avanskoye Chaussee, 3·5 km. north-west of Erevan. This park covers 105 hectares (262 acres) and is open from 9–5.

Akhtanak (victory) Park, Kanakev Chaussee. These gardens cover 70 hectares (175 acres) of hilly territory. The Victory Monument which can be seen from the city and which was built by architect Israelyan is 35 m. high. It used to be topped by an enormous 16 m. statue of Stalin but it was demolished and replaced by one of a woman with a sword. The monument is decorated with stone carving in national style and inside it is the Modern Armenia Exhibition.

Komitas Park, Ordzhonikidze Prospect 130. In the park is the Pantheon of outstanding figures in the world of Armenian literature and art, including Komitas, Iannisyan, Shirvan-Zade, Toramnyan, and Abelyan.

Komsomol Park, Marx St. 227

26-Kommissars Park, Shaumyan St. 2

Armenia (Intourist) Hotel and Restaurant, Amerian St. 1, TEL. 52–38–29.

Ani (Intourist) Hotel and Restaurant, Sayat Nova Prospect 19, TEL. 52–07–75.

Erevan Hotel, Abovyan St. 24, TEL. 52–50–61, 52–23–80.

Sevan Hotel and Restaurant, Shaumyan St. 18

Restaurant Arabkir, Komitasa St.

Massis (the Armenian name for Mount Ararat) Restaurant, Krasnoarmeiskaya St.

Egnik (deer) Restaurant, Spandriyan Square

Aragil (stork) Restaurant, in Victory Park

Zephyr Café, Kievskaya St.

Lyre Café, Komitasa St.

Anait Café, Nalbandyan St.

Garni Shashlik Bar, Nork region

Cocktail Bar, Abovyan St. 24, in the Armenia Hotel

Foreign Currency Shop, Amerian St.

Souvenirs, Abovyan St. 24, in the Armenia Hotel

Art Salon, Lenin Prospect 44

The environs of Erevan contain a wealth of interesting sights, but the following are probably the most important for those with limited time.

Oshakan

6·5 km. from Erevan, to the north-east. Oshakan was the home of Mesrob Mashtotz, the 4th-century monk from Echmiadzin who invented the Armenian alphabet which is still in use today. Here, in the crypt of a church rebuilt in the 19th century, is his tomb.

Just outside Oshakan is a Memorial Stele in the shape of an open book upon which the Armenian alphabet is carved; it was erected in 1962 to mark the 1600th anniversary of the alphabet.

Echmiadzin

15 km. from Erevan, to the west. At the end of the 3rd century B.C. a settlement called Vardkesavan was established here. Later its name was changed to Vagarshapat, but the story of Echmiadzin really has its beginnings in Rome. When the Roman Emperor Diocletian was seeking a bride, he chose as fairest in the land a Christian girl called Rhipsime. She refused him because he was a pagan and fled to Armenia with a number of other Christians. They sought refuge in the vineyards of Vagarshapat and preached their religion there. Tridates III was Armenia's ruler at that time and the Roman Emperor asked him to send Rhipsime back, but Tridates himself was also eager to marry the beautiful maiden. Again she refused, for he too was a pagan and in anger he had her and her friends driven out from the palace grounds and stoned to death. This however is not the end of the story, for Tridates went out of his mind and believed himself to be a wild boar. Help was sought from a certain prisoner named Gregory, who not only cured the tsar's madness but also converted him to Christianity. Thereupon this was adopted as the state religion and chapels were built to commemorate the untimely deaths of Rhipsime and Gayane, one of the girls martyred with her.

Gregory, later canonised and thereafter known as St. Gregory the Enlightener, and Tsar Tridates III had literally to fight to convert the people from paganism. Very often the splendid new churches were built over pagan temples to gods of fire, water, and other popular deities. It is said that St. Gregory saw a vision of Christ descending to the earth and on the spot he struck with a golden hammer, an image of a church appeared. It was in this place that in A.D. 303 St. Gregory founded *Echmiadzin Cathedral*, its name meaning 'the descent of the Only Begotten', to commemorate the conversion of the tsar and his people. Under the main altar is a room containing a fire-worshipping altar from pagan times. Other traces of paganism can be found in some of the rites of the Armenian Church; it is still customary to make sacrifices, and in the inner courtyard of Echmiadzin Cathedral is a place where sheep, lambs, cocks, and doves are slaughtered.

The cathedral has been repeatedly remodelled and rebuilt, and the present ground plan dates from the 7th century. The belfry was constructed in 1653 and the sacristy, now housing the treasury, was added behind the choir in 1868. Surrounding the cathedral are monastic buildings, a seminary, printing works, offices, and the episcopal palace built at the beginning of this century, but decorated with stonework using classic motifs. Echmiadzin has been the seat of the Catholics of all Armenia since the 14th century, and the Supreme Patriarch, Vazgen I, resides here today. The old palace has an impressive throne-room with finely ornamented walls and ceilings.

The *monastic museum* was built in 1869 and is a real treasury of church vessels, silver and gold work, jewellery, and embroidery. The museum also lays claim to a piece of Noah's ark and of the Cross, relics of saints, including St. Gregory the Enlightener, and the lance which pierced the body of Christ, long preserved in Gueghard Monastery (see below, p. 105). Also in the museum are illuminated manuscripts and miniatures and a famous collection of coins.

In the eastern outskirts of the town of Echmiadzin stands *Rhipsime Cathedral* (A.D. 618) built on the site of the original chapel and a classical example of an Armenian church with a central cupola. Here also is *Shogakat Cathedral*, built in 1694 also to commemorate the virgin martyrs and replacing a 7th-century church. Although built much later than the other cathedrals, it is nevertheless one of the finest examples of Armenian ecclesiastical architecture. Shogakat means 'ray' and derives from the story that a ray of light was said to have fallen on the broken bodies.

Gayane Cathedral is in the southern part of the town, near the monastic pond and dominating the ecclesiastical cemetery. It was built in A.D. 630 and, like Rhipsime Cathedral, stands on the site of the commemorative chapel. In 1652 restoration work was carried out and in 1683 a gallery was added in front of the entrance to house the tombs of the monks, but its simplicity is unspoiled, and it stands on a remarkable site with Mount Ararat as its background.

Zvarnots

18 km. from Erevan, and just 2 km. from Echmiadzin. Here are the ruins of the three-storey Cathedral of St. Gregory which was built in the 7th century but collapsed in the 10th century from faulty stonework. The large pool in the centre was for adult baptism, while a monolithic stone font for infants stands behind the chancel apse. In the

museum is a model reconstruction of the cathedral.

Garni

28 km. to the east of Erevan. On the way to Garni the road passes a *monument* to the famous Armenian poet, Egishe Tcharents (1897–1937). It is in the form of a stone arch designed by Raphael Israelian. From here a good view of the Ararat Valley and the snow-capped peak of Mount Masis (Greater Ararat) opens out. Carved on the arch are words taken from a poem by Tcharents: 'My love for Masis in my wanderings is as precious to me as the arduous path of fame.'

Garni is one of the most famous fortresses of ancient Armenia. It was built in the 3rd century B.C. and is mentioned by Tacitus. It was virtually impregnable and a number of Armenian kings took refuge here during their civil wars. Garni was first destroyed by the Romans in the year A.D. 59. However in A.D. 77 it was restored by Tridates I who defeated the Romans and then travelled to Rome to receive a crown from Nero and compensation of 150,000,000 dinars. It is said that the proud king refused to part with his sword as was demanded by etiquette in the presence of the Roman emperor. Garni was again destroyed when the Arabs conquered Armenia but was rebuilt at the beginning of the 10th century. Its final destruction came in 1638 during the Turkish invasion, and then a violent earthquake in 1679 buried what remained of it.

Since excavations were started here in 1949, the fortress walls and 14 towers have been unearthed. On a plateau high above stand the *remains of a temple* built by sun worshippers in the 1st century. Some richly carved stone decorations and the 24 Ionic columns which surrounded the temple can be seen there, and restoration work is in progress. After their conversion to Christianity at the beginning of the 4th century, the Armenian rulers used the temple as their summer residence, and it was known as the Cool Palace. King Khosrov often stayed here as this valley was his favourite hunting ground.

50 m. north-west of the temple are the remains of the *royal baths* (1st–3rd century A.D.). These were in Roman style and had separate rooms with cold, warm, and hot water while a system of ceramic pipes circulated hot air below the floors. In the baths a priceless piece of mosaic flooring has been discovered. Multi-coloured local stones were crushed and set into patterns featuring sea gods, fishes, and mythological creatures. On one piece of mosaic (almost 3 sq. m.) can be seen the figures of Oceanus and Thalassa (the sea). Above their heads a Greek inscription reads: 'We worked without pay.' Its meaning is still uncertain; some ascribe it to the artists who were proud to work for art's sake while others explain it as a comment upon the work of the seas.

Among the medieval buildings of Garni are the *ruins* of a circular, four-altared church (7th century) and houses from the 12th–17th centuries.

Gueghard

38 km. from Erevan and just 10·5 km. further along the road from Garni. First called Airivank, or the *Monastery of the Caves*, the history of this place probably goes back to pre-Christian times, but nothing has survived from then except perhaps the small cave-chapel to the west of the monastery.

The present buildings here date from the 10th–13th centuries when the monastery was re-named Gueghard, meaning 'lance' in Armenian. The name comes from the legendary lance, supposedly the one used to pierce the body of Christ, which was long kept here but is now in the museum of Echmiadzin Cathedral. Besides the main church with its impressive narthex and other monastic buildings, there are three churches here cut into the solid rock. The main church is the oldest building in the complex. It was constructed in 1215 and belonged to the Princes Ivane and Zakhare Dolgorukii. These were brave and talented warriors who served the Georgian Queen Tamara. They won most of Armenia back from the Seljuk Turks, were crowned Kings of Armenia, and established the Zakharides dynasty. The most interesting buildings date from a few years later, after Prince Prosh had purchased Gueghard from the Zakharides.

Avazan Church (1283) is carved right into the rock and is an incomparable work of art. It leads to a rectangular portico, believed to have served as the Proshyan family mausoleum, and then to another church deeper in the rock. In 1288 a columned portico was carved in the upper part of the rock. One large bas-relief is thought to be the Proshyan coat-of-arms; it depicts the head of an ox with two lions tied to ropes, while between the lions is an eagle with a lamb in his claws. Other bas-reliefs represent the sun, a mythical bird called Sirin with the head of a woman, and figures stemming from the folk art of pagan times. Connoisseurs say that the rock churches are best seen when the sun is directly above the window in the cupola; then the stone figures come to life and begin to move, the lions show their teeth, and the eagle spreads his wings. They are, however, very impressive at any time of day. Inside the rock church to the north-west of the main building a clear spring wells up from the ground; it is said that in pre-Christian times this was the site of a temple to the god of water.

Along the southern and eastern walls of Gueghard Monastery, high above the valley, are *medieval communal buildings* and dwellings which are well preserved. The monastery withstood all manner of assaults during a period of seven hundred years. Its walls stood firm and in times of danger sheltered many scholars so that it was revered throughout Armenia as one of the country's greatest spiritual and cultural centres.

Amberd Fortress

40 km. from Erevan, and 10 km. from the village of Burakan, where the observatory is. Amberd Fortress stands high upon the southern slope of Mount Aragats. It is an outstanding example of Armenian secular architecture and, as it was protected by thick walls and placed almost inaccessibly on the crags overlooking the two deep ravines of Arshakhyan and Amberd, it repulsed nearly every attack launched upon it during more than seven centuries. Today asphalt roads wind up the sides of Mount Aragats, but they do not lead right up to the fortress, and the last part of the climb must be made on foot.

Amberd Fortress is believed to have been founded in the 7th century A.D., during the rule of the Kamsarakan princes. It was rebuilt four centuries later by Vakhram Pakhlavuni, one of Armenia's most famous warriors; he added thick stone walls and three bastions along the ridge of the Arkhashyan ravine where there were no natural defences. The church inside the fortress was built at the same time, as is proved by the date, 1026, inscribed over its door.

Later on Amberd was taken over by Armenia's ruling princes, the Bagratids, and made into their most important forepost against enemies from the south. It was taken in the 11th century by the Seljuk Turks, but in 1200 Zakhare Dolgoruki, who served the Georgian Queen Tamara, drove out the Turks and flew Tamara's banner from the main bastion of the fortress. In the 13th century Amberd was ravaged by a fire which must have raged over the entire territory surrounding it.

Lake Sevan

70 km. from Erevan. Lake Sevan is often called Armenia's pearl. It is certainly a lake of great beauty and has served as the theme for many songs and poems. It lies 1900 m. above sea level and is one of the largest mountain lakes in the world. Its name comes from the Urartu word 'siunna', meaning 'the country of the lake', and in biblical times it was also called the Sea of Gegham. On the lake shore ten years ago an archaeological expedition discovered traces of a highly developed civilisation dating back to 2000 B.C.

Surviving monuments include *Sevan Monastery* built in A.D. 874 at the order of King Ashot I and his daughter, Miriam. At that time Armenia was part of the Arab khalifate, but the monastery is free from any influence from Arabian architecture. It was built on an island so as to serve as a fortress, but the waters of the lake receded and now it stands on a peninsula. The Arakelots' (apostles') Church within the monastery had a wooden structure built on to the western side, embellished with unique, carved wooden pillars; these are now in the Historical Museum in Erevan. Above the monastery is *Astvatsin Church*, larger than the monastery church and built of more carefully polished stone.

Lake Sevan lost much of its water because of a number of power stations and irrigation canals built on the R. Razdan which is fed by the lake. To save it from drying out further, a tunnel is being drilled in the basalt rocks to lead the waters of the river Arpa into Lake Sevan.

Akhtamar Intourist Hotel stands high on a cliff overlooking the lake and has three good restaurants. The place is famed for 'ishkhan' (king trout), a variety of trout only found in Lake Sevan. There is another good restaurant nearer the monastery which is appropriately called *Ishkhan Restaurant*. Near the hotel, boats can be hired for trips on the lake or for fishing for the same fine trout that is served in the restaurants.

Dilijan

110 km. from Erevan. This resort town has many curative mineral springs in the vicinity, some similar to those at Vichy in France. The climatic conditions are recommended for the treatment of tuberculosis.

The Armenians say that if there are woods, mountains, and mineral springs in paradise, then paradise must look like Dilijan, and the most picturesque spot near Dilijan is indisputably *Agartsin Gorge*. Here there stands an architectural ensemble from the 11th–13th centuries which is a classical example of Armenian medievai building. Most worthy of note is the refectory of *Agartsin Monastery*. It was built by a certain Minas in 1248, on the eve of the Mongol invasion. Outside, it is a simple, unpretentious building of smooth stone, but inside it is splendidly spacious with an ingeniously designed roof support. It was built following the traditions of secular architecture, repeating and developing the elements of a peasant house. These characteristics appear also in *St. Grigori's Church*, dating from the 11th century and probably the oldest building in the monastery. Agartsin's main cathedral was built in 1281 and, with lavish decorations of carved stone, is typical of Armenian church architecture of that period. It is almost an exact copy of the small family *church of St. Stephanos* nearby which was built in 1244.

Agartsin was in the territory belonging to the princes Ivane and Zakhare Dolgorukii. Legends tell of vast treasure hidden somewhere in the monastery walls and in the surrounding rocks. One of the rocks is even known as Treasure Rock. Beside the refectory are the ruins of an old kitchen. Some interesting tombstones are to be seen in the long grass on the premises; two of them stand near the southern wall, one bearing the inscription 'King Smbat' and the other, 'This is the grave of King Gaghki.'

ESSENTUKI

See Mineralniye Vody, p. 191

ESTONIA

See Tallinn, p. 288

FERGANA

See Tashkent, p. 301

FRUNZE

(Until 1926, Pishpek)

Population—431,000 (1970)
Capital of the Kirghiz Soviet Socialist Republic

KIRGHIZIA

Population—3,000,000, 40% of which is Kirghizi, belonging racially to the southern Siberian Mongoloids, while their language is related to the Turkic group. The percentage of Russians in the republic is gradually increasing and is now as high as 31%. There are many other nationalities to be found here, the Uzbeks (11%) and the Ukrainians (7%) being the next most numerous.

Kirghizia is one of the smallest republics in the Soviet Union; its territory is less than 1% of the total territory of the U.S.S.R. It shares its southern borders with China, and is very mountainous. Almost half lies at more than 3,000 m. above sea level. Highest of all is Pik Pobedy (Victory Peak) which soars to 7439 m. above sea level. Almost 6600 sq. km. of Kirghizia's territory is perpetually covered with snow and ice, the source of rivers, which empty either into the Aral Sea or into Lakes Balkhash and Taryma. The climate is extremely varied; in the mountains dry, subtropical areas are found lying beside zones of temperate climate and very cold regions. Kirghizia has many lakes; most of them are small, except Issyk Kull (Warm Lake) which is one of the largest in the U.S.S.R. It is 182 km. long and 58 km. wide and in places as much as 702 m. deep. The mountain slopes are lush with walnut, apple trees, barberry, and pistachio. There is also the wild nut of Kirghizia which is found nowhere else in the world.

The Kirghiz tribes came very long ago to the Tien Shan mountains from the upper reaches of the Siberian R. Yenisei. They soon discovered that their new territory was not very peaceful because it was crossed by the east-west trade routes and many other nations wished to control it. The Kirghizi had to fight new-comers from China, Central Asia, and the Arab potentates. They also suffered from the Mongol invasions. Until the end of the last century the Kirghiz tribes were headed by feudal lords, 'manaps', who claimed descent from a famous khan and led a nomadic life. A saying is still used today: 'My home is round my camp fire, my pasture round my horse's tether.' In 1855 Borombei Bekmuratov, chief of the Bugu tribe, which roamed the area east of Issyk Kul, was the first to become dependent on the Russian Empire. The other tribes were still ruled by the Kokand Khanate (now Uzbekistan). When the Russian troops entered this region, they attacked the Kokand fortresses one by one until by 1870 northern and central Kirghizia became part of the Russian Empire. After the 1917 revolution, the establishment of Soviet rule in this area was assisted by the poor settlers who had come from Russia and the Ukraine. In 1926 the Kirghiz Autonomous Republic was set up and ten years later it was declared a Union state.

The distribution of the population is very uneven. The majority live in the valleys which cover only one-sixth of the area while only 2% live in the mountains. Considerable efforts have been made in the past few decades to bring civilisation to the mountains, but many age-old customs still survive. One of the greatest problems is the status of women, which officially is equal to that of the men but in reality is far from it. Moslem influence is still very strong. Early marriages and payment, called 'kalym', from the bridegroom are still practised.

The mountains here are rich in non-ferrous ores which has led to significant industrial development. Kirghizia is the prime source of mercury and antimony. The latter is so pure that it is respected as a standard on the international market. The republic has also great resources of hydro-electric power. The R. Naryn, one of the republic's many waterways, has a potential of 35,600,000,000 kilowatts per hour. There is construction work in progress on a whole chain of power stations. The communication problem is very acute, for it often happens that two neighbouring districts only a dozen miles apart are entirely cut off from each other by impenetrable mountains.

Folk games and contests are very popular in Kirghizia. There is 'zhamby-atmai', an archery contest, 'kuresh', which is free-style wrestling, and apart from 'at-chabysh' (horse racing) there are a number of other diversions designed to test the skill of horsemen. 'Kuz-kuumai' is a horse race in which a 'bride' gallops away from her 'groom' who has to catch her and receives a kiss as his reward. 'Oorarrysh' is wrestling on horseback and 'tyiyn engmei' entails picking up coins from the ground at full gallop. These occasions bring in crowds of people dressed in national garments which consist of a padded coat, felt boots with leather overshoes, and a white felt hat with black flaps. Married women often wear the 'echelek', a great white turban made from a scarf 15 m. long.

National dishes of Kirghizia include 'sharpo' (mutton and potato soup), 'manti' (thin-skinned dumplings filled with peppery meat and onions), 'besh-barmak' (spaghetti and mutton), 'tukachi' (flat bread rolls) and 'konina' (horse meat).

A few words of the Kirghiz language:

hello	salaam matszbe
I am a tourist	bis tourist
thank you	rakhmat
yes	oh-a
no	dzho
good	yakshe
bad	dzhaman
I don't understand	men bil bame
Please fetch me an interpreter	bizgai kerek perevochik
good-bye	koshumuss
how do you do?	kandai turasass

Frunze

The capital city of Kirghizia is situated in the valley of R. Chu which flows down from the Tien Shan Mountains. It is also irrigated by two smaller rivers, the Ala-arch and the Ala-medin. The city stretches 20 km. from north to south and 16 km. from east to west, but it stands at a point where the valley slopes considerably, and so there is a difference of as much as 200 m. in the height of the southern and the northern suburbs.

The climate here is of an extreme continental type. It is sometimes –40°C. (–30°F.) in January and 40°C. (104°F.) in July. The hot, dry weather starts in May but the nights are always pleasantly cool because of the nearness of the mountains. The moderate temperatures of autumn make this a particularly good time of year for a visit.

The earliest settlements here grew up in the valley along the old caravan route from China, known as the Silk Road. Remains of a fairly prosperous trading settlement of the 8th–12th centuries A.D. have been found on the site of present-day Frunze. 10th-century travellers said that the route was so densely populated that 'cats could walk the rooftops all along the valley'. That was at the time when the Kirghiz people moved into the valley en masse.

In the early 19th century Kirghizia was taken by Kokand Khan and among the fortresses built by the order of Madali Khan (1821–42) was that of Pishpek. The name is said to come from the tool with which the nomad women whip up kumys (mares' milk). It is a small wooden stick with a little wheel on the end. The story goes that when a nomad family had moved on, someone left her pishpek behind. When in 1825 it was decided to build a fortress in that very place, the forgotten pishpek was found and the name, Pishpek, was given to the fortress.

Pishpek fortress was built of clay with gates in the western wall only. It was first stormed by the Russians in 1860, then again in 1862 and was finally ruined in 1866. As it had not been built of stone, nothing remains of it today except a small clay hill near Karpinsky St.

Russian peasants soon settled here and a posting station was opened in 1870. The Ukrainians who moved in a little later brought with them the Ukrainian look which many of the white-washed houses have even today. After the collapse of the Kokand Khanate in 1878 a Russian military settlement was founded and Pishpek became an administrative and trading centre of local importance. After a space of two years there were 500 people living there and then in 1883 a thousand Chinese Muslim refugees, known as Dungans, came from China to settle. Although it stood on the road between Tashkent and Verny (now Alma-Ata), it was more like a large village than anything else.

By the outbreak of the First World War the population had risen to 15,000, the majority being Russian as indeed they are today. Soviet power was established in 1918, and Pishpek's importance as an administrative centre was increased in 1924 when it was linked by rail to the rest of the country. Its name was changed in 1926 to Frunze

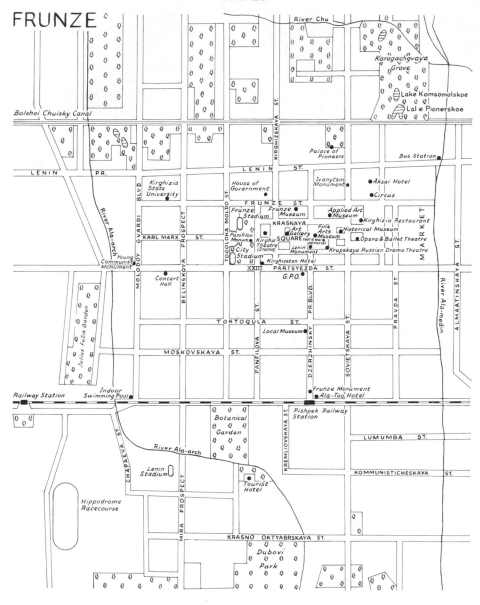

FRUNZE

River Chu

Karagachgvaya Grove

Lake Komsomolskoe

Lal e Pionerskoe

Bolshoi Chuisky Canal

KIRGHIZSKAYA ST.

Palace of Pioneers

Bus Station

LENIN　PR.

LENIN　ST.

Kirghizia State University

House of Government

Ivanytsin Monument

Aksai Hotel

Circus

GVARDI BLVD

TOGOLOKA MOLDO ST.

F R U N Z E　ST.

Frunze Stadium

Frunze Museum

Applied Art Museum

Kirghizia Restaurant

KARL MARX　ST.

BELINSKOVA PROSPECT

KRASNAYA

Panfilov Monum.

Kirghiz Theatre (Drama)

SQUARE

Art Gallery Museum

Fine Arts Museum

1941's War Memorial

Historical Museum

Opera & Ballet Theatre

Young Communist Monument

City Stadium

Lenin Monument

Krupskaya Russian Drama Theatre

MOLODOY

Kirghizstan Hotel

XXIII　PARTSYEZDA　ST.

Concert Hall

G.P.O.

PR. BLVD.

PRAVDA ST.

ALMAATINSKAYA ST.

River Ala-medin

M A R K E T

SOVIETSKAYA ST.

DZERZHINSKY ST.

Julius Fučik Garden

T O K T O Q U L A　ST.

Local Museum

PANFILOVA ST.

MOSKOVSKAYA　ST.

Railway Station

Indoor Swimming Pool

Frunze Monument

Ala-Too Hotel

CHAPAEVA ST.

Botanical Garden

KREMLIOVSKAYA ST.

Pishpek Railway Station

LUMUMBA　ST.

River Ala-arch

Lenin Stadium

MIRA PROSPECT

Tourist Hotel

KOMMUNISTICHESKAYA　ST.

Hippodrome Racecourse

KRASNO OKTYABRSKAYA　ST.

Dubovi Park

River Ala-arch

after Mikhail Frunze (see below). After the formation of the Kirghiz Republic in 1936, Frunze was made the capital, sizeable building projects were undertaken, and the Kirghiz population increased as workers moved into the young city. Many impressive buildings were put up at the end of the 1920s and the beginning of the 1930s. Two of them are now occupied by the *Praesidium* and the *Russian Drama Theatre*. Some were designed in the Constructivist style which was later criticised and banned entirely. Local industry only really began to develop when evacuated factories were set up here during World War II. Now the local industries include the manufacture of agricultural machinery, textiles, food, and tobacco products.

Frunze is well planned and the square blocks are set off by the rows of poplar and plane trees which run throughout the city. In summertime the smaller houses can hardly be seen because of the foliage, and it is estimated that a fifth of the city's area is taken up by gardens, parks, and orchards. All the streets that run from north to south have a wonderful panoramic view onto the snowy sunlit peaks of the Kirghiz Mountains. Because of their trees, some of the streets, particularly Lenin and Dzerzhinsky, would be best described as boulevards, and in fact the latter was originally called Boulevard St. Part of it was planted by schoolchildren in 1902 and the trees have been allowed to mature unhindered. Dzerzhinsky Boulevard runs northwards from Railway St. to a point near the Great Canal. On it, in the centre, stands the grey building of the *House of Government* and the *Council of Ministers*. Here also are *Dubovi Park* and the building of the *Academy of Sciences* (founded in 1954). *Respublikanskaya Sq.*, where the Kirghiz Theatre also stands, is the place where demonstrations are held. The central street is called after the 23rd Party Congress, *XXIII Partsyezda St.*, and *Sovietskaya St.* is the principal shopping street. Frunze is the home of a number of institutes and of the *Kirghizia State University* which dates from 1951.

Voskresenski (Resurrection) Cathedral, Lenin St. 479. Built in 1946–7 and open for services; the entrance is from the side street.

Synagogue, Lenin St. 290

Mosque, Gogolya St. 53. Built in the 1930s.

Historical Museum, Pushkin St. 78. Open 10–8, closed Mon.

Frunze Museum, Frunze St. 364. Mikhail Frunze, the Bolshevik revolutionary and civil war commander, was born here in 1885 and lived here until he was seven. There is a monument to him in front of the museum. Open 10–6, closed Mon.

Fine Arts Museum, Pervomaiskaya St. 90 and Dzerzhinsky Boulevard 50. There is a collection of classical Russian paintings (including Repin and Vereschagin) and of the works of modern local artists (e.g. Chuikov and Akilbekov). Open 11–6.30, closed Mon.

Zoological Museum, Pushkin St. 78. Open 10–4, closed Mon.

Toktogul Satylganov Monument, in front of the Opera and Ballet theatre. Toktogul Satylganov (1864–1933), known affectionately here as Toko, was a famous Khirghiz poet, composer and philosopher. The monument by Gapar Aitier was unveiled in 1974.

Ivanytsin Monument, Dzerzhinsky Boulevard. Alexei Ivanytsin (1870–1925) was a revolutionary and one of the organisers of the first Bolshevik groups here.

Young Communist Monument, Molodoy Gvardi Boulevard. This monument dedicated to Young Communists of the 1920s by Komsomol members of the 1960s was made by Pusyrevsky and unveiled in 1963.

Lenin Monument, Dzerzhinsky Boulevard. Designed by Neroda and unveiled in 1948.

Bust of D. Bokombayev, Dzerzhinsky Boulevard. Bokombayev was a local poet.

Panfilov Monument, in Panfilov Park, Panfilov St. Gen. Ivan Panfilov (1893–1941) was a hero of World War II, killed in battle. The division he led is known for its brave part in the defence of Moscow in 1941.

War Memorial Obelisk in the centre of Dubovi Park. This commemorates the fallen of the Second World War.

Opera & Ballet Theatre, Sovietskaya St. This theatre can seat about one thousand.

Krupskaya Russian Drama Theatre, Krasno-Oktyabrskaya St., Dubovi Park

Kirghiz Drama Theatre, Pervomaiskaya St. 61

Circus, Kirova St.

Dubovi (Oak) Park, Krasno-Oktyabrskaya St. This part was planted in 1898 and was much used for promenading by the nobility. The cathedral building in the park is used now by the Fine Art Museum as an exhibition hall.

Karagachevaya Grove, in the northern suburbs. This is another popular park with an amusement ground. The oaks, maples, and poplars were planted in 1881.

Julius Fucik Garden, Trudovaya St.

Botanical Garden

Hippodrome Racecourse

Ala-Too (Intourist) Hotel and Restaurant, Dzerzhinsky Boulevard 1, TEL. 6–14–50.

Tien-Shan Hotel & Restaurant, Dzerzhinsky Prospect, opposite the railway station, TEL. 3–38–24.

Kirghizstan Hotel & Restaurant, at the crossing of Panfilova St. and XXIII Partsyezda St.

Kirghizia Restaurant, Kirova St.

Susamyr Restaurant, Kirghizia St.

Bank, XXIII Partsyezda St.

G.P.O., Dzerzhinsky Boulevard

Central Telegraph Office, Dzerzhinsky Boulevard.

Department Store, Dzerzhinsky Boulevard.

Art Salon, Dzerzhinsky Boulevard, opposite the *Ala-Too Cinema*

Markets, Shapkova St. and at the crossing of Sovietskaya and Frunze Streets

Taxi ranks, railway station, bus station, and Ivanytsina St.

Lake Issyk-Kul lies about 150 km. from Frunze. It is a salt lake fed by about 50 small rivers. Some travellers have compared it to Lake Geneva for the dark sapphire colour of its water, although it is many times larger and the surrounding mountains even grander than the Alps. The water is heated by volcanic action, and the lake never freezes over.

GAGRA
See Caucasian Coastal Road, p. 76

GATCHINA
See Leningrad, p. 181

GEORGIA
See Tbilisi, p. 303

THE GEORGIAN MILITARY HIGHWAY
The Highway runs south from Ordzhonikidze through the Caucasus Mountains to Tbilisi, capital of Georgia. This part of the country is well worth seeing, but it is certainly not easy driving and it would be best to check any suspected faults in one's car before leaving Ordzhonikidze.

The route became very important from the time the Russians first appeared in the North Caucasus. In 1766 the Russian army under Count Totleben was sent this way through the mountains to help the Georgians in their battle against the Turks. After the unification of Georgia and Russia in 1801 it was important to have a reliable route to Georgia as the easiest connection between the two countries. The road was accordingly built, with the help of 'iron and powder'. It involved the use of much labour and a great deal of money, but by 1817 it was already open to the public. It is 207 km. long and derives its name from its strategical importance. The towers and fortress guarding the highway, the ruins of which can still be seen, were built at the same time.

The mountain section of the road crosses five mountain ridges. The first is Forest Ridge; at the beginning of the road, Mount Lisaya (bald) (1037 m.) rises in the west, and to the left is Mount Tarskaya (1224 m.). 9 km. farther on, the highway crosses the second ridge, Pasture Ridge, and to the right is Mount Fethur (1736 m.) while on the left stands Mount Izvestkovaya (lime) (1270 m.). The first village on the highway is Balta.

After 1·5 km. following the wide valley of the R. Terek, a route known to Pliny and Strabo in ancient times, the road reaches the Balta Gorge which crosses Rocky Ridge.

The pipeline running beside the road is the Stavropol-Ordzhonikidze-Tbilisi gas pipeline which was completed in 1963.

Ordzhonikidze

(Formerly Vladikavkaz and Dzaudzhikau)
Population—236,000 (1970)
The town was founded on either side of R. Terek on the site of the 18th-century Ossetian village, Dzauga. It is guarded by the rocky cliffs of Table Mountain (3008 m.) whose silhouette from the side resembles the sleeping princess in this local legend:

Long ago the Cyclops lived in caves in the thick forests. Each year one came down to the kingdom that lay to the north of where Table Mountain now stands, and demanded that the most beautiful seventeen-year-old girl be given him to eat. The people found out that the spell would be broken if the loveliest girl would sacrifice herself voluntarily. At last came the turn of the princess to be devoured. Her father locked her away but she learned of the trouble and escaped. She rushed forward to sacrifice herself to the Cyclops and there was a howl, a flash, and a cloud of smoke. When the air cleared the people saw the princess had turned into a mountain—but the monster had gone.

The princess's suitor, a brave shepherd called Kazbek, heard the sound and looked down from the hills upon the scene. He could not sacrifice himself as his beloved had done but turned immediately into the mountain now called Kazbek.

(There are some more legends of Mount Kazbek in the section describing the village of Kazbegi which lies further along the road, up in the mountains.)

A fortress was built here in 1784 to subdue the mountain peoples but in fact it was never used. In the second part of the 18th century the place became especially important for Russian trade with the Caucasus and Iran, and later because of its position on the Georgian Military Highway leading south through the mountains to Tbilisi. In 1860 it was proclaimed as the town of Vladikavkaz (Mistress of the Caucasus) but was renamed in 1931 in honour of Ordzhonikidze. Grigory 'Sergo' Ordzhonikidze (1886–1937) was a prominent communist, a Georgian who concerned himself with the political life of the whole of the Soviet Union. When he was posthumously held in disgrace from 1944–54, the town was known as Dzaudzhikau, but was changed back to Ordzhonikidze when the revolutionary was rehabilitated.

During World War II the German army was as close as 6 km. to the town.

Ordzhonikidze is the capital of the North Ossetian Autonomous Republic. The Ossetian people themselves are a mixture of Caucasian and Persian; their predecessors were called the Alani and lived here at the beginning of the 1st century A.D. Today the population is mainly Russian and Ossetian, although there are also Armenians, Georgians, Persians, and other minority groups.

The town's main thoroughfare is *Mir (formerly Alexandrovsky) Prospect*. It runs for 1 km., lined with many of the original old houses and with an avenue of fine lime trees. There are shops, hotels, and restaurants here and it is a favourite strolling place.

Local industry includes metallurgy based on zinc and silver, a rolling stock repair station, factories producing tractor and car equipment, textiles, sewing machines, food products, and the local mineral water known as 'Karmadon'. Before the revolution considerable Belgian capital was invested here and it was a Belgian company that installed the first trams. Among the town's educational establishments are mining, medical, teacher's training, and agricultural colleges. Not far distant are hunting reserves where bears can be found. It is planned to extend the local hunting facilities and to organise fishing on Lake Bekan and pony-trekking expeditions.

St. George's Church, Armyansky Pereulok 1. This Armenian church was built in the 1840s.

Local Museum, Muzeinyi Pereulok 5. Open 10–6.30; closed Tues. The building was constructed in 1902–6 but the museum itself was founded in 1897. This section contains the History Department.

Natural History Museum, Katsoyev St. 64. Open 10–6.30; closed Tues. The Natural History section of the local museum is housed here in one of the most impressive buildings in Ordzhonikidze. It is the Mukhtarov Dzhuma Mosque, a Sunnite mosque built in 1906–8 with money donated by a Baku oil magnate called Mukhtarov. (The 'Dzhuma' part of the mosque's name comes from the Arabic word for Friday.) It was designed as a small-scale copy of a famous mosque in Cairo, as were the mosques built in St. Petersburg and Kazan. It was closed by the state in the 1930s but over 300 inscriptions from the Koran still adorn the walls. The majority of believers in Ordzhonikidze now are either Christian or Mohammedan.

Kirov and Ordzhonikidze Museum, Kirov St. 48. Open 9–5; closed Wed. These were both well-known Bolshevik revolutionaries.

Kosta Hetagurov Museum, Voikov St. 20. Open 10–6; closed Thurs. Hetagurov (1859–1906) was called the Leonardo da Vinci of the Ossetian people. He was poet, artist, writer, and playwright and is venerated as the founder of the Ossetian literary language. This museum which bears his name illustrates the development of this literature. The museum is housed in a 19th-century Ossetian church and in the churchyard outside is Hetagurov Grave where there stands a black marble bust of the poet by Sanokoyev. Nearby is the *grave of Arsen Kotsoyev* (1872–1944), another Ossetian writer, who also worked as a translator.

Art Gallery, Mir Prospect 12. There are some works by the Russian realists, Repin and Levitan. Open 10–6; closed Wed.

Lenin Monument, Lenin Sq. This statue by Azgur stands 12 m. high and was unveiled in 1957.

Pushkin's Bust, in Pushkin Garden, Tsereteli St. The Russian poet stayed here in a hotel, now demolished, on his way down to the Caucasus in 1829.

Pliyev Bust, in a garden on Mira Prospect. General Issa Pliyev (1902–75) was twice acclaimed a Hero of the Soviet Union during World War II.

Kosta Hetagurov Statue, Karl Marx Sq. The 13-m. statue by Tavasiyev was unveiled in 1955.

Ordzhonikidze Monument, Svobody Sq. By Ditrikh, 13 m. high and unveiled in 1949.

Grey Marble Obelisk, Kitaiskaya Sq., at the entrance to the town. This is in memory of the Chinese soldiers who died here during the civil war in 1918. Bitemirov was the architect, and the obelisk was unveiled in 1960.

Granite Obelisk, Tbilisskoye Chaussee. In memory of 17,000 Red Army soldiers who fell during the civil war in 1919. The obelisk by Dziova and Poluyektov stands 24 m. high and was unveiled in 1957.

Ossetian Music and Drama Theatre, Naberezhnaya 18. The theatre was founded in 1935 but the building was only completed in 1958.

Russian Drama Theatre, Lenin Sq. 1. The theatre was founded in 1869, and the building in 1872.

Puppet Theatre, Lenin Sq. 3

Open Air Theatre, Kirov Park

Green Theatre (open air), Tbilisskoye Chaussee. Seats 10,000 people.

Planetarium, Kirov St. 14, in an old mosque

Kosta Hetagurov Park, Mir Prospect. This park is pleasantly situated beside the Terek. There are artificial lakes with islands linked by miniature bridges, and there is a puppet theatre here.

Children's Park, Kirov St.

Dynamo Stadium, Tramvainaya St.

Spartak Stadium, Shmulevich St.

Daryal (Intourist) Hotel and Restaurant, Mir Prospect 19, TEL. 3–25–52

Terek Hotel, Mir Prospect 56

Iriston Hotel, Mir Prospect 24, TEL. 32–74

Kavkaz Hotel and Restaurant, Vatutin St. 47, TEL. 49–26

Terek Restaurant, Mir Prospect 32

Otdykh (rest) Restaurant, Hetagurov Park

G.P.O., Gorky St. 14

Bank, Kuibyshev St. 4

Department Store, Mir Prospect 31

Souvenirs, Mir Prospect 33

Filling Station, Pozharsky St., on the left side of the road when entering the town from Rostov.

Service Station, at the same address; both provide round-the-clock service.

Camping Site and Motel. 7 km. from Ordzhonikidze towards the Georgian Military Highway are the camping site and the motel. They stand beside an artificial lake with a boating station and a bathing beach. A by-pass runs around the west of the town to this point. Here are the Redant Restaurant, an eating house, garage, filling station, and service station with carwash; TEL. 11–64 and 21–00; there is round-the-clock service.

Gorny Orel (mountain eagle) Restaurant, on the slopes of Mount Lysaya, 11 km. from town. There is an excellent view of Ordzhonikidze and of the mountains. There is also a dendrarium here, a swimming pool, and a boat-hiring station.

Stalactite Cave, 15 km. from town, in one of the northern spurs of Mount Stolovaya. The cave is 6 m. high.

Dargavs

Situated in the Dargava Ravine, 38 km. from Ordzhonikidze, and about 3 km. walk from the road, in the foothills of Mount Shau-Khokh (4646 m.). The name means 'town of the dead'. The Ossetians buried their dead in stone tombs because of the shortage of good arable land. It was an old Ossetian saying that every piece of good land big enough for a cow to stand on is worth a cow. So the villages were built only on poor ground, and nearby grew up a second settlement, for the dead. Each house of the living in the village had its corresponding mausoleum in the 'town of the dead', and each mausoleum had its own character, just as the ordinary houses had. Beside the bodies were placed the things their owners might need—knives and tobacco for the men and needles, beads, and mirrors for the women.

Nizhny Koban
Another interesting village on the way to Dargavs. It is best known for its burial places typical of the Koban Culture of the two thousand years B.C. Excavations began here in 1876 and the graves were found to have been made in eight distinct layers, over a territory of two hectares (5 acres). This particular Bronze Age culture is distinguished by special axes, long, narrow, and curved, as well as by a variety of ornaments including wide plaited belts. These people had been hunters and primitive herdsmen. Items from this site are on exhibit in museums abroad as well as in the Soviet Union and there is naturally a good selection on display in the Ordzhonikidze Museum.

Tatartup
On the left bank of the R. Terek, near the village of Elhotovo. In this ancient town there is a *14th-century minaret* 35 m. high. The place is now deserted, and special permission from Intourist is required to go there.

Nuzal
In Alaghir Ravine. Here there is a *12th-century church* with frescoes of St. George and St. Eustace.

Redant
7 km from Ordzhonikidze. This small village marks the beginning of the Georgian Military Highway and the name, Redant, properly belongs to the local tower, which is the first guard tower of the many along the route.

Chmi
This is the third village on the Georgian Military Highway after leaving Ordzhonikidze. 'Chmi' is the Ossetian word for dogwood.

To the west stands Mount Arau-Hokh (2600 m.) and to the east Stolovaya Gora (Table Mountain) (3008 m.). When there is snow on the mountains the flat granite plateau of Stolovaya Gora looks as though it is covered with a white tablecloth.

The stalactite caves near the village are a tourist attraction.

Larsy
This village is 1100 m. above sea level; the remains of an old Russian fortress called Lars lie here, dating from the time of the 19th-century Caucasian wars and built to defend the road.

The *Yermolovsky Kamen (Yermolov Stone)* blocks the R. Terek just to the south of Larsy. It takes its name from General Alexei Yermolov (1772–1861), who was appointed ruler of Georgia by Alexander I, and who is believed to have used the stone for a resting place. It weighs 1500 tons and measures 29 m. long by 15 m. wide by 13 m. high. It was brought down the mountains by an avalanche in 1832 which blocked the traffic for 2 years and the amount of ice and snow was so great that it had to be blasted away, and in fact only finished melting in 1839.

Beaten by jagged rocks to steam,
Before me pours the boiling stream;
Above my head the eagles scream,
The pinewood speaks,
And through the mist there faintly gleam
The mountain peaks.
(From *The Avalanche* by Lermontov, trans. by W. Morison.)

After Larsy and Chertov Most (this marked the border between Ossetia and Georgia; 'cherta' meaning 'border') the highway passes through *Darialskoye Usheliye (Darial Ravine)*, or 'the Gate of the Alani'. In old Persian the name means 'gate', and according to Pliny the Caucasian Gates

---

(Porta Caucasia or Portae Caspiae) were here. They were of wood plaited with iron and closed the mouth of the 8-km. gorge, the rocky sides of which tower perpendicularly to a height of 1798 m.

> The cliffs in serried masses seem,
> Replete with some mysterious dream,
> To bend their heads above the stream
> And watch the waters as they gleam.
> (From *The Demon* by Lermontov, trans. by
> A. C. Coolidge.)

One cannot help but be impressed by this stretch of road. Some have said that this is not a road at all but a thrilling fairy tale; the narrow and curiously shaped rift is like a gigantic grave, and the traveller feels a poor helpless creature at the bottom. Everything in the ravine is dim, and the southern sky looks like a narrow blue ribbon high up above.

The Darial Gorge has also been compared to the banks of the Rhine where similar romantic castles perch on the rocks. In the middle of the ravine on a small rock are the ruins of a particular old castle called Tamara's Castle which has, however, nothing to do with the famous Georgian Queen. It was mentioned in Lermontov's poems:

> Perched on the rock, the castle tower,
> That stands on Caucasus to wait,
> A giant guardian at the gate,
> Seems sternly through the mist to glower.
> (From *The Demon*, trans. by A. C. Coolidge.)

Some historians believe that it was built in 150 B.C. by King Mirian and restored by King David in the 12th century. The legend of the castle is as follows:

The castle was inhabited by the beautiful but wicked Queen Tamara, who enticed handsome young travellers into her castle with promises of love and happiness, but after a single night of pleasure the unfortunates were beheaded and their bodies thrown into the Terek.

It is this legend that Lermontov related in verse.

It is interesting to note that the home of the Amazons of whom the ancient Greek and Roman writers told was supposed to be here beside this very R. Terek.

Gveleti

Just before the village of Gveleti is *Gveleti Bridge* over the R. Terek. This marks the narrowest part of the gorge known as Chortovy Vorota (Devil's Gate) and also the beginning of the republic of Georgia. From here southwards the road passes successively through three ethnographical regions, Hevi, Mtiuleti, and Kartli.

At this point the highway could be built only by cutting into the rock face. Some of the overhanging rocks have a threatening aspect, and most resemble some object from which their interesting names derive, such as the Sphinx, Sentry, and Bat. Another rock is known as 'Carry us through, O Lord'.

Nearby, in the valley of the R. Kabakhi, are the remains of a 12th–13th-century *church* with fragments of frescoes, and also the ruins of a fortress.

Kazbegi (known in the 19th century as Stepan-Tsminda)

> Kasbek above with diamond light
> Of everlasting snow shines blinding;
> And deep below, a streak of night,
> Like some dark cleft, the snake's delight,
> In endless curves the Darial's winding.
> And Terek, like a lion springing
> With bristling mane, in fury roars;
> The beast of prey, the bird high winging
> Its flight in azure, where it soars,
> Have heard the cry his waves give forth.
> (From *The Demon* by Lermontov, trans. by
> A. C. Coolidge.)

Kasbegi is the centre of Mokhavia, a mountain region of Georgia, and the birthplace of the 19th-century Georgian writer, Alexander Kazbegi (1848–98). From the town there is a good panoramic view of Mount Kazbek (5047 m.), and, to the left of the road, Mount Kuru (3790 m.).

On the mountain slope is the *village of Gergeti* and the *Tsminda Samebo (Holy Trinity) Church.* This was built in the 12th century in the time of Queen Tamara on the spot where it was believed the Apostle Andrew erected a cross. It was built to complement the surrounding mountains and snowy Kazbek itself.

Church. In the main square of Kazbegi is a church built in 1801 in Roman style. It belongs to a private family.

Kazbegi Restaurant, on the main road.

Local Museum, on the main square. Open 9–5. The museum occupies the house where the writer Alexander Kazbegi lived. It contains a section about him as well as some arms and national costumes. There is a statue of Kazbegi in the Square which was unveiled in 1960 and nearby is his grave, with a tombstone carved out of solid marble in the shape of the two-peaked Mount Kazbek. Alexander Kazbegi was of a princely line, and the mountain was called after his family.

In the Ossetian language Mount Kazbek is called the Mountain of Christ. According to legend the top of the mountain is inaccessible, and God dwells on the summit. Anyone approaching it will be stopped by unseen forces or by a terrible storm. Abram's tent is said to be there, and a cradle supported by unseen hands with a sleeping child in it. There is also a tree surrounded with scattered treasure which no-one has ever seen. The only people able to see these marvels were an old priest

PLATE OPPOSITE
Rock churches and shrines in Gueghard, Armenia.

and his son, both being pure in body and spirit. The old man died on the return journey, but the son brought back a bit of unknown wood from the tree and a piece of material from the tent, and the soles of his boots were stuck with silver coins.

In spite of the legends, members of the London Alpine Club (Freshfield, Tucker, and Moore) managed to climb to the top of the mountain from the south-east slope in June 1868. From 1900 onwards the Russian mountaineer Mrs. Preobrazhenskaya made the ascent nine times, obviously finding it a pleasant walk. In 1913 at a height of 3962 m. ruins of a church with a cross on the top were found.

Here is another picturesque description of the mountain:

'He turned to stone and like a wise old man sat silent for centuries, his snow-white curls falling in a single mass, fringed with the delicate hairs of the mountain streams. The crown upon his royal head twinkles and sparkles with diamonds under the bright rays of the sun, or turns to pale opal under a transparent silver veil and then begins to shine again. At sunset his crown is covered with blood, burning with the last sad lights before dying and being extinguished by the darkness. Kazbek is great as only the ruler and master of the world can be.'

Sioni

In this village there are mineral springs of the Narzan type, and amidst the picturesque woody scenery stands an 8th–9th-century domeless *church*.

From Sioni the road climbs steeply along the side of Mount Kabardzhin (3141 m.) towards Kobi.

Kobi

Kobi lies at 1932 m. above sea level at the junction of four ravines. Nearby is a building with a mineral water bath.

After this village the road climbs again. In 3 km. one can cross a stone bridge over the R. Baidarka and climb a mountain where there is a mineral lake so rich in gas that it looks as though it is boiling. The lake overflows, and the rocks have turned yellow from the high iron content of the water. Above the lake are alpine meadows full of forget-me-nots, harebells, mountain violets, and cornflowers.

From this point the road climbs on its final ascent to *Krestovi Pereval* (Cross Pass) (2388 m.) the highest point on the road, marked by an obelisk. The pass used to be so dangerous that sometimes people preferred to get out of their carriages and walk, and it is recorded that a certain foreign ambassador was so frightened that he asked to be blindfolded and was then led through by the hand. When the bandage was taken from his eyes he fell down on his knees to thank God for his survival. From here there is a wonderful panorama of the Caucasus. To the left is the old part of the road, where at a distance of about 1 km. one can see a cross of red stone which was, according to legend, placed there by King David the Builder (grandfather of Tamara) and repaired by General Yermolov in 1824. The tops of the mountains Nepis-Kalo (3536 m.) and Shvidi-Dzma (Seven Brothers) (3150 m.) among others can be seen.

After this point the slope down to the valleys of Georgia begins, and the road winds in zig-zags through heaps of rock known as the Stone Chaos. Then it runs above the Gudaur Abyss (500 m.) and affords a good panoramic view over the southern mountains.

Gudauri

At 2158 m. this is the highest village on the Highway.

Legend runs that long ago a daughter, Nina, was born to a poor family living in this village. She was the most beautiful baby that had ever been in the whole of Ossetia and as she grew up the villagers and anyone who happened to be travelling through the mountains loved her for her beauty. Not least among her admirers was the spirit of Mount Gud; when she walked on the slopes he smoothed her path, and when she tended her father's five sheep he made sure that no harm came to them.

Nina grew up into an incomparably lovely girl and the ancient Gud, who in all his many years had never seen anyone like her, became more and more devoted to her. He wondered whether a powerful spirit could take on the form of a poor Ossetian peasant, but Nina herself was already attached to Sasiko, the good-looking son of a neighbouring family.

In his jealousy, Gud tried to harm the young man by sending him hunting in the most difficult places and giving him bad weather. This was of no avail, but then, when Nina and Sasiko were alone together in a hut, he buried them beneath an avalanche of snow. As the days passed their love was overshadowed by hunger. Sasiko paced the hut and then turned suddenly and rushed at Nina, biting her on the shoulder like a starving beast. Her terrified screams were heard by the neighbours who quickly dug through the snow to release the young couple. Their lives were saved, but their love had died entirely and old Gud could not restrain his laughter and shook down a great mass of stones in his delight.

From Gudauri begins the *Zemo-Mletsky Spusk* which zig-zags 640 m. down the mountains in six great bends. After passing Kumlis-Tsikhe the road again runs along the edges of precipices to the bridge over the R. White Aragvi. 'Probably there is no other place on the Highway which can compare with this in its beauty and sharp changes of atmosphere.' The spusk is built on the sheer rocks of the left bank of the Aragvi, and is a rare example of skilful engineering. In some places one side of the road is supported over the slope by a high artificial wall, and there are 18 sharp corners. The road was built between 1857 and 1861 following the project of Colonel Statkovsky, and under his personal supervision.

On arriving in Mleti the tourist feels as though he has come from north to south, from the severe, cold mountain world into the joyful southern country.

Before him now another scene
Had living beauties to display,
Where Georgian valleys robed in green
Stretched outward like a carpet lay.
(From *The Demon* by Lermontov,
trans. by A. C. Coolidge.)

Mleti

This village stands at a height of 1412 m. After the previous quick descent one feels that it is impossible to go any lower, but still from here the road continues by easy slopes down to the R. Kura.

Kvesheti

On the rocks at the side of the road near the village is an *old signal and guard tower*.

This part of the Highway may be blocked by masses of sand and stones brought down from the mountains by the small streams which swell and rush across the road. It is wise to examine the flooded places as the road itself may have been washed away and one's car might be swept over into the river below.

Passanauri

In old Persian 'Passanauri' means 'Holy height'. The place is 1014 m. above sea level, in a narrow valley at the confluence of the Black and the White Aragvi Rivers. There is an interesting natural phenomenon here, in that the waters of the two rivers do not mix for some distance, until the village of Bibliani. The dark water of the Black Aragvi keeps to the left side of the stream and the light-coloured White Aragvi stays on the right.

The 19th-century Church is closed

Passanauri Hotel and Restaurant, beside the main road from the north

Restaurant, beside the main road from the south

Filling Station

Up in the valley of the Black Aragvi live three tribes of Caucasians which have puzzled ethnologists for many years. They are the Hefsurs, the Tushins, and the Pshavs, and are now considered by some to be descendants of the crusaders. Certain of the families still possess unusual national costumes which some Hefsurs wore even as late as the 1930s. These are decorated with a large white or coloured cross, and consist of chain-mail shirts, helmets with chain-mail, and broad-swords. The shields bear inscriptions in Latin letters, 'Vivat Stephan Batory' (a Polish king), 'Souvenir', 'Genoa', 'Vivat Husar' and 'Sollingen'. Some have images of eagles and crowns. Linguists, however, have discovered that the tribes belong to the Kartli peoples. The Hefsurs are good hunters and

are famed for their kindness and hospitality; the greatest dishonour is to beat a child or to insult a guest, and even if the offender is the host's own brother he risks his life.

After Passanauri a region of vineyards and orchards begins.

Ananuri

The name means 'Holy Mother'.

There is a *16th–18th-century fortress* and within its walls stands the *Assumption Church*, built in 1689. There is a fine carved cross on the outside of the west wall, and inside some 17th- and 18th-century frescoes remain. The iconostasis is of Moscow workmanship and dates from the 19th century. Nearby is the *16th-century Bteba Church* and the small buildings up the hill, to the left as one goes through the entrance gate, were bath houses. Below is a ridged-domed *Armenian Church* of the 19th century.

In 1737 this village was the scene of an exceptionally bloody battle between the members of two families, during which barricades were made of corpses. During the fray someone sought sanctuary for himself and his family in a church, but the building was surrounded with logs and burnt to the ground.

Zhinvali

In the vicinity of this village are the *remains of a 7th-century town* and a *castle* called Bebris-Tsikhe. The castle consists of two parts, the upper and the lower. In some places the thickness of the wall is as great as 2 m. No exact date is known for its foundation, but it is probably of the 9th or 10th century.

Natakhtari

On the hill nearby are the *ruins of Natskhor* (Girl's Tower), and on the other side of the river is a *monastery* of the 6th century called Dzhevris-Sandari.

Further on the road forks. The turning to the right leads to the Black Sea coast, but the Georgian Military Highway leading to Mtskheta and Tbilisi is the left fork. It is 30 km. from here to Tbilisi.

Mtskheta

Mtskheta stands at the confluence of the Aragvi and Kura rivers. On the right bank of the R. Kura, on the slopes of Mount Kartli, the mythological father of the Georgian people, Kartlos, was buried, according to legend. He was said to be a direct descendant of Japhet, and it was his son Mikhetos who founded this town and gave it his name. It became the cradle of Georgian culture, and up till the 5th century it was the capital, where the ancient religious and political life was concentrated. It was also the residence of the Patriarchs.

On Mount Kartli, which is a holy mountain, stood the shrine of an idol called Armaz, the Georgian version of the Persian god Ormuzd, the god of compassion and life. On the mountain-side east of Mtskheta above the left bank of the R.

Aragvi was the shrine of Zaden, another idol, these two being the chief gods worshipped by pagan Georgia. On the other hills around Mtskheta were shrines to less important gods with names and characters derived from the gods of the various peoples upon whom Georgia had depended at different times. At the entrance to the town, for example, stood a statue of Aphrodite. Armaz and Zaden, however, were the most highly esteemed, being the gods who spread the sun's rays and in general protected the country from all harm. They were the gods of fertility, too, and were sometimes offered human sacrifices.

The *Armaz Monastery* was so called because it was founded on the site of the pagan temple. Now only a bell-tower remains among the ruins.

The centre of the town was at the point where the two rivers converge; a fortress and the tsar's palace were built there and the rest of the town spread farther up the river valleys. From the 3rd century B.C. the citizens of Mtskheta had been highly cultured, and during the town's early history they had military and trade connections with Greece, Rome, Persia, and Parthia.

Sveti Tskhoveli Cathedral. This cathedral was dedicated to the Twelve Apostles but was also known as the Church of the Pillar of Life. According to legend a local Jew called Elioz was summoned to Jerusalem to participate in the trial of Christ. He was present at the Crucifixion and after the drawing of lots for Christ's garments he won the robe and brought it back to Mtskheta. There he was met by his sister Sidonia, herself a secret Christian. When she learned of the Crucifixion of Christ she fell down dead, clutching the robe. None could wrench it from her grasp, it was as though it had grown onto her flesh, and all the city was witness to the strange occurrence. That night during an earthquake a crevasse opened and Sidonia was buried together with the robe. Later a cedar tree grew up on the spot.

About 250 years after this there lived in Jerusalem a certain Nina, the daughter of a Roman general. She had been born in Capadocia, but when she was twelve her parents took her to Jerusalem. There she was taught by an old woman called Nianfora who told her that the robe had been taken to pagan Iberia (the old name for Georgia). Inspired by this story Nina prayed constantly to the Virgin asking to be able to go to the place where the robe had been taken, and finally she was told by the Virgin in a dream that she should go to Iberia and that Christ himself would help her.

Simply clad, and carrying a cross of vine-rods tied with her own hair, Nina set off on the long difficult journey to Mtskheta, arriving in A.D. 314. At the moment of her arrival King Mirian was about to go up to Kartli to offer a human sacrifice to Armaz, but Nina prayed to God and in a violent storm the idol was overturned. She erected a cross on the slope of the mountain and then went down to begin her missionary work in the city. Even King Mirian himself came to the door of her hut to hear the story of Christ, and after ten years her sermons and her own holy life persuaded the King, his wife and children, and with them the whole population of the town, to be baptised.

The pagan temples and the idols were destroyed. According to the Georgian chronicles King Mirian said of his former religion, 'I am the thirty-sixth King, and the first Christian king of Georgia. My fathers sacrificed children to idols. The mountains of Armaz and Zaden deserve to be destroyed by fire.'

Among her other miracles Nina cured the queen of sickness, and when Mirian was blinded by lightning she restored his sight. After her death Nina was canonised and is today, like Queen Tamara, remembered as one of the great people of Georgia.

In the year 328 King Mirian had the great cedar tree chopped down, and beneath it, still held in Sidonia's hands, the robe of Christ was found. Mirian built a wooden cathedral over the spot. This was rebuilt in stone in the 5th century, but was robbed and damaged several times and finally destroyed during Timur's invasion, by his own order. The site of the legendary cedar tree is still marked by a *stone column* reputed to ooze holy oil. The column, which stands in the southern part of the cathedral, was decorated by Grigori Guldzhavarisshvile in the 17th century with themes from the history of early Christianity in Georgia, and was originally embellished with gold and silver.

Christ's robe was kept in Mtskheta until the 17th century when Shah Abbas captured the town and sent the robe as a gift to the Russian Tsar Mikhail Fedorovich, who in turn placed it with great ceremony in the Uspensky Sobor in the Moscow Kremlin.

The present building of the *Sveti Tskhoveli Cathedral* is a perfect example of Georgian 15th-century architecture surrounded by a great crenellated fortress wall with batteries and towers built in the 18th century. The cathedral itself was erected in 1440 during the reign of Alexander I of Georgia, and under the supervision of Patriarch Melchisadek. The upper dome of the cathedral was restored in the 17th century, and in the 19th century some small outbuildings were pulled down and most of the frescoes whitewashed. The interior decorations still to be seen date from the 16th and 17th centuries. The iconostasis is 19th-century work. On the southern wall is a 17th-century fresco illustrating the words of Psalm 150, 'Let everything that hath breath praise the Lord.'

The façade of the cathedral is carved. Over the arch of the northern façade there is a hand holding a set square, and the architect's name, Arsukidze, is inscribed there.

The coronation of the Georgian kings took place in this building and near the altar are the tombs of the last Georgian kings, Erekle II and Giorgi XII. In the south-east corner of the central aisle is the patriarchs' stone throne decorated with 17th- and 18th-century frescoes. Also inside the cathedral is a small chapel, a copy of the Chapel of Christ's Sepulchre in Jerusalem. The stone font is that in which the King Mirian is said to have been baptised. The tombs include those of members of the royal and noble houses of Georgia. Services are held in the Cathedral between 10 am and 12 on Sat. and Sun. and on all Church festivals.

Samtavra Convent. The main church is dedicated to St. Nina, 'the Enlightener of Georgia', who was buried there, and it is similar in form to the Cathedral of the Twelve Apostles. It was built at the beginning of the 11th century in medieval Georgian baroque style, on the site of a 4th-century church erected by King Mirian. Its name comes from 'mtavara' meaning 'ruler'. Beside the cathedral to the north-west there is a three-storey *16th-century belltower*, and a small and ancient *chapel* on the place where St. Nina's hut once stood.

The graves of King Mirian and of his wife, Queen Nana, are still in the cathedral but the sepulchres date from the 19th century and are of little historical interest. The site is surrounded by walls. The cathedral was restored at the same time as the rest of the convent in 1903. There are now fifteen nuns in the convent.

Dzhvari Church. Up on the hill on the other side of the R. Aragvi are the ruins of a church built in 585–604, its name meaning 'cross'. It is designed to catch one's attention, and from many points can be seen to dominate the town. When Christianity was adopted in the 4th century a cross was erected here as a symbol of the religious victory. The present church was built to enclose the older one completely.

During its 1400 years of existence Dzhvari Church was damaged only once: in the 10th century, when it was set on fire by invading Arabs. The eastern and southern façades are lavishly decorated with reliefs, including images of patrons and people who gave money for, and organised, the building. There is a legend that this church and the Sveti Tskhoveli Cathedral were linked by an iron chain, and that the monks used to leave their cells on the hilltop and climb down for services in the cathedral, but when faith grew weaker among the people the chain broke and was lost.

This church, which is very old, has served as the prototype of many other Georgian churches.

The Bedris Tzikhe Tower. This is another remnant of Mtskheta's past. Its name means 'old man's fortress'.

An ancient *cemetery* was found in 1871 beside the highway near Samtavra Convent. It had been used from the Iron Age until the 11th century, and during the excavations some coins of the time of Caesar Augustus were found. The upper row of graves are in the form of stone boxes.

Today Mtskheta is famous for the *garden* of one of the inhabitants named Mamulanshvili, who has a very rich collection of plants and flowers.

Mtskheta Restaurant, near Samtavra Convent, open from 9 am until midnight.

By the road leading out of Mtskheta, where the R. Kura joins the R. Aragvi, is the *Zemo-Avchalskaya dam and hydro-power station*, opened in 1927 and designed to generate 26,500 kilowatts. A large *monument* to Lenin stands here.

After passing through the Saburtalo suburb of Tbilisi the road comes to the capital of Georgia and so to the end of the Georgian Military Highway.

GORI

Population—50,000 (1970)

The town stands on the left bank of the R. Kura, at the point where it is joined by the R. Leakhvi and the R. Lidzhudi. There is a fruit cannery and textile manufacture here. The local white wine, Atenuri, can only be drunk in Gori as it travels badly. There is also a pedagogical institute in the town.

The *ruins of the castle of Goris-Tsikhe* stand above Gori on a hill. The name Gori itself means 'mountain' in Georgian. The castle, which dates from the 12th century, contains a church. In 1123 it was inhabited by refugee Armenians. In the 16th century the Turks captured it, and then it continually changed hands between the Turks, the Georgians, and the Persians until it was taken by Russia in 1801. It was restored in 1900, but suffered considerably in the earthquake of 1920.

Near the fortress is the *Armenian Church of St. Stephan*, founded in the 12th century and restored in the 17th century.

Synagogue, Cheluskintsev St.

Local Museum, Stalin St.

Stalin's House, open 9–6; closed Tues. Stalin was born in Gori on 21 December 1879, and lived here until 1894. His father, Vissarion Dzhugashvili, was a local cobbler. The museum was opened in 1939, and is in the form of a special pavilion which was built to protect the hut where Stalin was born. All the surrounding buildings were demolished.

Historical-Ethnographical Museum

Stalin Monument, Stalin Sq. This is now the only big monument to Stalin in the whole of the Soviet Union.

Bust of Chavchavadze, Chavchavadze St. Chavchavadze was a Georgian writer.

Drama Theatre, Chavchavadze St.

Intourist Hotel and Restaurant, Stalin Prospect 22, TEL 30–91.

Kartli Hotel and Restaurant, Lenin St.

Department Store, Stalin St.

Gift Shop, Stalin St.

Goris-Dzhavri (Cross of Gori) Monastery, 3 km. from the town centre, on a hill above the right bank of the R. Kura.

The 16th-century church is dedicated to St. George. The legend of its foundation is as follows:

Queen Tamara was hunting in this region when her favourite falcon flew away and settled on the top of the mountain where the monastery now stands. In dismay she asked that the man in her party who loved her best should swim across the R. Kura and recapture the bird for her. The river was in full spring flood and the young men hesitated to show their loyalty, but at last one plunged in. He reached the opposite bank, caught the falcon and began to swim back again, but halfway across he got into difficulties and it seemed that he would drown. Tamara prayed to St. George for help, promising to found a monastery if her prayer were answered. Apparently it was, for she late · founded the 'monastery on the mountain top where her falcon had alighted.

At the end of the last century it was a tradition of the cathedral that those women who wanted either a husband or a child should put an iron chain weighing more than 50 kg. (more than a hundredweight) around their necks, and if they were then able to walk around the building three times their wish would be granted.

Uplis-Tsikhe Cave Town, 7 km. from Gori along a very bad road. Also known as the Troglodite Town, this was inhabited before the time of Christ. Some scientists say it belongs to the period of Persian and Parthian influence in Georgia. The name means 'the castle of Uplis'; Uplis was the son of the founder of Mtskheta, and was said to be a direct descendant of Japhet. The caves of this town rise up in tiers, and streets, a market place, swimming pools, and houses of different sizes can be recognised. Some of the caves closely resemble churches. Also underground is the so-called Palace of Tamara; there is no evidence that Tamara ever lived there, but the Georgians are fond of calling anything unusually splendid after her.

Atenski Sioni (Athenian Sion) Cathedral, 11 km. from Gori along a very bad road. The cathedral was built by Bagrat IV in the 11th century and is considered to be one of the best examples of the architecture of its time. The village of Ateni stands on the site of a town founded in the 2nd century B.C. On the rocks on the other side of the ravine can be seen the *ruins of the Sativis-Tsikhe Monastery*, standing 274 m. above the R. Tana. The walls of the cathedral in this monastery are covered with carving, and have marble columns and good frescoes.

HERSONES

See Sevastopol, p. 282

IRKUTSK

Population—420,000 (1970)
This city is situated among beautiful scenery on the R. Angara and its tributary, the Ushakovka. It is 65 km. west of Lake Baikal where the Angara begins. It has plenty of sunshine, its extreme climate being tempered by the proximity to the lake. There are warm springs nearby. This couplet in its praise dates from 1846:

Our Irkutsk, a splendid city, is indeed a gift of God
Although freezing cold in winter and in summer monstrous hot.

Chekhov, who was here in 1890, wrote, 'Of all the towns of Siberia, the best is Irkutsk', and one of the names by which it is known in contemporary literature is the pearl of Siberia.

The Irkutsk area, of which the city is the centre, is equal in size to the territory of pre-war Germany, plus Austria, Switzerland, and Italy. Its gold mining industry is the largest in the Soviet Union.

The *Trans-Siberian railway* runs through Irkutsk, linking it with Moscow, 5031 km. to the west, and with Vladivostok, 4141 km. to the east. It was founded in 1652 as a Cossack encampment by a nobleman, Ivan Pokhabov. The first settlement was on Dyachy Island, opposite the mouth of the Irkut. Nine years passed before the local Buryat tribesmen had been subdued and only then was a fort built on the mainland.

Irkutsk became a town in 1686 and after a further ten years was granted the coat-of-arms of a panther on a silver field, running on green grass holding a sable in its jaws. The first school in Eastern Siberia was opened in 1725 by the order of Peter the Great. It was in *Voznesensky Monastery*, 6 km. from the town. The main purpose of the school was to train Mongolian-speaking interpreters and to prepare missionaries to convert the Mongols and Buryats to Christianity. In 1736 Irkutsk became a provincial capital and it was made capital of Eastern Siberia in 1822. In this area, remote from the rest of Russia, the local authorities often acquired immense power. The reputations of the Governors of Irkutsk were not always of the best. Peter the Great in 1721 ordered that Governor Gagarin be hanged for 'unheard-of theft'. He was accused of punishing and then pardoning just for monetary gain. His carriage wheels were of silver and his horses were shod with silver and gold.

From 1698 Irkutsk was important for its place on the Russian trade route to China and Mongolia when furs, hides, silk, and tea passed this way. Later, as Russian territory expanded eastward, it stood at the gateway to the trans-Baikal region. In the 1750s a new school opened, teaching geodesy, navigation, and Japanese. Those who failed their examinations were sent to the army. It was notable for having 80- and 90-year-olds among its students. In 1792, with the first attempts to establish regular trade relations with Japan, a special Japanese school was opened. Two Japanese sailors rescued from a shipwreck near the Aleutian Islands were appointed as teachers. They had first been converted to Orthodoxy and given Russian names. When Russia received the left bank of the R. Amur and the territory as far as the Pacific Ocean after the Peking Treaty of 1860, the Amur Gates were erected with the inscription, 'The Road to the Great Ocean'.

The town was a place of exile from the 17th century onwards. Some participants in the 1825 (Decembrists') revolt were sent here and played an important role in the development of the town. After the Polish uprising of 1863, 18,600 Poles were sent to Siberia from their own country. Part of their number settled down in Irkutsk. Among them were doctors, teachers, and artists who added to the cultural development of Irkutsk.

They included the zoologists B. Dybowski and V. Godlewski, the geologists I. Cherski and A. Chekanowski, the archaeologist N. Witkowski, and artists Wronski and Zenkowski. Skilled workers and technical specialists from Warsaw and other big Polish cities also shared their knowledge with local Siberians. The Poles gave lessons in music and foreign languages and the far away, provincial town turned quite suddenly into something like a European cultural centre, with an unusually high percentage of intellectuals.

Those who had participated in the uprising of 1863 were allowed to return home only after 20 years had passed. By that time large numbers had settled down properly and had married Siberians, so they stayed on with no thought of leaving. There are still many families in Irkutsk with Polish names, but they have been completely assimilated.

By 1885 exiles comprised one third of the local population. Among the Marxists who were sent to Irkutsk in the 1890s was Leonid Krasin, a well-known communist who later became Commissar for Foreign Trade. Between 1922 and 1926 he was twice Ambassador to Britain and once to France. Later still the exiles included Stalin and Dzerzhinsky. Another well-known communist sent here was Kirov, in 1909. Frunze was banished to the village of Manzurka, in the Irkutsk area, in 1914 and Molotov followed him in 1915. Kuibyshev was sent to the village of Tutura. They all managed to escape. Electricity and water supplies were laid down at the very beginning of this century, but it is relevant that in 1912 the town's budget for public utilities was almost entirely spent on prison construction.

The Trans-Siberian railway was built as far as Irkutsk in 1898, but, for the 7 years until the round-Baikal line was completed, trains crossed the lake in a specially equipped icebreaker, the 'Baikal'. The ship had been built in England, brought here in sections and reassembled on the lake. She was 4200 tons, 88 m. long and 17 m. wide, the second largest icebreaker in the world at the time. Irkutsk began to grow rapidly after the completion of the railway. In 1897 the town had 51,473 inhabitants and by 1919, 90,800. In 1910 there were 18,187 houses in Irkutsk, all but 1190 of them built of wood.

During the civil war there was exceptionally bitter fighting here. The town changed hands and was held by the counter-revolutionaries but it was here that Admiral Kolchak met his end. Alexander Kolchak (1870–1920) called himself the Supreme Ruler of Russia but he was captured and shot. At the same time a great part of Russia's gold was recaptured from the Czech ex-prisoners-of-war at Irkutsk. There were 29 railway truckloads of gold in 1678 sacks and 5143 boxes and, in addition, a further 7 truckloads of platinum and silver. After the Civil War the reconstruction of the town was delayed until 1924.

Irkutsk's importance as a railway junction has increased until now nearly one fifth of the local workers are employed by the railways. Timber, grain, building materials, and other goods transported on the Angara pass through Irkutsk, and it has become a centre for fur-purchasing and gold trans-shipment. The first direct Moscow-Irkutsk flight took place in 1929 and now the city's air traffic is also considerable.

Besides being both the administrative centre of the region and the chief cultural centre of Eastern Siberia, Irkutsk is also the home of a special branch of the U.S.S.R. Academy of Sciences which was established to deal with the scientific problems of industrialising Eastern Siberia. It has institutes of geology and chemistry and departments of biology, power, economics, and geography. Numerous expeditions set out from here annually to the remotest parts of the area. Local geologists found the important diamond fields in Vilnya.

The seven local higher educational establishments take 20,000 students; besides having faculties of physics, mathematics, chemistry, geology, philology, geography, and law, the university on Gagarin Boulevard trains Buryat-, Mongolian- and Russian-speaking teachers for East Siberian schools. There are separate colleges for mining, economics, agriculture, medicine, teacher training, and foreign languages with polytechnical and engineering colleges planned for the near future.

Local industries produce heavy machinery for the mining and metal industries, machine tools, mica, soap, flour, and macaroni among other things. There are also plants for tea packing, agricultural machinery repairs, ship repairs, and woodworking besides a number of brick yards and timber yards. Electrical power comes from the 660,000 kilowatt power station, which was built on the Angara in 1959, and from Bratsk.

Many of the impressive old buildings still to be seen were put up between 1830 and 1890, including the *town hall*, the *theatre* (1897), the *banks* and the *museum* in Moorish style. There were plenty of well-to-do merchants in Irkutsk until as late as the 1880s, because it was they who were the principal owners of the famous Lena goldfields, and naturally part of their wealth was spent on the construction of public buildings. An example is the *Central Telegraph Office* which belonged to the goldmine owner Nemchinov; it was reconstructed in the 1930s. On the records is the great two-day fire of 1870 when much of the town, including ten churches, burned down. Local inhabitants compared the catastrophe with the last days of Pompeii. One big bell melted from the heat and turned into a large lump of copper on the ground.

Wooden houses, typical of old Siberia, can still be seen on Krasnogvardeiskaya St. as well as in many other places. They are gradually disappearing and making room for new buildings. The busiest and most central part of the town is *Karl Marx St.* (formerly Bolshaya St.) and the best shops and cafés are to be found there. The big bridge across the river was completed in 1936.

The *Znamensky Convent*, which is still used by the Church, was founded in 1762. A prelate has his headquarters here. The main *Cathedral*, dedicated to the Apparition of Our Lady, was built in 1757 and the iconostasis and frescoes were restored in 1950. Within the convent walls are the graves of some of the Decembrists and also of Ekaterina Trubetskaya, the first wife to accompany her husband in his exile from St. Petersburg. Here also is a monument marking the grave of Grigori Shelek-nov, known as the Russian Columbus and the conqueror of Russian America (Alaska) because he founded the first Russian settlements in North America and in the Aleutian Islands in 1783. He died in Irkutsk in 1795.

The Church of Our Saviour, near the Children's Park by the R. Angara. This two-storey, stone church is Irkutsk's oldest building.

Church of Our Lady of Kazan, Barrikad St. 34. This church has been closed and is now used by a school of cine-mechanics.

Catholic Church, near Kirov Sq. This church was designed at the end of the 19th century but is now closed.

Krestovozdvishenskaya (Erection of the Cross) Church, Sedova St. Built in Russian baroque style in 1758, decorated with some fine stonework, and still in use.

Preobrazhenskaya (Transfiguration) Church (1798), Timiryazeva St., near Volkonsky's house

Local Museum, Karl Marx St. Founded in 1782, the museum has departments of natural resources and of history. The building was designed by Rozen and it is open 10–6; closed Mon. and Tues.

Humpbacked House, 5th-Armii St. Preserved as an example of 18th-century architecture.

The White House used to be the Governor-General's residence and at the time of the revolution it served as the Bolshevik headquarters. Its portico and six Corinthian columns date from the 19th century and mark it as an example of Russian empire style. Today it houses the university's scientific library.

Kirov's House, Stepan Khalturin St. Sergei Kirov lived here after the failure of the 1905 revolution and here, in 1909, he carried on party work in secret.

Fine Arts Museum, Karl Marx St. The collection began with 250 pictures which belonged to Mayor Sukachev before the revolution. There are over 600 Chinese articles on display.

The Museum of the Biological and Geographical Institute has a good display of the flora and fauna of Lake Baikal.

Planetarium, 5th-Armii St. In the building of the Troitskaya (Trinity) Church.

There is an excellent view over both the old and the new parts of the city from Znamenskaya Hill; here, near Radischeva St. is a *monument* marking the grave of historian Afanasii Schapov (1830–75).

Obelisk to the conquerors of Siberia, Gagarin Boulevard. This stands on the site of a monument to Alexander III. The bas-reliefs show Ermak, Count Speransky, and Muraviev-Amursky.

Revolutionary Fighters' Monument, near the White House. This monument designed by Rya-shentsev stands on the communal grave of those who died in December 1917. It was unveiled in 1965.

Civil War Memorial, Kommunarov St. A statue of three partisans with a flag.

T-34 Tank, Sovietsky Sq., on the way into the town from the airport. Commemorating the tank columns which were formed to serve in World War II using money collected by Siberians.

Lenin Statue, Lenin St. By Tomsky, and unveiled in 1952.

Musical Comedy Theatre, Lenin St. Originally designed in the 1890s by Rassushin as a club, it has served as a theatre since 1941.

Circus, opposite the Central Telegraph building. Built in 1965 with seats for 1745.

Drama Theatre

The Children's Railway in Irkutsk is called the Small East-Siberian Line.

Angara Hotel & Restaurant, Ul. Sukhe Bator 7, TEL. 4–60–64

Almaz (diamond) Restaurant, Lenin St. 46

Baikal

Lake Baikal lies 450 m. above sea level. It is reached from Irkutsk by a drive along 70 km. of good road or by a 45-min. journey in a hydroplane.

Its name perhaps derives from the Mongolian 'Bai-Gal' (big fire) or possibly from the Turkic 'Bai-Kul' (rich lake). It is described in the words of an old song, hardly great literature but nonetheless popular:

Holy Baikal—glorious sea,
An old fish barrel—my glorious ship.
Ho, North Wind, stir the waves for me,
And hasten a brave lad's trip.

The 'brave lad' is a fugitive convict, working his way westwards, back to freedom.

The crescent-shaped lake is the deepest in the world; it measures 1620 m. in the deepest part and is only seconded by Lake Tanganyika's 1435 m. 636 km. long and varying between 24 and 80 km. in width, Baikal contains 5513 cubic miles of water, so that if no more water flowed in and the R. Angara continued to flow out at its fairly constant rate of 1982 cu. m. per second, the supply would last for 500 years.

The R. Angara, itself a tributary of the R. Yenisei, is in fact the only outflow, while the lake is fed by 336 rivers and streams. An old legend relates that Baikal had 337 daughters, as quiet and obedient as any father could wish with the exception of one, the headstrong Angara who fell in love with Yenisei. Baikal forbade their marriage, and so the young couple eloped and as they fled Baikal hurled after them the great Shaman Stone which stands where R. Angara leaves Lake Baikal, hurrying down to be united with her Yenisei.

Olkhon is the largest of the lake's 22 islands. Storms are frequent and violent, and earthquakes still occur here. Only 100 years ago the 190 sq. miles of the Gulf of Proval was formed. The water of the lake is very cold and freezes over in December. The surrounding mountains may already be snow-covered in October.

Perhaps the most interesting feature of Baikal is its flora and fauna. It is believed that most of the indigenous species originally came from the sea. Because there are seals and salt-water types of fish among them, the local fishermen still say that there is an underground tunnel linking the lake with the Arctic Ocean, although this theory has been scientifically disproved. Altogether 1700 different types of animals and plants are to be found in the waters (compared with only 400 in Lake Tanganyika) and of these, more than 1000 are not to be found anywhere else in the world. Another feature of the lake is that it is free of plankton and instead (as is usual) of being able to see 2–3 m. down into the water, it is possible to see down to a depth of 40 m.

There are plans to build a large aquarium at the *Limnological Institute's Museum* near the lake.

A local delicacy, besides the famous Siberian 'pelmeni', is the Baikal 'omul', a species of salmon exclusive to this lake.

Bratsk
Population—155,000 (1970)

The history of the old town of Bratsk goes back to 1631. Formerly a quiet town in the Siberian taiga, where the winters are extremely cold, Bratsk changed beyond recognition during the 1960s.

It is now well-known as the site of a hydro-power station which was the largest in the world when it was completed in 1964. It stands on the river Angara, 600 km. downstream from Irkutsk. The *high dam* is 127 m. high and almost 5 km. long. 20 aggregates of 225,000 kilowatts produce 4,500,000 kilowatts, and between 22 and 24 billion kilowatt-hours annually.

Bratsk is also a port on the huge Bratsk reservoir which was formed from the confluence of the Oka, Iya, and Angara rivers and was completed in 1965. Besides hydro-electricity, Bratsk is the centre of an important timber and iron-ore area.

ITKOL
See Nalchik, p. 237

IVANOVO
(1871–1932: Ivanovo-Voznesensk). Population— 419,000 (1970)

This textile town lies 318 km. north-west of Moscow and is probably best visited between April and August. It is situated on either side of R. Uvod, a tributary of the Klyazma, and 65 km. from the Volga. The little river runs through it from the north-west to the south-east, dividing the town into two parts; on the right is the older part

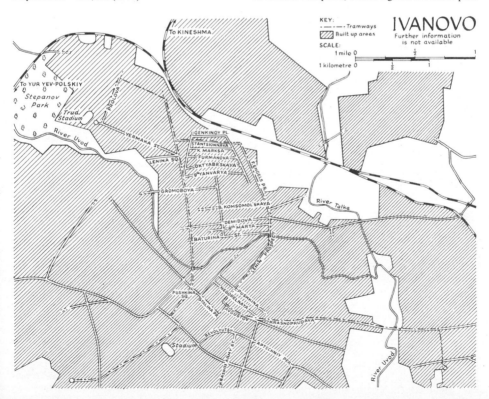

of the town, formerly the village of Ivanovo, and on the left is the part that was once the village of Voznesensk, but was incorporated into Ivanovo together with other nearby villages when it was declared a town in 1871.

Ivanovo was first mentioned in 1561 when Ivan the Terrible gave it to the princely family of Temrukovich-Cherkassky. In 1741, when one of the princesses married into the well known Sheremetiev family, Ivanovo passed to the Sheremetievs. The first linen mills had been founded near Ivanovo by the order of Peter the Great in 1710, then weaving mills were opened and textile printing factories, until by the middle of the 19th century the locality was known as the Russian Manchester. Until the abolition of serfdom in 1861, not only the workers but many of the factory owners as well were Count Sheremetiev's serfs. In fact, Ivanovo owes its development as a textile centre largely to the activity in the 1740s of two serf factory owners named Grachev and Butrimov. The damage caused in Moscow by fires in 1812 was an important factor in Ivanovo's further growth while the other villages nearby benefited from Count Sheremetiev's policy whereby he permitted the construction of factories in Ivanovo itself only on the condition that should the owners leave the village, the property would pass to the Sheremetiev family. Naturally many people preferred to build their factories outside the village boundary and so the neighbouring villages, particularly Voznesensk on the opposite side of the river, began to expand rapidly in the 1840s.

The town is known for its revolutionary activities, including strikes in 1883, 1885, and during the 1905 revolt. After the 1917 revolution it was called 'the third proletarian capital of the Soviet Republic' after Leningrad and Moscow, and many of its streets still bear the names of local Bolsheviks: Afanasiev St., Gromoboya St., Yermaka St., and Stanko St.

Ivanovo was never properly planned. Local architects explain that the winding river Uvod dictated the form the town has taken. Many sections are still more like villages than parts of a town. Among the older buildings can be seen some put up in the 1930s in 'formalist' style; one of these is an apartment house in the centre known locally as 'the ship' because of its shape. Rapid construction of new buildings began in the 1950s and is still going on. A number of houses and office blocks are designed by the local architects, Kadnikov, Mende, and Panov.

Local industry is still mainly concerned with textiles. 15% of the country's cotton cloth is produced here by 40,000 workers in twelve different types of mills and factories, but there are also clothing factories, textile and turf-cutting machine-building plants, food factories, and a piano factory. The six institutes include those specialising in medicine and textiles.

Wooden Church, Mineyevo, Frunze St. Built in the 17th century and reconstructed in 1904.

Local Museum, Baturina St. 11. Open 12–6, closed Fri.

Local Museum, Lenin Prospect

Art Gallery, in the building of the Drama Theatre

Pioneers' Palace, Baturina St. The murals were painted by artists from the well-known village of Palekh.

Obelisk commemorating the first revolution of 1905–7—in a park beside the R. Talka. It was unveiled in 1957.

Monument on the grave of thirty workers killed during a demonstration on 10 August 1915, in a park on 10-August St.

Lenin Monument, Dvorets Truda Sq. This was sculpted by Fridman and unveiled in 1956.

Frunze Monument, in the Town Garden near the circus. Frunze worked here after the revolution (1918–19) in the regional party organisation. The sculptor of the statue was Neroda and it was unveiled in 1957.

Drama Theatre, built in 1940

Musical Comedy Theatre, Krasnoi Army St. 8/2. There is also an amateur symphony orchestra and two choirs here.

Puppet Theatre

Circus

Stepanov Park, Yermaka St. This park was opened in 1936 and has a dance hall, a planetarium, and a boating station, as well as an open-air theatre.

Pobeda Park, beside R. Talka

1905 Park

Trud Stadium, Yermaka St. Seats 15,000.

Tsentralnaya Hotel and Restaurant, F. Engels St. 1, TEL. 9–02–35.

Zarya Restaurant, Lenin Prospect

IZBORSK
See Pskov, p. 262

IZMAIL
Population—65,000 (1971)

This Ukrainian town beside the Danube has a long history. A Slav settlement called Smil existed here well over a thousand years ago. In the 14th century, increasing trade brought prosperity and the town, now large and renamed Sinil, was an important centre of the grain and food trades.

In 1538 the whole area was seized by the Turks. They called it Sinil Ishmail, meaning 'Hear me, O God!', and later on re-named it Izmail. During the Russo-Turkish wars of the second half of the 18th century the town was first taken by the Russian troops in 1770 but it was returned to the Turks who then made it a strategic fortress reinforced with 300 guns, manned by a garrison of about 35,000 and encircled by a rampart 6·5 km. long and 8·5 m. high.

In the second Russo-Turkish War (1787–91) Russian troops twice failed to recapture the fortress. In December 1790 Suvorov took command of the Russian troops engaged here and although the total number of 31,000 included 15,000 irregulars he prepared to attack the fortress. The Turks fought desperately as the sultan had decreed death without trial for survivors should the stronghold fall. Nevertheless the Russian troops were victorious after a 10-hour battle and took Izmail. Suvorov reflected, 'It is only once in a lifetime that one can dare such an assault.'

During the succeeding hundred years Izmail again twice changed hands between Russia and Turkey, being returned at last to Russia in 1877 in compliance with the Treaty of San Stefano.

After the 1917 revolution a nationalist government called Spatul Tserii (the Land Council) proclaimed the formation of a Moldavian Republic which was immediately taken over by Rumania and held until 1940 when Bessarabia was returned to the Soviet Union. Now the greater part of Bessarabia is included in the Moldavian Soviet Republic while the northern and southern areas (with non-Moldavian populations) are part of the Ukraine. Izmail was under Rumanian occupation during World War II.

Today Izmail is an important southern port of the U.S.S.R. with well developed food industries, ship-repair yards, and brick works. There are several technical colleges and a pedagogical institute. The town is also the seat of the Soviet Shipping Administration for the Danube.

The remains of the *old Turkish fortress* can be seen not far from the town, 2 km. to the west. There is also a *16th-century mosque* which was reconstructed in 1810 and turned into an orthodox church, renamed Krestovozdvizhenskaya, The Erection of the Cross. On Trubayevsky Hill where Suvorov's tent stood there is an *obelisk*.

Suvorov Memorial Museum, Pushkina St. 33. Exhibits concerning the life and deeds of the general and some related to the history of Izmail.

Suvorov Monument, Suvorov Sq., in the centre of the town. The sculpture by B. Edwards was made before the First World War and kept outside the Odessa picture gallery. It was placed on its present foundation of metal plates in 1945.

Pokrovsky (Intercession) Cathedral, Suvorov Prospect. Built in 1833 following the design of Professor Melnikov of St. Petersburg Academy of Arts. Services are held here.

Lenin Monument, Suvorov Prospect

War Memorial, Suvorov Prospect. To the memory of Soviet soldiers who perished at Izmail during the revolution.

Shevchenko Drama Theatre, Suvorov Prospect
Hotel and Restaurant, Suvorov Prospect

Reni

Population—16,000

Founded in the 12th century, Reni was the first Soviet town and port on the Danube.

There are railway connections with both Odessa and Kishinyev. The port grew after the Second World War.

Palace of Sailors

KAKHOVKA

See Kherson, p. 137

KALININ

Population—345,000 (1970)

An old song tells of 'Tver, wonderful and charming and dear to my heart . . .'. Tver, supposedly derived from the old Russian word 'tverd', meaning 'stronghold', was the name of this ancient town until it was renamed in 1931. Mikhail Kalinin (1875–1946) was born in this region. An old Bolshevik, he played an important role in establishing Soviet rule in Central Asia and was Soviet President until 1946.

A Novgorodian trading post originally stood here on the bank of the R. Volga, at its confluence with the R. Tvertsa and the R. T'maka. The town was really founded by Grand-Prince Vsevolod of Vladimir in 1134–81. The main part of the town lay at that time on the left bank of the R. Volga and it was not until 1240 that Grand-Prince Yaroslav Vsevolodovich built the wooden kremlin fortress on the right bank. The kremlin stood on the place where the Khimik Stadium is today.

In 1246 Tver was separated from the Vladimir Principality and became independent, its first ruler being Yaroslav, the brother of Alexander Nevsky. In 1327, when the kremlin had grown to be really large and well-fortified, Tver organised the biggest uprising against the Tatars in the whole of Russia at that time. The local Tatar chief, Chol Khan, was torn to pieces; this action cost most of the local population their lives because Khan Uzbek gave 50,000 soldiers to Moscow's ruler Ivan Kalita, and ordered him to punish Tver. This was thoroughly done, and Kalita even brought Tver's largest church bell back to Moscow, the greatest possible humiliation in those times.

Tver survived nevertheless, and in the 14th and 15th centuries was well known for the high level of its craftsmanship. The townsmen not only built their own churches, but sent their craftsmen to build churches in other towns too. They made bells and armaments, and at the beginning of the 15th century the local artillery was among the strongest in Russia. Tver minted her own coins and her craftsmen were famous for their jewellery and fine metal work.

The town was represented at the Conference of Churches in Florence in 1439, when the question of inter-church unity was being discussed, and decided not to submit to the authority of Rome. After Novgorod was joined to Moscow in 1478 Tver was surrounded by Moscow's territory, and had no choice but to yield to Moscow when in 1485 Ivan III came with his army to the town. Ivan Mikhailovich, the last prince of Tver, fled to Lithuania. It is hard now to believe that Tver was ever the rival of Moscow and had fought her for nearly 200 years for the leadership of the surrounding territory.

When Ivan IV passed through Tver on his campaign against Novgorod in 1569 he sent Maluta Skuratov, a trusted member of his bodyguard, to the Metropolitan Philip (then exiled from Moscow to a monastery in Tver) to ask a blessing

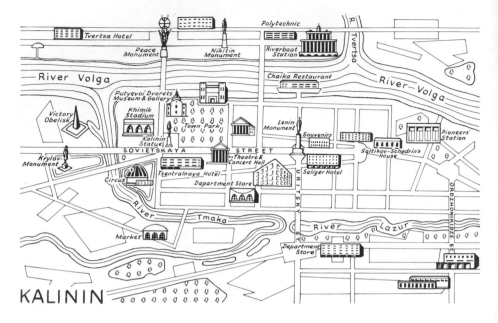

before his journey north to punish the citizens of Novogorod. The priest said that he felt able to bless those with good intentions only; Skuratov was frightened to bring such a reply to the tsar and accordingly strangled the old man with his own hands before reporting that he had not found him alive. Ivan the Terrible then lived up to his name and delivered Tver's inhabitants up to the brutality of his soldiers. Over 90,000 people were murdered. Afterwards he put a Christian Tatar, Simeon Begbulatovich, to rule over those who remained alive.

Tver was ruined by the Poles during the Time of Troubles, and in 1763 there was a disastrous fire which demolished most of the buildings. Catherine the Great sent architects to rebuild the town, among them the famous Matvei Kazakov (1738–1813). As a result Tver became a well-planned town, a 'provincial Petersburg' and Catherine the Great herself wrote in a letter, 'The town of Tver, after Petersburg, is the most beautiful in the empire.' In the 18th century and the first part of the 19th century it was the biggest town on the way from Petersburg to Moscow, and the court used to stop here, thus encouraging a certain degree of sophistication. This was very evident between 1809 and 1813, a time of real prosperity and growth for the town, when Prince Georgy Oldenburgsky (married to Catherine, Alexander I's favourite sister) was Governor General. In 1860–2 the post of Vice-Governor was held by the famous Russian satirist Mikhail Saltykov-Shchedrin, who had published his 'Provincial Sketches' four years earlier. Feodor Dostoyevsky lived here also for some time after his return from exile.

Following the 18th-century plan of the town,

there are still three main streets radiating from the centre. The central street used to be Millionaya St., where the rich people lived and which is now a shopping street. It is still the main Leningrad-Moscow road, but is now called *Sovietskaya St.* Along it there are three squares, *Pushkinskaya*, *Pochtovaya* (post office), and *Lenina*. The latter, formerly Fountain Sq., is the most interesting in the town; it contains the *Town Hall* (1770–80), the *House of Nobles* (1766–70, now the local Party headquarters), and a school built in 1786 which is now the *Youth Theatre*. In the centre of Kalinin is *Sovietskaya Sq.*, where demonstrations and parades take place.

Kalinin is the centre of a flax-growing region and is also an industrial centre especially concerned with light industry. There is a cotton mill over a hundred years old, and much of its production is exported. The town also produces rolling stock and textile machinery and there is a large printing works. There are pedagogical, medical, and peat research institutes, several technical colleges, and a Suvorov Military Academy. A new part of the town is now under construction on the left bank of the R. Volga. After World War II, when much reconstruction had to be done in the old parts of the town, most of the houses in the centre had two or three storeys added but the 18th-century style was preserved.

White Trinity Church, Engels St. Founded in 1563–4, this is the oldest building in the town. There is a plaque on the wall saying the church was built in the time of Ivan the Terrible; some of the icons in the iconostasis date from the 17th century. High up in the building there were secret rooms, and it is said that the blood of those found there and killed long stained the pillars and walls of the church below; this is probably true because it could have trickled through the ventilation holes. The church is open for services.

Transfiguration Cathedral. This Cathedral was built in 1689–96 following the lay-out of the Uspensky (Assumption) Cathedral in the Moscow Kremlin; like the Moscow Cathedral it has five domes. The *bell tower* standing near it was built between 1739 and 1758.

Convent of the Nativity, on the banks of the R. T'maka. The convent dates from the 16th century.

Church of Elijah the Prophet, Pervomaiskaya Naberezhnaya. This church was constructed in the late 18th century.

Local Museum, Sovietskaya St. 3, in the left wing of the Palace. Closed Tues. This museum was founded in 1866.

Picture Gallery, in the Church of the Ascension. The church was built in 1813.

Putyevoi Dvorets, Sovietskaya St. 3. This was built in 1763–75 by Kazakov as a coaching palace for Catherine the Great. It was partly reconstructed in 1809 by Rossi. The central façade is reminiscent of Leningrad's Winter Palace, but is simpler in design. The Palace used to contain a church dedicated to St. Catherine. The Regional Executive Committee offices are now housed in the building.

There is a group of *old houses* built by Kazakov on Pervomaiskaya Naberezhnaya, near the Church of Elijah the Prophet and the building of the theological college, now used as a technical college.

The new *bridge* over the R. Volga was completed in 1956.

Kalinin Statue, in front of Putyevoi Dvorets

Nikitin Monument, on the bank of the R. Volga. Afanasi Nikitin was a globe-trotter and merchant who went to India via Persia between 1466 and 1473, 30 years before Vasco da Gama. He spent three years there, and died in Smolensk on his way back home to Tver. He wrote a book of his travels called 'The Crossing of Three Seas'. His 8-m. bronze statue designed by Orlov and Zakharov stands on a red granite pedestal with a Russian ship's figurehead; it is on the left bank near the jetty, supposedly on the spot where he first set sail. It was unveiled in 1955.

Obelisk, in the garden in front of Putyevoi Dvorets. This obelisk commemorates those who fell during the revolution.

Lenin Monument, Lenin Sq. This statue by Kenig was unveiled in 1959; near it are the graves of those who fell during the Second World War.

Krylov Monument. Ivan Krylov (1769–1844) was a writer of fables who spent his childhood and adolescence in Tver. The monument by Shaposhnikov was unveiled in 1959; it stands 7 m. high, and around it are eight separate bas-reliefs illustrating his fables.

Peace Monument, Mira (Peace) Sq. This sculptured group in the town's newest square was unveiled in 1959.

Theatre and Concert Hall, Svobodny Pereulok 43/18

Puppet Theatre, Svobodny Pereulok 43/18

Youth Theatre, Sovietskaya St. 44 This building was formerly a school built in 1786.

Circus, on banks of R. Tmaka.

Khimik (Chemist's) Stadium, Revolyutsiyi Sq. The stadium, which can hold 11,000 people, stands on the one-time site of Tver's kremlin.

Hotel Tsentralnaya, Pravda St. 33/8, TEL. 3–81–57

Seliger Hotel and Restaurant, Sovietskaya St. 52, TEL. 3–27–21

Volga Hotel and Restaurant, Uritsky St. 37/60

Orel Restaurant, Naberezhnaya Stepana Razina

Chaika (Seagull) Restaurant

Bank, Sovietskaya St. 56/35

G.P.O., Sovietskaya St. 56/35

Central Market, Kommuny Sq.

Department Stores, Sovietskaya St. 84 and Uritsky St. 35

KANEV
See Kiev, p. 147

KAUNAS
(Formerly Russian Kovno) Population—270,000 (1975)

Kaunas is situated in the hollow formed by the confluence of the Nemunas and the Neris (the Viliya). It is the second biggest town in Lithuania and was founded in 1030 by a man of the same name, a hero of Lithuanian mythology, the ancestor of the Princes of Lithuania. In the old chronicles the place was described as Caonia, Cawonia, and Cowna. It was first mentioned in documents in 1280. During the 14th century the town was invaded several times by the Teutonic Knights. Throughout the years it was reduced to ashes thirteen times.

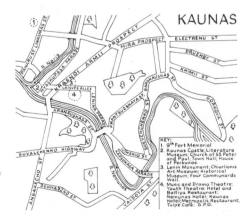

In 1408 the town received the Freedom of Magdeburg which gave it self-government and other privileges. It became the hub of Lithuania's export trade; the Hanseatic League had warehouses here, and there was a trading centre for other merchants. The town, together with the rest of Lithuania, fell into Polish hands in 1569, and so remained until the Third Partition of Poland in 1795 when it passed to the Russian Empire. Gradually the Lithuanian language was suppressed and trading only took place in Russian, although in the 16th and 17th centuries there had been trading stations run by the Dutch, English, Prussians, Swedes, and Venetians with an annual trade turnover of one million ducats.

Napoleon's army passed through the town twice in 1812; Kaunas was badly damaged and only 3000 inhabitants remained alive. In 1842 Kaunas became a provincial capital with a governor.

By 1914 nearly half of the population of 88,000 were Jewish. The Germans occupied the town in 1915–18 and again in 1941–4. After the Polish occupation of the ancient Lithuanian capital of Vilnius in 1919, Kaunas became the de facto capital of the country till 1939 when Vilnius was returned to Lithuania. In 1940 Kaunas became Soviet, with the rest of Lithuania.

There is an excellent view over the town from a nearby hill which is still known as *Napoleon's Hill*. It is 42 m. high. According to a story, Napoleon stood here to observe his army crossing the river. A small funicular railway takes one up to the hilly parts of the town.

It is also pleasant to wander about in the Old Town to see the medieval houses and romantic corners, the old warehouses, and *Napoleon's House*.

There are five institutes in Kaunas of which the largest is the *Polytechnical Institute* with about 10,000 students. It was founded in 1951 after Kaunas University was reorganised. There are also a number of scientific research institutes and a Catholic seminary there.

Many new apartment houses have been built recently in the centre of the town, along Pergale Embankment, and on the outskirts, on Jaunoji Gvardija St., as well as in the districts of Vilijampole, Petrasiunai, and Panemune.

The town has light and food industries as well as metal and woodworking industries.

A number of the town's Roman Catholic churches were converted for Russian Orthodox use in the 19th century. One of them was called after St. Nicholas by special order of the Russian Tsar Nicholas I after he escaped drowning in R. Neman in 1853.

The Church of SS. Peter and Paul, Aleksotas St., the largest Roman Catholic church in Lithuania, is also known as the Church of Vytautas. It stands beside R. Nemunas, and is the oldest church in the town. It was built by Grand Prince Vytutas in the 15th century of red brick in Gothic style. Legend has it that he wished to commemorate his safety after his army was defeated by the Tatars in a battle by R. Vorskla in 1399; in this battle his dreams of the conquest of Moscow and the destruction of the Golden Horde also perished. The church belonged at one time to the monks of the

Augustinian order. It is open for services.

Kaunas Basilica (early 15th century) has a single tower, and somehow looks unfinished. Originally Gothic in design, it was reconstructed by Italian builders in Baroque style and only the windows remain Gothic.

The Evangelist Church in Pergales St. was built in the 17th century but is now closed.

Ogel Yakob Synagogue, Ozeskienes St. 13; built in the early 19th century.

There is a *Catholic seminary* in Kaunas near the Church of SS. Peter and Paul, and the *Archbishop's Palace* is near Trinity Church.

Ruins of the 14th-century *Kaunas castle* can still be seen at the confluence of the Neris and the Nemunas. The first castle on the site was ruined by the Baltic Knights in 1362 and a new one was built in 1384 in the course of six weeks when 60,000 people and 80,000 horses were employed upon the job. A canal was dug so that the castle stood upon a small island. It was named Ritters-Werder. It was taken back by the Lithuanians in October of the same year. The Church of SS. Peter and Paul near the castle was built in 1895.

In the Old Town are a number of old houses, the most famous being the *House of Perkunas*, Aleksotas St. 6, opposite the Church of Vytutas. Perkunas was the god of thunder and lightning, the Thor of the ancient Lithuanians. This is a 16th-century Gothic building which stands on the site of Perkunas's temple.

The former *Town Hall*, originally built in the 16th century, was rebuilt in 1771 with a tower. At one time it served as a theatre.

Historical Museum, Donelaichio St. 64

Literature Museum, Rotushes Sq. 13, near the former Town Hall. This is a two-storey building in baroque style.

Petras Cvirka Memorial Museum, Donelaichio St. 13. Cvirka (1909–47) was a writer who lived in the cellar of this house. His bust, sculpted by Palis, stands in the garden.

Chiurlionis Art Museum, Neries St. 29. Mikalojus Chiurlionis (1875–1913) was both artist and musician. He tried to transmit sounds and melodies by means of paint. There are folk arts and crafts on display here, as well as Chiurlionis's work. Open 10–5; closed on Mon.

Music and Drama Theatre, Laisves Allee 74

Youth Theatre, Laisves Allee 39/41

Puppet Theatre

Zoo, Sixteenth Divizijos Pl. 21

Botanical Garden, A. Freda, Botanikos Pr.3

Stadium

Palace of Sport

Vytautas Park. In the park is a bust of the poet Vytautas Motvila.

In a garden near the Historical Museum is a *monument* by Buchas marking the grave of the prominent poetess, S. Neries (Salomea Bachinskaite-Buchene, 1904–45). Other monuments here are the *busts of Felix Dzerzhinsky* (1877–1926), the well known revolutionary who published an underground newspaper here in 1897, and of

Vincas Mickevicius-Kapsukas (1880–1935), head of the Communist Lithuanian government in 1919. In a wall is the *Four Communards Wall*, having memorial plaques to K. Pozhela, J. Greifenbergeois, K. Giedrys, and R. Garnas, who were shot on 27th December 1926, after the coup d'état by the Fascist organisation, the Iron Wolf. There is also a tank here, the first one to enter the town in 1944.

Hotel and Baltiya Restaurant, under construction

   Kaunas Hotel, Laisves Allee 21, TEL. 24–53

   Nemunas Hotel, Laisves Allee 64

   Metropolis Restaurant, Laisves Allee 44

   Gintaras (amber) Restaurant, Liepos St. 21

   Tulpe Cafe, Laisves Allee 25

   Egle Café

   Medziotoju Uzeiga (hunters' cafe), Rotushes St. 10, near the Rathaus

   G.P.O., Laisves Allee 74

There are a number of beautiful spots near the town; among them are:

Azhuolynas (oak grove) and *Panemune* with pine forests and beaches. The annual song festival is held here in the Valley of Songs.

Pazhaislis Cloister is located in a pine wood. The Baroque church and other buildings are 17th and 18th century. There are a number of frescoes, some of them of Italian workmanship. The church cost 'eight barrels of gold to build'. It was used by Roman Catholics and by Russian Orthodox and the last owners before the war were Roman Catholic nuns of the order of St. Casimir.

The 9th Fort Memorial was formerly a prison but was converted after World War I. During World War II the Germans used it as a death factory where more than 80,000 people were killed. Most of the Lithuanian Jews lost their lives during the German occupation. The walls of the fort still bear the victims' inscriptions in many different languages.

In *Mitskewitch Valley* is a stone with the initials 'A. M.—1823' and a few lines from a poem. Adam Mitskewitch was a famous Polish poet who worked in 1819–23 as a teacher in Kaunas, at School No. 9. He described this valley as the most beautiful in the world.

Kaunas Sea was formed 12 km. up the R. Nemunas when the hydro-power station was built in 1955–60. It is 64 sq. km. in area. The power station has four aggregates of 22,500 kw. each.

KAZAKHSTAN
See Alma-Ata, p. 47

KAZAN
Population—869,000 (1970)

   Sing to me, O harp, all about Kazan . . .

                        Derzhavin

Kazan has been called 'the Beauty of the East'. It is located on the left bank of the Volga, near the entry of the R. Kazanka. The central part of the town stands on hills which are 60–90 m. above sea level. The climate is continental and the summer temperature averages 22°C. (71·5°F.).

The Tatar word, 'kazan', means 'cauldron'. The first Kazan was founded in the second half of the 13th century by Tudai-Menghe, Khan of the Golden Horde, who was also known as Kazan-Khan, at a place some 45 km. from the present Kazan. It was later known as Iske-Kazan (Old Kazan) but no trace of it can be found. Legend has it that while one of Tudai-Menghe's servants was preparing a bath for his master, he dropped a golden cauldron into the river and the new town was later founded nearby.

Kazan was transferred to its present position in the middle of the 15th century. The new site was better both geographically and strategically. There are a number of Tatar legends connected with the construction of the new Kazan. One of these tells of a rich man from old Kazan who often visited his apiaries in the forest near Jilan-Tau (Snake Hill) and who usually took his daughter with him. When this young lady got married she lived in old Kazan and had to go quite a distance to R. Kazanka for water. She blamed the founder of the town for his bad planning. Ali-Bei, ruler of Kazan, learned of her complaining and sent for her. She told him that the founder of the town, who had water brought to him by servants, could not have realised how difficult it would be for the poor women, especially those expecting babies, to carry jars of water up the hill. The woman told Ali-Bei about the advantages of a place near the mouth of R. Kazanka where her apiaries were situated. The khan replied that Jilan-Tau was notorious for the great numbers of snakes there and that the place near the mouth of the Kazanka was inhabited by wild boars. The woman argued that both snakes and boars could be dealt with by wizards. As it happened, the khan himself was dissatisfied with the position of his town, so he sent his son with two nobles and a hundred warriors to the mouth of the Kazanka to search for a better place for the town, and gave them sealed instructions to be opened at the moment when the envoys came to an agreement about the place for the new Kazan. A site was finally found, the instructions opened, and the nobles read the khan's order to bury alive one member of their party on the place of the future city. Lots were cast and it fell to the khan's son to die. But the servants hid him and buried a dog instead. When the khan came to inspect the site he was grieved to learn of his son's fate, but his servants soon told him the truth. Although he was much relieved, he still regretted that his command had not been obeyed and remarked sadly, 'This means that our new city and kingdom will eventually fall into the hands of the enemies of our true religion, whom we call unholy dogs.'

In the autumn a wizard drove all the snakes into a certain place and gave orders that wood and straw be piled around them. This was done and the following spring all the snakes were burnt. However a dragon survived on Jilan-Tau and long

KEY
1 N.I. Lobachevsky Monument.
2 House of Nobles
3 Cathedral of the Annunciation.
4 St. John the Baptist's Monastery. (17th cent.).
5 Mikhailov's House (17th cent.). Peter 1st stayed here in 1722.
6 Cathedral of St. Peter and St. Paul.
7 Broadcloth Factory. Founded by Peter I in 1714.
8 Bronnikov's House. (18th cent.). Wooden mansion.
9 Baratinsky's House. (19th cent.).
10 Trader's Row (1800). Designed by Emelyanov.
11 Former Public School, (early 19th cent.). Designed by Smirnov.
12 Former Military Commander's House. (early 20th cent.).
13 Apanaev's House. (early 20th cent.). Tatar style.
14 Press House, 1930's constructivist style.

KAZAN

held the whole area in terror until it too was killed by a wizard. Probably it is to this legend that Kazan owes its coat-of-arms which first appeared at the beginning of the 17th century. The final version of the design was approved in 1730: 'Kazan's coat-of-arms, a black dragon with red wings under the golden crown of Kazan on a white field.'

After the disintegration of the Golden Horde, Kazan became the centre of a 'new Horde', an independent khanate. In the period between 1445 and 1477 Kazan troops made frequent incursions into Russian lands, attacking Murom, Galich, Vladimir, and other cities. In 1487, in a massive retaliation campaign, Russian troops under Ivan III entered Kazan and put a pro-Russian khan,

Mohammad Emin, on the throne.

At the end of the 15th and the beginning of the 16th century the economic ties between Kazan and Russia grew considerably. Kazan had a population of about 30,000. The city centred around the high, oak-walled kremlin, inside which stood stonebuilt mosques, mausoleums, and the khan's palace.

Kazan was the centre of a typical feudal Moslem state where internal strife resulted in frequent changes of khans. In the 1520s anti-Russian tendencies gradually developed, the policies of Mohammad Emin were forgotten, and in 1521 a pro-Turkish group placed Sahib-Ghirey, a brother of the Crimean khan, on the Kazan

---

PLATES OPPOSITE
December snow at the Yekaterinsky Palace in Pushkin (formerly Tsarskoye Selo, Tsars' Village). It was built by Rastrelli for Catherine, wife of Peter the Great, after whom the palace was named.

throne. Kazan became a tool in the hands of the Turkish sultan and his vassal, the Crimean khan, in their struggle against Moscow. Sahib-Ghirey and his successor, Safa-Ghirey, made several raids into Russian territory.

In self-defence Russia waged two unsuccessful campaigns (in 1547–8 and 1549–50) and finally the Russian fortress of Sviyazhsk was built near Kazan. The people living on the right bank of the Volga refused to serve Kazan and swore allegiance to Moscow. An uprising in 1551 in Kazan brought the pro-Russian Shah-Alei to the throne but he was without the support of his chief vassals and in the early spring of 1552 they asked the Russian Tsar, Ivan IV (the Terrible), to make Kazan a Moscow protectorate. Before negotiations were complete a pro-Turkish group once more seized power and closed the city gate. They invited Prince Yedigher of Astrakhan to take the Kazan throne. In the summer of 1552 the Russian army rose to the attack. By 25 August the city was surrounded, and the siege lasted for a month. Russian engineers mined the city walls and on 2 October blew them up in two places. The fortress fell after fierce fighting. In 1555 the first archbishop of Kazan, St. Guriy, arrived from Moscow with instructions to 'convert the Tatars with love and not with force'.

By the second half of the 16th century Kazan was much changed. The Tatars had been moved out of town and the centre of the city was repopulated with Russians. It had become a military settlement. In the 17th and 18th centuries Kazan served as a stronghold of government troops against rebellious peasants. In 1612 volunteers went from Kazan to help Minin and Pozharsky's forces liberate Moscow from the Poles. They took with them their own icon of Our Lady from the convent of the same name. The wonderworking icon was reputed to have been found buried in the earth and one of the convent's churches was specially built to mark the spot. After the victory in Moscow it was generally believed that the good fortune was due to Our Lady of Kazan, as the icon was called. In gratitude the royal Romanov family built a church in Moscow dedicated to Our Lady of Kazan. The icon was held in great veneration and was claimed to have helped stop the spread of the city fire of 1737. In the 19th century the famous Kazan Cathedral was built in St. Petersburg to house the icon.

In 1708 Kazan was declared the centre of the province of the same name, and soon all the trade and industry of eastern Russia focussed upon it. In spite of the policy of religious freedom followed earlier, the Tatars were now forced to adopt Christianity at the point of the sword. The first organised industry in Kazan itself appeared at the order of Peter the Great. A shipyard and admir-

alty building were established and 342 ships were built for the Persian campaign. During this period the wool and leather industries also developed. Peter, who visited Kazan in 1722, thought of it as a trade centre between Siberia, China, and Persia. When Catherine the Great visited the town in 1767 she wrote of it, 'this town is no doubt the first in Russia after Moscow', but times were still far from peaceful. In 1774 it was seized and burnt by Pugachev, Cossack leader of a popular revolt.

The first provincial Russian grammar school was opened in Kazan in 1759. It was run as a branch of Moscow University. In 1804 Kazan's own university was opened. From 1827 until 1846 the famous Russian mathematician, Lobachevsky, was rector (see below). It was at this time also that the Department of Oriental Languages was opened. In the 1840s the University of Kazan was an important scientific centre, and a centre of progressive social thought in the Volga basin and the Urals. In the late 1840s one of the first underground groups in Russia was established here. For years the University of Kazan was considered as the centre of liberal ideas in eastern Russia, especially after 1866 when a former student, Karakozov, made an unsuccessful attempt upon Tsar Alexander II's life. At the end of the 19th century the first Marxist groups appeared in Kazan and Maxim Gorky called it his 'spiritual birthplace'. Lenin, who was at that time studying at the University, was an active member of the group and was sent down for taking part in student riots in 1887.

Before the 1917 revolution, the Bolshevists were both strong and influential in Kazan. Soviet power was established there on 26 October 1917, at the same time as the uprising in Petrograd. In March 1918, Tatar nationalists established their short-lived Trans-Bulak Republic (so called because the Tatar population of Kazan lived near the little R. Bulak). On 6 August 1918, Kazan was seized by the Czech Corps, the ex-prisoner-of-war troops assisting the counter-revolutionaries on their way westwards from Siberia, but Soviet power was re-established on 10 September. In 1920 the Autonomous Tatar Republic was formed with Kazan as its capital.

Today Kazan spreads 20 km. from north to south. It is one of the Volga basin's largest industrial centres with sizeable chemical, engineering, food, leather, and fur industries. Local products include photographic film, typewriters and synthetic rubber and more than half Russia's furs are processed in Kazan.

There are a musical conservatoire, a local branch of the Academy of Sciences, and a number of scientific and research institutes, including those connected with the republic's oil and gas fields. Kazan is also an important transport centre

---

PLATES OPPOSITE

Pavlovsk, near Pushkin, was given to Paul (I) by his mother, Catherine the Great. *Below left*, statue of Paul in the courtyard of the palace and, *right*, the Temple of the Three Graces built in 1800 by the Scottish Palladian architect, Charles Cameron.

with an airport, a big railway junction, and a river port.

It is best to start a sightseeing tour of Kazan with the *kremlin*. It is possible to climb the Spassky tower and from the north side of the kremlin there is a good panoramic view. After leaving the kremlin, follow *Lenin St.* towards the *University. Bauman St.* is the main shopping centre.

The kremlin walls, at the end of the 15th and the beginning of the 16th century, consisted of two rows of thick oaken logs with the space between filled in with earth and stones. During the Russian siege of 1552 the wooden walls were burned down and blown up. In 1556 Ivan the Terrible sent 200 masons from Pskov to 'break the stone and build a new stone town in Kazan'. Part of the wall was built of limestone, but the remains of the oak logs were only replaced in the 17th century by a red brick wall. The architect Postnik, who was later responsible for the famous St. Basil's Cathedral on Red Sq. in Moscow, was in charge of the reconstruction.

After that the walls and towers of the kremlin were damaged by fire many times and each time the reconstruction was different. Now the walls are two-storeyed. The lower part is 4–5 m. thick. Of the original 13 towers, eight are still to be seen: the Spassky Gate (with clock), Preobrazhenskaya and Nameless Towers, the Tainitskaya and Pyatnitskaya Gates, and Konsistovskaya, South-east and South-west Round Towers.

Inside the kremlin, entering through the Spassky Gate, the white, three-storey building on the right used to be a guard house and, like many of the other buildings in the kremlin, is now used to house governmental and administrative offices. Some of the administrative buildings were built for that same purpose in the 19th century. The *Cathedral of the Annunciation* was originally wooden and founded by Ivan the Terrible on the day he triumphantly entered Kazan. Between 1556 and 1561 the masters from Pskov, Postnik and Ivan Shiryai, were responsible for an edifice of white limestone slabs, typical of the architecture of Pskov and Novgorod. Now the eastern part of the building is the only part left unchanged. Nearby is the former *Archbishop's Palace*.

A little further on is the former *Governor's Palace*, built in 1845–8 by Thon (who also built the Grand Kremlin Palace in Moscow). The 18th-century church was restored at the time of the construction of the palace and linked to it by a covered gallery.

The *Suyumbeka Tower*, to the left of the palace, is perhaps the most interesting structure in the kremlin. It is 57 m. high and has seven stages. The first three are cubes while the plans of the upper stages are octagonal. The top of the tower has tilted over 1·5 m. and the lean is quite noticeable. The date of construction is unknown but it is supposed to have been built in the 17th century as a watch tower. It closely resembles Moscow Kremlin's Borovitsky Tower,

which dates from that period.

There are plenty of other theories about its history. Some historians think it was the minaret of a large mosque which was converted into the Russian Orthodox Vvedenia Church after the Russian conquest and was later used as a gunpowder depot. Others think that it was built entirely by the Russians or alternatively by Tatar Prince Mur-Alei who was ambassador to Moscow during the negotiations with Ivan the Terrible. Other historians have come to the conclusion that at least the first three storeys were built by the Tatars long before, some saying that part was the remains of the khan's palace or that under the tower a holy man lies buried, from whose skull flows a spring of water. One of the least likely theories is that it was built by Princess Suyumbek and was called after her.

Suyumbek was the wife of three successive Tatar khans. Folk legends depict her as a wise and beautiful woman who lived in luxurious royal surroundings and yet suffered much misery, finally falling into the hands of her enemies and seeing her kingdom collapse. She was the daughter of the Nogai Tatar Prince Usuf. At 13 she was married to the 15-year-old Tatar Kazan-Khan Yen-Alei. His immaturity made him a weak ruler and his nobles plotted against him and killed him. She then married Khan Safa-Ghirey who died in a drunken fight leaving her with two baby sons. Finally she was forced to marry Shah-Alei whose pro-Moscow policies displeased her; she prepared some poisoned food and an enchanted shirt for him but he gave the food to a dog and the shirt was put upon a condemned criminal. Both died immediately and in 1551 Shah-Alei sent his wife and elder stepson to Moscow where they died.

Although it seems that the tower was built nearly a century and a half after Suyumbek died, it may have been called after her because perhaps the site was formerly that of a mosque which she had built. Certainly the legend that she jumped to her death when the army of Ivan the Terrible came to Kazan has no historical foundation.

A copy of the tower can be seen near the Leningradskaya Hotel in Moscow, on the building of the Kazan railway station.

Cathedral of SS. Peter and Paul, Dzhalilya St. 17. The merchant Mikhlyaev built this church in 1723–6 to commemorate Peter the Great's visit to Kazan. Both the cathedral and the nearby bell tower in Baroque style were designed by a Florentine architect. They are decorated with patterns of vine leaves, peaches, pears, and flowers and inside are fine tiles depicting white and yellow flowers on a blue background.

St. Nicholas's Cathedral, Bauman St. 5. The cathedral was built in 1885 and contains a miracle-working icon of St. Nicholas. Both this and the *Pokrovskaya Church* (1703) nearby are open for services.

There are a number of other monasteries and churches in the city, all closed. Among them is *Bogoroditsky Convent*, near the Kremlin, on Krasina St. It was founded in 1579 but all the buildings which remain today were constructed in the 19th century. It was from this convent that the icon of Our Lady was taken to Moscow in 1612.

Mardzhani Mosque, Nasiri St. 17. Built in 1766. The national Tatar motifs in the decoration show some influence of contemporary Russian baroque style. It is open for services.

Apanayevskaya Mosque, Nasiri St. 29. Built in the 1760s.

Other buildings of interest include the *Town Hall*, Lenin St. 1 and the former *House of Nobles*, Svobody Sq. This was built in the 1840s and there is a commemorative plaque saying that Soviet power was declared here on 26 October 1917. It is now the House of Officers.

Lenin Library, Lenin St. 33. Built in 1910 by architect Mufke for factory owner Ushkov, each room was decorated in a different style. The entrance is Japanese, the hall Empire, the room next to it Moorish, the study is an imitation grotto, and the dining room is Gothic.

At *Kuibysheva St.* 14 is the house where the famous Russian singer, Feodor Chaliapin (1873–1938), was born.

Tatar State Museum, Lenin St. 2. Open 10–5. The collector Likhachev was responsible for the opening of the original local museum in 1895. Now there are departments of History and Art and of Natural History. Of interest in the former is a coach used by Catherine II in 1767, the desk that belonged to the Classicist poet, Gavril Derzhavin (1743–1816), who lived in Kazan, Derzhavin's wife's harp, a New Testament dated 1606, and a collection of national costumes.

Gorky's House, Gorky St. 10. Open 10–7, closed Tues. The Russian writer lived and worked here in 1886–7. The bakery where he was employed is in a cellar.

Lenin Museum, Ulyanovykh St. 58. Open 11–6, closed Mon. Lenin lived here with the rest of the family in 1888–9 when he was permitted to return to Kazan after his banishment to the village of Kokushkina, 40 km. away, for participation in student riots.

Kamala Museum, Ostrovsky St. 15. Open 10–4, closed Fri. Here the Tatar writer, Sharif Kamal (1884–1942), whose real name was Baigildeyev, lived between 1928 and 1942. On show are his personal belongings, books, etc.

Kazan University, Lenin St. 18. The University was founded in 1804 and the buildings were constructed in the 1820s and the 1830s by architects Pyatnitsky and Korinfsky. There are four museums supervised by the university authorities, and special permission is required to visit some of them.

Ethnographical Museum, open 10–4, closed Sun.

Zoological Museum, open 4–5, closed Sun. Founded 1838. (Special permission required.)

Auditorium Museum, open 10–5 every day. Lenin attended this university from August till December 1887. On view is one of the auditoriums of the law faculty, reconstructed following photographs taken in the 1890s.

Geological Museum, Lenin St. 4, entrance from Dzhalila St. Open 8–4, closed Sun.

Industrial and Agricultural Exhibition, Orenburgsky Trakt. Open in summer only from 10–6; closed Mon.

Lenin Monument, Svobody Sq. Yatsyno was the sculptor of this statue which was unveiled in 1954 and which, together with the pedestal, stands 12 m. high.

Lenin Statue, in front of the University. This monument depicts Lenin as the student Ulyanov (his real name). It is by Tsigal and was unveiled in 1954.

Lobachevsky Monument, near the main building of the university. Nikolai Lobachevsky (1793–1857) was a great Russian mathematician who pioneered the modern non-Euclidean geometry and who was rector of this university for 19 years. The bust by Dillon was unveiled in 1896.

Monument to the Russian warriors who fell capturing Kazan in 1552. The monument has been on an island since the Volga was dammed lower downstream and can best be seen from the northern part of the kremlin. This combination of Egyptian pyramid and classic Greek forms was built in 1823 by Alferov; it stands 20 m. high and inside is the Spasa Nerukotvornova Church.

Bauman Monument, Ershova St., in front of the Veterinary Institute. Nikolai Bauman (1873–1905) studied at this institute before he began his career as a professional revolutionary in Kazan.

Kirov Monument, Marx St., near the former Industrial College from which Kirov graduated. Sergei Kirov (1886–1934) was another famous revolutionary.

Tukai Monument, near Lake Kaban. Gabdulla Muhammed Tukayev (1886–1913) was a poet. This statue by Akhun, Kerbel, and Pisarevsky stands 10 m. high and was unveiled in 1958.

Leo Tolstoy Monument, in a garden on the corner of Marx St. and Tolstoy St., near a house where the writer lived when he was a student. The bust was designed by Pinchuk.

Stolyarov Monument, in a garden on Tsetkina St. This bust of the Kazan-born war hero was by Mukhina.

Musa Dzhalil Monument, 1st May Sq. Musa Dzhalil (1906–44) was a local poet whose real name was Zalilov. He died in a Nazi concentration camp and was proclaimed a Hero of the Soviet Union. This 7-m. bronze statue by Tsigal was unveiled in 1966.

Musa Dzhalil Opera and Ballet Theatre, Svobody Sq. The theatre company was founded in 1939 after the graduation of performers from a special Tatar Studio in the Moscow Conservatoire. The building was designed by Gainutdinov and Skvortsov in 1956, and seats 1025 people.

Kamala Tatar Drama Theatre, Gorky St. 13. This theatre is called after the Tatar playwright,

Galiasgar Kamal (1879–1933), whose real name was Kamaletdinov.

Kachalov Russian Drama Theatre, Bauman St. 48. This theatre is called after Vasily Kachalov (1875–1948), a famous Russian actor who began his career here and who played at the Moscow Art Theatre from 1900.

Lenkomsomol Youth Theatre, Ostrovskova St. 10

Puppet Theatre, Lukovskova St. 21

Gorky Park, Ershova St.

Lenin Stadium, Kremlevskaya Damba

Spartak Stadium, Tukayevskaya St. 30

Zoo and Botanical Gardens, Taktasha St. 112. This was founded as a botanical garden in 1834 and the zoo was transferred here in 1931.

Kazan Hotel and Restaurant, Bauman St. 9, TEL. 20091. The Intourist office is in Room 212, TEL. 90–212.

Tatarstan Hotel and Restaurant, Bauman St. 86, TEL. 22–324

Hotel Soviet, Universitetskaya St. 7

Restaurant Vostok (east), Kuibysheva St. 13

Restaurant Mayak (lighthouse), Dekabristov St. 185/17

Restaurant Parus (sail), on a houseboat anchored near Lenin Bridge

Café of Tatar Cuisine, Bauman St. 31

Milk Bar, Bauman St. 58

Bank, Bauman St. 37

Department Store, Bauman St. 13

Bookshop, Bauman St. 19

Gifts, Bauman St. 78

Art Salon, Dzerzhinskova St. 27

Jeweller's, Bauman St. 58

Lebyazhye (swan) Lake is a popular recreation place 10 km. (6 miles) from the town. The *Berezka (birch tree) Café* is here.

KHABAROVSK

Population—437,000 (1970)

This town is named after Erofei Pavlovich Khabarov, a Russian explorer who made several expeditions to the R. Amur region in the middle of the 17th century. With a group of seventy hunters he conquered the area beside the river and in recognition of this he received the honourable title of 'Son of a Boyar'. On the occasion of his second expedition he took 138 people and three guns with him to help him subdue the local tribes. He achieved this largely by wholesale slaughter of the inhabitants and by devasting their land.

Long ago it was supposed that this part of the country rested on the backs of three great whales; today they are hardly discernible, but the city of Khabarovsk does in fact stand upon the 'backs' of three long hills which lie side by side as they drink for ever the waters of the Amur. The hills and the generous width of the streets both add to the town's pleasant appearance.

Khabarovsk stands on the right bank of R. Amur at the point where its tributary, R. Ussuri, flows into it and where the Trans-Siberian Railway crosses it. It is 769 km. by rail from Vladivos-

tok and its average annual temperature is only half a degree above freezing. The majority of the population are Russian, but there are also some Ukrainians and Koreans.

It was founded in 1858 as a military outpost by Count Muravyev, Governor of Eastern Siberia. At one time it was a trading centre for sable pelts, but it grew into a sizeable town and replaced Nikolayevsk-on-Amur as capital of the Maritime Province in 1880. The opening of the railway connection with Vladivostok in 1897 proved of great importance in the development of the town's economy. It soon became the main transit point for cargoes to and from China, Manchuria, and the Upper and Lower Amur. The description, 'three hills, two holes and 40,000 briefcases', summed up neatly both its geographical features and its flourishing business at the beginning of the 20th century.

During the civil war, from April until October in 1920, Khabarovsk was occupied by the Japanese army, but between 1918 and 1922 was mainly held by the White Russians. From 1926 to 1938 it was the capital of the whole of the Soviet Far East. Now it is the largest city and the main transport and political centre east of Lake Baikal. It is also the biggest industrial and cultural centre of the Soviet Far East and covers an area of over 300 sq. km.

There are ship-repairing, engineering, oil-refining, food, and other industries, and seven higher educational establishments. Local research institutes include the Institute of Oceanography.

Lenin Sq., covering nearly 5·6 hectares (14 acres), is the focal point of Khabarovsk. It was the scene of revolutionary meetings and demonstrations by striking workers before the establishment of Soviet power, and parades and demonstrations on public holidays are still held there. On either side of the large statue of Lenin there are stands for 2,500 people.

Two *parks*, the *Amur Steamship office*, and the *regional library* face onto *Komsomolskaya Sq.*, and from it a wide flight of steps leads down to the river embankment. The library, founded in 1894, contains 1,200,000 books including the best collection of literature on the Russian Far East. The main shopping street of the city, *Karl Marx St.*, begins in Komsomolskaya Sq. No. 23, Karl Marx St., once the Merchants' Duma, is now the Palace of Pioneers.

Khristorozhdestvenskaya (Nativity) Church, Leningradskaya St. 65. This church was built at the beginning of this century and is open for services.

Local Museum, Shevchenko St. 21. The museum was founded in 1896 and the stone tortoise in front of the building weighing 6¼ tons has been there since that date. The exhibits illustrate the region's history, geography, geology, and natural history. On the first floor are interesting costumes and items of handicraft made by the primitive peoples of the north and Kamchatka which are worth seeing. On the second floor is an exhibition showing progress in Soviet time. On the wall of the building is a memorial plaque to Vladimir Arsenyev (see below) who worked here for many years. Under a protecting roof outside in the garden is the 20-m. skeleton of a whale caught in 1891. The museum is open 10–5, closed Tues.

Fine Arts Museum, Frunze St. 45. There are some good icons, Russian classics including Repin, Shishkin and Levitan, a West European section including a Rembrandt etching, a Rubens drawing, and a painting by Monet, and a collection of Chinese and Japanese works of art besides paintings and drawings by Soviet artists.

Arsenyev's House, Arsenyev Lane 9. Vladimir Arsenyev (1872–1930) was an ethnographer who explored the Far East and wrote many books about its flora and fauna. His house is marked by a memorial plaque.

Narodny Dom (People's House), Pushkin St. 37. This house was built in 1899 to mark the centenary of Pushkin's birth.

Tower, beside R. Amur. Here, in 1918, a number of Hungarian and Austrian prisoners-of-war were shot. They were musicians who refused to play the imperial Russian anthem.

Volochayevka Battle Museum, Volochayevka 1st Station. The three-day battle of Volochayevka in February 1922, was a turning point in the civil war in the Far East. The memorial building which stands on Mount Ijun-Koran where there was a White Russian fortress, was constructed in 1928 over the grave of 118 soldiers who fell in the battle. On the top of the building is a statue of a Red Army soldier brandishing his rifle above a barbed-wire entanglement.

Lenin Monument, Lenin Sq. The metal monument on its granite pedestal was created in 1925 by Manizer.

The tombstone in Lenin Sq. marks the grave of four soldiers killed in a Russian-Chinese conflict in 1929 concerning the ownership of the eastern end of the Trans-Siberian Railway. The tombstone decorated with laurels, banners and a star was set up in 1950.

Khabarov Monument, Vokzalnaya Sq. Yerofey Khabarov was responsible for bringing the first Russian settlers to the R. Amur in 1649. He reported to the government that 'by the R. Amur is much goodly arable land and meadow and fishing and all kinds of virtues.' The monument by A. Milchin was unveiled in 1958, when the city was celebrating its centenary.

Amur Sailors' Memorial, Vokzalnaya Sq. The memorial in front of the railway station commemorates the detachment of 150 sailors who died here in 1920 during the civil war.

Civil War Victims' Memorial, Chornorechenskoye Chausee. The monument, easily seen from the road to the airport, was erected in 1953 over the ravine where mass executions took place.

Seryshev Monument, Seryshev St. Stepan Seryshev was an eminent military leader during the civil war of 1918–22. As Commander-in-Chief of the eastern front in 1922 he led the victorious attack on Volochayevka. His bust by A. Malinovsky was unveiled in 1958.

Civil War Heroes' Memorial, Komsomolskaya Sq. The obelisk of grey hewn granite is crowned with a laurel wreath and a five-pointed star. The three bronze figures on the pedestal form a group 7 m. high, symbolising the revolutionary forces. The architect was Professor Barsh and the sculptor Faidysh-Krandievsky, and the work was unveiled in 1956.

Pushkin Monument, Karl Marx St. 64, in front of the main building of the Pedagogical Institute

Arsenyev Monument, in the city park

Nevelskoy Monument, at the crossing of two walks in the city park. Admiral Gennadi I. Nevelskoy (1813–76) was exploring the Russian Pacific coast when he discovered that Sakhalin was in fact an island.

A second *monument to Lenin* stands in the city park, marking the spot where the city was supposed to have been founded.

Drama Theatre, Dzerzhinsky St. 92. The building, the auditorium of which seats 840 people, was completed in 1959.

Musical Comedy Theatre, Shevchenko St. 17. Opened in 1926.

Youth Theatre, Karl Marx St. 14. The theatre was opened in the former Merchants' Hall in 1945.

Philharmonic Society, Volochayevskaya St. 156

Circus, Leo Tolstoy St.

City Park, Komsomolskaya St. The park stretches along the high rocky bank of the Amur with a view across the valley to the Khekhtsir Mountains. Chekhov was enchanted with the view and wrote, 'I wish I could stay and live here for ever.' In the park are a summer threatre, cinema, sports facilities, and a children's playground. A flight of steps leads down to the river embankment.

Children's Park, Karl Marx St. 69. Here there are 8 hectares (20 acres) of woodland with an open-air theatre and playgrounds.

Children's Railway, Zheleznodorozhny Rayon. The Small Far Eastern Railway runs from Karl Marx St., near the Agricultural Research Institute at No. 143, to a vegetable farm in the suburbs and back again in a 3400 m. circle. The railway operates four days a week. It was opened in 1958 as part of the town's centenary celebrations.

Lenin Stadium, Serysheva St. Designed by M. Sorokin and opened in 1957 the stadium which seats 25,000 stands in a territory of 34.2 hectares (85½ acres). The complex also includes a football field, tennis courts, gymnasia, a Palace of Sports seating 6000, and a heated open-air pool which is used all the year round.

Botanical Garden, Volochayevskaya St. 71. On an area of 11·5 hectares (nearly 29 acres) the collection of 1300 trees and shrubs is claimed to represent all the types that grow in the Soviet Far East. The garden belongs to the Far East Institute of Forestry Research which has done much to improve forestry in the Far East.

Amur Hotel & Restaurant, Lenin St. 49, TEL. 33–50–43.

Tsentralnaya (Intourist) Hotel and Restaurant, Pushkin St. 52, TEL. 33–67–31.

Dalni Vostok (far east) Hotel, Karl Marx St. 20, TEL. 33–14–34. Hotel residents should dial 9 before the town number they require.

Sever (north) Hotel, Volochayevskaya St. 108, TEL. 33–14–32.

While in a Khabarovsk restaurant, one should try the 'ukha', which is fish soup of Siberian salmon and ruffe.

Ussuri Café, Karl Marx St. 34

Dalni Vostok Café, Karl Marx St.

Bank, Karl Marx St. 44

G.P.O., Karl Marx St. 24

Central Telegraph Office, Lenin Sq.

Department Store, Karl Marx St. 31

Central Bookshop, Karl Marx St. 23

Taxi Ranks, on Vokzalnaya Sq. and Komsomolskaya Sq., by the Department Store, by No. 1 Grocery Store at Karl Marx St. 13, and by the Amur and Sever Hotels. To call a taxi, dial 33–19–58.

Khabarovsk Airport is only 9 km. out of town, and there are two more hotels and a new restaurant there also.

KHARKOV

(Pronounced 'harkov')

Population—1,223,000 (1970)

The city is built on a plateau in the midst of the black earth region of the Ukraine. Three rivers flow through it, the Lopan, the Udy, and the Kharkov. Although it probably took its name from the R. Kharkov, legend records that a certain Cossack called Kharko or Khariton lived here, until he was drowned in the R. Donets, and that it was called after him.

The town of Kharkov dates from about 1656, when the fortress was built to protect Russia's southern border, particularly from the Crimean Tatars. There was probably some sort of settlement here before this, but no evidence of it remains. During the Cossack insurrection, Kharkov remained loyal to the tsars, who in return granted the town various privileges. Later, at the end of the 18th century, an earth wall with towers was built to surround the expanding town.

Before the foundation of the university in 1805, two men in particular were closely concerned with the problems of education in the Ukraine. They were Grigori Skovoroda (1722–94 whose name means 'frying-pan') a philosopher who spent most of hs life as an itinerant teacher of morals and was one of the chief sources of modern Russian Intuitivism, and Grigori Kvitka-Osnovyanenko (1778–1843; 'kvitka' means 'flower' in Ukrainian), an author and playwright. The present-day university has 10 faculties and over 100 Chairs. 12,000 students study in it and it contains 200 fully equipped laboratories. Kharkov has a total of 100,000 students because, besides the university, there are 22 other higher educational estab-

lishments and 57 scientific research institutes.

Kharkov has one of the most picturesque entrances of any Russian town. Approaching the town from the direction of Moscow, a wide tree-lined road leads to *Sumskaya Street* which is lined with cafés, restaurants, shops, and old buildings, and leads to the centre of town. One of the oldest parts of the city is *Universitetskaya Gorka*. This was originally surrounded by a wooden palisade, and at the end of the 17th century brick buildings were erected: the *Pokrovsky Cathedral* and the *Uspensky Cathedral*. *Dzerzhinsky Square* is one of the largest in the world and covers an area of 11 hectares (27¼ acres). The buildings around it were constructed between 1929 and 1933 and form an interesting complex. One of them is known as the *House of Projects* and was designed by S. Serafimov; another, the *House of Industry*, built by the architects S. Serafimov and S. Kravets, is, with its 18 storeys, the first Soviet skyscraper. It was badly damaged during the Second World War, when the city changed hands five times, and is now occupied by the university.

Until 1934 Kharkov was the capital of the

KHARKOV

Ukraïne, but this honour was then restored to ancient Kiev. It has long been one of Russia's major railway junctions and is the administrative centre of the great iron and coal mining industries of southern Russia. Its huge engineering industry produces locomotives, tractors, aircraft, agricultural machinery, and turbines, and there are various light industries as well.

Pokrovsky Cathedral, Universitetskaya St. The basic plan of this cathedral, built in 1689, is that of the old wooden Ukrainian churches, but the details are Russian. Its domes are coloured blue.

Uspensky Cathedral, Universitetskaya Gorka. This stands on the site of a 17th-century cathedral which was destroyed by fire in 1733. The present cathedral was erected between 1821 and 1841 by the architect Vasiliyev, and is 89·5 m. high. It was badly damaged during World War II, but has since been restored.

Bell-tower, Universitetskaya Gorka. The architects Vasiliyev and Thon designed this picturesque tower in 1841 to commemorate Russia's victory over Napoleon. It is 89.5 m. high and the foundations are 30 m. deep.

Annunciation Cathedral, Engels St., down the hill from the old town and across the river. This cathedral was built in 1901 on the site of earlier churches, and was restored in 1950. It is built of brick in neo-Byzantine style after St. Sophia in Istambul. It holds 4000 people.

Three Saints' Church, Zaikovskaya St. This church was built in 1915, and services are held here; part of the church is used by the Old Believers and contains some old icons.

Roman Catholic Church, Gogol St.

There are, besides those mentioned, a number of other churches, mostly of the 19th and 20th centuries, of no particular historical interest.

Yekaterinsky Palace was built between 1767 and 1776, in Russian classical Empire style. It is now used as an administrative building of the university and stands in Universitetskaya St.

Historical Museum, Universitetskaya St. 10 and another nearby building. Open 10–6; closed Tues. The displays illustrate the past history of the city and the more recent development of its flourishing industry. Other sections are devoted to the civil war and to World War II.

Fine Arts Museum, Sovnarkomovskaya St. 11. Open 11–7; closed Fri. This museum contains works of Repin, who was born nearby in Chuguyev, including his 'Zaporozhe Cossacks writing a letter to the Sultan'. The museum has 19 halls, with the first section devoted to Russian and Ukrainian pre-revolutionary art. It also shows icons of the Novgorod, Pskov, and other schools dating from the 16th century. The second section covers Soviet art.

Planetarium, Kravtsov Pereulok 13

Pushkin Monument, Teatralnaya Sq. The monument was erected in 1904, and designed by B. Edwards.

Karazin Monument. This monument was built in 1905 and designed by Andrioletti. Vasili Karazin (1773–1842), 'the Lomonosov of the Ukraine', founded Kharkov University in 1805. It was the first university in the Ukraine and the second in Russia, and Karazin first received permission from Tsar Alexander I to organise it. He collected the necessary money from the nobles and merchants of Kharkov. Having left a letter in the palace at the time of the accession of the tsar explaining his ideas and hopes for the future of Russia, he was then summoned to St. Petersburg where he discussed educational problems with him.

Gogol Monument, Sumskaya St. This monument was erected in 1909; the author's autograph is on the lower part of the pedestal.

Kotsubinsky Monument, in the garden at the crossing of Pushkinskaya and Chernishevsky St. Mikhail Kotsubinsky (1864–1913) was a Ukrainian writer.

Shevchenko Monument, Sumskaya St., at the main entrance to Shevchenko Park. The 16.5 m. high statue and its base by M. Manizer were erected in 1935. The 16 subsidiary statues represent the history of the Ukrainian people.

Lenin Monument, Dzerzhinsky Sq. Monument by Oleinik and Vronsky unveiled in 1963.

Monument to Revolutionaries, Sovietskaya Sq. Unveiled in 1957.

Rudnev Monument, Rudnev Sq. Nikolai A. Rudnev (1894–1918) was a hero of the Civil War.

Lysenko Opera House, Rymarskaya St. 19

Musical Comedy Theatre, Karl Marx St. 28

Krupskaya Puppet Theatre, Krasin St. 3

Pushkin Russian Drama Theatre, Chernyshevsky St. 11

Regional Drama Theatre, Sverdlov St. 18

Shevchenko Ukrainian Drama Theatre, Sumskaya St. 9

Circus, Krasnovo Militsionera St. 17

Philharmonia Concert Hall, Sumskaya St. 10

Ukraina Concert Hall, Shevchenko Garden. This modern building, seating 2000, was opened in 1965.

Hippodrome Racecourse, Pervomaiskaya Sq.

Avangard Stadium, Plekhanovskaya St. 65

Dynamo Stadium, Dinamovskaya St. There is a swimming pool in the stadium.

Zoo, Sumskaya St. 35

Gorky Park, Sumskaya St. 81. There is a monument to Gorky here, and also a children's railway.

Botanical Garden, Klochkovskaya St. This garden belongs to the university.

Shevchenko Park, Sumskaya St.

Intourist Hotel and Restaurant, Lenin Prospect 21, TEL. 47–38–28, 47–32–68

Kharkov Hotel, Restaurant, and Café, Trinkler St. 2.

Spartak Hotel and Restaurant, Sverdlov St. 4.

Lux Restaurant, Sumskaya St. 3

Teatralnaya Restaurant, Sumskaya St. 2

Dynamo Restaurant, in the Dynamo Stadium

Vareniki (Dumplings) Bar, Sumskaya St. 14. These small dumplings are a national Ukrainian dish. They may be filled with various things including cottage cheese, potato, and fruit.

G.P.O., Privokzalnaya Sq. 1

Bank, Teatralnaya Sq. 1

Department Store, Rosa Luxemburg St.

KHATYN
See Minsk, p. 196

KHERSON
Population—261,000 (1970)

The town stands on the high right bank of the R. Dnieper, about 24 km. upstream from where it empties into the Black Sea. In the spring the river floods nearby to a width of 25 km. and forms numerous small rivers so that the area is known as Kherson's Venice. The population of the town is mainly composed of Ukrainians, Russians, and Jews.

Like Odessa, Kherson stands above a maze of catacombs which vary in depth from 4 to 11 m. It is believed that these date from the time of the greatest activity of the Zaporozhye Cossacks. They were then used by smugglers and members of religious sects, and finally served as emergency exits from the fortress above.

Kherson was founded in 1778 at the instigation of Prince Gregori Potemkin, from 1774 to 1776 the favourite of Catherine II. The town was laid out on the site of old fortifications and called Kherson after the ancient Greek colony of Khersones, in spite of the fact that the latter did not stand here at all. Its ruins were found near Sevastopol in the Crimea and have been excavated. The initial work on Kherson was conducted by General Ivan Hannibal (1737–1801), grandfather of the poet Alexander Pushkin. After a few years a fortress was constructed as well as a large shipyard. The building went ahead so quickly that when Catherine the Great visited the town eight years after its foundation she wrote, 'There is a mass of people, apart from the military, and they speak almost all the languages of Europe.' The speed of Kherson's growth was accelerated after Potemkin's idea of making it a free port was adopted.

The present-day Black Sea Fleet can trace its origins back to the old shipyard. The 66-gun frigate 'Glory of Catherine' was completed here in 1783, and Kherson itself was the fleet's first base. In 1783–4 the shipyard was run by the famous Russian Admiral, Fyodor Ushakov, and it was from here that in 1787 and 1792–4 Generalissimo Alexander Suvorov conducted Turkish operations.

In 1803 Kherson was designated provincial centre and grew in importance through being the point of export of corn and wool. It enjoyed the unique advantages of being close to the Black Sea and also beside a large navigable river. Russian merchants and foreign firms opened their offices here and until the foundation of other ports— Nikolayev and more particularly Odessa— Kherson grew and prospered. Then the new ports took a great deal of its trade and only after 1890, when the river had been deepened allowing ocean vessels to call in, did Kherson really revive.

For a long time the town's industries were of secondary importance but now Kherson has a highly developed shipbuilding industry. There are also agricultural machinery factories (combine harvesters for maize are their most important product) and large food-producing plants, among them the largest food cannery in the Ukraine. The textile combine, one of the biggest in the whole country, covers an area of 100 hectares (250 acres) near R. Dnieper. Part of the town's industry is located on Quarantine Island, where there are also a variety of sports facilities including boat hiring stations.

Modern Kherson is one of the Ukraine's regional centres. New buildings line the main street, Prospect Ushakova, as they do Suvorova St. and Pobedi Sq. *Prospect Ushakova* is divided into two equal parts by Svobodi (liberty) Sq., and among the new buildings along its length still stands the *old 17th-century fire-watching tower.*

Suvorova St. is closed to traffic. It was a market street in the old days and now most of the ground floor accommodation is used for shops. The street is a popular place for strolling in the evening. On the corner of Lenin and Kommunarov Streets are the impressive buildings of the one-time *Duma* (town hall), built in 1906 and now used as the local Party headquarters. Also here is the old *law court* (1893). Another venerable thoroughfare that has retained its importance is *Perekopskaya St.,* which runs beside the Dnieper for 12 km. Some old aristocratic mansions remain here, including the two-storey house formerly used by the Governor. It is marked by a plaque commemorating the revolutionary events which took place here. Among the town's larger establishments are the *Naval School* (1834), the *Tsuryupa Agricultural College* (1874), and the *Krupskaya Pedagogical College* (1917).

Kherson was occupied by the Germans from August 1941 until March 1944, but after the war it was quick to recover. The town's holiday facilities are good and it is said to have 300 sunny days a year. The fame of the local melons and watermelons is an additional attraction to visitors.

The *Fortress*, Perekopskaya St., by the river, a little to the north-west of the town. It was abandoned as a military stronghold in 1835 but the earth walls, the Mosovskiye and the Ochakovskiye Gates are preserved as examples of 18th-century fortifications. Besides the building of the former arsenal there also remains here the *Church of Our Saviour* (1781). One of the inscriptions reads: 'Dedicated to the Saviour of Mankind by Catherine II'. The empress's favourite, Prince Potemkin, was buried here but her son, Paul I, ordered that the tomb be secretly opened in 1798. Potemkin's remains were removed and the vault blocked up again. There are a number of valuable icons in this church, two of which by the portrait-painter Borovikovsky (1757–1825) represent Catherine II and Prince Potemkin. The building is now used to store books belonging to the local library, but with special permission it can be visited. The six sculptures set in niches in the outside wall are by Zamarayev (1758–1823). Most of the monuments and tombstones are of those who fell during the 1788 siege of the nearby Turkish fortress, Ochakov.

Greko-Sofiiskaya Church, Krasnoflotskaya St. 13. This church is dedicated to the Nativity of the Virgin but usually referred to as the Greek Church. Its iconostasis of carved walnut, made in Cyprus, is famous although four rows of new icons have taken the places of the originals. The church was built in 1780 and is open for services.

Svyatodukhovsky Cathedral (of the Holy Spirit), Dekabristov St. This cathedral is also open for services. It was built in 1835 and is often called Privoznaya (brought-in) Church because it stood near the market where goods were sold that had been brought in to town.

Local Museum, Prospect Ushakova 16. Open 10–5, closed Wed. Among other items are objects which belonged to the Scythians and Sarmatians from the ancient Greek colony-town of Olvia. A more modern treasure is the Key of the City of Potsdam, a Soviet Army trophy.

Natural History Museum, Gorky St. 5. Open 10–5, closed Wed.

Art Pavilion, Svobody Sq.

Yuri Gagarin Planetarium, Suvorova St. 29. Built in 1960.

Howard's House, Suvorova St. 14. John Howard (1727–90) was an English philanthropist and prison-reformer who caught typhus while visiting a local hospital here and never recovered. In 1890, on the centenary of his death, a memorial plaque was affixed to the house on the second floor of which he used to live. As well as the house, an obelisk of grey granite on Ushakova Prospect remains here to his memory. It was erected on the order of Alexander I in 1828 and bears a plaque saying, 'Howard died on January 20th 1790, in his 55th year.' Howard was once Mayor of Bedford; there is a bust of him in Westminster Abbey.

Lenin Monument, Lenin St.

Karl Marx Monument, in Marx Garden

Bust of Suvorov, Suvorova St. The bust, a copy of an old one by Rukavishnikov, was unveiled in 1950. The two-storey house where the General-issimo lived from 1792–4 stands at Suvorova St. 3.

Bust of Shevchenko, in the Oak Grove, the trees of which were planted in 1964 to commemorate the 150th anniversary of his birth.

Ushakov Monument, Ushakova Prospect. The monument to Admiral Fedor Ushakov (1744–1817) is by Kravchenko and Chubin and was unveiled in 1957.

Musical and Drama Theatre, Gorky St. 7

Lenin Park, Ushakova Prospect. This is Kherson's oldest park. It was laid out at the end of the 18th century and known as Alexander Park. An ancient oak stands in the centre and outside the main gate is a statue of Lenin.

Lenkomsomol Park, Perekopskaya St., near the old fortress. The 19-m. obelisk honours the first Young Communists of the town. There is an amusements area here and the Otdikh (rest) Café.

Kiev Hotel & Restaurant, Ushakova Prospect 47, TEL. 286–12

Pervomaiski Hotel and Kherson Restaurant, Lenin St. 26,

Kherson Restaurant, Lenin St. 26

Dnieper Restaurant, at the seaport

G.P.O., Gorky St. 54

Bank, Komsomolskaya St. 21

Telegraph Office, Druzhby St. 4

Department Store, Ushakova Prospect 26/2

Market, Perekopskaya St

The *Avangard Stadium* can seat 30,000.

On Quarantine Island is one of the oldest *yacht clubs* in the Ukraine, founded in 1907. Also on the Island is a good *bathing beach*, just as there is on either bank of the river.

Not far from Kherson, but on the opposite side of the Dnieper, is the small holiday resort of *Tsurupinsk*.

From Kherson it is a drive of 129 km. to reach the *wild life reserve* of Askania-Nova. The road there passes through Novaya Kakhovka and Kakhova, lying first of all beside R. Dnieper and then crossing it by running over the top of the dam of the hydro-power station.

Novaya Kakhovka

Population—30,000 (1970)

In 1950 the decision was taken to build a new hydro-power station on R. Dnieper 10 km. away from the old town of Kakhovka. So it was that on the site of the little village of Kluchevoye, where only a few fishermen used to live, New Kakhovka was founded.

Construction of the hydro-power station began in 1951 and continued for five years. The gigantic reservoir, now known as the Kakhovka Sea, was not completely filled until 1957. It covers an area of 2150 sq. km., has an average depth of 8·4 m. and a maximum depth of 36 m. and its capacity is 18·2 cu. km. The reservoir stretches from Novaya Kakhovka to Zaporozhye and is used for the irrigation of the southern Ukraine and the northern part of the Crimea.

The hydro-power station is of 312,000 kilowatt capacity, and supplies the Dnieper area and the Donbas coal-mining region. It is situated on the Dnieper Rapids, 90 km. upstream from the mouth of R. Dnieper.

The town stands on the river's left bank, connected by rail and road via the dam with the opposite bank. It was built as an example of a new type of planning; the streets follow the sweep of the river and are lined with two- and three-storey houses. The residential, working, and shopping areas are on the higher ground, while the lower slopes leading down to the river consist of parks. Wide stone steps lead down from the impressive Palace of Culture through the park to R. Dnieper where there is a bathing beach and boats can be hired.

The town's principal street is Dneprovsky Prospect and the chief local industries are food production and electro-machine building.

War Memorial, Dneprovsky Prospect. Commemorating those who fell in the civil war and during World War II.

Civil War Memorial, near the dam, on the Novaya Kakhovka side

There is a *Summer Theatre* in the park; *Energiya Stadium* can seat 5000.

Druzhba (friendship) Hotel & Restaurant, Dneprovsky Prospect 14, TEL. 3–09, 3–10

Tavriya Restaurant, Dneprovsky Prospect

G.P.O. & Telegraph Office, Lenin St. 24

Bank, Dneprovsky Prospect 15

Kakhovka

Population—25,000 (1970)

Kakhovka also lies on the left bank of R. Dnieper. It was founded in the 18th century on the site of the Tatar fortress of Islam-Kermen.

In Soviet times it was of greatest importance

during the civil war when it was used as the bridge-head before the capture of the Crimea in 1920, when the Crimean peninsula was the last strong-hold of the anti-Bolshevik army.

The principal industries are car-repairing, food production, and the manufacture of electro-welding equipment.

Chapel, Pushkinskaya St. 94

Local Museum, Lenin St. 12. Open 10–7 Tues., Thurs., and Sat. Most of the exhibits illustrate the story of the attack on nearby Perekop in November 1920, which preceded the taking of the Crimea by the Red Army.

Bust of the Poet Pushkin, Pushkinskaya St. Pushkin visited Kakhovka in 1820, and the bust was unveiled in 1937.

Frunze Monument, on the embankment of the lake (which is in fact a reservoir). Mikhail Frunze was a famous Bolshevik who was a commander on the southern front during the civil war. The monu-ment, with an inscription reading, 'From the In-habitants of Kakhovka', was unveiled in 1957.

There is a bathing beach and boats can be hired.

Tavriya Hotel & Kakhovka Restaurant, Karl Marx St. 138

Tourist Restaurant, outside the town, beside the road leading on to Novaya Kakhovka

G.P.O., Karl Marx St.

Bank, Karl Marx St. 118

Department Store, Lenin St.

Filling Station, by the road leading out of town

Askania-Nova

Population—6,000 (1970)

This village lies 61 km. by a good road from Novo-Alekseyevka. It is best known for its wild life reserve.

The territory of 50,000 hectares (125,000 acres) was purchased in 1828 by a German noble, Duke Angalt-Ketenski, and he founded a small settle-ment there in 1841, naming it after his native estate of Askania in Germany. The steppe was used for breeding sheep and horses. But the estate really became profitable when it was sold to another German family, the Falz-Feins, who, with up to 400,000 sheep, became known as 'sheep-breeding kings' in the southern Ukraine.

In 1874 Friedrich Falz-Fein founded a little zoo which was called the Tierpark. Soon he began to buy animals from different parts of the world—ostriches from Africa, emus from Australia, zebu and antelopes from India. Then, from being a simple collection, the zoo took on scientific aims: the acclimatisation of animals and the preserv-ation of rare species from extermination.

The Ivanov Institute of Hybridisation and Ac-climatisation was founded in 1932 and called after Mikhail Ivanov (1871–1935), an Academician who was responsible for breeding fine-fleeced sheep and also a variety of pig which does well on the Ukrainian steppe. The Institute's main work is the domestication of valuable wild animals and cross-breeding them with other domestic animals. Wars have taken a heavy toll of the zoo's popula-tion. During the civil war the zebra hybrids were used to pull gun carriages and after the German occupation (1941–3) only 20% of the animals were left.

Now there are about 100 different species of animals and birds including 4 kinds of zebra, 6 dif-ferent antelopes, 3 types of ostrich, 5 kinds of swans, and both American and European bison. The animals are all either cloven-hoofed or mem-bers of the horse family, pride of place belonging to the Przevalsky wild horse from Mongolia. Ani-mals and birds are handed over to other zoos in the Soviet Union and exchanges are made with zoos in foreign countries. The local hospital is making useful experiments with antelope milk in curing ulcers and various other illnesses.

Special permission is required to see the animals living free on the open steppe.

Natural History Museum and Zoo, Askania-Nova, both open from 8–4.

Botanical Garden, open from 9–7. The garden was laid out between 1887 and 1902 when seeds and plants were brought mainly from Odessa and Riga. The landscaping was by Dufresne, a French landscape gardener, and the territory covers 68 hectares (170 acres) including a beautiful lake with an island and a grotto of stone. 120 different trees and bushes have been acclimatised on the dry Tavrida steppe and the garden is often called an 'emerald oasis'.

At the entrance stands a water-tower built in 1892–3 in Gothic style. Here also is a monument to 16 paratroopers shot on this spot in 1941.

Askania Hotel & Cafe, Krasnoarmeiskaya St.

KHIVA

See Urgench, p. 314

KHVALYNSK

Population—17,000

This town is situated in the extreme north of the Saratov region, in an area known for its sanatoria and rest homes.

The first settlement appeared in 1606 in place of a sentry post. It was a village called Sosnovy Ostrov (Pine Island) because of a large pine wood which belonged to Moscow's Chudov (Miracle) Monastery. The main occupation of the villagers was fishing. They sent their sturgeon to the monastery and even to the tsar's court.

In 1699 a fortress was built here upon the orders of Peter the Great to protect the settlement from the nomads across the Volga.

The place became known as a hide-out of those people, like the Old Believers, who did not accept the Russian Orthodox Church reforms carried out by Patriarch Nikon in the middle of the 17th cen-tury.

In 1720 Peter the Great gave this area to the Tatar nobles in reward for their frontier services. In 1780 the Saratov Province was formed by de-cree of Catherine II, and Sosnovy Ostrov became a town. It was called Khvalynsk, the old name for the Caspian Sea.

Mikhail Suslov, member of the Politburo of the Central Committee of the Communist Party, was secretary of the local branch of the Young Communist League till 1920; his father had been local party secretary in 1918.

Now Khvalynsk is a district centre, a pleasant town with plenty of trees and flowers. It has food and electrical industries, and also large canneries.

There is a local museum and a picture gallery, and theatrical performances are given in the House of Culture.

KIEV

Population—1,632,000 (1970)
Capital of the Ukrainian Soviet Socialist Republic

UKRAINE

In Ukranian: Ukrayina
The Ukraine is situated in the south-west of the European part of the U.S.S.R. and shares its western frontier with Rumania, Hungary, Czechoslovakia, and Poland. After the Russian Federation, its population of 47,136,000 (1970) is the second largest in the U.S.S.R., and in size it is the third largest republic (after the Russian Federation and Kazakhstan) covering an area of 601,000 sq. km. Forty-six per cent of the population is urban. The majority are Ukrainians (76%), then come Russians (18%), Jews (2%), and others (4%). By nationality the Ukrainians are Eastern Slavs, closely related to the Russians and the Belorussians.

Since the Kievan period of Ukrainian history some distinctive features have developed in local speech. Now the Ukrainian language which is similar to Russian and Belorussian is used. With the exception of Lvov, Russian is spoken mostly in the big cities.

The Ukraine was the cradle of the Kiev state. It was in Kiev that Christianity was introduced into Russia, when Prince Vladimir had his subjects baptized in the R. Dnieper in 988. After the Tatar invasion and the decline of the Kievan State (13th–14th century) the Ukraine changed masters several times, being held by Russia and Poland. Then it was devastated by the Crimean Tatars. In the 16th century Ukrainian hatred rose against the Polish landlords who were unpopular because they took the most fertile land for themselves and tried to introduce Catholicism. In 1654 the Cossacks, the most militant members of the Ukrainian population at the time, led by Hetman (Cossack military leader) Bogdan Khmelnitsky, won independence from Poland and established a state of their own which occupied the central part of the present-day Ukraine. Then, as the new state could not possibly stand alone, it chose to unite with Muscovy, the agreement being signed at the end of 1654.

Nationalist feelings and demands for the autonomy of the Ukraine developed at the beginning of the 20th century. During the civil war of 1918–22

the Ukraine was one of the most fiercely contested areas. It was under both German and White Russian occupation, and had different nationalist governments. The Ukrainian Soviet Republic was first proclaimed in December 1917 and in 1922 it was one of the four original republics to form the U.S.S.R.

In 1939 the western part of the Ukraine was included in the republic, followed by Transcarpathia in 1945 (formerly part of Hungary and Czechoslovakia) and the Crimea in 1954 (formerly part of the Russian Federation).

The Ukraine can be divided into three soil and vegetation zones: (1) mixed forests on the Belorussian boundary in the north, (2) wooded steppe with oak and beech forests, and (3) steppe. The steppe zones are notable for their predominantly fertile black earth. The moderate continental climate is much warmer than that of central Russia, and the southern coast of the Crimea has a Mediterranean climate.

The Ukraine is highly developed both industrially and agriculturally. The main crops are wheat, barley, rye, oats, sugarbeet, and sunflowers. Between 1910 and 1914 the Ukraine yielded 80% of Europe's sugar. There are also many orchards. The main industries include engineering, metallurgy, coal-mining, and chemicals. It is also very rich in natural deposits which include coal, iron-ore, natural gas, manganese oil, and mercury.

The major cities are Kiev (capital), Kharkov, Lvov, Odessa, Donetsk, Dnepropetrovsk, and Lugansk.

Some words of Ukrainian:

hello	dobri dyen
I am a tourist	ya toorist
please	bood laska
thank you	dyakooyoo
yes	tuk
no	nee
good	dobri
bad	poháno
I don't understand	ya ne razoomayoo
I need an interpreter	meni potriben tloomach
goodbye	do pobáchenya

Kiev

The Ukrainian capital has long covered a series of wooded hills on the right bank of the R. Dnieper.

Away above me, towering high,
Old Kiev guards her river.
At the steep wood's foot doth Dnieper lie,
His water rippling silver.

The city now has an area of over 75,000 hectares which also includes the industrial district of Darnitsa which has grown up on the left bank of the river. This region is connected with the rest of Kiev by the Paton Bridge.

Kiev is said to have got its name from the first

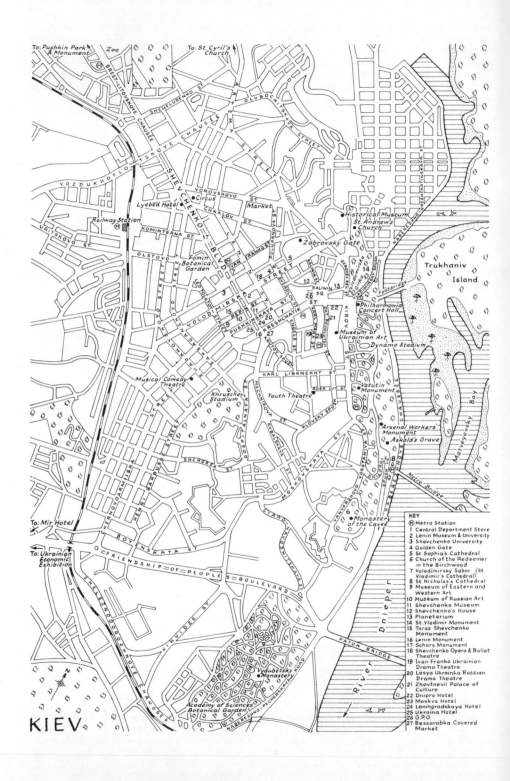

prince of the Slav tribe, the Polyani, who lived in this area. He was called Ki, and with his brothers he founded the town. In 864 Askold and Duir made themselves masters of the region and the city-state of Kiev grew and prospered from 882 until 1169. Mostly due to the hilly site, the town's early development was unusual. It consisted of three separate settlements. The Upper City (Staro-Kiev) overlooked the Podol, meaning 'low', which was the trading area close to the Dnieper. The third settlement was also on high ground above the river, but set at some distance behind Staro-Kiev; this was Pechersk, where vast natural caves are to be found. Hermits first lived in them. Later the Monastery of the Caves was founded, using them. In spite of these divisions, Kiev was strong enough to become the capital of the country and the trading centre of Eastern Europe. Situated on the navigable River Dnieper, Kiev had trading relations with the countries of Western Europe and the Baltic as well as Armenia, Constantinople, and Arabia. Its importance gave rise to a Russian proverb, reminiscent of 'All roads lead to Rome', saying, 'Your tongue will lead you to Kiev.'

But it is with the reign of Prince Vladimir (978–1015) that the 'Golden Age' of Kiev begins. In 988 Prince Vladimir introduced Christianity into Russia, but his choice of Christianity as the national religion was not an easy one. According to the chronicles he was a violent man, 'insatiable in vice' and a fanatical heathen who had offered thousands of human sacrifices. But he was also a thinker, and although there is no record of his reasons for seeking a new religion, it is fairly clear that as an intelligent monarch he saw that the peoples who remained outside the world's great religions never achieved any degree of culture, civilisation, or political power. The legend runs that Vladimir considered many religions before finally choosing Christianity. The Jewish faith was admirable, but the thought that its followers had been scattered throughout the earth for their sins distressed the Russian prince. Islam he rejected on the grounds that total abstinence was incompatible with survival in a cold climate. Roman Catholicism he could not accept because he himself would have become subservient to the Pope. The emissaries Prince Vladimir sent to find out about the Greek Orthodox Church reported on their return: 'the Greeks led us to the edifices where they worship their God; and we knew not whether we were in heaven or on earth. For on earth there is no such splendour or beauty, and we are at a loss how to describe it. We only know that God dwells there among men, and their service is fairer than the ceremonies of other nations. We can never forget that Beauty.' Accordingly, Vladimir was baptized, married the Princess Anna, sister of the Greek Emperor, and adopted Christianity as the religion for the country as a whole. Mass baptisms took place in the R. Dnieper even in mid-winter, and Prince Vladimir was canonised for his part in the conversions.

The acceptance of Christianity brought Kiev into closer contact with Byzantium and Kiev adopted both the autocratic government and the architecture of Constantinople.

There were many rival city-states and constant wars raged between them. In 1169 Kiev gave way to the city of Vladimir, and the title of capital was lost (at this early date Moscow was still a small settlement of no consequence). After its early period of glory Kiev fell into a decline. A series of fires devastated the city during the 12th century, and in 1240 Kiev was plundered by the Tatars. An Italian traveller who visited the city six years later wrote that most of the churches had been burnt and that only 200 houses remained. Kiev remained under the Tatar yoke until 1320 and was invaded again in the 15th century. It was also badly damaged by Lithuanian and Polish forces and was under Lithuanian rule from 1320 to 1455.

Kiev only recovered again after the unification of the Ukraine and Russia in 1654 when it was proclaimed that they 'should be one for ever'. It then became a city of merchants, and many magnificent buildings were erected in the 17th and 18th centuries, a large number of them in Baroque style. It spread along the river and its original three settlements were quickly surrounded by houses and other buildings, but it was not until the 19th century that Kiev was elevated to the status of provincial centre, and in 1798 the first of the annual contract fairs was held there. These brought merchants to Kiev from all over Europe, but the city's growth was temporarily halted by a series of fires, the most disastrous of which was in 1811. It raged for several days and Podol, the most densely inhabited part of Kiev, suffered particularly badly. This is one reason for the lack of ancient monuments in that region; the other is that it was an area never surrounded by adequate defences and which had always been subject to terrible devastation by invaders.

In May 1812, the general reconstruction of the city began, and by the middle of the 19th century the central part of Kiev had wide, well-planned streets with plenty of attractive buildings lining them. Kiev became modernized and a number of factories were built. In 1848–53 one of the largest bridges in Russia was built over the Dnieper by an English engineer. In 1892 the first trains in Russia (the second in Europe) began to run from Kiev, and by 1888 a telephone service was in operation. As well as being the administrative and economic centre of the south-west part of the Russian Empire, Kiev was also the hub of the Ukrainian literary and national movement. By 1917 its population had reached half a million.

After the October Revolution and during the 1917–20 civil war, Kiev was the seat of several transitory Ukrainian governments. It was occupied by the Germans for a short while in 1918. When the Ukraine joined the Soviet Union in 1922, Kharkov was made the capital and the seat of government was only transferred to Kiev in 1934.

In spite of severe damage during the Second World War, when 195,000 Kievans lost their lives, and despite the drastic rebuilding necessary after it, the three old divisions of the city still exist, and they have retained their individuality.

Kreschatik is the city's central street, and its busiest. In the old days the site of the street was a deep, wooded valley crossed by ravines. It was known as Kreschata, meaning 'crossed', and from this the street's present name is derived. The street is less than 2 km. long but over 350 buildings were destroyed in this part of Kiev during the war. Afterwards its width was doubled and it was completely rebuilt. Very few of the old houses remain. No. 8 was the Petersburg bank and was designed by Benois. No. 10 was the Volgo-Kama Bank, and No. 15 was, and still is, an arcade of shops. Both the latter were designed by Andreyev and all three were built in 1911–14.

Kirov St. runs through the Staro-Kiev part of the city, between Kreschatik and the riverside parks. Here the building of the *Ukrainian Parliament* stands out with its six-columned portico and its great glass dome. It was built in 1939 and designed by Zabolotny. Next to it, behind ornamental iron railings, is the former Tsar's Palace, built in 1742 following Rastrelli's designs but enlarged and reconstructed in 1870. It is used partly by the Supreme Soviet and partly as a guest house for important visitors to the Ukrainian capital. This area is still known by its ancient name of Lipki (lime trees). It used to be the old aristocratic quarter and a number of the nobility's ornately decorated mansions remain.

Volodimirska St. runs parallel to Kreschatik on the side furthest from the Dnieper. Most of the ancient monuments of Kiev are to be found here. Apart from the best known, including the Golden Gate and St. Sophia's Cathedral (see below), there is a fine *mansion* built in the 1850s by Beretti. It is now No. 54 and is the seat of the Praesidium of the Ukrainian Academy of Sciences. No. 57, now the *Lenin Museum*, was built as a pedagogical museum by Alyoshin in 1911 and reconstructed in 1938. The *university building, No. 58*, was designed by Beretti and constructed in 1837–42.

Apart from the usual forms of public transport, a *funicular railway* runs down from Volodimirska Girka to Podol. It was first built in 1905. Kievans are also proud to have the Soviet Union's third metro. It was opened in November 1960, and the stations already operating are called Vokzal, Universitetskaya, Kreschatik, Arsenalnaya, Dnieper, Polytechnical Insitute, and Bolshevik.

Kiev is unlike most of the ancient cities and towns of Russia in that there are no obvious remains of a kremlin or a fortified citadel. The ruins of the Golden Gate are almost the only reminders of the way the city had to fight for its very existence.

The *Golden Gate* is in the centre of the town. The two parallel walls which one can see today were built in 1037 by Yaroslav the Wise to support the main entrance arch into the earthen-walled city of Kiev. The arch was surmounted by the small Church of the Annunciation and its construction is said to have been inspired by Constantinople's Golden Gate.

St. Sophia's Cathedral (Sofiisky Sobor), Volodimirska St. 24. Open 10–6, closed Thurs.

The cathedral was dedicated in 1037 by Yaroslav the Wise in gratitude for the victory he gained on this site (then an open meadow outside the city walls) over the Pechenegi, an invading tribe from the east. It was here that the country's earliest historical chronicles were written and the first library organised.

The design of the cathedral was influenced by St. Sophia in Constantinople, but the Kievan cathedral also contains elements of early wooden architecture. When first built, the cathedral was a large five-aisled building with an open gallery on 3 sides, and 13 cupolas. The first Metropolitan of Kiev, Ilarion, wrote of the cathedral in 1037 that 'this church has roused the astonishment and praise of all peoples around, and nothing like unto it can be found in the breadth of the land from east to west.'

Interesting mosaics and frescoes are to be seen in the central part of the cathedral and in the main dome. The latter contains a mosaic representation of Christ the All-Ruler, the Pantokrator; not the realistic Christ of the Gospels, but a being very closely akin to the other two members of the Trinity. The archangels surrounding him are dressed in the costume of the imperial court at Byzantium and hold the symbols of the imperial office, the orb and standard. In the apse of the cathedral is the magnificent Virgin Orans, another symbolic figure in mosaic. She is neither the Queen of Heaven nor the Mother of God, but a symbol of the earthly Church interceding for mankind. Both the figure and the splendid golden background survived the ups and downs of the cathedral so that a legend grew up about the wall's indestructibility and the Virgin Orans became an increasingly important object of worship. Below the Virgin Orans are depicted the twelve apostles receiving the eucharist and below them are the Fathers of the Church.

In the cathedral's central aisle is a portrait of the family of Yaroslav the Wise and on the walls of the southern and northern towers are pictures of entertainment, hunting, and battle scenes. In the north-eastern part of the cathedral is a marble tomb wherein 1054 Yaroslav the Wise was buried. The iconostasis was installed in 1754 and is the work of local craftsmen.

The cathedral was partly ruined by Tatars and Mongols and was further damaged while the Poles and Lithuanians were ruling the region. It was restored in 1636 and reconstructed at the beginning of the 18th century when six new domes were *added. After the* unification of the Ukraine and Russia in 1654, it was in this cathedral that the Kievans pledged their oath of loyalty. It was also here that Peter the Great celebrated his victory over the Swedish army in 1709.

Of the 18th-century buildings, the most outstanding is the 4-tier *bell-tower* near the main entrance. It was erected between 1744 and 1752 and is 78 m. high. Also of interest is the *Zabrovsky Gate*, built in 1746 as the main entrance to the Metropolitan's house. It is decorated with elaborate detail and stucco ornament, but has lost its original proportions as the ground level has risen considerably during the past 200 years. *The Metropolitan's House* was built at the beginning of the 18th century in the style of Ukrainian baroque. To the south of the cathedral is the *refectory*, built in 1722–30.

The wall surrounding the cathedral was built in the 1740s.

The Sophia Cathedral is now a museum which also displays the architecture of the other old Russian towns of Novgorod and Chernigov and local archaeological finds. All its precincts are kept as an architectural and historical monument.

The *Monastery of the Caves* (Pecherskaya Lavra, so called from the word 'peschera' meaning 'cave'), Sichneve Povstannya St. 21. Open 10–5, closed Tues. The caves are only open from 12–5.

Every visitor to Kiev should certainly try to see this monastery, described as the place

Where the darkness of the silent caves
Is lovelier than the royal halls.

It was founded in 1051 by two monks, Antony and Theodosius, and through the centuries underground churches were built. In some cases the caves were natural and then the monks themselves excavated further. Some of the members of the community lived their lives there underground and when they died their bodies remained in their cells. Due to the chemical properties of the soil and the temperature, the bodies became mummified and they are still to be seen. 'The whole Orthodox world bows before the relics of the saints of the monastery; in times past and today, undiminished their blessing emanates upon all who come to their tombs in faith and love.'

From the time of Peter the Great and throughout the 18th and 19th centuries almost all the tsars and tsarinas came to Kiev and made lavish gifts to the Lavra, the other monasteries, and the churches of the city. The monastery became exceedingly wealthy and in the 18th century it owned 13 smaller monasteries, 7 towns, 189 villages, and three glass factories.

The entrance gate is surmounted by the *Trinity Church*, which was built in 1108 and contains frescoes and a wooden iconostasis dating from the 18th century. The walls of the *Upper Monastery*, built between 1698 and 1701, run from this gateway.

Inside, a little way on from the entrance gate, a much smaller archway on the left leads through to an enclosed corner of the monastery grounds surrounding the 17th-century Church of St. Nicholas, built in Ukrainian Baroque style. It now serves as a lecture hall, but its appearance is good; it was restored in 1956–7, right up to its blue, star-bedecked dome.

The five-domed *All Saint's Church* by another gateway was built in the 17th century by the architect Aksamitov. The main court of the Upper Monastery centres around the ruins of the *Cathedral of the Assumption (Uspensky Sobor)*, built in 1073–89 and blown up by the Germans during the Second World War. Most of the surrounding houses date from the 18th century. In some of these houses were the printing works of the monastery which printed its first book in 1617 and continued to function until the revolution. The architectural complex of the Upper Monastery is completed by the *bell-tower* which was built in 1731–45 by the St. Petersburg architect Shedel. It is 96.5 m. high and the highest bell-tower in Russia. The four tiers of the tower are all decorated with pillars and pilasters. A flight of 374 steps leads to the top of the tower. In spite of the fact that the tower was constructed in comparatively recent times, there is nevertheless a legend about its construction. It is supposed to have been built by twelve brothers who are now buried in the caves. During construction the tower sank slowly into the earth, thus obviating the use of ladders or scaffolding. When it was completed it sprang out of the earth again in a single night.

The way down to the caves leads past the *refectory church* which was built in 1893 on the site of an older stone building. It was restored in 1956 and is used as an anti-religious museum at present.

Near the walls of the refectory are the graves of the Cossack leaders Kotchubei and Iskra, who were executed in 1708 by Ivan Mazepa because they informed Peter the Great of the Ukrainian Hetman's plan to separate the Ukraine from Russia with the help of Charles XII of Sweden and the Zaporozhye Cossacks; the plan was defeated the following year when the Russian army won the Battle of Poltava.

The last diversion before going down to the caves is to walk onto a wide stone terrace on the right which has a most impressive view over the wooded slopes, the wide river, the spreading suburbs of Kiev, and the countryside beyond.

The *Nearer Caves*, sometimes referred to as *St. Antony's Caves*, contain 73 tombs and 3 underground churches. In the *Further Caves*, or *St. Theodosius's Caves*, there are 3 more churches and 47 tombs. They are quite separate from each other and both are reached by walking along covered galleries. The *Belfry of the Further Caves* was built in the 18th century by a serf-architect named Stefan Kovnir who also designed one of the houses in the Upper Monastery.

From 1926 to 1964 the whole territory was open to the public as a museum, with monks caring for it and acting as guides. On entering the caves visitors were asked to purchase a small candle instead of an admission ticket. Now, however, the monks have gone, there is electric light throughout and the insides of the caves have been painted. It is now only possible to visit the Nearer Caves. The mummified bodies still have their names attached, but many of them are further described on new anti-religious plaques. The most famous tomb of all is probably that of the chronicler Nestor who died in 1115.

A little to the north of the monastery stands the early 12th-century *Church of the Redeemer in the Birchwood (Tserkov Spasa-na-Berestove)*. The eastern part dates from 1640–3 and contains frescoes of that time. The older part was formerly a sepulchre for the princes of Kiev and in 1157 Prince Yuri Dolgoruki, who had founded Moscow ten years earlier, was buried here. The grey marble tomb now commemorating him was installed in 1947. It weighs six tons. The church is open as a museum.

Vydubetsky Monastery is situated on the higher bank of R. Dnieper, south of the Monastery of the Caves and in part of the land belonging to the Academy of Sciences' Botanical Garden. This architectural complex was founded in 1070–7 by Prince Vsevolod, and there is a story attached to its unusual name. After the mass conversion of Kievans to Christianity, the powerful pagan idol, Perun, was thrown into the Dnieper. He was carved out of wood but his head was silver and his beard was gold, and apparently the weight of the metal kept him underwater. For some time his distressed followers ran along the river bank shouting, 'Vydubai, come out of the water, O God!'; a mile further down he did in fact rise to the surface but there was much confusion and fighting on the bank as the newly baptised Christians were all for letting him continue his journey downstream. It was from the shouts of 'vydubai' that the whole area was thereafter known as Vydubichi, as was the monastery also.

Of *St. Michael's Cathedral* (1070–88) only the western side remains but it has good frescoes. The other side of the building fell into ruins in the 15th and 16th centuries following a landslide. *St. George's Church* (1696–1701) is a five-domed masterpiece of Ukrainian architecture. The refectory dates from the beginning of the 18th century and the belfry was built in 1730. Between St. Michael's and St. George's is the grave of Konstantin Ushinsky (1824–70), Russian teacher and educationalist. The buildings have recently been restored and some are used as storehouses.

Mikhailovsky-Zlatoverkhii Monastery (St. Michael-with-the-Golden-Roof), Geroyev Revolutsii St. The monastery was founded in 1051. Its cathedral, founded by Prince Svyatopolk in 1108, is Kiev's second most important construction of this period after Sofiisky Sobor. Part of a mosaic of the Last Supper remains.

St. Andrew's Church, Andreevsky Spusk. This church was built in 1744–53 in Baroque style by Rastrelli, renowned court architect of St. Petersburg and master of the Baroque. It stands on Andreevsky Hill, the highest point of Old Kiev, overlooking Podol, the river and the plain to the east, where according to tradition the Apostle Andrew, who first preached the Gospel in Russia, erected a cross.

The church stands on a platform reached by a broad flight of steps. It was built at the command of Peter the Great's religious daughter, Elizaveta. It is outstanding for its perfect proportions as well as for the way in which it makes use of the hilltop upon which it stands. Today the domes are silvered and the walls washed in turquoise and white. Inside the iconostasis is interesting; it was made under the guidance of portrait-painter Antropov who was also responsible for the frescoes.

Services are held in the church.

Volodimirsky Sobor (St. Vladimir's Cathedral), Shevchenko Boulevard 20. This cathedral with seven cupolas was built in Byzantine style in 1863–96 by Beretti and Gernhardt to commemorate the 900th anniversary of Christianity in Russia. Sparro was another architect who participated in the church later. The completed building shows a diversity of styles which resulted from frequent changes of plan. The original idea was to follow the lines of ancient Russian architecture. It is 49 m. long, 28 m. wide and 50 m. in height. The windows are framed with fine stone ornamentation. The walls bear some interesting murals in imitation of Byzantine style. The decorations were carried out under the supervision of Professor Prakhov, a specialist in the history of art, and include some paintings by famous Russian artists, Vasnetsov and Nesterov among others. In the central aisle is a painting called 'The Christening of Russia', showing Prince Vladimir and Princess Olga. The paintings were restored after the Second World War. It is worth while attending a service here to hear one of the best church choirs in Russia.

St. Nicholas's Cathedral, near Askold's grave (see below) overlooking the Dnieper, but situated a little higher and nearer to the Monastery of the Caves. The cathedral was built in 1696 and is a good example of 17th-century church architecture.

St. Cyril's Church, Frunze St. 103. This church was founded in the northern outskirts of Kiev in 1146 as the main church of St. Cyril's Monastery, itself founded in 1140 by Prince Vsevolod. It has been restored several times and its present shape dates from the 18th-century reconstruction by Beretti. The 12th-century frescoes were restored by Prakhov and Vrubel. It now serves the Pavlov Mental Hospital and is closed to visitors.

St. Flor's (Florovsky) Convent, Podol, Florivska St. 6/8. This convent dates from the foundation of the Church of St. Flor and St. Laura near Kiselevka Hill in the 16th century. It was exceedingly prosperous at the end of the 18th century but a disastrous fire in 1811 burned down most of the buildings.

The *Church of the Ascension (Voznesenskaya Tserkov)* is open for services. Opposite stands the 17th–18th-century refectory. The bell-tower was built between 1740 and 1821. The *Resurrection*

Church which is white with six columns, was built in 1824 by Melensky for the use of the hospital. Both this church and St. Nicholas's Church are now closed.

Convent of the Intercession (Pokrova), Bekhterevsky Pereulok 15, near Artyema St. The convent was founded in 1889, and in the same year the Pokrovsky Church was built. In St. Nicholas's Church, built in 1896–1911, is the miracle-working icon of Our Lady of Pochayev. Today the convent is the home of 140 nuns and some of the buildings on the convent's territory are used by a state hospital.

There are two other churches in Podol, the *Bratskaya*, or *Epiphany Church* (1710), which is closed, and the *Church of the Prophet Elijah*, which is open for services.

Roman Catholic Church, Chervonoarmeiskaya St. 75. Built in 1913 and recently restored.

Synagogue, Schekovitskaya St. 29. The building was constructed in the mid-nineteenth century and is still open for services.

Museum of Eastern and Western Art, Repin St. 15. Open 10–5, closed Fri. The collection includes Byzantine painting of the 6th to 8th centuries; Italian Renaissance art including works by Bellini, Tiepolo, and Guardi; Flemish and Dutch art of the 15th to 18th centuries including works by Frans Hals and Rembrandt; and works by Velasquez, Goya, Bouchet, and David.

Museum of Russian Art, Repin St. 9. Open 10–5, closed Thurs. The section on Russian art from the 12th to 17th centuries includes icons of the Novgorod, Moscow, and Stroganov schools. The 18th–19th-century section contains works by Brullov, Ivanov, Shishkin, and Repin. The first quarter of the 20th century is represented by Vrubel, Serov, and Korovin among others. Another section shows Soviet art. There is an interesting collection of 18th–20th-century porcelain, glass, and crystal.

Museum of Ukrainian Art, Kirov St. 29. Open 11–6, closed Fri. The museum was built under the supervision of Academician Nikolayev in 1898–1900. It was supposed to resemble an ancient Greek temple and the huge granite steps, over 17 m. wide, which lead to the main façade have lions at each side. The six-columned portico in antique style is decorated with a sculptured group called 'The Triumph of Art'. The first section of the museum is devoted to Ukrainian art of the 15th–19th centuries, and the second section to works by Soviet Ukrainian artists.

Historical Museum, Volodimirska St. 2. Open 10–6, closed Wed. The museum contains over 500,000 exhibits dating from prehistoric times to the present day. Of particular interest are the sections on the Scythians and Kievan Rus. A branch of the historical museum is housed in the Monastery of the Caves. Open 10.30–5, closed Tues. Here are examples of 17th- to 20th-century fabrics and 16th- to 19th-century handwork. There are also wood carvings, metalwork, and ceramics on view, all displayed to demonstrate Ukrainian art

work. Particularly interesting are the krashenki, intricately painted eggs to be exchanged at Easter time. Some rooms here are reserved for temporary art exhibitions.

Shevchenko Museum, Shevchenko Boulevard 12. Open 10–5, closed Mon. The museum, which was opened in 1949, contains 24 halls with over 800 works of art by the poet Shevchenko who was trained at the St. Petersburg Academy of Arts. Also on display are editions of his literary works and a number of his personal possessions.

Shevchenko's House, Shevchenko Lane 8a. Open 10–5.30, closed Fri. Shevchenko lived in this small house during the spring and summer of 1946. The display is very similar to that of the Shevchenko Museum and mostly includes his personal possessions and editions of his literary works. There is a bust of the poet in the garden.

Lenin Museum, Volodimirska St. 57. Open 10–6, closed Mon. The museum, which was opened in 1938, is situated in one of the finest houses in Kiev.

Planetarium, Cheluskintsiv St. 17. This is housed in what was formerly a Roman Catholic church.

Saint Vladimir Monument, in the park on Volodimirska Girka at the northern end of the main street, Kreschatik. Overlooking the river is a statue of Prince Vladimir, erected in 1853. He is holding aloft a cross. The statue was cast in bronze by Klodt (famous for his horses on the Anickhov Bridge in Leningrad) after a design by Demut-Malinovsky. Prince Vladimir is shown in the dress of an ancient Russian warrior, standing bareheaded in thanksgiving as he gazes at the water of the Dnieper below where he was instrumental in the mass baptism of his people. The statue is 4.5 m. high and weighs about 6 tons. The unusual chapel-like pedestal is covered with cast-iron plates. On the pedestal above the bas-relief depicting the baptism of Rus is the old seal of Kiev. The height of the statue and pedestal together is 20.4 m.

At the bottom of Volodimirska Girka is another *monument* dating from 1802 and commemorating the conversion of Russia to Christianity.

Bogdan Khmelnitsky Monument, in the centre of Bogdan Khmelnitsky Sq. opposite St. Sophia's Cathedral and near the spot where the Kievans took their oath of loyalty to Russia in 1654. Bogdan Khmelnitsky (1593–1657) was the Cossack Hetman who freed the Ukraine from the Poles and later subjected it to the Moscow State. The equestrian statue was cast in bronze in St. Petersburg by Mikeshin in 1880 and transported to Kiev. It was erected in 1888. The statue is 10.85 m. high and so placed that it can be seen from three different directions. The mace Khmelnitsky holds is a symbol of his power as Hetman and it points to the north, to Moscow.

Taras Shevchenko Monument, in the park bearing his name in front of the university. The monument was unveiled in 1939 on the 150th anniversary of the poet's birth. It was designed by Manizer and is 6 m. high. On the pedestal is a quotation from one of his most famous poems:

And in the great family,
The new, free family,
Do not forget me.
Remember me
With a kind, quiet word.

Lenin Monument, Shevchenko Boulevard. The statue, designed by Merkurov, was unveiled in 1946.

Ivan Franko Monument, Franko Sq., near the Ivan Franko theatre. The statue of the writer and public figure was unveiled in 1956.

Schors Monument, at the crossing of Shevchenko Boulevard and Kominterna St. Nikolai Schors (1895–1919) was a Red Army commander who became a hero of the civil war. The equestrian statue which stands 6·5 m. high was made by Lysenko, Sukholodov, and Borodai and unveiled in 1954. The upper edge of the red granite pedestal bears a bronze cornice and a frieze depicting episodes from the history of the Red Army.

Arsenal Worker's Monument, at the crossing of Kirov St. and Sichneve Povstannya St. The cannon mounted on a pedestal of red granite was unveiled in 1922 to commemorate the workers of the Arsenal Plant who fell during the civil war of 1917–22. There is another monument to these workers in Radyansky Park; it takes the form of a red granite urn hung with crepe and standing on a black marble pedestal which bears the inscription: 'To the eternal glory of the fighters for freedom.'

Askold's Grave and War Memorial. These are in one of the most beautiful parts of Kiev in the park which is also called Askold's Grave. In 1909–10 the architect Melinski built a rotunda where, according to legend, Askold, Prince of Kiev, was buried in 882. In the upper part of the park, near the rotunda, is the grave of an unknown warrior of the Second World War, and as a memorial there is a tall obelisk and an everlasting torch. The obelisk stands 27 m. high and the memorial was completed in 1957. A good road runs through the park.

Vatutin Monument, in Radyansky Park, Kirov St. General Nikolai Vatutin (1901–44) died, heavily wounded, in Kiev after the liberation of the city. The monument by Vuchetich was unveiled in 1948. The 4·7-m. sculpture is of grey granite and stands over the General's grave. On the pedestal is an inscription reading: 'To General Vatutin from the Ukrainian People.'

Pushkin Monument, in front of the entrance to Pushkin Park. The bronze sculpture by Kovalyev stands 3·5 m. high and the total height of the monument is over 7 m. The black granite pedestal carries the inscription: 'To Pushkin from the Ukrainian People.' The monument was unveiled in 1962.

Shevchenko Opera and Ballet Theatre, Volodimirska St. 50. This building was designed in 1901 by Schretter. It seats 1650. The company was formed in 1926.

Ivan Franko Ukrainian Drama Theatre, Franko Sq. 2. The theatre was built in 1898 and reconstructed in 1960.

Lesya Ukrainka Russian Drama Theatre, Lenin St. 5. Lesya Ukrainka (1871–1913) was a well-known Ukrainian poetess.

Musical Comedy Theatre, Chernovoarmiiska St. 51a

Youth Theatre, Rosa Luxembourg St. 15/17

Puppet Theatre, Rustaveli St. 13. This theatre, which can seat 316, was once a synagogue.

Philarmonia Concert Hall, Kirov St. 16. This was built in 1882 by Nikolayev as the Merchants' Hall.

Zhovtnevii (October) Palace of Culture, Zhovtnevoi Revolutsii St. 1. This building was built by Beretti in 1838–42 as a School for Girls of Gentle Birth. It has a classical colonnade and stands on a hilltop. It was restored and enlarged in 1953–7 and its hall, which can seat over 2000, is one of the largest in Kiev and is used for concerts.

Circus, Peremoghi Sq. The circus was built in 1958–60 and can seat 2100.

Cinerama, Rustaveli St. 19. Built in 1958, this was the first cinerama in the Soviet Union.

Hippodrome Racecourse, Suvorovskaya St. 5

Dynamo Stadium, Kirov St. 3. This was built in 1934–6 to accommodate 30,000 spectators. There is a restaurant.

Tsentralny Stadium, Chervonoarmiiska St. 51b. This occupies a territory of 53 hectares (130 acres) and the main stadium seats 60,000. Nearby is a Palace of Sport, opened in 1960 and locally called 'Crystal Palace'. With accommodation for 12,000 it is the largest covered arena in the Soviet Union.

Zoo, Brest-Litovskoye Pr. 80

Swimming pool, Vozdukhflotskoye Chaussee 32

Academy of Sciences Botanical Garden, Vidubetska St. 11. The garden is situated on the bank of the R. Dnieper to the south of the Monastery of the Caves, and it covers an area of 180 hectares (450 acres).

Fomin Botanical Garden, Komintern St. 1. The garden, which is situated behind the university, covers an area of 22 hectares (54 acres). It was laid out in 1841 on a stretch of wasteland, and its present name comes from a botanist who fought for its preservation just after the revolution.

Ukrainian Economic Exhibition, Sorokorichya Zhovtnya Prospect. This is a permanent exhibition in the southern suburbs of the city. It is laid out in grounds of 300 hectares (750 acres), more than half of which is parkland.

Kiev is lucky to have another beautiful stretch of natural parkland close to the centre. It runs along the hilly wooded slopes above the river. There are really a number of parks here, but they run into each other imperceptibly. The most northerly is *Volodimirska Girka (Vladimir's Hill Park)* where there is the St. Vladimir Monument and an open-air cinema seating 1500. *Pionersky (Pioneer) Park* is reached by a flight of steps from

Lenkomsomola Sq. and contains amusements, a cinema, and a concert platform. *Pershotravnevy (First of May) Park* was laid out in 1747–55 as the tsar's park adjoining the palace. There is a bandstand with 2000 seats, an open-air theatre, amusements, and the Cuckoo Restaurant. *Radyansky (Soviet) Park*, laid out in the 19th century, is opposite the tsar's palace and contains a children's village and a playground. The last of the parks is called *Askold's Grave* (see above).

Lower down, beside the river, runs *Park Lane*, which is closed to motor traffic on summer evenings when it is usually crowded with pedestrians. In the autumn the local fruit and flower show is held here near the statue of the horticulturist, Michurin. Also on Park Lane is an open-air theatre with a seating capacity of 4000. Its amphitheatre makes use of the 19th-century wall of Kiev fortress. Higher up the slope, but still in the park area, runs a good motor road with an excellent view across the river. One can get on to it by driving from the clover-leaf at Paton Bridge along the embankment road and taking the first large left fork up the hill.

Trukhaniv Island. This island in the R. Dnieper is reached by a suspension bridge for pedestrians which was opened in 1957. It is Kiev's most popular bathing beach.

Pushkin Park, Brest-Litovskoye Chaussee. This park was opened in 1899 to mark the 100th anniversary of the poet's birth. There are groves of beech, pine, birch, and other trees.

Lenkomsomol Park, also on Brest-Litovskoye Chaussee. There is a monument to the young Communists of the 1920s, and boats can be hired on the pond.

Babi Yar. Drive out of the centre of the city along Artemov Street towards the television tower; just the other side of the tower, on the left of the main road a granite block marks the site of a monument to be dedicated to 'the Victims of Fascism—1941–1943'. Babi Yar is the name of the wooded gulley that runs back from the road at this point and which was the scene of gruesome mass murders during the time of the occupation of Kiev. Now planted with young birches, rowans, and firs and criss-crossed with winding footpaths, its very simplicity and silence are deeply moving.

Goloseyevo Forest, on the left of the main road leading to the Ukrainian Economic Exhibition. There are lakes and ancient trees, and also a 160-hectares (400-acres) park with sports grounds and an open-air theatre. In the summer a restaurant and a café are open here.

Children's Railway, in the Syrets district of Kiev. The engine and six coaches run for 3 km. along a track that was opened in 1953. The railway is staffed by schoolchildren.

Lyebed (Swan) Hotel and Restaurant, Pobeda Sq. TEL. 74–32–06

Dnipro Hotel and Restaurant, Kreschatik 1/2, TEL. 29–65–69

Moskva Hotel, Restaurant and Café, in the skyscraper near Kalinin Square, TEL. 29–00–15

Intourist Hotel and Restaurant, Lenin St. 26, TEL. 25–11–21

Mir Hotel and Restaurant, Goloseyevsky Forest

Leningradskaya Hotel and Restaurant, Shevchenko Boulevard 4, TEL. 25–71–01

Kiev Hotel and Restaurant, Volodimirska St. 36

Ukraina Hotel and Restaurant, Shevchenko Boulevard 5, TEL. 24–50–19

Teatralnaya Hotel and Restaurant, Lenin St. 17, TEL. 25–50–45

Pervomaiskaya Hotel and Restaurant, Lenin St. 1/3, TEL. 4–10–15

Abkhaziya Restaurant, Kreschatik 42

Dynamo Restaurant, Kirov St. 3, at the Dynamo Stadium

Metro Restaurant and Café, Kreschatik 42

Leipzig Restaurant, Volodimirska St. 30, (specialises in German dishes.)

Poplavok (fishing float) Restaurant, Naberezhnoye Chaussee

Priboy (surf) Restaurant, Rechnoi Vokzal

Cuckoo Restaurant, Pershotravnevy Park

Riviera Restaurant, Park Lane

Kashtany (foreign currency) Shop, 11 Syres, Kolotovskovo St.

Polish Legation, Karl Liebknecht St. 28

Czech Legation, Polupanova St. 3

G.P.O., Kreschatik 22

Main Department Store, Lenin St. 2, at the corner of Kreschatik

Podarki (gift) Shop, Karl Marx St. 9 and at the corner of Kreschatik and Shevchenko Boulevard

Kashtany (foreign currency) Shop, Lesya Ukrainka St. 27/26

Ukrainian Handicrafts, Chervonoarmiiska St. 23 and Kirov St. 93

Book Shop, Kreschatik 30

Bessarabka Covered Market, Shevchenko Boulevard. The building was designed by Gai and erected in 1910.

Market, Vorovskov St. 17

Taxi Ranks, Chervonoarmiiska St. 7/18, Peremoghi Sq., Station Sq., and Chernova Sq.

Kanev

This town is 149 km. down river from Kiev. The way passes pretty Ukrainian villages including Tripillya where a settlement of primitive man of 4th-2nd century B.C. was discovered, giving rise to the term Tripolyan Culture. Another village of historical interest is Vitachiv which was once a strongly fortified point where merchant vessels assembled in armed convoys to sail on down the river to the Black Sea. Kanev itself was first mentioned in 1149 and its St. George's Church dates from the time of Kiev Rus. The Cathedral of the Assumption was built in the early 12th century. The town's chief claim to fame, however, is that 4 km. away is the burial place of Taras Shevchenko, who is often simply called Kobzar which is the Ukrainian for 'bard'. The celebrated poet visited this place in 1859 and thought of settling down here but his plans never materialised and he died in St. Petersburg in March 1861, and was buried there. Shortly after the funeral, his friends, carrying out his last wish, conveyed his remains to Kanev where he was reburied in May 1861, on the picturesque slopes of the right bank of the Dnieper.

The grave and the surrounding area of 1360 hectares (3400 acres) of woodland now form a national park. The bronze monument to Shevchenko by Manizer was unveiled in 1939. There is also a two-storey museum where in ten halls are displayed documents, pictures, and sculptures connected with Shevchenko, copies of his publications, and some of his water colours.

Taras's Hill Hotel and Restaurant

Cherkassy

Population—150,000 (1973)

The place has been known since the 14th century and was one of the Cossack centres. It was from here that the Cossack leader, Bogdan Khmelnitsky, sent his first letter in June 1648 proclaiming the Ukrainians' wish to unite with Russia.

Taras Shevchenko lived here in 1843 and again in 1859 and wrote some of his poems here.

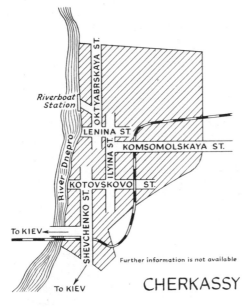

CHERKASSY

Local industry is mostly concerned with food production.

Local Museum. The pride of the collection are the flags of the regiment which fought the Turks at the Battle of Schipka in Bulgaria in the last century.

Lenin Monument, Proletarsky Garden

Cherkassy Hotel, Novaya St. 6

Tourist Centre, by Kremenchug Reservoir

Bathing Beach, at the resort of Sosnovka not far from town

Kozlets

Population—7500

Kozlets is picturesquely sited on the banks of R. Ostra, on the road from Kiev to Chernigov, and was known from the 17th century onwards as a well fortified town. The focal point today is the *Uspensky Cathedral* (Komsomolskaya St. 46) which was built in 1763 by Rastrelli. The large central dome is surrounded by four smaller ones and each of the three curving stairways leading up to the main entrances is housed in a graceful pillared rotunda with a conical roof. The ground floor of the cathedral building is occupied by the *Church of SS. Adrian and Natalie* and the *Razumovsky family crypt*.

It was Count Alexei Razumovsky (1709–71) who paid for the construction of this cathedral and his exciting career is worthy of mention. The son of the Cossack Grigori Razum, Alexei started life as a shepherd. Then the young boy was singled out by a local priest for his extraordinarily lovely singing voice. By 1731 he had earned a place among the court singers in St. Petersburg and there his good looks and his outstanding voice caught the attention of Empress Elizabeth. In 1741 he was made a general and the following year he married the empress, becoming known as Count-Fieldmarshal.

Alexei's younger brother, Kirill (1728–1803), has his own claim to fame. Apart from going down in history as the last of the Ukrainian Hetmans, after teaching in Berlin he returned to Russia to become, at the tender age of 18, President of the Academy of Sciences.

Beside the Uspensky Cathedral soars a magnificent three-storey *belfry*, 77 m. in height, which was built in 1784. Both buildings were restored in 1973. In the park behind the cathedral and next to the Pokrovskaya Church, now serving as a sports centre, is the 18th-century *Magistrat* building.

Past the cathedral, the main road runs along to the town's central square where there is a *statue of Lenin*. Near the department store is *Vozneseniya Church*, while *St. Nicholas's Church* lies back from the road on the right.

Prolisok Restaurant & Café

There is a filling station just outside Kozlets.

Chernigov

Population—150,000 (1970)

Intourist organises tours to Chernigov, starting from Kiev.

This ancient town was first mentioned in records of 907, but its foundation was very much earlier and the derivation of its name, according to legend, is from that of a certain Black Prince, 'cherny' meaning black. It stands upon R. Desna of which a tributary, the Strizhen, divides the town.

In 992, a few years after this part of the country was converted to Christianity, a bishop was established here and soon the bishopric was second in importance only to Novgorod. Chernigov became the capital of a princedom and it was at this time that Spaso-Preobrazhensky Cathedral was founded by Prince Mstislav on the site of a pagan temple. The territory of the princedom was very large, stretching as far as the boundaries of the Moscow and the Vladimir regions.

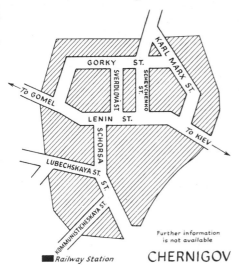

Further information is not available

■ Railway Station   CHERNIGOV

The town lost its importance after being sacked by the Tatars in 1239. At first the inhabitants defended themselves bravely by rolling big boulders down the steep bank of R. Desna upon the heads of the invaders. Chernigov's last prince, Mikhail Vsevolodovich, was taken prisoner and along with a faithful follower called Fedor he died a martyr's death. They were both canonised and their bodies were carried to Moscow in 1572 upon Ivan the Terrible's order, and laid to rest in the Kremlin's Arkhangelsky Cathedral.

Subsequently Chernigov changed hands several times and was under Polish-Lithuanian rule for 328 years. The churches which have survived successive wars and the passage of the years tell the history of the place; some were converted into Roman Catholic churches and then back again to Russian Orthodox.

In 1941 the town was heavily bombed and most of the present-day buildings and the abundant trees and gardens date from after the war. The town planners did their best to preserve what they could of ancient Chernigov and a notable achievement is the boulevard planted along the line of the old earth wall which until the 18th century surrounded the Kremlin, Detinets. It is decorated with strategically placed cannons. Lenin St. was completely new, laid out across the ruins. Most of the administrative buildings are located here. Shevchenko St. runs out of the wide expanse of Kuibyshev Sq.

Local industry includes the production of up to 25,000 pianos annually and a variety of textiles and synthetic fibres; the textile mills are mostly in the Shovkograd region of the town.

Spaso-Preobrazhensky Cathedral, inside the Kremlin area, is one of the country's oldest stone buildings. It was designed in 1030 as a cathedral,

and is still most impressive. It also served as a princely sepulchre; Prince Mstislav, his wife Anastasia, their son, and a number of other princes were buried here. The original cathedral has been rebuilt and embellished many times and the present building is a 1792–8 reconstruction. The iconostasis is of the same date. This, like most of Chernigov's churches, is open as a museum 10–5.30, closed Thurs.

The yellow building with a six-columned portico near the approach to the cathedral used to be the Governor's residence built in 1803; it is now a polytechnical college.

Near the cathedral stands *SS. Boris and Gleb Cathedral* (1123), originally part of a monastery of the same name. The cathedral was burnt in 1511 and taken over and rebuilt by a Dominican monastery. At about this time a silver idol was unearthed nearby. It was melted down and the silver used to make a pair of altar gates depicting in very fine work Isaiah on the left and David on the right; the gates are now in Danzig. The church was again ruined during World War II but it has since been rebuilt.

A little farther on stands a *belfry* which suffered from fire during the last war but was restored in 1954. Adjoining the belfry is the *Collegium* which dates from 1702 when the education problem was recognised as being in urgent need of solution and many schools and 'collegia' were built. It stood within the monastery walls until the monastery closed. The original building was later added to, and now houses the town archives.

Pyatnitskaya Church (or the Church of St. Paraskeva), Shevchenko Boulevard, behind the theatre. This was founded in the 12th century but was almost completely destroyed when it received a direct hit during a World War II raid. It was rebuilt in 1962.

Voskresenskaya Church and belfry (1772), in the old part of the town, near the market. The belfry is a copy of that in the Kirillovsky Monastery in Kiev. The church is open for services.

St. Catherine's (Ekaterinenskaya) Church (1715) stands near the road on the way into the town from Kiev. It was built as a memorial by Colonel Yakov Lizogub, hero of the storming of the Turkish fortress at Azov. The colonel's own house, built in the 1680s, is inside the Detinets territory. It is open as a museum 10–6; closed Wed. The colonel himself was buried in the family crypt in the cathedral of Eletsky Monastery (see below).

The war left but few old buildings of interest in Chernigov. Among these are a bank at 25th-Anniversary St. 16, at the end of the garden on Kuibyshev Square, located in the former Magistrat (late 19th century) which once also served as a prison and then as a police station; an old red-and-white brick hospital at Lenin St. 36, now a polyclinic; a printing works with a tall tower at Lenin St. 34, and the original post office building at Lenin St. 28.

History Museum, Revolutsii St. 16. There is a good collection of Cossack arms here and among the icons note the 17th-century Our Lady of Elets from Uspenskaya Church in the local Eletsky Monastery.

Kotsubinsky Museum, Kotsubinsky St. 3. Mikhail Kotsubinsky (1864–1913) was a famous Ukrainian writer and translator. He lived here from 1898 until his death. He was buried nearby, on Boldin Hill.

Troitsky Monastery, L. Tolstova St., opposite No. 111. The monastery's principal building is Troitsky Cathedral, built in Baroque style in 1679–85. Beside it, to the south, stands *Vedenskaya Refectory Church* (1677). The belfry and the entrance gate were built later, in 1775, to complete the ensemble. Near the cathedral stands a *monument* to the poet, Baikar, the pseudonym used by Leonid Glibov (1827–93).

A short walk down a narrow path from Troitsky Monastery leads to *Ilinskaya Church* at Uspensky St. 33. This marks the entrance to the *Antoniev Caves* where there are three underground *churches* dedicated to SS. Antonia, Feodosia, and Mikola.

Eletsky Monastery, south-west of the town. *Uspenskaya Church* was founded by the local Great Prince Svyatoslav in 1069 after a vision of the Virgin appeared there in a tree. The existing building can be traced back to the 12th century although it was burnt and rebuilt many times. It was restored again in 1960 and now appears as it did in 1679. The iconostasis and some of the frescoes are still under restoration. The 17th-century icon of Our Lady of Elets was taken from this church and now hangs in the local history museum.

The belfry stands 36 m. high and both this and the other buildings of the monastery date from the 17th century.

Opposite the entrance to the monastery is the *Black Grave*, one of the many barrows in this area. It is thought to be a 10th-century prince's burial mound.

Taras Shevchenko Monument, in Detinets

Bogdan Khmelnitsky Monument, Teatralnaya Sq. Schevchenko St.

Lenin Monument

Popudrenko Memorial, in the garden by the Regional Council building. Popudrenko was a partisan leader and local hero. The memorial marks his grave.

War Memorial, in the Kremlin

Tank Monument, Schors St. opposite the pre-war railway station building

Shevchenko Music and Drama Theatre, Lenin St.

Concert Hall, Lenin St.

Gagarin Stadium

Ukraina Hotel & Restaurant, Lenin St. 33

Desna Hotel & Restaurant, Lenin St.

Vesna Restaurant, Kuibysheva Sq. 1

G.P.O., Lenin St. 28

KIRGHIZIA
See Frunze, p. 106

KISHINEV
(Pronounced Kishinyov) Rumanian: Chisinau
Population—357,000 (1970)
Capital of the Moldavian Soviet Socialist Republic

MOLDAVIA
Moldavian: Moldova

This republic of the Soviet Union is situated to the north-west of the Black Sea, on the Rumanian frontier. It is 33,700 sq. km. in area, and its population numbers 3,572,000 (1970), 22% of which lives in the towns. The people are mostly Moldavians, but other nationalities include Ukrainians (15%), Russians (10%), Jews and Gagauz (3.3% each), and others (4.4%). With 85 people per sq. km. the country has the densest population in the Soviet Union.

The Moldavians, once called the Volokhs by the Russians, speak a Romance language very similar to Rumanian, but use the Cyrillic alphabet. As much as 40% of the language consists of words of Ukrainian origin.

The country has been inhabited since prehistoric times. It is supposed that the Moldavians are descendants of the ancient Thracians, and the Greeks, Romans, and Turks had colonies in the area and influenced the country for a considerable time. The Moldavian principality was formed in the 14th century, but from the 16th century the country was under Turkish rule. After the Russo-Turkish war of 1806–12 Moldavia was joined to Russia.

The country is divided in two by the R. Dniester, and the territory on the right bank of the river up to the border (formed by the R. Prut) came to be known as Bessarabia. From 1918 until 1940 this area was under Rumanian rule and a small autonomous Moldavian republic was created in 1921 within the Ukraine on the left bank of the R. Dniester. The Soviet Union never accepted the annexation of Bessarabia and in 1940 she demanded that the Rumanian army leave Bessarabia within four days. Subsequently the Union Republic of Moldavia was formed, comprising both parts of the country.

Moldavia's soil is fertile and the climate very mild, so the country is mainly agricultural and grows wheat, maize, sunflowers, etc.; in viniculture it ranks second in importance in the U.S.S.R.

The country's food and light industries are well developed; its mineral resources are only lignite and stone. The main towns are Kishinev (capital), Beltsy, Tiraspol, and Bendery.

Useful expressions in Moldavian

hello	norok
I am a tourist	ayoo sint tourist
please	poftim
thank you	mooltsoomesk
yes	da
no	noo
good	beene

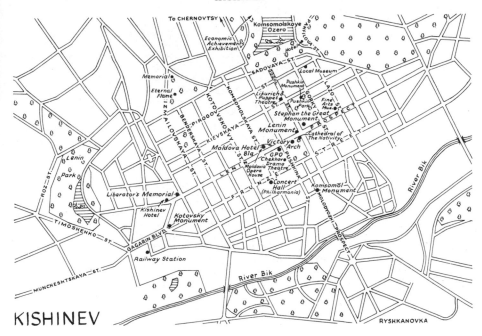

KISHINEV

bad	rayoo
I don't understand	noo intseleg
please fetch an	kemats ve rog
interpreter for me	oon interpret
good-bye	la revedere

Kishinev

The name of the capital of Moldavia is supposed to come from Kishla Noue ('kishla' means 'sheep-fold'). The city was founded in 1420, and was for a long time the property of the Holy Sepulchre Monastery and it is sometimes thought that the name might have come from the Turkish word for 'monastery village'.

The city stands on the R. Bik. It has an average summer temperature of 20–23°C. (68–74°F.) and is warm in the autumn.

In 1812, when Moldavia was united with Russia, there were only 7000 people living in Kishinev. The population decreased again when from 6–8 April 1903 there was a severe Jewish pogrom, but it has since increased greatly.

Kishinev is divided into two parts, the old town with small, winding streets down by the R. Bik, and the new town, which occupies the upper part of the territory beginning from Lenin Prospect, which was formerly called Alexandrovskaya St. after Tsar Alexander II. In this part of the town the streets are better planned and the houses, which are mostly one-storey buildings, were the private mansions of merchants and businessmen.

Kishinev was in Rumanian hands from 1918 until 1940 and during World War II 76% of the residential buildings were destroyed. In 1953 the 3·5 km.-long Lenin Prospect was reconstructed and office blocks of three and five storeys were put

up. The building with a statue of Mercury (the god of trade) on the façade is the State Bank. The central part of the Prospect, between Pushkinskaya St. and Gogolevskaya St. was extended to five times its original width and was called Pobedy (Victory) Sq. A monument to Lenin was erected, and it became the Red Sq. of Kishinev, where parades and demonstrations take place. The new Moldavian government building is under construction in this square.

The suburbs of Kishinev, especially Benderskaya and Skulyanskaya, have become the industrial regions of the capital and account for half Moldavia's industry. The food industry is the most important, but there are also factories for the tobacco, textiles, and machine building industries. A new part of the city was built in the suburbs after the war. Kishinev has a branch of the U.S.S.R. Academy of Sciences (opened 1961), some scientific research institutes, a university with eight faculties and 7000 students, medical, agricultural, and pedagogical institutes, and a conservatory.

Cathedral of the Nativity, Lenin Prospect, opposite the Lenin Monument in the city centre. The cathedral was built in 1836. The cathedral's bell-tower (1840) was designed by architect Zaushkevich, who was also responsible for the *Victory Arch* nearby. Originally known as Holy Gate, the arch is decorated with 16 Corinthian columns and supports the town clock. The big bell weighs almost 7 tons and was cast from melted-down Turkish guns captured during the Russo-Turkish wars. It was only renamed Victory Arch after World War II, when commemorative plaques were added.

Mazarakievskaya Church of the Nativity of the Virgin, in the old part of the town. This church, built in 1152, is called after a Greek, Vasilyi Mazaraki, a Greek Christian in the service of the Turkish sultan. At one time he was suspected of disloyalty to his master, but throughout his troubles his faith remained unshaken, and he vowed that if only his innocence could be proved, he would show his gratitude by providing the money to build a church. This one that still bears his name owes its existence to Mazaraki's donation; it must have been a handsome gift, judging by the solid construction, for the walls of the church are 1·4 m. thick.

Synagogue, near Armyanskaya St.

Pushkin's House Museum, Antonovskaya St. Open 11–6, closed Mon. Pushkin lived in exile in Kishinev between 1820 and 1823, and it was here that he began to write 'Eugene Onegin'.

Fine Arts Museum, Lenin Prospect 115. Closed Tues. The 5000 exhibits are displayed in 14 halls, and they include Russian art dating from the end of the 18th to the beginning of the 20th century, and also Soviet, Moldavian, Western European (16th to 19th centuries), and applied art. The Western European section has examples of Italian, Dutch, Flemish, and German masters.

Local Museum, Pirogov St. 82. Open 12–7, closed Wed. The museum, founded in 1889, is located in a house built in 1905 in Mauritanian style; it has a good collection of carpets and national costumes.

Iskra Museum, Podolskaya St. 39. Open 11–6, closed Wed. Iskra (spark) was the name of the first Bolshevik newspaper, published illegally here in 1901–2 by the Social Democratic Party.

Kotovsky and Sergei Lazo Museum, Komsomolskaya St. 31. Open 11–6, closed Tues. These were heroes of the Civil War, both born in Moldavia.

Lenin Monument, Pobeda Sq., just opposite the Cathedral. This 12-m.-high monument is by Merkurov and was unveiled in 1949.

Kotovsky Monument, Kotovsky Sq. This equestrian statue by the Moldavian sculptors Dubinovsky and Kitaika was unveiled in 1954. Grigori Kotovsky (1881–1925) was a hero of the civil war, born in Moldavia, in the village now called Kotovskoye after him.

Stephan the Great Monument, at the entrance to Pushkin Park where Gogol St. crosses Lenin Prospect. Stephan was called 'the Great' despite his small stature, for his victories over the Turks. He was Moldavian Gospodar (ruler) between 1457 and 1504, and during that time the country remained independent. This monument by Plamadeala was unveiled in 1927.

Pushkin Monument, in Pushkin Park. Unveiled in 1885, this bust is by Opekushin who designed the Pushkin statue in Moscow.

Komsomol Monument, Molodezhi Prospect. This 15-m.-high statue is by the sculptor Dubinovskii and the architect Naumov. During World War II this part of the town was the region of the Jewish ghetto.

Moldavia Opera House, Lenin Prospect 79

Pushkin Music and Drama Theatre, in the same building as the Opera House. All performances here are in Moldavian.

Chekhov Drama Theatre, Yunya St. 28. This theatre used to be a synagogue.

Concert Hall (Philharmonia), at the corner of Komsomolskaya St. Performances are given by symphony orchestras, the famous Doina choir, the Zhok National Dance Ensemble, and the Fluerash Orchestra of National Music.

Likurich (glow-worm) Puppet Theatre, Fontanaya St. 7.

Youth Theatre, at the same address as the Puppet Theatre

Pushkin Park, in the centre of the town. This Park is famous for its Writers' Walk with statues of Rumanian and Moldavian classical writers. The main gates of the park are on Lenin Prospect.

Komsomolskoye Ozero (Young Communist League Lake). Here there is a bathing beach and a boat hire station. An impressive flight of 250 steps with waterfalls leads down to the water. In the park is an open-air theatre for 7000 and also a parachute tower, a dance floor, and other attractions. There are two restaurants, the Otdykh (rest) and the Chaika (seagull)—the latter on a floating raft. The park covers 96 hectares (240 acres).

Economic Achievements Exhibition, on the banks of Komsomolskoye Ozero

Botanical Gardens, Boyukansky Spusk

Republikansky Stadium, Benderskaya St. The stadium seats 30,000 people.

Kishinev Hotel and Restaurant, Negruzzi Boulevard 7, TEL. 2–25–69

Moldova Hotel and Restaurant, Lenin Prospect 8a, TEL. 2–26–52

Dniester Café, Komsomolskaya St. 56

Druzhba (Friendship) Café, Lenin Prospect 62. A national dish worth trying is 'mititeyi', small sausages containing spice and onions.

G.P.O., Lenin Prospect 134

Kołhoznyi Rynok, at the corner of Benderskaya St. and Lenin Prospect. This newly-built market in the centre of the town sells peasant ware and national handicrafts as well as food.

Department Store, Lenin Prospect 136, at the corner of Pushkinskaya St.

Podarki (Gift) Shop, Komsomolskaya St., at the corner of Lenin Prospect

Main Taxi Ranks, Gogol St., at the corner of Lenin Prospect, Zhukovskaya St., at the corner of Lenin Prospect, and by the hotels and the railway station

KISLOVODSK
See Mineralniye Vodi, p. 192

KIZHI
See Petrozavodsk, p. 256

KLIN
Population—70,000 (1970)

The name of this town which stands on the R. Sestra ('sister') is first recorded in 1234. In 1482 it became part of Muscovy, and in 1572 Ivan the Terrible left it to his son, Ivan, after which it passed to the Romanovs. Klin was made a district town in 1785. It has factories making synthetic fibre, glass, and thermometers.

There is an old arcade of shops in the town.

18th-Century Church, on the territory of the Uspensky (Assumption) Monastery, which was closed in the 18th century. The church, built in the style of Moscow Baroque, dates from 1712.

Tchaikovsky Museum, Tchaikovsky St. 48. Open 11–5, closed Wed. The composer Peter I. Tchaikovsky lived in this region from 1885 until 1893, and his home was actually in this house between 1892 and 1893. He himself wrote of his affection for the place, 'I have become so attached to Klin that I cannot imagine myself living anywhere else. . . . I am unable to do justice to the charm of the Russian village, the Russian landscape and this silence which I need most of all.' He wrote his 6th (Pathetic) Symphony, the 3rd Piano Concerto, and the music for the 'Nutcracker' and 'Sleeping Beauty' ballets here.

When the composer died, his brother, Modest, decided to make the house a museum, so it was first purchased from the owner by Tchaikovsky's servant, Sofronov, and then bought by Modest Tchaikovsky and the composer's nephew, V. Davydov. The former died in 1916 and the house passed to the Russian Musical Society; it was protected by government charter and became state property in 1921. It was looted by the Germans during World War II, but anything of value had previously been evacuated, and the house was restored in 1944.

The two-storey building is furnished and decorated as it was in the composer's lifetime, and contains his books, paintings, grand piano, and other personal possessions. Modest Tchaikovsky wrote a three-volume biography of his brother, and the material he collected for this purpose formed the basis of the Tchaikovsky archives now amounting to almost 50,000 items and still used for research.

There is a *restaurant* in the town.

KOBULETI
See Batumi, p. 63

KOLA
See Murmansk, p. 236

KOLOMENSKOYE
See Moscow, p. 231

KRASNAYA POLYANA
See Caucasian Coastal Road, p. 76

KURSK
Population—284,000 (1970)

'Kursk' comes from 'Kuropatka', the Russian word for partridge, and three of these birds were pictured on the old coat-of-arms.

The town is situated on two hills on the right bank of the R. Tuskari, a tributary of the R. Seim. It was founded in the 9th century and was first mentioned in a document of 1095. The Mongols destroyed it in 1240; later it belonged to Lithuania for many years and an important trade grew up in grain, linen, leather, and apples. It was eventually annexed to the principality of Moscow, and in the 16th century became another of the defence points on Russia's southern border.

At the beginning of the 18th century when the Russian border was moved farther south Kursk fortress lost much of its importance. Administrative buildings were built upon its site and in 1798 Kursk became a provincial capital. There are still many houses of typical 19th-century Russian architecture, among them the former House of Nobles at 4, Verkhne-Naberezhnaya St. and the *manège* (now a cinema) at Dzerzhinskova St. 51. An even older part of Kursk can be seen on Pionerskaya and Zolotorevskaya streets where Romodanovsky House (1649–80) and the 17th-century Trinity Church stand. There might have been more to see had it not been for the fighting and enemy occupation here during the Second World War.

Lenin St. is the main thoroughfare and the road followed by motorists passing through the town. The best shops are here and it leads into Krasnaya (red) Sq. where there are the hotel and the impressive buildings of the House of Soviets (1948), the town-hall, and the Local Economical Council. The monument to Lenin by Manizer was unveiled in 1956. There are pedagogical, medical, and agricultural institutes in Kursk and local factories produce electrical apparatus, synthetic fibre, rubber, glass, textiles, and food products. The Kursk region is famous for its nightingales and for its Antonovka apples which ripen at the end of September.

Local delicacies include Kursky Salat (salad of chicken, butter, and apple) and Gavyadina Po-Kursky (rolls of beef stuffed with egg, rice, and butter and then deep-fried).

St. Serge's Cathedral, Gorky St. The cathedral was built in 1752–78 following a project by Rastrelli. Inside is a carved iconostasis, 18 m. high, and a Bible dated 1693.

Church of the Sign of Our Lady, formerly the cathedral church of the Znamensky Monastery, 43 m. high and built in 1816–28. The distinctive silver dome stands out clearly as one drives down Lenin St. The round brick tower nearby which dates from the 1790s was part of the monastery wall. The church now houses the October Cinema.

Trinity Convent, Gorky St. 13. Here remain the bell-tower and Upper Trinity Church (1695). The buildings are now used to house the local archives.

St. Nikita's Church, near Moskovskiye Vorota. This church is open for services.

St. Catherine's Church, Engels St. 7, behind the filling station

Local Museum and Planetarium, Lunacharsky St. 4. Open 10–4.

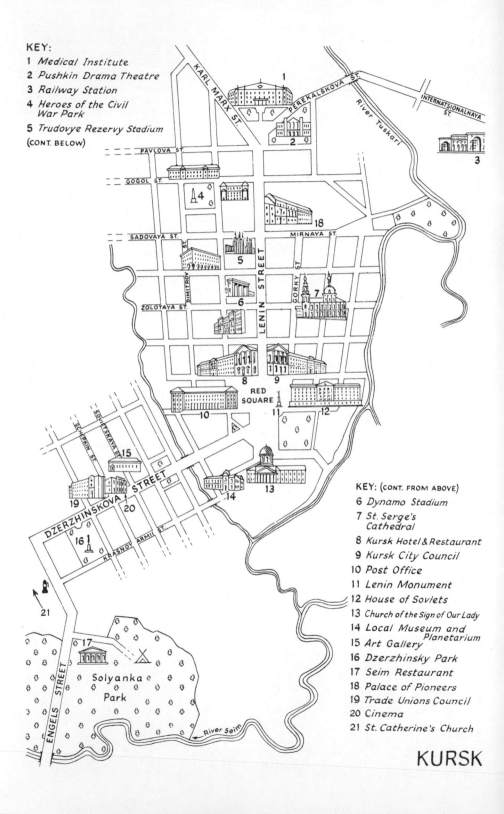

KEY:

1 Medical Institute
2 Pushkin Drama Theatre
3 Railway Station
4 Heroes of the Civil War Park
5 Trudovye Rezervy Stadium

(CONT. BELOW)

KEY: (CONT. FROM ABOVE)

6 Dynamo Stadium
7 St. Serge's Cathedral
8 Kursk Hotel & Restaurant
9 Kursk City Council
10 Post Office
11 Lenin Monument
12 House of Soviets
13 Church of the Sign of Our Lady
14 Local Museum and Planetarium
15 Art Gallery
16 Dzerzhinsky Park
17 Seim Restaurant
18 Palace of Pioneers
19 Trade Unions Council
20 Cinema
21 St. Catherine's Church

KARL MARX ST.

PEREKALSKOVA ST.

River Tuskari

INTERNATSIONALNAYA ST.

PAVLOVA ST.

GOGOL ST.

SADOVAYA ST.

MIRNAYA ST.

LENIN STREET

GORKY ST.

DIMITROV ST.

ZOLOTAYA ST.

RED SQUARE

SOVIETSKAYA ST.

SCHEPKIN ST.

DZERZHINSKOVA STREET

KRASNOY ARMII ST.

ENGELS STREET

Solyanka Park

River Seim

KURSK

Moskovskiye Vorota, Karl Marx St. at the entrance to Kursk on the main road from Moscow. The name means Moscow Gates, and originally there was a triumphal arch here to commemorate the visit of Alexander I in 1823, but now only the gateposts remain.

Ufimtsev Museum, Semenovskaya St. 13. Anatoli Ufimtsev (1880–1936) was a Kursk-born inventor and aeroplane engine constructor. His first claim to fame was when in 1898 he blew up a miracle-working icon in the cathedral of the Znamensky Monastery with a time-bomb. He was sent to Siberia and the monks set up a copy of the original icon in the hopes that it would also work miracles. Ufimtsev built the windmill that stands beside his house and the house itself is used as a club for young technicians.

Art Gallery, Sovietskaya St. 3

Dzerzhinsky Monument, Dzerzhinsky Sq.

Heroes of the Civil War Park, containing *Borovykh's Bust*, a memorial to the pilot, Andrei Borovykh, Kursk-born and twice made a Hero of the Soviet Union.

Pushkin Drama Theatre, Perekalskova St. 1

Summer Theatre, Lenin St., in the 1st-May Garden opposite the Kursk Hotel

Puppet Theatre, Lenin St. 99

Dynamo Stadium, Lenin St. 36

Trudovye Rezervy Stadium, Lenin St. 58. There are places for 17,000. The local Agricultural Exhibition is open between September and November. It is near the Camping Site.

Tsentralnaya Hotel, Lenin St. 2, TEL. 338–74

Kursk Hotel and Restaurant, Lenin St. 4, TEL. 3–31–92. There is an Intourist bureau at this hotel.

Seim Restaurant, Solyanka St. 6, near the Camping Site

G.P.O. and Telegraph Office, Krasnaya Sq.

Bank, Lenin St. 83. Kursk's coat-of-arms with the partridges can be seen on the façade.

Department Store, Lenin St. 12

KUSKOVO

See Moscow, p. 231

KUTAISI

Population—161,000 (1970)

Kutaisi is located on either side of the R. Rioni, at the place where it leaves a ravine to flow over the Colkhidian Plateau. There is an excellent panoramic view from the height of the right bank where the remains of one of the world's most ancient cities can still be seen. Some archaeologists are of the opinion that Kutaisi was in ancient times the town of Ea or Kitea, residence of the legendary King Aietes of Colchis who owned the Golden Fleece and whose daughter was Medea. With its great age of more than 3000 years, it is five centuries older than Rome itself and the classical geographers wrote of its importance. To start with the town was in the colony of Miletus, and then in the 6th century B.C. it became the capital of the ancient empire of Colchis. It stood in the most beautiful and fertile part of the country, on the cross road of three important trade routes, one from Iberia (the old name of Georgia), one from the south, and one from the Black Sea coast. Later it became the capital of Imeretia and the residence of the king.

In the time of the Eastern Roman Empire this territory was known by the name of Lazica and was nominally a dependant of the Greek emperors. The fortress was known as Ukhinerioni. At the beginning of the 6th century Imeretia was for about forty years the battlefield for the forces of Emperor Justinian and the Persian Shah Hozroi. In the first part of the 7th century it was devastated by the Arabs and only recovered when it was united by Bagrat III (975–1014). Tbilisi at the time remained in enemy hands and so Kutaisi became the political and administrative centre and the capital of the whole of Georgia. It retained its position until 1122 when Tbilisi was finally recaptured. David the Builder transferred the capital from Kutaisi to Tbilisi and at the same time he founded the Gelati Monastery at Kutaisi. Bagrat III, Bagrat IV, David the Builder, and the famous Queen Tamara each did much to rebuild the country in the period of their reigns, and a great deal of their construction remains to be seen. Kutaisi has suffered much but the ruins of towers, churches, bridges, and chapels in the Kutaisi region mostly belong to this time.

In 1510 the Turks burnt the town and the monastery too, and they seized the Kutaisi fortress again in 1666. It was only in 1770 that Russian and Imeretian forces under Solomon I liberated Kutaisi from the Turks who had held it for 102 years. Kutaisi became an important trade centre, and when in 1810 Imeretia was joined to Russia it became the seat of the governor. After 1840 trade increased rapidly and industry began to develop. In the middle of the 19th century it was the centre of the revolutionary movement in the southern Caucasus.

Today Kutaisi is the second most important cultural centre in Georgia. There is the Tsulukidze Pedagogical Institute, an agricultural institute, the Balanchivadze Musical School, and the Chavchavadze Library, founded in 1894 and now possessing 270,000 books. Kutaisi has inspired many Georgian writers, both by its beauty and its heroic past. The town's industrial position is also second only to Tbilisi. There is a lorry and bus factory and an electro-mechanical factory; mining equipment, silk cloth, chemicals, and food products are also manufactured. The market is interesting as people gather there from the farthest parts of the Caucasus.

Part of the ruined walls of *Kutaisi fortress* can be seen on the high right bank of the Rioni. The road up to the top starts from Tsepnoy (chain) Bridge. Here, in the old town, is a most impressive and ancient *cathedral* built by Bagrat III in 1003. King Bagrat paid great attention to its construction which was intended to symbolise the unification of Georgia. It was built in the shape of a cross. For seven centuries visitors marvelled at its splendour. It was partly ruined in 1691 during the Turkish attack and was damaged again in the war of 1770. Now some restoration work is in progress to prevent further dilapidation.

At *Mtsvanekvavila*, not far from the fortress but on the left bank of the river, is a well preserved *17th-century tower* and a number of churches, mostly dating from 17th–20th centuries. Among them, however, are the remains of a church built in 1013. Since 1956 the cemetery here has been re-organised as a burial place (pantheon) for prominent people.

Tsulukidze Garden, on the left bank of the Rioni, was the garden of Alexander III of Imeretia. The royal buildings stood here, but only one has survived. It is famous for its hall called *Okros Chardakhi* (golden tent) which was built in the 17th century and was completely reconstructed in the 1830s. It was used for receiving ambassadors, holding feasts, and other important occasions. In the garden is a great plane tree, its trunk 10·6 m. in circumference. According to tradition, the Imeretian kings conducted trials and executions beneath its branches. Also in the garden is a monument to Tsulukidze (see below, Tsulukidze Museum) by Tvavadze and Merabishvili, which was unveiled in 1935.

St. Peter and Paul Cathedral, 26-Kommunarov St. 9. The cathedral is open for services.

St. George's Church, Asatiani St. This church built in 1890 is not far from the cathedral; it is open for services.

Tavar-Angelogis (Archangel) Church, Tkibuli St. This was built in the 16th century.

Roman Catholic Church, Telmann St. The building has now been put to secular use, but its very existence points to the fact that the foreign colony here must have been of considerable size.

Synagogues, Shaumyan St. These are located in the old quarter of town which has long been inhabited by Jews. The synagogues stand close to each other. They were built about 150 years ago and are in good condition.

History and Ethnography Museum, Tbilisi St. 1. Open 10–6, closed Tues. In the museum's rich collection are 10th–13th century icons; some of them of gold and silver came from Gelati Monastery as did many manuscript books. There are 700 manuscripts dating from the 11th to the 19th century and including an 11th-century gospel. Other items include armour and old musical instruments.

Tsulukidze Museum, Tsulukidze St. 21. Open 10–6, closed Mon. Kutaisi was the birthplace of Alexander Tsulukidze (1876–1905), a Georgian revolutionary. The Museum is located in the house that used to be his home. The monument to him that stands in the museum courtyard is by Nikoladze.

Lenin Monument, Lenin Sq. The 6·40-m. bronze figure by Merabishvili was unveiled in 1958.

1905 Revolution Obelisk, Town Garden. This was unveiled in 1955 to mark the 50th anniversary of the 1905 revolution. It stands on the place where demonstrators clashed with the Cossacks.

Kikvidze Monument, Avtozavodskaya St. Vasili Kikvidze (1895–1919) was a hero of the civil war. Unveiled in 1959, the 2·5-m. bronze figure is by Mizandari and Nikoladze.

Meskhishvili Drama Theatre, Rustaveli Sq. The theatre was founded in 1861.

Puppet Theatre, Revolutsiya St. 11

Open-air Theatre, in the park

Park, on the banks of the Rioni

Central Stadium, Engels St.

Tbilisi Hotel and Restaurant, Tsulukidze St., TEL. 26–29

Kutaisi (Intourist) Hotel and Restaurant, Rustaveli St. 5, TEL. 5–85–01

Gelati Restaurant, on the left of the main road, at the 46/204-km. milestone

Imeretia Restaurant, Rustaveli St. 15

G.P.O., Kirov St. 64

Bank, Pushkin St. 18

Department Store, Paliashvili St. 18

Market, Paliashvili Pereulok 2

Geguti, to the south of the town, near Rioni Railway Station. Ruins of Geguti Palace which was built during the reign of Georgi III (1156–84) as a winter and hunting palace. It had twenty-one rooms. Excavations have been going on since 1953.

Rioni Power Station, 5 km. from the town. The Rioni was dammed here in 1934 and the very attractive reservoir is known locally as the Sea of Kutaisi. The power station has a capacity of 50,000 kilowatts. Two more power stations were completed in 1956 in the nearby village of Gumati, and they have a joint capacity of 66,500 kilowatts.

Sataplia lies 6 km. to the south-west of the town and is accessible by road. The name means 'honey-bearing' and refers to the wild bees that nest in the hills there. Sataplia is a reservation of 500 hectares (1250 acres), famed since 1933 when a local scientist, Peter Chabukiani, found traces of dinosaurs here. There is a huge karst cave, about 600 m. long, with stalactites and stalagmites; another, with an open arch, is called Yazom Grotto. In 1914 some tools belonging to Paleolithic Man were found in the Sakazhia Cave.

Motsameta (Martyr) Monastery, 6 km. to the east of Kutaisi, standing upon a cliff above the right bank of the Tskhaltsitela (red river). The road is not very good, but one can get there by train and it is only two stops from Kutaisi.

The story of the monastery's foundation tells how in the middle of the 8th century there were in the royal house of Mkheidze two princely brothers called David and Constantine. They ruled this territory and were famed for their nobility and courage. When they were attacked by the Arabs they and their army defeated the vanguard of the invaders, but later fell before the main force. The Arab emir, surprised by their youth, bravery, and uncommon beauty, offered them their freedom and honour if they would accept the Mohammedan faith. This they refused to do and so they were tortured and then with heavy stones around their necks they were thrown into the Rioni. The river cast the bodies up on the shore where they were found by a peasant. He laid the brothers on his bullock cart and then gave the bullocks freedom to wander. The beasts made their way up the hills to where the monastery now stands. The princes were buried there and in 1040 the monastery itself was founded, while the sacred remains were the object of pilgrimage of the faithful.

Gelati Monastery, 7 km. from Kutaisi on the road to Tkibuli and accessible by car. Open 10–6, closed Tues.

The monastery was founded in 1106 on the left of the R. Tskhaltsitela by King David II of Georgia (1089–1125), often referred to as David the Builder. He built the monastery in gratitude for his first victories and he was later canonised by the Georgian Church. From the day of its foundation King David and his successors always cared for the monastery and gave many presents of gold, silver, and rare manuscripts so that at one time it was the richest in the Caucasus. The monastery complex is a good example of Byzantine and Georgian architecture of the Georgian Golden Age, although much has crumbled away owing to the softness of the sandstone blocks used in the construction. Inside the thick wall are three churches, the main one dedicated to the Nativity of the Virgin. It is from this that the monastery itself takes its name, the Georgian word 'genati' having changed to Gelati. Other buildings include the bell-tower and the refectory, which until the 16th century was the academy hall.

King David was well versed in both Christian and Islamic culture and was at the same time a champion of Georgian culture. Besides founding Gelati, he assisted older Georgian monasteries, both in Georgia and abroad. When the monastery was founded, King David invited scholars from Georgia and from other countries too to come and join the brotherhood, and he endowed it well. The academy soon became a centre of learning and art; histories, philosophic and scientific works were written here and almost all the most important literature in the world at that time was translated into Georgian. The mosaics and the work in precious metals created here were noted for their beauty. Even in the time of David the Builder the academy was called the New Athens and the New Jerusalem. The academy school was run on the lines of similar schools in Byzantium and geometry, arithmetic, music, rhetoric, philosophy, and astronomy were taught. The monastery was sacked and burned by the Turks in 1510 but was soon rebuilt and restored and became the residence of the Patriarch of Western Georgia. The academy, however, did not survive, and the academy hall was rebuilt as a refectory. In 1759 the monastery was again pillaged, this time by the Lezgins, and the cathedral was burned again. However it was rebuilt and the monastery tradition continued until Gelati was closed in 1923.

Construction of the *Church of the Nativity of the Virgin* took 19 years (1106–25). It was consecrated

in 1126 on the order of King David's son, Demetre. It is built in the shape of a cross and measures 29·2 m. long, 20·2 m. wide and 36·3 m. high. The 13th–17th-century frescoes inside the cathedral show the saints and portraits of various Georgian kings including on the north wall one painted in the 16th century which is the only surviving portrait of David the Builder himself; he is depicted as a giant dressed as a king with a crown and carrying a model of the church in his left hand. At the corner of the apse is a large 13th-century mosaic of the Virgin and the Archangels Gabriel and Michael. Gelati Monastery was the burial place of both the Georgian and the Imeretian kings. It is believed that the famous Queen Tamara who ruled from 1184 to 1212 is buried on the right side of the cathedral. On the left are buried King Bagrat IV, Solomon I, and others.

David the Builder's grave is in the two-storey building, a combined chapel and entrance gate, which stands to the south of the main church. His tomb is covered with a stone slab bearing the inscription in Georgian: 'This is my resting place for all eternity. And I would not wish for anything more.' The slab of stone was set in the floor so that all who passed might tread it underfoot; it is said that this was David's own wish and a sign of his humility. Another of his epitaphs reads: 'There was a time when seven kings were guests at my feasts; and I was so mighty that I swept the Persians, the Turks, and the Arabs away from my borders and let the fish of one sea into another— but being so mighty, still I lie here with my hands folded upon my chest.'

St. George's Church stands to the east of the main church and measures 11 m. long, 5·5 m. wide and 21·4 m. high. Built in the 13th century, it was damaged in 1510, when the main church was burned by the Turks, but Bagrat III restored them both and he and his wife are buried here. The frescoes are of the 16th and 17th centuries and Bagrat III's portrait is on the south wall.

St. Nicholas's Church is to the west of the main church. It was built in the 14th century and has two storeys. It is 8·5 m. long and 6·5 m. wide. The bell-tower dates from the 12th–14th century; there is a spring of water under it. To the west of St. Nicholas's are the ruins of the academy building founded in the 12th century. It is roofless but inside the 10-m. walls the stone benches remain. The other buildings in the compound are of the 19th and 20th centuries. Outside the monastery walls, near the eastern entrance, is a church over a spring; it was rebuilt in 1903. To the north-east are the ruins of the Sokhasteri (hermitage).

Tskhaltubo

Tskhaltubo is 12 km. by road to the north-west of Kutaisi. The name of this spa means 'warm water'. It is said that once, long ago, an old shepherd stopped to rest beside an unknown stream. He bathed his feet as he sat there, and enjoyed the surprising warmth of the water. When at last he got up to continue on his way, he was amazed that all the aches and tiredness to which he had long been accustomed had gone from his legs. He returned as quickly as he could to his village to tell his story, and the fame of the water soon spread far and wide. This may be only a legend but the collections of crutches and discarded walking sticks left behind by patients that have been cured at the various sanatoria here is proof of the water's powers.

The first written reference to Tskhaltubo dates from the 12th century. In ancient times it was a royal bathing place and many came to benefit from the water. Some thought that the longer they spent in the water, the quicker the cure, and they settled there for the night, comfortably warm and tied to a low hanging tree so that they would not drown or drift downstream while they slept.

Although it has been known for centuries, it only became a proper spa in the 1930s. The place is located in the picturesque valley of the R. Tskhaltubo, surrounded by hills and mountains and protected by them from the wind. It is only 70 km. from the Black Sea coast. The river now flows through two canals which meet again near the railway station and then it flows in the Gubis-Tskhali. The river is dammed not far from its source and forms a reservoir of 5 hectares (12·5 acres). Visitors come here all the year round, but the best time is October and November. The winter is mild. The water maintains a steady temperature of 33–35°C. (92–96°F.) summer and winter because the river is fed by many warm springs which flow straight into it. The chemical content of the water is also constant; it contains rodon and nitrogen and is slightly radio-active (from 3 to 30 Mache Units) and is recommended for the cure of rheumatism, disorders of the metabolism, gynaecological diseases, and diseases of the circulatory and nervous systems. Since 1965 Intourist have organised special courses of treatment lasting 20 days at Tskhaltubo. There are a number of sanatoria and bath-houses here.

Theatre

The Park of 80 hectares (200 acres) contains some sub-tropical flora. There is an open-air stage.

Tbilisi Hotel and Restaurant

Cafés

LATVIA
See Riga, p. 264

LENINGRAD
Population—3,513,000 (1970)

Leningrad is the second largest city in the Soviet Union. From 1712, nine years after its foundation by Peter the Great, until 1918 it was the capital of the Russian Empire. Originally named St. Petersburg after its founder (and affectionately called 'Peter' by its inhabitants), it has since been twice renamed. In 1914 after the beginning of the war with Germany its name was changed from the Germanic-sounding Petersburg to the Russian equivalent Petrograd ('grad' meaning city or town), and in 1924 after the death of Lenin it was renamed Leningrad in his honour.

Situated on a flat plain at the mouth of the R. Neva in the Gulf of Finland, at a point 59°57'N. lat. and 30°20'E. long., 640 km. north of Moscow, the city covers an area of over 500 sq. km. The numerous canals, spanned by 620 bridges, take up one-sixth of the total area of the city and altogether there are 101 islands in Leningrad: these include the Vasilyevsky, Krestovsky, Yelagin, and Dekabristov islands, which are formed by canals and various streams of the Neva. The R. Neva itself is 67 km. long, 13 km. of which are within the boundaries of the city, its width within which varies from 337 m. to 592 m.

Leningrad is undoubtedly among the best-planned and most attractive cities in the world, and has deservedly earned its many titles such as 'Northern Palmyra' and 'Venice of the North'. From the beginning the city layout conformed to strict planning under the personal direction of Peter I, whose memory lingers at every step. Even today his planning is evident for, on the left side of the river, the three main streets converge upon the golden-spired building of the Admiralty where the first shipyard used to be, while a series of canals form concentric semi-circles around it, flowing into the river on either side. The right bank of the main stream of the river is at this point formed by many islands. Spreading behind the Peter and Paul Fortress is Petrogradskaya Storona and nearer the sea is the expanse of Vasilyevsky Ostrov (Island), where Peter I founded the Academy of Sciences and where Lomonosov, Popov, Mendeleyev, and Pavlov all worked. Peter's heirs and successors faithfully continued his work of constructing and embellishing the city, which now forms an admirable and harmonious ensemble of classical Russian architecture.

Moreover, there are few skyscrapers or very tall buildings to disturb this harmony, at least in the old central districts of the city, where four- or five-storey buildings predominate. In 1844 Nicholas I, wishing to stress the difference in station between the tsar and his subjects, decreed that all new buildings in St. Petersburg should be at least a sazhen (about seven feet) lower than the Winter Palace. Only the churches, with their domes, spires, and crosses, rose higher than the palace. This tradition was enforced for many decades. The highest landmark in Leningrad today is the new television tower, completed in 1962, which stands on the Petrogradskaya Storona. It rises to a height of 316 m. Although it is taller than the Eiffel Tower, its total weight is calculated to be seven times lighter.

Since the Revolution Leningrad has retained its position of importance in the spheres of administration, industry, trade, and the arts in the Soviet Union. It remains the administrative capital of the region of the same name, and is still one of the biggest seaports in the country. Its strategic position on the Baltic makes it an essen-

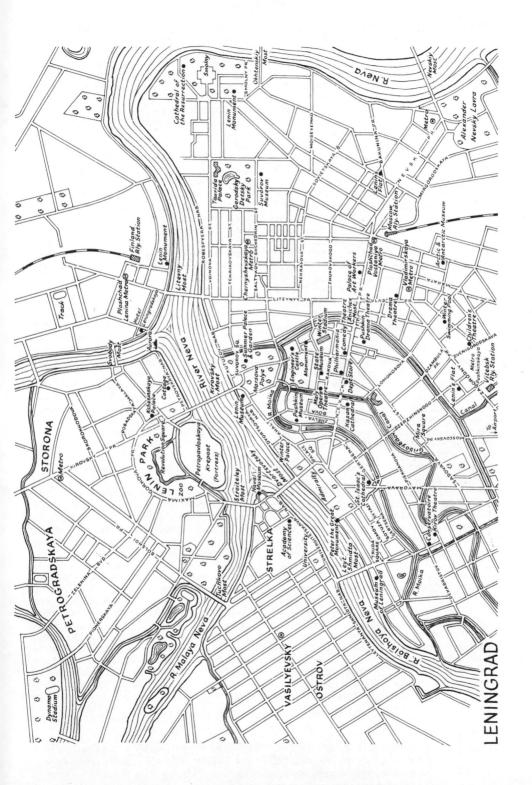

LENINGRAD

tial link in trade and communication between the interior of the Soviet Union and Finland, the Baltic countries and the West. It is also one of the most important industrial centres of the country, the main products being machinery, metals, and ships, chemicals, electrical goods, and textiles. Besides the university, there are about 270 scientific research centres, over 40 institutes of higher education, a conservatoire, 13 theatres, and 7 concert halls. The city boasts over 1000 architectural and historical monuments, and immense artistic and cultural riches are housed in its 50 museums and 2000 libraries. The largest of these is the Saltykov-Shchedrin Library, which has a collection of over 13,000,000 books and manuscripts.

The climate is quite mild in comparison with that of the central regions of the Soviet Union, but tends to be rather damp and misty. The average temperature for the year is 4°C. (39°F.); for July it is 18°C. (63°F.), and for January −8°C. (17°F.). From mid-November to April the river is frozen. The city is seen to its best advantage in May and June, during the famous 'White Nights', celebrated by so many poets, when only 40 minutes of semi-darkness occur in 24 hours.

Leningrad is a young city in comparison with many towns of the Soviet Union and Europe, but it has achieved an unprecedented historical significance. However, although St. Petersburg was only founded in the 18th century the history of the area around the city goes back many centuries.

It is often said that St. Petersburg was founded in the midst of uninhabited swamps and forests. It is true that these did exist but the place was inhabited. The area around the mouth of the Neva, at the point where the Baltic Sea penetrates deepest on its eastern shore, was of importance long before the building of St. Petersburg. The earliest settlers appear to have been the Finns, and up to the time of Peter the Great the various parts of the Neva delta retained their Finnish names. The Finns were followed by the Swedes and the Novgorodian Russians, who built castles and founded settlements which changed hands several times during the long struggle for permanent possession, for this area soon became an object of hot dispute.

In the earliest times of which there is any record of this part of Russia, the Neva served as an artery of trade between Europe and Asia; according to Arabian and Persian chronicles, the Persians and even the Hindus received goods from the West along this route. It was the starting-point for the great trade-routes running from the Varangians to the Greeks, through the Volkhov and the Dnieper, and from the Varangians to the Arabs along the Volga. Evidence of this ancient traffic

has been brought to light in discoveries of large numbers of Saxon and Arabian coins dug up in several places at the mouth of the Neva and on the shores of Lake Ladoga. Nestor, the 11th-century Russian chronicler, recorded that 'The Neva served as a means of communication between peoples of the West and Novgorod through the Volkhov; by the Neva they went into the Varangian Sea, and by that sea to Rome.' Thus for Novgorod, the most important Russian trading centre at this time, the Neva was a vital natural outlet to the Western sea, while on the other hand, for the sea-faring Swedes, the Neva delta was the key to Ingermanland, the southern shore of the Gulf of Finland, where trade with the inhabitants of the spreading plain was being developed. Considerable strife gradually sprang up between Slavs and Scandinavians over the command of the Neva. In 1143 the Swedes, assisted by the Finns, attacked the Russians at Ladoga and were repulsed, but from that time the contest became serious and, in spite of several peace treaties, it went on intermittently for 600 years. The strife was finally put an end to in 1743 by the Treaty of Abo, which confirmed Russia's possession of the whole area of the Neva and the Gulf of Finland.

Besides the Swedes and the Danes on one hand, who began to approach through the Baltic provinces, on the other the most important contestants for this region were the Knights of the Teutonic Order, who tried to extend their conquests into the Neva region. The struggle with these invaders took place in the south-western part of the present region of Leningrad, and lasted about 400 years. The ostensible purpose of these German and Livonian knights was to spread Christianity, by which was meant Catholicism, among the 'Baltic heathen and the Russian schismatics'. They were joined in this purpose by the Swedes, by whom a holy crusade was organised and undertaken at the behest of Pope Gregory IX, conveyed in a Bull to the Archbishop of Uppsala in 1237. This resulted in the famous battle of 1240 between the invaders and the inhabitants of Novgorod under the leadership of their Grand Duke Alexander. The Swedes, led by Jarl Birger, brother-in-law of King Erik of Sweden, encamped at the mouth of the Izhyora, a tributary of the Neva, were taken completely by surprise and were totally routed by the Russian forces who, according to legend, were inspired by a vision of the Russian saints Boris and Gleb. For this exploit Grand Duke Alexander was canonised under the name of St. Alexander Nevsky, and one of the first things which Peter the Great considered it his duty to do, when he began the foundation of St. Petersburg, was to have St. Alexander Nevsky made the

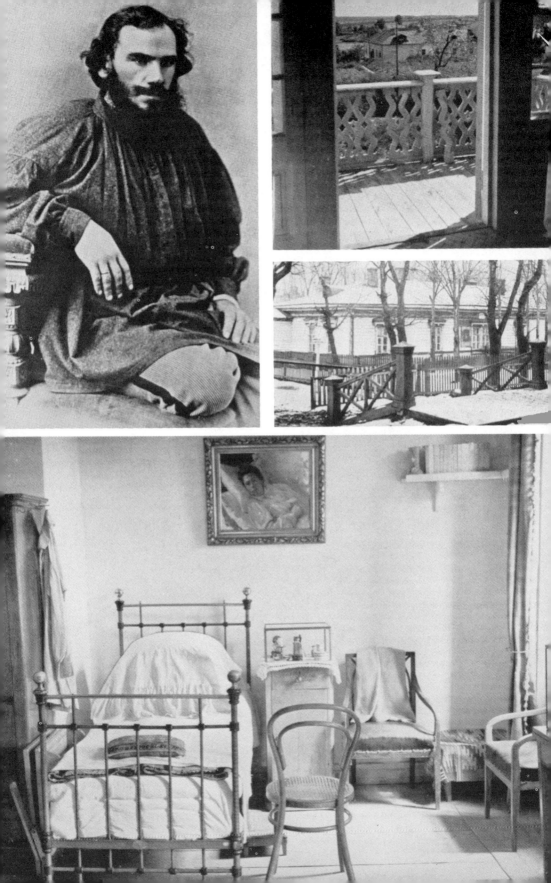

patron saint of his new capital, and cause a magnificent monastery to be built for the reception of the saint's remains.

In 1300 the Swedes established the castle of Vyborg and re-appeared on the Neva. This time they built a fortified position, Landskrona, at the mouth of the R. Okhta in the Neva delta, but this fortress—the first attempt to establish a Swedish town within the limits of the present Leningrad—was soon destroyed by the inhabitants of Novgorod. In order to be able to offer greater resistance to these continual encroachments, the Russians in 1323 built a fortress at Ladoga, on a small island at the head of the Neva. However, during the succeeding 300 years this fortress was continually taken and retaken by the Swedes. At last, at the end of the sixteenth and beginning of the seventeenth centuries, circumstances became particularly favourable for the Swedes. Novgorod had lost its independence to Moscow, and Russia's national power was greatly weakened by sedition and rivalry for possession of the throne. During this 'Time of Troubles', the Swedes took advantage of the opportunity to settle themselves firmly on the Neva and Lake Ladoga. After the first Romanov had been elected to the Russian throne, they were confirmed in possession by the Treaty of Stolbova, signed on 27 February 1617, and remained masters of the situation until the advent of Peter the Great.

During this time the most important undertaking of the Swedes on the Neva was undoubtably founding the settlement of Nyenshantz on the site of the former Landskrona. A small fortress was first built on the right bank of the Neva in 1632, and a tiny, flourishing town soon grew up around it. Today this same site is occupied by the region of Leningrad called Okhta, which lies opposite the former Smolny Institute. In the 17th century the Smolny district was a colony of Russian tar-distillers, from whom it derived its name ('smola' meaning tar or pitch). The colony was dependent upon Nyenshantz, both politically and economically, and came under the control of the Swedish authorities. There is evidence that the commercial community of Nyenshantz was a wealthy one: it carried on considerable trade with Lubeck and Amsterdam (during the summer of 1691 over 100 foreign vessels discharged their cargoes on the Neva, the goods probably being sent up the R. Volkhov to Novgorod), and one of the town's merchants, by the name of Frelius, was able to lend a large sum of money to Charles XII in his war against Russia. Besides the town itself, some 45 villages and farmsteads are marked on Swedish maps from the year 1670, dotted over the area now occupied by Leningrad. There was good pasture-land, an abundance of water-fowl, and plenty of game, including elk, in the surrounding woods. Many Swedish noblemen had extensive game reserves here. Thus in pre-Petrine times, the region was far from being uninhabited swamp.

After his return from visiting England and Holland, Peter the Great began to turn his attention to the Neva. At that time Russia had no access to the sea, as Turkey still held the Black Sea. So it was of the utmost importance for the development of Russia's economic, technological, and cultural contacts with the West that she gain control of this area. Thus, after his unsuccessful attempt to wrest Narva from the grasp of the Swedes, Peter resolved to attack and capture Noteburg and Nyenshantz. In the autumn of 1602 he was successful in forcing the surrender of Noteburg: the key of the fortress, surrendered by the Swedish commandant, was nailed by Peter's orders to the top of the principal bastion, and the fortress itself was renamed Schlusselburg, from the German word for a key. In the following year Nyenshantz too was forced into submission.

After the capture of Nyenshantz, Peter lost no time in beginning to carry out his project of establishing a commercial town in order to utilise the mouth of the Neva. Nyenshantz itself was not suited to the purpose, as it was situated a little too far up the river. Therefore a spot nearer the sea was selected, at the point where the Neva, before entering the Gulf of Finland, branches into three main channels, with several minor streams which form a number of islands of different shapes and sizes. On the first of these islands—a very small one, known by the Finnish name of 'Janni-saari' or Hare Island—Peter started the building of the fortress of St. Petersburg. Immediately behind Janni-saari was the large island called 'Koivu-saari' or Birch Island, now the Petrogradskaya Storona (Petrograd Side), on which the first buildings outside the fortress were erected. On 16 May, 1703, only 16 days after the conquest of Nyenshantz, Peter the Great laid the foundation stone of the fortress, and commanded a cathedral dedicated to the apostles Peter and Paul to be built within the walls.

Wooden barracks and houses were rapidly put up to accommodate the troops from Nyenshantz and the chief officers and civil officials. For himself Peter had a small hut with only 3 rooms, built of logs just outside the fortress on the adjoining island of the Petrogradskaya Storona so that he could supervise the construction work. In general Peter disliked large and luxurious buildings, and the palaces which were built for him in St. Petersburg were all mere cottages in comparison with the magnificent structures raised by his successors. He preferred to give his money and attention to the commercial and military aspects of building the city. He resolved to ensure the safety of the city by fortifying the island Kronstadt, some 18 miles upstream, and constructing a mid-water fort to protect the navigable passage. Kron-

---

PLATE OPPOSITE
The author and playwright, Anton Chekhov, photographed in April 1897 on his estate at Melikhovo where he lived from 1892 to 1898 and wrote 'The Seagull'.

stadt in effect rendered the Peter and Paul Fortress redundant, but nevertheless it was reconstructed with more solid material some six or seven years later. Its ramparts and six bastions were at first built of wood and earth, which was subsequently replaced by stone revetments and masonry.

Next to the construction of these fortifications, Peter gave the greatest attention to the building of the Admiralty and shipbuilding yards on the opposite side of the Neva. In fact, the left bank of the Neva, on which the principal quarter of the city eventually developed, was largely peopled in the first instance by shipwrights—Dutch and other foreign experts in naval construction—together with great numbers of workmen.

Estimates as to the precise number of workmen involved in the building of the new city vary enormously, but it is said that over 10,000 people died during the course of the operations (hence the melancholy saying that the town is 'built on bones'). Workers were sent by force to St. Petersburg from all parts of the Empire and were employed in laying the first foundations in the marshes and digging the canals. In the unhealthy climate and under the terrible conditions of work, they were killed off almost wholesale by disease and exhaustion. The mortality rate was further increased in the early days by frequent flooding: during Peter's reign there were no less than seven inundations, and it seems miraculous that the town was not washed away in its infancy. It was only the tenacity and determination of the tsar himself which ensured the eventual success of the city, for it appears that everyone else, nobleman and peasant alike, hated the place. Many of the soldiers and workmen deserted whenever the chance arose, but most were soon caught and dragged back. Nor could people be persuaded to come and live here, in spite of the fact that incentives were offered. Thus Peter was forced to resort to drastic measures of compulsion. In 1710 he ordered 40,000 workmen a year for 3 years to be sent to St. Petersburg from the provinces and, with a view to attracting masons, he further commanded that no stone buildings should be erected anywhere in the Empire except St. Petersburg under penalty of banishment to Siberia. One of Peter's decrees, dated 26 May 1712, reads as follows: '1. One thousand of the best families of the nobility are required to build houses of beams, with lath and plaster, in the old English style, along the bank of the Neva from the Imperial Palace to the point opposite Nyenshantz. 2. Five hundred of the best-known merchant families and five hundred traders less distinguished, must build for themselves wooden houses on the other side of the river, opposite to the dwellings of the nobility, until the Government can provide them with stone houses and shops. 3. Two thousand artisans of every kind— painters, tailors, joiners, blacksmiths, etc.—must settle themselves on the same side of the river, right up to Nyenshantz.'

Under such pressure the progress of the city was naturally very rapid. Within eight or ten years of its foundation there were a dozen streets and about 1000 houses. The paving of the streets was begun in 1717 and in 1725 Peter ordered lamps to be put up. By 1725 the city contained 75,000 inhabitants.

After Peter the Great's death, his widow Empress Catherine I and his grandson Peter II did nothing for the advancement of St. Petersburg. On the contrary, Peter II transferred his court to Moscow and entertained the idea of divesting Petersburg of its rank as capital. The mere attempt led thousands of people thankfully to desert the city, and before the next ruler who took up residence in St. Petersburg, the Empress Anna, could reinstall her court on the Neva, more compulsory measures had to be taken to bring back deserters. Then the city had to contend with an epidemic of incendiarism: in 1737 over 1000 houses were destroyed by arson. Nevertheless, under Anna and her successor the Empress Elizabeth, the town grew rapidly. Anna built the Admiralty Tower, with its gilded spire, and also began the Winter Palace; Elizabeth erected the Anichkov Palace. However, the real successor to Peter the Great, as far as the continuation of his building work was concerned, was Catherine II (the Great). Many of the finest buildings date from her reign (1762–96). On her invitation many well-known foreign architects came to St. Petersburg during this period and designed not only single houses but complete 'architectural landscapes', in which all the buildings were regarded as parts of a great whole. It is largely owing to her encouragement of such building that the city, even today, has numerous architecturally harmonious squares and streets.

Not without reason is Leningrad frequently called 'the Cradle of the Revolution', for the whole history of the revolutionary movement in Russia is intimately connected with this city. The first strike broke out in St. Petersburg as early as 1749, in the form of a weavers' uprising, and since that time the workers, students and intellectuals of the city were always in the fore-front of revolutionary activity. In 1825 the Decembrist uprising, an attempt by a group of officers of the Guards to overthrow the tsar and establish a constitutional form of government, broke out here but was quickly suppressed. Here too, in the 1870s and 1880s were concentrated the terrorist activities of the Narodnaya Volya (People's Freedom) Group, which on 1 March 1881 succeeded in assassinating Tsar Alexander II. Here too, the first Marxist group of workers in Russia, the Northern Workers Association, was formed. On 9 January 1905 the first Russian revolution received its bloody baptism here, when a huge demonstration of workers, led by the priest Father Gapon, was fired upon by the Imperial guards in the square in front of the Winter Palace. After the ensuing strikes and disturbances the tsar was forced into calling a limited form of parliament, a consultative body called the State Duma. At this time too, the first Soviet (Council) of Workers and Soldiers was formed in St. Petersburg and Soviets subsequently sprang up all over the country.

By the outbreak of the First World War in 1914, the population of Petersburg, then renamed Petrograd, had reached 2 million, of whom approximately 250,000 were industrial workers. After the February revolution of 1917, which overthrew the monarchy and established a Provisional Government, Lenin returned to Petrograd from his exile abroad and upon his arrival at the Finlyandsky (Finland) Station was greeted by, and himself addressed, a huge crowd of workers, soldiers, and sailors. Except for a short period in July/August when he went into hiding in Razliv and Finland, Lenin was constantly in Petrograd, planning the Bolshevik takeover of the government. On 25 October (or 7 November as it became when the calendar was revised) 1917 the Soviet government was proclaimed and the Red Guard of the Petrograd workers, with the help of the Baltic Fleet, broke down the resistance of the provisional Government.

Naturally after the transfer of the seat of government to Moscow, the city's political significance to a certain extent diminished, but it continued its previous development as an industrial and commercial centre. In 1924 it was again the victim of serious flooding, but even this could not restrain its growth. Disaster again struck Leningrad during the Second World War, when the city was under siege by the Germans for almost 900 days. In August 1941 Nazi troops reached the outskirts of Leningrad and it became part of the front line. Food supplies ran short, water and electricity supplies were cut off, fuel stocks ran out, and public transport came to a standstill. About 650,000 people died in Leningrad during the blockade and more than 10,000 buildings were destroyed or damaged by bombs or artillery fire. However, the blockade could not succeed in starving Leningrad into surrender, for a constant flow of lorries brought to Leningrad provisions, fuel and ammunition along the so-called 'road of life', laid across the ice of Lake Ladoga a few miles from the front line. In January 1943 the ring of the blockade was broken, and a year later a victory salute was fired over the city to celebrate its liberation. Leningrad was subsequently awarded the title 'Hero City'.

Work was immediately started on repairing the damage caused by the war. By 1948 Leningrad's industry reached its prewar level of production and soon surpassed it. In particular electrical and radio-electronic industries were developed here, and the technical level is especially high in these fields. Recently the first atomic ice-breaker in the world, the 44,000 h.p. 'Lenin', which can sail for more than a year without refuelling, was built here as was, more recently, the 'Artica'.

Reconstruction and repair of the buildings damaged during the war was faithfully carried out, inspired by the past, and has now been com-pleted. Much new building also went on, and there are many modern blocks of flats, such as those along Moskovsky Prospect, and even whole new residential regions such as Avtovo.

Petrogradskaya Storona (Petrograd Side).

The name 'Petrogradskaya Storona' applies to part of Leningrad which includes the Zayachy, Petrogradsky, Aptekarsky, and Petrovsky Islands. To the north are the Kirovsky Islands and the sections of the city known as Staraya Derevnya (old village) and Novaya Derevnya (new village). The Neva is at its broadest at the point where it divides the centre of the city, on its left bank, from the Petrogradskaya Storona, and it was here that the building of St. Petersburg began. Here stands the oldest building of the city:

Peter and Paul Fortress (the Petropavlovskaya Krepost). The fortress was founded in May 1703, and by the autumn of that year there were emplacements on the earthworks round the fortress and 300 guns barred the Swedish Fleet's approach to the site of the new city. In 1706 builders began to replace the original earthworks with powerful brick fortifications, according to the plans of Domenico Trezzini. The new walls were 12 m. high and took 35 years to complete. However, by the end of that century the brick had begun to look shabby in comparison with the other buildings erected on the banks of the Neva, and in the reign of Catherine II the walls were faced with granite slabs which gave them the appearance they have today.

Gradually, as the fortress lost its military importance, it was used for other purposes, notably as a prison for political offenders. Many of the most famous opponents of the tsarist régime were imprisoned here at one time or another. The first prisoner of the fortress was the Tsarevich Alexei, the son of Peter I, who was tortured to death by order of his father in 1718. In 1790 the writer Alexander Radishchev was imprisoned here before his exile to Siberia by Catherine II for writing about the horrors of serfdom and autocracy in his book 'Journey from St. Petersburg to Moscow'. After the Decembrist uprising of 1825, the leaders of the conspiracy were confined in the Alexeyevsky Bastion to await judgement: the majority were sentenced to many years of hard labour, but five were sentenced to death and were executed outside the fortress, to the north of it, on 13 July 1826. Throughout the nineteenth century the list of prisoners reads like a catalogue of the revolutionary movement in Russia: after 1849, members of the Petrashevsky Circle (which included Dostoevsky) before their exile to Siberia; in the 1850s the anarchist Mikhail Bakunin; in 1862 the writer Dmitri Pisarev and in July of the same year Nikolai Chernyshevsky (who wrote his famous novel 'What is to be done?' here); in 1866 Karakozov, who made an unsuccessful attempt on the life of Alexander II, before his subsequent execution. In the 1870s and 1880s the cells of solitary confinement in the Trubetskoy Bastion held many of the most prominent members of the 'Zemlya i Volya' (Land and Liberty) and 'Narodnaya Volya' (People's Freedom) groups, including Lenin's elder brother, Alexander Ulyanov. In January 1905 the writer Maxim Gorky was imprisoned here for issuing a revolutionary proclamation. However, in October 1917 the garrison of the fortress came over to the side of the revolutionaries and the arsenal, containing nearly 10,000 rifles and large supplies of ammunition, was used to arm the insurrection. In 1924 the Peter and Paul Fortress was opened as a museum.

The fortress is entered through the outer *Ivanovskiye Vorota* (the John Gate) and the *Petrovskiye Vorota* (the Peter Gate). The latter is of particular interest, as it is the only building in the fortress that has remained practically unchanged since it was first built. It was designed by Trezzini, built 1717–18, and adorned with bas-reliefs by Konrad Osner representing the miracle of the Apostle Peter. In the niches there are statues of Mars and Venus. In the centre of the fortress stands the *Petropavlovsky Sobor* (Peter and Paul Cathedral). This is a domed building, in the Dutch style, and was erected between 1712 and 1721 by Domenico Trezzini. Later it was reconstructed by Rastrelli and Chevakinsky in 1750 after a fire, and again altered under Nicholas I. It is 64 m. long and 30 m. wide; the extremely slender gilded spire, which stands 120 m. high, is crowned by an angel bearing a cross, the work of Rinaldi. The clock in the tower was brought from Cologne in 1760. Of particular interest inside the cathedral are the pulpit, dating from the time of Peter the Great, a rare occurrence in a Russian church, and the carved and gilded wooden iconostasis made in the 1720s by carvers Ivan Telegin and Trifon Ivanov and artist Andrei Merkuryev. This cathedral is the burial place of all the Russian tsars, from Peter I to Alexander III, with the exception of Peter II: the imperial tombs are of white marble, with gilded eagles at the corners. However, the sarcophagi of Alexander II and his wife are carved out of Altai jasper and Ural red quartz respectively; work on these tombs took 17 years.

To the right of the cathedral stands a small house, built by the architect Zomtsov in 1730 and adorned with a statue of a nymph holding an oar, which used to house a little boat belonging to Peter the Great—the so-called 'Grandfather of the Russian Fleet'.

To the west, opposite the cathedral, is the *Monetny Dvor* (the Mint). This was originally founded in 1724, but the present building by Voronikhin dates from the 19th century.

Also near the Cathedral stands the *Nevskiye Vorota* (the Neva Gate), built by Lvov in 1787. It was through this gate that prisoners were led at night from the fortress dungeons on to the granite Commandant's Wharf, to be sent to the Schlusselburg Fortress or to Lisy Nos (fox's nose), a remote spot on the shore of the Gulf of Finland, where the death sentences were carried out.

On the crownwork of the fortress is situated the *Arsenal*, the old building of which was established on the site of the former outer fortifications of the fortress in 1706. It now houses the *Military museum*. This museum was founded by Peter the Great himself with the purpose of representing the whole history of weaponry, particularly in Russia. The collection has over 50,000 exhibits, including weapons (dating from the Paleolithic Age to the present day), military uniforms, and documents.

The park on the bank of the Kronverksky (crownwork) Sound was planted in 1845 and has since 1923 been called the *Lenin Park*. It stretches from the sound to Gorky Prospect, where the writer Gorky lived from 1914 to 1921 at No. 23. On the park side of the Prospect stands the *Lenin Komsomol Theatre*, built in 1939 but damaged during the siege and restored after the war. Next door (at 4, Lenin Park) is the *Planetarium*, opened to the public in 1959. Adjoining the Planetarium is a three-dimensional cinema and then the *Vulkan*, the largest cinema in Leningrad, seating about 2000. Further round to the west of the crownwork are the Zoological Gardens (founded in 1865), which have a collection of about 250 types of animals and birds.

On the opposite side of the fortress, on the Petrovskaya Naberezhnaya (Embankment), stands the *Cottage of Peter the Great* (Domik Petra Velikovo). This was built in 3 days in May, 1703, in Dutch style, as the first house of the city. From here the tsar directed the building of St. Petersburg. As Peter lived in the cottage only in summer, it had no stone foundation, no stoves, and no chimneys. The cottage is about 12 m. long and 6 m. wide, and contains two rooms and a study. The doors and windows are all different sizes, and the biggest door is only 5' 9" high, while Peter was 6' 6". It is built of pine logs, painted to resemble bricks, a device frequently employed in the city's early years, when the hastily erected wooden structures were given the appearance of solid brick buildings. When the Summer Palace across the river was completed, Peter stopped using the cottage altogether and it was preserved only as an interesting historical relic. In 1784 Catherine II had a stone shelter built around it to protect it.

Inside the cottage is the boat in which the tsar saved the lives of some fishermen on Lake Ladoga in 1690. It is said to have been built by Peter himself. There is also an exhibition devoted to Russia's victory in the Northern War and the first years of St. Petersburg.

The granite wharf on the embankment in front of the cottage is decorated with two mythical Shih Tsa (lion-frog) carvings, brought to St. Petersburg from Manchuria in 1907. There is a bronze bust of Peter I in the garden.

A little further along the embankment, near the Nakhimov Naval College, is moored the famous cruiser '*Aurora*', which gave the signal for the start of the revolution. The ship was built in 1903 and took part in the Russo-Japanese War; in October

1917 the crew went over to the side of the revolutionaries and took command of the ship. On the night of the 25 October, on instructions of the Revolutionary Military Committee, the 'Aurora' sailed up the Neva and fired a blank shot as a signal for the beginning of the attack on the Winter Palace. The gun which fired the shot and the radio room from which the fighting orders of the Revolutionary Military Committee and Lenin's manifesto announcing the victory of the revolution were transmitted are still to be seen, and the ship is open to the public.

Returning along the Petrovskaya Embankment, past Peter the Great's cottage, one comes to *Revolution Sq.*, formerly called Troitskaya (trinity) Square. This is the oldest square of the city, for it was here that the first houses of St. Petersburg were built. Here too were the first harbour, the Exchange, the Customhouse, and the Market. The Troitsky Cathedral, built after the victory in the Battle of Poltava in 1710 and in which Peter I took the title of Emperor in 1721, stood here. Little, however, remains of these very early buildings.

On the corner of Gorky Prospect stands the palace which formerly belonged to the ballerina Matilda Kshesinskaya, mistress of Nicholas II. This very elegant building, with its tiled facade, was built in 1902 by the architect A. I. Gogen. In 1917 the *Kshesinskaya Palace* was the headquarters of the Central and Petrograd Committees of the Bolshevik Party and Lenin spoke here several times. It and the building next to it now house the *Museum of the October Revolution*.

Adjoining the palace is a mosque, built in 1912. It has two minarets and its grey stone is decorated with gaily coloured tiles. S. Krichinsky, the architect who designed it, took as his model the tomb of Timur in Samarkand, dating from the beginning of the 15th century.

Here in Revolution Sq. begins one of the main thoroughfares of the city, *Kirovsky Prospect*, which runs through the Petrogradskaya Storona to the Kamennoostrovsky Bridge.

At No. 10 are the Lenfilm Studios, one of the most famous and important film studios in the country.

In *Kirovsky Prospect* there are several examples of early 20th-century Russian architecture making use of classical forms. One of these is No. 19, a stone-faced building designed by S. Minash.

Next to this house stands the oldest building in the street, No. 21. It was to this building that, in 1843, the *Tsarskoye Selo Lyceum*, a school for the sons of the gentry at which Pushkin had been a pupil, was moved. It was then renamed the Alexandrovsky Lyceum.

A little further along the street broadens into the *Lev Tolstoy Sq.* The focal point of this square's architecture is a building known as 'The House with the Towers'. This strange building was erected in 1914 by Byelogrud; above a roughstone and ceramic façade, its hexahedral towers

rise high over the square, giving the impression of a medieval castle.

At *No. 42 Kirovsky Prospect* stands the Leningrad Soviet Palace of Culture, a building dating from 1934 and designed by Levinson and Munts.

Crossing the R. Karpovka, one reaches the part of the Petrogradskaya Storona known as *Aptyekarsky Ostrov* (apothecary island). It received this name in the time of Peter the Great, when, in 1713, a large plantation for cultivating medicinal herbs was laid out on the island and called the 'Apothecary's Garden'. A hundred years later the plantation was converted into a botanical garden. In 1931 a Botanical Institute, attached to the Academy of Sciences, was founded here. The institute has a Botanical Museum whose herbarium, with over 3 million samples, is one of the largest in Europe.

Continuing down *Kirovsky Prospect* one comes to a timber house (No. 62) which belonged to the architect A. N. Voronikhin. It was built in 1807–8, probably by the architect himself, and it was here, until his death in 1814, that he spent the last years of his life.

A little further along are the *Dzerzhinsky Gardens*. Here the Kirovsky Prospect ends in a broad bridge (Kamennoostrovsky Most) which crosses the Malaya Nevka and leads to the *Kirovskiye Ostrova* (Kirovskiye Islands). This is the collective name for the islands in the north of the Petrogradskaya Storona; they consist of Yelagin Island, Krestovsky Island, and Trudyashchikhsya (workers') Island, formerly called Kamenny (stone) Island.

The first island one comes to is the *Trudyashchikhsya*, which has an area of 103 hectares (260 acres). It was first owned by a foremost statesman of Peter the Great's reign, Golovkin. He was succeeded by the Chancellor, Bestuzhev-Ryumin, who had thousands of serfs brought from the Ukraine to improve his estate here. These peasants settled around the island, thus founding those parts of the city now known as the Staraya Derevnya and the Novaya Derevnya (the old and new villages). During the 18th century canals were dug on the island, and their banks lined with limestone and granite. Many of the leading families of the gentry built magnificent summer houses and hunting-lodges here. On the eastern side of the island stands the *Kamennoostrovsky Dvoryets* (palace), which was built for Paul I who owned the island before his accession to the throne. The palace was probably designed by the distinguished 18th-century Russian architects Bazhenov and Felten, and the latter was certainly responsible for the design of the Maltese Chapel attached to the palace.

At *No. 1, Bekhterev Embankment* stands the former villa of Prince Dolgorukov, built in 1831–2 by Shustov in the shape of a domed cube.

The wooden building of the *Kamennoostrovsky Theatre*, which stands at No. 26, Bolshaya Nevka Embankment, was also the work of Shustov. It was erected within 40 days in 1827 and was restored later in the 19th century after damage by fire. This theatre was particularly popular for its performances during the summer season when the back walls were opened and the grove in which it stands was used as a natural backdrop.

The poet Pushkin was a frequent visitor to the island and owned a house here which has unfortunately not survived. It was replaced in 1913 by a mansion built for the senator Polovtsev by the architect Fomin. This building, in strict classical style, with rooms richly decorated with marble, Italian silk, moulding, and gilt and painted ceilings, is considered the most beautiful on the island.

On Krestovka Embankment stands *Peter the Great's Oak Tree*, planted by the tsar in 1709, and nearby (at No. 2) is a villa built for the industrialist Vurgaft, again by Fomin. This and most of the other large mansions on the island were converted after the revolution into sanatoria and holiday centres, which remains their function today.

Crossing the waters of the Srednaya (Medium) Nevka, one comes to *Yelagin Island*, which has an area of 95 hectares (230 acres) of park. It was first owned by Shafirov, a noted diplomat of the beginning of the 18th century, but in 1780 passed into the hands of the nobleman Yelagin, whose name it still bears. Under his ownership, the marshy land was drained, and broad dykes, which still survive, were built to prevent flooding. In 1817 Alexander I purchased the island from Count Orlov, and gave the young but brilliant architect K. I. Rossi the task of building a palace there for his mother, the widow of Paul I. The *Yelagin Dvoryets* built between 1818 and 1826 in the classical Russian style, was the result. It stands on a broad stone terrace, girdled with an elegant grille, and has two façades. The main one faces the park, which is laid out in English style, and is very impressive: a broad flight of steps decorated with lion carvings leads up to the six-columned portico of the main entrance. The other façade overlooking the river is more restrained: its central section consists of the convex wall of the Oval Hall, beautifully proportioned columns, and an elegant frieze above the windows of the ground floor. Also outstanding are the colossal white marble vases with bas-relief groups of nereids and tritons, designed by Rossi himself. Of the surrounding buildings the semi-circular kitchen, the Pavilion (on the embankment of the Bolshaya Nevka), and the Musical Pavilion are also of interest.

The extreme western tip of the island, which runs out into the Gulf of Finland, the so-called Strelka, was replanned and laid out in 1927 by Ilyin. It has a terrace of pink marble with lion carvings on stone pedestals.

The rest of Yelagin Island is taken up by a recreation park with various amusement and sports facilities. Celebrations are held in this park in June and July to see the white nights in and out.

The largest Kirovskiye Island, with an area of 415 hectares (1037 acres), is *Krestovsky Island*. This is the sports centre of Leningrad, for in the western part of the island lies the huge *Kirov Stadium*, with a seating capacity of almost 100,000 people. It was built in 1950 (architect A. S. Nikolsky) mainly of earth: many million cubic metres of soil were raised from the bed of the Gulf of Finland to form the mound on which the stadium rests. The liquid mud was pumped through pipes to the construction site, where it was allowed to harden in the required shape. The stadium has a large central arena with facilities for most spectator sports.

Also on Krestovsky Island is the *Victory Park*, laid out in 1945 to celebrate and commemorate victory in the Second World War.

If one continues further to the north of the Petrogradskaya Storona, through the Novaya Derevnya and along the Kolomyazhskaya Chaussee, one reaches the site where Pushkin fought the duel in which he was mortally wounded on 27 January 1837. The spot is marked by an *obelisk* of pink granite, roughly 20 m. high, with a bronze bas-relief, commemorating the poet.

The Left Bank of the Neva

Much of the best architecture in Leningrad is to be found on the banks of the Neva. Here there are many squares and buildings, even complexes of buildings, of great artistic and historical importance. Beginning at the eastern end of the embankment, the most striking building here is the whole complex of the *Smolny*. Before the founding of the city the Swedish fort Sabina stood on this site (facing the fortress Nyenshantz on the right bank of the river) and later there arose a colony of tar-distillers, from whom the district derived its name. In the 18th century under Peter the Great, the Smolny Dvor (Tar Yard) was built here to store tar for the ships being built further along the river in the shipyards of St. Petersburg. In 1723, the Smolny Dvor was moved to another part of the city and a summer residence for the daughter of Peter the Great, the Tsarevna Elizabeth, was built in its place. When the main building of the palace was burnt down in 1744, Elizabeth, now Empress, decided to found a convent here in which to spend her last days. In 1748 building was begun to the designs of Rastrelli, in the Baroque style, with the convent buildings grouped around a central cathedral, the *Cathedral of the Resurrection*. This has five domes, the central one of which is almost 80 m. high and is surrounded by four smaller differently shaped domes. The whole group is reminiscent of the style of early Russian church architecture.

On her accession to the throne Catherine II decreed that a school for young ladies of noble birth be founded in the convent, and at the same time it was decided to build a house for widows next door to the convent. The plans for the latter were entrusted to the architect Giacomo Quarenghi and the building was erected between 1806 and 1808 in a strict classical style. Set well back from the street, its long façade is relieved by two projecting wings and the elaborate central part. Above the raised arcade of the front entrance there is a portico of eight Ionic columns with a pediment and a loggia behind the columns. The white and yellow façade has no moulded ornaments at all, except for the capitals of the flat pilasters. The interior decorations are even more simple, but nonetheless impressive; particularly attractive is the enormous assembly hall, which takes up the first and second floors of the entire south wing.

When this building was completed, the school (the Smolny Institute) was moved here, and the occupants of the Widows' House accommodated in the convent. In August 1917 the building was taken over by the Petrograd Soviet and the Central Executive Committee and in October 1917, when the Revolutionary Military Committee began working here, it became the headquarters of the revolutionary forces. After the overthrow of the Provisional Government the first Soviet Government was formed here. The room in which Lenin lived and worked here has been turned into a museum.

From the Smolny there is no through road along the embankment, and so one must follow the parallel Voinova St. Here, at the junction with Stavropol St., stands one of the oldest buildings in the city, built in 1714. In the early years of St. Petersburg it was the home of the boyar Kikin, who conspired with the Tsarevich Alexei in a plot against Peter the Great. After the exposure of the plot and Kikin's execution in 1719, the house was given over to the collections of the Kunstkammer, the first Russian science museum, founded by Peter. Entry was open to all, free of charge, and to attract the public all those who visited the museum were given refreshments, including a glass of vodka. In 1727 the Kunstkammer was moved to another building, and this building now houses a children's club.

A little further on, on the opposite side of Voinova St. at No. 47, stands the *Taurida Palace* (Tavrichesky Dvorets) built in 1783–9 by Starov on the orders of Catherine the Great and presented by her to her favourite, Prince Potemkin of Taurida, after his conquest of the Crimea. The interior in particular was decorated with great splendour, but after Potemkin's death in 1791 the palace was resumed by the crown, and the mad Paul I, out of sheer hatred for Potemkin, had it turned into barracks. The famous Oval Hall with white marble columns was used as a stable. At the beginning of the 19th century, after Paul's death, the palace was restored by Rusca, and in 1906 it was slightly reconstructed so that it could be used for the sessions of the State Duma. It was here that, after the overthrow of the monarchy in February 1917, the Provisional Government was formed.

Behind the Taurida Palace lies the 75-acre park the *Tavrichesky Sad* (Taurida Garden) where in the days of Catherine II magnificent entertainments were given. Part of the park is now used as Leningrad's largest nursery garden.

Towards the end of *Voinova St.*, at No. 6, is a house where, from 1860–70, lived the composers Rimsky-Korsakov and Mussorgsky. Here Mussorgsky worked on his opera 'Khovanshchina'. 'Pictures from an Exhibition' was written in 1874.

At the end of the street stands a house, faced entirely with marble, which used to belong to the uncrowned wife of Alexander II, Princess Yuryevskaya.

Turning right here brings one onto the *Kutuzov Embankment* (Naberezhnaya Kutuzova) and beyond the steeply arched bridge over the R. Fontanka lies a large park, of nearly 30 acres.

Summer Garden (Lyetny Sad). On the side of the Neva the garden is enclosed by a fine wrought-iron railing, designed by Felten and erected in 1770–84. The pillars of greyish-pink granite, decorated with vases and urns, are linked with extremely delicate iron tracery work.

The garden itself was laid out in 1704–12 by Leblond in geometrically precise Franco-Dutch style. The avenues were lined with clipped trees and the park was decorated with many fountains fed by the Fontanka. Peter the Great dreamed of making it a Russian Versailles and spared no expense in bringing rare trees and plants, and even sculptures, from all parts of Russia and Western Europe; for the Summer Garden he acquired an ancient statue of Venus (300 B.C.) discovered during excavations in Italy. (Subsequently the statue was housed in the Taurida Palace—and hence became known as the Venus of Taurida—and now stands in the Hermitage museum.) There are now altogether 79 statues in the Summer Garden, many of which have stood here for more than 200 years. The sculpture *Peace and Plenty* was carved by special order of Peter the Great by P. Baratta (1722) to be placed before the southern façade of the Summer Palace, and is an allegorical representation of the Russian victory in the Northern War (1700–21). Other statues are by such Italian masters as Bonazzo, Gronelli, Tarzia, and others. To the left of the main avenue stands a statue of the famous Russian fabulist Ivan Krylov, a seated bronze figure sculpted by Klodt in 1856. On the granite pedestal are four bronze reliefs with animals and birds and other figures from his fables by A. Agin. Krylov himself loved to visit the garden as did many other writers, artists, and musicians, including Pushkin, Zhukovsky, Mussorgsky, and Repin. In the 18th and 19th centuries the garden was a centre of social and political life in St. Petersburg.

In the garden stands the unpretentious two-storey building known as the *Summer Palace* (Lyetny Dvoryets). Built in 1710–12 for Peter the Great in the Dutch style by Domenico Trezzini, and decorated with statuary by Schluter, this palace was not usually inhabited, but was used during the festivities which took place in the garden. The lay-out of the two floors is identical: each has six halls, a kitchen, a corridor, and a servants' room. Particularly noteworthy are the kitchen (with its walls covered with Dutch tiles), the entrance hall (with a bas-relief in carved oak, representing Minerva, by Schluter), the Green Study upstairs, and the numerous blue-and-white tiled stoves. The paintings on many of the ceilings are still in very good condition.

Also very attractive are the *Coffee House*, built by Rossi in 1826 and with bas-reliefs by Demut-Malinovsky, and the *Tea House* by Charlemagne, 1827.

In the southern part of the garden stands a huge porphyry vase, presented in 1839 by Charles XIV of Sweden.

A little further along the embankment of the Neva, opposite the Kirovsky Most (Bridge) which leads to the Petrogradskaya Storona, is the small *Suvorov Sq.* In the centre of the square stands a monument to the famous 18th-century Russian general by the sculptor Kozlovsky, in which Suvorov is depicted as the god of war. An effective background for the statue is formed by the broad open space of *Marsovo Polye* (The Field of Mars), which borders the square on the south side.

The Field of Mars, now a beautiful 25-acre park, was formerly used as a vast drilling-ground where great military parades and splendid firework displays were held on special occasions. In the city's early years the site of the park was a sedgy marsh, but Peter the Great had the whole area drained by two canals. When he had a palace built for his wife Catherine to the south of what is now the Field of Mars, the area came to be called Tsaritsin Lug (Tsaritsa's Meadow). The park received its present name at the end of the 18th century or possibly at the beginning of the 19th, when the Suvorov statue was erected. For over two centuries the Field of Mars remained a completely bare stretch of land, without trees, bushes, or lawns. It was known for its dustiness in summer, and was often described as the 'St. Petersburg Sahara'. Now, however, it has been laid out with flower-beds and avenues. In the very centre of the garden, where the walks meet, stands a massive quadrilateral block of granite, designed by Rudnev in 1919 as a monument to the victims of the February Revolution, and 180 revolutionaries lie buried here in a common grave. On the eight stone blocks of the tomb are inscribed epitaphs in blank verse written by Lunacharsky. Ore of them reads:

By the will of tyrants
The nations were tearing each other.
You rose, St. Petersburg toilers,
And were first to wage a war
Of all the oppressed
Against all the oppressors, thus to destroy
The very seed of war itself.

In 1957, on the 40th anniversary of the October Revolution, an eternal flame was lit in the centre of the monument.

The Field of Mars is surrounded by a number of buildings of outstanding architectural interest. Almost the whole of the western edge of the park

is taken up by a building of enormous length, the former Barracks of the Pavlovsky Regiment. This was built by the architect Stasov in 1817–20 after this regiment had distinguished itself in the Patriotic War against Napoleon in 1812. A stepped attic rises above the twelve-columned portico of the main entrance; it is decorated with a composition of banners and military arms.

In the south-east corner of the Field stands the *Mikhailovsky Zamok* (Mikhailovsky Castle) or *Inzhenerny Zamok* (Engineers' Castle), built at the close of the 18th century by Bazhenov and Brenn on the orders of Paul I. The building has an interesting history, for Paul sought refuge here from the conspirators in his court who were plotting against him, and ordered the castle to be constructed with secret passages, moats, and drawbridges. However, this was all to no avail; when he had lived here for little more than 12 days Paul was strangled by his own courtiers in the castle on 11 March 1801. Subsequently a school for military engineers was opened in the castle, and since 1819 it has been known as the Engineers' Castle. Many famous men at one time or another studied here, among them the future writers Dostoyevsky and Grigorovich. The castle is also interesting from the architectural point of view, for each of its four façades was treated in a different way by the architects. The main, south façade looking over a great square on which parades took place, is relieved by groups of Ionic columns supporting a pediment adorned with reliefs of historical scenes. The square entrance arch is framed by huge obelisks of dark stone let into the wall and extending up all three storeys of the building. The north façade with its colonnade of pink marble faces the Summer Garden.

At the main entrance to the castle stands an equestrian *statue of Peter the Great*, cast in the reign of Elizabeth from designs by K. Rastrelli (father of the architect) and set up under Paul I, on whose orders the pedestal was inscribed with the words: 'To great-grandfather from great-grandson 1800.' The statue portrays Peter as a victorious general, and the pedestal is decorated with bas-reliefs in bronze by Kozlovsky, depicting the decisive battles of the Northern War (Poltava, 1709 and Cape Hango, 1714).

On the opposite corner of the Field of Mars, in the north-west, is the *Mramorny Dvoryets* (Marble Palace), built in 1768–85 from the plans of Rinaldi and presented by Catherine II to Count Orlov. Thirty-two kinds of marble were used for the facing and the interior decoration of the palace, which was carried out by the two best Russian sculptors of the day, Shubin and Kozlovsky.

At this point begins *Khalturin St.* in which there are several interesting buildings: *No. 22–24* is particularly old, dating from 1710, and *No. 30*, which used to belong to the Princess Golitsina.

Parallel to Khalturin St., along the river bank, runs the *Dvortsovaya Naberezhnaya* (Palace Embankment). *No. 18* is a house built by Stakenschneider in the middle of the 19th century for a member of the tsar's family, and at *No. 26–28* stands another ducal palace, built by Rezanov in 1867–72 in the style of a 15th-century Florentine Palace. Further along the embankment is crossed by the *Zimnaya Kanavka* (Winter Canal), dug in 1718 along the old Winter Palace. On the corner stands the *Ermitazhny Teatr* (Hermitage Theatre), completed by G. Quarenghi in 1787 as a court theatre and now used as a lecture hall for the State Hermitage. The hall is built in classical style in the form of an amphitheatre without boxes or stalls. It stands on the site of the former Winter Palace in which Peter the Great died in 1725.

The Hermitage Theatre is connected by a small covered bridge to the building of the *Hermitage* (Ermitazh). This in fact consists of three separate but adjoining buildings: the oldest is the so-called *Small Hermitage*, a two-storey pavilion which Catherine II had built by de la Mothe in 1764–7 to house her collections of paintings. The Hall in this building is notable for its decor, and from its windows can be seen the *Hanging Garden*, so-called because it is laid out on a platform supported by vaults, and thus seems to hang in the air. The layer of earth on the platform is 2 m. deep. In 1775–84 another building, known as the *Old Hermitage* and notable for its interior decoration, was added by Felten, Director of the Imperial Academy. Here, in 1788, Quarenghi constructed the *Raphael Gallery*, an exact replica of the Raphael Gallery in Rome and now of particular interest as the original is in poor condition. On the Khalturin St. side, the Old Hermitage adjoins the building of the *New Hermitage*, to which it is connected by a system of corridors. This was constructed in 1839–52 by the architects Klenze and Yefimov on the orders of Nicholas I, and contains several points of interest, including the *Hall of Twenty Columns*, with pillars of Karelian granite, and the white marble Roman courtyard. Its portico is supported by granite figures of the Atlantes. In these buildings are housed Leningrad's world-famous collections of paintings and other priceless art treasures (see p. 175).

From here opens up a splendid view of the *Palace Square* (Dvortsovaya Ploschad). This is the most impressive square in the city, designed to form one harmonious architectural whole. The oldest building is the *Winter Palace* (Zimny Dvoryets), a grandiose edifice in Baroque style which stands on the north side of the square. It was built in 1754–62 by Rastrelli, and after the fire of 1837 reconstructed by Stasov and Bryullov, and was the largest and most splendid building in St. Petersburg. Each of its four façades has a character of its own: the design of the eastern façade is a canopy on pylons, and its projecting wings form the main courtyard opening into the city towards the *Admiralty*; the northern façade, facing the Neva, is quieter in style but with a double tier of white columns which give an impressive effect of light and shade; whereas the main southern façade is richly decorated. The latter, looking onto the *Palace Sq.*, has three arched entrances; the walls

are of a light green colour which sets off the white of the columns. The cornices and window mouldings, with their Baroque cupids' heads, lions' faces and scrolls, are intricately cast, and on the roof are 176 sculptural figures interspersed with vases. The whole building is of impressive size: it contains more than 1000 rooms and reception halls, and has 1945 windows, 1786 doors, and 117 staircases. Many of the rooms, with their ornamentations of Russian semi-precious stones—malachite, jasper, agate—afford unique examples of interior decoration. One of the richest in the palace is the Small Throne Room, with its beautiful panels and painted ceiling, its walls adorned with silver-embroidered velvet, consoles of coloured stone, parquet flooring of rare varieties of wood, silver chandeliers, and Peter the Great's throne.

Almost next door is the *Gallery of the 1812 Patriotic War*, the walls of which are almost entirely covered with 332 inset portraits of the generals who took part in the war. The majority of the portraits are by the English portrait-painter George Dawe, and were painted from life, as the subjects were commanded to appear in the artist's studio, each at an appointed day and hour. Adjoining the gallery is the *Georgievsky Hall*, or Large Throne Room, in which the tsar used to receive visitors; here too the first Russian parliament, the Duma, was opened in 1906. The parquet flooring (with an area of 800 sq. m.) is composed of 16 different sorts of wood and its pattern repeats that of the ceiling. The balcony round the hall is supported by 48 Corinthian columns of pure white Italian marble, and the walls and balcony are faced with marble blocks. All the columns, as well as the 52 pilasters, have capitals of gilded bronze, and the decor is completed by the 28 chandeliers and the bas-relief of Georgy Pobedonosets (St. George), the patron saint of Russia. The throne, which is now in the Small Throne Room, also used to stand here. At the back of the hall there is now a large mosaic map of the Soviet Union, made from stones and jewels from the Urals. Moscow, as the capital, is executed entirely in rubies. On the same floor is the Malachite Hall, so-called because all the 8 columns, 8 pilasters and the 2 fireplaces are faced with Urals malachite of a deep silken hue. More than 2000 kg. of malachite were used for the columns alone. The inlaid parquet floor is made up of 9 different sorts of wood, including rosewood, ebony, mahogany, palm, and amaranth. It was in this hall that the ministers of the Provisional Government were gathered for conference on the eve of the October Revolution, before being arrested by the revolutionary troops. The main white marble staircase of the palace, with its magnificent sculptures, gilding, painted ceiling, and moulding, is a masterpiece of 18th-century Baroque.

At the beginning of the 19th century the government decided to make Palace Square into one complete architectural unit, and therefore bought up all the private buildings on the south side. In 1819 K. Rossi was commissioned to design an administrative building, the *Glavny Shtab* (General Headquarters), and the result was a severe classical building, almost totally devoid of decoration, completed in 1829. At one time it housed the offices of the Ministry of Finance and the Ministry of Foreign Affairs. The horse-shoe-shaped façade, 585 m. in length and with 768 windows, centres on the Winter Palace and is broken by a large archway. This triumphal arch is surmounted by a bronze six-horse victory chariot, by Pimenov and Demut-Malinovsky, which symbolises the victory of Russia over Napoleon in 1812. The arch, which is 28 m. high, is further decorated with coats-of-arms and martial figures, and is now called the Triumphal Arch of the Red Army.

In the centre of the square stands a triumphal column, the *Alexandrovskaya Kolonna* (Alexander's Column), which also commemorates the Russian victory in the 1812 war. It was designed by Montferrand and erected in 1834 on the orders of Nicholas I in memory of Alexander I and bears the inscription 'To Alexander I from a grateful Russia'. The column of polished red Finnish granite stands 30 m. high and weighs 600 tons, and was quarried out of a cliff in the Gulf of Finland, a task which took three years. It was brought to St. Petersburg on a specially constructed barge, and it took 2000 soldiers, aided by a complicated system of pulleys, to raise the column into position. After erection the column was given its final polishing and crowned with the huge figure of an angel by Orlovsky representing the peace that was established in Europe after the victory over Napoleon. The base of the column is ornamented with coats-of-arms and bas-reliefs of an allegorical nature.

On the eastern side of the square are former barracks, built in 1840 by Bryullov for one of the Guards regiments.

The square itself was the scene of the massacre of 'Bloody Sunday' in January 1905, and it was from here that the revolutionary troops and workers attacked the Winter Palace, then the headquarters of Kerensky's Provisional Government, in October 1917.

To the west of the Winter Palace lies the huge building of the *Admiralty*. This was founded originally in 1704 by Peter the Great as a fortress and a shipyard, and was one of St. Petersburg's most important enterprises in those days. In the U-shaped yard opening on to the Neva, there were storehouses, workshops, and ten large covered slipways. Here were built the large warships with which Peter founded and built up his navy. The present building, also in a broad 'U'-shape, dates from the years 1806–23 and was built to the designs of A. Zakharov. The central block is 150 m. long and each of the two wings, turned towards the Neva, are 65 m.; there are several porticos to relieve the monotony of such a huge façade. The building is also adorned with 56 sculptures and 11 large reliefs, all with the common theme of the sea or the Russian navy. The haut-relief over the arch of the main entrance, dedicated to the foundation of the navy, depicts Neptune presenting Peter the Great with a trident in the presence of Minerva and Mercury. This was the work of Terebenev. To the right and left are groups by Shchedrin of three sea nymphs bearing the terrestrial globe, and at each of the four corners is a figure of a seated warrior, also by Shchedrin. Over the gateway rises the Admiralty Tower, visible from almost all parts of the city. It is 70 m. high, ending in a tapering gilded spire, and surmounted by a weather-vane in the form of a crown and ship.

From the west wing of the Admiralty stretches *Ploshchad Dekabristov* (Decembrists' Sq.), which takes its name from the conspirators, mainly tsarist officers, who in December 1825 attempted a coup d'état and gathered here outside the Senate and the Council of State.

In the centre of this grassy square stands the celebrated *Peter the Great Monument*, the work of the great French sculptor E. M. Falconet. Unveiled in 1782, the statue portrays Peter on horseback, his face turned to the Neva and his right hand pointing towards the scene of his labours. The horse is balanced on its hind-legs and tail, while its hoofs trample on a writhing snake, said to be an allegorical representation of Sweden. Pushkin, in his poem 'The Bronze Horseman', wrote of it:

There, by the billows desolate,
He stood, with mighty thoughts elate,
And gazed.

Work on the statue took several years, and Falconet was aided in this by his pupil Marie Collot, who sculpted the head of the rider. The snake was the work of the Russian sculptor Gordeyev. The enormous solid block of granite which forms the pedestal weighs nearly 1500 tons, and was transported part of the way to St. Petersburg on an ingeniously constructed platform running on wheels. The pedestal bears the inscription in Russian and Latin 'Petro Primo Catharina Secunda 1782'.

On the opposite side of the square to the Admiralty stand the twin buildings of the *former Senate* and the *Holy Synod*. The Senate House was designed in 1763 by Rossi; in 1829–34 it and the Synod were reconstructed and connected by a gallery spanning the street in between them.

In the south-west corner of the square stands a *manège*, or former riding school, built by Quarenghi in 1804–7 and decorated with marble figures.

To the south of the square stands the magnificent structure of the largest church in Leningrad, *St. Isaac's Cathedral*. This church, with its impressive columned porticos, beautiful bronze sculpture, and famous golden dome, took the French architect Auguste Montferrand over forty years (1819–59) to build. Constructed of granite and marble, in the shape of a cross, it is 111 m. long and 96 m. wide, and has a total height of 110 m. The enormous dome is visible from afar, and there is a magnificent view of the city and the river from here. (Permission is needed to take photographs.)

The main entrances on the north and south sides have beautiful porticos imitating those of the Pantheon in Rome. Each has 16 monolith columns of polished red Finnish granite, 16 m. high and 2 m. thick, with bronze bases and capitals. The columns are surmounted by pediments adorned with large bronze reliefs, and above these are statues of the evangelists and apostles: the statues of angels at the corners of the roof are by Vitali. Altogether on the roof there are more than 350 sculptural decorations, some of them by Klodt.

The interior height of the dome from the floor is 82 m. compared with St. Paul's in London (69 m.) and St. Peter's in Rome (123 m.). 562 steps lead to the top of the dome, and from the dome swings a pendulum weighing 54 kg. (over a hundredweight) which moves round 13° each hour. The interior of the cathedral is decorated with nearly 200 valuable paintings, many of them by Bryullov, Bruni, and Bassin. The iconostasis, 68 m. long, is of richly gilded marble, and has 33 large mosaics of saints; the Holy Door in the centre is again the work of Vitali, and is flanked by columns veneered with malachite and lapis lazuli. The four colossal beaten bronze doors, richly adorned with sculptures by Vitali, each weigh 10 tons.

On the haut-relief of the pediment on the western façade is depicted the figure of Montferrand holding a model of the cathedral.

The building, which can hold 13,000 people, is open now as a museum.

St. Isaac's Square, on which the cathedral stands, contains buildings dating mainly from the 19th century. No. 9, however, in the north-west corner, was built in the 1760s for Myatlev, a friend of Pushkin's, and the French philosopher Diderot lived here from 1773-4 during his stay in St. Petersburg.

On the opposite side of the square stands the building, decorated with lions, which until 1917 housed the War Office.

On the south side of the square, beyond the *Siny Most* (Blue Bridge), the broadest bridge in the city, which used to be used as a serf market, stands the former *Mariinsky Dvoryets* (Palace), built in 1839-44 by Stakenschneider for Maria, daughter of Nicholas I, and subsequently used for sessions of the State Council.

In 1859 a statue to Nicholas I by P. Klodt was erected at the southern end of the square. The tsar is represented on a prancing horse, and the sculpture has only two points of support (the hind legs). The pedestal is adorned with bronze trophies and four reliefs depicting memorable events in the tsar's rule. At the corners are allegorical figures of Faith, Justice, Wisdom, and Strength which are portraits of the tsar's wife and daughters.

From the northern end of the square the *Bulvar Profsoyuzov* (Trade Union Boulevard) runs westwards for almost half a mile to *Truda (Labour) Sq.* In the early days of the city this square was one of the outlying districts adjoining the Admiralty Yard. However, upon the expansion of the city, and particularly of the shipbuilding activities, it became part of the central districts. Its increasing importance was marked by the building there in 1853-61 of a palace by Stakenscheider for the eldest son of Nicholas I. This palace is a monumental building on the eastern side of the square, surrounded by a fine railing on a granite pediment, and is now occupied by the Regional Trade Union Council.

On the opposite corner of the square, to the south-west, lies the triangular-shaped island known by the name of *Novaya Gollandiya* (New Holland). This is a man-made island, formed by the R. Moika and the Kryukov and New Admiralty Canals, which were dug in the reign of Peter the Great to connect the Admiralty with its subsidiary enterprises further along the embankment. Surrounded by water, Novaya Gollandiya was a useful place for storing inflammable materials and as early as the 1730s timber for shipbuilding was stored here. It was decided to build a whole complex of stone buildings for this purpose, and the project was entrusted to the architect Chevakinsky. In 1780 the buildings on the side of the Moika were completed, but the rest was not finished until the 1840s. In the centre was built a dock, connected to the outer canals, which could accommodate 30 barges at one time for unloading. The subsidiary canal leading to the Moika is spanned by a beautiful decorative arch. At the end of the 1820s, the building of a new naval prison, designed by Shtauberg in the shape of a ring with a circular inner court, was added to the complex.

The street leading southwards from Truda Sq. brings one to the old *Most Potseluyev* (Bridge of Kisses), decorated with granite obelisks. From here one can see, on the left, on the opposite bank of the Moika (at No. 94), a yellow building with white columns which is the former palace of Prince Yusupov. Built at the end of the 18th century by Quarenghi, it was here, in one of the basements, that Yusupov and his fellow-conspirators killed Rasputin in 1916.

Beyond the Most Potseluyev lies *Teatralnaya (Theatre) Sq.* The oldest building here is St. Nicholas' Cathedral, a splendid Baroque turquoise and white building with a soaring belltower, erected in 1753-62 and decorated in traditional Russian style by Chevakinsky. It is open for services.

This square has long been a centre of entertainment in Leningrad, hence its name. As early as 1765 a wooden theatre was constructed here for performances by amateur companies, and in 1782 it was replaced by a brick building known as the Bolshoi (Big) Theatre. In this, the largest theatre in Europe at that time, were performed operas, ballets, and plays. However, in 1886 the theatre closed down, and its premises were converted to accommodate the St. Petersburg Conservatoire, which had been founded in 1862 on the initiative of the composer Anton Rubinstein as the first higher musical institution in Russia. It is now known as the *Rimsky-Korsakov Conservatoire*, and its famous graduates include Tchaikovsky, Glazunov, Prokofiev, and Shostakovich.

Opposite the Conservatoire stands the building of the *Kirov State Theatre of Opera and Ballet*, formerly called the Mariinsky Teatr in honour of the Tsaritsa Maria, wife of Alexander II. Designed by the architect Kavos in 1860, this theatre was one of the most important centres of Russian opera and ballet. Both Fyodor Chaliapin and Anna Pavlova performed on its stage, and more recently Galina Ulanova started her career here before leaving in 1944 to join the Bolshoi Ballet Company in Moscow.

In Teatralnaya Sq. stand monuments to *Glinka* (sculpted by Bakh in 1906) and *Rimsky-Korsakov* (Bogolyubov and Ingal, 1952).

The Strelka of Vasilyevsky Ostrov (Island)

This is the name given to the eastern tip of the island nearest to the Peter and Paul Fortress, the largest one in the delta of the Neva (8300 hectares: 27,170 acres). Its principal fame now lies in the many institutes of higher education and research which are concentrated here.

The central position on the Strelka is occupied by the former *Exchange*, designed by Thomas de Thomon in 1810–16, and surrounded by 44 white Doric columns in imitation of the ancient temple of Paestum in southern Italy. The building stands on a massive granite foundation, with a broad staircase leading up from a semi-circular court to the main façade. On this façade (the eastern) stands a figure of Neptune in a chariot drawn by sea-horses, with the Russian rivers Neva and Volkhov flowing symbolically round him. On the opposite pediment stand the goddess of seafaring and the patron saint of trade, Mercury, surrounded by nymphs. One of the most beautiful views of Leningrad is that obtained from the semi-circular space between the columns. On the left-hand side is the spire of the cathedral in the Peter and Paul Fortress, and to the right the former palaces along the Neva embankment.

The *Exchange building* now houses the *Central Naval Museum* (see page 178).

In front of the Exchange stand two 32-m. high *Rostral Columns*, designed by Thomson in 1806 and decorated with beaks of galleys and figures of naiads. The figures at the foot of the columns personify Russia's commercial waterways, the Neva, the Volkhov, the Volga, and the Dnieper. Besides being decorative, the columns also served as beacons for ships entering the commercial port between 1733 and 1885. Oil was poured into the copper cups at the top and, when it was lighted at dusk, the columns turned into gigantic flaming

torches. Now on national holidays gas jets are lit and the heat from them can be felt by those standing nearby.

The assembly of buildings here was later completed by the addition of warehouses on either side of the Exchange and the construction of the Customs House. Since 1886 the southern warehouse has accommodated the *Zoological Institute and Museum of the Academy of Sciences*, and the northern warehouse is now the *Academy's Geological Museum*.

The Customs House, at 2a Naberezhnaya Makarova, is adorned with a severe portico and statues of Fortune and Mercury. From its dome watchers used to give signals of ships approaching the port. The building now houses the Academy of Sciences, Institute of Russian Literature, and the museum known as Pushkin House.

No. 3 Universitetskaya Naberezhnaya is the *Kunstkammer* (see p. 178), a massive two-storey building with a tower, a protruding central section and arched façade built in Baroque style in 1718–34 by Mattarnovi, Kiaveri, and Zemtsov. The upper part of the building used to be an astronomical observatory. It was here that the Academy of Sciences, planned by Peter the Great with the help of Leibniz and Christian von Wolff, first began its work, and its round conference hall still retains its original appearance. Here the great Russian scientist Mikhail Lomonosov worked from 1741–65. However, the building was chiefly the home of Peter the Great's Kunstkammer, the first Russian natural science museum, which Peter referred to as his cabinet of 'curiosities, rarities and monsters'. His collection formed the basis of the *Museum of Anthropology and Ethnography* which is housed here in the Kunstkammer. Also in the Kunstkammer is the *Lomonosov Museum*.

By the end of the 18th century space in the Kunstkammer had become too cramped for the Academy, and it was decided to erect a separate building next door. The main building of the *Academy of Sciences* was completed between 1783 and 1788 and is one of the architect Quarenghi's best works. Its noble classical proportions are embellished only with a fine eight-columned portico and a double flight of steps projecting on to the pavement.

Also on the embankment, but divided from the Academy building by the street called the Mendeleyevskaya Liniya, are the premises of the *University*, a group of 12 identical buildings designed by Trezzini in 1722–42 to house various government institutions. It was placed at the disposal of the university in 1819. Many brilliant and distinguished men in all fields of study were once students here, among them Mendeleyev, Popov, Pavlov, Turgenev, and Chernyshevsky.

Near the university, and today forming part of it, is the three-storey, red and white building which was formerly called the *Menshikov Palace*. It was built by the architects Fontana and Schedel for General Menshikov in 1707, when Peter the Great presented the whole of Vasilyevsky Ostrov to him. (The gift was withdrawn again, however, in 1714.) In the second half of the 18th century the building was used as a military college by the First Cadet Corps, and a new long wing added. In front of the ex-college stands a monument to Field-marshal Rumyantsev, which was originally erected in 1799 by Brenna on the Field of Mars.

Adjacent on the embankment, and facing the Neva, is the *Academy of Arts*, a large building by de la Mothe and Kokorinov (built 1764–88), whose inner courtyard forms a circle set in a huge rectangle of surrounding buildings. The central section has a dome and portal decorated with sculptures of Hercules and Flora. When, in 1947, the Academy was moved to Moscow, the Repin Institute of Painting, Sculpture, and Architecture was accommodated here.

The embankment in front of the Academy is interesting for its classical quay with Egyptian sphinxes, granite seats, and bronze torches. The sphinxes are carved out of pink granite, obtained from the Aswan quarries nearly 3500 years ago, and the hieroglyphs on them glorify the Pharaoh Amenophis III, whose palace they once adorned. They were bought by the Russian Government in 1831 and transported to St. Petersburg.

Nevsky Prospect

This is the main street of the city and one of the oldest. It was built in 1710 to link the Admiralty Yard directly with the Great Novgorod Road leading to Novgorod. Beginning at the Admiralty building, it runs to the Moscow Railway Station and then stretches on further to the Alexander Nevsky Lavra (Monastery), covering a total of 4·5 km.

Here, in tsarist times, were built all the largest banks, the best shops, and the palaces of the nobility.

Building No. 9, on the corner of Gogol St., was once the Wavelburg Bank, built in 1912 by Petryatkovich in imitation of the Doge's palace in Venice and the Medici Palace in Florence. Its granite facing stone was imported ready for building from Sweden.

In *Gogol St.*, house *No. 13* was for a long time the residence of the composer Tchaikovsky, who died there on 25 October 1893. *No. 17* was occupied by the writer Gogol from 1833–6, and it was here that he wrote 'The Inspector-General' and 'Taras Bulba'.

The next side-road is *Herzen St.*, where, in house *No. 25*, the famous writer lived from 1840–1. The part of Herzen St. to the north of Nevsky Prospect was built by the architect Rossi straight along the Pulkovo meridian, and at noon on a sunny day one can check one's watch by it—the fronts of the houses cast no shade.

No. 15 Nevsky Prospect is one of the oldest in the street. It was built in 1768–71 by Kokorinov for the chief of the St. Petersburg police Chicherin, and is now a cinema. The elegant classical building at *No. 20* was once the Dutch Church

built in 1837 by Jacquot, and is now a library.

On the corner of the Moika Embankment is the white-columned *Stroganov Dvoryets* (Palace), built in 1752–4 by the architect Rastrelli, and constituting one of the best examples of the Russian Baroque style.

No. 22–4 is the former Lutheran Church of St. Peter and St. Paul, built in the Romanesque style by the architect Bryullov in 1833–8.

Almost opposite stands the impressive *Kazan Cathedral*, which is approached by a semi-circular colonnade of 136 Corinthian columns, modelled on that of St. Peter's in Rome. It was designed by Andrei Voronikhin (1760–1814) and at the time of its construction in 1811 was the third largest cathedral in the world. It is 79 m. high, 72 m. long and 55 m. wide, built in the shape of a Latin cross in the Greek neo-classical style. Huge bas-reliefs on biblical themes adorn the end walls of the colonnade, and the niches of the façade contain enormous statues of Russian warriors. The small square in front of the main entrance is surrounded by beautiful ironwork, also designed by Voronikhin. To the right of the entrance is the tomb of Field-Marshal Kutuzov, and on either side hang the keys of the towns and cities he captured during his campaigns. Nearby is a memorial to the architect of the cathedral. The building takes its name from the wonder-working icon of Our Lady of Kazan, which used to be here but has now been transferred to the Russian Museum. It is worthwhile going down into the crypt to see the exhibits there. The cathedral is no longer open for services, but houses the *Museum of the History of Religion and Atheism*.

In the square in front of the Cathedral stand statues, designed by Orlovsky in 1831–2, of Kutuzov and of General Barclay de Tolly, who led the Russian army to victory in the 1812 campaign. At their feet lie the banners of Napoleon's defeated army.

On the corner of Nevsky Prospect and the Griboyedov Canal stands a building faced with polished granite, with a glass tower and a 3 m. glass globe, which was built in 1907 and formerly belonged to the Singer sewing-machine company.

On the left, some distance along the embankment, stands a church built in 1883–1907 by Parland on the spot where in 1881 Alexander II was assassinated by members of the Narodnaya Volya (People's Freedom) group. The church is in the old Russian style, with ornate decorations, and was modelled on St. Basil's Cathedral in Moscow. It is called the *Church of the Resurrection*.

No. 30 Nevsky Prospect was once owned by a friend of Pushkin's, Engelhardt, and later, in the 19th century, was used for concerts by the Philharmonic Society. Performers there included Berlioz, Wagner, Liszt, and Strauss. Today it is the Small Hall of the Leningrad State Philharmonic Society.

Next door (*Nos. 32–4*), was formerly the Roman Catholic Church of St. Catherine, built by de la Mothe in 1763–4 in the shape of a Latin cross.

The corner building on the opposite side was built in 1784 by Quarenghi and before the Revolution was used for sessions of the city council. The pentagonal tower by Ferrari (1802) was used originally as a firemen's watch-tower, then as a semaphore station linking St. Petersburg with such country residences as Tsarskoye Selo and with Warsaw. Between the Winter Palace and Warsaw there were 149 such towers, all of them over 15 m. high.

Here the side-street to the left, Brodsky St., links Nevsky Prospect with the Iskusstv (Arts) Sq. The most striking building here is the large *Mikhailovsky Dvoryets* (Palace) built in 1819–25 by Rossi for Nicholas I's brother, the Grand Duke Michael. The main building stands at the back of a courtyard formed by subsidiary blocks. High iron railings separate the courtyard from the square, which is entered through three gates, decorated with coats-of-arms. The palace stands on a socle and there are arches under the protruding eight-columned portico which enabled carriages to drive straight up to the palace doors. There is also a broad granite staircase decorated with bronze lions. On both sides of the portico, between the high oval windows of the first floor there are elegant Corinthian pilasters. Rossi is said to have likened the palace to the building of the Louvre in outward appearance. Decorative sculpture was much used on the façades and interiors of the palace and the best artists of the time collaborated in this work and that of painting the ceilings and walls. The original decoration of the vestibule, main staircase, and White Hall, which has survived to this day, is one of the best examples of the Russian classical interior. In 1890–5 the palace was converted into the *State Russian Museum*.

The painter Isaak Brodsky lived and worked in *Iskusstv Sq.*, at *No. 3*, from 1924–39, and after his death his flat was turned into a museum.

Next door stands the *Maly (Small) Opera*, built in 1833 by Bryullov, following Rossi's general project for the whole square. It was first called the Mikhailovsky Theatre, and up to 1918 it was occupied on a more or less permanent basis by a French drama company. After that date an opera company worked here, and was joined by a ballet company in 1933. Lavrovsky was in charge of the ballet in this theatre before he became the chief choreographer at the Bolshoi Theatre in Moscow.

On the other side of the square, in a building on the corner of Brodsky St. originally erected by Jacquot for the Dvoryanskoye Sobraniye (Assembly of Nobles), is the *Leningrad Philharmonic Society*.

Back on Nevsky Prospect, No. 35 is the 230-m. frontage of the Gostiny Dvor *department store*, a two-storey building with a row of arches and arcades along each floor. It was built in 1761–85 by de la Mothe, and numerous shops were built into galleries forming a square 1 km. around. The interior has now been reconstructed to form the largest department store in the city.

Opposite, at Nos. 40–2, is the small but elegant former *Armenian Church* built in the 1770s, probably by Felten, and a little further down is another big arcade of shops founded in 1848 and reconstructed in 1900, now turned into another large department store.

At the corner of Sadovaya St. is the *Saltykov-Shchedrin Library*, built partly by Sokolov in 1796–1801 and partly by Rossi in 1828–32 and decorated with bas-reliefs and carvings of orators, philosophers, and writers of ancient times. It is one of the largest libraries in the world.

At this point Nevsky Prospect is joined by Ostrovsky Sq., on the south side of which stands the *Pushkin Drama Theatre*. Called the Alexandrinsky Theatre until the Revolution, in honour of Tsaritsa Alexandra, wife of Nicholas I, it was built by Rossi in 1832. The main façade is decorated with a six-columned loggia, raised above the ground floor, and the whole building is girdled with a frieze of theatrical masks and garlands. The attic is crowned with a chariot of Apollo, executed by Pimenov.

Southwards from the theatre runs an interesting street named after Rossi, who designed it in 1828–34. On either side lie identical buildings, painted yellow and decorated with white columns, whose walls are exactly the same height as the width of the street. The length of the street is exactly ten times its width.

In the centre of the gardens in Ostrovsky Sq. stands a statue of *Catherine II*, erected in 1873 by Mikeshin. Round the base of the statue are grouped the distinguished figures of 18th-century Russia.

On the eastern side of the square stands the *Anichkov Dvoryets*, built in 1741–7 to the designs of Rastrelli, by order of the Empress Elizabeth for her favourite, Count Razumovsky. From Nevsky Prospect only the northern side, which is devoid of decoration, is visible; the front of the palace faces the Fontanka, as, at the time of its building, this embankment was a more fashionable area than Nevsky Prospect.

At the point where Nevsky Prospect crosses the R. Fontanka is the famous *Anichkov Most* (Bridge). The present bridge was built in 1839–41, with railings designed by Montferrand. It is chiefly noted for its statues of youths with horses by Peter Klodt; these were begun 10 years before the present bridge was completed. Originally there were two statues, each cast twice and placed at the four corners of the bridge. Then one pair was sent by Nicholas I to the King of Prussia as a present and plaster casts, painted in imitation of bronze, were erected in their place. New casts were made, but in 1846 Nicholas again sent them away as a present, this time to the King of Sicily. In 1850 Klodt made two different statues to complete the set, and they were eventually erected on the bridge. They have stood here since then, except for a time during World War II, when they were buried in the nearby gardens for protection.

The rest of Nevsky Prospect, from the Fontanka to Vosstaniya (Uprising) Sq., was built mainly at the end of the 19th century, and there is little of very great architectural interest here. However, *No. 68* was the residence of the famous Russian critic and writer Vissarion Belinsky in 1842–6 and he was often visited here by Dostoyevsky, Goncharov, and other well-known writers. In 1851 Turgenev lived in the same building.

The cross-road of Nevsky Prospect with Liteiny Prospect and Vladimirsky Prospect is one of the busiest in the city.

In the Vosstaniya Sq. stands the *Moscow Railway Station* building designed by Thon and opened in 1851 when trains started running between St. Petersburg and Moscow.

From the square it is just a little over half a mile to the *Alexander Nevsky Lavra*. A 'lavra' in Russian is a monastery of the highest order, one which is also the seat of a Metropolitan. There are only four of them in Russia, and the Alexander Nevsky Monastery was raised to this status in 1797. After the Monastery of the Caves in Kiev, it was the largest lavra in Russia. According to legend it stands on the spot where Grand-Prince Alexander won his great victory over the Swedes and the Teutonic Knights in 1240, although actually the battle was fought much higher up the Neva. Peter I built a small church on this spot in 1713, and in 1724 had the remains of St. Alexander brought here from Vladimir; a bas-relief illustrating this event can be seen in St. Isaac's Cathedral. In 1750 a silver sarcophagus was made in the St. Petersburg Mint for the ashes of the saint; this was transferred to the Hermitage in 1922.

The lavra, which contained 11 churches and 4 cemeteries, as well as church offices, an ecclesiastical academy, and a seminary, is surrounded by a stone wall. The central entrance is adorned with an elegant *Gate-Chapel*, designed by Starov in 1783–5. Beyond this main entrance lie the cemeteries, known as necropoles, which can be seen on admission by ticket. On the left is the 18th-century *Lazarevskoye Cemetery*, where Peter the Great's sister, Natalya Alexeyevna, was buried in 1716, soon after the foundation of the monastery. Also buried here are the scientists Lomonosov and Euler, and the architects Voronikhin, Rossi, and Zakharov. On the right of the main entrance is the *Tikhvinsky Cemetery*, where are buried the fable-writer Krylov, the composers Glinka, Tchaikovsky, Mussorgsky, Rimsky-Korsakov, and Borodin, the architects Stasov and Klodt, the writer Dostoyevsky, and the poet Zhukovsky. The buildings of the lavra were designed by Trezzini, Starov, and others. The oldest part (1722) is the two-storey tower to the left of the main gate; here there are two churches. On the upper floor is the *Church of Alexander Nevsky*, and below it is the *Church of the Blagoveshcheniye* (Annunciation). Here a marble slab set in the floor and bearing the simple inscription 'Here lies Suvorov' marks the grave of that famous Field-Marshal. Other monuments in the church were carved by such sculptors as Martos and Gordeyev. This building also houses the *Museum of Urban Sculpture*, where the original models of many of the works of art that decorate the city are on display. The *Troitsky Sobor* (Trinity Cathedral) was founded in 1724 by Peter I to house the remains of St. Alexander Nevsky, and was completed in 1778–90 by Starov. It is in classical style, with sculptures by Shubin. The *Mitropolichny Korpus* is a fine example of Russian Baroque, designed in 1756–9 by Rastorguyev.

Former Palaces etc.

Peter and Paul Fortress, Revolution Sq. Open daily (except Wed.) 11–6; Tues. 11–4.

Cottage of Peter the Great, Petrovskaya Naberezhnaya 1. Open May–November daily (except Tues.) 12–7.

Summer Palace, Lyetny Sad. Open May–November daily (except Tues.) 12–8.

Winter Palace, Dvortsovaya Ploshchad. (Opening hours as for the Hermitage.)

Art Museums

The Hermitage, Dvortsovaya Naberezhnaya 34–36. Open daily (except Thurs.) 11–6, Mon. 11–4. The State Hermitage contains one of the largest and most valuable collections of paintings in the world, including priceless examples of works by the greatest Western European masters. Although it is often claimed that Catherine II was the real creator of the Hermitage collections, several paintings which hang here today were in fact purchased earlier, in the reign of Peter the Great. Peter's interest in art was mainly of a practical nature; in particular he recognised the value of art as a propaganda instrument in his struggle for the modernisation of Russia, and this explains his predilection for the work of such Dutch painters as Adam Silo which depicts the ships and shipyards of the Netherlands. However, we also know that in 1716 Peter purchased for the Hermitage one of its Rembrandts, 'David's Farewell to Jonathan'. Peter also began collections of Russian antiquities by issuing an order prescribing the careful preservation of all ancient objects found in the ground; as a result of this arose the Siberian collection, mainly of gold objects, to be found in the Hermitage today.

It was Catherine II, however, who began collecting art, mainly Western art, for its own sake, on a large scale. She systematically bought up whole collections of paintings which came on to the market, such as that of Gotkowski, which comprised 225 pictures, including several Rembrandts, a Frans Hals, a Van der Helst, and two Gotzius. Her Ambassadors throughout Europe, and particularly in Paris, were ordered to keep her constantly informed of interesting sales, and in

1769 she pulled off a major coup by acquiring for 180,000 roubles the collection of the recently deceased Count de Bruhl of Dresden. This contained many masterpieces: 4 paintings by Rembrandt, 4 Ruisdaels, 21 Wouwermans, 5 Rubens, and several Bellottos and Watteaus. It was Catherine too who had the actual buildings of the Hermitage constructed to house her collections of paintings, and such were the numbers of the pictures that she purchased that the high walls of the buildings were closely covered from the floor to the ceiling. On Catherine's death it was estimated that the Imperial collections totalled 3926 pictures.

The process of collecting was continued, to a greater or lesser degree, by succeeding monarchs; in particular Nicholas I greatly expanded the collection, and did much to rectify the preponderance of Dutch and Flemish paintings by purchasing works of the Spanish and Italian schools. Hitherto the collection had been an entirely private one, open only to a few privileged guests and visitors. It was Nicholas I who, in 1852, opened the Hermitage as a public museum, and from this time the Hermitage became an independent administration under the direction of Curators; now the acquisition of paintings no longer depended as before on the individual caprices of the tsar, but on the decisions of a public body. Apart from works purchased abroad, the Hermitage also benefited to a large extent from the collections of members of the Russian aristocracy who, following the fashion set by Catherine II, had become prodigious collectors of Western art. After the Revolution the private collections which remained in Russia, such as those of the Stroganov and Yusupov families, were all taken over by the State and went to swell the Hermitage collection. Thanks to such discriminating collectors as Sergei Shchukin and Ivan Morozov, who both purchased and also commissioned works from contemporary artists such as Bonnard, Cézanne, Picasso, and Matisse, the Hermitage has one of the richest collections in the world of Impressionist art, although many of these paintings have now been transferred to the Pushkin Museum in Moscow.

The exhibits in the Hermitage Museum fall into 7 main sections, and are subdivided into 40 smaller sections:

1. HISTORY OF RUSSIAN CULTURE

7th–13th centuries	1st floor, rooms 5–10
17th–early 18th century	1st floor, rooms 13–18
	(Includes a bronze bust and a wax mask of Peter the Great by Rastrelli)
Malachite objects (early 19th century)	1st floor, room 19 (Malachite Hall)
Second half of 18th century	1st floor, rooms 20–34
Early 19th century	1st floor, rooms 35–9, 48
Russian Silverware (17th–20th century)	1st floor, room 60 (includes the silver tomb of Alexander Nevsky made in the St. Petersburg mint in 1750–3)
Russia's Heroic Military Past	1st floor, rooms 65–7
1812 Patriotic War	1st floor, room 67
Mosaic map of Soviet Union (in precious and semi-precious stones)	1st floor, room 68 (St. George's Hall, or Small Throne Room)

2. HISTORY OF PRIMEVAL CULTURE
(Relics of primeval culture found on the territory of the U.S.S.R.)

Scythian culture and art (7th–2nd centuries B.C.)	Ground floor, rooms 6–12
Culture and art of primeval nomads in the Altai area (Western Siberia)	Ground floor, rooms 15–21

3. HISTORY OF ORIENTAL CULTURE
(Within the Soviet Union)

Central Asia (6th c. B.C.–19th c. A.D.)	Ground floor, rooms 1–16
Caucasus (10th c. B.C.–8th c. A.D.)	Ground floor, rooms 17–22

4. ORIENTAL CULTURE AND ART
(Outside the Soviet Union)

Ancient Egypt (4000 B.C.–6th c. A.D.)	Ground floor, rooms 1–12
Babylon and Assyria (4000–1000 B.C.) and Palmyra (2nd–3rd c. A.D.)	Ground floor, rooms 13–17
Byzantium (4–15th c.)	2nd floor, rooms 39–40
Near and Middle East	2nd floor, rooms 41–55
China (2000 B.C.–20th c.)	2nd floor, rooms 18–35

India (17th–20th c.)   2nd floor, rooms 36–38a
Japan (17th–19th c.)   2nd floor, room 26a

5. ANTIQUE CULTURE AND ART

Ancient Greece (8th–2nd c. B.C.)   Ground floor, rooms 1–4, 8, 10

Greek colonies on the northern shore of the Black

Sea (7th c. B.C.–3rd c. A.D.)   Ground floor, rooms 5–7, 9, 10, and 21

Ancient Italy (7th–2nd c. B.C.)   Ground floor, room 13

Ancient Rome (1st c. B.C.–4th c. A.D.)   Ground floor, rooms 11–12, 14–18

6. WEST EUROPEAN ART

Medieval European Applied Art (11th–15th c.)   1st floor, room 1

Italian Art (13th–18th c.)   1st floor, rooms 4–33. Room II has two paintings by Leonardi da Vinci, room 25 seven Titians, and room 26 several Veroneses and Tintorettos.

Spanish Art (16th–18th c.)   1st floor, rooms 34–5. El Greco and Velàzquez are in room 35.

Dutch Art (15th–16th c.)   1st floor, rooms 37–40. Painting 'The Fair', attributed to Pieter Brueghel, and two drawings by Brueghel in room 39.

Flemish Art (17th c.)   1st floor, rooms 41–4. In room 42 are most of the 42 paintings by Rubens which the Hermitage possesses, including 'The Descent from the Cross', 'Venus and Adonis', 'Perseus and Andromeda', and 'Union of Earth and Water'. Room 43 contains many works by Van Dyck, including 'The Holy Family', 'Self-portrait', 'Charles I of England', 'St. Peter', and 'Rubens with his son Albert'.

Dutch Art (17th–18th c.)   1st floor, rooms 46–54. In room 46 are two Frans Hals, a Pieter de Hooch, several Ruisdaels, and a Hobbema. 21 works attributed to Rembrandt hang in room 50, including 'The Holy Family', 'Parting of David with Jonathan', 'Portrait of Saskia as Flora', 'Danae', and 'Descent from the Cross'.

Belgian Art (18th–20th c.)   2nd floor, rooms 121–3

Dutch Art (19th c.)   2nd floor, rooms 124–5

German Art (15th–19th c.)   1st floor, rooms 55–60. Rooms 55–6 contain several woodcuts and engravings by Dürer, and paintings by Holbein.

2nd floor, rooms 61–9. Room 64 was the Small Throne Room, also known as Peter's Hall.

Finnish Art (19th–20th c.)   2nd floor, room 70

Austrian Art (18th–19th c.)   2nd floor, rooms 71–3

French Art (15th–20th c.)   1st floor, rooms 74–89a, 93–7. Room 80 contains several works by Poussin and room 85 Watteau. Rooms 93–7 contain an exhibition of articles of applied art.

2nd floor, rooms 98–114. Rooms 111–14 contain works by Renoir, Monet, Pissarro, Sisley, Degas, Rodin, Cézanne, Gauguin, Bonnard, Matisse, Picasso, and Toulouse-Lautrec.

Swedish and Danish Art (18th c.)   1st floor, rooms 90–2

English Art (17th–19th c.)   1st floor, rooms 115–18. Works by Peter Lely, William Hogarth, Godfrey Kneller, Reynolds, Gainsborough, and others.

History of Western European Arms (15th–17th c.)   1st floor, room 36

Western European Silverware (17th–18th c.)   1st floor, room 83

Western European Decorative China   1st floor, room 120

7. RUSSIAN AND FOREIGN MEDALS, BADGES, AND ORDERS   2nd floor, room 2

The State Russian Museum, Inzhenernaya St. 4/2 (Mikhailovsky Palace), open daily (except Tues.) 11–6. Mon. 11–4.

The museum, which is housed in the former Mikhailovsky Dvoryets (Palace) is the second largest depository of Russian art after the Tretyakov Gallery in Moscow. It has about 300,000 exhibits in all, dating from the 10th century to the present day. They include priceless specimens of Russian 12th- and 13th-century icon painting by Rublev and Ushakov, and works by such well-known 18th- and 19th-century artists as Ivanov, Levitan, Repin, and Bryullov. The post-revolutionary section of the collection is on show in another building, facing the Griboyedov Canal, built in 1912–16 by Benois and reconstructed after extensive damage in the Second World War.

Museum of Urban Sculpture, Alexandrovo Nevskovo Sq. 1 (Alexander Nevsky Lavra). Open 1 May–30 September; Mon., Tues., and Fri. 11–7, Sat. and Sun. 11–8, Wed. 11–4. 1 October–30 April. Open daily 11–6, Wed. 11–4.

Brodsky Museum, Iskusstv Sq. 3. The museum is housed in the flat where Brodsky lived from 1924–39. 80 of his works are on display as well as his own collection of paintings, and sketches by other artists.

Historical Museums

Museum of the October Revolution, Kuibysheva St. 4, (Kshesinskaya Palace). Open daily; Mon. and Fri. 12–8, Wed. 11–5, Tues., Sat., Sun. 11–7.

The museum contains over 5000 exhibits pertaining to the October Revolution. They are displayed in 35 halls of the former Kshesinskaya Palace.

Museum of the History of Leningrad, Naberezhnaya Krasnovo 44, Flota. Open daily (except Wed.). Fri.–Sun. 11–7; Mon., Thurs. 1–9; Tues. 11–5.

The museum was founded in 1918 and has many exhibits illustrating the history of Leningrad; among them are detailed models portraying such scenes as Nevsky Prospect in the middle of the 18th century, the transporting of the rock for the statue of the Bronze Horseman, and a firework display in the early years of the 18th century. Among the more modern exhibits is a scroll presented to Leningrad by Franklin D. Roosevelt on behalf of the people of the United States of America in honour of the city's gallant defence during the Second World War blockade.

Lenin Museum, Khalturin St. 5, (Marble Palace). Open daily (except Wed.) 11–6, Tues. 11–4.

Museum of the History of Religion and Atheism, Kazanskaya Sq. 2 (Kazan Cathedral). Open daily. Mon. 1–7; Tues. 12–4; Thurs.–Sat. 12–6; Sun. 11–6.

Cruiser 'Aurora', Petrovskaya Naberezhnaya. Open daily (except Wed. and Sat.) 11–5

Military Museum, Peter and Paul Fortress (see p. 178

Central Naval Museum, Pushkinskaya Sq. 4, Vasilyevsky Island. Open daily (except Sat.) 11–6; Thurs. 1–6: Fri. 11–4.

The museum is housed in the building of the former Exchange (see p. 000). The collection was started by Peter the Great in 1709, who ordered models of ships to be kept here. It now has about 200,000 exhibits, amongst them a 3000-year-old oak dug-out canoe and Peter the Great's boat which was the foundation of the Russian navy.

Museum of Artillery History, Lenin Park 4. Open daily (except Thurs.) 11–6; Sun. 10.30–6; Mon. 11–3.

Suvorov Museum, Saltykov-Shchedrin St. 41b. Open daily (except Wed.) 11–7.

The museum is housed in a building erected for this purpose by Gogen with money collected by public subscription. It has nearly 4000 exhibits pertaining to the 18th-century Russian general—his personal belongings, documents, and trophies captured by the Russian army during his campaigns.

Scientific Museums

Kunstkammer (Museum of Anthropology and Ethnography), Universitetskaya Naberezhnaya 3. Open Thurs. and Sun. 11–4. In summer also open Tues.

The building of the Kunstkammer was the first home of the Academy of Sciences in the reign of Peter the Great. The collection of the museum of anthropology and ethnography developed from art works which Peter purchased in Holland in 1716; these were predominantly of Chinese and Indian origin. Added to these were anatomical specimens and a collection of 'monsters', mostly freak human and animal embryos. Also on display are Peter I's surgical instruments, porcelain, lacquerwork, bronzes, wood-, stone-, and ivory-carvings, and a large globe made in 1754. The collection has since grown into one of the biggest anthropological and ethnographical museums in the country.

In the same building is the *Lomonosov Museum*. Mikhail Lomonosov worked here from 1741–65 and the exhibition includes documents and relics relating to his life and many-sided work in science, history, philology, and literature.

Zoological Museum, Universitetskaya Naberezhnaya 1. Open Wed., Fri., Sat., Sun. 11–5.

Geological Museum, Naberezhnaya Makarova 2. Open daily (except Mon. and Sat.) 11–5.

Arctic and Antarctic Museum, Marat St. 24a. Open Wed.–Sat. 11–7.

Literary, Musical and Theatrical Museums

Literary Museum (Pushkin House), Naberezhnaya Makarova 4. Open daily (except Tues.) 11–5; Sat. 11–4.

The museum is housed in the Customs House. The collection includes rare ancient manuscripts, first editions, archives, and letters and a unique collection of phonographically recorded folk lays, legends, and songs. The museum exhibits give a broad picture of the development of Russian literature from the first edition of the ancient Russian 'Lay of Igor's Host' to the present day, and there are also on display a number of personal articles which belonged to Russian writers such as Tolstoy, Chekhov, Dostoevsky, Gogol, and Blok.

Pushkin Museum, Naberezhnaya Reki Moiki 12. Open daily (except Tues.). Sun., Wed., Fri. 11–6; Thurs., Sat. 1–8; Mon. 11–4.

The poet Alexander Pushkin lived here from 1836 until he died on 29 January 1837 from wounds incurred during a duel. His flat is kept as it was during his lifetime and there are many of his personal belongings amongst the exhibits. In the courtyard is a monument to the poet by Didikin.

Nekrasov Memorial Museum, Liteiny Prospect 36, Flat 4. Open Sun., Wed., Fri. 11–6; Thurs., Sat. 1–8.

Theatrical Museum, Ostrovskovo Sq. 6. Open daily (except Tues.) 12–7; Mon. 12–5.

Exhibition of Musical Instruments, Isaakievskaya Sq. 5. Open daily (except Tues.) 12–6.

Saltykov-Shchedrin Library, Nevsky Prospect. One of the largest libraries in the world. Of particular interest are old collections which include ancient Slavonic and Russian manuscripts (including the 11th-century 'Ostromirovo Gospel'), West European editions printed before 1500, the original manuscripts and papers of Peter the Great and Suvorov, the letters of Catherine de Medici and Henry IV, and 6814 volumes of Voltaire's personal library.

Gardens

Botanical Gardens, Professora Popova St. 2. Open daily (except Sat.). In summer: 9–5; Fri. 9–2. In winter: 11–3; Fri. 11–2.

Zoological Gardens, Lenin Park 1. Open daily. May–August 10 am–10 pm. September–April 10–5.

Planetarium, Lenin Park 4. Open daily (except Wed.), 3–8; Sun. 12–8.

Churches

St. Nicholas' Cathedral, Kommunarov Sq. 3. This cathedral was built in 1753–62 by Chevakinsky. St. Nicholas' Cathedral and the following two churches are open for services.

Church of the Transfiguration, Radishchev Sq. 1. The architect of this church was Stasov.

Church of Saint Vladimir (or *Church of the Assumption*), Petrogradskaya Storona, Blokhin St. 16.

Kazan Cathedral, Kazanskaya Sq. Open daily (except Wed.) 11–6; Tues. 11–4.

Saint Isaac's Cathedral, Isaakyevskaya Sq. Open as a museum 10–5; closed Tues.

Alexander Nevsky Lavra, Alexander Nevsky Sq.

Open 1 May–30 September. Mon., Tues., Fri. 11–7; Sat., Sun. 11–8; Wed. 11–4. 1 October–30 April: Open daily 11–6, Wed. 11–4.

Cathedral of the Resurrection, Smolny

Church of the Resurrection, North side of Nevsky Prospect

Baptist Church, Bolsheokhtinsky Prospect 5

Roman Catholic Church, Kovensky Pereulok 7

Synagogue, Lermontovsky Prospect

Mosque, At the beginning of Kirovsky Prospect. Open Fri.

Statues and Monuments

Peter the Great (The Bronze Horseman), Dekabristov Sq.

Peter the Great, Inzhenerny (Mikhailovsky) Zamok

Catherine II, Ostrovskovo Sq.

Nicholas I, Isaakyevskaya Sq.

Pushkin, Iskusstv Sq. Sculptor Anikushin, 1957

Pushkin, Pushkinskaya St. Sculptor Opekushin, 1884

Pushkin, Novaya Derevnya

Rimsky-Korsakov, Teatralnaya Sq.

Glinka, Teatralnaya Sq.

Krylov, Lyetny Sad

Griboyedov, Zagorodny Prospect, Vitebsky Railway Station. Sculptor Lishev, 1959

Suvorov, Suvorov Sq. This monument, designed by Kozlovsky in 1809, shows the Russian general as the god of war.

Chernyshevsky, Moskovsky Prospect. Sculptor Lishev, 1947

Lenin, by Finland Railway Station. This monument by Yevsyev, 1926, is perhaps the best of the many of Lenin, who is shown standing on an armoured car.

Kirov, at the entrance to the Kirov Stadium, Krestovsky Island. Pinchuk designed this monument in 1950 in honour of Sergei Kirov (1886–1934), a Communist leader who for some time headed the Leningrad Party organisation.

Moscow Triumphal Gates, Moskovsky Prospect. These gates were built by Stasov in 1833–8.

Narva Triumphal Gates, Stachek Prospect. These gates were planned by Quarenghi and reconstructed by Stasov in 1827–34. They commemorate those who defended the country in the 1812–14 war. The arch is decorated with allegorical figures of Glory and with inscriptions enumerating the Guards' Regiments that had distinguished themselves during the war, and the places where decisive battles had been fought.

War Memorial, Serafimovsky Cemetery. This memorial, unveiled in 1965, is dedicated to the memory of the defenders of Leningrad.

War Memorial, Piskarevskoye Cemetery, by the main gate. There are two pavilions in the cemetery, with a museum showing life in Leningrad during World War II. At the end of the avenue of graves is a sculpture, by Isayeva and Taurit, of a woman symbolising the Motherland.

Theatres, Concert Halls, etc.

Pushkin Drama Theatre, Ostrovsky Sq. 2. (See p. 174). Modern and classical drama.

Kirov Theatre, Teatralnaya Sq. 2. Opera and ballet.

Maly Opera Theatre, Iskusstv Sq. 1.

Gorky Theatre, Fontanka Naberezhnaya 65. This building was constructed in 1879 by the architect Fontan. Maxim Gorky was responsible for the foundation of the present theatre company in 1919.

Komsomol Theatre, Lenin Park 4.

Comedy Theatre, Nevsky Prospect 56. This theatre has the reputation of being one of the best comedy theatres in the country.

Musical Comedy Theatre, Rakov St. 13. Opened in 1929, this was the only theatre in Leningrad which gave performances throughout the Second World War, even during the siege of Leningrad.

Youth Theatre, Zagorodnyi Prospect 46. This theatre was founded in 1921 by A. Bryantsev.

Leningrad Puppet Theatre, Nekrasova St. 10. (Performances for adults at 7 pm; for children at 11 am and 3 pm).

Theatre of the Music and Drama Institute, Mokhovaya St. 35

Circus, Fontanka Naberezhnaya 3. This building was designed by Kennel in 1876. (Performances at 8 pm)

Philharmonia Concert Hall, Brodsky St. 2. (Main Hall). Nevsky Prospect (Small Hall).

New Concert Hall, Lenin Sq. 1

Glinka Kapella (Choir Hall), Moika Naberezhnaya 20. The building was constructed in 1880 by L. Benois, but the choir itself was founded by Peter the Great in 1713. Glinka and Rimsky-Korsakov performed here, as did other famous musicians.

Rimsky-Korsakov Conservatoire, Teatralnaya Sq. 3.

Hotels

Astoria Hotel, Gertsen St. 39, TEL. 12–36–05

Baltiiskaya Hotel, Nevsky Prospect 57, TEL. 12–64–31

Yevropeiskaya Hotel, Brodsky St. 1/7, TEL. 11–91–49

Rossiya Hotel, Moskovsky Prospect 163, TEL. 98–76–49

Leningrad (Intourist) Hotel, Pirogovskaya Naberezhnaya 7

Leningradskaya Hotel, Maiorov Prospect 10/24, TEL. 12–68–66

Moskovskaya Hotel, Ligovsky Prospect 43/45, TEL. 17–72–81

Neva Hotel, Tchaikovsky St. 17, TEL. 72–14–86

Oktyabryskaya Hotel, Nevsky Prospect 118, TEL. 14–62–50

Severnaya Hotel, Vosstaniya St. 2, TEL. 72–04–97

Vyborgskaya Hotel, Byeloostrovskaya St. 136,

TEL. 42–68–24

International Seamen's Club, Griboyedov Nabereshnaya 166

Restaurants and Cafés

All Leningrad restaurants stay open until 12 pm.

Astoria Restaurant, in the Astoria Hotel

Yevropeiskaya Hotel Restaurant, Brodsky St. 1/7

Rossiya Hotel Restaurant, in the Rossiya Hotel

Vostochnyi Restaurant, in the Yevropeiskaya Hotel

Kavkazky Restaurant, Nevsky Prospect 25

Metropol Restaurant, Sadovaya St. 22

Sadko Restaurant, Brodsky St. 1/7

Moskva Restaurant, Nevsky Prospect 49

Primorsky Restaurant, Petrogradskaya Storona, Bolshoi Prospect 32

Severnyi Restaurant, Sadovaya St. 12

Universal Restaurant, Nevsky Prospect 12

Chaika Restaurant, Griboyedov Naberezhnaya 14

Avtomat (Self) Service Café, Nevsky Prospect 45

Neva Café, Nevsky Prospect 30

Sever Café, Nevsky Prospect 44

Uyut Café, Liteiny Prospect 28

Festivalnoye Café, Stachek Prospect 57

Sputnik Café, Moskovsky Prospect 171

Fantosia Café, Ivanovskaya St. 7

Buratino Café, Vosstaniya St. 35

Progress Café, Nevsky Prospect, at the corner of Suvorovsky Prospect

Youth Café, Poltavskaya St. This café, where young poets recite, is open in the evenings only.

Shops

Foreign Currency Shop, Makarova Naberezhnaya

Foodstuffs (Foreign Currency Shop), Baltyiskaya St. 2/14

Bolshoi Gostinnyi Dvor Department Store, Nevsky Prospect, between Sadovaya and Dumskaya Streets

Passage Department Store, Nevsky Prospect 48

Apraksin Dvor Department Store, Sadovaya St., from Lomonosov St. to Apraksin Pereulok

Dom Leningradskoi Torgovli Department Store, Zhelyabova St. 21/23

Novinok (Novelties) Shop, Nevsky Prospect 23

Gift Shop, Nevsky Prospect 26

Souvenir Shop, Nevsky Prospect 100

Antiques, Nevsky Prospect 58

Bookshop, Nevsky Prospect 28

G.P.O., Soyuza Svyazi St. 9

Central Telegraph Office, Soyuza Svyazi St. 15

Petrodvorets

Can be reached by road or by boat from Leningrad. It is about 34 km. from Leningrad on the low southern shore of the Gulf of Finland. Petrodvorets was founded by Peter the Great, who gave it the German name Peterhof, in commemoration of the victory of the Russian army over the Swedes at Poltava and the gaining of an outlet to the Baltic.

Petrodvorets is mainly famous for its system of fountains which begins 21 km. away on the Ropshinskiye Heights. It was Peter the Great's intention to make Petrodvorets the Russian equivalent of Versailles; he himself drafted the original layout of the park and gave numerous instructions on the decoration of the pavilions and the design of the fountains. Over 4000 soldiers and peasants dug canals for the fountains and all of them together use nearly 30,000 litres (7500 gallons) of water each second. The system was designed by hydro-engineer Tuvolkov, and the water-supply is sufficient to enable the fountains to work 10–12 hours out of every 24.

The *Grand Palace* was begun in 1715–24 according to plans by Le Blond, but its modest dimensions could not hold the large imperial court. It was reconstructed and enlarged for the Tsaritsa Elizabeth by Rastrelli in 1746–51. The main building has three storeys and is connected to the wings by galleries. The façade is 268 m. long and at the eastern corner of the palace is a church in Rococo style with five gilded cupolas built by Rastrelli in 1751. These buildings were burned down during World War II and are under reconstruction, the work proceeding in accordance with drawings, photographs, and other documents so that the reconstructed ensemble will be as like the original as possible. The grounds also suffered during the war when 25,000 trees were felled.

The Grand Palace stands on a terrace about 12 m. high. The surrounding park and gardens cover approximately 120 hectares (300 acres). From the grounds in front of the palace there is a wonderful view of the Nizhny (Lower) Park which stretches between the ridge of hills in the background and the shore of the Gulf of Finland. The façade of the palace facing the sea towers over the *Grand Cascade*, a great system of fountains which descends in broad steps to the park below. The most famous of the 129 fountains now operative is directly in front of the palace façade, at the head of the Grand Cascade; this is the *Samson Fountain*, where Samson is portrayed tearing open the jaws of a lion from which a jet of water rises 20 m. into the air. The lion represents Sweden defeated by Russia at the Battle of Poltava on St. Samson's Day in 1709. Other sights of interest include the *Chessboard Cascade*, and the *Zontik* (little umbrella) and the *Dubok* (little oak), surprise fountains which shower any unsuspecting visitors who come near.

The *Hermitage* is a two-storey pavilion built for Peter the Great. The walls of the dining-room on the first floor are lined with Dutch paintings, and part of the table can sink to the floor below to be cleared and relaid. To the right of the Hermitage is a statue of Peter, made by Antokolsky in 1883.

The small villa in Dutch style, built in the early 18th century, where Peter the Great lived while the Grand Palace was under construction, is known as *Mon Plaisir*. The stone wing of this miniature palace was built by Rastrelli and reconstructed by Quarenghi, and inside it is decorated with numerous paintings. The Dutch-style garden contains small flower beds and exotic trees. *Marly* is the name of the small two-storey house in Louis XIV style built in 1714 by Peter the Great.

The pavilions which stand on either side of the canal were designed by Voronikhin in about 1800.

Gatchina

48 km. south of Leningrad. The Gatchina estate was originally owned by Peter I's sister, Natalia; it changed hands before belonging to Count Orlov, for whom Rinaldi built a palace in 1776–82. The park with the White Lake in its centre was also laid out at that time.

The whole estate was subsequently purchased by Catherine II, and her son Paul who lived there turned the palace into a medieval castle with help from the architect Vincenzo Brenna. It acquired moats, drawbridges, battlements, and a parade ground in front. The castle was badly damaged by the Germans in the Second World War, and has not been rebuilt.

The main entrance to the park is through Admiralty Gate. This gate with Corinthian columns was built in 1796 by Brenna. The private garden in formal French style with a statue of Flora in the centre was added at the end of the 18th century. The Priory with an octagonal tower and tapering spire was built by Lvov in 1797–8 on the shore of Black Lake. It was intended for a prior of the Knights of Malta, whose Order enjoyed Paul's special patronage.

Chesma Obelisk at the edge of the White Lake commemorates the victory of the Russian fleet at Chesma, as does the obelisk at Pushkin. It was designed by Rinaldi and is of many different shades of marble.

At the end of the lake is the Island of Love with a Temple of Venus on it.

Pushkin

22 km. south of Leningrad. Visitors can also reach Pushkin by train from Vitebsky Station in Leningrad. There are buses and taxis from the station to the Yekaterinsky Palace. The *Yekaterinsky Palace* is open daily (except Tues.) from 11–6. The *Hermitage* is open daily (except Mon.) from 11–6.

Formerly Tsarskoye Selo (Tsar's Village), the village was called Detskoye Selo (Childrens' Village) after the revolution because the buildings were used as kindergartens, children's hospitals, sanatoria, and schools. In 1937 it was again renamed, this time after Alexander Pushkin on the occasion of the 100th anniversary of the poet's death.

The so-called *Egyptian Gates* mark the entrance to the village. They were designed by the English architect, Adam Menelaws, and built in 1828; Menelaws also built a ruined 'chapel' and a Turkish elephant house for the zoo. By the Egyptian

Gates stands a *monument to Pushkin* (1911) by Bernstam.

Yekaterinsky Palace was built during the reigns of Elizabeth, the youngest daughter of Peter the Great, and Catherine II. It takes its name from the wife of Peter the Great, Catherine I, to whom the village was given by her husband. The small two-storey palace which was first built here in the reign of Peter was later incorporated into the main palace.

The palace was begun by the architects Kvasov and Chevakinsky, and completed by Rastrelli. With its azure façade over 300 m. long with gold ornamentations and ornate pilasters and sculptures, it is one of the finest examples of Russian Baroque architecture. It was badly burnt during the Second World War, but has since been restored in accordance with the original plans.

Part of the palace is now open as a museum. In a number of halls which have not yet been completely restored there is an exhibition relating the history of the palace, of its furniture and china. Other halls which have been completely restored and which are open include the *Green Dining-room*, the *Light Blue Parlour*, and the *Chinese Light Blue Parlour*. The *Amber Room*, in which all the decorations were of amber, was completely gutted by the German troops during the war, and the decorations have never been found. It is thought possible that the amber still lies under the ruins of Kaliningrad, then Königsberg. The *Hall of Paintings* contains 130 paintings, 114 of which were in the palace collection before the Second World War.

In the former Church Wing of the palace is the *Pushkin Museum* which contains over 700 pages of the poet's manuscripts as well as a number of his personal belongings, rare books, a collection of portraits painted during his lifetime, and several portraits of his contemporaries.

Yekaterinsky Park covers 592 hectares (1482 acres). The land was given to Catherine I by her husband Peter the Great and subsequently gardens, a hothouse, ponds, and a zoo were laid out. The gardens were laid out over the course of fifty years and include many buildings of different styles.

An obelisk, unveiled in 1771, commemorates the Russian victory over the Turks near the Danube.

The Orlov Column, on an island in the middle of the lake, was erected in 1778 by Rastrelli to commemorate Prince Orlov's victory at Chesma; this was a sea battle where the Russians again beat the Turks.

Cameron's Gallery, built in 1779–93 by the Scottish architect Charles Cameron, is adorned with busts of Greek and Roman philosophers.

The *Grotto* was designed by Rastrelli who, together with Chevakinsky, was also responsible for the *Concert Hall* on the island.

The *Hermitage* was built in 1744 by Kvasov and completed in 1759 by Rastrelli. It was used as a place for relaxation by the imperial family. The

fantastically curved façade is decorated with 64 columns and a mass of ornamentation. The ingenious cross-shaped lay-out of the building fits well into the surrounding gardens.

The *Agate Rooms*, a two-storey building so named because of the interior which was fitted out by Cameron with jasper and marble to give the effect of agate, is being restored. The upper floor of the building is open in summer. Both the Agate Rooms and the Hermitage were used as stables by the Germans during the Second World War.

Also open is the *Upper Bath House* which was built in 1777–9 by Neyelov and was used by the imperial family. The Lower Bath House, built at the same time, was used by courtiers.

The *Marble Bridge* was designed in 1770–6 by Neyelov, and built from Siberian marble which was carved in Siberia and transported here ready for erection.

Alexander I's Triumphal Arch was built by Stasov in 1817–21 in honour of the Russian victory of 1812.

Vechernyi Zal (Evening Hall) near the Yekaterinsky Palace was designed by Neyelov in 1796–1810.

The *Granite Terrace* was planned by Luigi Rusca in 1809.

The *bronze fountain*, 'Girl with a Pitcher', was made by Sokolov in 1810. It was mentioned by Pushkin in one of his poems.

The *Alexandrovsky Palace* was built by Quarenghi in 1792–6 for the grandson of Catherine II, Alexander I. Nicholas II lived here almost permanently after the 1905 revolution. The palace is not open to the public. In the Alexandrovsky Park are the Ruined Kitchen (built of real pieces of ancient ruins brought from Italy), many chinoiseries (the Chinese village and the Chinese summer-house, for example) and the Grande Caprice built by Neyelov in 1770–3.

The *Lycée* is linked to the Yekaterinsky Palace by an arch over the road. Neyelov erected the building in 1791, and a school for the nobility was opened here in 1811; Alexander Pushkin, who spent his schooldays here, was one of the first pupils. The school moved to Kirovsky Prospect in Leningrad in 1843, after which time it was known as the Alexandrovsky Lycée. The garden was relaid under the direction of the architect Stasov at the beginning of the 19th century. The monument to Pushkin was made by Bach in 1909. The Lycée building is open from 11–6, closed Tues.

By the Lycée is the *Znamenskaya Church*, which was built in 1734–47 by the Moscow architect, K. Blank, and was the first stone building in the village.

Pavlovsk

25 km. south of Leningrad and 3 km. from Pushkin. The entrance to the town on the road from Pushkin is marked by cast-iron gates designed by Rossi in 1826. Visitors to the *palace*, which is open from 11–6 (closed Thurs. and Fri.), should leave their cars by the wooden bridge; it is a short walk

across the bridge and up the drive to the palace itself.

This territory was originally the hunting ground attached to the imperial estate of Tsarskoye Selo, 3 km. away. In 1777 Catherine II gave the land, including two villages and their serfs, to her son Paul as a site for a country residence, and they then received the name of Pavlovskoye, Paul's Village.

The Scottish architect Charles Cameron, who was invited to Russia by Catherine II, was responsible for the original planning of Pavlovsk, which is one of the finest palaces in Russia. The Grand Palace was later enlarged and decorated inside by Voronikhin, Quarenghi, Brenna, and Rossi.

It now has three storeys and a central dome which rests on 64 columns. The palace was badly damaged during the Second World War, but it has since been restored according to the original plans. The *statue of Paul I* in the middle of the main courtyard was designed by Klodt in 1872.

Four halls on the ground floor, the ballroom, drawing room, billiard room, and dining room, have been restored according to the designs of Cameron. All the rooms on the first floor, which is approached through the Egyptian vestibule, were built for receptions and were never in daily use. They now contain a fine collection of paintings, furniture, and china. The collection of antique sculptures is one of the largest after the Hermitage in Leningrad. Many of these were bought by Catherine from the British collector Lord Hamilton. All the furniture in the Greek Hall was carried by hand from St. Petersburg by soldiers during the reign of Paul I.

In twelve halls on the third floor is a permanent exhibition of Russian costumes and portraits of the 18th and 19th centuries. The collection of paintings is based on the palace collection which was removed from the palace during the Second World War.

Cameron was also responsible for the first plans of the surrounding park; with 600 hectares (1500 acres), it is one of the largest landscaped parks in Europe. The R. Slavyanka was dammed to form a lake, and the trees were planted with special attention to their autumn colours. The park is intersected by avenues and winding paths which lead to pavilions and statues, and which constantly reveal new views of the beautifully landscaped estate. Unlike Petrodvorets, where the fountains and other objects of interest are so arranged that they can easily be seen from afar, the architectural sights of Pavlovsk are mostly cleverly concealed in the park in order to afford a series of surprises.

At the end of the 18th century the park was extended, mainly by the architect Brenna. The sections which were added under his direction were the Old Sylvia and the New Sylvia, to the north-west of the palace. In the New Sylvia (furthest from the palace) is the *Mausoleum of Paul I*, a pavilion in the form of an ancient temple. It was never used as a burial place and its function is purely decorative. It was built in 1807–8 by the architect Thomas de Thomon with sculptures by Martos.

Adjoining the palace, between the lime avenue and the Slavyanka valley is the section called the *Grand Circles*, which takes its name from two large circular stone terraces, also by Brenna. In the centre of each stand marble sculptures on granite pedestals. These statues, representing Justice and Peace, were carved in Italy by order of Peter the Great, long before the building of Pavlovsk. All the statues in the park were buried during the Second World War.

Apollo's Colonnade on the left bank of the R. Slavyanka was built by Cameron in 1780–3, and in the centre is a bronze copy of the Apollo Belvedere. Part of the colonnade collapsed during a flood in 1817, but it was decided to leave the fallen stones to create a more ancient effect.

The Pavilion of the Three Graces, a stone terrace with 16 columns supporting the roof, is also by Cameron (1800–1) and the central statue was carved out of a solid block of marble by Trisconni.

Cameron's *Temple of Friendship* on the bank of the river is a graceful domed rotunda in Doric style with sixteen white columns, built in 1780–2.

There is a boating station and an open-air café in the park.

LENINSKIYE GORKI
See Moscow, p. 232

LITHUANIA
See Vilnius, p. 320

LIVADIA
See Crimean Circular Road, p. 87

LVOV
Population—560,000 (1971)
Ukrainian: Lviv, Polish: Lwow, German: Lemberg.

The town of Lvov stands near the R. Poltva, a tributary of the R. Bug, and the river also flows under part of the town.

It was founded in 1256 by Prince Danil Romanovich, who named it after his son, Lev. Lev is the Russian word for lion, and as well as being featured on the coat-of-arms of Lvov, lions were constantly used in the decorative metal- and stone-work of the town. Little is known about the appearance of the town in the 13th century, but it is thought that the first walled fortress was built under Prince Danil Romanovich. At the foot of the hill, where Bogdan Khmelnitsky St. runs today, were a trading centre and the houses of nobles, and along the banks of the R. Poltva were the houses of merchants and craftsmen.

From the beginning of the 14th century Lvov was an important centre on the Black Sea—Baltic trade route. Lvov also had trading connections with Cracow and Nuremburg, and many foreigners settled in Lvov. As well as Russians there were Poles, Armenians, Germans, Hungarians, Tatars, Greeks, Jews, Moldavians, Italians, and Saracens.

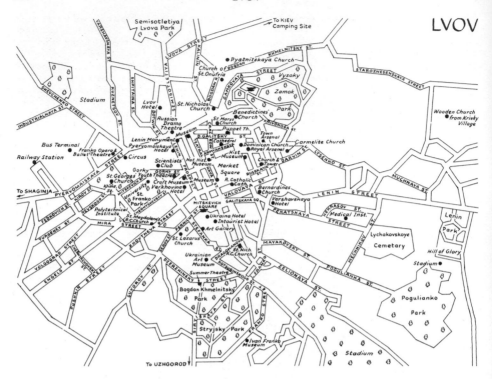

LVOV

In 1387 Lvov was captured by Roman Catholic Poland and it remained part of that country until the First Partition of Poland in 1772 when it was incorporated into the Austro-Hungarian Empire. It was made the capital of the province of Galicia and grew considerably in commercial importance.

At the end of the First World War it was returned to Poland and in 1939, with the rest of Eastern Poland, was annexed by the Soviet Union.

Most of the Polish people have now been repatriated, so the greater part of the town's inhabitants are Ukrainians and the language spoken is Ukrainian.

The main industries of the town, besides the manufacture of buses, are connected with machine building, radios, and food products. There is also an interesting pottery; the greater part of its products are sold in Moscow and Kiev, but it is possible through Intourist to visit the factory and to purchase articles there.

The old part of the town has narrow streets lined with old houses, many dating from the 16th century. Of particular interest is *Market Sq.* (Rynok) and the streets leading off it. The newest and largest building here is the *Rathaus*, which was built in 1828–35. The heraldic lions of Lvov can be seen over the main entrance of the building which is now used by the Town Council. Of particular interest on the Market Sq. are Nos. 4 and 6 which now house the Historical Museum. No. 4 is known as the *Black House* (Czarna Kamienica in Polish) and belonged to Marzin Anczowski, sec-

retary to the Polish king, Jan Sobiesski. The house was built from 1577–84 in Renaissance style and the façade is very similar to that of the Palazzo dei Diamenti in Ferrara. *No. 6* was built by Pietro di Barbona in 1574–80 for a Greek merchant, Constantine Korniakt, who financed the building of several churches in Lvov. In the middle of the 17th century the house was bought by Jan Sobiesski himself. In 1686 an 'eternal peace treaty' was signed here between Poland and Russia in which Poland renounced her claims to Kiev.

On the other side of the Black House is another *16th-century house*, also built in Renaissance style. In 1637 the first post office in Lvov was opened here by the Italian owner of the house, Robert Bandinelli.

Above the main entrance of *No. 14* is a winged stone lion with a Latin inscription and the date of completion, 1600. The lion can be seen on the coat-of-arms of Venice for the house once belonged to the Venetian Consul Massari. There are 44 houses dating from the 16th to 18th centuries altogether on Market Sq., the latest being those on the northern side of the square which were almost all built during the last half of the 18th century.

In the square near the Rathaus are *four fountains* which were designed at the end of the 18th century by Gartman Vitver. They depict Neptune, Amphritrite, Diana, and Adonis.

There are a number of other interesting secular buildings in Lvov, many of them built by members of the Polish nobility.

The Gunpowder Tower (Porokhovaya bashnya),

Podvalnaya St. 13, was built in 1554–6 and was one of four towers on the outer walls of the town. During times of peace it was used for storing grain. It is now the House of Architects.

In the same street is the *Town Arsenal* (Gorodskoi arsenal) which was built in 1554 and was used as a prison in the 18th century. On the south wall is a coat-of-arms which was taken from the demolished town walls in 1799.

The Royal Arsenal in Krivonosa St. was built in 1630 by Pavel Grodzitsky. The town archives are now kept here.

Count Pototski's Palace, Kopernik St. 15, was built in the 19th century and is now used by the Geological Institute.

The Local Government Offices in Universitetskaya St. were built in 1877–81 by Gochberger. They have housed the university since 1918.

The Polytechnical Institute, Mir St., was built in 1872–7 by Zakharevich.

There is a wealth of cathedrals and churches in Lvov, some dating from the 14th century. Owing to the mixed population, there were Armenian and Greek churches as well as Roman Catholic and Russian Orthodox.

St. Yuri's Uniate Cathedral, Bogdan Khmelnitsky St. This Baroque cathedral was designed in 1744 by the Italian architect Bernard Merettini, and completed in 1770. The statue of St. Yuri (George) on the façade is by Pinzel who was also responsible for most of the other statues adorning the cathedral. In the bell-tower is the oldest bell in the Ukraine which was cast in 1341 for a church which was built on the site in that year. The cathedral was converted for Russian Orthodox use in the 20th century. Opposite is the former residence of the Archbishop of the Uniate Church. It was built in 1761 in the same Baroque style, and is now occupied by the Lvov-Ternopol episcopal offices.

Roman Catholic Cathedral, Rosa Luxemburg St. The foundations for the cathedral, which is the only example of Gothic architecture remaining in Lvov, were laid in 1360 on the order of King Casimir III. The cathedral, which was completed in 1471, has been considerably altered throughout the centuries. It contains 18th-century frescoes and many decorative carvings and statues of the 17th and 18th centuries.

The tower was added in the late 16th century after the original tower had been ruined by fire. In the 16th and 17th centuries a number of chapels were added, many of them in the graveyard of the cathedral. In 1765 an order was issued forbidding graveyards in the centre of the town, and many of the chapels were destroyed. One of the remaining chapels is the Boim chapel which was built in German Renaissance style in 1609 and has a richly carved façade in sculptured stone. The Boim family was of Hungarian origin and one of its members was private secretary to the Polish King, Stephan Batory. The chapel is open as a museum 11–5, Tues., Thurs., and Sat.

Another remaining chapel is the Kampianow chapel on the northern wall of the cathedral. Kampianow was a ruthless pawnbroker who became Mayor of Lvov at the beginning of the 17th century. It was built of red, pink, white, and black marble by Paolo Romano in 1619 in Renaissance style.

The Church of the Assumption (Uspenskaya Tserkov), Russkaya St. is one of the most beautiful churches in Lvov. In 1527 the original church was burnt down and a new one was built; this was in turn burnt to the ground in 1571 and money was collected to rebuild it. It is recorded that the Russian Tsar Fyodor gave 200 sables, 200 martens, 50 gold coins, and 35 roubles because it was a stronghold of the Russian Orthodox Church in Poland.

The present building was erected in 1596–1629 by the Italian architect Paolo Romano. In the design are reflections of both the Renaissance and old Ukrainian architecture. In the yard is a 66-m. bell-tower dating from 1572–8 which is known as the *Korniak Tower* after the rich Greek merchant who financed its construction. In the tower is a bell called Cyril which was cast locally in 1783 and which weighs nearly 5 tons.

On the outside walls of the church is a sculptured frieze of Biblical scenes. In the main dome inside are the carved stone coats-of-arms of Russia, Moldavia, and Poland. There are also 18th-century sculptures and 17th- and 18th-century icons. The stained glass windows were installed recently. The altar in Rococo style dates from the 18th century. Among its many other treasures, the church has a silver cross made in 1638.

The Chapel of Three Saints adjoining the cathedral was built in 1578–91 with money from the Greek merchant Korniak. In the chapel are Ukrainian murals and icons dating from the 17th century.

St. Magdalene's Roman Catholic Church, Mir St. 10, was built at the beginning of the 17th century on the site of an earlier wooden church, but it was rebuilt in 1784. The statues on the main façade and the decorative towers were added in the 18th century. Inside the church are some interesting carving and sculptures of the 18th century.

Church of St. Nicholas, Bogdan Khmelnitsky St. 28, was built in the 17th and 18th centuries on the foundations of a 13th-century church which had been the church of the Princes before it belonged to the Guild of Shoemakers. The cupola was added in 1880 after the original cupola had been destroyed by fire in 1783. The interior was decorated in Rococo style in the 18th century.

Church of St. Onufria, Bogdan Khmelnitsky St. 34, was built in the 16th century on the site of a 13th-century church, and originally stood in the grounds of the St. Onufria Monastery which was destroyed by fire in the 16th century. It was rebuilt in the 17th and 18th centuries. Ivan Feodorov, the first Russian printer, is buried here. He produced his first book in 1563 in Moscow, and then fled from there to continue his work in Lithuania and Poland. He died in 1583.

All the above churches are open for services.

Armenian Cathedral, Armyanskaya St. 7, was built in 1363–70 and is thought to have been designed by a German architect from Silesia named Doring. This is doubted by many, however, who do not believe that a West European could have built the cathedral which is a blend of both Gothic and Armenian architecture. The belltower and the residence of the Armenian Archbishop date from the 16th century. The domed entrance of the cathedral, which is now two metres lower in the ground than it was at the time of construction, is decorated with Byzantine mosaics and frescoes. In the courtyard of the cathedral is an 18th-century statue of St. Christopher.

Pyatnitskaya Church, Bogdan Khmelnitsky St. 63, was built in 1645 on the foundations of an earlier church from which there used to run an underground passage to the Prince's fortress on the hill. It contains a carved wooden iconostasis with over 70 icons by unknown masters dating from the 16th and 17th centuries.

Roman Catholic Church of Maria Snezhnaya, Snezhnaya St. The history of this church is not certain. It is known, however, that there was a Catholic church serving the German population of Lvov on this site at the end of the 13th century. Some historians think that the present church was built in the 16th century from the materials of an earlier church. At any rate, it was rebuilt at the end of the 19th century when the interior was redecorated in Rococo style. By the church is an 18th-century statue of the Madonna.

Church of the Dominican Monastery, Stavropigiskaya Sq. This impressive church in Baroque style was founded in 1748. The architect was Jan de Witt. It was reconstructed at the end of the 18th century after a fire, and again in 1956. Its dome is a copy of that of St. Peter's in Rome. Inside are some 18th-century sculptures and a bas-relief made by the Danish sculptor, Thorvaldsen, in 1816. The grave of the Polish artist, Artur Grottger (d. 1880), is here too.

The building now houses an atheist museum and in the centre hangs a Foucauld Pendulum of the type developed in Paris in 1851 to prove that the earth rotates on its axis. A globe of the moon stands where the altar used to be. Attached to the church is another museum displaying a wide range of articles from churches of many different denominations and also from local synagogues. Near the church are some 16th-century Gothic buildings belonging to the monastery which once stood here.

Church and Convent of the Benedictines, Vechevaya Sq. The church and convent of the Benedictines were erected at the end of the 16th century by Paolo Romano. They were rebuilt after a fire in 1623.

Jesuit Monastery and Church, Teatralnaya St. 11/13. Work on the church began in 1613, two years after the foundation of the Jesuit college in Lvov. Inside there are 18th-century woodcarvings, and frescoes dating from the 17th and 18th centuries. The monastery was built in Baroque style in 1723–8.

Bernardines' Church, Vossoedineniya Sq. The monastery was built between 1600 and 1630. In the church are some frescoes and 18 wooden altars with decorative carving, all dating from the 18th century.

Saint Lazarus' Roman Catholic Church, Kopernik St. 27. This church was built in 1635–40. Near the church in Kopernik St. is a dried-up well guarded by two stone lions from the former Mayor's house.

Casimira Roman Catholic Church, Krivonosa St. 1, was built in 1660 in Baroque style. The building adjoining the church was built at the same time as an orphanage.

The Church and Monastery of the Barefoot Carmelites, Sovietskaya St. 20, were founded in 1634 and were enclosed in thick defensive walls, the remains of which can still be seen. In the church are some 18th-century frescoes, and wooden sculptures dating from the 17th and 18th centuries.

Clarissa Roman Catholic Church, Lenin St. 2, was founded at the beginning of the 18th century.

St. Nicholas' Roman Catholic Church, Sherbakov St. 2, was built in 1739–45 and belonged to the Trinitarian order. It was later converted for Russian Orthodox use. In the chapel of St. Florian to the left of the main altar is a carved marble altar, dated 1595, which was originally in the Roman Catholic Cathedral.

St. Bridget's Roman Catholic Convent, Chapayev St. 24. This 17th-century convent was turned into a prison in 1792.

Wooden Church, Krivchitskoi St., was built in 1763 and brought here in 1930 from the Ukrainian village of Krivky as an example of folk architecture.

Historical Museum, Rynok 4/6. Open 11–6, closed Wed. The museum is housed in two of the oldest houses on Market Sq. (see above). The former throne room of No. 6 is now used for a display of present-day industry.

Ukrainian Art Museum, Dragomanov St. 42. Open 11–7, closed Mon. There is a good collection of 14th–18th-century icons here.

Art Gallery, Stefanik St. 3. Open 11–7, closed Mon. The collection of about 10,000 paintings includes some works by Rubens, Titian, Goya, Tintoretto, and the Russian classics.

Lenin Museum, Lenin Prospect 20. Open 10–7, closed Mon.

Craft Museum, Lenin Prospect 15. Open 11–6, closed Mon. The museum building was built in 1874–91 by Zakharevich.

Natural History Museum, Teatralnaya St. 18. Open 11–5, closed Mon.

Ivan Franko Museum, Franko St. 152. Open 10–7, closed Tues. Ivan Franko (1856–1916) was a famous Ukrainian writer.

Yaroslav Galan Museum, Gvardeiskaya St. 18. Open 12–5, closed Wed., Fri., and Sat. Galan was a Ukrainian political writer who was murdered in 1949 at the age of 47.

Open Air Museum of Wooden Architecture, in a beautiful park in the suburbs of Lvov. Open 11–7, closed Mon. There are wooden houses and churches here and peasant huts of the 18th and 19th centuries. The church with the belfry was built in 1863 and was brought here, as were all the other buildings, from various parts of the Lvov Region.

Miczkiewicz Monument, Mitskevich St., opposite the Intourist Hotel. The sculptors of this statue of the Polish poet Adam Miczkiewicz were Popiel and Parashuk, and it was unveiled in 1905.

Ivan Franko Monument, in front of the University. This monument of the Ukrainian writer was unveiled in 1964.

Lenin Monument, Lenin Prospect. This monument by Merkurov was unveiled in 1952.

Kilinsky Monument, by the pond in Stryjsky Park. Kilinsky was a revolutionary Warsaw cobbler and hero of the Polish uprising of 1794. The monument was erected in the 1890s.

Tank Monument, Lenin St. The T-34 tank commemorates the Soviet Tank Corps which liberated Lvov in 1944.

Kholm Slavy (Hill of Glory), near Lychakovske Park. Here, marking the graves of those who fell during the Second World War, is an eternal flame accompanied by an architectural and sculptural complex, constructed in 1946–52.

Franko Opera and Ballet Theatre, Torgovaya Sq. The theatre was built between 1897 and 1900 and designed by Gorgolevsky in a mixture of Baroque and Renaissance styles. On top of the façade are bronze statues of Glory, Victory, and Love by Piotr Voitovich. The theatre seats 1100 and is very decorated inside.

Zankovetskaya Ukrainian Drama Theatre, Ukrainskaya St. 1. This theatre was built in classical style in 1837–42 by Pikhl and Zaltsman.

Russian Drama Theatre, Gorodetskaya St. 6

Gorky Youth Theatre, Gorky St. 11

Puppet Theatre, Galitsky St.

Circus, Pyervomaiskaya St.

Summer Theatre, Khmelnitsky Park, Dzerzhinsky St. 43

Concert Hall, Franko St. 25. The choir of Lvov is called 'Trembita'.

Library, Stefanka St. This building was designed by Nobile and Biema and erected in 1826–49.

Franko Park, Universitetskaya St., opposite the main university building. The park dates back to the 16th century. There is a restaurant here in summer.

Stryjsky Park, on the road leading to the town of Stryj. Stryjsky Park is one of the most beautiful in Europe, and its 56 hectares (140 acres) also take their place among the richest arboreta in the Soviet Union. The park, which has a children's railway and permanent exhibition halls, was opened to the public in 1877. There is a café in the park.

Bogdan Khmelnitsky Park, Dzerzhinsky St. In the park are a summer theatre seating 6000, a restaurant, exhibition pavilions, and a monument to Lenin.

Prince's Hill. The remains of the 14th-century Vysoky Zamok (high castle) fortress, built by Casimir III on the site of an earlier wooden fortress, can be seen here. The fortress was in ruins by the end of the 18th century and a park was laid out here in 1835–9. There is also a stone monument to Maxim Krivonos, the Cossack colonel who seized the fortress in 1648.

Lenin Park encloses the graves of Russian soldiers who fell in the First and Second World Wars, and has an eternal flame which has burned on the Hill of Glory war memorial since 1958. There are several statues here, including one of a woman symbolising the motherland.

Lychakovskoye Cemetery, Mechnikov St. Since the 16th century many monuments to the nobility have been erected in this cemetery. There is one to Ivan Franko, and also the graves of other Polish and Ukrainian writers and artists.

Botanical Garden, Scherbakov St.

Hippodrome Racecourse, Stryjskoye Chaussee

Spartak Swimming Pool, Instrumentalnaya St. 49

Komsomolskoye Lake, 3 km. from Lvov on the road to Vinniki

Glinovnavaria Lake, 16 km. from Lvov. This lake has a sandy beach.

Intourist Hotel and Restaurant, Mitskevich Sq. 1, TEL. 79–90–11

Lvov Hotel, Lenin Prospect 13, TEL. 79–90–11

Pervomaiskaya Hotel and Restaurant, Lenin Prospect 21, TEL. 79–90–31

Ukraina Hotel and Restaurant, Mitskevich Sq. 4, TEL. 79–99–21

Kiev Hotel, Chapayev St. 15, TEL. 74–21–05

Dnieper Hotel, Pervomaiskaya St. 45, TEL. 74–21–02

Varshavskaya Hotel, Vossoedineniya Sq. 5, TEL. 72–59–64

Prikarpatskaya Hotel, Nalivaiko St. 6

Narodnaya Hotel and Restaurant, Kosciusko St. 1

Kolkhoznaya Hotel, Trekhsotletiya Vossoedineniya Sq. 14

Vysoky Zamok (high castle) Restaurant, TEL. 72–25–22. There is a beautiful view over the city from this restaurant. It stays open until 2 am and puts on a floorshow. There is an entrance charge of 1·50 roubles and it is best to make a reservation.

Leto (summer) Restaurant, Gorky St. 17

Moskva Restaurant, Mitskevich Sq. 7

G.P.O., Slovatsky St. 1

Kashtan Foreign Currency Shop, Rudenskova St. 3, TEL. 74–10–64

Gift Shop, Kopernik St. 1

Souvenirs, Galitskaya St.

Arts and Crafts, Mitskevich Sq., near the Intourist Hotel

Taxi Ranks, Komsomolskaya St. 5, Lenin Prospect 22, and at the Railway Station

MAKHINDZHAURI
See Batumi, p. 62

MARGILAN ·
See Tashkent, p. 302

MELIKHOVO
See Yasnaya Polyana, p. 342

MIKHAILOVSKOYE
See Pskov, p. 262

MINERALNIYE VODY
There are over a hundred mineral springs in the Caucasus, but the most important are the group known as the Caucasian Mineral Waters. Here, within a distance of about 40 km. can be found all the cures which would otherwise have to be sought all over Germany and France. Some of the types of water here are even unique of their kind.

The territory is located in steppeland not very far from Mount Elbruz. It is on the same latitude as Genoa in Italy and it lies considerably farther south than Yalta, but as it is separated from the warm Black Sea by the main Caucasian mountain range it has a continental climate, and the summer here is cooler than in the southern part of the Steppes. One of the first explorers of the geology of the Caucasus, Abikh, called this region the 'cliff archipelago'. Now it has been confirmed that the isolated mountains here were in fact once islands when the low-lying steppeland to the north of the Caucasus was under the sea.

The first Russian records of the people living in the Pyatigory (five hills) region date from the middle of the 16th century. After Kazan had fallen to Ivan the Terrible, in 1552, the local population (now known as Kabardintsi, but then called the Cherkessi of Pyatigory) asked the tsar's protection from the Turks and Tatars. A few years after this Ivan the Terrible married a local Cherkess princess, Maria, and the first Russian fortress, Terki, was built in 1567. However, it was only after the peace treaty with Turkey in 1774 that Pyatigorsk and the region surrounding it passed to Russia.

Russia had been searching for health resorts of her own since the time of Peter the Great, and in 1773 an Academy of Sciences' expedition confirmed the healing qualities of Pyatigory's mineral springs. It was noticed that wounded soldiers recovered much more quickly when they used the springs here; so the first Russian residents of Pyatigory were retired soldiers who stayed on, and in fact all the main buildings of the future spas were built by the soldiers.

Only in 1803 was Caucasian mineral water proclaimed to be of national importance. Two resident doctors were then appointed and the present spas really date from 1803. In 1810 Dr. Gaaz quite by chance discovered the springs at Zhelezno-vodsk and Yessentuki because local people reported that in some places their horses drank especially greedily. Pyatigorsk was proclaimed a town in 1830.

Now over 70 springs have been developed in this region, yielding up to 6,000,000 litres (1,300,000 gallons) a day of 12 different types of water; Pyatigorsk is famous for its hot carbonic hydrogen sulphide springs, and it takes first place among the spas because of its greater variety of waters. Pyatigorsk alone has 34 springs yielding up to 2,000,000 litres (450,000 gallons) of water a day.

In spite of the different qualities of the waters from the various springs, all the towns in the vicinity are known collectively as the spas of the Northern Caucasus, and all share the same emblem which is depicted everywhere; it shows an eagle with wings spread, perching on a mountain peak. There are statues of this eagle in the hilly parks that rise above each spa.

Zheleznovodsk
Zheleznovodsk lies 7 km. off the main road to the right. It has a mountainous climate like that of the central Alps, and the average annual temperature is 10°C. (50°F.). The 23 springs give up to 1,000,000 litres (250,000 gallons) of water a day, and the water includes carbonic acid, hydro-carbonate-sulphate, sodium, and calcium. The springs have temperatures varying from 10–55°C. (50–130°F.). The town now has about 15 sanatoria, some located in old villas and some in new buildings.

The Zheleznovodsk waters are particularly useful in the cure of metabolic, digestive, and kidney diseases, and since 1965 Intourist have organised special 26-day courses of treatment for foreign visitors.

Mount Zheleznaya (iron) is of typical laccolit rock. A famous park lies in the southern foothills of the mountain adjoining the natural forest. A spiral path leads up the mountain side and from the entrance of the park an attractive flight of steps leads up to *Verkhnaya Ploshchadka* (upper square) and the *Pushkin Gallery*. A chestnut avenue leading to the right from the gallery brings one to the springs. A little farther on and to the left under a small bridge is a statue of a group of bears; this is the point at which to turn either up the mountain or around the ring path. Alternatively the same avenue leads on the *Slavyanovsky Istochnik* (Professor Slavyanov's Spring, discovered in 1913) located in a pleasantly designed pavilion. The spring itself looks like a foaming fountain, and has a temperature of 50°C. (122°F.); water is served there.

Farther on, in the *Bolshaya Ploshchadka* (large square), is the colonnade of the three *Smirnov Springs* (45·5°C./114°F.). Down from this point run the *Cascade Stairs*, a double staircase with mineral water running down the centre. At the bottom of the stairs, through the trees, the surface of a large artificial pond can be seen. On the slope of the mountain to the left of the stairs is *Nyezlobinsky Istochnik* with pleasant tasting and fairly cold water (19°C./66°F.). To the right are some other springs, and baths looking like small swimming pools, filled with mineral water.

The uphill spiral path, by which one circles the mountain twice, leads past three springs: *Kegamovsky* (16·5°C./62°F.), *Vladimirsky* (26°C./79°F.) and *Spring No. 1*. The route is 3600 m. in length. The second path leading to the top of the mountain (852 m.) is 3300 m. one way and takes about 1 hr. 15 min. to climb. From the top of the mountain there is a good view of Mount Beshtau, and to the left Mount Mashuk can be seen.

Theatre, in Pushkin Gallery, in the park

Kavkaz Hotel, Gorky St. 3

Druzhba (Friendship) Hotel and Restaurant, along the main road

Beshtau Restaurant, Chaikovsky St.

Café, Pushkin St., in the park

Bank, Lenin St. 55

G.P.O., Lenin St. 53

Bookshop, Chaikovsky St. 9

Pyatigorsk

Population—80,000 (1970)

This spa lies at 514 m. above sea level on the left bank of the R. Podkumok. Its name means 'five mountains', and the peaks referred to are: Lysaya Gora (bald mountain) (758 m.), Mashuk (994 m.), Zmeika (snake) (994 m.), Beshtau ('five hills' in Turkish), and Zheleznaya Gora (iron mountain) (854 m.). All these are of volcanic origin and, with the exception of Beshtau, have a layer of limestone over the lava. Other mountains in the vicinity are Razvalka (930 m.), Byk (bull) (821 m.), Verblud (camel) (902 m.) and Goryachaya (hot).

There are pedagogical and pharmaceutical colleges in Pyatigorsk and also Institutes of Physiotherapy and Oil. There are food, textile and associated light industries, and an agricultural machinery repair plant.

The town is mainly located on the southern and south-western slopes of Mashuk. It has about 50 springs which can be divided into four types: carbonic acid-hydrogen sulphate, carbonic acid, salt-and-alkaline, and radon. Their temperatures range from 14–60°C. (57–140°F.). The majority of the springs are at the foot of the mountain, but another part of the resort, Proval, is on a terrace on the southern slope of the mountain.

The waters are particularly valuable in the cure of muscular, circulatory, digestive, metabolic, nervous, skin, and gynaecological diseases and since 1965 Intourist have organised terms of treatment lasting for 26 days.

The *Lermontov Baths*, near Tsvetnik (the Flower Garden), were formerly called the Nikolaevsky Baths; they are fed by the Alexandro-Yermolovsky spring. The temperature of the water is 42°C. (107°F.) and it contains natronchloride, bicarbonic lime, sulphuric natron, free carbonic acid, and sulphuric hydrogen. The bathhouse was built in 1826–31 and is the oldest of its kind in Russia.

Mikhail Lermontov (1814–41), after whom the baths were named, was a Guards officer of Scottish ancestry, and is famed for his novels and poems which earned him his position as the greatest Russian Romantic and which cost him his life.

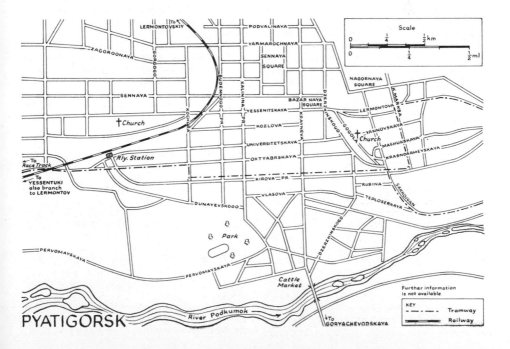

There are many mementos of Lermontov in Pyatigorsk, the more important of which are described below.

Proval is a great grotto, 27 m. deep, on the slope of Mashuk. It was carved out many years ago by a subterranean sulphuric stream; later a hole formed in the roof of the grotto and a lake 14 m. deep was formed. It has a warm sulphur spring and the water is blue in colour from the sulphuric combinations. In the past it was one of the sights for visiting society to see, and in 1837 a suspension bridge was put up upon which six couples could dance a quadrille. The bridge only lasted for four years. Local legend says that Lermontov was cured of rheumatism by swimming in the Proval Lake. The grotto is entered by a 45 m. gallery. Open 11–6, closed Tues.

On the road to Proval from the town is an imposing *stone monument* by Svetlitsky; it stands on the spot overlooking the valley where four Soviet commissars were shot in 1918. There is a pleasant walk which starts from Proval and leads around Mount Mashuk, passing Lermontov's duelling place and ending near the Tyoply (warm) Narzan spring.

Another walk, which follows the arrows saying 'Marcheroute 10', climbs gently to the top of 4600 m. Mount Mashuk from where there is a superb view. The mountain is now crowned by one of the highest television aerials in Europe.

Lermontov Museum, Buachidze St. 9

Lermontov's House, Lermontovskaya St. 18. The writer lived here for two months, and after the duel his body was brought back here.

The duel in which Lermontov was killed took place on the foothills of Mashuk, 4 km. from the centre of Pyatigorsk. Lermontov was challenged by a certain Martinov for mocking him in the presence of ladies. When they met at the appointed time Lermontov explained that he never intended to insult Martinov and what he had said had been meant as a joke; he said that if Martinov would not be offended he was ready to ask his pardon, not only there but at any other place he chose. Martinov replied 'Shoot! Shoot!' Lermontov was to fire first and he fired into the air, but Martinov came closer and shot him through the heart so that he died instantly. The writer had been opposed to the tsar and sent to the Caucasus as punishment for his verses, especially those devoted to the death of Pushkin, who was also killed in a duel. 'Butchers of freedom, genius and glory' was how he described the members of the government in the offending poem, referring to Pushkin's death. When Nicholas I learned of Lermontov's fate he said, 'A dog deserves a dog's death' and Martinov, instead of being sentenced to hard labour (the punishment for duelling at that time) was simply ordered to seek religious absolution. Lermontov's death was understood by many Russians to be a murder planned by the authorities. Lermontov was buried in Pyatigorsk and later his body was transferred to his birthplace, Moscow.

Lermontov Statue, Lermontov Garden, Andzhiyevsky St. This bronze statue by Opekushin was unveiled in 1889. The terrace in front of it commands a fine view of the mountains with the snow-capped summit of the twin-peaked Elbruz (white breasts) 97 km. distant as the crow flies.

Lermontov Grotto, opposite the Akademicheskaya Gallery in the Park. This cave was called after the writer following his death. During his lifetime he visited it several times, and he has described it in 'A Hero of Our Time'. A marble sign marks the entrance.

Lermontov Monument, on the site of the duel. The monument, which takes the form of a bust of the poet surrounded by mourning griffons on stone posts connected by chains, was designed by Mikeshin and unveiled in 1915.

Church, on the hill top at the end of Andzhiyevskova St. It was built at the end of the 19th century.

Local Museum, Sacco-and-Vancetti St. 2; open 10–4.30; closed Tues. There are natural history and art sections. The museum was founded in 1905.

Akademicheskaya Gallery, on the top of Goryachaya Mountain. This white pavilion built 1847–9 has a good view of Pyatigorsk. It used to be known as the Elizabeth Gallery but was renamed in 1925 to celebrate the 200th anniversary of the Academy of Sciences.

Restauratsia, Kirov St., near Tsvetnik. In Lermontov's time this used to be a very grand restaurant with frequent balls and dances. Now the building houses the Physiotherapy Institute.

Eolova Arfa (Aeolean Harp). This monument was built in 1830–1 and called after the Greek god of the winds, Aeolus. Originally there was a wooden column with two harps; when the wind blew a weather vane plucked the strings and made music. This was replaced by the present small pavilion in ancient Greek style which has the best view over the town and surrounding region. It stands on the spot where, even in Lermontov's time, Cossack guards kept watch to protect patients from sudden attack from the peoples living in the mountains.

Health Resort Exhibition, Proval St. 2, in the Mikhailovskaya Gallery which was built in 1848.

Obelisk, on the top of Mount Mashuk, commemorates the topographer, Pastukhov.

Kirov Monument, Kirov Sq. This monument to the revolutionary and statesman is by Kondratev and was unveiled in 1959.

Bust of Andzhiyevsky, in the park on Kirov Prospect. Shotskikh made this bust in memory of the first local party chairman.

Musical Comedy Theatre, Kirov St. 17

Philharmonia Concert Hall, in Lermontov Gallery, Tsvetnik Park. This gallery was brought from the fair in Nizhni-Novgorod (now Gorky) in 1899.

Diana Grotto, in Tsvetnik (flower garden) Park. This big artificial cave named after the goddess of hunting was excavated in 1830–1. It is cool inside, even on the hottest day. It was designed by Bernardazzi.

Kirov Park, Dunayevsky St. 5. Here are the planetarium, an open-air theatre, amusement grounds, a dance floor, and a boat hiring station.

Hippodrome Racecourse, Kursovaya St. 219. Open from 2 May until October; racing Sat. at 4 and Sun. at 12 noon. There is a totalisator and a restaurant.

Bathing Beach, beside the reservoir. There is a snack bar here, sunshades and changing cabins, and at the far right-hand end of the reservoir is an area of shallow water reserved for children.

Mashuk Hotel and Druzhba (Friendship) Restaurant, Kirov St. 26. The hotel was formerly known as the Bristol. The Intourist office is here, TEL. 73–60.

Pyatigorsk Hotel and Restaurant, Krainyev St. 43a, TEL. 39–31.

Kolos (Ear of corn) Restaurant, Shoseinaya St. 101

Tsentralnaya Restaurant, Kirov St. 27a

Yug (South) Restaurant, Universitetskaya St. 34

Mashuk Restaurant, Kirov St. 60

Tourist Restaurant, Kirov St.

Lyesnaya Polyana (Glade) Restaurant, at Lermontov's duelling place

Kavkaz Restaurant, near Proval

Gorka (Hill) Café, Anisimov St. 3

Otdikh (Rest) Café, Kirov St. 32

Proval Café, in the Proval area

Yunost (Youth) Café, Kirov Prospect 56

G.P.O., Kirov St. 52

Bank, Kirov St. 25

Department Store, Oktyabrskaya St. 1

Taxi Ranks, at the central bus station, the railway station, the upper market, and Proval.

Filling Station, Naberezhnaya St. 15, by the central bus station. Round-the-clock service.

Service Station, at the same address as the filling station, TEL. 35–13. Open 8 am–6 pm; closed Sun.

Motel, Kalinin St. 2, Belaya Romashka region; on the right side of the road coming into town from Mineralniye Vody. Also at Lumumba St. 17, on the way into town, is a new building under construction which will supplement the existing facilities.

Camping Site, beside the Motel

From Pyatigorsk a side road branches off to the right and leads to *Essentuki* (17 km.) and then on to *Kislovodsk* (a further 20 km.).

Tambukanskoye Lake is about 11 km. along the main road from Pyatigorsk. The road passes by the shores of this famous lake, the mud of which is used for curative mud-baths at the spas.

Essentuki

This spa lies off the main Intourist road, 17 km. to the right from Pyatigorsk, in a valley watered by two streams, the Bugunty and the Essentik. It was founded as a military settlement in 1798, and after 1826 it was known as a Cossack settlement. It was developed as a spa in the late 1880s.

There are springs yielding a total of 500,000

litres (110,000 gallons) of water daily. All the springs are cold and either carbonic ferruginous or alkaline. The best are No. 4 and No. 17, both of which have a high degree of mineralisation. The water cures here are augmented with mud baths, and are recommended for the treatment of digestive and metabolic disorders. Intourist organises courses of treatment lasting 26 days.

The main street, Internatsionalnaya St., runs down from the railway station and leads to a small square, unofficially known as 'Pyatachok' meaning '5-kopek coin' and indicating its small size and its liveliness; it is the real heart of the spa. The best hotel, the Mayak, and the entrance to Staryi Park which has a territory of 40 hectares (100 acres) and contains the springs, are in this square.

Just inside the park is a theatre, and nearby there stands a *pavilion* where the water from springs No. 17 and No. 19 is used for drinking in summer. Spring No. 17 is open 7–10, 12–3.30 and 5–8 so that one can drink before meals. When it was discovered over 100 years ago it was called the 'pearl of Caucasian mineral waters, and the pride of the motherland'. Its temperature is about 13°C. (56°F.). Behind the theatre is the main bath-house supplied by these springs. There is a memorial plaque here with the dates of their discovery.

An asphalted avenue, Alkalichesky Prospect, leads down through the park. To the right, opposite the theatre, is the building of the *Lower Baths* with 34 bathrooms, and birch trees in front of it. Further on, to the left of the avenue, is the summer pavilion of Spring No. 4 and on the right side is the corresponding winter pavilion. This spring is less mineralised than No. 17 and has a temperature of 10–12°C. (50–54°F.).

The avenue finally leads to the domed and columned *Pavilion No. 1*, which is still less mineralised than Nos. 4 and 17. To the right is a pile of stones with the local emblem of an eagle killing a serpent, and to the left, on the slopes of Alkali Hill, is a sculpture depicting a Russian peasant seated with a drinking cup in his hand, commemorating the first use of these waters. Above him can be seen a semi-circular colonnade from which there is a good view across to Mashuk and Pyatigorsk. Further on the path leads past flower beds to stone steps and a small bridge. The big sanatorium, one of the oldest buildings in Essentuki and formerly a restaurant, is situated here. Nearby is the building of the *Upper Baths*, built in 1898 with a fountain in front of it. This has 60 bathrooms, each bath being of solid marble. Not far away along another avenue are other baths which are used only in summer.

The avenue leads on to the centre of the park where there is a *concert platform* and a *library*. The metal column with a figure of a dove on it marks the place where the water of Spring No. 17 was first tapped. A little aside from this an avenue of palms leads back to the lower park.

Three walks begin from the east gates of the park. The first is 1820 m. in length and is a gentle slope climbing up 23·5 m.; the second, more hilly than the first, is 2515 m. and rises to 42·4 m. The third walk is of 2436 m., and is more hilly still, going up to 61·8 m. The park was planted out in 1849. In the northern part of Essentuki is another park on higher ground, originally known as English Park.

Semashko Mud Baths, Semashko St. These baths were built in 1913–15 by Academician Shreter, and are called after Dr. Nikolai Semashko, Soviet Commissar of Health, 1918–30. The building is in the style of ancient Greek public buildings, decorated with lions, columns, and statues of heroes from Greek mythology.

Memorial Obelisk, in front of the railway station. This small obelisk is dedicated to those who fell during the Revolution.

Theatre, in the park

Essentuki Hotel, Karl Marx St. 26

Mayak (Lighthouse) Hotel, Internatsionalnaya St. 3

Yalta Hotel, Internatsionalnaya St. 18

Kavkaz Restaurant, Internatsionalnaya St. 26

Eating Houses, Lenin St. 12 and Vokzalnaya Sq., in front of the railway station

Mechta (Dream) Café, at Pyatachok

Bank, Kislovodskaya St. 5

G.P.O., Kislovodskaya St. 18

Department Store, Internatsionalnaya St. 11

There is good bathing in the R. Podkumok, near the town at Byeli Ugol ('white coal', called after one of the oldest power stations in Russia) railway station.

Kislovodsk

This spa lies off the main road to the right from Pyatigorsk; it is 20 km. past Essentuki, and 37 km. away from Pyatigorsk itself.

Kislovodsk is 822 m. above sea level, and lies at the bottom of a mountain valley crossed by the R. Olkhovka and the R. Berezovka. Surrounded by forestless mountains, it is protected from all winds, and late summer and autumn are its best seasons. Its winters are warm, in fact it has more sunny days in winter than Davos, and only 60 or 70 rainy days in the whole year. The average annual temperature is 10°C. (50°F.), and the average winter temperature 2°C. (35·5°F.). The town is surrounded by terrace-like slopes of hard limestone which contain many caves.

There are 7 springs in Kislovodsk, the *Narzan spring* being the most famous of all in the region. It is the richest carbonic spring in the world and the Circassians called it the 'drink of heroes'. It is 818 m. above sea level and its temperature is 13°C. (55°F.). The spring has been known since the 18th century, and in 1848–58 a gallery was built in English Gothic style to house it. The *Narzan Bathhouse* was built later in Indian style. In the centre of the town there is a factory where the water is bottled. The other springs in the town, including

Dolomitic Narzan and *Sulphate Narzan*, are of similar type. The volume of water yielded daily by the Kislovodsk springs is only exceeded by those of Pyatigorsk.

The waters here have been found most effective in the cure of circulatory diseases, mild bronchial asthma, and chronic (but non-tubercular) diseases of the respiratory organs. Since 1965 Intourist have organised 26-day courses of treatment for foreign visitors.

The Russian writer and Nobel Prize winner, Alexander Solzhenitsyn, was born here in 1918.

St. Pantilemon's Church, Uritsky St. 16. Built in 1905 in a good position with an excellent view over the town.

KISLOVODSK

KEY:
1. Yaroshenko Museum.
2. Narzan Spring, Gallery.
3. Steklannaya Strunya, (Glassy Stream).
4. Krasnye Kamni, (Red Stones).
5. Serye Kamni, (Grey Stones).
6. Sosnovaya Gorka, (Pine Hill).
7. Narzan Hotel.
8. Kavkaz Hotel.
9. Excursions Office.

Yaroshenko Museum, Yaroshenko St. 3. Open 11–6; closed Tues. Nikolai Yaroshenko (1846–98) was a prominent Russian painter.

Sergo Ordzhonikidze Museum, in the Sergo Ordzhonikidze Sanatorium

Statues of Lenin and Dzerzhinsky, by Lenin Prospect

Gorky Theatre, Krasnoarmeiskaya St. 5

Concert Hall, in Verkhny (upper) Park

Kurortnyi Park. Following the right bank of the R. Olkhovka the main path leads to a pool. A small pavilion stands here, and from under it the water flows from the pool in a steady stream. It is crystal clear and so much resembles molten glass that it is often called *Steklannaya Struya* (Glassy Stream). From here the path goes on to *Sosnovaya Gorka* (Pine Hill), where there is a rosarium and an open air stage. Further along through shady avenues the path comes to *Krasnye Kamni* (Red Stones), which are coloured by the iron content of the water and many have been eroded by the weather into strange mushroom shapes. A bas-

relief of Lenin has been carved on one of the stones. A flight of steps runs down from this point to Leninsky Prospect.

The path leads on to *Serye Kamni* (Grey Stones) which stand at a height of 942 m. From this point there is a good view of Kislovodsk, and in fine weather the summit of Elbruz can be seen. Further on is *Pyervomaiskaya Polyana* (Mayday Field), a meadow surrounded by mountain slopes to form a natural amphitheatre with room for 60,000 people. It is occasionally used as such. Nearby is *Khram Vozdukha* (Temple of Air).

Krasnoye Solnishko (Red Sun) gets its name from being the usual place to watch the sun rise and set. From here the road leads to *Siniye Gori* (Blue Mountains), so called because at sunset they take on a blueish colour. The spot commands a good view of Kislovodsk and Elbruz. It is prescribed for people with weight to lose walk on from this point up to Maloye and Bolshoye Sedlo.

Verkhnyi Park (Upper Park) is usually at its liveliest in the evening. The Gorky Theatre, a cinema, and a concert platform which is acoustically unique are all in it. The floor of the concert platform contains a layer of broken glass to reflect the sound, and the shell-shaped roof is double-layered and itself resounds like a musical instrument.

Stadium, Pyervomaisky Prospect 34, on the left side of the road leading into town

Kavkaz Hotel and Restaurant, Dzerzhinskova St. 24, TEL. 5–18–00

Narzan Hotel, Mira Prospect 14

Zarya (dawn) Restaurant, Gertsen St.

Chaika (seagull) Restaurant, Pervomaisky Prospect 4

Khram Vozdukha (Temple of Air)

Restaurant, Nizhni (lower) Park

Tourist Café, by Lake Kislovodsk, just outside the town and near the Motel

Cosmos Café, by the railway station

G.P.O., Krasnaya St. 3

Bank, Mira Prospect 24

Motel, 3 km. from the centre of the town, beside Lake Kislovodsk, which covers 10 hectares (25 acres). Here there are facilities for bathing and boating. There is a *café* and a *shashlik bar*, and the *'Tourist' Restaurant* is nearby, and also a *Service station*, *carwash*, and *filling station*. 3 km. farther on is the *'Zamok' (Castle) Motel*, where a two-storey building built to resemble an old castle is used as an annexe to the main Motel; it also has a restaurant, the *Zamok Restaurant*, which specialises in Caucasian dishes.

Camping Site, beside the lake

Filling Station, at the entrance to the town, on the right-hand side

Lermontov Cliff, 4·5 km. from Kislovodsk. This cliff is described in 'A Hero of Our Time'. 430 m. from here is the *Lermontov Spring*.

Kovarstva i Lubvi (The Castle of Cunning and Love) is 6 km. from Kislovodsk. This is really the name of a cliff strongly eroded by the weather. The actual castle which stands there and which is now used as a motel was built long after the cliff got its name. The story about it runs thus:

Once upon a time the daughter of one of the mountain princes fell in love with a simple shepherd boy. Her father was angry at this and betrothed her to a rich relative of his own. When the young couple learned of his plans they decided to commit suicide by leaping from the cliff. The young man jumped first, and the girl was so terrified at the sight of his battered body that she thought better of her intention and returned home to marry the man of her father's choice. The cliffs alone were witness to the tragedy.

Medovyi Vodopad (Honey Waterfall) is 10 km. past the castle, following the same beautiful road with gorge and valley landscapes.

Dolina Narzanov (Narzan Valley), 33 km. from town. It is so called because there are 17 Narzan-type springs here. The valley, which has the mountain rivers Khasaut and Mushta rushing through it, can be reached by car.

Bermamuitskaya Skala, 34 km. from Kislovodsk. Skala means 'cliff'. This point should be visited, because from here Elbruz can be seen in its entirety.

MINSK

In Belorussian: Mensk
Population—916,000 (1970)
This city is located in the centre of the Republic of Belorussia, of which it is the capital.

BELORUSSIA
(White Russia)

In Belorussian: Belarus
This republic of the Soviet Union is situated in the west of the European part of the country and shares its borders with Poland.
Area: 207,600 sq. km.
Population: 9,003,000 (1970), of which a quarter live in the towns. The people are a mixture of Belorussians (80%), Russians (9%), Poles (7%), Jews (2%), and others (2%). The Belorussians are closely related to the Great Russians and the Ukrainians, and they trace their origin from the East Slav tribes, the Krivichi, Dregovichi, and others. The language spoken is Belorussian, which is closely akin to Russian and Ukrainian. The inhabitants of the major cities speak mostly Russian.

Until the 12th century the area was under the authority of the Kievan state; later the new principalities of Turov-Pinsk, Smolensk, and Volynia emerged, and these were incorporated in the 13th and 14th centuries into the Grand Duchy of Lithuania. Russian was the official language

PLATES OPPOSITE
Above: A corner of Riga, ancient capital of Latvia. *Below*: Trakai, a 14th-century Lithuanian castle near Vilnius.

spoken until Lithuania's union with Poland in 1569. The whole of Belorussia was taken over by Russia after the Polish partitions of 1772–95.

The first demands for autonomy occurred at the beginning of the 20th century when the revolutionary Hromada (community) Party (later called the Socialist Hromada Party) was formed. This, however, gained little popular support. Strong Polish and Zionist movements were also active at that time. In 1918, during the German occupation, an independent Belorussian Republic was proclaimed; in 1920 the country was temporarily occupied by Poles, who later partly withdrew, while remaining in possession of the western part. In 1921 the Soviet Belorussian Republic was formed, and it joined the Soviet Union in 1922. The size of the republic was increased in 1924–6 by the addition of adjacent territory to the east, and, in 1939, by the inclusion of Western Belorussia. It suffered a great deal during the First, and especially the Second, World Wars.

Approximately 25% of the area of Belorussia is covered with forests and about 10% with marshes. The climate is moderate continental.

Belorussia's agricultural products are chiefly grain, potatoes, and dairy products. There is pig-breeding too and Belorussia is also the most important flax-growing area in the Soviet Union.

The country's main industries are food production and light industry, wood-processing, and engineering. The country also has large resources of peat (about 5,000,000,000 tons), which constitute the main source of fuel for its many power stations. Other mineral resources include lignite, potassium, and rock salt.

A few words of Belorussian:

hello	dóbraga zdarovya
I am a tourist	ya toorist
please	kali laska
thank you	dzyakooi
yes	tuk
no	nye
good	dóbra
bad	dréna
I don't understand	ya nye razoomeyoo
I need an interpreter	mnye pateeben peravodchik
goodbye	da pabáchenya

Minsk

Minsk stands on the R. Svisloch, 20–30 m. wide at this point, and unnavigable, and at the same time it is situated at the crossing of important railway lines between Moscow–Brest and Vilnius–Kiev. Its name comes from the word 'menyat' (to change) and refers to its importance as a trading post.

The town is one of the oldest in Russia. Its first known mention dates from 1067, when it belonged to Prince Vseslav of Polotsk and stood on the ancient river trade route which linked the Black Sea to the Baltic. The R. Svisloch was navigable at that time. From the beginning of its history Minsk has been ruined again and again. In 1084 it was utterly demolished and, according to an old chronicle, 'not a single body nor a single beast' remained alive. This devastation was the work of Vladimir Monomakh, who was wreaking revenge on the citizens of Minsk for having burned down Smolensk. Minsk was under Polish rule, and then under Kiev's, but in 1101 it became the capital of an independent principality. In 1326 it became subject to Lithuania and in 1499, when it had already risen to being an important commercial and cultural centre of that state, the Magdeburg Law was introduced into the local city government. In 1505 it was invaded and ruined by the Tatars. Later, in 1569, it formed a part of Poland after Lithuania's union with that country, and in 1793 the region passed to Russia. In 1796 Minsk was proclaimed the provincial capital and then was again ruined, this time by Napoleon. In 1835 Nicholas I signed a decree which stated the few places in which Jews were allowed to live; Minsk was one of these, and until the Second World War the population was in fact half Jewish. Not only was Minsk many times in history devastated by wars and invasions, but it was also ruined by recurrent fires; in 1881, for instance, half the city was burned to the ground. These catastrophes, however, did not halt its ever increasing economy. Development was especially rapid after the completion in 1874 of the railway which followed the old trade routes. Minsk soon grew to be one of the centres of trade with the West.

On 1 January 1919, the Belorussian Soviet Republic was organised and Minsk was proclaimed its capital. During World War II 80% of the houses were destroyed. Russians call Minsk 'the town of partisans', for during the war partisans killed many German officers in command of the region, including their leader.

Minsk is unique among the capital cities of the Soviet Union for having been ruined over and over again, and yet still dominating the region. It is now a completely new town, rebuilt on the wartime ruins. As there were no outstanding valuable historical monuments, no attempt was made to try to restore the old parts of the town, as was done in Warsaw. The territory of Minsk, covering 9000 hectares (22,500 acres), is about twice the size it was before the war. The central street of the town, *Leninsky Prospect*, called Zakharievskaya St. before the Revolution, crosses Minsk from northeast to south-west. As it was utterly destroyed during the war, it was widened from 14–19 m. to 48 m. when it was reconstructed. It is about 8 km. long. The governmental houses, theatres, museums, shops, hotels, and institutes are concentrated in the centre of the town. Crossing the main prospect are the streets most worthy of note: Lenin St. and Engels St. Like the other central thoroughfares, they are lined with 4- and 6-storey buildings. On the same prospect are Pobedy (victory) and Tsentralnaya Squares, where the Minsk counterparts of the Moscow Red Square parades (which take place on the national holidays of 1 May and 7 November) are usually held. On Tsen-

MINSK

tralnaya Sq. is the *Trade Union Palace of Culture*; this has a Hall of Columns and also contains a theatre, the stage of which is a replica of that of Moscow's Bolshoi Theatre. Close to the square is a big, old garden with a *monument* to Yanka Kupala (1882–1942), Belorussia's most popular poet, usually known by his pseudonym (his real name was Ivan Lutsevich); the monument by Azgur was unveiled in 1949. When the central streets were rebuilt they were planted with 20- and 30-year-old trees, and this has helped to give them a more mellow look than they would otherwise have had.

The *Belorussian Government House* is an 11-storey building on Lenin Square, designed in 1935 by Langbard. The *Belorussian Academy of Sciences* was founded in 1922 and reorganised in 1929. Minsk is also a university town; Lenin university, which has eight faculties, was opened in 1921. Besides this there are 12 different institutes and a total of about 35,000 students. The Polytechnical Institute is the second major educational establishment.

The Belorussian Film Studio is in Minsk, and

the capital of the republic is also one of the biggest industrial centres of the Soviet Union. When it was reconstructed after the war, over 100 big industrial enterprises were built, and Minsk now produces 25% of all Belorussian manufactures. These include the biggest Russian lorries (40- and 60-tons), tractors, motor-cycles, radios, watches, textiles, leather, and food products.

The population is now mainly Belorussian, Jewish, and Russian.

There are in Belorussia many burial mounds and barrows, which date mainly from the 10th–12th centuries. In a field by the village of *Grushevski*, near Minsk, there are some excavations made between 1945 and 1951. Here the old territory of a fortress (Zamchishche) was discovered; part of the main street is discernible with traces of some houses and a 12th-century church.

Bernardine Convent, Bakunin St. 4. Built in the 17th century and situated in the oldest part of Minsk, this convent is now used to house the town archives.

Cathedral of the Holy Spirit, Bakunin St. 3. This is one of the four churches open for religious service in Minsk, and is where the Bishop officiates. The cathedral was built in the 17th century. Its most precious possession is a miracle-working icon of Our Lady; the age of the icon is uncertain, but according to legend it was placed by Prince Vladimir in the Desyatinaya Church in Kiev, where it remained for 500 years. Then, in the 15th century, when the town suffered one of its periodic raids by the Tatars, it was thrown into the river Dnieper. In 1550 an unusual radiance was noticed by the inhabitants of Minsk in their own river Scisloch, and the icon was found and rescued.

The Church of St. Catherine, Ostrovsky St. Built in 1611 and at first known as the Church of SS. Peter and Paul, this church is also now used to house the town archives.

Calvary Cemetery Gates, at the end of Opansky St. These gates were built in 1830 and are decorated with sculptures.

The Governor's House, Svobody Sq. The Jesuits had a college in Minsk from 1650 until they were expelled in 1820; and they used this building during the 18th century. Since 1932 it has been the building of Minsk Conservatoire.

Synagogue, Shkolny Pereulok

Mason's Lodge, Muzikalnyi Pereulok 5. This 3-storey house was built in the 18th century; in the second part of the 18th century it was the meeting place for the Northern Torch Lodge. This was declared illegal in 1822, as were all Lodges in Russia.

World War II Museum, Svobody Sq. 23. Also known as the Museum of the History of the Great Patriotic War, this museum has 25 halls.

Belorussian Art Museum, Lenin St. 20. Here are canvases by Ivazovsky, and also by Shiskin and Repin, both of whom lived and worked in Belorussia for some time. The Museum is open 11–7, closed Thurs.

Local History and Folklore Museum, Revolyutsionnaya St.

Yanko Kupala Museum, Yanko Kupala St. The Museum is open 10–5, closed Fri.

Yakub Kolas Museum, Lenin Prospect 66. The Museum is open 9.30–3.30, closed Sat.

First Congress Museum, Lenin Prospect. This building is a replica of that in which the Social Democrats met in 1898; the original was burned down. The Museum is open 11–6, closed Fri.

The Minsk Lenin Library, this Library has 2·5 million books on its shelves.

Lenin Monument, on Lenin Sq. in front of the Belorussian Government House. The monument was designed by Manizer.

War Memorial, Pobedy Sq. This great obelisk was erected in memory of the soldiers and partisans who fell in World War II. It was built in 1954 by Zaborsky and Korol. It stands 38 m. high, and on top is a model of the highest Soviet military award, the Order of Victory. At its foot burns the Eternal Flame.

Bolshoi Theatre, Parizhskoi Kommuny Sq. 7. This opera house was built in 1935, and was designed by Langbard who was also responsible for the Belorussian Government House. Besides opera and ballet, it also shows performances of the Capella Belorussian Choir and the Belorussian Folk Choir. The Puppet Theatre is located in the same building.

Yanko Kupala Theatre, Engels St. 23. This was built in 1890 by Kozlovsky.

Gorky Russian Drama Theatre, Volodarsky St. 5. This was once a synagogue.

Youth Theatre, Engels St.

Puppet Theatre, Lenin Prospect 23

Trade Union Palace of Culture, Lenin Prospect 25

Circus, Lenin Prospect

Dynamo Stadium, Kirov St. This stadium seats 40,000 people.

Winter Swimming Baths, near Kolas Place

Gorky Park, Pervomaiskaya St. 17. This park was founded in 1880 as the Governor's garden and covers 26 hectares (65 acres). It contains fountains, a monument to Maxim Gorky, an exhibition hall, and an open-air theatre seating 1800.

Cheluskintsev Park, Lenin Prospect, beside the main road to Moscow. This park was founded in a pine forest in 1930. It has an area of 45 hectares (112 acres) and contains a children's railway, an open-air stage, a café, and war graves decorated with the statue of a mourning woman.

Botanic Gardens, Lenin Prospect 80. The gardens cover 106 hectares (265 acres).

Victory Park, Zalivnaya St. With a territory of 204 hectares (510 acres), this is Minsk's largest park. It has two boat-hire stations, a restaurant, and billiard hall.

Yubileinaya (Intourist) Hotel and Restaurant, Parkovaya Magistral 19, TEL. 29–80–15

Beloruss Hotel and Restaurant, Kirov St. 13, TEL. 22–59–81

Minsk Hotel and Restaurant, Lenin Prospect 11, TEL. 29–23–63

Sputnik Hotel and Restaurant, Chvalov St. 34

Pervaya Sovietskaya Hotel, Komsomolskaya St. 13

Vtoraya Sovietskaya Hotel, Volodarsky St. 6

Neman Restaurant, Lenin Prospect 22. This restaurant is called after a Lithuanian river.

Zarya (dawn) Restaurant, Lenin St. 2

Raduga Restaurant, Privokzalnaya Sq.

Chaika (seagull) Restaurant, Tolbukhina St. 3

Leto (Summer) Restaurant, Pervomaiskaya St. 8

Vesna (Spring) Café, in the department store, Lenin Prospect 21

G.P.O., Lenin Prospect 10

Central Telegraph Office, Engels St. 44

Department Store, Lenin Prospect 21

Podarki Gift Shop, Volodarsky St. 22

Minsk Sea, 16 km. from town. This reservoir was completed in 1956; it is possible to bathe here.

Khatyn

60 km. to the north of Minsk, on the site of a former village is a memorial to the victims of Nazi occupation. The village of Khatyn was

burned to the ground together with all its inhabitants by the Germans during World War II. Symbolic chimneystacks, each topped with a bell, now mark the positions of the peasants' cottages before the burning. The Khatyn Memorial was conceived as a place to commemorate all who perished in Belorussia during the war and it was opened in 1968. Urns with ashes from 136 Belorussian villages that suffered a similar fate have been brought here and beside the cemetery of the villages stands a Memorial Wall honouring those who died in Nazi concentration camps.

MOLDAVIA

See Kishinev, p. 150

MOSCOW

Population—7,061,000 (1970)

Moscow, the population of which was recorded as over 7 million in the 1970 census, is by far the largest city in the Soviet Union. It is the capital of the Russian Federation as well as of the Soviet Union and the headquarters of the East European Economic Community, Comecon. As well as the seat of government, it is an important cultural and industrial centre with diverse industries.

Originally a small defence post on the Moskva river, from which it takes its name, Moscow owes its importance largely to its geographical position. The policy of the early princes of Muscovy was to gain control of the main waterways with an outlet to the sea by conquering the neighbouring principalities. It became an important point on the Baltic–Volga–Caspian trade route, by which goods were transported from the south to the Baltic and thence to Europe. Today it is the main junction of all the road and rail arteries.

Moscow has always remained on the perimeter of Europe and its isolated position, supported by the descriptions of the winter in Russian novels, have led to the belief that it is much colder and more distant than it actually is. Its latitude of 55° is no more northern than that of Copenhagen or Edinburgh and it is nearer to London than is Athens. The winter is certainly cold, with an average temperature of 14°F. (−10°C.) in January, and odd days as cold as −22°F. (−30°C.), but the summer is usually hot with an average temperature in July of 66°F. (19°C.).

Various legends account for the name Moscow, but perhaps the most appealing explanation is that Moscow was founded by Japhet's sixth son, Mosokh. Mosokh's wife was called Kva and so the name Moskva was chosen. Mosokh and Kva had a son and daughter, whom they named Ya and Vuza. It is said that from these names the R. Yauza, Moscow's second largest river, took its name.

Long ago Moscow was known as the sacred city of the Russians and the city of 'white walls'. In poetry and songs it was often referred to as 'Matushka Moskva', Mother Moscow. During the last century it was sometimes referred to as

'Brides' Fair' because of the society marriage market.

The official date for the founding of Moscow is accepted as 1147. It was in this year that Moscow was first mentioned in the Russian chronicles when Prince Yuri Dolgoruky wrote to his friend Prince Svyataslov inviting him to Moscow to attend a banquet in honour of Prince Chernigov saying, 'Come to me, brother, in Moscow.' Eight hundred years later a statue was erected to Yuri Dolgoruky, whose name in Russian means 'Yuri with the long arms', and who was the Prince of Rostov-Suzdal and founded Moscow as a southern border settlement. Prince Yuri, who undoubtedly played an important role in Russian history, had a certain amount of foreign blood, his mother being the daughter of the Swedish king, Ing. Prince Yuri Dolgoruky's Moscow estate consisted of a few wooden buildings and a church on a wooded hill at the confluence of the Moskva and Neglinnaya rivers, where the Borovitsky Gate of the Kremlin stands today.

A wooden fence was built around the settlement in 1146 but in 1238 the whole fortress was burnt down by the Tatar hordes of Batu Khan. During the rule of the 'Golden Horde' of the Tatars Moscow actually grew in prosperity in spite of its vassal state. The princes of Moscow acted as tax-collectors for the Tatars and even used Tatar soldiers in their campaigns against neighbouring principalities.

Ivan I, known as Ivan Kalita (Ivan the money bags) for the way he accumulated treasure, became the first Grand Duke of Moscow in 1328. A few years earlier the Metropolitan of the Church had moved his seat to Moscow from the old church capital of Vladimir, an act which added to the already growing importance of Moscow. After the fall of Constantinople in 1453 a monk in Pskov wrote that 'Two Romes have already fallen, but the third remains standing and a fourth there will not be' and Moscow became known as the Third Rome. This occurred during the reign of Ivan III (1462–1505), also known as Ivan the Great, who married Sophia, the niece of the last Byzantine Emperor. Ivan thus considered himself the heir of the Byzantine emperors and adopted their arms of the double-headed eagle which remained the arms of the Russian state until 1917. During his reign the first stone and brick buildings of the Kremlin were built, including the walls and the Cathedrals of the Assumption and Annunciation which still stand today. They were built by foreign architects, mostly from northern Italy, who were all given the surname of Friasine, meaning Franc, but with workmen and influences from the Russian towns of Vladimir, Pskov, and Novgorod. In this way the original form of Moscow architecture developed.

The prosperity of Moscow continued to grow but the city was periodically raided by the Tatars who made their last attack in 1591 under Kara Girei. Territorial gains from nearby principalities, the final collapse of Novgorod in 1570 when Ivan

MUSEUMS

1 Marx and Engels Museum
2 Lenin Museum
3 Lenin Funeral Train at Paveletsky Rly. Station
4 Museum of the Revolution
5 Kalinin Museum
6 Museum of History
7 St. Basil's Cathedral Museum
8 Kolomenskoye Estate Museum, 16ᵗʰ-17ᵗʰ cent.
9 Novodevichii Monastyr
10 Battle of Borodino Museum
11 Museum of the History of Moscow
12 Soviet Army Museum
13 Frunze Club of Aviation
14 Planetarium
15 Polytechnical Museum
16 University Museum of Geography
17 Zoological Museum
18 Botanical Garden. Ostankino
19 Zoo
20 Tretyakov Art Gallery
21 Pushkin Fine Arts Museum
22 Museum of Eastern Cultures
23 Shchusev Architectural Museum
24 Donskoi Monastery Architectural Mus.
25 Ostankino Palace Museum of Serf Art
26 18ᵗʰ c. Kuskovo Estate and Mus. of Ceramics
27 Andrei Rubiyov Museum of Ancient Art
28 Pushkin Museum
29 Leo Tolstoy Museum
30 Leo Tolstoy Estate Museum
31 Gorky Museum
32 Mayakovsky Library-Museum
33 Chekhov Museum
34 Nikolai Ostrovsky Museum
35 Museum of Literature
36 Bakhrushin Theatrical Museum
37 Glinka Museum
38 Skryabin Museum
39 Central Exhibition Hall
40 Armoury

THEATRES

41 Bolshoi Theatre
42 Palace of Congress
43 Moscow Arts Theatre
44 Moscow Arts Theatre (New building)
45 Maly Theatre
46 Branch of Maly Theatre
47 Vakhtangov Theatre
48 Moscow Soviet Theatre
49 Mayakovsky Theatre
50 Stanislavsky and N.D. Theatre
51 Soviet Army Theatre
52 Lenin Komsomol Theatre
53 Pushkin Drama Theatre
54 Stanislavsky Drama Theatre
55 Drama and Comedy Theatre
56 Yermolova Theatre
57 Gogal Drama Theatre
58 Operetta Theatre
59 Satire Theatre
60 Sovremennik Theatre
61 Drama Theatre in Malaya Bronnaya
62 Central Children's Theatre
63 Central Puppet Theatre
64 Romany Theatre
65 Variety Theatre
66 Moscow State Circus

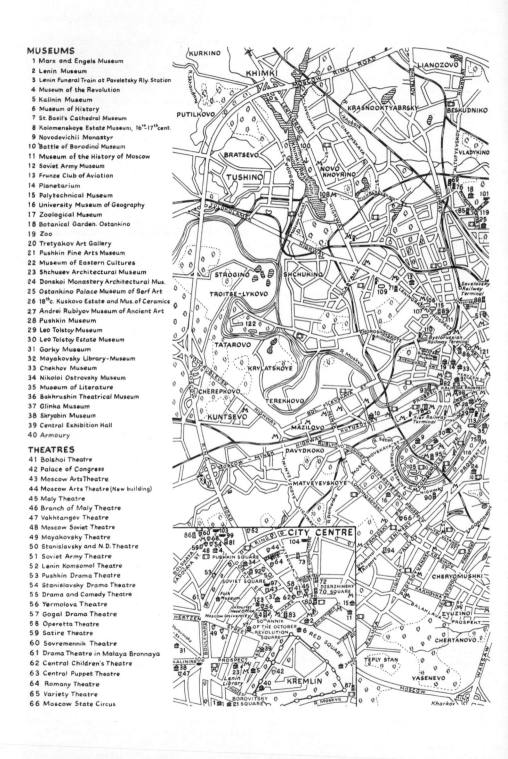

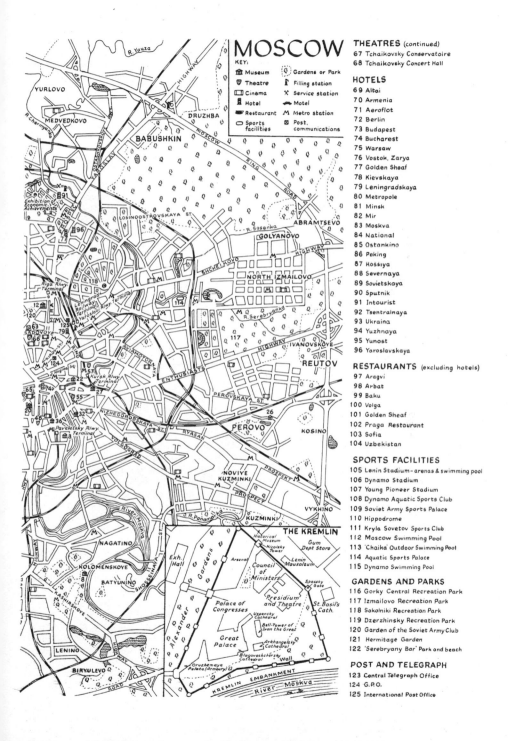

MOSCOW

KEY:

🏛	Museum	⊕	Gardens or Park
▽	Theatre	⌐	Filling station
▭	Cinema	✕	Service station
⬚	Hotel	⬅	Motel
○	Restaurant	M	Metro station
○	Sports facilities	⊠	Post, communications

THEATRES (continued)
67 Tchaikovsky Conservatoire
68 Tchaikovsky Concert Hall

HOTELS
69 Altai
70 Armenia
71 Aeroflot
72 Berlin
73 Budapest
74 Bucharest
75 Warsaw
76 Vostok, Zarya
77 Golden Sheaf
78 Kievskaya
79 Leningradskaya
80 Metropole
81 Minsk
82 Mir
83 Moskva
84 National
85 Ostankino
86 Peking
87 Rossiya
88 Severnaya
89 Sovietskaya
90 Sputnik
91 Intourist
92 Tsentralnaya
93 Ukraina
94 Yuzhnaya
95 Yunost
96 Yaroslavskaya

RESTAURANTS (excluding hotels)
97 Aragvi
98 Arbat
99 Baku
100 Volga
101 Golden Sheaf
102 Praga Restaurant
103 Sofia
104 Uzbekistan

SPORTS FACILITIES
105 Lenin Stadium - arenas & swimming pool
106 Dynamo Stadium
107 Young Pioneer Stadium
108 Dynamo Aquatic Sports Club
109 Soviet Army Sports Palace
110 Hippodrome
111 Kryla Sovetov Sports Club
112 Moscow Swimming Pool
113 'Chaika' Outdoor Swimming Pool
114 Aquatic Sports Palace
115 Dynamo Swimming Pool

GARDENS AND PARKS
116 Gorky Central Recreation Park
117 Izmailovo Recreation Park
118 Sokolniki Recreation Park
119 Dzerzhinsky Recreation Park
120 Garden of the Soviet Army Club
121 Hermitage Garden
122 'Serebryany Bar' Park and beach

POST AND TELEGRAPH
123 Central Telegraph Office
124 G.P.O.
125 International Post Office

the Terrible is said to have massacred 60,000 Novgorodians, and the opening of the trade route to Western Europe from the White Sea in the 16th century, all added to the importance of Moscow. In 1547, Ivan IV, known as Ivan the Terrible for his persecution of the 'boyari' (barons), was crowned in Moscow with the royal diadem and assumed the title of Tsar of all the Russias. During his reign the last of the other principalities fell and the kingdoms of Kazan and Astrakhan were conquered. The power of the tsar became absolute and Ivan the Terrible increased the crown lands by confiscation as had Henry VIII of England.

The turn of the 17th century is known as the time of troubles in Russian history, but the growth of Moscow continued almost uninterrupted. When Ivan IV's son, Feodor I, died in 1598 he was succeeded by his brother-in-law, Boris Godunov, who died mysteriously in 1605. Boris Godunov had been opposed by two false Dmitris, both supported by the Poles, who both claimed to be Ivan's youngest son who had died in 1591. At one point the Poles were threateningly near to the Kremlin but they were driven from the country in 1612 by an army of volunteers led by a meat merchant, Kosma Minin, and Prince Pozharsky, whose statue stands in Red Square. In the same year was the first of the Romanovs, Mikhail Romanov, was elected tsar by the National Assembly in Moscow.

In 1712 St. Petersburg became the capital, but Moscow retained the status of Russia's second capital. Pushkin wrote:

And Moscow bowed to the new capital
As the Queen Dowager bows to the young
Queen . . .

Nevertheless, Moscow lost much of its former glory and an order of Peter the Great in 1714 which forbade any building in stone except in St. Petersburg reduced the status of Moscow still further. Even during this period, however, a few fine buildings were erected which, although of wood, were given the appearance of stone by stucco on the wood. Peter's successors mostly preferred the old capital and the reigns of Elizabeth (1741–61) and Catherine II (1762–96) were times of active building and many of the finest houses in Moscow appeared. The university, two large hospitals, and numerous mansions along the boulevards and in the fashionable district of the Arbat were built by the architects Bazhenov and Kazakov, and slightly later, by Ghilardi, Quarenghi, and Bovet. Several large estates were built near Moscow, some by serf craftsmen, such as Archangelskoye, Kuskovo, and Ostankino.

The fire which ravaged Moscow for three days and nights in 1812 is well known. When the French troops under Napoleon were forced to evacuate the city, three quarters of the houses had been destroyed by fire but an order to blow up the Kremlin on departure was only carried out in part. Over a quarter of the 100,000 men who had entered Moscow with Napoleon had been taken prisoner or died from hunger. The following year the reconstruction of the city began and was completed by a special commission for the reconstruction of Moscow set up by Alexander I in 1825. Most of the new building was in brick and whole new streets, such as Kropotkinsky and Vorovsky, appeared. Several magnificent buildings in the imperial style were erected, such as the Manège and the Bolshoi theatre by Bovet.

During the last half of the 19th century the population of Moscow grew particularly rapidly, from 350,000 in 1863 to 1,039,000 in 1879. Moscow had been an important trade and craft centre since the middle ages and was affected more than other Russian towns by industrialisation and the industrial boom of the 1890s. By the eve of the Revolution Moscow was the financial, commercial, and industrial capital of Russia. The first Russian Revolution of 1905 was famous for its battles here, especially that in the Presnaya region. It was of this that Vladimir Lenin wrote, 'It trained the ranks of the fighters who were victorious in 1917.'

By a decree of the government on 16 November 1917 Moscow was re-established as the capital of the country and the government moved to the Kremlin in March 1918. It has been the seat of the government since then except for the winter of 1941–2 when the government moved to Kuibyshev because of the threat of German invasion. The German army came dangerously close to Moscow and in 1965 Moscow was acclaimed a Hero City, sharing the honour with Odessa, Sevastopol, Volgograd, Kiev, Leningrad, Novorossisk, Kerch and Brest Fortress.

Since the Revolution, reconstruction of the city has been carried out on a large scale. Many of the old buildings, including half of the churches, have been demolished and large new suburbs have been built. The first plan for the reconstruction of Moscow, which was drawn up in 1935, called for radical new building and alterations in the centre of the city. Gorky St. was widened and the Moskva Hotel and the Lenin Library built. Building work was held up by the war, but was later continued on an even grander scale. New avenues lined with vast buildings, such as Prospect Mira and Leninsky Prospect, were constructed and a few huge sky-scrapers with a somewhat gothic appearance—the Ministry of Foreign Affairs and the new university are good examples—were built.

The second plan, drawn up in 1951 and put into effect from 1954, called for fewer prestige buildings with rich ornamentation and for more plain blocks of flats as an effort to solve the housing shortage. Building is continuing at an astonishing rate, both in the suburbs and in the centre, where it is planned that new wide roads will converge.

Moscow has developed outwards from the Kremlin in concentric circles which have been formed on the line of the old fortifications. The *Bulvarnoye Koltso* (boulevard ring) and *Sadovoye Koltso* (garden ring) serve as easily recognisable landmarks to the visitor. The Bulvarnoye Koltso, which has a line of trees and gardens in the centre, is the nearest to the centre and in fact forms a semi-circle on the northern banks of the R. Moskva. The Sadovoye Koltso is a very wide busy street which intercepts all the main streets radiating from the centre.

The boundary of Moscow is marked by the circular by-pass which lies at an average distance of 25 km. from the city centre. No new building is allowed at present beyond this ring which is 109 km. long and which crosses 14 main roads leading from the city. The territory within the by-pass ring is 87,500 hectares (218,750 acres), while the area of Greater Moscow (including the green belt) is 265,000 hectares (662,500 acres).

The centre of Moscow

Red Sq. (Krasnaya Ploschad) is the main square of the city where demonstrations and military parades take place. Its name dates from the 17th century, the word 'krasnaya' meaning 'beautiful' in Old Russian. The square is 695 m. long and 130 m. wide. The best view of the square is to be obtained from the windows of the *Museum of History* which is on the northern side. To the south stands *St. Basil's Cathedral* with the *Minin and Pozharsky Monument* in front, to the west the *Kremlin* wall and the *Lenin Mausoleum*, and to the east *GUM*, pronounced 'goom', the State Department Store.

Close to St. Basil's Cathedral is the *Lobnoye Mesto*, a round platform of white stone which was constructed early in the 16th century. The Russian name for this platform, which is derived from the word 'forehead', has come to mean 'execution place'. Executions were not carried out on the platform, however, but near it. The first historical mention of the Lobnoye Mesto is when Ivan the Terrible used it to make a public confession of misdeeds to the assembled people. At that time it was a round brick structure with a roof supported by pillars and surrounded by a wooden fence. In 1786 it was faced with rough stone and the roof was removed. Until the reign of Peter the Great all edicts and decrees were read aloud here. The tsar used to present himself to his people here once a year and he also presented his heir-apparent when the latter reached the age of sixteen. All religious processions stopped by the Lobnoye Mesto while the chief clergyman present blessed the people from the platform.

The statue of Minin and Pozharsky (see above, p. 200), by Ivan Martos in front of St. Basil's Cathedral was erected in 1818 from money collected by public donation. The two bas-relief ornaments on the pedestal of the monument depict episodes from the war of liberation. The monument originally stood in the middle of Red Sq.

Two streets run out of Red Sq. to the East. They pass through the old part of Moscow called *Kitai-Gorod*. The name is thought to have been derived from the Mongol word 'Kitai' meaning 'central'. In the 14th century Kitai Gorod was surrounded by an earthen wall, but this was replaced in the 16th century by a fortified wall, remains of which can be seen from Sverdlov Sq. near the Metropole Hotel and from Kitaisky Proezd which leads off Marx Prospect. In the 14th century Kitai Gorod was a busy district of small shops and markets, and later banks and offices appeared here and the area became the financial and business centre of Moscow.

25th October St. (formerly Nikolskaya St.) runs from the north-east corner of Red Square into Kitai Gorod. No. 9 in this street is the *Zaikono-Spassky (Behind-the-icon-of-the-redeemer) Monastery* which was founded by Boris Godunov in 1600. It has been much altered and enlarged since then, but a few of the old chambers and the cathedral which was built in 1661 are still standing. They can be seen from the courtyard of No. 7 in the same street. The Slavic-Greek-Latin Academy, the first higher educational establishment in Russia where Lomonosov, the famous 18th-century Russian scholar, studied, was housed here from its foundation in 1682 until 1814. No. 15, the *Institute of History and Archives*, was formerly the Synodal Printing Plant which was built in 1814 by Bakarev. The façade is covered with intricate carvings in white stone and there is a sundial above the portal. The Synodal Printing Plant was built on the sight of the Tsar's Printer's Yard, the first printing plant in Russia which was founded by Ivan Feodorov in 1563. The timber buildings were later destroyed by fire and only one now stands in the courtyard behind the institute.

Kuibyshev (formerly Ilyinka) St. runs out of Red Sq. at the other end of GUM and forms the main thoroughfare of Kitai-Gorod. Banks, offices, and several ministries are situated here. Half way along the street on the right-hand side is the building of the former Moscow Stock Exchange which was built in 1873–5 and now houses the All-Union Chamber of Commerce.

Razin St. (formerly Varvarka St.) runs out of Red Sq. behind St. Basil's Cathedral parallel to the two streets already mentioned. To the right is the large *Rossiya Hotel* which was built by Chechulin and completed in 1967. It has accommodation for 6000 and a number of restaurants, including one on the top floor from which one has a very good view over the Kremlin. Beside the hotel stand several monuments of 16th- and 17th-century architecture. At the beginning of the street on the right side is the *Church of St. Barbara*, which was built in 1514 by Alevisio Novi and rebuilt in 1796 by Kazakov. It has recently been restored. Next on the same side is the *Church of St. Maxim* which was built in the 17th century.

In front of the hotel are a group of buildings of historical and architectural worth which had been totally neglected until the hotel was built, but which have now been restored. One of the oldest of these is the first *English Embassy* in Moscow which was built in the 16th century by Russian craftsmen. The building is at present being excavated and restored. *The House of the Boyars*

Romanov was built in 1565–7. This low house with thick walls and small windows was the birthplace of Mikhail Feodorovich Romanov, the first Romanov tsar. In 1859 the house was reconstructed by Richter who added stairways, galleries, and a small superstructure. The mansion now houses an exhibition of chattels of the 17th to 19th centuries. Behind the House of the Boyars Romanov stands the *Monastery of the Apparition.* The five-domed cathedral was built in the late 17th century and the belfry, designed by Matvei Kazakov, was added in 1789.

Further on near Nogina Sq. is the *Church of St. George* which was built in the middle of the 17th century. Down the side of the Rossiya Hotel, near the river, is the 15th-century *Church of the Conception of St. Anne.* It was altered in the 16th and 17th centuries, but is soon to be restored to its original state.

Revolution Sq. adjoins Red Sq. to the north. It is bounded by the Lenin Museum, a metro station, and the back of the Moskva Hotel. Adjoining Revolution Sq. is *Sverdlov Sq.* (formerly 'Teatralnaya' or 'Theatre' Sq.). Yakov Sverdlov (1885–1919) was a prominent Bolshevik and one of Lenin's closest collaborators. During the last years of his life he was titular head of the Soviet state. On the east side of Sverdlov Sq. is the *Metropole Hotel* which was built by Walcott in 1899–1903 in the fashionable 'modern' style of the period. It is decorated with a mural, 'Dream Princess', which is a replica of the famous drawing by Vrubel of the same name. Above the second floor is a curios rebus inscription of intertwining letters which reads 'The old story again—on completing a house you discover that you have learnt something'. The fountain in the centre of the square in front of the hotel was installed here in 1826–35 and is decorated with a sculptural group 'Cupids at play' by Ivan Vitali. On the other side of Marx Prospect the square is surrounded by three theatres and a metro station. To the north is the *Bolshoi Theatre*, built in 1824 by Bovet, to the east the *Maly Theatre* with a statue of the 19th-century Russian playwright Ostrovsky in front, and to the west the *Children's Theatre.*

Marx Prospect (Prospect Marksa) is a new name, given in 1961, to some of the oldest streets in the city. It runs downhill from Dzerzhinsky Sq. through Sverdlov Sq. and Manezhnaya Sq. to the Lenin Library at the bottom of Prospect Kalinina. Passing Sverdlov Sq. in this direction one sees the imposing building of the *Trade Unions House* on the right-hand side. It was built in 1784 for Prince Dolgorukov-Krymsky and later became the Bobles Club. Inside it, the Hall of Columns, where concerts are now held, was at one time one of the largest and most fashionable ballrooms in Moscow. A little further down on the same side is the building of the *Council of Ministers*, which was built in 1932–5 by Langmann. Behind the building of the Council of Ministers is a small street, *Georgyevsky Pereulok.* It was once one of the most fashionable residential streets in Moscow. No. 4 is

a 16th century mansion once belonging to the boyar Troyekurov and now housing the *Glinka Museum.* On the opposite side of Marx Prospect is the *Moskva Hotel* which was built by Schusev in 1932–5. On the 15th floor is an open-air café, *The Lights of Moscow*, from which one can obtain a good view of the city. This part of the street was formerly known as Okhotnyi Ryad (Hunters' Row) and was a very busy market. On the right one passes the bottom of Gorky St. and on the far side of Gorky Street, next to the *National Hotel*, is the head office of *Intourist.* It was built by Ivan Zholtovsky in 1934 in a style imitative of 16th-century Italian architecture and once housed the American Embassy.

In front of the Intourist building is *Manezhnaya Sq.* where open-air cinema, music, and folk dancing displays take place on national festivals. Before Marx Prospect was constructed in the 1930s this whole area was a mass of small shops and houses. On the far side of the square beneath the Kremlin wall is the *Alexandrovsky Garden.* The R. Neglinnaya used to run here, forming a natural moat of which the stone bridge leading up to the *Trinity Tower* is a reminder. The garden was designed by Bovet in 1821–3 during the reign of Alexander I after whom it was named. The grotto 'Ruins' near the *Middle Arsenal Tower* was also designed by Bovet. The *obelisk* beneath the wall was erected in 1913 in commemoration of the 300th anniversary of the Romanov House (see p. 200). Near the Sobakin Tower is the *Grave of the Unknown Soldier.* The tomb, enclosed in red and black granite, was placed here in 1967 during the 25th anniversary of the Battle of Moscow. The inscription reads: 'Thy name is unknown, thy exploit immortal. To the fallen 1941–45.' Beside the Intourist head office is the oldest building of the university (see p. 000). In the centre of the square is a small monument which was erected in 1967 on the 50th anniversary of the Revolution. The large building in the square is the *Manège*, which was built in 1817 by Augustin Batancourt and decorated by Bovet. When first built, it was considered an engineering feat because, despite its size of 167 × 47 m., the roof was supported by the walls alone with no stanchions. Until the Revolution it was an equestrian centre for officers of the Court. After the Revolution it was used as a garage for government cars until it was restored in 1957. It is now the Central Exhibition Hall where large art exhibitions are often held. Marx Prospect ends at the bottom of Prospect Kalinina with the Lenin Library and a metro station of that name on the corner. Between Marx Prospect and the Bulvarnoye Koltso are a number of small shopping streets which are an interesting contrast to the main streets such as Gorky St. and Prospect Kalinina. One of the busiest of these streets is *Kuznetsky Most (Blacksmith's Bridge).* During the 14th and 15th centuries the blacksmiths from the Royal Arms Foundry lived here. Later aristocratic mansions were built here and when Catherine II (1762–96) issued an edict permitting trade outside the walls of Kitai-Gorod, Kuznetsky Most became a fashionable shopping street with a number of French shops.

Neglinnaya St. runs from Prospect Marksa to the Bulvarnoye Koltso, intercepting Kuznetsky Most. It took its name from the R. Neglinnaya which was bricked over at the beginning of the 19th century and now runs under the street. No. 12, the State Bank of the USSR, was built in 1894 by Professor Bykovsky and rebuilt in 1930–1 by Zholtovsky.

The Bulvarnoye Koltso (Boulevard Ring)

The area between the Kremlin and present Boulevard Ring was known as the White Town during the 16th and 17th centuries. During the reign of Boris Godunov (1598–1605) this area was fortified with a brick wall and 28 towers and gates. Many of the squares which were made when the gates were removed still bear the names of the gates. The walls were demolished between 1750 and 1792 when the boulevards were planted. The Boulevard Ring, although called a ring, does not in fact form a circle but ends on the northern bank of the R. Moskva.

Starting from the western end of the boulevard on the embankment, the ring leads to Kropotkinskaya Sq. The *Moscow open air swimming pool*, open all year, is on the right. On this site stood the *Cathedral of Our Saviour (Khram Spassitelya)* which cost 14 million roubles to build during the last century. It was designed by the architect Konstantin Thon and was erected on the site of the Alexeevski Abbey in 1837–83 in commemoration of the liberation of Russia after the Napoleonic invasion.

From Kropotkinskaya Sq., Gogolevsky Boulevard (formerly Prechistenskaya—Immaculate Virgin Boulevard) leads up to Arbatskaya Sq. where it crosses Prospect Kalinina. A *monument to Gogol* stands at the end of the boulevard. The small narrow streets to the left of the boulevard form the largest part of the old residential district of the nobles which remains. Many of the old houses are now being demolished, but many fine examples of Russian architecture can be seen here as well as some old wooden houses. The *Praga Restaurant* which stands at the end of Arbat St. is famous for its small dome, said to be one of the finest in the city.

The next part of the boulevard is called Suvorovsky Boulevard after the famous Russian Field Marshal. No. 8 on the right-hand side is the *House of Journalists* which was built in 1760. No. 7 on the opposite side is the house where Gogol died in 1852 and where he burnt the second volume of his novel 'Dead Souls' two days before his death. A monument to the author by Nikolai Andreyev stands in the courtyard. No. 12a, known as *Lunin House*, was built in 1818–23 by Dementy Ghilardi in the Russian empire style. The façade of the house is covered with inset sculptures of musical instruments in honour of the owner's wife, who was a well known singer.

The junction with Gertsen St. at the end of Suvorovsky Boulevard is known as *Nikitskie Vorota (Gates)* after the old gate and tower which once stood here. The next section of the boulevard ring, Tverskoi Boulevard, was once the most fashionable promenade in Moscow and is mentioned in a number of 19th-century Russian novels, including Tolstoy's 'Anna Karenina'. At the beginning of the boulevard is a *monument* to the botanist Timiryazev, showing him wearing a gown of Oxford University from where he received an honorary doctorate. No. 25, built at the beginning of the 19th century, was the birthplace of Alexander Herzen, the famous revolutionary philosopher. A memorial stands in front of the house.

Tverskoi Boulevard leads to Pushkinskaya Sq. where it crosses Gorky St., formerly Tverskaya St. as it led to the town of Tver. A *monument to Pushkin*, erected in 1880, stands in the centre of the square. Admirers still bring tributes here on the anniversaries of the poet's birth and death, fulfilling his prophesy that:

> My verses will be sung throughout all Russia's vastness,
> My ashes will outlive and know no pale decay . . .

Behind the *Rossiya cinema* on the far side of the square, Chekhovka St. is to the left and Pushkinskaya St. to the right. On the left of the square are the offices of the newspaper *Izvestia* which were designed in 1927 by Barkhin.

Strastnoi Boulevard starts behind the cinema and leads down to *Petrovskie Vorota (Gates)*, from where Petrovka St. on the right runs down to the Bolshoi Theatre. No. 25, built by Matvei Kazakov in the 1790s, is a good example of Russian classical architecture. Near the boulevard is the former *Petrovsky Abbey* with a cathedral built in 1691. No. 15/29 Strastnoi Boulevard, now a hospital, is known as the *Gagarin house*. It was built by Matvei Kazakov and has the largest twelve-column portico in Moscow. It was once the home of the family of the tsar's chamberlain and from 1802–12 housed the famous English Club. It was damaged considerably during Napoleon's invasion but was later restored and slightly altered by Bovet. To the left of Strastnoi Boulevard is Karetnyi Ryad (Coachbuilder's Row) where the small and popular *Hermitage Garden* is situated.

The next square, *Trubnaya Sq.*, was formerly renowned for its bird market which was transferred to Konnaya Square. The R. Neglinnaya flows beneath the square and the street to the right bears its name. Down this street on the right-hand side is the popular *Uzbekistan Restaurant* which in summer has tables out in the garden.

Rozhdestvensky (Nativity) Boulevard, the steep hill which forms the next part of the boulevard ring, was once a real problem for horse-trams. The walls of the old convent, founded in the 14th century, from which this part of the boulevard ring takes its name, can be seen on the right.

At Sretenskie Vorota the boulevard ring is crossed by *Sretenka St.*, another busy shopping street. The gardens on this part of the boulevard are always crowded with children and old people. In winter there is skating here and in summer it becomes an informal open-air club for playing chess and dominoes.

Kirov St. crosses the next square. To the right is the *Central Post Office* and, almost opposite the post office, an unusual *tea and coffee shop* built in 1890 in Chinese style. Nearby in Telegrafnyi Pereulok is the tower of the former *Church of the Archangel Gabriel*. It was built in 1704–7 by Ivan Zarudnyi at the request of Alexander Menshikov, a favourite of Peter the Great and after whom it has always been known as the *Menshikov Tower*. It is said that Menshikov ordered a tower to be built which would be taller than the Bell Tower of Ivan the Great in the Kremlin. It was originally topped with a flying archangel, but this was destroyed by lightning in 1723. A new vault and a cupola, topped this time with a cross, were added later and for a long time it was the second tallest building in Moscow.

At the beginning of the next section of the boulevard ring, *Chistoprudnyi (clear pond) Boulevard* is a *monument* to the writer Griboyedev. This is the widest part of the boulevard ring and has a *café* and a *rectangular pond* where boats can be hired.

From Pokrovskie Vorota, Bogdany Khmelnitsky St. runs down on the right to *Staraya Ploschad (Old Sq.)*. In Chernyshevsky St. on the left of the boulevard ring is a rococo building erected in 1766 and known as the '*Chest-of-drawers' house* because of its abundant decoration.

The wide space along the boulevard was formerly a parade ground in front of the *Pokrovski Barracks* which were built in the 1830s.

The last section of the boulevard ring, the *Yauzsky Boulevard*, is named after the R. Yauza. The 22-storey block of flats at the end of the boulevard was built in 1949–52 by Chechulin and Rostovsky. The 32-storey tower is 173 m. high.

One can return to the beginning of the boulevard ring near the Moscow swimming pool by going along the embankment of the R. Moskva to the right of the sky-scraper. Opposite the Kremlin are the restored bell-towers of churches and a well-preserved merchant's house with iron gates which now houses the *British Embassy*. One of the best views of the Kremlin is to be obtained from the *Bolshoi Kammenyi (large stone) Bridge* which crosses the river at the far end of the Kremlin wall.

The Sadovoye Koltso (Garden Ring)

This, Moscow's widest street, was formed along the line of the old earthen wall which was pulled down at the beginning of the 19th century. The gardens in front of the small houses along the street gave it its name, the Russian word *sad*

meaning 'garden'. Trees were planted along the middle of the street in the last century, but these were removed and the gardens destroyed in the 1930s when the street was widened. The Sadovoye Ring forms an almost perfect circle with the *Bell Tower of Ivan the Great* as the central point. It is roughly 16 kms. in circumference.

Crossing the river by *Krymsky Bridge*, a 700 m. suspension bridge and one of the best designed bridges in Moscow, the Sadovoye Ring runs (going in a clockwise direction) under an overpass towards Zubovsky Sq. To the left is the beginning of Komsomolsky Prospect and to the right Metrostroevskaya St. which leads towards the Kremlin. The long white-washed buildings on the right were constructed by Stasov in 1832–5 as a food depot and in spite of their utilitarian purpose are one of the finest examples of Russian classical architecture standing today. The road to the left from Zubovsky Sq. leads to Novodevichy Convent. To the right is *Kropotkinskaya St.* with many nobles' houses of the last century still standing. The area between this part of the Sadovoye Ring and the inner Boulevard Ring was the old aristocratic district of Moscow, and the narrow winding streets with their quiet mansions retain the atmosphere of the old city.

Further along the Sadovoye Ring on the right is a green painted house, *No. 18*. This was once the home of the millionaire Morozov. The 27-storey building on the right houses the *Ministries of Foreign Trade and Foreign Affairs*. It was designed by Gelfreikh and Minkus in 1951 and is 171 m. high. The square in front of the ministry is *Smolenskaya Sq.*, formerly Sennaya (Hay) Sq. To the right is *Arbat St.*, now often known as the Old Arbat, which is one of the busiest shopping streets in Moscow. There are two *antique shops* here selling old furniture, china, and paintings and on the left hand side at the far end is a shop selling posters.

The Sadovoye Ring then passes under Prospect Kalinina, often referred to as the New Arbat. The large building on the left after the underpass is the *American Embassy*. Next door is the house where the famous singer Chaliapin lived. The 22-storey block of flats on the same side was built by Posokhin and Mndoyants in 1954. It is 160 m. high, comprises 452 flats and has a group of food shops on the ground floor. The square in front of this sky-scraper is called *Vosstanaya (insurrection) Sq.* because of the heavy fighting which took place here during the revolutions of 1905 and 1917. It was formerly called Kudrinskaya Square after the village of Kudrino which stood here in the 14th–17th centuries.

The next section of the Sadovoye Ring still bears this name. To the right is *Vorovsky St.*, once one of the most fashionable streets in Moscow. At one time no shops were allowed in this part of the city and even today it is relatively quiet. No. 52 Vorovsky St. once belonged to Countess Sollugub and is said to be the house on which Tolstoy based his description of the Moscow home of the Rostovs in 'War and Peace'. It now houses the *Board of the Union of Soviet Writers*. A *monument to Leo Tolstoy* stands in the courtyard. No. 25 was built by Ivan Ghilardi in the 1820s. It now houses the *Maxim Gorky Museum* and a *monument* to the writer stands in front of the building. Further down on the right hand side is the *Cinema Actors Club* which was built in 1931–4 by the Vesnin brothers.

Leading down the hill on the far side of the skyscraper in Vosstanay Sq. is *Barrikadnaya St.* which takes its name from the barricades erected here during the 1905 revolution. On the right is a two-storey building with a portico and classical colonnade. It was built in 1775 by Ghilardi and restored by his son after the fire of 1812. After the restoration it became an almshouse for the widows and children of government officials and military officers and it is still known as the *Widow's House* today. It was once the home of the writer Alexander Kuprin and now houses a medical institute.

On the right-hand side of the Sadovoye Ring past Vosstanaya Sq. is a small red house which is easily noticeable among the tall blocks. It was the home of Anton Chekhov during the 1880s and is now the *Chekhov Museum*. On the opposite side of the street is the *planetarium* with instruments in the grounds to observe planets and stars. *No. 15*, a mansion with a four-column portico, is one of the few wooden buildings to have survived the fire of 1812. It belonged to Princess Volkonskaya and later to the poetess Rostopchina. On the left of the Sadovoye Ring near the underpass under Mayakovsky Sq. is the *Peking Hotel* which is easily recognised by the Chinese-style writing. On the opposite side is the *Satire Theatre* and the *Tchaikovsky Concert Hall*. In the middle of the square is a *statue* of the poet and playwright Mayakovsky by A. Kibalnikov.

After the underpass, the Sadovoye Ring runs down to *Samotechnaya Sq.* To the right is Tsvetnoi (Flower) Boulevard, once a flower market, where the *circus, panorama cinema*, and *central market* are now. The boulevard to the left of the Sadovoye Ring leads to the *Soviet Army Theatre* and *Museum*.

The next square on the Sadovoye Ring is *Kolkhoznaya Sq.* To the left Prospect Mira leads to the *Economic Achievements' Exhibition* and *Ostankino Palace*. To the right is *Sretenka St.*, one of the oldest shopping streets.

Further along the Sadovoye Ring on the left is an impressive *hospital* building. It was begun in 1794 by Nazarov for Count Sheremetev, but when Count Sheremetev's wife died in 1803, he decided to put the building to public use. After alterations carried out under Quarenghi, it opened as a guest house in 1807 and later became a hospital. On the same side is a Corbusier-style building designed by the Russian architect Schusev in 1933 which now houses the *Ministry of Agriculture*. To the right is Kirov St. with a genuine Le Corbusier building, the *Central Statistical Administration of*

the U.S.S.R. It was built from 1929–36 with the assistance of the Russian architect Kolly, and in the original design had no ground floor, the space between the supporting piers being used for cars. A ground floor was added at a later date. There are few houses of interest in this street, the most notable being *No. 42* which was designed by Matvei Kazakov.

The next square on the Sadovoye Ring is *Lermontov Sq.* which is still known by its old name of Krasnye Vorota (Red Gates). The 24-storey office block was built in 1952 by Dushkin and Mezentsev and is 133 m. high. The road to the left leads through Komsomolskaya Sq. to *Sokolniki Park*. The *Leningradskaya Hotel*, a 26-storey skyscraper 136 m. high, which stands in Komsomolskaya Sq. was built in 1953 by Polyakov and Boretsky. Here also are the three busiest *railway stations* in Moscow; Leningradsky, Yaroslavlsky, and Kazansky. It is from Yaroslavlsky Station that trains leave for Siberia and Vladivostok.

From Lermontov Sq. the Sadovoye Ring turns to the right towards *Kursk Station*. This part of the Sadovoye Ring is named Chkalovsky and *No. 47* was once the home of Tchaikovsky. On the left is the *Naidyonov Estate*, a beautiful mansion built by Ghilardi in 1829–31 with extensive grounds leading down to the R. Yauza. It is now a sanatorium.

The Sadovoye Ring then crosses the R. Yauza, passes through a tunnel, over the R. Moskva and on through a district where petty merchants used to live.

The road leading to the left from Dobryninskaya Sq., the next square on the Sadovoye Ring, is the *Varshavskoye Chaussée* which leads to the south and the estates of Tsaristsino and Kolomenskoe.

At the next square on the Sadovoye Ring, *Oktyabrskaya Sq.*, the Sadovoye Ring goes through an underpass. On the square is the *Warsaw Hotel* and two hotels belonging to the *Academy of Sciences*. The largest *cinema* in Moscow, with a seating capacity of 4000, is to be built here. On the left after the underpass is an impressive arch, the entrance to *Gorky Park*, which, as well as other entertainments, has a *boating pond* and a *fun fair*. The Sadovoye Ring then crosses the R. Moskva at the Krymsky Bridge.

The main streets of Moscow

A brief description of the main streets, radiating from the centre of Moscow.

Gorky St. (Ulitsa Gorkovo). Gorky St. is considered by many to be the main street of Moscow and has a number of shops and other buildings which may be useful to the visitor. There are three *metro stations* on Gorky St.; Prospect Marksa station at the foot of Gorky St. opposite the Kremlin, Mayakovsky station on Mayakovsky Square, where Gorky St. crosses the Sadovoye Ring, and Byelorusskaya station at the end of Gorky St.

Gorky St. was formerly known as Tverskaya St. because it was the road which led to Tver (now

Kalinin) and thence to St. Petersburg. It was reconstructed in the 1930s and now has little in common with the old Tverskaya St. Very few of the old buildings remained after reconstruction, during which the street was straightened and considerably widened to its present width of 40 m.

On the left-hand side at the bottom of Gorky St. is the *National Hotel* and beside it the new *Intourist Hotel* which was opened in 1970. The *café* of the National Hotel, which is situated on the ground floor and is approached from the entrance in Gorky St., is to be recommended to those wishing to eat more quickly than in a restaurant. Slightly further up on the left is the *Central Telegraph*, designed by Rerberg in 1927. International telephone calls can be made from the office which is entered from the side street. Opposite the Central Telegraph is *Teatralnaya (Theatre) Proezd* with the *Moscow Arts Theatre* on the left.

Some of the small streets now join Gorky St. through arches in the large buildings which line it on both sides. On Sovietskaya Sq. is a *monument* to Yuri Dolgoruky, the founder of Moscow. The *Aragvi*, the popular Georgian restaurant, is on the right-hand side of the square as one faces the monument. The *City Hall* on the other side of Gorky St. was built in 1782 by Matvei Kazakov for the Govenor-General of Moscow. In 1946, under the architect Chechulin, the main edifice was moved back 11 m. and two more storeys were added. Opposite is the *Marxism-Leninism Institute* which was designed in 1927 by Chernyshev. Beside the entrance is a *statue of Lenin* by Sergei Merkurov.

Further up Gorky St. on the right is the best *baker* in Moscow, built in 1912, and formerly known as Philippov's. No. 14 on the same side is *Gastronom No. 1*, probably the only shop in Moscow which is still unofficially known by the name of its former owner, Yeliseyevsky. Its ornate decorations deserve a visit and it is open until 10 pm (8 pm on Sun.).

Gorky St. crosses the Boulevard Ring at Pushkinskaya Sq. The garden with the *statue of Pushkin* was laid out on the site of the former Strastnoi Abbey which was built in the 17th century and demolished at the end of the last century. At the end of the square is the *Rossiya Cinema* which has a seating capacity of 2500 and is one of the largest cinemas in this country. Nearby in Chekhov St. to the left of the cinema is the *Church of the Nativity* which was built in the 17th century by the walls of Belyi Gorod (White town) which ran along the line of the present Boulevard Ring.

When Pushkin described Tatiana's arrival in Moscow in his poem 'Eugene Onegin', he mentioned the lions on the gates of No. 21 Gorky St. Built in 1780, the house was badly damaged during the 1812 fire and was then rebuilt in the classical style by Adam Menelaws. It became the residence of the aristocratic English Club and since 1926 has housed the *Museum of the Revolution*.

Mayakovsky Sq., with a *statue* of the poet, lies where Gorky St. crosses the Sadovoye Ring. This square contains the *Tchaikovsky Concert Hall* built in 1940 by Chechulin and Orlov.

At the end of Gorky St. in Byelorusskaya Sq. is a *monument* to the poet and playwright, Gorky. The street was renamed after him in 1935 and the statue unveiled in 1951. On the left is the *Byelorusskii station*, the terminus for trains from Western Europe, which was opened in 1870. Beyond the bridge is the beginning of Leningradsky Prospect.

Leningradsky Prospect, which starts from Byelorusskii station, is the road leading to *Sheremetevo international airport* and towards Leningrad. Many new buildings were erected here before the Second World War when it was developed as a residential area.

The *Sovietskaya Hotel and Restaurant* on the right was once known as Yar and was the best restaurant outside the city. It has now been partly reconstructed. The road to the left almost opposite the hotel leads to the race-course (see p. 226).

Further on is the *Dynamo stadium*, the second largest stadium in Moscow, which was built in the park of the Petrovsky Palace. The *Petrovsky Palace*, which looks like a battlemented fortress, was built in 1775–82 by Matvei Kazakov, and is one of the few remaining examples of Russian-Gothic architecture. The imperial family often used it as the last staging-point on their way to Moscow from St. Petersburg, and Napoleon stayed here for a few days after abandoning the Kremlin during the fire of 1812. It now houses the *Zhukovsky Air Force Academy*.

Further along on the left side of the Prospect is the *central air terminal, helicopter terminal*, and *Aeroflot Hotel*.

Near the Sokol metro station is *All Saint's Church*, which was built in 1736, and is open for services.

The road to Leningrad bears right further on while the road through the underpass leads to Archangelskoye. Near the underpass is a 25-storey sky-scraper, the offices of *Gidroproekt*, the organisation responsible for designing hydropower stations.

The Leningrad road now has the name Leningradskoe Chaussée and passes through the new residential area of Khimki-Khovrino. To the left is the Northern River Port from which one can take boat trips down the Moscow canal and R. Moskva.

Before one reaches Sheremetevo airport there is an unusual *monument* on the left of the road in the form of three crosses, like part of an anti-tank barricade. This is the spot the German army reached in the Second World War, when approaching Moscow.

Gertsen St. runs from Manezhnaya Sq., between the two old buildings of the university, to the Sadovoye Ring. It was formerly known as Bolshaya Nikitskaya. On the left is the *Moscow Conservatoire* which was founded by Nikolai Rubinstein in 1866. The present building was erected in 1901 by Zagorsky. The *statue of*

Tchaikovsky among the birch trees in front of the Conservatoire was designed by Vera Mukhina and erected in 1954. On the right-hand side of Gertsen St. is the former *Church of the Ascension* which was designed by Bazhenov in the 1820s and built by his pupil, Matvei Kazakov. Pushkin was married here. In the small garden behind the church is a *statue* of the writer Alexei Tolstoy.

Prospect Kalinina runs from the Lenin Library, near the Trinity Tower of the Kremlin, westwards to the R. Moskva where it leads into Kutuzovsky Prospect. The first part of the prospect used to be called Vozdvizhenka and still contains a few 18th-century buildings. No. 5 on the left is known as the *House of Golitsyn*. It was mostly built in the 18th century but contains an older part dating from the reign of Ivan the Terrible. No. 7 is the former *Monastery of the Holy Cross*. No. 16 on the other side is an unusual building which stands out clearly on account of its Moorish style. It once belonged to the textile-king Morozov who is said to have wanted an ancient Spanish castle and who sent the architect, Mazarin, to Spain to form ideas for the plan. Since 1959 it has been the *House of Friendship* where delegations from foreign Friendship Societies are entertained. There is a café in the basement where all foreigners can get a quick meal.

Arbat Sq. divides the old part of Kalinin Prospect from the new. This was reconstructed in the 1960s when an underpass was built and a number of buildings demolished. Arbat is the old name for this area and is derived from the Eastern word 'Arbad' which means 'beyond the city walls'. When the walls of Byely Gorod (white town) were built, the name was moved to the street running down to the left of the Praga Restaurant which still bears this name.

On the right is a new *telephone exchange* where one can make visual calls to a number of towns within the Soviet Union for as little as 2–3 roubles (approximately £1.00). On the left are four 25-storey office blocks with shops in front. The first shop is the largest *food store* in Moscow and has a self-service department on the first floor. Further along on the same side is a large *gift shop* and at the very end the *Arbat Restaurant* which can seat 2000. There are a number of shops on the other side of the street too, including a very large *bookshop* which sells posters and postcards on the first floor. Further along is the largest *record shop* in Moscow. On the same side is the *October Cinema*, the largest cinema in Moscow with a seating capacity of 3000 in the two auditoriums. There are a number of *cafés* on both sides of the street including an 'ice cream parlour' which has tables outside in summer and, despite its name, sells alcoholic drinks and other refreshments as well as ice-cream. Prospect Kalinina then passes over the Sadovoye Ring and down to the R. Moskva. On the right are the headquarters of *Comecon*, the East European Trade Community. The thirty-storey building, which was built with materials from all the participating countries, was designed

by Posokhin and Mndoyants. Behind is the *Hotel Mir (Peace)* which is used by Comecon delegates.

Kutuzovsky Prospect starts from the Kalinin Bridge at the end of Prospect Kalinina. It is named after the famous Russian Field-Marshal who conducted the campaign against Napoleon.

On the right is the *Ukraina Hotel*, which has 1025 rooms and is 32 storeys high. In the garden in front of the hotel is a *monument* to the Ukrainian poet Taras Shevchenko (1814–61). There is a *coffee bar* (standing only) at the rear of the ground floor of the hotel.

New blocks of flats have replaced the old suburbs of Dorogo-milovo. On the right side of the street is a large *toy shop*, and on the left two *gift shops*, one dealing only in foreign currency. The part of the street by the underpass was mostly built before the Second World War. In Bolshaya Dorogomilovskaya St., very close to the junction with Kutuzovsky Prospect by the underpass, is a shop selling *wines, spirits, and cigarettes* as well as groceries for foreign currency only.

At the end of Kutuzovsky Prospect is the *Triumphal Arch* which was recently re-erected here. Once it stood at the end of Gorky St. where it had been built in 1827–34 in celebration of the Russian victory in the 1812 war. (It was in fact down Kalinin Prospect, then Smolensk Road, that Napoleon marched into Moscow and many people thought the old site, on the road along which the victorious Russian soldiers returned to Moscow, a more suitable one.) Beside the arch is the *Battle of Borodino Museum* which was built in 1962 to display canvases of the battle painted by Roubaud (1856–1912). Nearby is *Kutuzov's Hut Museum*. It is situated in the peasant house where Kutuzov held the war council at which he ordered the Russian troops to retreat from Moscow.

To the right of Kutuzovsky Prospect is Fili-Mazilovo, a new residential district which has one important architectural monument, the *Church of the Intercession*. This church was built in 1693–4 by Lev Naryshkin, uncle of Peter the Great, and is a fine example of what is known as Naryshkin or Russian Baroque. Peter the Great is said to have visited the church a number of times and one of the icons reproduces his portrait as a young man.

Kutuzovsky Prospect eventually leads into the Moscow-Minsk road. A *motel* and the *Mozhaisky camping site* are situated on the corner where it crosses the circular by-pass. Here also is the Mozhaisky Hotel which has a bar where foreign currency is accepted.

Volkhonka St. leads south-west from the centre, starting opposite the Borovitsky Tower of the Kremlin. It contains several old buildings, but none of particular merit. On the right is the *Pushkin Fine Arts Museum* which was built in 1912 as a museum of plaster models and became the Museum of Fine Art in 1924. Volkhonka St. ends in Kropotkinskaya Sq. To the right and left is the Boulevard Ring and opposite, Kropotkinskaya and Metrostroevskaya Streets.

Kropotkinskaya St. to the right was once a very

fashionable street lined with aristocratic mansions, many of which are museums today. No. 12
on the right was built in 1814 by Afanasy Grigo-
rev in Empire style. It now houses the *Pushkin
Museum*, not to be confused with the Museum of
Fine Art in Volkhonka St. which is also often
called the Pushkin Museum. No. 11, almost
opposite, was designed by the same architect and
now houses the *Leo Tolstoy Museum*. No. 17 was
the home of the poet Denis Davydov and No. 19
was built by Matvei Kazakov in 1790 for Prince
Dolgoruky. It was badly damaged during the fire
of 1812 and later restored. No. 21, which now
belongs to the *Academy of Arts,* is a good example
of early 19th-century Russian architecture. No.
22 further down on the right was built by Matvei
Kazakov in the late 18th century and was the
home of General Yermolov, a General in the 1812
War. It later became a police station where Alexander Herzen was held in 1834.

Metrostroevskaya St., which runs slightly left
from Kropotkinskaya Sq., leads into Komsomolsky Prospect. The only building of note is near
the far end on the right. It was built in the beginning of the 19th century and at one time housed
the tsar's Law Courts. It was later the home of
Mikhail Bakunin and is now the *Institute of
Foreign Languages*.

Metrostroevskaya St. passes over the Sadovoye
Ring into Komsomolsky Prospect.

Komsomolsky Prospect, which leads out to the
new university building and the south-west residential areas. On the right is the brightly painted
Church of St. Nicholas, which was built in 1682.
On the same side are military barracks which were
built from 1807–9. On the right before the bridge
over the R. Moskva is a fair, selling a wide variety
of goods, which is very crowded in the summer.

To the right of the bridge is the *Lenin Stadium*
where the main sporting events are held in
Moscow. In winter the tennis courts become
popular skating rinks where skates can be hired.
The bridge over the river is on two levels, the
upper level for cars and the lower level for the
metro. The *metro station*, Leninskie Gory (Lenin
Hills), is on the bridge itself and has glass walls
from which one can look over the river. The area
beyond the bridge is known as *Lenin Hills* (formerly Sparrow Hill). The best view of Moscow is
to be had on a fine day from the look-out point in
front of the university. People also gather here on
national festivals to watch the firework display
over the city. There is a very steep ski jump down
to the river where competitions are held in winter.
Nearby is the small *Church of the Trinity*, built
1811, which is open for services.

Beyond the river, Komsomolsky Prospect leads
into *Prospect Vernadskovo* which is named after
the famous Russian scientist. On the left is the new
circus building which seats 3000.

Leninsky Prospect, which leads out of Oktyabrskaya Sq. on the Sadovoye Ring, follows part
of the old road to Kaluga. The *Kaluga Gate*, which
stood on the site of the present square, was an important entrance in the earthen wall and the ambassadorial court of the Crimean Khan was
situated here. Many armies retreated along this
road, including that of Khan Kazy-Girei in 1591,
the Polish interventionists in 1612, and the army
of Napoleon in 1812.

At the beginning of Leninsky Prospect on the
right-hand side are the buildings of the *Mining,
Steel*, and *Oil Institutes*. No. 8 on the same side is
the *Town Hospital* which was built by Bovet in
1828–32. No. 10 is the former Prince Golitsyn
hospital, designed by Kazakov in 1796–1802.

Beyond the hospitals on the right is a side entrance to Gorky Park through the *Neskuchnyi Sad*
which is now part of the main park. Neskuchnyi
Sad, meaning 'not boring' garden, was originally a
botanical garden containing almost unknown
foreign plants in the grounds of the Alexan-
drovski Palace. The palace was first built in 1756
for the factory- and mine-owner Demidov. In
1830 the palace passed into the possession of
Nicholas I and it was then rebuilt by Yevgraf
Turin. The sculptures 'Seasons of the Year' on the
gates are by Ivan Vitali. The palace park stretches
down to the river and is one of the most pleasant
spots in Moscow. The palace is now used by the
Academy of Sciences, and this street is popularly
known as the Prospect of Science because so many
research institutes are located here.

The next turning to the left off Leninsky Prospect leads to the Donskoi monastery (see p. 222).

A little further on, the older part of Leninsky
Prospect ends at the crescent which was designed
by Arkin and marked the city limits in 1940. The
area beyond, the site of the old Kaluga turnpike,
has been renamed *Gagarin Sq.*, after the first
Soviet cosmonaut, and a statue is to be erected
here. Since the end of the Second World War extensive building has been carried out in this part of
the city and when it is completed, the area beyond
Gagarin Sq. will be nearly equal to the whole area
of old Moscow. The blocks of flats are built in
separate neighbourhood units for 25,000 inhabitants, each on an area of 36–50 hectares (90–125
acres).

The road to the right from the square leads to
the university and the south-west part of the city.
To the left of this road is the *Pioneers' Palace*
which stands in grounds of 54 hectares (135 acres)
and which, amongst other amenities, has an observatory, auditoriums, a library, and various
sports facilities.

A number of large shops have been built on the
new part of Leninsky Prospect, such as the *House
of Shoes, House of Fabrics*, the *Moskva Department Store* and, much further on, the *House of
Furniture*. At the far end of the Prospect is the
Patrice Lumumba Friendship University where
foreign students study. Further on, Leninsky Prospect runs into the Kievskoe Chaussée which leads
to Vnukovo airport.

Prospect Mira, which starts from the Sadovoye
Ring at Kolkhoznaya Sq., was renamed at the time
of the 1957 Youth Festival in Moscow. Once

populated by middle-class merchants, it still has some old buildings but they are overpowered by the huge apartment blocks. Prospect Mira follows the line of the old road from Kiev to Rostov-Veliki and Suzdal.

Two houses which are of interest are *No. 14* built at the end of the 18th century and *No. 16* built by Bazhenov in the 1770s. At No. 28 are the oldest *Botanical Gardens* in Moscow. Once known as the 'Apothecary's Garden', it was transferred here in 1706 by the order of Peter I from its former site beside the Kremlin wall.

On the left side of Prospect Mira is the *Church of the Metropolitan Philip* which was built by Kazakov in 1777–88 in Baroque style.

Riga railway station, designed by Diderix in 1899, once marked the end of the city. The whole region beyond the bridge was very much altered during the late 1930s when the Agricultural Exhibition, now known as the *Exhibition of Economic Achievements*, was laid out. Since 1964 the soaring space-rocket monument by the main entrance to the exhibition has formed a landmark which is seen from far along the street.

The turning to the left as one approaches the exhibition leads to Ostankino and the new *television centre*. The television tower, which is 537 m. high, transmits to all parts of the Soviet Union. During gale force winds it sways as much as 42 m. At a level of 328 m. is the *Seventh Heaven Restaurant* which slowly revolves.

To the right of Prospect Mira one can see an 18th-century *aqueduct* and *Tikhvinskaya Church*. Past the exhibition the Prospect becomes Yaroslavskoye Chaussée, which leads to Zagorsk and the town of Yaroslavl, on the Volga.

The Kremlin

Before visiting the Kremlin, it is advisable to check the opening hours of the museum at an Intourist office.

Kremlin is a translation of the Russian word 'kreml' or 'kremnik' which means fortress. There are kremlins in a number of old Russian towns but none so well known as the Moscow Kremlin which is often used as a synonym of the Soviet state and government.

The Kremlin stands on an irregular triangle of ground covering 28 hectares (69 acres) above the R. Moskva. From the Kremlin an advancing enemy could be seen and a bell would be rung to warn those outside the walls of the fortress to take protection inside. It used to be surrounded by water: the R. Moskva on the south, the R. Neglinnaya (now bricked in) on the north-west, and a deep moat which was dug in the early 16th century along the east wall. The main entrances of the Kremlin, the Spassky, Nikolsky, Trinity, and Borovitsky Gates, were all entered by a drawbridge on the far side of which was a portcullis.

The first wooden walls around the Kremlin were built in the 12th century under Prince Yuri Dolgoruky, the founder of Moscow. At that time it was a much smaller fortress at the confluence of the R. Moskva and R. Neglinnaya. In the 14th century, during the reign of Prince Ivan Kalita, the area of the Kremlin was considerably enlarged and surrounded by a strong oak fence. During Ivan Kalita's reign the first two stone buildings were erected—the *Cathedral of the Assumption (Uspensky Sobor)* and the *Cathedral of Archangel Michael (Arkhangelsky Sobor)*.

In 1367 the wooden fence was replaced by white limestone walls which protected the Kremlin from the fires which constantly ravaged Moscow, but these walls soon crumbled and were replaced at the end of the century with the battlemented brick walls which stand today. The circumference of the walls is over 2 km. and in some places they are as high as 19 m. They are from 3·6 to 6·4 m. thick and are reinforced with 20 towers, 5 of which are also gated to the fortress. The towers were originally surmounted by battlements and each tower contained a firing platform. A platform for bowmen runs along the inside of the walls. The timber roofing which used to cover the platform was burnt down in the 18th century.

In the following description those towers which since 1937 have been decorated with illuminated red stars in place of the tsarist double-headed eagle are marked with an asterisk*. The main gate to the Kremlin is the gate opposite St. Basil's Cathedral on Red Sq. It is known as the *Spassky (Redeemer's) Gate*, and was built in 1491 by Pietro Antonion Solario of Milan. It used to be entered by a drawbridge over the moat. In 1625 the Scottish architect, Christopher Galloway, added the Gothic tower and steeple, and a clock was installed. The present clock dates from 1851 and was made by the Butenop brothers. The chime of the largest bell in the tower clock is broadcast on Moscow Radio, as is that of Big Ben on the B.B.C. The bell, which weighs over two tons, was cast in 1769 by Semon Mozhukin. Before the Revolution there was an icon of the Redeemer above the gate, hence its name, and it was a strictly observed custom that everyone entering the Kremlin by this gate should bare his head and enter on foot.

The next large tower (moving in an anticlockwise direction) is the *Nikolsky Tower* near the *Historical Museum*. It was built in 1491 at the same time as the Spassky Tower, but was blown up in 1812 by Napoleon and rebuilt in 1820 by Bovet. It is named after the icon of St. Nicholas which used to hang over the gateway. The white stone decorations were added by Rossi at the beginning of the 19th century.

At the corner of the wall is the *Sobakina Tower* which was built particularly solidly with walls 4 m. thick, partly because it contained a secret well, important in time of siege, and also because it concealed a way out to the R. Neglinnaya which used to flow along the Kremlin wall. *The Trinity Gate* was built in 1495 and at 80 m. is the highest of all the Kremlin towers. It is approached by a bridge over the Alexandrovsky Gardens, constructed in place of the R. Neglinnaya, from the Kutafia Tower. This was one of the first stone bridges in Moscow and was built in 1516. The mounds beside the wall further along the garden are the remains of earthworks constructed by Peter the Great in 1707 when Charles XII of Sweden planned to attack Moscow.

The next large tower is the *Borovitskie (Forest) Tower** which was built in 1490 by Pietro Antonio Solario, the upper half being added at the end of the 17th century. It was through this gate that Napoleon entered the Kremlin. At the corner nearest the Kameny (Stone) Bridge over the R. Moskva is the round *Water-Hoist Tower**, so named in 1663 when craftsmen found a way to raise water from the river and convey it along an aqueduct to the Kremlin palaces and gardens. It was built in 1488 by Antonio Friasine, but was blown up in 1812 and rebuilt by Bovet in 1817. Along the river are five smaller towers. The first is the *Blagoveshchenskaya (Annunciation) Tower*, named after a church which was attached to it. During the reign of Ivan the Terrible this tower was used as a prison. The next tower is the oldest of all and was built in 1480 by Antonio Friasine. It is called the *Tainitsky Tower* (Tower of Secrets) because of a secret underground passage which led from here to the R. Moskva. It was partly demolished during the reign of Catherine II when plans were made to build a large palace on the site. The palace was never built and the present tower was built on the model of the old one in 1771–3. In 1930 the gates were bricked up but they can be seen from the road below.

Next come the *First and Second Nameless Towers* and then the *Petrovskaya Tower*, named after the Church of St. Peter the Metropolitan, which was destroyed and rebuilt several times. On the south-west corner is the *Beklemishev Tower* which was built by the Italian Marco Ruffo in 1487. The next tower is the *Tower of St. Constantin and St. Helen* which was attached to a church of the same name. The next is the *Nabatnaya (Alarm) Tower*, which was so called because it was here that a bell was rung in times of danger to warn the people to take refuge inside the Kremlin. During the rebellion of 1771, the insurgents rang the bell in order to summon the people of Moscow to the Kremlin. After the rebellion had been quashed, Catherine II was so angry when the culprits could not be found that she ordered the clapper of the bell to be removed. In 1821 the bell was transferred to the Armoury where it can be seen today. The last tower is the *Tsar's Tower* which was added in 1860. It is said to have been named the Tsar's Tower because Ivan the Terrible used to watch ceremonies in Red Sq. from a platform near the site of the present tower.

The central square of the Kremlin is *Cathedral Sq.* where the three principal cathedrals are situated.

The *Uspensky (Assumption) Cathedral*, on the north side of the square, is the largest of the Kremlin cathedrals. It was built in 1475–9 by the Italian architect Aristotle Fioravanti, who had spent many years in Russia studying the architecture of old Russian cities. The five-domed cathedral was built in the style of the 12th-century Uspensky Cathedral in Vladimir and it became Russia's principal church. The tsars were crowned here and the cathedral served as the burial vault of the Moscow metropolitans and patriarchs.

The walls of the cathedral are of white limestone and the drums beneath the domes and the vaulting are of brick. The exterior is divided into panels set off by columns and gables. On the west, south, and north façades is a belt of arcature and pilasters halfway up the walls.

The interior surprised visitors in the 15th century by its size and lightness. The Chronicle of Nikon recorded that the cathedral 'is amazing by virtue of its majesty and height, its lightness and spaciousness; such a church has never been seen before in all the land of Russia, save the Church at Vladimir'.

The walls of the cathedral are covered in frescoes dating from the 16th to 19th centuries. These were considerably damaged by fires and were touched up in oils in the 19th century, but they have recently been restored. On the west wall is a mural of the Last Judgement and in the Chapel of Praise on the right side of the cathedral are some frescoes which are attributed to Dionisy.

The five-tiered iconostasis, which was covered in chased silver gilt at the end of the 19th century, includes some valuable icons of the 14th to 17th centuries. The icon of the Virgin of Vladimir is a copy of the 11th-century Byzantine icon which used to be in the cathedral but which is now in the Tretyakov Gallery. Originals still here, however, include the icon of St. George (early 12th-century Novgorodian school) and the icon of the Trinity (14th century).

Near the main entrance is the Tsar's Throne, which was carved in walnut in 1551 and which belonged to Ivan the Terrible. Known as the Throne of Monomakh, it is covered in carvings and inscriptions depicting Vladimir Monomakh's Thracian campaign. In the south-east corner is a shrine encased in cast bronze openwork. It contains the relics of Patriarch Hermogen who was killed by the Polish invaders in 1612.

During the Napoleonic invasion the French soldiers turned the cathedral into a stable, using the icons as firewood. They took away with them as much as 288 kilograms (5·25 cwt.) of various gold articles and about 5000 kilograms (5 tons) of silver, much of which was lost during the subsequent retreat and which has not yet been recovered. The central chandelier, however, is made from silver captured from the French troops.

The *Blagoveshchensky (Annunciation) Cathedral* was designed as a chapel for Ivan III in early Moscow style in 1484–9. It was built on the foundations of a 14th-century stone church which had become unsafe. It had three cupolas at first, but, after a fire, was rebuilt in 1562–4 with additions by builders from Pskov. The vaults, galleries, four single-domed corner chapels, and two new domes were added. The domes and roof were covered in gilded copper and the nine-domed cathedral became known as the 'Golden-domed'. In 1572 a new porch and steps were added which are known as the *Steps of Ivan the Terrible*. The heavily ornamented portals on the west and north façades date from the 1560s and only that of the southern façade dates back to the 1480s when the cathedral itself was built.

The floor of the cathedral is of polished tiles of agate jasper and the walls are covered in frescoes dating from the 16th century. The pillars bear portraits of Greek philosophers and all the Moscow Princes from Prince Daniel to Vasily III. The second and third tiers of the iconostasis include icons painted by Theophanes the Greek, Prokhor from Gorodets, and Andrei Rublyev. Six of the icons in the third tier are attributed to Andrei Rublyev: 'The Transfiguration', 'The entry into Jerusalem', 'The purification of the Blessed Virgin', 'The Nativity', 'The Epiphany', and 'The Annunciation'. Other works of art which can be seen in the South gallery include the 13th-century 'Golden-Haired Christ', the 14th-century 'Cloaked Christ', and the 16th-century 'Our Lady of Vladimir'.

A narrow staircase in the north wall leads up to the choir where women members of the tsar's family used to sit during services.

The *Arkhangelsky (Archangel Michael's) Cathedral* was built on the site of a 14th-century church in 1505–9 by an Italian architect from Milan, Alevisio Novi. Two single-domed chapels, the Chapel of St. Var and the Chapel of St. John the Baptist, were added at the very end of the 16th century. The cathedral was designed in Russian style with only traces of Italian influence, particularly in the exterior. The north and south façades are divided into three sections, the east and west into five. Each section is made to stand out by pilasters and is surmounted by gables or fluted niches. The five domes are painted silver. Originally only the central dome was gilded and the four outside ones covered in white iron. The decorative white limestone portals on the north and west façades show the Italian influence in the cathedral.

The walls inside the cathedral are covered in murals painted in 1652–66 by a large group of artists from several Russian towns. They depict scenes from every-day life and battle scenes as well as paintings of a religious and historical nature. On the south-west pillar is a portrait of Alexander Nevsky who defeated the Teutonic knights in 1242. The gilded carved wooden iconostasis is 13 m. high, and contains icons dating mostly from the 15th to 17th centuries. The icon of the Archangel Michael is attributed to Andrei Rublyev.

From 1340 to 1700, first the smaller church which stood on this site and then the cathedral served as the burial vault of the grand princes of Moscow and the Russian tsars.

There are portraits of many of the monarchs on the walls above the tombs. All the tsars from Ivan Kalita to Peter the Great, except for Boris Godunov whose body was exhumed in 1606, are buried here. The only tsar to be buried here later was Peter II, grandson of Peter the Great, who died in Moscow in 1730. The bronze encasements were added in 1903.

The *Bell-Tower of Ivan the Great*, which unites the various buildings of the Kremlin into a single architectural ensemble, is one of the most remarkable structures to be built in the 16th century. The lower part was built in 1532–43, and the belfry and cupola added in 1600 as famine relief work carried out under Boris Godunov. Below the cupola are three rows of Slavonic script which relate the circumstances under which the work was carried out.

The bell-tower is 81 m. high, and when it was first built, it served as a watch-tower from which all Moscow and the vicinity within a radius of 30 km. could be observed. Inside the walls are 575 steps which lead in three stages up to the dome. There are 21 bells in the tower. They date from the 16th to 18th centuries and are embossed with bas-reliefs and inscriptions relating the history of the bell and when and by whom it was cast. The main bell, known as the *Bell of the Assumption*, weighs 63 tons.

In 1812 Napoleon, believing the cross on top of the dome to be pure gold, ordered it to be removed. However, it was found to be iron and those who had spread the rumour were shot.

At the foot of the Bell-tower of Ivan the Great is the *Tsar Kolokol* (Tsar Bell), the largest bell in the world. It weighs over 200 tons and the fragment on the ground weighs 11·50 tons. It is 6 m. high and 6·6 m. in diameter. The bell was cast in 1733–5 in a special casting pit inside the Kremlin by Ivan Motorin and his son Mikhail. They used both new metal and an old broken bell dating from the reign of Boris Godunov. After its completion the bell remained in the casting pit, but during the Kremlin fire of 1737 several cracks appeared and a large piece was broken off. The damage is thought to have been caused by the uneven cooling of the bell when cold water, used to extinguish the fire, fell on the bell. Almost a century later in 1836 the bell was raised from the casting pit and placed on the pedestal designed for it by Montferrand. The surface of the bell is decorated with bas-reliefs by Rastrelli representing Tsar Alexei and Tsaritsa Anna Ivanovna. There are also five icons on the bell and two inscriptions describing the history of its casting. The decorations are the work of Kobelev and Galkin.

Not far from the Tsar Bell is the *Tsar Cannon* which has the largest calibre of any gun in the world. It was cast in 1586 by Andrei Chokhov at the Cannon Yard on the bank of the R. Neglinnaya where the Teatralny Proezd is today. It weighs 40 tons and is 5·3 m. long with a calibre of 890 mm. and a barrel 15 cm. thick. It used to stand outside the Kremlin in Kitai-Gorod where it covered the approaches to Spassky Gate and the ford across the R. Moskva. A special carriage was required to fire it, but the present carriage was cast in 1835 especially for display purposes. It is said to have been named after Tsar Feodor Ivanovich, the son of Ivan the Terrible, whose picture is carved on the barrel, but it is more likely that it was called Tsar Cannon on account of its size.

Behind the Blagoveshchensky (Annunciation) Cathedral is the *Church of the Twelve Apostles and the Patriarch's Palace*. The Patriarch's Palace consisted of the Church of the Twelve Apostles, the Krestovy Chamber, the personal chambers of the patriarch, and the monks' cells. The present buildings were completed in 1656 for Patriarch Nikon, but the first stone chambers for the Metropolitan (later called Patriarch) were built in 1450. In 1473 they were completely destroyed by fire and rebuilt, only to be looted during the Polish invasion and then destroyed again by fire in 1626. The present church and four-storey palace, which includes part of the older residence of Boris Godunov, were built by Okhlebib, Konstantinov, and Makayev in the Moscow style of the time which was still heavily influenced by the architecture of Vladimir and Suzdal. The Krestovy Chamber in the Patriarch's Palace is a large hall where the patriarchs received tsars and foreign ambassadors and where church councils were held. The Church of the Twelve Apostles served as a private church for the patriarchs. It was first called the Church of St. Philip the Apostle, but was given its present name in 1680 when it was rebuilt after a fire. The church and palace now house a museum of 17th-century applied arts. The exhibits were taken from the reserve of the State Armoury Museum and include books, domestic utensils, household linen, and clothing. In the church is a 17th-century carved wooden iconostasis which was formerly in the Kremlin Monastery for the Ascension, demolished in the 1930s.

The *Church of the Deposition of the Robe* (Tserkov Rizpolozhenya) is a small, single-domed church standing between the Cathedral of the Assumption (Uspensky Sobor) and the Palace of Facets. It was built in 1484–6 by masons from Pskov on the site of an older church of the same name. This church served as a private chapel for the patriarch before the Church of the Twelve Apostles was built. The interior of the church is decorated with frescoes painted in 1644 by Osipov and Borisov, court painters who had also helped to paint the frescoes in the Cathedral of the Assumption. The silver chandelier was made in 1624 and the iconostasis was painted in 1627 by a group of icon painters under Nazary Istomin.

Behind the Church of the Deposition of the Robe one can see the eleven gilded domes of the *Upper Saviour's Church* (Verkhospaskaya Tserkov). The Upper Saviour's Church, which can be entered through the Great Kremlin Palace, was built in 1635–6 by Ogurtsov, Konstantinov, Sharutin, and Ushakov over the Tsarina's Golden Room in the Terem Palace. The church, which was used by the royal family, is also known as the Church behind the Golden Rail (Tserkov za zolo-

toi reshetkoi) because of a railing around the terrace near the church which was cast in 1670 from copper coins; these had been withdrawn from circulation after the 'Copper Revolt' of 1668 which broke out because of the debasing of copper coins. Inside the church are 17th-century frescoes and an 18th-century chased silver gate leading through the iconostasis to the altar. This church is very picturesque amongst the other more austere churches and cathedrals. The cupolas have long red brick drums which are decorated with blue and green tiles set by Osip Startsev after designs by the Elder Ippolit, a famous 17th-century carver. The copper roof of the church dates from the 18th century.

The *Granovitaya Palata* (Palace of Facets) on the west side of the Cathedral Sq. is the oldest public building in Moscow. Its name derives from the shape of the stone facings on the side looking onto Cathedral Sq. It was built in 1473–91 by the Italian architects Marco Ruffo and Pietro Antonio. The ground floor was designed for administrative rooms and the upper floor as a single chamber for receptions. The chamber, 500 square metres in area, has four cross vaults supported by one central pillar. The hall is lit by four large 19th-century chandeliers. The walls of the chamber were originally painted with religious frescoes. These were destroyed in a fire in 1682. Another fire ruined the decorations in 1696 and the present murals were painted in the 1880s by the Belousovs from the town of Palekh after the designs of 1683. The iron ribs of the vaulting are gilded and there are inscriptions in slavonic lettering on the vaulting. Above the carved portal is a 'look-out' room from which the tsarinas and their daughters watched the receptions as custom forbade any women to be present.

The *Great Kremlin Palace* was built in 1838–49 by a team of architects under the supervision of Konstantin Thon on the site of an earlier palace built by Rastrelli in the 18th century. It was the residence of the imperial family during their visits to Moscow. It is now a government building where the Supreme Soviets of the U.S.S.R. and of the Russian Federation meet, and where official receptions are held.

Although the palace appears to have three floors, it in fact has only two, the upper floor having two tiers of windows. The grandest of the old halls is the Hall of St. George, named after the tsarist military order of St. George. Along the walls are marble plaques inscribed in gold with the names of officers and military units decorated with the Cross of St. George, the highest order in tsarist Russia. The 8 alcoves are fronted by 18 zinc columns supporting an allegorical figure of Victory, all the work of Ivan Vitali.

The doors in the centre of the Hall of St. George lead into the Hall of St. Vladimir, named after the Order of St. Vladimir. One can then pass into the *Terem Palace* (Palace of Chambers) which was built in 1635 by Ogurtsov, Konstantinov, and Ushakov. The palace contains the old private chambers of the tsar and was built on the site of older chambers built for Vasily III and Ivan the Terrible. In the palace are the reception rooms, bedroom, and prayer room of the tsar. In the Throne Room, where the tsar worked and where very few boyars were admitted, stands the tsar's throne which was upholstered in velvet during the 19th century. The windows and entrances are decorated with fine carvings and all the chambers are covered in paintings done in the 19th century by Kisilev.

The *Oruzheinaya Palata* (Armoury) is the oldest Russian museum, where the tsar's regalia and ambassadorial gifts are kept. It is usually open for group excursions only and tickets are best obtained through Intourist.

The museum exhibits the treasures of the tsars which were collected through the centuries. In the reign of Ivan III (1462–1505) there were already so many treasures that they had to be housed in a special building called the Treasure Court which was built for this purpose between the Annunciation and Archangel Cathedrals. Military weapons and armoury were also made in the same building, which gave the collection and the present building its name. Most of the treasures were made in workshops of the Kremlin. The collection grew particularly large under Ivan the Terrible and, when Moscow was threatened by the Crimean Tatars under Devlet Girei, 450 sledges were needed to move the treasure to Novgorod. During the 16th and 17th centuries the treasure was augmented by gifts from foreign monarchs and ambassadors. During the reign of Peter the Great the Kremlin craftsmen were moved to the new capital of St. Petersburg and work in the Kremlin workshops almost came to a halt. At the beginning of the 19th century the treasures were moved into the Imperial Palace Museum which was housed in a building erected for this purpose by Yegotov opposite the Arsenal and Senate buildings. The collection was evacuated to Nizhny Novgorod during the Napoleonic invasion of 1812, but was moved back in the following year. In 1851 it was moved to the present building which had been built earlier in the same year by Konstantin Thon. The façade of the building is decorated with carved white stone columns and ornate window frames in the Russian style of the 17th century. A white marble staircase with gilt banisters leads up to the first floor where the tour of the exhibits begins. The walls are lined with marble bas-reliefs depicting Russian princes and tsars, the work of the Russian sculptor Shubin.

HALL I: WEAPONS AND ARMOUR OF THE 13TH TO 18TH CENTURIES. Of special interest is the collection of helmets on Stand 1. One of the earliest helmets is that of Yaroslav Vsevolodovich, the father of Alexander Nevsky. The helmet, which is covered in embossed silver, was found on the site of a battle on R. Koloksha which took place between Suzdal and Novgorod in 1216 and the name of the owner is inscribed on the front. Another 13th-century helmet, believed to be of Byzantine origin, is decorated with images of the Virgin

Mary, Christ, and John the Baptist and is covered with a net of very fine silver. Also on show here is the small helmet of the little Prince Ivan, the son of Ivan the Terrible, who grew up to be killed at the age of 28 by his father in an outburst of anger. It bears an inscription saying that it was made for the prince, who was then four years old, by order of his father in 1557. On the same stand are examples of Russian chain mail, the oldest type being the 'kolchuga' which was made from thousands of small iron rings linked together and weighing about 18 kg. There are also some fine breastplates on show, including those of the Tsars Mikhail and Alexei, which are gilded and embossed. Some of the battle-axes and maces on show were made in the 17th and 18th centuries when they were already obsolete as battle arms and only used for dress purposes. Some of the axes made by Kremlin craftsmen in the 17th century have blades covered in gold inlay.

On Stand 2 are Russian arquebuses and Dutch and German muskets of the 16th and 17th centuries. The earliest arquebus in the collection dates from the time of Ivan the Terrible and belonged to the Boyar Belsky, Ivan's Chief Armourer.

On Stand 3 is a collection of ceremonial armour and Russian and oriental sabres. Of special interest is the helmet of Tsar Mikhail Romanov, which has a finely polished surface inlaid with gilt and decorated with diamonds, rubies, and emeralds. Among the sabres on display are lavishly decorated gold and silver sabres studded with precious stones which were worn by the tsars on ceremonial occasions. Also here are the sabres of Minin and Pozharsky who headed the army which drove the Poles out of Moscow in 1612. These sabres, made in Egypt and Persia respectively, are outstanding because of their simplicity.

On Stand 4 is a collection of armour and weapons of the second half of the 17th century. The breastplate in the centre was made in 1670 by Titov and Vyatikin. The large quiver and bowcase set in gold and gems were made in Constantinople and given to Tsar Alexei in 1656 by Greek merchants. Also here is Tsar Alexei's oriental sabre with a hilt and golden sheath. The heavy golden mace (1·2 kg.), cast out of pure gold with gold crests, was presented to Tsar Alexei by Shah Abbas II of Persia in 1658.

Stand 5 displays Russian arms of the reign of Peter the Great and trophies from the Northern War (1700–21). In the centre of the stand is a bas-relief of Peter the Great beaten in pewter by the architect Rastrelli who was responsible for many of the imperial buildings in St. Petersburg. Among the Swedish trophies from the war are a silver mace bearing the crest of Gustavus Adolphus Vasa and a bible published in Stockholm in 1703 bearing the monogram of Charles XII.

Stand 6 has a display of 16th-century pistols and European suits of armour of the 15th to 17th centuries. In the centre is a suit of equestrian armour cast by Kunz Lochner and presented to

Tsar Feodor by the Polish ambassador in 1584 as a gift from the Polish king, Stefan Batory. To the right of the stand among the suits of armour are three which were made for the royal children in the 17th century. These were only worn on ceremonial occasions.

HALL II: RUSSIAN GOLD AND SILVER, 12th to 17th centuries. One of the earliest pieces of silver on display is a 12th-century chalice which was given to the Cathedral of the Saviour in Transfiguration in Pereslavl-Zalessky by Prince Yuri Dolgoruky, the founder of Moscow. It is engraved with figures of the saints. Another 12th-century cup here belonged to Prince Vladimir Davydov of Chernigov, as is related on the inscription beneath the rim. The fine work of Kievan craftsmen is shown here in the so-called Ryazan treasure which dates from the 12th or 13th century and was discovered in Old Ryazan in 1822. The treasure includes two heavy necklets decorated with coloured enamel and filigree, a bracelet, rings, ear-rings, and images of the saints. Novgorodian work is represented by a 14th-century jasper chalice in a silver filigree case studded with precious stones, and 14th-century silver dippers in the shape of a sauce-boat. Also on display are gold and silver dippers made by Moscow craftsmen in the 16th century, including a dipper smelted out of a single nugget which belonged to Boris Godunov. The extremely decorative gospel was given to the Cathedral of the Assumption in 1571 by Ivan the Terrible. The gold cover is picked out with enamel and precious stones with pictures of Christ and the saints linked by inscriptions in blackened gold. There is a large collection of various drinking vessels on display. Besides dippers, which were used for drinking mead, there are 'bratinas', a tall round bowl used as a toasting cup and for drinking beer and kvas, 'korchiks', small dippers on a saucer with a goblet for strong drinks, and 'endovas', a low lipped vessel usually used for pouring drinks. One of the finest 'bratinas' is the silver-lidded one which was made in Moscow in the first half of the 17th century and belonged to Tsarina Irina Mikhailovna. There is also a very small 'bratina', decorated with coloured enamel and studded with jewels, which belonged to the Tsarina Yevdokia Dukyanona. There is one particularly fine 'endova' on display which was made in 1644 in Moscow and belonged to the boyar Streshnev. The articles on display dating from the second half of the 17th century are particularly lavish with bright enamel work studded with precious stones, including two emeralds Tsar Alexei Mikailovich which is covered in green enamel painted with bright flowers, the gold mounting for the icon of the Virgin Vladimir studded with previous stones, including two emeralds weighing 100 carats each, and two gold-covered gospels with emerald- and ruby-studded enamel.

Also on display in this hall are boxes, knives, forks, cups, and caskets, and a collection of Russian and foreign clocks and watches of the 16th to 18th centuries. The gilded copper watch in the form of a book belonged to Ivan the Terrible and the wooden watch was made in the 19th century by Russian craftsmen.

HALL III: SILVER AND JEWELLERY, 18th to 20th centuries. At the beginning of the 18th century St. Petersburg, the new capital, became the centre of the Russian silver and gold trades. In the middle of the 18th century the predominant style was that of Russian Baroque and Rococo with very lavish ornamentation and brightly painted enamel. One of the finest exhibits dating from this period is the pair of silver candelsticks made in St. Petersburg by Liebmann. They are mounted on tall cast stems with intricate ornamentation and scrollwork. Although the Rococo style gave way to Russian Classicism at the end of the century, the large silver beaker displayed in a separate case, which was made by Ratkov in Moscow in 1788, has a Rococo finish. Also on display is a collection of snuff-boxes made of gold, silver, mother-of-pearl, tortoise-shell, ivory, and porcelain. Many of them are decorated with precious stones and enamel portraits. The flat snuff-box bearing an enamel portrait of Peter the Great was made in 1727 by Andrei Osov, one of the first Russian miniaturists. Also here is a large, round, gold snuff-box with a plated bas-relief portrait of the Empress Elizabeth which is believed to have been made by Pozier, one of the most famous craftsmen of the last century. Further on is a collection of silver dating from 1770 to 1825, the period of Russian Classicism. These articles are much plainer in decoration, such as the silver samovar shaped like a Greek urn made by Unger and Eckert in 1801. On the same stand is a silver children's tea service made by Johann Blohm in St. Petersburg in 1784. In the centre of the stand is a gold oval dish, made by F. Sebastian in 1788, and presented to Catherine II by Prince Potemkin. Further on are two small crowns woven out of silver laurel leaves which are said to be the crowns used during the ceremony of Pushkin's marriage to Natalya Goncharova in 1831. The last section in this hall shows examples of the work of the famous jewellers' firms which grew up in Moscow and St. Petersburg after 1830. The Sazikov Jewellers' is represented by a silver sculpture 'Warrior on watch' made in St. Petersburg in 1852. The work of Fabergé, probably the most famous of all Russian jewellers, is represented by a number of works. One of the most fascinating is a silver Easter egg, on the outside of which is engraved a map of the Trans-Siberian Railway. Inside is a gold clockwork model of a Trans-Siberian express with a platinum engine with a ruby headlamp. The carriages are inscribed with the usual inscriptions, such as 'Smokers', 'Ladies Only', and 'Clerics' and have windows made of crystal. There is also a nephrite egg which contains a model of the Alexandrovsky Palace in Tsarskoye Selo (now Pushkin) near Leningrad. Another egg contains a gold model of the royal yacht, 'Standard'. The yacht is set in a sea of rock crystal and the crystal egg has two pear-shaped pearl pendants. Another fascinating exhibit is a vase of rock-crystal with a pansy decoration. If a button on the flower stem is pressed, the petals open revealing miniature portraits of the children of Nicholas II in frames of small diamonds.

HALL IV: VESTMENTS. This hall contains vestments of silk, velvet, and brocade, woven and embroidered with gold and encrusted with jewels and pearls. They belonged to the imperial family, patriarchs, and metropolitans. Before the 18th century no silk or brocades were made in Russia. Most of the articles on show in the first section of this hall were imported from West Europe or from the Middle East.

The oldest vestment on display is the 'sakkos' (robe) of Peter, the first Metropolitan of Moscow. It was made in 1332 of blue satin woven with gold stripes and crosses. Some of the robes, such as those of the Metropolitan Photius, are embroidered with portraits of the rulers of the time or with religious figures.

In the 17th and 18th centuries materials were particularly heavily embroidered with precious stones, pearls, and gold plates. One of the last vestments on display is a velvet cope which was presented to Metropolitan Platon of Moscow in 1770 by Catherine II There are altogether 150,580 pearls on the cope.

Beyond the vestments are examples of Russian pictorial embroidery on altar cloths and other church articles. These date from the 15th century.

HALL V: FOREIGN GOLD AND SILVER, 13th to 19th centuries. Most of the items on display in this hall were gifts to the tsars from ambassadors on behalf of their country. The first exhibits are of Dutch silver made in Amsterdam in the 16th century. They are remarkable for their simplicity and limited decoration. Many of the articles are decorated with tulips, the most common motif on 17th-century Dutch silver.

The next section is a collection of English silver, mostly made in London in the 16th and 17th centuries. In 1553 Richard Chancellor was received in Moscow by Ivan the Terrible and was the first of a long succession of English ambassadors to the Russian Court. The earliest item is a flat goblet, made in 1557, and thought to have been presented to Ivan the Terrible by the English merchant, Antony Jenkins. Other items of English silver on display are trays, cups, figured salt-cellars, wine flagons, pitchers, and chased livery pots.

Silver from Poland and Sweden is in the next section. Many of the gifts from Poland in the 17th century were made in Danzig, but a number of the items on show were made in Germany where they were bought by Polish tradesmen. The collection from Sweden is the largest of all and comprises about 200 items, all made in the 17th century. Some of these were made in Augsberg, such as the two oval basins which were a gift from Queen Christina to Tsar Alexei. The two globes, depicting the earthly and heavenly spheres and supported by the figures of Neptune and Atlas, were also made by German craftsmen and were brought to Moscow as gifts from Charles X. The work of Swedish silversmiths is represented by a number of pieces including candlesticks, flasks, tumblers, filigree cups, and a water bowl in the shape of a silver swan.

The next stand is a display of gifts from Denmark, also mostly made by German craftsmen.

Further on are silver and gold vessels made by craftsmen in Nurenberg in the 15th to 17th centuries. There is a large collection of drinking-cups and goblets in various shapes, some in the form of a fruit or an animal.

At the end of the hall are some foreign dinner and tea services. The large silver service is only part of one consisting of over 3000 pieces which was given by Catherine II in 1772 to Prince Orlov. It was ordered from Rottiers and Fils, but the order was so big that they were obliged to subcontract part of it. The Sèvres tea, coffee, and dessert services on show were presented to Alexander I by Napoleon when the Treaty of Tilsit was signed.

HALL VI: REGALIA OF THE ROYAL FAMILY. At the beginning of the hall on the left are the thrones of the tsars. The oldest throne on display is that of Ivan the Terrible which was made in Western Europe and is decorated with ivory carvings. The second throne was given to Boris Godunov by Shah Abbas of Persia. The throne is covered with thin plates of gold and studded with 2200 precious stones and pearls. The third throne was made in Moscow for Mikhail Romanov from a throne belonging to Ivan the Terrible of Iranian origin. The next throne was presented to Tsar Alexei Romanov by a group of American merchants. The throne, which was made in Persia, is decorated with 1223 precious stones and 876 diamonds which have given it the name of the 'Diamond Throne'. The last throne is that used in the first years of the reign of Peter the Great when he shared power with his elder brother, Ivan, and his sister Sophia was regent. The two seats in front were used by the two tsars and the hidden seat behind by Sophia who used to prompt the boys with the right answers to ambassadors' questions.

The oldest crown on display is the 'Cap of Monomakh' which was made by Oriental craftsmen in the 13th or 14th centuries and is thought to have been given to the Grand Prince Vladimir Monomakh of Kiev by the Emperor of Byzantium. It is made of finely wrought gold lace smelted onto a strip of gold leaf, surmounted by a pearl-tipped gold cross and edged with a band of sable.

The Kazan Cap was made in Moscow for Ivan the Terrible to commemorate the capture of Kazan. Also on show is the regalia made in Moscow for the coronation of Tsar Mikhail Romanov, the regalia brought to Moscow from Greece for Tsar Alexei Romanov, and the diamond coronets made in Moscow between 1682 and 1689 for Peter the Great and his brother Ivan. Only two crowns made in the days when Russia was an empire are in the armoury: the crown of Anna Ivanovna, which is encrusted with numerous diamonds and a large ruby, and the crown of Catherine I.

The last section of this hall contains a display of Russian costumes from the 16th century. Until the end of the 17th century the most usual garment was a long loose caftan. There are a number on display, including one belonging to Peter the Great. From the end of the 17th century shorter, closer-fitting clothes were worn with short breeches reaching just below the knee.

Beyond the men's garments is a display of accessories and jewellery. The single ear-rings were worn by men in Russia until the reign of Peter the Great. At the end of the hall are a number of dresses, including coronation dresses, which belonged to the empresses and tsars' wives.

HALLS VII & VIII: HARNESSES. The harnesses in these two halls are extremely exotic. Most of them were made in Russia but some were gifts to the Russian court from foreign countries, in particular from Poland which regularly sent saddles to the tsar.

The display begins with a collection of 16th- and 17th-century German, Polish, and English harnesses. The oldest saddles here were gifts to Boris Godunov from the King of Poland. The German saddles were made in the second half of the 17th century and are decorated with embroidery.

Further on are a number of Persian harnesses which were mostly gifts from the Shah of Persia. A particularly exotic saddle is that in a gold frame which is covered in velvet, embroidered with gold threads and decorated with rubies, emeralds, and turquoises.

The oldest Russian saddle on display was made during the reign of Ivan the Terrible. It is covered with velvet, embroidered with golden two-headed eagles. There are a number of childrens' saddles, no less ornate than those for adults, including one made in 1642 for the Tsarevich Alexei Mikhailovich.

HALL IX: CARRIAGES. The oldest carriage is a 16th-century English one thought to have been a gift to Boris Godunov by Elizabeth I.

The child's coach and closed sledge were made at the end of the 17th century for Peter the Great when he was a child.

An unusual carriage is that in which Empress Elizabeth travelled from St. Petersburg to Moscow for her coronation. It was drawn by 23 horses—one pair and seven threes. The most lavish of all, however, is the French carriage made in Paris in 1757 by Bourinhall. This one, with carved gilt wood made to represent sea foam and breaking waves, has panels painted by François Bouchet. It was presented to the Empress Elizabeth by Count Razumovsky.

A new section of the museum has been opened to show the presents made to the Soviet Union by foreign countries.

The new *Palace of Congresses* was completed in 1961 for the 22nd Soviet Communist Party Congress. It was designed by Mikhail Posokhin and built 15 m. down into the ground, the height of a 5-storey house, so that it would not be higher than the rest of the Kremlin ensemble. It contains over 800 rooms and halls and the main auditorium has a seating capacity of 6000. The acoustics in the auditorium are very good with 7000 loudspeakers concealed in different parts of the hall. During congresses the speeches can be heard in 29 languages. The praesidium seats and the rostrum can be lowered to form an orchestra pit. Above the main auditorium is a banqueting hall seating 2500. The Palace of Congresses is now also used for concerts, ballet and opera.

The *Arsenal* is the long yellow building forming a quadrangle between the Trinity and Nikolsky Towers. Work was started on the Arsenal under Peter the Great who planned it as a storehouse for arms and ammunition. It was completed in 1736 but was badly damaged by fire the following year. It was later rebuilt under the direction of the engineer, Gerard. In 1812 the wall of the Arsenal near to the Kremlin wall was blown up by Napoleon's troops and the whole building destroyed in the ensuing fire. It was rebuilt from 1816 to 1828, this time by Bovet. The final two-storey structure that emerged can be seen to combine features of Petrine architecture and the baroque of the 1830s. Plans were made in the 19th century to open a museum of the 1812 war in the building. 875 cannons which were captured from the French army were placed along the south-east wall where they remain today, for the plans for the museum were never fulfilled.

The building of the *Council of Ministers* faces the south-east façade of the Arsenal. It was built by Matvei Kazakov in 1776–88 on a piece of land which had belonged to the Trubetskoi family and the Monastery of the Miracle. Before the Revolution it was the Senate building and now houses the offices of the Council of Ministers. In the centre of the façade facing the Arsenal is an archway which leads into the courtyard. In the centre of the building is a large circular hall with a domed roof. Before the Revolution the hall was known as the White Hall or the Catherine Hall and was used for meetings. It is now used for plenary meetings of the Central Committee of the Communist Party.

Churches and Cathedrals

St. Basil's Cathedral, Red Sq. Open Mon., Wed.–Sat. 10.30–5.30. Closed 1st. Mon. in month.

The Cathedral of the Intercession (Pokrovsky Sobor), or St. Basil's as it is more usually called, was built in 1555–60 by order of Ivan the Terrible to commemorate the conquest of the Tatar City of Kazan on the Volga. Ivan the Terrible's first plan was for eight churches to be built on Red Sq., each church being dedicated to the saints on whose days he won his battles. One stone and seven wooden churches were built in 1552, but Ivan the Terrible was dissatisfied and ordered them to be demolished. The task of building new churches was given to Barma and Posnik, two architects whom recent historical evidence has shown were probably the same person, Postnik Yakolev, whose nickname was Barma. A new plan was drawn up, this time for one large cathedral surrounded by seven subsidiary churches. Seven small churches would have spoilt the symmetry of the design so the architect(s) built eight.

The central cathedral, the dome of which is 46 m. high, was named Pokrovsky Sobor (Cathedral of the Intercession) because the chief victory in the campaign fell on the day of the Intercession. The more popular name of St. Basil's was taken from a church built close to the cathedral in 1588 which was dedicated to the memory of a holy man named Basil, a Muscovite who had exercised a certain amount of influence over Ivan the Terrible.

Legend says that when the cathedral was completed Ivan ordered the eyes of the architects to be gouged out so that they could not build a similar cathedral elsewhere. It is known that when first completed the cathedral was painted in more subdued colours and that it was only in the 18th century that it was painted as it is now with all the details picked out in different colours. The exotic grandeur of the cathedral makes it one of the best and most striking examples of old Russian architecture.

The first room of the museum in the cathedral contains an exhibition relating the history of the building, the story of its construction and specimens of the materials used.

Among the more interesting sights in the cathedral are the iconostasis of the Trinity Church, the 'Entry into Jerusalem' icon in the same church and the interior decoration of the Church of St. Alexander of Svir.

In the 16th century the crypt was used as the State Treasury. In 1595 two nobles planned to rob it and started fires in different parts of the city in order to divert the attention of the city guard. Their plan failed, nevertheless, and they were summarily executed.

In front of the cathedral is the monument to Minin and Pozharsky (see pp. 200–201).

Novodevichii Monastyr (Novodevichy Convent), Bolshaya Pirogovskaya St. 2. (Near the Sportivnaya station.) Open 1 May—30 Oct. 11–6; 1 Nov.—30 Apr. 11–5; closed Tues. and 1st Mon. of each month.

Novodevichy Convent is one of the most interesting historical and architectural monuments in Moscow. It was founded in 1524 by Grand-Prince Vasili Ioanovich to commemorate the union of Smolensk and Moscow. It formed a stronghold on the road to Smolensk and Lithuania and was enclosed by fortified walls with twelve towers.

Novodevichy was a convent for ladies of noble birth and many historical figures ended their lives here. When Tsar Feodor died in 1598, his widow, Irina, and her brother, Boris Godunov, came to the convent. Tsar Feodor had been almost imbecile for a number of years before his death and power had been in the hands of his brother-in-law,

Boris, but he realised that if he assumed power immediately he would be faced with opposition. His calculations proved right as he was soon entreated by the Patriarch and a number of nobles to leave the convent.

Peter the Great's elder sister, Princess Sophia, was banished to the convent in 1679 by her brother. In 1698 the Streltsy, whom she had supported in their revolt against the tsar, were hanged along the walls of the convent with their hands clasped in a begging attitude. Sophia, who had become Sister Susanna in the convent, had her hair shorn and was banished to a tower where she died in 1704. Her sisters, Yekaterina, Maria, and Fedosia, also lived in the convent.

Peter the Great, unlike other Russian tsars, saw little good in monasteries and convents. At one time he turned the Novodevichy Convent into a home for abandoned babies and he later issued an order that war veterans should be offered shelter in the convent.

Napoleon visited the monastery in 1812, but left it untouched until the last day of the French occupation when he ordered that it should be blown up. Barrels of gunpowder were set up in the convent, but a nun named Sara succeeded in extinguishing the fuses just in time and the convent remained undamaged.

The *Preobrazhenskaya Tserkov (Church of the Transfiguration)* is the first church the visitor sees when entering the convent through the main entrance. It was built in 1687–8 in Moscow Baroque style over the gateway. The seven-tier iconostasis which was painted in 1687 by Kremlin craftsmen is of particular interest.

Nearby are the *Lopukhinskie Palaty (Lopukhin Chambers)*, a two-storey building erected in 1687–8 for the daughter of Tsar Alexei and sister of Peter the Great, Tsarevna Yekaterina. The first wife of Peter the Great, Evdokia Lopukhin, lived here from 1727 to 1731 and the building has been called after her ever since.

Smolenskii Sobor (Smolensk Cathedral) was the main church of the convent. It was dedicated to Our Lady of Smolensk, which was an icon of the Virgin Mary brought to Kiev from Greece by the Greek Tsarevna Anna and thence to the cathedral in Smolensk. In 1398 the icon was moved to the Cathedral of the Annunciation in the Kremlin and today it can be seen in the Tretyakov Gallery.

The cathedral was built in 1524–5 by the architect Aleviz Fryazin. The side aisles and galleries were added at the end of the 17th century. The brick walls of the cathedral are set off by the architectural details in white stone. Of the three arched entrances with carved cornices, also of white stone, those on the west and north façades remain in their original form.

The interior of the cathedral is covered in murals of the 16th century which have recently been restored. The carved wooden iconostasis is worthy of special attention. It has 84 intricately carved columns and was the work of about 50 craftsmen under Konstantin Mikhailov in 1685.

The icons date from the 16th and 17th centuries and were painted by the best Muscovite masters. The icon of Christ on the right-hand side of the first tier of the iconostasis and the icons on the doors of the sanctuary were painted by the famous 17th-century artist, Simeon Ushakov.

In the centre of the cathedral stands a large chalice which was made in 1685 and is decorated with brightly painted and embossed tulips and roses.

In the cathedral are the tombs of Princess Sophia, the first wife of Peter the Great, Evdokia Lopukhin, Tsarevna Anna, and the daughter of Ivan the Terrible.

The cathedral now houses a museum of Russian applied arts of the 16th and 17th centuries. The exhibits include embroidery, paintings, fabrics, woodwork, and metalwork. Along the south wall are exhibited the private possessions of Princess Sophia. There is also a large collection of 16th- and 17th-century books, beautifully illuminated and illustrated, bound in leather and decorated with gold, silver, and jewels.

The *Belfry* is situated near the east wall of the convent. This is contrary to Russian custom, in which belfries were always built on the western side of the main buildings, and the site was chosen as it was thought that the belfry would be more striking on this side of the convent.

It is indeed a fine example of the best architecture of the time and is considered by many to be superior to the Bell Tower of Ivan the Great in the Kremlin. The belfry was completed in 1690. It is 72 m. in height and consists of six octagonal tiers of varying width and height. Around the base of each tier is an open-arched gallery. The belfry, which was built of brick, is decorated with limestone details which give it an air of lightness in spite of its size.

Uspensky Tserkov (Church of the Assumption) was built in 1687, but was badly damaged in a fire in 1796 after which it was rebuilt and much altered. In place of the five cupolas only one was rebuilt. The church is now open for religious services.

Trapeznaya Palata (Refectory). The refectory was built at the same time as the Church of the Assumption which adjoins it. It is a large hall with no supporting pillars which was the refectory for nuns and the hall where guests were entertained on feast days. After the fire of 1796 the refectory was rebuilt, but without the open galleries which formerly ran along the western façade of the building.

Near the refectory is the *Palata Irina Godunov (The Chambers of Irina Godunov)*, the sister of Boris Godunov, who came to live in the convent after the death of her husband, Tsar Feodor, in 1598. The building was completed in the same year and was then surmounted by a wooden chamber with a lavishly painted roof. The building was considerably altered at the end of the 18th century.

To the south of the convent, but still within the walls, is a cemetery with the graves of many famous people. The writers Gogol and Chekhov are buried here, and also Stalin's wife Nadezhda Alliluyeva. Prominent statesmen, artists and military officers are still buried here in the new part of the cemetery.

The following churches are among those open for services in Moscow: daily services at 10 and 6.

The Patriarchal Cathedral of the Manifestation of Christ (often called Yelokhovskaya Church), Spartakovskaya St. 15. The cathedral was built in 1835–45 and contains, among other treasures, the Kazan Virgin icon, the Virgin of Tikhvin icon, and a sacred relic, the shrine of Saint Alexis, Metropolitan of Moscow in the 14th century, which was transferred here from the Assumption Cathedral in the Kremlin.

The Church of the Ascension (Tserkov Vozneseniya), Sokolniki Sq. This church was built in 1914, but it possesses many old icons, including the wonder-working icon of the Virgin of Iberia (Iberia was the old name for the country of Georgia).

The Church of the Transfiguration (Tserkov Preobrazheniya), Preobrazhenskaya Sq. Near Preobrazhenskaya metro station. This church was built in 1746 and contains the wonder-working icon of the Virgin of Healing.

Church of the Assumption, Novodevichy Convent (see p. 217).

The Church of St. Nicholas in Khamovniki (Tserkov Svyatova Nikolayav Khamovnikakh). At the corner of Komsomolsky Prospect and Timur Frunze St. This church was built in 1679 in the old weavers' district known as Khamovniki. The exterior is painted in white with bright decorations in red and green. Inside the church is the wonder-working icon of the 'Countenance of Sinners Virgin'.

The Church of the Lamenters, Bolshaya Ordynka 20. This church was built in 1787 and contains the wonder-working icon 'The Joy of All Afflicted'.

The Church of John the Warrior (Tserkov Ivana-Voina), Dimitrov St. 46. This church was built in 1709–13 on the order of Peter the Great in commemoration of the victory over the Swedes at the Battle of Poltava. It contains finely carved iconostasis and the icon of the Holy Martyr.

The Church of the Deposition of the Robe (Tserkov Rizpolozhenya), Donskaya St. 56. This church was built in 1701 in Moscow Baroque style. The interior walls are covered with inset sculptures.

The Church of the Resurrection (Tserkov Vosskresenskaya), Brusovsky Pereulok 20. This church was built in 1629.

The Church of the Resurrection (Tserkov Vosskresenskaya), Aksakovsky Pereulok 20. This church was built in 1683.

All Saints Church (Tserkov Vsekh Svyatykh), Leningradsky Prospect, near Sokol metro station. This church was built in 1736.

The Church of the Archangel Gabriel (Tserkov Arkhangela Gavriila), Telegrafnyi Pereulok 15a. This church was built in 1704–7 (see p. 204).

Church of St. Pimen (Tserkov Svyatova Pimena), Novovorotnikovsky Pereulok 3. This very small church near the old Arbat was built in 1848.

Church of the Resurrection (Tserkov Vosskresenskaya), Vtoroi Kadashevsky Pereulok 9. Not far from the Tretyakov Gallery. This church was built in the 17th century.

Trinity Church, Lenin Hills, in front of the new building of the University. This small church was built in 1811.

Evangelical Christians' (Baptists') Meeting House, Malyi Vuzovsky Pereulok 3. Meetings at 6 on Tues., Thurs., and Sat., at 10 and 6 on Sun.

Old Believers' Cathedral, Rogozhsky Pereulok 29

Armenian Church, Malaya Dekabrskaya St. 27

St. Louis's Roman Catholic Church, Markhlevsky St. 7. This church was designed by Ghilardi and was built in 1827–30.

Mosque, Vypolzov Pereulok 7. The midday service is recited Fr. at 1 pm.

Synagogue, Arkhipov St. 8. Daily services at 10 am and one hour before sundown.

Moscow University

Moscow University was founded in 1755 by Russia's great scientist and encyclopaedist, Mikhail Lomonosov, and is named after him. It is now the largest university in the country and has over 22,000 students attending its 14 faculties.

It is housed in many buildings in the city centre and since 1953 also in the large sky-scraper on Lenin Hills. The main buildings in the centre are the two opposite the Alexandrovsky Gardens on either side of Gertzen St. The oldest building, on the right as one faces Gertzen St., was built by Matvei Kazakov in 1786–93. It was badly damaged in the 1812 fire, after which it was restored and altered by Ghilardi. Ghilardi was responsible for the façade with the 8-column colonnade and also for the semi-circular assembly halls which is adorned with Ionic columns and murals. The *monuments* to Alexander Herzen and Nikolai Ogaryov by Nikolai Andreyev in front of the building were erected in 1922.

The building on the other side of Gertzen St., still known as the 'new' building, was built by Tyrin in 1836 in Classical style. Behind the 'new' building is the *Church of the Apparition (Tserkov Znamenskaya)* which was built at the end of the 17th century in Russian Baroque style. The *monument* to Mikhail Lomonosov in front of the university was made by Kozlovsky and erected in 1857.

The new building on Lenin Hills was designed by Rudnyev and built in 1949–53. It is used chiefly by the scientific departments of the university and for accommodation. The main building is 240 m. high, including the spire, and the main façade is 450 m. long. The whole university complex here, which is situated on a site of 415 acres, comprises 27 blocks and 10 ancillary buildings. To inspect all the premises here one would have to walk nearly 150 km.

The *monument to Lomonosov* in front of the main façade was made by Tomsky and was erected in 1954.

Libraries

Lenin Library, Kalinin Prospect 3. With an overall stock of 25,000,000 books, this is the country's largest library, and it always receives one copy of each book printed in the Soviet Union. The rare books and manuscripts section has a collection of early documents, and also many first editions and old manuscripts, both foreign (beginning with Gutenburg) and Russian, dating back to the time of Russia's first printer, Fedorov, in the 16th century. There are handwritten Slav and Russian manuscripts dating from the 11th century.

The library building was built in 1939–40 by Schuko and Gelfreikh. Along the façade are bronze relief portraits of famous writers and scientists.

Next to the new building in Kalinina St. is the magnificent old building of the library. It was built by Bazhenov in 1786 and is known as Pashkov House after its owner who was a descendant of the batman of Peter the Great. It once housed a museum which was bequeathed to the state by Count Rumyantsev.

Foreign Literature Lending Library, Ulyanovskaya St. 1. The library is housed in a new building completed in 1966. It was founded after the revolution and has over 3 million books in 127 languages.

Art Galleries and Museums general

Tretyakov Gallery, Lavrushinsky Pereulok 10. Open 10–8 (ticket office open until 7); closed Mon.

The Tretyakov Gallery consists exclusively of Russian art from early religious works of the 10th century until the present day.

The foundation of this collection was laid by the art collectors Pavel and Sergei Tretyakov, after whom the gallery is named. Pavel Tretyakov began his collection with a number of lithographs and engravings and only later turned to paintings, in particular contemporary Russian art, and then to icons. His brother Sergei collected West European paintings and Russian sculpture. When Sergei died in 1892, he bequeathed his whole collection to Pavel, who in the same year gave the whole collection, then comprising 3500 works of art, to the city of Moscow.

After the Revolution the works of West European artists were transferred to the Pushkin Museum of Fine Arts. Since then the collection has grown and, although a new wing was built to accommodate works of the Soviet period, the present building, designed by Vasnetsov in 1898 to house the collection, is far too small. A new gallery on the Krymsky Embankment opposite the main entrance to Gorky Park is at present being built.

In the forecourt is a copy of Yevgeny Vuchetich's sculpture 'Swords into ploughshares', presented to the United Nations by the Soviet Union.

HALL I: Portraits, 1700–1750

Ivan Nikitin (1690–1741)—Chancellor Golovin. Ivan Vishnyakov (1699–1761)—Empress Elizabeth.

L. Karavak—Empress Anna Ivanovna.

HALL II: Portraits, 1750–1800

Feodor Rokotov (1735–1808)—Princess Lanskaya; Catherine II; Rimsky-Korsakov, ancestor of the famous composer; A. Struiskaya.

Alexei Antropov (1716–1725)—Tsar Peter III.

A. Boutourlin (1716–1795)—A. Izmailova.

Mikhail Belskii (1753–1794)—composer Bortnyansky.

HALL III: 1750–1800

Dmitri Levitsky (1735–1822)—portraits of factory-owner Peter Demidov, 1773; the artist's father; Ursuna Mnishek.

Feodor Shubin (1740–1805)—marble bust of Prince Galitsyn.

HALL IV: small hall containing sketches of sculptures of end of 18th and beginning of 19th centuries.

HALL V: Portraits, 1750–1800

Vladimir Borovikovsky (1757–1825)—Princess Lopukhin, 1797; Catherine II during a stroll at Tsarskoe Selo; Madame de Stael.

HALL VI: 1750–1850.

The first half of the hall is devoted to landscapes. Of note are the works of Simen Schedrin (1754–1804) and a number of paintings by Feodor Alekseev (1753–1824) including 'Cathedral Square in the Kremlin', and 'A view of the palace embankment from the Peter and Paul Fortress'.

In the second part of the hall are portraits dating from the beginning of the 19th century. At this time Russian art became less formalistic and the subjects of portraits were extended beyond court figures to ordinary people.

Orest Kiprensky (1782–1836)—Countess Rostopchina, 1809; Alexander Pushkin, 1827.

Vasily Tropinin (1766–1857)—Self-portrait; the lace-maker; the artist's son.

HALL VII: 1800–1850

Alexander Ivanov (1806–1858)—'The appearance of Christ to the people'. Ivanov spent about 20 years on this canvas. Many of his preliminary sketches can be seen in this hall. Karl Bryullov (1799–1852)—'The rider'; Self-portrait.

HALL VIII: 1800–1850

Maxim Vorobev (1787–1855)—landscapes.

Mikhail Lebedev (1811–1837)—landscapes, mainly Italian.

HALL IX: 1800–1850

A. Venetsianov—(1780–1847)—various canvases depicting the life of the peasants.

Pavel Fedotov (1815–1852)—'The fastidious bride', 1847.

HALL XI: 1800–1900

Perov (1833–1882)—'Hunters at rest'; 'The Troika'; portrait of Dostoevsky.

HALL XII: Aivazovsky (1817–1900)—'The Black Sea'; 'The Seaside'.

Flavitski (1830–1866)—portrait of Princess Tarakanova.

HALL XIII: works by members of the 'peredvizhniki' group, the Society of Travelling Art Exhibitions.

Savitsky (1844–1905)—'Railway Repair Work'. Marble sculpture of a peasant in distress by Chiev (1838–1916).

HALL XIV: Works by Ivan Kramskoi

Kramskoi (1837–1887) was the leader of the 'peredvizhniki' group of wandering artists. Works in this hall include 'Christ in the Wilderness', 'The Stranger', portraits of Leo Tolstoy and Pavel Tretyakov, and a self-portrait.

HALL XV: Nikolai Ghe (1831–1894)—'Peter I questioning Tsarevich Alexei in Peterhof' and an unfinished canvas 'Golgotha'.

HALL XVI: A. Savrassov (1830–1897)—'The rooks have come'.

HALL XVII: Vladimir Makovski (1846–1920) —'Failure of a bank', 1881; 'The Boulevard', 1886.

HALL XVIII: Pryanishnikov (1840–1894)—'Episode from the 1812 war' (Russian women taking French soldiers prisoner).

Yaroshenko (1846–1898)—'Life everywhere' (pigeons feeding from a convict train); portraits of prisoners, workmen, and intellectuals.

HALL XIX: Ivan Shishkin (1832–1898)—'Morning in a Pinewood', 1872; 'A corn field', 1878.

Kuindzhy (1842–1910)—'Night on the Dnieper'.

HALL XX: Polenov (1844–1927)—'Granny's Garden'; 'Overgrown Pond'.

HALL XXI: Serov (1865–1911)—'Girl with peaches'; portrait of the actress, Maria Yermoleva.

HALL XXII: Victor Vasnetsov (1848–1926)—'The three heroes'; 'Ivan the Terrible'; 'Alyonushka' (illustration of a fairy tale).

HALL XXIII: Vasily Vereschagin (1842–1904) is best known as a painter of battle scenes depicting the war between Russia and Turkey in 1871. 'Deification of war'; 'Mortally wounded'; a number of landscapes of India and Eastern Asia where the artist travelled.

HALL XXIV: Paintings by Vasily Surikov (1848–1916) who concentrated on historical scenes. 'The execution of the Streltsi'; 'Boyarinya Morozova', 1887 (a scene depicting the Old Believer Morozova being taken for investigation during the religious split of the 17th century).

HALLS XXV & XXVI: Ilya Repin.

Ilya Repin (1844–1930) is perhaps the most famous of all 19th-century Russian artists. 'Ivan the Terrible and his son' (Ivan the Terrible clutching to him his son whom he had just killed in a fit of temper); 'Not expected' (a prisoner unexpectedly arriving home); 'Princess Sophia in Novodevichy Convent'; 'Religious procession in Kursk province'; portraits of Leo Tolstoy and

Kramskoi.

HALL XXVII: Isaak Levitan (1860–1900) was famous for his landscapes. 'Eternal peace'; 'Golden Autumn'; 'Evening on the Volga'.

Antokolsky (1843–1902), sculptor–'Ivan the Terrible' in marble and 'Peter I' in bronze.

HALL XXVIII: Ancient Russian Art (on the ground floor, down the steps in hall XXVI).

The ancient religious art of Russia was clearly definable by the different schools which grew up in the leading religious centres. The first works in this hall belong to the Kievan school and date from the 10th and 11th centuries.

The mosaic 'Dmitri Solunsky' dates from about 1060 and once adorned the Sofiisky Cathedral in Kiev which was built at the same time. Dmitri Solunsky was a warrior in Macedonia in the 3rd century and came to be represented in art as the epitome of strength and bravery.

The 12th-century icon of 'Our Lady of Vladimir' was brought to Kiev from Byzantium. In 1155 it was moved to Vladimir, whence its name, and in 1395 to the Cathedral of the Assumption in Moscow. It was revered as a miracle-working icon.

The next icons belong to the Novgorodian school and include 'The Annunciation' (12th century), 'St. Nicholas' (12th century, found in the Novodevichy Convent), 'St. George' (15th century) and 'The battle between Novgorod and Suzdal' (a good example of the epic style of icon painting).

HALL XXIX: Icons of the Moscow school, 14th to 17th centuries. Icons of Theophanes the Greek who came from Byzantium and worked in the Cathedral of the Annunciation in the Kremlin, including 'The Transfiguration' from Pereslavl-Zaleski and 'The Assumption' from the Kremlin in Moscow.

Andrei Rublyev (d. 1430)—one of the most famous of all icons, 'The Trinity' from the Troitsy-Sergei Lavra in Zagorsk. A number of icons attributed to the school of Rublyev, including 'The Apostle Paul' and 'The Archangel Michael'.

Simon Ushakov (1626–1686)—'Our Lady of Vladimir'.

HALL XXX: Vrubel (1856–1910)—'The Demon'; 'Pan'; 'Nightfall'.

Konenkov (1874–1973), sculptor—'Stone Crusher' (Bronze).

HALLS XXXI–LI: Works of Grabar, Konchalovskii, Rerich, Sariyan, Brodsky, Golubkina, Ioganson, Kustodiev, Yuon, Gerasimov, Reshetnikov, Neprintsev, and Prorokov among others. Political cartoons by Yefimov are displayed in Hall 43.

Pushkin Fine Arts Museum, Volkhonka St. 12. Near Kropotkinskaya metro station. Open 10.30–8; closed Tues. and last day of each month. The museum, first known as Alexander III's museum, opened in 1912. The building, which was largely financed by Madame Alekseevna, was designed by Academician Klein and completed in the same year.

After the Hermitage in Leningrad this is the largest museum in the country. It was first planned, however, not as a museum of original works of art, but as an educational museum serving the needs of Moscow University. For this purpose, many copies of Egyptian, Greek, and Roman works of art were made under the direction of Professor Tsvetayev, the first director of the museum.

The museum collection was greatly enhanced by a number of donations, most notably those by the collector Golenischev of Ancient Egyptian Art and Ancient Coptic Art. In 1925 the collection of West European paintings which had belonged to Sergei Tretyakov was moved here from the Tretyakov Gallery, and also the renowned collection of French art which had belonged before the Revolution to two patrons of art, Morozov and Schukin.

In the first hall of the gallery is the collection of Ancient Egyptian Art dating from the 4th century B.C. to the 1st century A.D.

Hall 2 contains works of art dating from the 3rd century B.C. to the 7th century A.D. from Babylon, Assyria, Persia, etc.

Spanish and Italian art (Halls 28 and 29) is represented by such artists as Murillo, José de Ribera, Botticelli, Romano, and Fetti.

Hall 30 is devoted to Dutch art of the 17th century, including works by Ruisdael, Rembrandt, Steen, and Ostade. The next hall contains works by Flemish artists including Rubens and Van Dyck.

One of the most treasured sections is the collection of French paintings in Halls 27 to 22. Artists included here are Poussin (Hall 27), Watteau and David (Hall 25), Delacroix, Rousseau, and Géricault (Hall 24), Cézanne, Courbet, Manet, Matisse, Gauguin, Van Gogh, Picasso, and Monet (Halls 23 and 22).

Andrei Rublyev Museum of Ancient Art, Pryamikov Sq. 10. Open Mon. and Thurs. 2–7; Tues. 11–3; Fri., Sat., Sun. 12–5; closed Wed. The museum is inside the walls of the former Andronikov monastery which was founded in 1359 by St. Alexei and Andronikov, who became the first abbot here and whose name the monastery bears. The monastery, which was originally made entirely of wood, was also a fortress on the road to Vladimir. The white stone walls and towers which stand today were built during the second half of the 17th century.

In the monastery is the oldest cathedral in Moscow, the Spassky Cathedral which was built in 1420–7. The cathedral was decorated by Andrei Rublyev, Russia's most famous icon painter, who was a monk in the monastery and who was buried here in 1430. Unfortunately all the decorations were destroyed except for fragments of the murals, believed to be the work of Rublyev, which were found around the windows which were once blocked up.

The refectory building, built of brick with a high sloping roof, was erected in 1504. In 1691–4 the Arkhangelskaya (Archangel) Church was built onto the northern and eastern walls of the refectory.

The museum, which was opened in 1960, contains a number of icons dating from the 15th to 17th centuries. Most of the icons were found in churches and monasteries in old Russian towns and have been restored. The collection is being constantly enlarged.

Museum of Eastern Cultures (Muzei Vostochnykh Kultur), Obukh St. 16. Open 11–6; Wed. and Fri. 2–9; closed Mon. The museum was opened in 1918 and comprised several private collections, including the Schukin collection, which had been taken over by the state. The collection has since been expanded and besides exhibits from India, China, and Japan, now has an interesting section of exhibits from the Soviet East.

The Chinese section includes stone bowls dating from the first millennium B.C., Chinese scrolls, wood and ivory carvings, and silk pictures.

Other exhibits of interest are the collection of miniature Japanese sculptures, Persian carpets, and Turkish gold-embroidered satin.

Exhibition of Russian Decorative Folk Art, Petrovka St. 28. Open 12–7; closed Tues. and the last day of the month. The choice collection is beautifully displayed and includes textiles, lace and embroidery, ceramics, wood carvings, decorative metal work, and tiles.

It is housed in the Naryshkin House of the Vysoko-Petrovsky Monastery. The monastery was found by Dmitri Donskoy in the village of Vysoko to commemorate his victory over the Tatars of Kulikovo. The name Vysoko-Petrovsky was bestowed during rebuilding by Grand Prince Vasily Ivanovich. Three additional churches and the Naryshkin House were built by Peter I at the end of the 17th century. The monastery is in a good state of preservation and forms one of the largest complexes of old Russian architecture in the centre of Moscow.

Handicraft museum (Muzei Narodnovo Iskusstva), Stanislavsky St. 7. Open 11–5; closed Sat. Samples of traditional lace and embroidery work, wood and bone carving, lacquer boxes, etc. can be seen in this museum. The exhibits are displayed in sections according to their geographical location. The museum building was designed in 1870 in the style of the 17th-century Russian architecture.

Exhibition of Russian chattels of the 17th–19th centuries, 18/2 Razin St. The exhibition is housed in the House of the Boyars Romanov (see p. 201–2).

Simon Ushakov Museum, Nikitnikov Pereulok 3 (off Razin St.). The Trinity Church in Nikitniki, which is now open as the Simon Ushakov Museum, was built in 1634 for Grigory Nikitnikov, a rich merchant and manufacturer. The church is notable for its murals on which Simon Ushakov worked together with other Moscow artists. Many of them portray parables, which hitherto had been seldom used as motifs for church decorations and which are explicit of the more worldly attitude brought into the Church by such

merchant patrons as Nikitnikov. Grigory Nikitnikov, together with his family, is portrayed in the mural on the southern wall of the church.

Shchusev Architectural Museum, Kalinin Prospect 5. Open 10–6; Wed. and Fri. 12–8; closed Tues. Academician Shchusev (1873–1949) was a well-known Soviet architect who designed, among other things, the Lenin mausoleum. The museum covers the principal trends in Russian architecture from 1037 to the present day.

Donskoi Monastery, Donskaya Sq. 1. A branch of the museum of Russian architecture is housed in the cathedral of this monastery. Open 11–6; closed Mon. and the last day of every month.

The fortress-monastery was founded by Tsar Feodor in 1592 to commemorate Moscow's deliverance from the Crimean Khan, Kasi-Gerei, in 1591. It is built on the camp site of the Russian troops who were sent to fight against the Crimean Khan as he approached Moscow.

The only building dating from the 16th century still standing is a small church, known as the 'Maly Sobor' (Small Cathedral). The rest of the present-day buildings were erected between 1680 and 1730.

The stone walls with twelve towers were built at the end of the 17th century. The Big Cathedral (Bolshoi Sobor) was built in 1684–98. The five-domed cathedral is a typical example of Moscow Baroque and contains a fine carved iconostasis which was made by Moscow craftsmen in 1693–8.

The museum is located in the cathedral. The display is very similar to that of the Shchusev museum. In the former private church and chapel of the Princess Golitsyn which was built in 1809 are Russian monumental sculptures of the 18th and 19th centuries.

The cemetery within the monastery walls contains many monuments to nobles, some of them the work of such renowned sculptures as Vitali and Martos.

Historical Museums

Lenin Mausoleum. On Red Sq. by the Kremlin walls. Open 1–4; Sun. 12–5; closed Mon. and Fri. To avoid standing in the long queue, tourists should ask Intourist to arrange a special time for an accompanied visit.

The body of Vladimir Lenin (1870–1924), founder of the Communist Party and the Soviet State, whose real name was Ulyanov, lies here. Stalin's body also lay in the mausoleum from his death in 1953 until 1961, when it was removed by popular demand and buried near the Kremlin wall among other Communist leaders, including Frunze, Kirov, Sverdlov, and Dzerzhinsky.

The building of the mausoleum was constructed in 1930 by Shchusev and is generally agreed to be well-planned, harmonising with the older structures surrounding the square. It is made of red granite with black and grey labradorite. The present building replaced a wooden mausoleum which was erected after Lenin's death in 1924.

Steps lead up on both sides of the mausoleum to the roof where members of the government stand to watch parades and demonstrations in the square.

Two guards stand at the entrance to the mausoleum. Steps lead down to the underground vault where the embalmed body lies in a glass sarcophagus. A railing surrounds the sarcophagus and four guards stand nearby.

Lenin Museum, Revolution Sq. 4. Open 11–7; closed Mon. The museum was opened in 1936 following a resolution taken by the Central Committee of the Soviet Communist Party.

It is housed in the Duma ('parliament') building which was constructed by Chichagov in pseudo-Russian style in 1890–2. It was built in red brick to blend with the earlier building of the Historical Museum alongside.

Over 7000 exhibits are displayed in the 22 halls of the museum. They cover the main periods of the life and work of the founder of the Soviet State, Vladimir Ilyich Lenin. Among the exhibits are some of Lenin's personal belongings such as a desk with secret drawers, a coat with bullet-holes (the result of an attempt on his life in 1918), and his car. In one of the halls is a replica of his study in the Kremlin.

A newsreel of 1917–24, in which Lenin appears and speaks, is shown. There are also numerous sculptures, paintings, carpets, carvings, and embroideries portraying the founder of the Communist Party.

Museum of History, Red Sq., on north side. Open Mon., Thurs., Sun. 10.30–5.30; Wed., Fri., Sat. 12–7. Closed Tues. and last day of each month. The building was constructed in 1874–83 by the architect Sherwood and the engineer Semyonov under the influence of 17th-century Russian architecture. The museum was initiated by Moscow University and the first 11 halls were opened in 1883. It now has 300,000 exhibits and is the biggest repository of historical material and documents tracing the origin and history of the peoples of the Soviet Union from ancient times until the 1917 Revolution.

The first seven halls carry the story up to the 1st century A.D. The painting 'Stone Age' on the ceiling of the second hall is the work of the artist Vasnetsov and was commissioned for this hall in 1883–5.

Hall 9 contains many archaeological finds from Novgorod dating from the 9th to 15th centuries. There are models of old Novgorodian churches as well as a collection of icons from Novgorod and Pskov dating from the 14th and 15th centuries.

Hall 13 contains a number of interesting exhibits relating the development of central Russia in the 14th and 15th centuries. There are a number of icons, including the icon of 'The Virgin Mary with Sergei Radonezh' which is attributed to the school of Andrei Rublyov. There are fragments of the wooden streets of Novgorod, which are thought to have been relaid 28 times in the course of 700 years, and part of the bows of a rowing boat dating from the 12th century. The fresco is a contemporary reconstruction of the Moscow Kremlin during the 16th century.

Hall 15 contains a number of beautifully illustrated manuscripts and the first book to be published in Russia, the *Apostle* of 1564.

Hall 20 relates the history of the beginning of the 18th century when St. Petersburg was founded by Peter the Great. There are many documents relating the reforms carried out by Peter and, in one of the show-cases, garments belonging to the tsar.

Hall 23 relates the history of the second half of the 18th century, in particular the Peasant's Revolt of 1773–4. Above a portrait of Catherine II (1762–96) is one of the peasant leader Pugachev painted by an unknown artist in 1774. Also on display is the iron cage in which Pugachev was brought to Moscow after the revolt had been supressed.

Hall 28, the walls of which are covered with banners captured from the French army and of the Russian regiments, contains varied exhibits pertaining to the 1812 war. On the right of the hall is a marble bust of Napoleon by an unknown artist which was brought to Russia in order to be erected on the main square of Moscow. Also here is the field kitchen and sledge which Napoleon used during the campaign.

The remaining halls illustrate the history of the 19th century, including the Crimean War and the abolition of serfdom. Halls 38 and 39 are devoted to scientific, literary, and artistic developments.

The last hall, 40, contains documents relating to the 1917 Revolution and the personal belongings and arms of the revolutionaries who stormed the Winter Palace in St. Petersburg.

Museum of the Revolution, Gorky St. 21. Open Mon., Wed., Fri. 12–8; Tues., Thurs., Sun. 10–6; Closed Sat. The museum is housed in the building of the former English Club (see p. 206). The six-inch gun in the forecourt was used by revolutionary troops to fire on the Kremlin in October 1917.

The museum, which was opened in 1926, has 11 halls, the exhibits of which trace the history of the revolution from 1915 until 1917 and also the evolution of socialism in the Soviet Union. Among the exhibits are battle-standards of the revolutionary troops, the horse-drawn machine-gun cart of the First Cavalry Army, texts of the first decrees of the Soviet government and many photographs, paintings, and sculptures. Some of the halls display presents to the Soviet Union from foreign countries, including many given on the 50th anniversary of the Revolution.

Marx and Engels Museum, Marx Engels St. 5. The museum exhibits relate to the life and work of Marx and Engels and include manuscripts, letters, photographs, and early editions of their works. Also on display are a number of personal belongings of Marx, including the chair in which he died.

Soviet Army Museum, Kommuny Sq. 2. Open Tues., Fri. 10–7; Wed., Thurs. 12–8. Closed Mon. The museum is devoted to the history of the armed forces of the Soviet Union, and the museum building was completed in 1965.

The periods most fully represented in the museum are the years of the Civil War and of World War II. The display starts with the story of the workers' combatant groups of the 1905 revolution. While preparing for the armed uprising of 1917, the Bolshevik party established the 'Red Guards', the core of the future Red Army. The appropriate decree was signed by Lenin on 28 January, 1918; the official celebration date is 23 February.

On display are hand-grenades, swords, and Maxim machine-guns (often the only weapons of the first Red Army units) and also some handmade weapons used by the Siberian guerrillas. The stands show personal belongings of some outstanding Red Army commanders, such as Chapayev, Frunze, and Budyonnyi. Among the exhibits of the years 1922 to 1939 are pictures of the first people to be awarded the title of Hero of the Soviet Union; these were pilots who rescued 100 members of the polar expedition on the icebreaker 'Chelyuskin'.

The remainder of the exhibits refer to the conflicts with the Japanese (1937) and the Finns (1939–40), and the greater part of the Second World War. The display ends with exhibits demonstrating the present state of the Soviet Armed Forces and includes modern small arms, models of modern tanks, and a self-propelled rocket launcher.

Outdoors, in the museum grounds, are an armoured train, some tanks, planes, and other large exhibits.

The museum used to be in the next-door building, founded in the 18th century and rebuilt following Ghilardi's plans in 1802. In 1812 it was damaged by fire, and was again reconstructed in Classical style by Ghilardi and Grigoryev housed Catherine the Great's school for young ladies of noble birth. It is now Soviet Army House.

Kutuzov's Hut Museum, Kutuzovsky Prospect 38. Open 10–7; closed Mon. Here in 1812 the Russian War Council, headed by Field-Marshal Mikhail Kutuzov, decided that it was necessary to retreat from Moscow in order to save the army. The painting by Kivshenko (1880) shows the council in session. In front of the hut is an obelisk, on which are inscribed the famous words of Field-Marshal Kutuzov: 'The loss of Moscow is not yet the loss of Russia. For the good of our fatherland I order a retreat.'

Battle of Borodino Museum, Near Kutuzov's Hut and the Triumphal Arch (see p. 207). Open 11–7; closed Fri. The first building for the panorama was built at the beginning of this century, but it was damaged by fire and the present building was completed in 1962 to commemorate the 150th anniversary of the historic Battle of Borodino in August 1812, when Napoleon's Great Army suffered a serious defeat. The cylindrical building is 42 m. in diameter.

The canvases of the panorama were painted in Munich by Roubaud (1865–1912), who came from Odessa and was also responsible for the Sevastopol Panorama. They are 14 m. high and the cylinder they form is 115 m. in circumference.

The Museum of the history and reconstruction of Moscow, Novaya Sq. 12. Metro Dzerzhinskaya. Open Mon. 10–3; Wed., Fri. 2–9; Thurs., Sun. 10–5; Sat. 10–6; closed Tues. and last day of each month.

The museum is housed in the former Church of St. John the Baptist, built in 1825. It was founded in 1896 and by maps, photographs, engravings, lithographs, and models gives an outline of the history of Moscow's rise, telling the part it played in different periods of Russian history.

The reconstruction section deals with the modernization of the public services, building programmes, and plans of how the city will look in the future.

The display of presents received by the City of Moscow on the 800th anniversary of its foundation in 1947 is of interest.

Literary, theatrical, and musical museums

Leo Tolstoy Museum, Kropotkinskaya St. 11. Open daily except Tues. Mon. 10–3; Wed. Fri. 2–8; Thurs., Sat., Sun. 11–5. The museum is housed in the former Lopukhin mansion (see p. 208). It contains a very full collection of the writer's manuscripts covered in his corrections, as well as part of his personal library and a number of paintings and papers illustrating his life. Of interest are the 17 sketches Tolstoy intended to illustrate 'Around the world in 80 days' by Jules Verne.

However, many people consider the museum to be less interesting than Tolstoy's Moscow home.

Tolstoy's Moscow Home, Lev Tolstoy St. 21. Open 10–4.30; closed Tues. Sixteen rooms of this house are preserved as they were during the time that Tolstoy lived here with his family from 1882 to 1909.

Chekhov Museum, Sadovo Kudrinskaya St. 6. Open Mon., Thurs., Sat. 11–6; Wed., Fri. 2–9; closed Tues. and Sun. Anton Chekhov lived here during the 1880s, and a brass plate reading 'Dr. A. P. Chekhov' can still be seen on the door.

Dostoevsky Museum, Dostoevsky St. 4. Open

Thurs., Sat., Sun. 11–6; Mon. 10–4; Wed. and Fri. 1–9; closed Tues.

Gorky's House, Kachalova St. 6/2. Maxim Gorky lived here from 1931 to 1936.

Gorky Museum, Vorovsky St. 25a. Open Tues., Fri. 1–8; Wed., Thurs., Sun. 10–5; Sat. 10.30–4; closed Mon.

The house in which the museum is situated was built in the 1820s by Ivan Ghilardi. The museum was opened in 1937 and contains books, letters, manuscripts, and photographs illustrating the writer's life. The monument to Gorky in front of the museum was designed by Vera Mukhina.

Pushkin Museum, Kropotkinskaya St. 12/2. Open Sat. 1–7.30; Sun. 11–5.30. This mansion was built in 1814 (see p. 208). The exhibits include manuscripts, letters, first editions, and paintings relating to the life and work of the poet.

Bakhrushin Theatrical Museum, Bakhrushin St. 31/12. Near Paveletskaya metro station. Open 12–7; Wed., Fri. 2–9; closed Tues. This museum was founded in 1894 by the theatre-lover and collector whose name it now bears and is located in his house. The exhibits relate the history of Russian drama, opera, and ballet theatres from the 18th century to the present day. The exhibits include portraits of actors, manuscripts, playbills, programmes, personal belongings, and photographs.

Glinka Museum, Georgievsky Pereulok 4. Open 9–5.30; closed Sun. The museum is housed in the Boyar Troyekurov's Mansion (see p. 202).

The display includes scores, letters, photographs, and recordings of famous composers and performers. Of special interest is the collection of musical instruments.

Skryabin Museum, Vakhtangov St. 11. Open Mon., Thurs., Sun. 1–5; Tues., Fri., Sat. 3–7; closed Wed. The well-known Russian composer and pianist Alexander Skryabin (1871–1915) lived and died here.

Economic, scientific, and technical museums and exhibitions

The U.S.S.R. Exhibition of Economic Achievements. This is located in the north-western part of Moscow, the main entrance being on Prospect Mira, on the way to Ostankino. The exhibition occupies a site of 216 hectares (553 acres) and includes about 80 large pavilions and many smaller structures. There is a 5-km. circular road with various forms of public transport, including small buses, open car-trains, and motor-bike taxis.

There are pavilions built in the architectural styles of the different Soviet republics, and also many large pavilions devoted to different branches of agriculture, industry, and science.

Among them are the pavilions 'Atomic Energy', 'Education', 'Science', 'Radio-Electronics', and 'Machine-Building', a domed pavilion where there is a display of Russian cars. One of the largest pavilions is the pavilion 'Cosmos'. In front of the pavilion there is a multi-stage rocket which is a replica of the one which launched Yuri Gagarin on the first manned space flight.

Also in the exhibition grounds are a circus, a circorama cinema, and an open-air theatre. There are many restaurants and cafés, but the best is probably the Zolotoi Kolos (Golden Ear) restaurant.

By the main entrance to the exhibition is a monument to commemorate Soviet space exploration. The monument, which is 90 m. high, was erected in 1964 and there is a museum inside. In front of the monument is a statue of Konstantin Tsiolkovsky. A number of busts of leading scientists and cosmonauts line the avenue from the space monument to Prospect Mira.

In front of the North Gates entrance is a stainless steel statue 'Worker and Farm-Woman' by Vera Mukhina, which was designed for the Paris Fair of 1937.

Polytechnical Museum, Novaya Sq. 3/4. Open on Tues., Thurs., Sat. 1–8; Wed., Fri., Sun. 10–5; closed Mon.

This museum contains a large collection of technical and scientific exhibits, including some on space exploration. It also has a technical library.

The building itself was constructed in Russian style in the 1870s from plans by Monighetti.

Natural History Museum, Gertsen St. 6. Open 9–4; closed Sun.

Timiryazev Biological Museum, Malaya Gruzinskaya St. 15. Open 10–6; Wed., Fri. 12–8; closed Mon.

The museum is named after Kliment Timiryazev (1843–1920), who championed Darwinism in Russia. His work as a botanist was chiefly concerned with photosynthesis.

The exhibits of the museum illustrate plant and animal life, and the origins and development of life on Earth.

Darwin Museum, Malaya Pirogovskaya St. 1. Open 10–5; closed Sun.

Durov's Corner, Durov St. 4. Open 11–5; Thurs. 10–3; Sun. 10–5; closed Fri.

Durov's Corner is named after the famous Russian animal tamer and circus clown, Vladimir Durov (1863–1934). About 200 trained animals and birds are kept here. They can be seen in their cages and performing on the stage of the Animal Theatre (seating 120) on Sat. at 1 pm and on Sundays at 11, 1, and 3. More than 50 animals can be seen in 'Terem-Teremok', a fairy tale. There is

---

PLATES OPPOSITE

Above, the blue-domed Gur Emir Mausoleum which contains the tomb of Timur (Tamberlaine), the Tatar conqueror of Samarkand and Bukhara, whose Kalan Mosque, *below*, can accommodate 10,000 people in its courtyard.

also a production called 'The Story of How the Animals of Grandfather Durov's Corner Flew to the Moon'.

Planetarium, Sadovaya-Kudrinskaya St. 5. Open 9–8.30; closed Tues.

Zoo, Bolshaya Gruzinskaya St. 1.

Botanical Garden, Academy of Sciences, Ostankino, Botanicheskaya St. 4. The botanical garden was opened in 1959 and occupies a site of 360 hectares (900 acres), which includes an attractive park and some forest land where elk may be encountered.

Botanical Garden of Moscow University, Prospect Mira 26. This botanical garden was founded in 1706 and was originally known as Apothecary Garden (see p. 209).

Parks and Recreational Facilities

Gorky Park, Krymsky Val 9. Near Oktyabrskaya and Park Kultury metro stations. Open from 9 to midnight (see p. 205). In the park there are amusements, sports grounds, a boating station, a chess club, a shooting gallery, a restaurant, cafés, a beer hall, and an open-air theatre seating 12,000. In winter many of the paths of the park are flooded and used for skating.

Sokolniki Park, Sokolniki metro station. Sokolniki Park is named after the falconers (sokolniki) who used to live here and attend the tsars' hunting parties. For over a hundred years it was a popular place to go for picnics, and the nobility used to drive their coaches along the avenues. It has become widely known for the American, Japanese, British, French, and other national fairs held here. Each country has added to the exhibition site's equipment and accommodation.

In the park are also an open-air theatre seating 5000, an amusement park, a shooting gallery, bicycles for hire, restaurants, and cafés. In winter the park which covers an area of 612 hectares (1530 acres) is a popular place to ski and one can hire skis here.

Izmailovo Park, Izmailovskaya metro station. Open 10 am–11 pm. The park covers 1180 hectares (2950 acres) and includes large stretches of pine forest. It was once the manor of the Romanov family and a favourite resort of the tsars. Here, in a disused storehouse, Peter the Great found the old English boat which is now known as the 'grandfather of the Russian fleet' and kept in a museum in Leningrad. There is an amusement park, an open-air theatre, and several cafés.

Hermitage Garden, Karetnyi Ryad 3. Open 10–10. This small garden has retained its popularity since the 1890s. During the summer season there are concerts and performances by variety and puppet theatres, and there are several cafés and a restaurant.

Hippodrome Racecourse, Begovaya St. 22. Races on Wed., Sat., and Sun. at 5 pm and Sun. also at 1 pm.

The racecourse was founded in 1883. Its gates are decorated with figures of people and horses by K. Klodt, the grandson of the architect P. Klodt, which resemble the latter's famous sculptures on the Anichkov Bridge in Leningrad.

There are about 500 horses in the stables, and there is a totalisator and a restaurant.

Lenin Stadium, in Luzhniki, near Komsomolsky Prospect and Leninskiye Gory metro station. The complex was built in 1955–6 by Vlasov, Rozhin, and other architects. Major national and international sports events are held here. The large arena can seat 103,000. There is also a Children's Sport Area and many different sections for swimming, tennis, basket-ball, and other sports.

Dynamo Stadium, Leningradsky Prospect (see p. 206). This is Moscow's second largest stadium and can seat 60,000.

The Moskva Open-air Swimming Pool, opposite Kropotkinskaya metro station.

The pool is open all the year and is heated to a temperature of 28–30°C. in winter. It is covered in a cloud of steam in cold weather which protects bathers from the cold air.

Bathing beaches. There are bathing beaches at Serebryanyi Bor (Silver Grove), Khimki, and the recreation area beside the Klyazma Reservoir.

Transport

The Metro. Open 6 am–1 am. The metro is the pride of the city. Its three main lines crossing in the centre are linked by a circle line crossing them each in turn and forming a junction with four newer lines which serve the suburbs. This basic spider-web plan follows the layout of the city itself.

The metro works perfectly from a technical point of view; the escalators, air-conditioning, and the passenger tunnels are all well planned. During the rush hour trains leave the stations at intervals of 90 seconds and the maximum speed is 90 km.

The decor of each station is a separate work of art; some give the impression of a palace, with soft lights shining on the marble columns and intricate mosaics. Each line has its characteristic features; the noble simplicity of the Sokolniki-Yugo-Zapadnaya line is in contrast to the extravagant grandeur of the Circle Line. One of the most impressive stations is Mayakovskaya, named in honour of the poet Mayakovsky whose statue stands in the square above. Here the columns are of stainless steel and red marble, and the mosaics on the ceilings were made from paintings by A. Deineka, a well-known artist in the Soviet Union. The first line of the metro was opened in 1935, and new construction is always in progress. The newer stations, however, are much plainer.

There is a standard fare of 5 kopeks. To enter the metro one must drop a 5-kopek piece into the turnstile on one's right hand side and wait for the yellow light to change.

Boat Trips. Boat trips along the river operate

from May or June until September or October depending on the weather.

Route 1: From the Kiev terminal (in front of the Kievsky Station) eastwards to the Novospassky Bridge. On this route one passes the Novodevichy Convent, Lenin Hills and stadium, and the Kremlin. The trip lasts 1 hour 20 minutes and the fare is 15 kopeks.

Route 2: From Kiev terminal westwards to Kuntsevo-Krylatskoye. This route goes to the Fili-Kuntsevo Park and the river beach. The trip lasts 1 hour and the fare is 15 kopeks.

There is a standard fare on *buses, trolley-buses, and trams* of 5, 4, and 3 kopeks respectively. On most routes the last run is made at 1 am.

Monuments

Dzerzhinsky Monument, Dzerzhinsky Sq. This statue of Felix Dzerzhinsky (1877–1926), revolutionary and statesman, was designed by Yevgeni Vuchetich in 1958.

Feodorov Monument, Teatralnaya Proezd. Ivan Feodorov was the first Russian printer, and the date on the pedestal, 19 April 1563, is that on which the printing of the first Russian book was begun. The statue is by Sergei Volnukhin and was erected in 1909.

Gogol Statue, Arbatskaya Sq. This statue of Nikolai Gogol (1809–52) by N. Tomsky was erected in 1952.

Gorky Statue, by the Byelorussky railway station. Designed by Ivan Shadr and made from his sketches by Mukhina, Zelenskaya, and Ivanovia, the statue was unveiled on 10 June, 1951.

Grenadiers of Plevna Monument, Ilyinskiye Vorota. This monument, designed by V. Sherwood, was erected in 1887. It was built with funds collected by the survivors of the grenadiers who fought at the Battle of Plevna (1887) during the liberation of Bulgaria from the Ottoman Empire.

Griboyedov Monument, Kirovskiye Vorota, Chistoprudnyi Boulevard. Alexander Griboyedov (1798–1829) is famed for his single play, 'Woe from Wit', which was rejected by the censor and only staged two years after he was murdered while serving as Ambassador to Persia. The statue of him by N. Manuilov was erected in 1959.

Karl Marx Monument, Sverdlov Sq. This monument to the philosopher by Lev Kerbel was unveiled to mark the 22nd Soviet Communist Party Congress in 1961. The street in front of it was renamed Marx Prospect at the same time.

Lenin Monument, Sovietskaya Sq., in front of the Marxism-Leninism Institute. This statue by S. Merkurov was exhibited at the New York World Fair in 1939 before it was erected here in 1940.

Lermontov Monument, Lermontov Sq. This 5 m. statue by Brodsky was unveiled in 1965 to commemorate the 150th anniversary of the poet's birth.

Lomonosov Monuments, in front of the Old University building, Marx Prospect and in the courtyard of the New University building on Lenin

Hills. Mikhail Lomonosov (1711–65), was the scientist and encyclopaedist who founded Moscow University in 1755. The statue on Lenin Hills is by N. Tomsky and was erected in 1954.

Mayakovsky Monument, Mayakovsky Sq. This statue of Vladimir Mayakovsky (1893–1930), poet and playwright, was designed by A. Kibalnikov and erected in 1958.

Minin and Pozharsky Monument, on Red Sq., in front of St. Basil's Cathedral (see pp. 200–201).

Obelisk, in Alexandrovsky Gardens, beside the Kremlin Wall. This obelisk was erected in 1913 in commemoration of the 300th anniversary of the House of Romanov and was engraved with the names of the Russian tsars. After the Revolution these and the double-headed eagle were eradicated, and replaced with the names of Marx, Engels, Marat, Plekhanov, Spartacus, and other revolutionaries and philosophers.

Ostrovsky Monument, Sverdlov Sq., in front of the Maly Theatre. Alexander N. Ostrovsky (1823–86) was a popular satirical playwright, and is regarded as the founder of Russian drama. The monument to him by Nikolai Andreyev was erected in 1929 in front of the theatre where his plays were, and still are, staged.

Pirogov Monument, Bolshaya Pirogovskaya St. This monument to Nikolai Pirogov, surgeon and scientist, by V. Sherwood, was erected in 1897.

Pushkin Monument, Lermontov Sq. This statue by A. Opekushin was erected to the poet's memory by popular subscription in 1880.

Repin Monument, Bolotnaya Sq. This statue of artist Ilya Repin was created by M. Manizer in 1958.

Sechenov Monument, Bolshaya Pirogovskaya St. 2/6. Ivan Sechenov (1829–1905) is known as the father of Russian physiology; he was a professor of both St. Petersburg and Moscow universities. This statue, which was erected in 1958, is by Lev Kerbel.

Shevchenko Monument, in front of the Ukraina Hotel, Naberezhnaya Shevchenko. Taras Shevchenko is the best known Ukrainian poet (1814–61) and this statue was unveiled in 1964 to mark the 150th anniversary of his birth.

Tchaikovsky Monument, Gertsen St., in front of the conservatoire. This seated statue of the composer was designed by Vera Mukhina and erected in 1954.

Timiryazev Monument, Nikitskiye Vorota. This monument to the naturalist and follower of Darwin was designed by Sergei Merkurov and erected in 1923.

Tombstones of the Soviet Union's Outstanding Leaders. Beside the Kremlin wall, on Red Sq. Here lie Sverdlov, Frunze, Dzerzhinsky, Kalinin, Stalin, and others.

Tsiolkovsky Monument, at the foot of the soaring rocket monument on Prospect Mira. Konstantin Tsiolkovsky (1857–1935) was a pioneer in the theory of cosmic travel and rocketry.

Vorovsky Monument, at the crossing of Kuznetsky Most and Dzerzhinsky St. The memorial to the literary critic and diplomat, who was assassinated in Switzerland in 1923, was erected in the year following his death by M. Kats.

Worker and Farm-Woman Statue, at the entrance to the Exhibition of Economic Achievements. This gigantic statue created in 1937 by Vera Mukhina was on show at the Soviet Exhibition in Paris in that year.

Yuri Dolgoruky Statue, Sovietskaya Sq., Prince Yuri Dolgoruky founded Moscow in 1147, and the foundation of this commemorative equestrian statue was laid to mark the 800th anniversary of the event. It is by Sergei Orlov.

Theatres, concert halls, and cinemas

Bolshoi Theatre, Sverdlov Sq. This theatre was formerly known as the Great Imperial Theatre. It was built by Bovet in 1824 and restored after a fire in 1854 by Cavos. The statue of Phoebus in the Sun Chariot above the ionic portico is famous.

The theatre company is known all over the world for its incomparable ballet, and Russian and foreign operas are also in the repertoire. The orchestra, too, is one of the best in the country.

Maly (Little) Theatre, Sverdlov Sq. 1/6. (Affiliated theatre, Bolshaya Ordinka St. 69). This theatre, built by Bovet in 1824 and reconstructed by Thon in 1838–40, was formerly known as the Little Imperial Theatre.

It has been well known for many years for its staging of Russian classical plays, especially those by the satirist Ostrovsky, a statue of whom stands by the entrance. Plays by other Russian and Soviet playwrights as well as those translated from other languages are in the current repertoire.

The Moscow Arts Theatre, Proyezd Khudozhestvennovo Teatra 3. This theatre was founded in 1898 by the famous Russian actor and director, Stanislavsky (1863–1938), and Nemirovich-Danchenko (1858–1943). They staged Chekhov's and Gorky's plays here and it was here that Konstantin Stanislavsky developed his theories, based on the realistic traditions of the Russian theatre, which became known as the Stanislavsky method. After the production of Chekhov's 'The Seagull', they chose the bird as their emblem and it now decorates the curtain, tickets, and programmes.

The Moscow Arts Theatre, New Building, Tverskoy Boulevard 24. (Opened 1973).

Stanislavsky and Nemirovich-Danchenko Musical Theatre, Pushkinskaya St. 17. This theatre, which has a repertoire of classical and modern operas, operettas, and ballets, is named after the popular Russian actor and director.

Palace of Congress, Kremlin, entrance for performances through the white-washed Kutafia Gate (by the Manège) which leads to the Trinity Gate (Troyitskiye Vorota) (see p. 209). Performances by the Bolshoi theatre and visiting companies are held here.

Operetta Theatre, Pushkinskaya St. 6

Central Puppet Theatre, Sadovo-Samotechnaya (and in the summer often in the Hermitage Garden Summer Theatre).

This theatre is often known simply as Obraztsov's Theatre after its founder and present director. The performances for adults are well worth seeing.

Central Soviet Army Drama Theatre, Kommuny Sq. 2. This theatre, designed by Alabyan and Simbirtsev in 1934–8, is built in the shape of a huge five-pointed star.

Lenin Komsomol Theatre, Chekhov St. 6

Mayakovsky Drama Theatre, Gertsen St. 19

Moscow Theatre of Drama and Comedy on Taganka, Chkalov St. 76. Opposite the Taganskaya metro station. This theatre is considered by many to be the most progressive and lively in Moscow. Most of the performances involve music, and such pantomimes as 'Ten days that shook the world' are to be recommended to those who do not understand Russian, as well as the productions of foreign playwrights including Brecht and Molière.

Pushkin Drama Theatre, Tverskoi Boulevard 23

Romany Theatre, Pushkinskaya St. 20. This is the only gipsy theatre in the world, and many of the performances include gipsy songs and dances.

Satire Theatre, Bolshaya Sadova St. 18

Sovremennik (Contemporary) Theatre, Chistoprudny Boulevard 19

Vakhtangov Drama Theatre, Arbat St. 26. This theatre is named after Stanislavsky's pupil, Evgeny Vakhtangov (1883–1922).

Variety Theatre, Bersenevskaya Naberezhnaya 20/2

Yermolova Drama Theatre, Gorky St. 5. This theatre is called after the most famous Russian actress, Maria Yermolova (1853–1928).

Tchaikovsky Conservatoire, Gertsen St. 13

Tchaikovsky Concert Hall, Mayakovsky Sq.

Kolonnyi Zal (Hall of Columns), in the House of Trade Unions, Pushkinskaya St. 1 (see p. 202)

Circorama Cinema, at the exhibition of Economic Achievements.

Cosmos Cinema, Prospect Mira 109

Mir Panorama Cinema, Tsvetnoi Boulevard 11

Octyabr Cinema, Kalinin Prospect

Metropole, Sverdlov Sq. 2. Foreign language films are sometimes shown here.

Rossiya Cinema, Pushkinskaya Sq.

Circus, Tsvetnoi Boulevard 13 and Prospect Vernadskovo 7

Hotels

Altai Hotel, Gostinichnaya St. 12, TEL. 482–58–79

Armenia Hotel, Neglinnaya St. 4, TEL. 290–06–90, 295–08–59

Belgrad Hotel, Smolenskaya St. 5, TEL. 203–77–91

Berlin Hotel, Zhdanov St. 3, TEL. 22–04–77. This Intourist hotel was formerly called the Savoy.

Bucharest Hotel, Balchug St. 1, TEL. 233–00–29, 233–09–88

Budapest Hotel, Petrovskiye Linii 2/18, TEL.

294–88–20, 294–05–41

Intourist Hotel, Gorky St. 3–5, TEL. 203–40–08
Kievskaya Hotel, Kievskaya St. 2/16, TEL. 243–40–00, 243–50–18
Leningradskaya Hotel, Kalanchovskaya St. 21/40, TEL. 225–53–00. This hotel is near the Leningrad, Yaroslavl, and Kazan railway terminals.
Metropole Hotel, Marx Prospect 1, TEL. 225–66–73 & 225–66–77. Service Bureau TEL. 225–66–54. This is an Intourist hotel.
Minsk Hotel, Gorky St. 22, TEL. 299–12–11, 299–12–15. This is an Intourist hotel.
Moskva Hotel, Marx Prospect 7, TEL. 292–60–88, 292–21–21
Mozhaisk Hotel, Mozhaiskoye Chaussée 165, TEL. 447–34–34
National Hotel, Marx Prospect 14, TEL. 203–65–39, 203–59–89. This is an Intourist hotel.
Ostankino Hotel, Botanicheskaya St. 29, TEL. 219–28–80. Situated at some distance from the city centre, this hotel is near the Ostankino Palace.
Peking Hotel, Bolshaya Sadovaya St. 1/7, TEL. 253–83–35, 253–82–47
Rossiya Hotel, Moskvoretskaya Naberezhnaya 1, near Red Sq., TEL. 298–54–01. This is an Intourist hotel.
Sovietskaya Hotel, Leningradsky Prospect 32, TEL. 250–23–42
Tsentralnaya Hotel, Gorky St. 10, TEL. 229–89–57
Ukraina Hotel, Kutuzovsky Prospect 10/9, TEL. 243–30–30, 243–31–95. This is an Intourist hotel.
Warsaw(Varshava) Hotel, Oktyzbrskaya Sq. 2/1, TEL. 231–12–05, 233–00–32

Restaurants

Aragvi Restaurant, Gorky St. 6, TEL. 229–37–62. This restaurant specialises in Georgian cuisine. The following may be recommended:
Satsivi—poultry in spicy sauce
lobio—butter beans in spicy sauce
Kharcho—spiced meat soup
Osetrina na vertelye—spit-roasted sturgeon
tsiplyata tabaka—roast spring chicken, flattened between hot stones
shashlik po kharski or po kavkazsky—pieces of mutton roasted on a skewer
koopati—Georgian sausages
Arbat Restaurant, Prospect Kalinina, TEL. 291–14–03
Ararat Restaurant, Neglinnaya St. 4, TEL. 223–57–46. This restaurant has Armenian cuisine, including:
Solyanka—soup
forel' v tyestye—trout in pastry
shashlik—mutton grilled on a skewer
chebooreki—large, succulent, and spicey cornish pasty
tolma—vine leaves stuffed with rice, meat, and prunes
Baku Restaurant, Gorky St. 24, TEL. 299–80–94.

This restaurant specialises in Azerbaijani cuisine, which is similar to Turkish, including:
dovta—sour milk and meat soup
piti—thick mutton broth with potatoes, Caucasian peas and herbs
pilaff—a choice of up to 23 different kinds
golubtsy—meat balls wrapped in vine leaves
Berlin Restaurant, Zhdanov St. 6, in the Berlin Hotel, TEL. 228–25–88
Budapest Restaurant, Petrovskiye Linii 2, in the Budapest Hotel, TEL. 221–57–67. The restaurant has mainly Hungarian cuisine.
Dubrava, 50 km. from Moscow along Kievskoye Chaussée.
Hermitage Restaurant, Karetnyi Ryad 3
Iveria, 45 km. from Moscow along the Minskoye Chaussée, TEL. 443–41–59. Georgian cuisine, as at the Aragivi Restaurant.
Metropole Restaurant, Sverdlov Sq. 2, in the Metropole Hotel, TEL. 228–40–60
Moskva Restaurant, Marx Prospect 2, in the Moskva Hotel
National Restaurant, Gorky St. 1, in the National Hotel, TEL. 203–55–95. The bar upstairs serves whisky and other drinks for payment in any convertible currency.
Peking Restaurant, Bolshaya Sadovaya St. 1/7, in the Peking Hotel, TEL. 253–83–65. The restaurant sometimes has Chinese food.
Praga Restaurant, Arbat St. 2, TEL. 290–61–52. This restaurant, with a pleasant open-air terrace on the roof, specialises in Czech cuisine.
Rossiya Restaurant, Moskvoretskaya Naberzhnaya 1, in the Rossiya Hotel, TEL. 298 05–52
Russkaya Izba, 30 km. from Moscow, in Ihnskoye near Arkhangelskoye, TEL. 253–75–04/44.
Slavyansky Bazaar, 25th October St. 13, TEL. 228–48–45. This restaurant specialises in traditional Slav cooking.
Sovetsky Restaurant, Leningradsky Prospect 32, in the Leningradsky Hotel, TEL. 250–74–50
Sofia Restaurant, Gorky St. 32/1, TEL. 251–49–50. This restaurant specialises in Bulgarian cuisine.
Tsentralynyi Restaurant, Gorky St. 10, TEL. 229–72–35. All sorts of traditional Russian dishes are served here.
Ukraina Restaurant, Kutuzovsky Prospect 10, in the Ukraina Hotel, TEL. 243–32–97. Ukrainian cuisine is a speciality of the restaurant and includes:
Ukrainian borsch
vareniki—tiny dumplings filled with meat, fruit, vegetables, or cottage cheese.
Uzbekistan Restaurant, Neglinnaya St. 29, TEL. 294–60–53. This restaurant, which has some tables in the open-air, is extremely popular. The Uzbek cuisine includes:
logman—meat and noodle soup
maniar—soup of minced meat, eggs, and dumplings
mastava—meat and rice soup
muntyi—large dumplings filled with meat

tkhum-dulma—Scotch eggs
shashlik—meat grilled on a skewer
pilaff

Warsaw (Varshava) Restaurant, Oktyabrskaya Sq. 2/1, in the Varshava Hotel, TEL. 236–80–63 ext. 23. The restaurant specialises in Polish cuisine.

Shops

Gum (pronounced goom) Department Store, Red Sq. Open Monday to Saturday 8–9. *Gum* was built in 1888–94 by Pomerantsev in pseudo-Russian style as commercial arcades for nearly 1000 small shops. It is now the country's largest shop. There is a souvenir shop by the fountain in the middle of the central aisle and the record department is also on the ground floor.

Tsum (pronounced tsoom) Department Store, Petrovka St. 2. Open Monday to Saturday 8–9. Before the Revolution this shop was called Muir and Merrilees. It was built in Gothic style by Klein in 1909. There is a souvenir counter and a record department.

Moskva Department Store, Leninsky Prospect 56. Open Tues.–Sat. 8–9; Mon. 11–9.

Detsky Mir (Children's World) Department Store, Marx Prospect 2. Open Mon.–Sat. 8–9.

Souvenir Shops

Beryozka Souvenir and jewellery shop, Gorky St. 12

Souvenir shop, Kutuzovsky Prospect 9

Gift shops: Gorky St. 4, Stolenshnikov Pereulok 13/15, Leninsky Prospect 10, and Prospect Kalinina

Handicrafts: Petrovka St. 10 and Kutuzovsky Prospect 17; also Ukrainsky Boulevard 6

Embroidered goods: Stoleshnikov Pereulok 11

Jewellery: Petrovka St. 8 and Stoleshnikov Pereulok 14

Antiques: Gorky St. 46, Arbat St. 19, and Sretenka St. 31; also Dimitrova St. 54

Posters, pictures, graphics, etc.: Gorky St. 46, Arbat St. and the first floor of the book shop in Kalinin Prospect

Records: Kirov St. 17, 6/2 Arbat St., and Prospect Kalinina

Sheet music: Neglinnaya St. 14, Gertsen St. 13, and Arbat St.

Books in foreign languages: Kuznetsky Most 18

Secondhand books in foreign languages: Kachalov St. 16

Cameras and photographic goods: Gorky St. 41 and 25, Petrovka St. 12 and 15, Leninsky Prospect 62/1 (ciné shop), and Prospect Kalinina

Wines and Spirits: Stoleshnikov Pereulok 7

Central Market: Tsvetnoi Boulevard

Food shop, accepting payment in any convertible currency: Dorogomilovskaya St. 60. Whisky, gin, American cigarettes, etc. are on sale here, as well as meat and groceries.

Bank and Post Offices

USSR Bank for foreign trade, Neglinnaya St. 12

G.P.O., Kirov St. 26. Telegrams and poste-restante deliveries around the clock, other transactions until 10 pm.

Central Telegraph Office, Gorky St. 7. Open until 10 pm. Entrance to the international telephone office around the corner at No. 10. Open 24 hours.

International Post Office, Komsomolskaya Sq. 1. Open 9–9.

Ostankino Palace Museum

Pervaya Ostankinskaya St. 5. Open 11–6; closed Tues., Wed.

When Count Sheremetiev inherited the Ostankino estate through his marriage with Princess Cherkassaya in 1743 it was already one of the richest estates in Russia, having 210,000 serfs and an annual income of 1,500,000 roubles.

The palace, which is wooden although it appears to be built of stone, was built in 1792–7 by the serf architects Argunov, Mironov, and Dikushin under the supervision of Quarenghi, Camporesi, Nazarov, and Blank, all prominent architects of the time. The interior decoration was also the work of serfs and is particularly notable for the intricate wood carving around the doors and ceiling cornices. The parquet flooring is beautifully finished and every room has a different design, executed in various costly materials such as amaranth, rosewood, and ivory.

There is a fine collection of 17th- and 18th-century paintings, engravings, rare carvings, crystal, porcelain, and fans.

In the 18th century the theatre in the centre of the palace was particularly renowned and its company included about 200 actors, singers, dancers, and musicians. The stage is very large in comparison with the auditorium and could hold the whole company at once. At the end of a performance the armchairs in the auditorium could be removed in a matter of minutes by a special device, thus turning the theatre into a ballroom. It also had very advanced lighting, scenic, and sound effects, all designed by serfs. The most popular of all the actors was a serf-actress, Parasha Kovalyova, who had been taken into the company as a girl. She came from a blacksmith's family and was unusual for her beauty, great talent, and good-heartedness. Count Sheremetiev fell in love with her and later married her. One of the streets in Ostankino bears her name.

When the palace was built the existing park and lands were replanned. The palace was so grand and striking by contrast to the shabby peasant huts of a nearby village that on one occasion when many guests were invited, the huts were hidden by huge screens on the top of which burning torches were placed.

On the left of the main entrance to the palace is the *Trinity Church* which was built in 1683 by the serf-architect Pavel Potekhin.

There is a *café* behind the palace, and two places where boats can be hired.

Kolomenskoye

Kashirskoye Chaussée. Kolomenskoye was once the favourite summer residence of the Grand-Dukes of Moscow and later of the Russian tsars. Situated on a hill overlooking the R. Moskva, the first historical record of Kolomenskoye was in 1339 when it was mentioned as the estate of Ivan Kalita. In the second half of the 17th century a large wooden palace was built and Peter the Great spent some of his childhood here. The palace was demolished in 1767 by Catherine II because it was in a state of decay. (There is a model of it in the museum.)

One of the earliest buildings still standing is the *Church of the Ascension*, built in old Russian 'tent' style in 1532. At the time of its construction it was the tallest church in Russia. Hector Berlioz, the French composer, wrote after a visit to Russia in the 1840s, 'Nothing has impressed me more than this relic of ancient Russian architecture in the village of Kolomenskoye.'

The *Kazan Church*, with five onion-shaped domes, was built in 1660. It is open for services in the mornings.

Of the original royal estate only the *Main Gate*, the *Clock Tower*, and the *Water Tower* are now standing.

The museum is housed in the former domestic quarters of the estate. There are exhibitions of Russian wood-carvings, metalwork, ceramics, and displays illustrating the peasant war waged by Ivan Bolotnikov in 1606–7 and the 'Copper' Mutiny of 1662, so-called because of the tsar's decree that copper coins be accepted for the value of silver.

In the park are a number of wooden buildings from different parts of Russia, including the *log cabin* in which Peter the Great lived in Archangelsk (1702), a *prison tower* from Bratsk in Siberia (1631), a *defence tower* from the White Sea (1690), and a 17th-century *mead brewery* from the village of Preobrazhenskoye near Moscow. There is an open-air *café* in the park in summer.

Kuskovo Palace Museum

About 10 km. from Moscow along the Ryazanskoye Chaussée. Open 10–7; closed Tues. and the last day of each month.

First mentioned in 1510, the present architectural ensemble of Kuskovo dates to the 18th century when it was the summer residence of the Sheremetiev family, one of the oldest Russian noble families whose members were statesmen and soldiers.

The palace was built in 1769–75 by the Moscow architect Karl Blank in place of a smaller two-storey house. It was built in early Russian Classical style, but is unusual for its walls of pine logs faced with painted boards. It contains about 800 objets d'art, including one of the best collections of 18th-century Russian art in the country. The rooms of most interest are the White Hall, the dining room, the children's room, the Crimson drawing room with a large stove covered with coloured tiles, the oak-panelled study, the main bedroom, and the ballroom.

In front of the palace is a small square flanked by a *church* built in 1737 and a *belfry* built in 1792 by the serf-architects Mironov and Dikushin.

The park was laid out in French style under the direction of Andrei Vogt, a landscape gardener, and Yuri Kologrivov. The park which has been preserved is much smaller than the original one which included a zoo and was surrounded by woods.

There are a number of interesting buildings in the park. Near the palace is the *kitchen building* which was built by the serf-architect Argunov. Argunov was also responsible for the *grotto* and the *greenhouse*. The grotto was built in 1755–61 and is faced in sea-shells. The greenhouse was built in 1761–5 and includes a two-storey concert hall in the centre.

The *Dutch house* was built in 1749. The interior is decorated with pink and blue Delft tiles.

The *Italian house* was built in 1754–5 by Kologrivov in the style of a 17th-century Italian villa.

The *Hermitage* was built by Karl Blank in 1765. The table in the dining room on the first floor was lowered to the ground floor after each course to be cleared and reset, thereby avoiding the need for servants to be present throughout the meal.

Also known as the State Museum of Ceramics, Kuskovo houses one of the best collections of Russian porcelain. There is also china, majolica, and glass, and a considerable number of the exhibits are of Chinese, French, Dutch, and English origin.

Tsaritsyno

About 20 km. from Moscow, along the Kashirskoye Chaussée passing Kolomenskoye and Domodedovo airport.

The palace of Tsaritsyno, where Catherine II intended to live as a 'simple country woman', was never completed. Work began on the palace in 1775 under Bazhenov. Ten years later it was nearly completed but Catherine was not satisfied with it and ordered that it be pulled down. It is said that she only did this to punish Bazhenov for his association with Nikolai Novikov, the eminent educator who had earned Catherine's disapproval, but when work on the palace was resumed under Kazakov, it was in any case again built in the same rare Russian Gothic style which Bazhenov had designed. The war with Turkey and subsequent financial difficulties prevented its completion during Catherine's reign and work was stopped on her death in 1796.

Besides the half-ruined palace, one can see the *Entrance Bridge* and some *pavilions* scattered in the park. The most remarkable are the round Temple of Ceres, the Milovida Pavilion, and the Ruined Tower.

Tsaritsyno is situated in one of the most beautiful spots around Moscow, in hilly country intersected by ravines. In the English-style park there are numerous lakes and ponds. Boats can be hired and there is a *café*.

Arkhangelskoye

16 km. from Moscow. Motorists should leave Moscow by Leningradsky Prospect, then pass under the tunnel into Volokolamskoye Chaussée and then fork left to Petrovo-Dalniye Chaussée.

The museum is open from 11–5; closed Mon., Tues.

The park of Arkhangelskoye, overlooking the R. Moskva, is one of the most pleasant spots near Moscow and, together with the exterior of the palace, merits a visit even when the museum is closed.

The main complex of the estate was built at the end of the 18th century for Prince Golitsyn by the French architect, Chevalier de Huerne. In 1810 it was bought by Prince Yusupov, one of the richest Russian landlords and a descendant of the Tatar Khans. He was the director of the Imperial Theatre and Hermitage Museum and used his frequent trips abroad, during which he bought works for the Imperial family, to build up his own collection. There are in the palace many pictures by old European masters, including Hubert Robert, Van Dyck, and Roslin, and also tapestries and numerous marble sculptures. A number of portraits of the royal family hang in the study. Also on display are examples of fabrics, china, and glassware which were manufactured on the estate.

The park was laid out in French style and the avenues are lined with numerous statues and monuments. There is also a monument to Pushkin who visited Arkhangelskoye a number of times. In the western part of the park is a small pavilion known as the *Temple to the Memory of Catherine the Great*, here depicted as Themis, goddess of justice.

The two buildings at the end of the park were built in 1934–7 as a sanatorium. There is a delightful view over the R. Moskva from the balustraded terrace at the end of the park between the buildings of the sanatorium.

The Serf Theatre, on the right side of the main road a little beyond the main entrance, was built in 1817 by the serf-architect Ivanov. It is now sometimes open as a museum. The well-preserved stage decorations are the work of the Italian artist, Gonzaga. At the beginning of the 19th century the company was one of the largest and best known companies of serf actors.

There is a *restaurant* opposite the main entrance to the park.

Instead of returning to Moscow by the same road, motorists can drive further on to Ilyinskoye (there is an eating-house here on the left side) and take the turning to the left which leads to the Mozhaisk-Moscow highway, and continue straight on when the Minsk-Moscow road joins this road. The road leads into Kutuzovsky Prospect.

Leninskiye Gorki, Lenin Museum

34 km. from Moscow. The museum is open from 11–7, closed Tues.

The house was built in 1830 and stands in a park of 70 hectares (175 acres), which has old oak trees and a number of ponds. Just before the Revolution the estate belonged to Reinbolt, Mayor of Moscow. Lenin and his family lived here from time to time from September 1918 until his death here on 21 January 1924.

Many of the rooms in the museum have been kept as they were during Lenin's lifetime. In the garage are old motor cars, including Lenin's Rolls-Royce which was adapted for use in heavy snow by the addition of caterpillar wheels.

Abramtsevo

60 km. from Moscow, along the Yaroslavskoye Chaussée. The museum is open from 11–6; closed Mon., Wed.

This country estate, built in the 1770s, became well known when it was the home of the writer Sergei Aksakov from 1843 to 1859. Many eminent writers, including Gogol and Turgenev, visited Abramtsevo and it is mentioned in many of their letters.

In 1870 the wealthy industrialist and art connoisseur Savva Mamontov bought the house and it then became a meeting place and refuge for artists and actors. Repin, Vrubel, Serov, Nesterov, Chaliapin, Stanislavsky, and Maria Yermolova were all guests here.

A small church in old Russian style was built near the house. It was designed by the artists Vasily Polenov and Victor Vasnetsov, and decorated by Repin, Polenov, and the sculptor Antokolsky. Vasnetsov also built the 'Hut on Hen's Legs' which is based on a Russian fairy tale and stands in the park. After 1882 a number of workshops for pottery and various other forms of applied art were built.

The museum is laid out to describe the two eras of the house, the first rooms relating the time when the house was owned by Aksakov and the last rooms showing the house as it was after 1770 when it was an active arts centre. There are a number of portraits and paintings in the museum as well as colourful majolicas by Vrubel.

Borodino

128 km. from Moscow, near Mozhaisk on the Moscow-Minsk road. The museum is open from 10–6.

The Borodino museum, on the site of the famous 15-hour battle between the French and Russian armies on 26 August 1812, at which Napoleon's army suffered a heavy defeat, was founded in 1903. A new building for the museum was built in 1912 to commemorate the 100th anniversary of the battle. In front of the building are busts of the Russian generals, Barclay de Tolli and Bagration, which were made by Azgur in 1948. The monument to Kutuzov, the Russian commander-in-chief, by N. Tomsky was erected in 1966.

The collection in the museum includes guns, pictures, portraits, uniforms, and personal relics.

There are 34 monuments scattered over the Borodino field. They were erected in 1912 and are dedicated to the various units of the Russian army which fought in the battle. There is also a monument to French soldiers and officers, and new memorials which commemorate the Russo-German fight which took place here in the autumn of 1941.

MTSKHETA

See Georgian Military Highway, p. 115

MUKACHEVO

See Uzhgorod, p. 319

MURMANSK

Population—341,000 (1973)

'Murman' in the local Saami language means 'the edge of the earth', which is a true description of the place if one looks at the map. Another theory as to the origin of the name is that it comes from 'normann' meaning Norwegian, although the Kola Peninsula has been in Russian hands since 1478. Until 1917 Murmansk was known as Romanov-na-Murmane, Romanov after the imperial family.

Murmansk is located on the east side of the Kola Gulf of the Barents Sea, 50 km. from the open sea. It is so far north that there are nine months of winter and the polar night lasts for 52 days, from 26 November until 16 January. In winter the temperature may fall to −50°C. but in spite of its position its average January temperature is only −12°C. and while Russia's southern ports in the Caspian and Azov seas are covered with ice in winter, Murmansk remains ice-free all year round. The mild winter is explained by the North Cape Stream, the last branch of the Gulf Stream, which warms all this part of the coast. The town is known for holding the last of the country's winter competitions each year; at the end of March and the beginning of April is the Festival of the North which includes reindeer racing. In summer it may be as warm as +35°C. and the midnight sun shines from 17 May until 27 July.

The town's importance as a trading port is considerable; it stands fifth in the U.S.S.R. for cargo turnover. The Soviet Union's largest atomic-powered ice-breaker, the 'Arctica', is based here, and Murmansk is the western terminus of the Northern Sea Route to Vladivostok. Besides the cargo vessels, the local fishing fleet numbers about 1500 boats, and there is a special fishing harbour. Cod, haddock, turbot, wolf-fish, flat fish, and eel make up the greater proportion of the catch, and sharks are also caught for medical and technical purposes. It is the Soviet Union's most important fishing port, and the local fish processing plant is one of the largest in Europe.

The town stretches out for 20 km. in a narrow line along the coast. It stands upon what was once part of the sea bed, worn out of the rock by ancient glacial action. Murmansk is bounded in the north by R. Rosta and in the south by the old settlement of Kola. The stony hills, called the 'stone sack', which prevent it spreading further inland, keep its width to about 1·5 km. from the sea.

In the 16th century the request of the King of Denmark to begin trading with the Kola area was turned down because the Russians considered the place inconvenient.

During World War I the Russians' need for a port which would open all the year round led them, under British instigation and with British assistance, to build the port. It was constructed in September 1915, and the following year, when Russia was still cut off from her allies because her usual southern route through the Black Sea was blocked, it was decided to build a railway up from Petrozavodsk to the Kola Peninsula. The line runs through 965 km. of marshland and dense forest and was completed with great difficulty by the end of 1916. The first houses in Murmansk were brought from England. The Russians were surprised by their semi-circular iron roofs and called them 'suitcases', referring to the traditional rounded shape of Russian trunks and chests.

The town played an important role during the war, handling supplies from the allies. After the 1917 Revolution, in March 1918, Royal Marines under Rear-Admiral Thomas W. Kemp landed here from the battleship 'Glory'. The Admiralty also sent the cruiser 'Cochrane', the French their heavy cruiser 'Admiral Aube', and the Americans their cruiser 'Olympia'. They were forced to leave the area in February 1920. The pretext for the occupation had been 'the defence of the Murmansk region from the power of the German coalition'.

The varying numbers of the local population reflect the state of well-being of the town. There were 30,000 inhabitants in 1917 but by 1920 this had dropped to 19,000. However by 1938 the figure had soared to a booming 300,000. It was in that year that the Norwegian writer, Nordahl Grieg, wrote of his visit: 'In Murmansk I noticed two huge buildings under construction in this newly-built town between the Arctic Ocean and the snowy mountains. One was a power station, the other a theatre; the hammer blows sounded in unison. This is the way the world of the future is built.'

During World War II Murmansk was again an important transit point for incoming supplies. The battle front was only 80 km. away from the town and in 1941 Murmansk was almost entirely ruined by German bombing attacks.

Nothing at all is left now of the old wooden Murmansk. Today's town is the largest inside the Arctic Circle. The main thoroughfare is Lenin Prospect; as the popular Soviet lyric writer, Stepan Schipachov, described it:

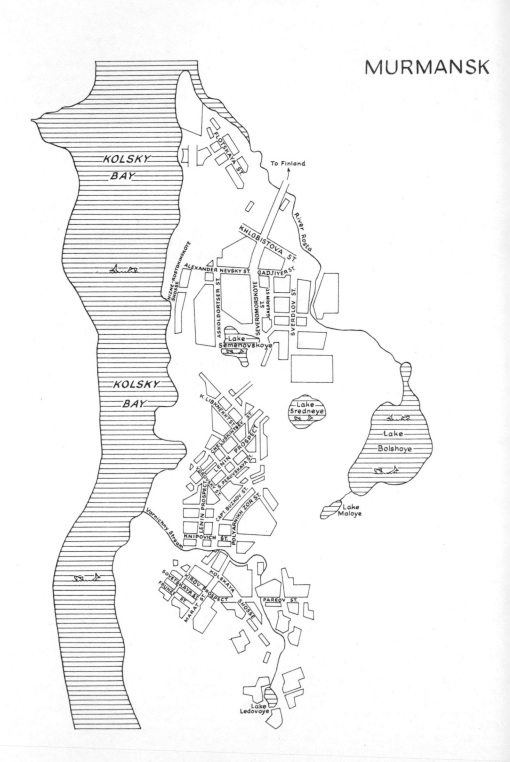

MURMANSK

A spacious street and straight—
This way it leads to Moscow;
That, to the Arctic sea.

(*trans.* J.M.Louis)

With the administrative buildings and the best shops, it is also the busiest street in Murmansk. It is divided into two parts by Pyat Uglov (five corners) Square, an architectural device reminiscent of Leningrad, and ends at the Gun Monument (q.v.). Karl Marx St. runs from the gulf to the hill. The town is laid out on three terraces: first the industrial zone and the bay, then the centre, and thirdly the Northern Region where the living quarters are. There is an observation point near the Panorama Restaurant in the Northern Region which has an excellent view over the town and the port. The port was subjected to 97 air raids during the war and was completely ruined. Allied ships came in and anchored under the protection of an overhanging cliff which can be seen from this point. 100,000 people, a third of the population of Murmansk, now live in the Northern Region where there is no industry at all. The buildings are mostly from 9 to 14 storeys high, in an area where but 30 years ago people used to go gathering golden cloudberries.

There is a pedagogical institute in Murmansk and a marine school as well as the Polar Institute of Fishery and Oceanology. The town has also a large ship-building industry.

A highway is under construction between Murmansk and Leningrad, and there are border crossings to Finland and Norway (see below).

Local Museum, Lenin Prospect 54. Open 11–5; closed Fri. It consists of three sections, the picture gallery on the ground floor, the natural history of the Kola Peninsula on the second floor, and the history of Murmansk section on the third floor. In the latter is an interesting display of wartime maps and plans showing the German advance and attack.

House of Soviets, Lenin Prospect
Regional Library, Perovskoy St.
New Library, Profsoyuznaya St., near the Sever Hotel. This was built in 1970 and holds a million books.
1918–20 Intervention Victims' monument, in a garden on Leningradskaya St. in the centre of the town. The monument was designed by Savchenko in 1927 in the Constructivist style of the time and is in the shape of a captain's bridge.
Obelisk, commemorating the 30th anniversary of the foundation of Murmansk port, unveiled in 1945.
War Memorial. An obelisk in memory of those who died during the air raids of World War II was unveiled in 1945.
Lenin Monument, Lenin Prospect. Tomsky was the sculptor and the statue was unveiled in 1957.
Sergei Kirov Monument, Pushkinskaya St. Sergei Kirov (1886–1934) was a famous Bolshevik. This statue by Vilensky was unveiled in 1940.
Anatoly Bredov monument, Lenin Prospect, in front of the House of Soviets. Bredov was a local docker who died at the Northern Front at Pechenga, near Murmansk, in October 1944. Rather than surrender, he blew himself up together with the advancing Germans, and was posthumously proclaimed a Hero of the Soviet Union. The monument, made jointly by Tatarovich and other sculptors, was unveiled in 1958.

The Gun Monument with an Eternal Flame, Kolskoye Chaussée, at the end of Lenin Prospect. This stands to the memory of the 6th Artillery Battery which, until it was annihilated in September 1941, bravely withstood the attacks of the approaching Germans in the valley of the Western Litsa river. The monument was unveiled in 1959.

Drama Theatre, Pyat Uglov Sq., Lenin Prospect. This was built in 1963 and has seats for 800.

Puppet Theatre, Perovskoy St. 21
International Seamen's Club, Karl Marx St. 1
Trud Stadium, Sport Sq. This stadium seats 15,000.
Winter Swimming Pool, part of the sports complex in the centre of town, which also includes football and hockey stadiums. The pool holds 3600 cu. m., has seats for an audience of 840, and was opened in 1966. It is one of the largest winter pools in the country.
Garden, Leningradskaya St. This is one of the most popular parks in the town. It has a good view over the gulf.
Severnaya (north) Hotel (Intourist) and Restaurant, Profsoyuznaya St. 20, TEL. 99–21. There is an Intourist office in the hotel, TEL. 78–29–13.
69th-Parallel Hotel, Sopka Varnichanaya St.
Polyarniye Zori Hotel and Restaurant, Knipovich St. 17
Dary Morya (ocean's gifts) Fish Restaurant, Lenin Prospect 26/9
Vstrecha (meeting) Restaurant, Oskoldovtsev St. 31
Panorama Restaurant, Northern Region. There is an excellent view from here. Nearby is a monument which was built to commemorate the town's wartime defenders.
Yunost (youth) Café, Lenin Prospect 50/7
Uyut (cozy) Café, Kominterna St. 15
Sport Café, Karl Marx St. 40
Theatre Café, Teatralnaya Boulevard
Bank, Profsoyuznaya St. 11
G.P.O. and Telegraph Office, Leningradskaya St. 27
Ingosstrakh Insurance Office, Pushkin St. 7
Rubin Foreign Currency Shop, Vorovskovo St. 4, opposite the railway station.
Department Store, Lenin Prospect 33
Children's World Department Store, Lenin Prospect
Bookshop, Lenin Prospect 23
Souvenirs, Lenin Prospect 34
Jewellers, Vorovskovo St. 4/22
Neptune Fishmonger's, Lenin Prospect 28. Most unusual and worth a sightseeing visit, this splendid shop stocks fish from the seven seas, from

wherever the Murmansk fishing fleet lets down its nets.

There is a *motor road* open *to Finland* for Scandinavian tourists, leading through the town of Padun and along the valley of R. Lotta (dolina Lotta) to Ivalo in Finland.

A railway runs from Murmansk to Nikel and it is only a short drive across the Soviet–Norwegian border to Kirkenes. This crossing is only for Scandinavians and Russians and two days' notice of a planned crossing is required.

Both Ivalo and Kirkenes are linked by regular transport services with Helsinki and Oslo respectively. The telephone number of the Tourist Office in Kirkenes is 917–82.

Kola

Population—10,000
Kola is located at the mouth of R. Kola on the Kola Gulf 12 km.,south-of Murmansk.

It was founded in 1264 and has been known for its importance as a trading port with foreign countries since the 16th century.

The remains of the old earth wall and the moat can still be seen, and there are still many old houses which belonged to local merchants. There is an interesting 19th-century wooden church which is now used as school workshops, and the old gun which is proudly pointed out to visitors was used in 1854 when British battleships sailed in close to the town. Since the foundation of Murmansk, Kola has lost much of its former importance and soon it will merge entirely with its growing neighbour.

The town produces furniture, plaster-of-Paris, and food products.

By the main road is a *church*, now closed.

The *wooden cross*, opposite the Volna Cinema, bears an inscription saying that it was erected 'in the summer of 1635, on the 12th day of June, to be revered of all Christian folk'.

NAKHODKA

Population—105,000 (1970)
The name of this new port means 'find' or 'godsend'. The bay in which it is located was discovered by Russian explorers in 1859 when after two stormy days their corvette 'Amerika' put in at a quiet bay. It is one of the most perfect bays on far eastern Russian territory, and opens on to the Sea of Japan.

It was decided before World War II to build a port here, but it was only at the end of the war that construction actually began. It has been a town since 1950 and lying 43 miles east of Vladivostok it is, after Vladivostok, the second most important port in the area. Since 1958 Vladivostok has been closed to foreigners, and Nakhodka serves as the transit point for travellers going to Japan, with which it is connected by regular sailings. One of its advantages over Vladivostok is that the Sea of Japan near Amerika Gulf never freezes over and near the port the ice is weaker than it is at Vladivostok.

The town is picturesquely situated in the amphitheatre of the shore of Amerika Gulf and now stretches for 19 km. around the bay. Intensive construction is in progress following a recently-approved twenty-year plan. The town around the Gulf is divided into three regions, north, central, and south.

The railway station, called locally Tikhookeanskaya (Pacific), is in the centre of town, close to the port, and terminates a branch line from the Trans-Siberian Railway.

Apart from its importance as a transport centre, Nakhodka has a ship-repairing yard and a considerable fishing industry. There is a club for foreign sailors here, a branch of the Far East Polytechnical Institute and a naval school.

Stadium

Vostok (east) Hotel (Intourist) and Restaurant, Central Sq. TEL. 65–02.

NALCHIK

Population—150,000 (1970)
This town lies on the left bank of the R. Nalchik at a height of 554 m. above sea level. Its name, meaning 'horseshoe', refers to the shape of the mountains around, for it is in the foothills of the northern spurs of the Black Mountains. It is famous for its picturesque environs and for its view of the Caucasus Mountains. One of the local sorts of mineral water, Nartan, takes its name from a nearby mountain.

During the Caucasian War of 1822 a Russian military fortress was founded here, and by the end of the 19th century the number of inhabitants had already increased considerably. Now the town is the capital of the Kabardino-Balkarian Autonomous Republic, and the republic's university was opened in 1957. It is also the central point for tourists and mountaineers going to the central Caucasus.

Local Museum, Lenin Prospect. Open 11–6; closed Sat.

Fine Arts Museum, Lenin Prospect 35. Open 11–6; closed Sat.

Lenin Monument, Sovietov Sq. Made by Posyada and unveiled in 1957.

Unification Monument, Lenin Prospect. This monument by Listopad and Makhtin was unveiled in 1957 to mark the 400th anniversary of the region's union with Russia.

Jabagi Kazanokov Monument, in Svoboda Garden. Kazanokov was a local philosopher of the 18th century.

Two busts, of *Bekmurza Pachev* (Kabara poet) and of *Kyazim Mechiyev* (Balkar poet), in the park. The sculptors Tkhakumashev and Krym-Shakhalov were responsible for them both and they were unveiled in 1961.

Drama Theatre, in the park

The large park begins immediately outside the town on the way to Dolinsk, and continues for 3 km. Occupying an area of 800 hectares (2000 acres) it is one of the biggest parks in the northern Caucasus. There is a collection of trees from the

Caucasus, Europe, and America and the avenue of pines and the rose gardens are especially worthy of note.

Spartak Stadium, Sovietov Sq.

Hippodrome Racecourse, Baksanskoye Chaussée

Rossiya Hotel and Restaurant, Lenin St. 32

Nalchik Hotel, Lermontov St. 2

Kavkaz Restaurant, Kabardinskaya St. 13

Dorozhny Restaurant, Osetinskaya St. 132

Nalchik Restaurant, Respublikanskaya St. 2

Elbrus Restaurant, in the park

Kosmos Café, Lenin Prospect 35

G.P.O., Teatralnaya St. 4

Bank, Teatralnaya St. 2

Department Store and Souvenirs, Kabardinskaya St. 15

Bookshop, Lenin Prospect 46

Popular short excursions are those from Nalchik to *Mount Nartan* (1009 m.) and *Mount Sarai* (1329 m.), while 40 km. away are the *Blue Lakes* and *Chegemski Waterfalls*. The largest of the lakes has an elliptical shape, and is 235 m. long and 125 m. wide. Its depth of 258 m. makes it the sixth deepest lake in the U.S.S.R.

Itkol

It is a short journey from Nalchik up into the Caucasus Mountains to this winter sports resort where there is good skiing.

NARVA

Population—75,000 (1968)

The name, Narva, appears to derive from that of the ancient Vep tribe which lived in these parts about 1000 years ago. It means 'waterfall' and is a fitting description of the rock-lined and turbulent R. Narova upon which it stands. In the 9th century Estonians settled here and Slavs moved in soon afterwards, but fires and wars devastated the city and little of historical value remains apart from the two castles.

The city grew from rival settlements on either side of the river. Narva, on the left bank, belonged to the Estonians and Ivangorod, on the right bank, was held by the Russians. Even today the republican boundary follows the line of the river and part of the city is in Estonia and part in the Russian Federation, with the Estonian part more industrially developed and predominant.

Narva proper was first mentioned in Russian chronicles of 1171 when it formed an important trading-point for the members of the Hanseatic League. Early in the 13th century it was captured by the Danes who then sold it to the Teutons. They, in turn, sold it to the Livonians. The Russians under Tsar Ivan III built their fortress of Ivangorod directly opposite Narva in 1492. The centuries of fighting between the Russians, the Poles, and the Swedes for influence in these regions went on until Peter the Great's victory over the Swedish forces in 1721, but there was little left of the city then for it had been almost entirely razed by fires in the middle of the 17th century. Its

important strategic and economic position aided Narva's revival but in 1944, as the Germans retreated, they blew up 98% of the buildings. Narva Castle and the fortress of Ivangorod are still under restoration.

Narva Castle was built in the 13th century and formed the nucleus of the city which sprang up around it. It stands on the river's high, rocky bank and its walls enclose three hectares (7¼ acres). The highest tower is known as Tall Hermann and the castle itself is sometimes called Hermann Castle. When the restoration work is complete, the museum will be housed in the castle.

There are local people who believe that Narva Castle is haunted. They claim that on certain nights one can hear shouts and moans coming from an underground passage. The story behind all this is that once upon a time a knight called Indrik von Berengaut lived here with his beautiful wife and their small son. The place was invaded by the Russians who saw von Berengaut's beautiful wife and rushed forward to capture her. The knight's followers fought fiercely in their master's defence but they were outnumbered, and to prevent his wife's capture, von Berengaut slew her with his own sword. Then fire broke out in the castle and as they fled, the Russians took the little boy with them. Desperate for revenge, the knight decided to tunnel his way beneath the river into Ivangorod and so, with his men, to take his enemies by surprise and kill them.

The construction of the tunnel took 30 years and the night before the surprise attack was scheduled to take place, von Berengaut crept alone into the Russian fortress and sought out his son to save him from the impending massacre. However the young man had grown up to feel himself a Russian in every way and refused to leave the fortress and the Russian girl that he loved and wished to marry. Von Berengaut returned alone to Narva and went ahead with his plans. At the appointed time he led his soldiers through the tunnel to wreak his revenge, but when only halfway through he was met by a body of Russian soldiers led by his own son. When the old man realised how he had been betrayed, he threw himself upon the young man who ran his father through with his sword and killed him. At this point, seeming to sense the tragedy, the tunnel collapsed and the waters of the Narova poured in, drowning everyone where they were, underground. The unhappy ghost is said to be that of young von Berengaut, still begging his father's forgiveness.

Ivangorod Fortress, on the other side of the river, was originally built to safeguard Russian trading interests. It was surrounded by walls 15 m. high and had 10 towers, but 6 of these were blown up by the retreating Germans at the end of the last war.

Peter the Great's House, Lidia Koidula Boulevard. This two-storey house where the tsar stayed whenever he visited the city was made into a memorial museum in 1726. It is in a bad state of repair at present.

The *City Hall* was built in 1668–71 in Baroque style. The three female figures decorating the portal represent Wisdom, Justice, and Temperance, these being the virtues which were to guide the city fathers in their work. A weather vane in the shape of a stork stands on top of the spire and beneath his feet is an apple inside which at the time of the hall's construction were put coins minted in Narva and a manuscript describing the contemporary rulers. The building was completely restored, both inside and out, in 1963 and is now the home of a local youth club.

War Memorial, in the city garden. A simple metal cross stands on a slab of grey stone with an inscription honouring the Russian soldiers who fell storming Narva in 1704.

War Memorial, 3 km. to the north of Narva. This monument was built in 1900 with money collected from two guards' regiments and it commemorates soldiers killed in battle in 1700.

Local Museum, Leningradskoye Chaussée 2

Lenin Museum, Anvelt St. 22

Narva Hotel, Pushkin St. 6, TEL. 27–00

Baltika Restaurant, Pushkin St. 10

Söprus Restaurant, Anvelt St. 5

Mayak (lighthouse) Restaurant, Narva-Iiesuu, Pargi St. 9

Ivangorod Restaurant, Gagarin St. 24

G.P.O., Tuleviku St. 3

Bookshop, Pushkin St. 5

NORTH OSSETIAN AUTONOMOUS REPUBLIC

See Georgian Military Highway, Ordzhonikidze, p. 110

NOVAYA KAKHOVKA

See Kherson, p. 137

NOVGOROD

Population—128,000 (1970)

The name Novgorod means 'New Town' in Russian, but it is actually one of the oldest towns in Russia and was founded over 1100 years ago by the Ilmen Slavs.

The town of Novgorod is situated on either side of the R. Volkhov which until recently was spanned by a single bridge. The two parts of the city have retained their medieval names of Sophia Side, after the Cathedral of St. Sophia in the Kremlin, and Market Side, the side of the town which was occupied by the important merchant class. The town stands on a hill and the surrounding lowlands are flooded in spring.

Novgorod played an important role in Russian history until the end of the 15th century when it lost its independence. An early chronicler writes that the northern Slavs, having combined forces and successfully driven out invaders, were overtaken by internal strife so great that in 862 Slavonic legates went beyond the sea to the Norse Rus and said, 'Our land is great and fruitful, but there is no order in it; come and reign and rule over us.' Three brothers came with their armed followers and the eldest, Rurik, settled in Novgorod. Russia is supposed to have been named after Rurik's tribe. It is considered more likely, however, that the Norse settlers in Novgorod were merchants who were exploiting the trade routes to the south.

In 1882 Prince Oleg with his Novgorodian army conquered Kiev and transferred his government there. Novgorod, now governed by a viceroy, continued to grow, and was given special concessionary privileges by the Princes of Kiev. Christianity was accepted in Novgorod in 990, scarcely later than in Kiev, and by the 12th century it was virtually independent of Kiev which it long outlived as an important trading centre. Largely on account of its important position on the trade route between the Baltic and Black Seas, Novgorod became known as 'Lord Novgorod the Great' and its power was expressed in the saying 'Who can resist God and Lord Novgorod the Great?' Novgorod also had the advantage over other Russian towns of not suffering the full weight of the Mongol invasion although the town did pay tribute to the invaders.

The sphere of trade covered by Novgorod was extremely wide. In return for silks and spices from the South and East, many of which were shipped on to Europe, furs and precious metals were sent to the East and Europe. In the 11th century there was a group of German merchants in Novgorod and in the last years of its independence, it was the eastern-most member of the Hanseatic League.

Novgorod was also the only Russian town where there was any real form of democratic power. The 'veche' in Novgorod (a 'veche' was a popular assembly of citizens which used to govern in most Russian towns) was extremely powerful and the Prince of Novgorod was little more than a military leader. His rights were strictly limited by a number of treaties and neither he nor his family were allowed to purchase land within the city domain. On more than one occasion the ruling Prince was removed at the will of 'Veche' and there is an old Novgorodian saying, 'If the Prince is bad, into the mud with him.'

Between 1100 and 1150 there are supposed to have been 230 churches in Novgorod. There were numerous struggles between the principalities of Novgorod, Suzdal, and Moscow and on one occasion Novgorod is said to have been saved by a miracle. Andrei Bogolyubsky, Prince of Suzdal, was besieging the town when the citizens hung an icon of the Virgin Mary on the gates. Arrows flew 'thick as rain' into the icon, but it remained unharmed and real tears ran down the face of Our Lady, so upsetting the attacking army that it fled. This event is commemorated by a famous icon 'The Battle between the Novgorod and Suzdal', which can be seen in the Kremlin museum.

In 1471, in a battle near Lake Ilmen, the armies of Novgorod were defeated by the combined forces of Ivan III of Moscow and the Tatars. Growing rivalry between the two principalities and a religious dispute involving allegations that the Novgorodians were defecting from the true

NOVGOROD

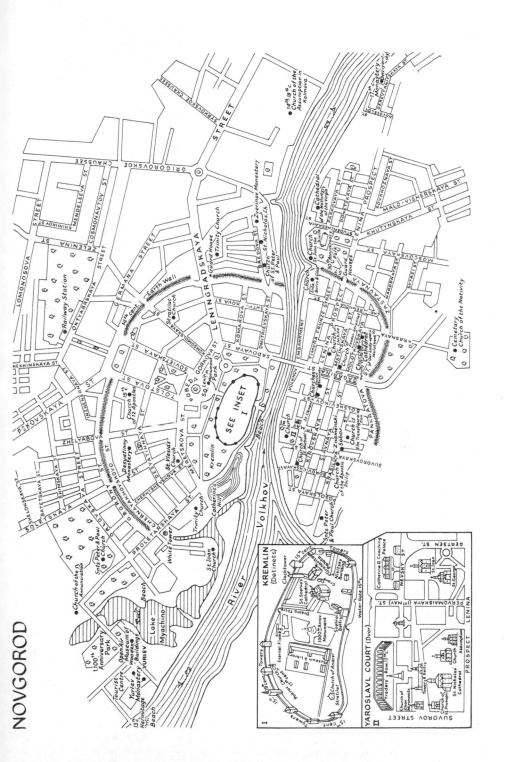

Orthodox faith to a latinised form of Christianity gave rise to the battle. The woman, Martha, who led the anti-Moscow faction in Novgorod is described in a Moscow chronicle of the time as a person wanting 'to seduce the whole people, to turn them from the right way, and to join the Latinism'.

After this date the prosperity of Novgorod steadily declined and suffered a final blow in 1570 when Ivan the Terrible is said to have butchered 60,000 citizens in order to suppress a plan to kill him. For six weeks there were tortures, murders, robberies, and fires and, according to an old chronicle, every day hundreds of Novgorodians were thrown into the Volkhov together with their wives and children. The river was choked with dead corpses and since then, the legend runs, it has never frozen at this point.

By the middle of the 17th century the population which had once totalled 400,000 had fallen to about 2000. It is written that after the Swedish war of 1627 there were only 850 people left alive in the town. The foundation of St. Petersburg at the beginning of the 18th century and a succession of fires completed the ruin of Novgorod.

65 out of the 66 more valuable monuments of the town were damaged during the Second World War, but over 40 churches and part of the 12th-century earthen wall of the town still remain. Massive building work has been carried on since the war and the name Novgorod seems appropriate for the present-day town. Many of the historical monuments have also been restored and no tall buildings or trees are allowed near the main historical buildings.

The three main thoroughfares of the town are Sadovaya (Garden) St., Leningradskaya St., and Gorkova St. There are all intersected by the main Moscow-Leningrad road. In Pobeda (Victory) Sq., on Gorkova St., are the buildings of the Palace of Soviets and the Communist Party School, and also a monument to Lenin.

The town's industries are mainly concerned with timber (particularly matches), ship repairing, and food. It is also the centre of an important agricultural area.

The Kremlin: The first Kremlin was built on this site in 864 by Rurik. It was known as the Detinets, a name given to the fortress in many Russian towns at that time. Since then it has been reconstructed many times in accordance with the defensive needs of the town.

The wall, which has nine towers, is 1386 m. in circumference, between 8·5 and 10·6 m. high and between 2·7 and 3·3 m. thick. The wall and most of the towers were built between 1484 and 1490 on the site of an earlier wall which had fallen into disrepair.

The main church in the Kremlin is *St. Sophia's Cathedral* (Sofiiskii Sobor), which was built in 1045–50. An earlier cathedral, built entirely of oak with thirteen domes, was destroyed by fire in 1045. The present cathedral was built on the order of Prince Vladimir and was intended to imitate the famous St. Sophia's Cathedral in Kiev. The design was simplified in many ways, however, with three apses instead of five, frescoes instead of mosaics, and stone and brickwork instead of marble. However, a new feature was the emphasis laid upon the apses which in subsequent Novgorodian architecture became the most important feature. At the beginning of the 12th century galleries were built onto the north, south, and east façades of the cathedral, thus enclosing within the walls the spiral staircase and tower which originally projected at the south end of the west façade.

The central dome of the cathedral is a gigantic copy of the helmet of an ancient Russian warrior, topped by a cross and bronze dove. According to legend, Novgorod will stand until the dove flies away.

At the west entrance are the Sigtuna or Korsun doors, thought to have been made by Master Riquinius of Magdeburg in 1152–4 for the Bishop of Plotzk and captured in 1187 from the ancient Scandinavian capital of Sigtuna where they served as town gates. They are about 3·5 m. high, and are made of oak overlaid by 48 plates of bronze. Three of these plates portray scenes from the Old Testament, 23 scenes from the New Testament, and 22 are of allegorical or mythological subjects. The inscriptions are partly in Slavonic and partly in Latin, but it is thought that the Latin inscriptions were added at the beginning of the 15th century.

The interior of the cathedral was not decorated until 1109, almost 60 years after the cathedral was built, because life was too unsettled in Novgorod at this time to allow continuous work on the cathedral. The original frescoes can be seen only in a few places because the cathedral was redecorated

---

PLATES OPPOSITE

The small Transfiguration Cathedral, at Pereslavl-Zalesky, built in 1152 and restored in the 19th century.

OVERLEAF

L/h page above: One of the many ancient Russian churches of Novgorod, St. Paraskeva Piatnitsa was founded in 1207. *Below*: Children in a Kiev kindergarten.

R/h page: Sveti Tskhoveli Cathedral in Mtskheta where the kings of Georgia were crowned. On the hill over the river is the Dzhvari church from which, according to legend, the monks would climb down on an iron chain which linked their hill-top cells with the cathedral below where they attended services. But faith grew weak, the chain broke and was lost.

with oil murals in the 1830s. Work was stopped by Nicholas I who occasionally passed through Novgorod on his way from St. Petersburg to Moscow, but the painting was renewed in the 1890s. The best frescoes that are left from the 12th century are in the southern part of the cathedral where there is a life-size frescoe depicting the Byzantine emperor Constantine and his mother Helen. The fresco in the drum of the main cupola was unfortunately almost completely destroyed during the Second World War and can only be seen in parts. It was painted in the 12th century and, so the legend says, first portrayed Christ with arm outstretched, blessing the people. The day after the fresco was completed, the craftsmen found that the hand was in a clenched position. The craftsmen repainted the hand three times, only to find that whatever they did the hand remained clenched. On the fourth day they heard a voice saying, 'Painters, painters! Do not draw me with a blessing hand, but with a clenched fist for I hold Novgorod the Great in my hand and when my hand will be outstretched, then the town will fall.'

The 11th-century mosaics which were originally behind the altar are now in the Kremlin museum. Fragments of the mosaic, thought to have been made by Byzantine craftsmen, can be seen in the main apse of the cathedral.

The iconostasis dates from the 16th century and is richly ornamented with silver and gold. Before it stand the painted and gilded thrones, also dating from the 16th century, of the Metropolitan and Tsar. There are a number of tombs in the cathedral, including the silver sarcophagus of John of Novgorod who died in 1186. Also of interest are the 'golosniki' (earthen-ware jars) built into the walls at certain points in order to improve the acoustics.

The *Sophia Belfry (Sofiiskaya zvonitsa)* is situated near the wall of the Kremlin. The present building dates from the 15th to 17th centuries, and was restored and slightly altered during the 19th century. The first historical mention of the belfry was in a chronicle of 1437 which stated that together with the Kremlin wall it fell into the river during a flood.

Along the wall from the belfry is the tiny *Church of Andrei Stratilat* (Tserkov Andreya Stratilata), which is reputed to have been built in one day in the 17th century.

Near this church in the centre of the Kremlin is the *museum* which is housed in a former office block, built in 1783. It has over 80,000 exhibits in its 35 halls, mostly from the churches of the Kremlin, Novgorod, and the surrounding area. There are over 550 icons, the oldest being an 11th-century icon of St. Peter and St. Paul which is thought to have been painted by a travelling Greek artist. There are also many icons dating

from the 12th to 15th centuries when there was a flourishing school of icon painting in Novgorod which was marked by its strong images and vivid colours. Many of the icons depict local saints.

Also in the museum are manuscripts dating from the 10th century and a collection of private letters written on birch bark dating from the 11th century.

In front of the museum is a *monument* commemorating Russia's 1000th anniversary. It was designed in 1862 by the sculptor Mikyeshin. On the imperial orb stands a figure of Russia, watched by her guardian angel who leans upon a cross. The six statues surrounding this centrepiece represent the six main periods of Russian history, the times of Rurik, St. Vladimir, Ivan III, Dmitri Donskoi, Peter the Great, and Mikhail Romanov.

Another museum is housed in the *Granovitaya Palata* (Palace of Facets), which was built in 1433 at the order of Archbishop Yefimy and was one of the first secular buildings to be built of stone instead of wood. It was intended for important receptions and meetings and in the last years of the town's independence the boyars' council used to meet here. The main hall of the palace is roofed with low arches supported by a central column. The museum collection contains icons and other articles of value from local churches and monasteries.

Next to the Palace of Facets is the *Church of Sergei Radonezh*, which was built in 1463 by the Archbishop Iona in the same style as many of the gate churches in the Moscow Kremlin. Contrary to custom, it was dedicated to a Moscow saint instead of a local saint as the Archbishop was an advocate of union with Moscow. The interior of the church was formerly covered in frescoes. The church as it looked at the time of building can be seen on one of the frescoes.

Next to the church is the *clocktower* (chasozvon) which was built in 1673 on the site of a 15th-century watch-tower.

Behind the clocktower are the remains of the *Archbishop's Palace* which was built in the 1430s by Archbishop Yefimy. This three-storey palace used to cover the whole area from the clocktower to the two-storey *Nikitsky building* which now houses the offices and library of the museum. This building, which is named after the Archbishop Nikita, was built in the 17th century on the foundations of a 12th-century wooden building.

In front of the Granovitaya Palata is the *grave* of the Russian poet Gavril Derzhavin (1743–1816). Derzhavin lived near Novgorod and was buried in the grounds of the Khutinsky Monastery. This was destroyed during the Second World War, and the coffins of Dzerhavin and his wife were later moved to their present site.

Also in the Kremlin is a *war memorial* commemorating those who fell during the liberation of the town in January 1944 after it had been held for 29 months by the German army.

Novgorod is renowned for its many churches, some dating from the 12th century. Many of these are situated across the river from the Kremlin on the Market (Torg) Side.

Opposite the Kremlin on the bank of the river is a group of old buildings on a site known as *Yaroslav Dvor* (Yaroslav Court). The first mention of Yaroslav Dvor was in a chronicle of 1113, and it is thought that this is where the Prince of Yaroslav resided until the end of the 14th century. The main building in this complex is *St. Nicholas' Cathedral* which was founded in 1113 and is the oldest church after St. Sophia's. It was for some years the only church open for services in Novgorod and was in fact only elevated to the status of cathedral because of this.

The principle icon, a circular one depicting St. Nicholas, is now in the museum in the Kremlin. According to the legend, Prince Mtislav of Novgorod was fatally paralysed and sent ambassadors to Kiev to fetch this icon which he believed could cure him. On the return journey, their ship was wrecked but the icon was found floating in the R. Volkhov. Prince Mtislav recovered his health and in gratitude built the church to house the icon.

The large church was built with five cupolas and three aisles in the style of Kievan churches of the same period. The present roof was added much later and so was the wooden staircase leading to the choir.

Inside the church are fragments of the original 12th-century frescoes.

The Church of St. Nicholas was a princely church, the priests being subordinated to the Prince of Novgorod rather than the Archbishop. When Archbishop Nifont refused to marry Prince Svyatoslav to a Novgorodian girl for political reasons the Prince was married in this church by his own priests.

The *Church of St. Prokopii* nearby was built in 1529 in the Moscow style.

The *Church of Zhon Mironosits*, also near the Cathedral of St. Nicholas, was built in 1510.

To the north-west of St. Nicholas' Cathedral is an old three-storey building with two entrance arches and an octagonal tower. It is commonly known as the *Vechevaya Tower*, the 'veche' being the popular assembly of citizens which used to govern the town. The assembly used to hold its meetings here in the tower, and it is an interesting example of early civil architecture.

On the other side of the Yaroslavl Dvor are two churches which were built in the 14th century. The nearest is the *Church of St. Michael* (Tserkov Mikhaila) in Mikhailov St. It was founded in 1300, but was rebuilt in 1454 and again in the 19th century. The *Church of the Assumption* (Tserkov Uspenia) in Bitkov Pereulok was founded in 1362 and, although rebuilt in 1466 and again in the 17th century, has retained its original appearance to a great degree.

The southern part of the Torg Side used to be known as Slovensky Kholm (Slav Hill). There are a number of old churches here. One of the earliest is the *Church of St. Ilya* (Tserkov Ilii) in Krasilova St. It was built in 1198–1202 and rebuilt in the 15th century. Only the lower part of the walls date from the 12th century.

In the same street is the *Church of St. Peter and St. Paul* (Tserkov Petra i Pavla) which was built in 1367. It was restored in the 1950s and the old portals on the northern and southern façades deserve attention.

Nearby in Nutnaya St. is the *Church of the Apostle Philip* (Tserkov Apostola Filippa) which was built in 1383–4 and rebuilt in 1526.

At the junction of Krasilova and Pervomaiskaya Sts. are two churches. The older one of the two is the *Church of the Transfiguration* (Tserkov Spasa) which was built in 1374. Inside the church are frescoes dating from the 14th century and attributed to the well-known icon painter, Theophanes the Greek.

The *Znamenski Sobor* in Pervomaiskaya St. was built in 1682–8 in the Moscow style. The tympana are decorated with colourful frescoes.

There are a number of churches in Lenin Prospect. The oldest of all is the *Church of the Assumption* (Tserkov Uspeniya) which was built in 1135–44 and founded by Prince Vsevolod shortly before he was driven out of Novgorod. It was considerably altered in the 15th century.

Of more interest is the *Church of Dmitri Solunsky* (Tserkov Dmitriya Solunskovo) which was built in 1381–2. The upper part of the southern and eastern façades is decorated with intricate stone work.

There are two churches of minor interest in Lenina Prospect, the *Church of St. Clement,* founded in 1386, and the *Church of Nikita the Martyr* (Tserkov Nikity Muchenika), founded in 1557.

One of the most outstanding churches of the Market Side is the *Church of Feodor Stratilat* (Tserkov Feodora Stratilata) in Feodorovsky Ruchei St. The church was built in 1360–1. Inside the church are frescoes believed to have been painted shortly after the church was completed.

A church which is renowned for its frescoes is the *Church of the Nativity* in the Rozhdestvenskoye Kladbische (Nativity Cemetery). The church was built in 1381–2.

In the northern part of the Torg Side are the remaining buildings of the Antoniev Monastery which was founded at the beginning of the 12th century by a monk, Antonia Romano, from Rome. The principal church of the monastery was the *Cathedral of the Nativity of the Virgin* (Sobor Rozhdestva Bogoroditsi) which was built in 1117–19. It was considerably altered in later centuries, however, when the large onion-domes were added. Inside the cathedrals are fragments of murals dating from the 12th century.

Below is a list of some of the other churches

remaining in the Torg Side of the town:

Church of St. Ioan, Gertsen St. This church was built in 1127–30 and rebuilt in 1453.

Church of St. George, Pervomaiskaya St. This church was built in the 13th century.

Church of Paraskeva Pyatnitsa. This church was founded in 1207 by a guild of Novgorodian merchants who traded abroad. It was rebuilt in 1345.

Church of St. John the Divine (Tserkov Ivana Bogoslova), by the R. Volkhov. Built in 1383–4, this is one of the best preserved churches.

Church of Ss. Boris and Gleb, beside the R. Volkhov. This church was founded in 1536 on the site of an earlier church.

Church of St. George, Pervomaiskaya St. 17th century.

In Gertsen St., on this side of the river, is a small *imperial palace* which was used by the tsars on their journeys from St. Petersburg to Moscow. It was built in the 18th century and is thought to have been designed by Matvei Kazakov. It is now a House of Culture.

There are also so many churches on the Sophia Side that, once again, it is impossible to describe them all fully. One of the oldest churches on this side is the *Church of the Annunciation* (Tserkov Blagovescheniya) on the way to the Yuriev Monastery. This church was built in the 12th century and belonged to the Arkazha monastery, the remains of which can be seen not far from the church. The church was rebuilt in the 16th century and only the lower part of the walls date from the 12th century. Fragments of the original frescoes of 1189 can be seen near the altar.

Another 12th-century church which can be seen in this part of the town is the *Church of St. Peter and St. Paul* (Tserkov Petra i Pavla) in St. Peter's Cemetery (Petrovskoye Kladbische). It was founded in 1185 and, unlike many 12th-century churches, still retains its original appearance.

An interesting 13th-century church is the *Church of Feodor Stratilat* in Komsomolskaya St. It was built in 1292–4 and rebuilt in 1682. The murals inside the church are well-preserved.

The *Church of the Trinity* (Tserkov Troitsy) in Proletarskaya St. was founded in 1365, but was radically reconstructed in the 19th century.

Just off Proletarskaya St. is the *Church of St. Ioan* which was founded in 1421. Nearby is the *Uvereniya Fomy Church* which was founded in 1463. An earlier church stood on this site and until recently it was thought that the present building contained elements of the older one. Recent research, however, has shown that the original church was completely ruined in the 15th century before the present one was constructed.

A good example of 15th-century Novgorodian architecture is the *Church of St. Peter and St. Paul* in Zverinskaya St. It was founded in 1406.

At one time there were over 20 monasteries in Novgorod. The churches of two of these can be seen on the Sophia Side. The *Zverinov Monastery* was first mentioned in a chronicle of 1148 when a wooden church in the monastery was hit by light-ning. The name Zverinov comes from the Russian word 'Zver' meaning wild animal, for in the 9th to 12th centuries there was a forest here which was one of the most popular hunting grounds of the Princes of Novgorod.

In 1339 the *Pokrov Church*, which can be seen today, was built on the side of the wooden church destroyed by lightning. It was repeatedly rebuilt in the ensuing centuries and almost eclipsed from view in the 19th century when a large church was built beside it.

Near the Pokrov Church is the *Church of St. Simon* (Tserkov Simeona) which was built in 1467 and has a large onion-shaped dome. The frescoes inside date from the 15th century and are in a good state of preservation.

The *Dukhov Monastery* (Monastery of the Holy Spirit) was founded in the 12th century. The principal church of the monastery, the Church of the Holy Spirit, has unfortunately not survived. Of most interest here is the *Church of the Trinity* which was built in 1557.

On the bank of the R. Volkhov just outside the town is the *Yuriev Monastery* which can be reached by boat. The principal church of the monastery was the *Cathedral of St. George* (Giorgievski Sobor). It was founded in 1119 by Prince Vsevolod and is considered the best architectural monument in Novgorod after St. Sophia's Cathedral which it was intended to surpass in grandeur. It was designed by a Russian architect named Piotr who is also thought to have been responsible for the Cathedral of St. Nicholas.

The cathedral was restored during the 1930s when additional structures were removed from the façades, thereby returning to the cathedral its severe and impressive lines. Unfortunately the original frescoes were almost all removed during the 1840s, but fragments have been found during recent restoration work. Of particular merit are the figures of saints in the tower of the cathedral.

Open Air Museum of Wooden Buildings, in the park near Yuriev Monastery. The collection here has been growing since 1960 and now consists of churches, houses and peasant huts of artistic or historical value from all parts of the Novgorod region. Particularly interesting is Kuritskaya Church (17th century) which was brought here from the shore of Lake Ilmen in 1965.

Novgorod Museum, in the Kremlin and in the Granovitaya Palata of the Kremlin (see above).

Lenin Monument, Pobeda Sq. near the Kremlin. This square was formerly called Sophia Sq. The bronze statue of Lenin was designed by Merkurov and erected in 1956 on an earlier pedestal constructed by Osipov in 1926.

Park of the 30th Anniversary of the October Revolution, in the Antonev region of the Torg Side. The Dynamo Sport Stadium, which can seat 30,000, is in the park.

Drama Theatre and concert hall, in the Kremlin

Volkhov Hotel and Restaurant, Nekrasova St. 24, TEL. 922 47

Sadko Hotel and Restaurant, Yuri Gagarin Prospect

Ilmen Hotel and Restaurant, Gorkova St.

NOVOCHERKASSK

See Rostov-on-Don, p. 273

NOVOSIBIRSK

(Until 1925: Novonikolayevsk)

Population—1,161,000 (1970)

Novosibirsk is the largest city in Siberia.

SIBERIA

Area: 10,000,000 sq. km., larger than either China or the U.S.A.

Population—approximately 25,500,000 which is small for such an area, averaging about 10–15 persons per square mile. The people are 94% Russian and the others include a wide variety of indigenous nationalities. There are Buryats, of Mongol origin, who live in the Buryat Autonomous Republic with Ulan Ude as their capital, the Yakuts of the Yakut Autonomous Republic whose capital is Yakutsk, and many others belonging to Turkic-speaking, Finno-Ugrian, and Tungus groups.

Siberia is the largest part of the Soviet Union in area and economically one of the most important. It stretches from the Arctic Ocean to the Mongolian steppes and from the Urals almost to the Pacific. Its mineral resources include coal, iron ore, gold, diamonds, and various non-ferrous metals. Also of great value are the timber resources and the power of the mighty rivers, Ob, Yenesei, and Lena, and their tributaries.

There are several theories as to the origin of the name Siberia. One is that it derives from the Russian word 'syever' meaning 'north' and this is quite in line with the impressions of Siberia gathered by the first travellers from Russia. There were people from Novgorod who reached the R. Ob at the end of the 11th century. The main attraction for the Russians at that time were the furs, and when the Grand Princes of Moscow imposed taxes on the inhabitants of the Ob region, they were paid in sable, mink, and other valuable furs.

The conquest of Siberia received new impetus after Ivan IV (The Terrible) had defeated the Kazan Tatars. However, even then the movement into Siberia was strongest in the east and the north while in the southern regions the Russians met with staunch resistance from the nomadic Tatars under the leadership of Khan Cochoum. The way to the southern part of the Ob basin was only opened after a campaign against the Tatars was won by the Russians under the leadership of the Cossack, Yermak, who himself died during the fighting.

At the end of the 16th century the first Russian towns were built in Siberia and in the course of about half a century the vast new continent was more or less colonised by Russians. The second period of colonisation started during the first half of the 18th century when the first attempts were made to utilise Siberia's mineral resources. Nevertheless the country's main use was as a place to which undesirable elements of society could be exiled and also as empty territory ready for the resettlement of surplus population from the European part of the country. In 1891–1900 the Trans-Siberian Railway was built, crossing the whole of Asia.

Since the late 1920s a great deal of research has been done regarding the utilisation of the immense wealth locked in the forests, steppes, and mountains of the country. The great rivers, Ob, Yenesei, and Angara, which were of enormous service as communication routes during the colonisation period, now constitute the source of electrical power and a whole network of hydro-electric stations has been established, among them those at Bratsk and Krasnoyarsk which are the largest in the world.

The fertile soil of southern Siberia was used during the virgin lands campaign at the end of the 1950s and today such cities as Novosibirsk, Irkutsk, and Vladivostok have become important scientific centres with Novosibirsk having its own branch of the Soviet Academy of Sciences.

Novosibirsk

In 1893 the village of Gusevka was founded during the construction of the Trans-Siberian Railway and ten years later it was already granted town status. It grew quickly for it was a transit point for settlers going into the Altai area or further on into Siberia. Along the banks of the rivers Ob and Kamenka wooden houses were springing up like mushrooms and at the point where the railway crossed the Ob both trade and transport encouraged the growth of the town.

The church of St. Alexander Nevsky was a landmark on the Siberian route eastwards and it welcomed new settlers. Novosibirsk has sometimes been compared to an American city for the way its population increased in 1897 there were 7800 inhabitants, 20 years later 69,800, in 1937 400,000, and now there are over a million. Between 1927–9 alone nearly 5000 buildings went up in the town.

Local industry took on its first real importance during the early five-year plans of the 1930s, and during World War II industrial plant evacuated from the European part of Russia increased local industry ten times over. Now the city is one of the country's biggest machine-building centres but there is also considerable metallurgy, and chemical, food, and light industries.

Since the Academy of Sciences opened its Siberian branch here in 1943 Novosibirsk has been the educational centre of Siberia. It has 13 higher educational establishments. It is also a vital railway junction where the Trans-Siberian joins the lines to the Altai and Kuzbas areas, and is an important river port.

Tourists to Novosibirsk are proudly shown many different things which are record-breakers—the railway station built in the 1930s which is the largest on the Trans-Siberian, the

Opera House which is bigger even than Moscow's Bolshoi Theatre, and one of the country's largest airports. In the Sovietsky Region of the city on the R. Ob is a hydro-power station built in 1950–9 with a total output of 400,000 kilowatts. The Novosibirsk Reservoir is 1070 sq. km. in area, 200 km. long, and 17 km. across at its widest point.

The city itself is the Soviet Union's third largest, after Moscow and Leningrad. Most of it lies on the right side of R. Ob and its tributaries, the Kamenka and the Yeltsovka, but new blocks of flats are going up on the left side too, in the industrial part of the city known as the Kirov Region, formerly the village of Krivoschyekovo.

NOVOSIBIRSK

KEY
1 Station
2 Stadium
3 Town Park
4 Musical Comedy Theatre & Planetarium
5 Souvenirs
6 Department store
7 Bank
8 Circus
9 Krasny Fakel Theatre
10 GPO
11 Novosibirsk Hotel & Restaurant
12 Tsentralnaya Hotel
13 Central Restaurant
14 Art Gallery
15 Local Museum
16 Opera & Ballet Theatre
17 City Council
18 Youth Theatre
19 Siberia Hotel & Restaurant
20 Regional Council

To Airport

The main thoroughfare is *Krasny (red) Prospect* which crosses the city from the mouth of the Kamenka to the airport. It serves as a shopping street and has administrative and office buildings too. The most outstanding are the buildings of the Regional and City Executive Committees, and also the banks and theatres, some of them built in Constructivist style, popular here in the early 1930s. The Academy of Sciences and the Drama Theatre are both on Lenin St. and from Sovietov Sq., which joins Krasny Prospect, there is a good panoramic view from the high bank of the Ob across the river to the Kirov Region on the left bank.

Local Museum, Krasny Prospect 7; open

11.30–6, closed Tues.

Art Gallery, Sverdlova St. 37

Kirov Museum, Lenin St. 6. Sergei Kirov (Kostrikov, 1886–1934), a well-known Bolshevik, lived here during the time he was working in the town.

A *monument to revolutionaries* who were shot in 1919 has been placed on their grave in a garden in the centre of the city. It is in the shape of a hand holding a burning torch.

Opera & Ballet Theatre, Krasny Prospect 38. The building was designed in 1931 by the architect A. Grinberg and it was intended to be the largest opera house in the world. A number of other architects took part in the work before it was completed. It seats 2000 and has a cupola 35 m. high. The attached concert-hall seats 1000. The bas relief 'Soviet Art' which decorates the main entrance was sculptured by Stein.

Krasny Fakel (red torch) Drama Theatre, Lenin St. 191. This theatre was built in 1912 in Empire style by Kryachkov.

Regional Drama Theatre, Kotovskovo St. 8

Musical Comedy Theatre, Michurina St. 12

Youth Theatre, Krasny Prospect 34

Puppet Theatre, Tramvainaya St. 31

Planetarium, Michurina St. 12

Botanical Garden, by the Academy of Sciences

Central Park

Spartak Stadium

Kirov Park, in Kirov Region

Park, Zayeltsevsky, 2nd Yeltsovka St.

Town Park, Michurina St. 12

Bathing beach, on left bank of R. Ob, near the railway bridge. Other popular recreation areas are Bugrinskaya Grove on the left bank and Zayeltsovsky Grove on the right bank of the river. The warmest time of its rather short summer is July with an average temperature of 18–20°C. (65–68°F.)

Siberia Hotel & Restaurant, Krasny Prospect 26

Novosibirsk Hotel & Restaurant, corner of Lenin St., TEL. 38313

Tsentralnaya Hotel, Lenin St. 1

Tsentralny Restaurant, Krasny Prospect 23

Snezhinka (snowflake) Café, Lenin St. 6

G.P.O. & Telegraph, Sovietskaya St. 33

Bank, Krasny Prospect 25

Department Store, Krasny Prospect 1

Art Salon, Krasny Prospect 15

Academgorodok

The name means 'Academy Town'.

It was decided in June 1957 that a scientific centre should be built in Siberia. Two academicians, Mikhail Lavrentyev and Sergei Khristianovich, were the initiators of the scheme because they pointed out that scientific development in Siberia was lagging far behind the current demand. In fact there was practically no scientific research work going on beyond the Urals at all.

Academician Lavrentyev found a good site for his dream city quite near Novosibirsk and many young scientists from Moscow and Leningrad moved into Golden Valley, as the first settlers called their new home. They even made up a song about it:

Moscow farewell! With Siberia round
We live as one happy family,
And our new home deserves its name—
We call it Golden Valley.

Academgorodok grew fast to become one of the most important scientific centres of the Soviet Union. Now it has a complex of research institutes, about twenty in all, and a university. It lies 30 km. from Novosibirsk on the bank of the Ob Sea, the reservoir which was formed after the completion of the hydro-power station.

History & Architecture Museum: This open-air museum displays examples of old architecture gathered from all over Siberia. Among the most interesting exhibits are the two towers from the Uilsky settlement in the north of the Tiumen Region. The northern and southern towers of the Uilsky settlement are the oldest surviving Russian buildings in Siberia. It took three months to transport them to the museum. Also interesting is the Zashiverskaya Church (1700) from Yakutia and a Buddhist temple from the Buryat Autonomous Republic.

ODESSA

Population—892,000 (1970)
Ukrainian: Odesa

Odessa is the Ukraine's third largest city. It is situated 30 km. north of the mouth of the R. Dniester, and the central part of the city stands on a plateau divided by three ravines, Quarantine, Military, and Water Ravine. The city now covers them all. Odessa's coat of arms bears St. George and the Dragon and a gold field and flower-fluked anchor on a red field.

In the middle ages the settlement and port of Kotsubievo sprang up on this site. It flourished because of its proximity to the mouths of the Dniester, Danube, Dnieper, and South Bug, rivers which brought goods from the steppes and the northern regions. It was chiefly important for exporting grain, mainly through Italian merchants. The city was destroyed by the Tatars and then rebuilt under the name of Khadzhibei. It regained its importance as a trading centre, and then the Tatars were succeeded by the Turks, who in 1764 built a fortress called Yeni-Dunia (new light). In 1789, during the third Russo-Turkish war, Russian troops led by the Neapolitan de Riba captured the fortress and the town together with the entire region between the R. Dniester and R. Bug. By the Yasi Peace Treaty of 1791 the captured area was finally declared to be Russian. Alexander Suvorov built a new fortress in 1792–3 and the foundations of the present naval port were laid in 1794 under the supervision of Vice-Admiral de Ribas and on the order of Catherine the Great. The following year the town was given its present name of Odessa after the ancient Greek settlement of Odessos then believed to have been

located on one of the estuaries (limany) near the R. Bug, although recent research denies the existence of such a settlement at any time. In 1803 some German colonists settled near Odessa to farm, and their successors lived there in the villages until the Second World War.

At this point the history of Duke Richelieu becomes interwoven with that of the city of Odessa. Duke Richelieu Armand Emmanuel du Plessis (1766–1822), a descendant of the famous cardinal of the time of Louis XIII, came to Russia at the beginning of the French Revolution, and remained a devoted follower of Louis XIV. At the end of her reign, Catherine the Great put him in command of her Cuirassier Regiment. He fell from favour under Paul I and went to Vienna. However, when the throne passed to Alexander I in 1801, the new tsar gave an order that the privileges given to Odessa by Catherine the Great be returned for a period of 25 years, and in 1803 the tsar recalled Richelieu and made him the Mayor of Odessa, with great independence of action and local power. Through him one fifth of all the Odessa customs duty was paid in to the town treasury; as a result banks, theatres, and institutes were built, street lighting was installed, and under his guidance the town grew five times larger.

When Louis XVIII became King of France in 1814 he offered Richelieu a high government post. The latter accepted, leaving his country house and his pension to the city of Odessa. The city was neglected after his departure and its development slowed down considerably, but Richelieu fully intended to go back again. On learning of his death in 1822, Alexander I told the French Ambassador, 'I mourn Duke Richelieu as a real friend who always spoke me the truth. His merits will be eternally commemorated by the gratitude of all honest Russian people.'

From 1816 Count Langeron was Mayor of Odessa. The new city grew rapidly because of the speed of building, the privileges afforded to the population, and the establishment of a *porto franco* in 1822. In 1854 the city was bombarded by the Anglo-French fleet for 12 hours but was successfully defended. Its development continued and it gradually acquired its European aspect. By 1881 it had risen to be Russia's greatest port through its trade turnover, which still consisted largely of grain. Its industrial growth was also considerable, and by 1900 it ranked third after Moscow and St. Petersburg in the number of its industrial concerns.

In 1875 the first Marxist working organisation, 'the South Russian Union of Workers', was formed; this was the first revolutionary political organisation in Russia. During the 1905 revolution the workers of the city were joined by the mutineers of the *Potemkin*, a battleship of the Black Sea Fleet. After the suppression of the uprising, the pogroms began, and as a result more than 13% of the total population of 600,000 (including many of Jewish origin) fled the city. Odessa suffered greatly during the Civil War of

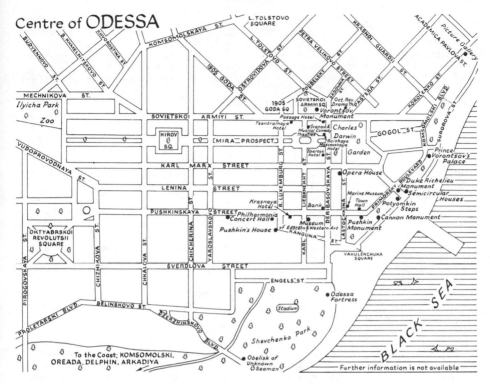

Centre of ODESSA

1917–20 when it changed hands several times. One third of the city's houses were destroyed and the population decreased considerably; it was not until after the famine of 1921–2, when at last renewed sea traffic brought back trade with foreign countries, that the city began to revive.

In 1941 Odessa endured a 69-day siege by Nazi troops, suffered heavy damage, and after World War II was, together with Leningrad, Sevastopol, and Volgograd (formerly Stalingrad), given the title of Hero City by decree of the Praesidium of the Supreme Soviet.

Today Odessa is able to boast 16 colleges and 23 technical training centres, more than 70,000 students making it the fifth largest educational centre of the Soviet Union. The city's heart is October-Revolution Sq.; in the past this was a place for merry-making on public holidays, and now parades and demonstrations take place. The suburbs of Moldavanka and Vorontsovka in the west, Melnitsy in the south-west, and Peresip in the north are now integral parts of the city.

Uspensky (Assumption) Cathedral, Sovietskoi Armiyi (or Preobrazhenskaya) St. This five-domed cathedral was built in 1855–69. Its façade is a mixture of Russian and Byzantine styles. The belltower is 47 m. high. A memorial plaque tells that during the German occupation in World War II a certain Georgi Dubakin raised a red flag on the top of the cathedral. Services take place in the cathedral which has a miracle-working icon of Our Lady of Kasperovskaya.

Ilya Proroka (Elijah the Prophet) Church, Push-kinskaya St. 79. This church, built in the second part of the 19th century, is also open for religious services.

St. Peter's Church, Khalturina St. 5. Services take place at this Roman Catholic church.

Kirche, The Lutheran Church, Ostrovidova St. Closed.

Greek Orthodox Church, Karl Marx St. Open.

There are other late 19th- and early 20th-century churches in Odessa, but they are of no historic interest, and are all closed.

Odessa Fortress, in Shevchenko Park (formerly Alexandrovsky Park). The old tower and wall remain from the military fortress built by Suvorov in 1793.

Prince Vorontsov's Palace. This building by Boffo in classical Russian style was built in 1826–7 and it became the Palace of Pioneers in 1936.

The white lighthouse in the port also bears Vorontsov's name.

Potemkin Stairs. This flight of stairs completed in 1841 was built narrower at the top than at the bottom to give an illusion of greater length. The first step is 21 m. wide and the top step (the 192nd) is 12·5 m. wide. From the top only the landings are visible and from the bottom only the steps. The stairs are called after the battleship which took part in the uprising of 1905. They lead to Primorsky (formerly Nikolayevsky) Boulevard which, at over a 100 years old, is one of Odessa's main streets and still its most popular promenade.

One of the cannons used in the Crimean War stands on it. It came from the English frigate Tiger, and was brought up from the bottom of the sea. Beside the stairs is a funicular railway.

Town Hall. This 19th-century building is decorated with statues of Mercury and Ceres, and the large clock on the main façade has figures of Day and Night.

Catacombs. There are many entrances and exits, but most are on the slopes of Mount Shevakhovo. Most of the caves were formed early in the 19th century when the sandstone was quarried to build up the growing city, and later they were used by smugglers. Numerous revolutionaries hid in the caves during the Civil War of 1917–20, and an underground printing shop was also hidden in them. During World War II the Catacombs were a headquarters for partisans. The tunnels run for a total of more than 800 km. In some places they are very narrow and in others several metres wide; even now new corners are still being discovered, with the remains of soldiers and their munitions in them.

Archaeological Museum, Kommunarov Sq. Open 10–8; closed Wed. This museum, dating from 1825, shows the history of the people living on the northern shore of the Black Sea from ancient times until the 13th century, and also has one of the largest collections of ancient Egyptian relics in the Soviet Union, as well as material from the ancient Greek settlements on the Black Sea.

Historical-Ethnographical Museum, Khalturina St. 4. Open 9–5, closed Sat. This museum is divided into two parts: the historical section at Khalturin St. 3, in the former Commercial Club, and the Geological and Natural History departments, Lastochkin St. 24.

Marine Museum, Lastochkina St. 6. Open 10–5, closed Tues.

Museum of Eastern and Western Art, Pushkinskaya St. 9 (formerly Italian St.). Open 11–5.30, closed Wed. This two-storey building was erected in 1856 by the architect Otton for a merchant called Abaza. It contains 18 halls, and the exhibits fall into 3 groups: antique, mostly copies; western European art, including original works by Rubens, Rembrandt, Veronese, and Murillo; and oriental art, Persian miniatures and handicrafts from China, India, and Japan.

Picture Gallery, Korolenko St. 5a. Open 11–4, closed Wed. Russian artists of 18th and 19th centuries, Soviet art, and graphics are displayed here.

Duke Richelieu Monument, at the head of Potemkin Stairs. This figure of the Duke, shown wearing a Roman toga, was cast in Paris in 1828 by Martoss, Dean of the St. Petersburg Academy of Art. Part of the pedestal was broken by a cannonball during the Anglo-French bombardment, and was restored with an artificial cannonball remaining for all to see. Inside the biggest stone inside the pedestal were placed the most important medals and coins minted during the reigns of Louis XVI, Catherine II, Paul, Alexander I, and Louis XVIII, all of whom Richelieu had served, as well as a medal of Napoleon I and a bronze medal cast in Paris to commemorate the great man's death.

Vorontsov Monument, Sovietskoi Armiyi Sq. This bronze statue was cast in 1863 in Munich by Brugger. The Prince is shown on a pedestal of Crimean porphyry decorated with bas-reliefs of battles.

Pushkin Monument, at the end of Primorsky Boulevard, opposite the *town hall*. Under the bust of the poet by sculptor Polonsky is written 'To Pushkin from the Citizens of Odessa'. The dates 1820–4 engraved on the upper part of the pedestal indicate the years when Pushkin lived in exile in Odessa. The monument was unveiled in 1888.

Grigory Vakulinchuk Monument, Tamozhnaya Sq., near the port. This monument commemorates one of the organisers of the mutiny on the Potemkin who was killed by one of the officers, and whose funeral became the excuse for a mass demonstration. The monument with his bust on a pedestal of red granite stands 6 m. high. It was unveiled in 1958.

Potemkin Uprising Monument, Karl Marx Sq. The monument by Bogdanov commemorates the uprising of 1905 and was unveiled in 1965.

Kotovsky Monument, Kotovsky St.

Obelisk to the Unknown Seaman, Shevchenko Park. An eternal flame burns beside the obelisk.

Opera House, Lastochkina St. 8. This theatre was designed in 1884–7 by Hellmer and Fellner, two Viennese architects and resembles the Vienna Opera House and the Dresden Court Theatre. On the Italian Renaissance style façade are busts of Glinka, Gogol, Griboyedov, and Pushkin. The interior is in Louis XVI style, and the ceiling of the auditorium is decorated with scenes from Shakespeare's 'A Midsummer Night's Dream', 'As You Like It', 'Hamlet' and 'A Winter's Tale'. The theatre seats about 1600. It was damaged by fire in 1925 and then restored. It suffered again with the rest of the city during World War II. Tchaikovsky, Rubinstein, Glazunov, and Rimsky-Korsakov all conducted here in their day.

October Revolution Ukrainian Drama Theatre, Paster St. 15

Ivanov Drama Theatre, Karl Liebknecht St. 48

Musical Comedy Theatre, Karl Liebknecht St. 50

Ostrovskii Youth Theatre, Chaikovsky Pereulok 12. This theatre is called after the Russian playwright.

Philharmonia Concert Hall, Rosa Luxemburg St. 15. This building, dating from 1899 and originally the merchant stock exchange, is one of the best pieces of architecture in Odessa. It was designed by Bernardazzi in Florentine Gothic style. The ceiling is painted to symbolise trade and industry.

Nezhdanova Conservatoire, Ostrovidova St. David Oistrakh, Emile Gilels, and many other leading Soviet musicians graduated from this conservatoire.

Circus, Podbelsky St. 25. This circus is one of

the best in the Soviet Union.

Shevchenko Park. Formerly Alexandrovsky Park and now named after the famous 19th-century Ukrainian poet, this 90 hectares (225 acres) park has an excellent view of the Black Sea and has its own bathing beach, *Komsomolskaya Beach.* There is a *monument to Bogdan Khemlnitsky*, who united the Ukraine and Russia in 1654. Also in the park are the *Avangard Stadium* which can seat 40,000 and is one of the largest in the Ukraine, an *open-air theatre, boat hire stations,* and the University *observatory* and *planetarium.*

Pobeda (Victory) Park, Perekopskaya Pobeda St. This park was formerly called Dukovsky Gardens. There is a swimming pool here, and a permanent local *Economic Achievements Exhibition.*

Charles Darwin Garden, near the Opera House. This garden was once known as Palais-Royale.

Zoo, near Ilyicha Park. Open daily.

Hippodrome Racecourse, Bolshoi Fontan, Chetvertaya Stantsiya

Odessa Hotel and Restaurant, Primorsky Boulevard 11, TEL. 21961. Formerly the London Hotel, this is now run by Intourist.

Krasnaya Hotel and Restaurant, Pushkinskaya St. 15, at the corner of Kondratenko St., TEL. 2–14–22. This is also an Intourist hotel.

Bolshaya Moskovskaya Hotel, Deribasovskaya St. 29, TEL. 24603

Spartak Hotel, Deribasovskaya St. 25

Passage Hotel, Sovietskoi Armiyi St. 34

Tsentralnaya Hotel, Sovietskoi Armiyi St. 40

Hotel Arcadia, Solnechnaya St. 1

Bank, Lenin St., at the corner of Deribasovskaya St.

G.P.O., Gorky St. 12

Central Telegraph Office, Sadovaya St. 3

Indian Legation, Kirov St. 31, TEL. 28–851

Department Store, Pushkin St. 75/73

Podarki Gift Shop, Deribasovskaya St. 33

Beryozka Souvenir Shop, Deribasovskaya St. 19

Odessa's estuaries (limany) are former river mouths which have become separated from the sea by sandbanks; through evaporation they have turned into saline-bitter lakes of varying degrees of salt concentration. The water contains more magnesium, lime, iodine, and bromine than sea water, and the mud is rich in sulphur, which is efficacious in the cure of rheumatic, nervous, and skin diseases. Besides these natural assets the sea itself is very shallow and is quickly warmed by the sun. There are over 30 sanatoria, and 15 rest homes in this part of the Black Sea coast.

Lermontovsky Resort

On Lermentovsky Pereulok. The resort is located within the city boundaries. It stands on a high plateau from which a 220-m. slope with terraces leads down to the sea. There is a large park and sanatoria for rheumatics.

Beyond Shevchenko Park and the Komsomolsky Beach the western resort region begins. Langeron, near Shevchenko Park, was called after

Count Langeron who took the place of Richelieu as Mayor of Odessa in 1816. There is a good bathing beach, and behind it, in Chernomorskaya St., are many sanatoria.

After Otrada comes the park of Arkadiya, running along the sea shore. This is the most popular place near Odessa and the most picturesque. Some parts of this region, along the shore, are known as Minor Fountain (malyi fontan), Middle (sredny) Fountain, and Major (bolshoi) Fountain—but these names have nothing to do with fountains. They simply indicate Odessa's problems with its fresh water supply in the 19th century. There were Artesian wells (fontany) here. Malyi Fontan region lies between 1st and 7th Stantsiya, Sredny Fontan between 7th and 9th, and Bolshoi between 10th and 16th. There is an exceptionally good beach at Bolshoi Fontan, called Golden Beach.

There is a summer theatre, a restaurant, and many sanatoria in what were formerly private villas. Near Primoriye Sanatorium are the Medicinal Baths. Here also is one of the entrances to the catacombs.

Uspensky Monastery, Mayachny Pereulok 6, Bolshoi Fontan. The monastery was founded in 1824 and today 40 monks live there while 50 students attend the seminary. There are vineyards in the grounds and the Patriarch usually spends the summer here. St. Nicholas's Church was built in the 1840s and the Uspenskaya Church in 1892.

Chernomorka

18 km. from Odessa. The name of this resort means 'Black Sea'; it was formerly the German settlement of Lustdorf. The beach of quartz sand is one of the best in the Odessa region and there are many sanatoria here, including a special one for children suffering from ossical tuberculosis. There is a café in the resort.

Malodolinsky was also at one time a German colony, known as Klein Liebenthal. The liman here is 10 km. long and 1 km. wide.

The road from Odessa to the eastern resorts leads through the seaside suburb of Peresip to Shevakhovo on Mount Shevakhovo. It is 11 km. from the centre of the city. Here, too, is Luzanovka with two parks, Verkhny and Nizhny. The beach is wide and sandy; at a distance of 50 m. the sea is not more than 2 m. deep. There is a large children's sanatorium called Ukrainian Artek at this point.

Kuyalnitsky Resort

13 km. from the centre of Odessa. Formerly known as Andreyevsky after Dr. Andreyev who founded the first medical establishment here in 1833, Kuyalnitsky stands beside Kuyalnitsky Liman. This is 30 km. long, up to 2–3 km. wide and 2·2 m. deep. It is divided from the sea by a 2-km. wide sandbank and has the most concentrated salt solution of any of the Odessa limany (4·5–27%). There is a summer theatre and a restaurant and also sanatoria, mudbaths, and a mineral spring used for bathing and drinking.

Near the village of Kholodnaya Balka, 21 km. from Odessa, is Khadzhibeyevsky Liman, 34 km. long, 2·5 km. wide and, in the southern section, 10·5–14 m. deep. The salt solution is weaker than that of many of the other limany (2·5–12%). There is a park, beach, café, and mudbaths on the liman.

ORDZHONIKIDZE
See Georgian Military Highway, p. 110

OREL
Pronounced 'ahr-yol' and meaning 'eagle'
Population—232,000 (1970)
The town stands at the confluence of the R. Oka and the R. Orlik. It was founded in 1564 in the reign of Ivan the Terrible when it was a border fortress of the Muscovite State against the Crimean Tatars. It was said that once, when a group of Tatar invaders were in these parts, an eagle fell like a stone onto the Khan who led them. After a short fight between them, the eagle, pouring blood, rose into the air and then folded its wings and plunged down into the river. The Khan, however, was also wounded and fled with all his men from the R. Oka. Ivan the Terrible heard this legend and decided to name the new fortress after the eagle.

OREL

To TULA and MTSENSK
also SPASSKOYE-LUTOVINOVO
Filling Station
GORKOVA ST.
R. Oka
MOSKOVSKAYA ST.
LENIN ST.
STREET
KOMSOMOLSKAYA
Camp site
To KROMY and KURSK
Further Information Not Available

Orel was an especially important border fortress because it was on the main route by which the Tatars came north to attack Moscow. It was ruined by the Poles at the beginning of the 17th century, and in the 1660s was again devastated by the Tatars; in 1673, after a tremendous fire, it was transferred to a new site known as Yamskaya Hill. It played a useful role in the extension of Russia's dominion further south, and after that life became more peaceful in Orel. The fortress remained until 1702.

On 7 June 1884, it is recorded that Orel was again badly damaged by fire. Its trade at this time

was in grain, hemp, eggs, and poultry. In the 1860s Orel served as a place of exile for Polish insurgents and later a central prison was built to accommodate prisoners on their way to Siberia.

The present layout of the town dates from 1779 when Orel became the district capital, and, according to new plans, was divided into three parts, each part containing a certain area where it was forbidden to build. Thus originated the three main squares, Komsomolskaya (formerly Kromskaya), Promyshlennaya (formerly Vozdvizhenskaya), and Poleskaya Squares. Near Lenin (formerly Market) Sq., arcades of shops were built in 1843 but were largely destroyed. When it was liberated on 5 August 1943 a salute was fired in Moscow; this was the first of such salutes which afterwards heralded the liberation of all the larger cities and towns in turn.

Orel now stretches 11 km. from the north to the south. From Lenin Sq. the main Moscow–Simferopol road runs along Moskovskaya St. and Komsomolskaya St. which are the busiest in town. Most of the buildings here are of post-war construction.

The quiet Normandiya-Neman St. is called after the French squadron who fought with the Russians for Orel in the Second World War.

Lenin St. is among the oldest in Orel with many pre-revolutionary houses. There is a pedagogical institute in the town, and the local House of Soviets stands on Lenin Sq.

Orel is an important railway junction and its industries include the manufacture of machinery for agriculture, road making, and the textile, footwear, and food industries. Leather, food products, watches, and clocks are also produced.

St. Nikita's Cathedral, Rabochy Pereulok 18. This church was built in 1775.

Church of the Archangel Michael, Sacco and Vanzetti Pereulok. This church was built in 1801 in Russian Classical style.

St. Nicholas-on-the-Sand Church, Normandiya-Neman St. This church was built in 1790, is closed, and of no particular historical interest.

Smolenskaya Church, Normandiya-Neman St. This church is also of little interest. It is of 19th-century construction.

Turgenev Museum, Turgenevskaya St. 11. Closed Fri. This museum is located in the house which belonged to landlord Trubitsyn. Turgenev never lived here although he was born in Orel.

Museum of Local Writers, 7-Noyabrya St. 24. Closed Fri. The building was the home of the historian and writer Timofei Granovsky.

Many of the streets of Orel are named after writers and poets who were born or lived here. Among them are Ivan Turgenev, Leonid Andreyev, Nobel prizewinner Ivan Bunin, Granovsky, Leskov, Fet, Prishvin, and others whose names mean much to any admirer of Russian literature. The Writers' Museum is in a hilly part of the town, and the region around is known as 'the nest of the gentry'. Many old houses typical of Russian nobles' homes have survived. Leskov, talking about the importance of Orel in Russian literature, said that his birthplace 'with its shallow waters nourished for the motherland more Russian writers than any other Russian town'. Local enthusiasts used to call Orel the literary capital of Russia.

Local Museum, Moskovskaya St. 1/3

Picture Gallery, Saltykov-Schedrin St. 33

Lenin Monument, Lenin Sq., in front of the House of Soviets. The sculpture by Tomsky was unveiled in 1949.

Polikarpov Monument, in the garden on Moskovskaya St. Nikolai Polikarpov (1892–1944), an aeroplane designer, was born in Orel.

Medvedev Monument, Moskovskaya St. Mikhail Medvedev (1897–1919) was a Civil War hero.

Tank Monument, Tankistov Garden. A tank marks the grave of those who fell here in World War II; an eternal flame burns here.

Gurtiev Monument, Gurtiev Sq. Major-General Gurtiev was killed during the liberation of Orel in 1943.

Turgenev Drama Theatre, Teatralnaya Sq. Founded in 1815, this is one of the oldest theatre companies in the country. It was organised as a theatre of serf-actors by Count Kamenskii on his estate 12 km. from Orel. The Count was a real tyrant, and used to sit in his box with a book in front of him in which he wrote down each mistake the actors made. Nearby hung an assortment of whips, and during the interval he would select one of these and go backstage to beat those who had displeased him. Their cries could even be heard by the audience. Nevertheless the company thrived and in 1817 it is recorded that during six months 82 productions were staged, including 18 operas, 15 dramas, 41 comedies, 6 ballets, and two tragedies; the playwrights included Shakespeare, Schiller, Beaumarchais, and the Russian classics, and there were also works by local serfs. Productions were extremely lavish, with costumes of silk and velvet. The theatre is described in the writings of Leskov. The building now used by the company was built in 1779 and was originally occupied by the Town Council.

Puppet Theatre, Moskovskaya St. 1–3, in the 18th-century building of the Epiphany Church.

Park, Gurtiev Sq., beside the R. Orlik. There is a summer theatre here.

Children's Park, in the centre of town where the R. Orlik and R. Oka meet and where the fortress once stood.

The region beside the R. Tson, a tributary of the R. Oka, called Botanika, 5 km. from the town centre, is one of the most beautiful in the area. The Orel Exhibition of Economic Achievements and a fruit-farming research station are here.

Hippodrome, near Troitskoye Kladbische

Orel Hotel and Restaurant, Pushkin St. 5, TEL. 32–89

Rossiya Hotel and Restaurant, Gorky St. 37, TEL. 745–50

G.P.O. and Telegraph Office, Gorky St. 43

Bank, Teatralnaya Sq.

Department Store and Souvenirs, Moskovskaya St. 5

Spasskoye-Lutovinovo
Turgenev's Home

Spasskoye-Lutovinovo lies off the main road north of Orel, past Mtsensk. The turning is at the 303 km. milestone where there is a bust of the writer, Ivan Turgenev, and a signpost indicating the way to his former estate, 6 km. from the main road.

The Turgenev family estate is now a branch of the Orel Museum. There are 8 halls of exhibits in the Exile's House, where Turgenev was exiled in 1852–3 by the order of Nicholas I for writing an unsuitable obituary on the death of Nikolai Gogol. Although after 1855 Turgenev spent many years abroad, mostly in Germany and France, this place, where his family had moved when he was three years old, was nevertheless his favourite. In a letter written in France to a Russian friend he said, 'When you are next in Spasskoye give my regards to the house, the grounds and my young oak tree—to my homeland.' Turgenev's oak tree is still to be seen.

The main part of the house was burned down in 1906, but the remaining side wings and other buildings have been restored to their appearance of 1881 when Turgenev was last here. Some of his works, including the novel 'Rudin', were written here, and 'Fathers and Sons' and 'A Nest of the Gentry' were completed here.

The park was laid out in 1808. Some of the avenues were planted in the figure 'XIX' signifying that it originated in the 19th century. The longest avenue is of lime-trees, forming the 'I' of the number.

Along the avenues there are wooden boards with quotations from the writer's works, for he is known in Russia as one of the most competent of nature writers. One avenue leads to a pond, called Savinsky Prud after Maria Savina (1854–1915), an actress who took part in his plays. On the estate are a church and a mausoleum, built at the beginning of the 19th century.

OSTANKINO
See Moscow, p. 230

PALANGA
Palanga is now the largest and best known Lithuanian seaside resort and its popularity is growing. It is 348 km. from Vilnius and 242 km. from Kaunas and is famous for its dunes. One of the explanations of its name is that it comes from the Lithuanian word 'palange' which means 'windowsill'; the fishermen's cottages stood so close to the shore that sometimes the waves reached the sills.

The R. Ronze flows into the Baltic Sea here and divides Palanga; the resort is on the left bank and the town on the right. The beach is 200 m. wide and stretches for several miles. The seabed here is sandy and flat, sloping very gradually, and there is amber to be found.

At one time Palanga was an important port, even rivalling Riga. In 1589 British merchants were permitted to build a proper harbour here. The stone breakwaters and the port were destroyed in 1701 by the Swedish army and were never rebuilt, but even today, when the sea is still, the remains of the port can be seen.

It has been known as a resort since the 18th century. At the turn of the century, the Polish noble family, Tyszkiewicz, made the place into a fashionable resort. Most of the villas belonged to the family as did the restaurant, the bath house, and other buildings. It is a local tradition to go out on to the breakwater to watch the sunset, the 'sun's farewell', as they say.

Amber Museum, Vytautas St. 140. This is located in the palace built by a French architect, E. André, for the count. There are about a thousand specimens of natural amber here and also many articles made of amber by local craftsmen. Perhaps most interesting of all are the chunks of amber containing insects which became stuck in the resin of prehistoric pinetrees and were fossilised together with the resin.

Lenin Monument, in front of the town hall; by Vuchetich.

Statue of Egle, Queen of the Grass Snakes, in the park; by Antinis.

Obelisk to Soviet soldiers who fell during the Second World War.

Jurate and Kastytis Statue, in the seaside garden; by Gaigalaite. This statue illustrates a favourite local legend which explains the origin of the amber. Once upon a time a handsome young fisherman of Palanga named Kastytis sailed out to sea and was far from home when night fell. On the bed of the Baltic, in an amber castle, lived the goddess, Jurate, daughter of the Lord of the Sea, and when she saw Kastytis she fell in love with him. He forgot his home and his mother awaiting his return, gazed long at the eyes clear as water and the skin whiter than foam, and kissed Jurate. Perkunas, god of thunder and lightning, was so angry at this violation of ali the laws of behaviour between gods and mortals that he summoned his thunder and lightning to drive Kastytis to the shore so that there the waves of the Baltic should kiss him to death. Now the moaning of the wind is said to be the crying of Jurate, and the amber tossed up on the beaches to come from her castle, ruined by Perkunas.

Palanga Park was laid out by the same French architect, E. André, who designed the palace. It is still one of the principal attractions of the resort. There are two picturesque ponds connected by canals and decorated with bridges. The park was planted with trees and bushes from different parts of the world. The grounds cover about 70 hectares (185 acres).

Besides the Amber Museum, the Painters' and Artists' Holiday Home is also in the palace.

Hotel, Basanavicus St. 9

Jura Restaurant, Basanavicus St. 3

G.P.O., Vytautas St. 29

One of the most popular excursions is the walk to the top of *Birute Hill*, once the site of pagan sacrifices but cleared by the Jesuits in the 16th century. They built a chapel here instead. The area was a stronghold of paganism even as late as the 16th century, when the rest of the country had already long been Christian and the people had become devoted Catholics.

PÄRNU

Pronounced Pyarnoo

Population—40,000 (1968)

(German: Pernau, Russian: Pernov).

Pärnu is Estonia's second most important seaport and one of the best resorts. It stands on both banks of R. Pärnu, where it flows into Pärnu Bay on the northern arm of the Gulf of Riga, 144 km. south of Tallinn. Old Pärnu lies on the right bank of the river and New Pärnu, which runs on into the resort area, on the left. The two parts are joined by a bridge, and the parts on the left bank stand on a narrow strip of land, 1–2 km. wide, between the Gulf of Riga and the river. The R. Pärnu flows parallel to the coast for about 5 km. and then turns south-west to the sea, cutting the town in two. Pärnu beach is 1.5 km. long and consist of coarse, clean sand. It is very level and slopes gradually to the sea. The best bathing season lasts from mid-June until September when the temperature of the water is between 17°–20°C. (63°–70°F.)

There are fish canneries here and local textile work includes flax.

Although the town is shown as a settlement on an Arab map dating back to the 12th century, the first written documentation is dated 1251 when the bishop of Saare Maa, Heinrich, declared that the existing church would become a cathedral, and the town a bishop's seat.

Because of its favourable situation, it soon became a flourishing trading port and in the 14th century joined the Hanseatic League. Owing to war and epidemics between 1483 and 1533 the town was almost entirely devastated four times.

In the 16th century it was occupied in turn by the Swedes, the Poles, and the Teutonic Knights. It was held by the Swedes from 1617 until 1710 when it was taken by the Russians. The Swedes built their fortress in the 1670s but of all the old fortifications, only *Punane Torn* (Red Tower) in Hommiku St. remains, together with parts of the town walls which run from Tallinn Gates to the Venus Bastion near the river and part of the moat of the fortress. The remains of another bastion, the Mercury Bastion, which collapsed in the 19th century, is now known as *Munamägi* (Egg Hill). During Swedish rule there was a Swedish University here called Academia Gustavo-Carolina.

The town became known as a resort in 1838 when an old tavern by the beach was turned into the first bathhouse. It contained six bathrooms and four apartments. The idea was taken up immediately and every year the mudbaths and the excellent beach attracted more and more people.

In 1863 stone breakwaters, 2·5 km. long, were built and now they are one of the most popular places to walk.

In 1882 the *Marine Park* was planted and in fact none of the greenery in the town is natural. Before the First World War the resort enjoyed international popularity, with especially large numbers of visitors from Finland and Sweden. Fashionable hotels were built there in the mid 1930s, the Ranna, now the *Estonia Sanatorium*, and the Vasa Hotel, now the *Soprus Sanatorium*, as well as a new house for mudbaths and restaurants and other public buildings.

A *Lutheran church* is open for services in Kingissepp St., as are also the *Estonian Orthodox Church* in Apa St. and the *Russian Orthodox Church* of St. Catherine in Vee St.

Among the few old buildings of interest are *Petiait (Betty's Barn)* near Old Pärnu Bridge, and the former *town hall* in the centre of Pärnu.

Local Museum, Kalevi St. 53, open 11–5

Lydia Koidula Memorial Museum, Silla St. 37, open 11–5

Lydia Koidula (1843–86) was a famous Estonian poetess and writer. This museum is in her parents' home and everything is kept as it was in their day.

Lydia Koidula Monument, Koidula St. This bronze sculpture of the poetess by Adamson was cast in Italy and was unveiled in 1929.

Koidula Drama Theatre, in the House of Culture. The company was founded in 1911 and its new home was completed in 1967.

The *Resort Club*, by the shore, has a concert hall and a cinema. Nearby is a shell-shaped open-air song theatre.

Kalev Stadium, Ranna Puiestee 2

Tennis Court, Ringi St.

Winter Swimming Pool, Silla St. 3

Kalev Hotel and Baltika Restaurant, Kalevi St. 45, TEL. 517

Voit Hotel, Kingissepp St. 25, TEL. 169

Sputnik Motel

Rannahoone Restaurant, Rannapuiestee 3. This restaurant is one of the largest in the country.

Bank, Kalevi St. 28

G.P.O., Kalevi St. 21

PAVLOVSK

See Leningrad, p. 182

PECHORY MONASTERY

See Pskov, p. 263

PERESLAVL-ZALESKY

The town was established at the mouth of the R. Trubezh in 1152 by Yuri Dolgoruky who had previously (in 1147) founded Moscow. In 1302 the Pereslavsky princedom was united with Moscow, and became a great trading centre, flourishing especially in the 16th and 17th centuries. Most of the surrounding lands belonged to the monasteries which then numbered more than 50. The English traveller Fletcher listed Pereslavl as one of the 16 greatest towns in Russia.

In 1688 Peter the Great, exploring as a boy, found an English boat in Moscow, and because there was not enough room to sail it there he went to the Plescheyevo Lake at Pereslavl. Here he organised a ship-yard, studied navigation, and within a few months had built other vessels which formed the basis of the future Russian navy. The first parade of the fleet took place in 1692 and Peter's relatives, foreign ambassadors, clergy, and a regiment of soldiers from Moscow came to the opening ceremony. Peter then went on to build sizeable ships in Archangel, Voronezh, and the Baltic, and when he returned to Pereslavl in 1721 he had to reproach the authorities for letting his ships get into a state of decay. They were looked after for another 60 years but in 1783, 87 of them were destroyed by a fire.

PERESLAVL-ZALESKY

Botik Museum, near the village of Veskovo, 3 km. from Pereslavl. Open 10–4, closed Tues. This museum was formerly part of the Botik Estate, where there is now a wooden palace, a triumphal arch at the entrance which was built in 1852, a monument to Peter the Great designed by Campioni in the same year, some of his naval guns, and a museum with relics of the flotilla. Only one ship, the *Fortune*, remains.

Goritsky Monastery, Kardovsky St., reached before entering the town on the way from Moscow; an arrow pointing to the left shows the way to the white-walled monastery. Open 10–4, closed Tues. A wooden monastery was founded here in the 14th century but nothing remains of it, and the present complex dates from the 18th century. The Holy Gates were built in the 17th century. The *Uspensky Sobor* (Cathedral of the Assumption) dates from 1757, as does also its iconostasis which is known to be of Moscow workmanship. The bell-tower was put up at the same time but the refectory is a little older. Both the *Local Museum* and *Picture Gallery* are housed in this monastery; the Gallery contains mainly the works of Academician Dmitri Kardovsky (1866–1943) who was born in this region. The Tsar Gates from Vedenskaya Church were exhibited in 1867 in Paris where they won a medal. The plaster mask of Peter the Great was taken from the living tsar in 1719 by Rastrelli. Falconnet's original model for the 'Bronze Horseman' is also in the museum.

Transfiguration Cathedral. This cathedral was built in 1152 and restored in 1894. At the beginning of the 13th century it was the burial place of the local princes. The frescoes were done at the time of the restoration and so are of little historic interest.

Convent of St. Nicholas. This convent was founded in 1392, and its principal church was built between 1690 and 1721.

Fyodorovsky Monastery. This convent was founded in 1551. The Cathedral of St. Theodore Stratilata was built in 1557 by order of Ivan the Terrible in memory of the birth of his son Fedor.

The *Vedenskaya Church* (1710), the *Kazan Church* (1714), and a *belltower* (1705) are also here.

Danilov Monastery, Bolshaya Krestyanskaya St. This monastery was founded in 1508, and its Trinity Cathedral with 17th-century frescoes was built in 1532. Other buildings include *All Saints' Church* (1687) and a *two-storey refectory* (1695). The little *Pokhvali Church* was completed in the same year as the refectory.

Many of the other churches around the town are all that now remain of the surrounding monasteries.

Smolenskaya Church, Hilovaya St. This church was built in 1697–1705.

Novi-Vladimirsky Cathedral. This cathedral was built in 1745 together with the Peter and Paul Church near it.

Simeonovskaya Church, Rostovskaya St. The church was built in the style of Rastrelli in 1771.

Sorokosvyatskaya (Forty Saints) Church, Rybnaya Sloboda (fish quarter). This church was built in 1775.

Pokrovskaya (Intercession) Church, Pleshcheyevskaya St. Built in the 18th century; this is the only church in Pereslavl at which services are still held.

Alexander Nevsky Church, Nagornaya Sloboda (village on the hill). This church was built in 1746.

Church of the Metropolitan Peter, Sadovaya St. 5. This church was built in 1585 and restored in 1889 and again in 1957.

The *Kremlin.* The town's earthen walled Kremlin was founded in 1152–7; the wall is 2·5 km. long.

Hotel and Restaurant, Rostovskaya St. 7.

Filling Station

Nikitsky Monastery, on the way out of the town on the road to Yaroslavl, in the Nikitskaya Sloboda. The monastery was founded in the 12th century, but the stone buildings were added only in 1561–4 on the order of Ivan the Terrible; the

Nikitsky Cathedral was built at this time. Close to the Cathedral is the *Blagoveschensky (Annunciation) Church* with a huge 17th-century refectory and a bell-tower built in 1668. Near the monastery by the road is a small cemetery with an octagonal chapel founded in 1702 on the site of the miraculous healing of Prince Mikhail of Chernigov in 1186.

Holy Cross Chapel. This chapel stands to the right of the main road southwards, from Pereslavl-Zalesky to Moscow, at a distance of 7 km. from the town.

It was erected on the order of Ivan the Terrible in 1557 when he was returning from the consecration of a new church in Pereslavl with Tsaritsa Anastasia, and she gave birth here to their son, Fedor. The chapel dates from that time, but was restored in 1889.

PETRODVORETS
See Leningrad, p. 180

PETROZAVODSK
Population—185,000 (1970)

Petrozavodsk is the capital of the Karelian Autonomous Republic and stands on the shore of Lake Onega, 306 km. north-east of Leningrad. The region had been known in the 16th century for its iron ore and metal industry and in 1703 Peter the Great ordered that a cannon foundry be built here. Some skilled workers were brought from England and even the coal was imported. Present-day Karl Marx Prospect was known as English Street, indicating that this was where the foreign specialists lived. In 1774 the Alexandrovsky Zavod was founded, so called after Catherine the Great's grandson, who became Tsar Alexander I. The foundries produced sea cannon, bombs, steam engines, and looms as well as artistic ironwork for decorating the streets, bridges, and buildings of St. Petersburg. The standard of work was of the highest quality and those responsible for examining the finished products declared that the local guns were certainly not inferior and were very often superior to those of English make. The foundry is now a tractor factory; it stands away from Marx Prospect, beyond the park.

In 1777 Petrozavodsk became a town. Its first governor was the poet, Gavriil Derzhavin (1743–1816), who praised the beauties of the north in his poetry in general and Kivach waterfall in particular in 'The Cascade'. The inhabitants of St. Petersburg considered that Petrozavodsk was really out in the wilds. They sometimes called it 'Siberia-near-the-capital' because it was a place of exile for those who had committed minor offences.

Lenin Sq., formerly known as Circular Place, is the oldest in the town. The two-storey, semicircular buildings make a pleasing ensemble. They were erected in 1775 in late Classic style by Nazarov, at the time the factory was under construction. They housed offices and store-

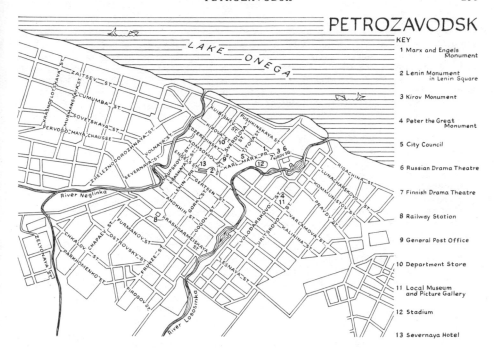

PETROZAVODSK

KEY

1 Marx and Engels Monument

2 Lenin Monument in Lenin Square

3 Kirov Monument

4 Peter the Great Monument

5 City Council

6 Russian Drama Theatre

7 Finnish Drama Theatre

8 Railway Station

9 General Post Office

10 Department Store

11 Local Museum and Picture Gallery

12 Stadium

13 Severnaya Hotel

houses. Some were reconstructed in 1839.

The central square of the town is Kirov Square where theatres and a monument have been erected on the sites of demolished churches. The building of the *Russian Drama Theatre* was designed in 1953–5 by Brodsky, and the sculptured group, 'Friendship', on the pediment is by Konenkov. The *Finnish Drama Theatre's* modern building occupies the west side of the square. Little of old Petrozavodsk has survived. The university was founded in 1940. Many of the town's original buildings were wooden and Petrozavodsk suffered severely during World War II. There are still some merchants' houses of no particular architectural interest in the central part, and on Kirov and Gertsen Streets can be seen Lutheran churches, now closed. There is much construction work in progress.

Krestovozdvizhensky (the Raising of the Cross) Cathedral (1880s), Volkhovskaya St.

Local Museum & Picture Gallery, Zavodskaya Sq. 1. This museum, founded in 1871, has a good collection of local wood carvings and embroidery. The gallery shows, among its other exhibits, an excellent collection of ancient icons (15th–18th century). Open 11–6.

Peter the Great Monument, Zavodskaya Sq. The bronze figure by Schröder was unveiled in 1873. The inscription reads, 'To Emperor Peter the Great, founder of Petrozavodsk', and the statue points towards R. Lososinka where the foundry was built.

Marx & Engels Monument, Kuibyshev St. This is by Belostoksky, Fridman, and Osipenko and it was unveiled in 1960.

Lenin Monument, Lenin Sq. The sculptor was Manizer, and the statue was unveiled in 1933 and restored in 1946. It stands 11 m. high, including the pedestal, and is made of 14 blocks of local grey granite weighing 140 tons.

Kirov Monument, Kirov Sq. This is also by Manizer and was unveiled in 1936.

Anokhin's Bust, Lenin Prospect/Anokhin St. Peter Anokhin (1891–1922) was a local revolutionary.

Fraternal Grave, at the corner of Karl Marx Prospect and Komsomolskaya Street. An obelisk marks the graves of those who fell during the Civil War and World War II. Another impressive memorial, near Lenin Sq., is that of the *grave of the Unknown Soldier* where there is also an Eternal Flame.

Finnish Drama Theatre, Kirov Sq. Founded in 1932.

Russian Drama Theatre, Kirov Sq.

Puppet Theatre, Karl Marx Prospect 19

Pohjola (north) Hotel, Prospect Lenina 21, TEL. 763–06

Kivach Restaurant, Prospect Lenina 52

G.P.O., Dzerzhinsky St. 7

Petrozavodsk now attracts tourists as the starting-point of their trip to the island of Kizhi, 80 minutes away by hydrofoil. The ancient wooden buildings there have a magic all of their own, and seeing them is certainly an experience that should not be missed by anyone visiting Karelia.

Martsialnye Vody

(Waters of Mars)

54 km. from Petrozavodsk

After his visit to Europe, Peter the Great wanted to have a spa of his own, and this spring which was discovered in 1714 immediately attracted his attention. The mineral water was very rich in iron and was appropriately called after Mars, god of war and iron; so the first Russian resort, the Waters of Mars, came into being.

Palaces were built in the vicinity, but nothing of these has remained. What can be seen however is the *wooden church* (1719–21) dedicated to the Apostle Peter which was built according to Peter's plans. There is also a giant candlestick inside made by the tsar. The icon of the Saviour is unusual in that Christ is holding a ship's wheel, has a halo in the form of a compass, and features that bear a strong resemblance to Peter the Great's.

After Peter I's death the resort was soon abandoned, but it revived in 1964 when a sanatorium was built here.

Opposite the church is a small *museum*. Open 11–6, closed Wed. One can sample the mineral water in a *pavilion* near the museum. The pavilion was built to commemorate the visit of Tsar Alexander II in 1858.

Kivach Waterfall
70 km. from Petrozavodsk

It is quite convenient to go on to Kivach after visiting Martsialnye Vody.

On its way down to Lake Onega, the R. Suna forms about 50 waterfalls. Those of Por-Porog and Girvas are well known, but Kivach is the most famous of all. Governor Derzhavin of Petrozavodsk sang of its beauty in his poem, 'The Cascade':

A hill of diamonds pours down
In a four-stepped cliff precipitate.
In the deep abyss pearl and silver
Boil below in seething mounds;
Spray shimmers in a hill of blue,
The roar flies far through distant woods . . .
O waterfall! All, all is drowned
In your crater's fathomless darkness!
Do the pines crash before the gales?
You splinter them in pieces;
Can thunder crack the mighty boulders?
You grind them into sand.
Thunder on, O waterfall,
As wonderful as you are precious!
Trans. J. M. Louis

Kivach is 17 miles from the mouth of the Suna. The river rises near the Finnish border, and flows 290 km. through 22 lakes before it reaches Onega. It is rightly called the 'mother of waterfalls'. At Kivach it drops 10·7 m. The best time to see it is in May or early June when the river is full. There is a local legend about its origin which goes as follows:

The lovely sisters, Suna and Shuya, rising from one and the same spring, flowed side by side for many miles, never tiring of each other's company. When they reached the rocks and bogs of the forests, they decided to rest a while. Kindhearted Suna, who always let her younger sister take the easiest path, fell fast asleep and in the meantime the ungrateful Shuya ran far ahead. When she awoke, Suna rushed angrily after Shuya, hoping to catch her up, but great rocks stood in her way. She threw herself against the boulders and began to force them apart. When at last she had broken through, she leapt down in three gigantic strides and so the waterfall was formed.

The area around the fall is a nature reserve of 10,500 hectares (26,250 acres), 12 km. from north to south and 14 km. from east to west. Some of the trees here are over 350 years old.

Kizhi
Kizhi parish was founded in the middle of the 16th century. The island's name came from *kizhasuari* meaning 'Island of Games' because it had traditionally been used for people's games in the past. In 1769–71 Kizhi was the site of the largest peasants' revolt in Karelia.

Now there is a collection of different examples of peasant architecture here. There are houses, barns, and both a water- and a windmill. The *house from the village of Oshevnevo* only 2 km. from Kizhi was built in 1876, and *Yelizarov's House* (1880) came from nearby Seredok. The latter has no chimney and the smoke from the stove had to find its own way out. *Sergeev's House* (1910) came from Logmoruchi, 13 km. outside Petrozavodsk.

The *three barns* are all of 19th-century construction. In the threshing barn, grain was dried as well as milled. This barn came from Beryozovaya Selga, as did also the *watermill* (1875), while the *windmill* is from Volkostrov. All the buildings were put together without nails, in the traditional style of wooden architecture in the north.

Preobrazhenskaya (Transfiguration) Church has 22 cupolas and was built in 1714. It has been called 'an incomparable fairytale of cupolas' and 'a miracle of miracles'. Some Russian artists consider it to be the ultimate in Russian church architecture and the equal of St. Basil's in Moscow's Red Square. Its total height is 37 m.

The interior of the church is remarkable for its unusual iconostasis. It is curved and the left and right ends follow the lines of the north and south walls with the result that the light falls differently on the various parts of it and the effect changes with the time of day. The icons in the lowest row are perhaps the most interesting. There is one de-

picting Abram and Sarah (third from the right) which is an excellent example of the colours typical of the icons of the north, making full use of rust-red and golden-toned ochres. The icon on the farthest left shows Zosima and Savvati, founders of the monastery on Solovetsky Island in the White Sea, and that third from the left illustrates the life of St. George. The fourth from the left is of Elijah being carried away to heaven in the chariot, always a favourite theme for icon painters. The iconostasis was dismantled during the Second World War before the occupation and was reassembled in 1945 when the icons, all dating from the 17th and 18th centuries, were restored. The large, wooden cross was originally a wayside one.

KIZHI

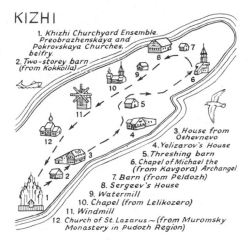

1. Khizhi Churchyard Ensemble.
   Preobrazhenskaya and
   Pokrovskaya Churches,
   belfry.
2. Two-storey barn
   (from Kokkoila)
3. House from
   Oshevnevo
4. Yelizarov's House
5. Threshing barn
6. Chapel of Michael the
   (from Kavgora) Archangel
7. Barn (from Peldozh)
8. Sergeev's House
9. Watermill
10. Chapel (from Lelikozero)
11. Windmill
12. Church of St. Lazarus ~ (from Muromsky
    Monastery in Pudozh Region)

Pokrovskaya (Intercession) Church was built in 1764. The 9 cupolas are each dedicated to a different saint and there is a tenth over the altar.

The church's original iconostasis was lost, but the present one was put together in 1951 to display local icons painted in the 18th century, many of them older than the church itself. The beautiful colouring of 'The Entry into Jerusalem' (sixth from the left) is worth noting and also the realistic detail of the costumes and horses in 'Frol and Lavr'. The variety of the collection gives a good idea of the richness of northern icon-painting in the 17th and 18th centuries.

The palistrade surrounding the churches was restored in 1959, following old illustrations and also the construction methods of existing wooden walls in other places in the north. The belfry was built in 1874.

Church of St. Lazarus (1390) is the oldest in Karelia. It has one dome and was brought here

from the former Muromsky Monastery and restored in 1961.

The *Chapel of Michael the Archangel* (late 18th century) was brought from the village of Lelikozero and restored in 1961.

The *Chapel of the Three Prelates* (late 17th century) was restored in 1962 after being brought here from the village of Kavgory.

PITSUNDA

See Caucasian Coastal Road, p. 78

POLTAVA

Population—220,000 (1973)

Poltava is picturesquely situated on three hills and a plateau on the right bank of R. Vorksla. It is one of the oldest settlements in the Ukraine, known since the 7th century. In the 12th century it was called Ltava or Oltava and was ruined several times by the Tatars. It was under Lithuanian rule until 1430 and was the headquarters of the Cossack Poltava Regiment until 1654 when, with the rest of the Ukraine, it was united with Russia.

Today Poltava is mainly famous for being besieged for three months in 1709 by the Swedish army under Charles XII before Peter the Great won his victory at the Battle of Poltava on 27 June. The defenders of the town were so resolute that when someone suggested in church that it was time to surrender, he was taken outside and stoned to death. The battle concluded the great War of the North and established the position of Russia in Europe. There were 25,000 men in the Swedish army and 42,000 in the Russian army; 9234 Swedes lost their lives and 1,344 Russians. Charles XII narrowly escaped being taken prisoner. He was wounded and had to be carried on a chair of crossed spears. When the Swedes fled, he was carried off too and only because the Russian generals were so delighted with their victory was no attempt made to pursue the retreating Swedes.

In 1787 Catherine the Great visited the battlefield, which is near the town, and soldiers demonstrated the manoeuvres of the two armies for her. She was much impressed and very moved by what she saw, commenting: 'Look upon what the fate of nations depends. A single day and a few hours decided their fate.' The manoeuvres were repeated thirty years later for the benefit of Alexander I.

In 1808 a group of 54 German families moved to Poltava to establish various factories. Their houses formed a German colony where Skovoroda, Balakina, and Boulevard Streets are today. It is recorded however that the mud in the unpaved streets of the town was so deep that ladies had to use oxcarts to go to a ball. Before World War II Poltava had a large Jewish population.

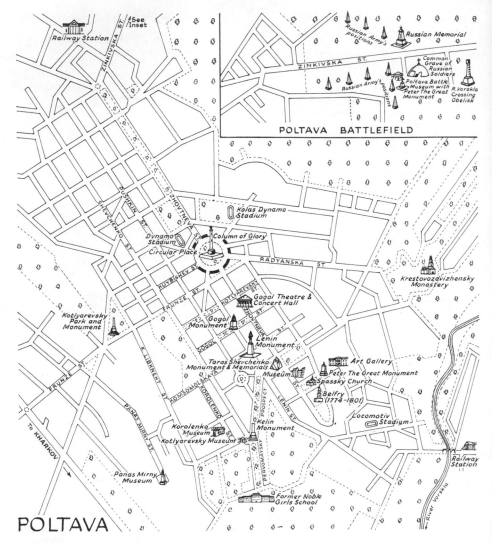

POLTAVA

The most impressive part of the town is the Circular Place where the *Column of Glory* stands. Here are the former buildings of the Cadet School, the District Court, and the Governor's Residence built in Russian Classical style by Zakharov at the beginning of the 19th century. The Institute of Construction Engineering is in the former Noble Girls' School.

Poltava is now an important educational and industrial centre and boasts one of the largest chemical machine-building factories in Europe.

Spassky Church (Church of Our Saviour), on the crossing of Parizhskoi Kommuny St. and Dzerzhinsky St. It is said that Peter the Great came here to give thanks to God for his victory over the Swedes.

Trinity Church (1750), Oktyabrskaya St.

Krestovozdvizhensky (Elevation of the Cross) Monastery, on the outskirts of the town. The Monastery was founded in 1650 by a certain local Colonel Pushkov to mark his victory over the Poles in that place. The belfry (1786) shows Italian influence.

There are a number of other churches in Poltava of no particular architectural interest.

Local Museum, Lenin Sq. 2. Open 10–6, closed Wed. The museum was built in 1906 in national style and decorated with the coats-of-arms of the towns of the region.

Art Gallery, Dzerzhinskovo St. 11. Open 10–6, closed Mon. The collection includes West European art of 15th–19th centuries as well as the work of local artists. The handcraft section is of special interest.

Korolenko Museum, Korolenko St. 1. Open 10–6, closed Mon. The Russian writer lived in this house for 18 years. His grave is in Peremoga Park, nearby, marked by a monument of black granite.

Kotlyarevsky Museum, Pervomaysky Prospect 18. Open 10–6, closed Fri.

Kotlyarevsky's House, Red Square. This was rebuilt following a drawing made by Shevchenko to commemorate the 200th anniversary of the birth of the Ukrainian writer, Ivan Kotlyarevsky (1769–1838).

Panas Mirny Museum, Panas Mirny St. 56. Open 9–5. The classical Ukrainian writer, Panas Mirny (1849–1920), whose real name was Rudchenko, lived here in 1903–20.

Poltava Battle Museum, 7 km. out of town. Open 9–6; closed Mon. Not far from the Battle Museum is a 7·5 m. granite cross unveiled in 1894 marking the grave of the Russian soldiers.

About ·5 km. from this cross is the *Russian memorial* to the Swedish soldiers who fell in the battle. This was unveiled in 1909 to commemorate the 200th anniversary of the battle. A second *monument to the Swedish soldiers*, brought from Sweden and unveiled on the same date, is to be seen 3 km. from the Battle Museum.

Column of Glory, in the centre of October Park in Poltava. This monument is 11 m. high and made of pig iron surmounted by a bronze eagle turning towards the battlefield. It was designed in the shape of an enormous gun-barrel by Tomon and unveiled in 1811. Nine Russian and nine Swedish guns are set into the base of the monument.

Kelin Monument, Pervomaysky Prospect. This monument was erected to Colonel Kelin, commander of the fortress, in commemoration of the 200th anniversary of the Battle of Poltava.

Peter the Great Monument, near Spassky Church. This Monument was erected on the spot where Peter the Great rested after the battle.

Gogol Monument (1915), by Pozen

Lenin Monument (1960), 9 m. high, by Kerbel

Taras Shevchenko Monument, Petrovsky Sq. Designed by Kavaleridze in 1926.

World War II Memorials, Kotlyarevsky Park. The Eternal Flame and the 22-m. granite obelisk commemorate those who fell in the last war. 3411 citizens of Poltava were killed here, in this very park.

Gogol Theatre, Zhovtneva St. 23

Concert Hall, Zhovtneva St. 21

Puppet Theatre, Zhovtneva St. 16

Kiev Hotel & Restaurant, Leningradskaya St. 2, TEL. 748–30

Poltava Hotel & Restaurant, Oktyabrskaya St. 19

Tsentralny Hotel & Restaurant, Zhovtneva St. 19, TEL. 729–12

Poltava Motel, Sovnarkom St. 31, TEL. 737–51

Poltavskaya Lesnaya Hotel, on the main road

Poltava Restaurant, Lenin St. 16

Lileya Restaurant, Red Sq.

Vorskla Restaurant, named after R. Vorskla, by the highway leading out of town to Kiev.

Poltavsky Galushki (Ukrainian dumplings) Café, Zhovtneva St. 25

Ukrainsky Stravy (dishes) Café, Frunze St. 25

Gift Shop, Gogol St. 20

Souvenirs, Zhovtneva St. 25

PSKOV

Population—127,000 (1970)

Pskov is an ancient Russian city situated southwest of Leningrad. It is not known when it was founded but it was first mentioned in Russian chronicles in 903. Excavations show that Slav settlements have existed there since the 6th century which means that Pskov is one of Russia's oldest cities.

Originally Pskov was an outpost of Novgorod the Great, but after the 11th century it became more and more important as a Russo-German trading centre. Its political organisation was similar to that of Novgorod, an aristocratic merchant republic where the work of the elected prince was mainly concerned with defence and justice. In all administrative, economic, and other respects the city was run by two commissioners who presided over the 'gospoda' (council of nobles) elected by the people's forum.

From the beginning of the 13th century the city waged an almost unceasing struggle against the Teutonic Knights. Invariably the Germans were beaten off and only once, in 1240, did they manage to seize Pskov for a short time, and that only because one of the city commissioners opened the gates for them. In 1242, after Alexander Nevsky, Prince of Novgorod, destroyed the military strength of the Teutonic Order in the Chudskoye Lake ice battle, the Germans were driven out of Pskov. In 1348 Novgorod officially recognised Pskov's independence and respected this for more than a hundred years. When Novgorod fell to the position of a province of the Moscow State in 1478, Pskov lost much of its independence.

The last Princes of Pskov were appointed by the rulers of Moscow. In 1510 Vasily III ordered the arrest of the leaders of the city's nobility who opposed Moscow's rule, had the Forum Bell removed and sent two governors to the city. To cement the union, the Prince of Moscow exiled three hundred influential families from the town and settled Muscovites in their stead. The nobles of Pskov did not submit easily to Moscow's domination and there were several uprisings, the last being ruthlessly suppressed by Ivan the Terrible. Rimsky-Korsakov based his opera 'The Maid of Pskov' on the story of this last uprising.

In 1581–2, during the Livonian War when Ivan the Terrible was trying to secure Russian access to the Baltic, the Poles besieged Pskov. They were utterly defeated although, under their king, Stephan-Batory, their army ranked among the best in Europe. In 1615 the same fate met the Swedish army under Gustav Adolph.

In the 18th century Pskov became a provincial centre. It was here, on 15 March 1917, that Nicholas II formally abdicated, in his train at Pskov railway station, and it was near Pskov that in 1918 the first battle of the newly formed Red Army was fought against the Germans.

During World War II Pskov was occupied by

PSKOV

KEY:

the Germans and reduced to ruins, but there has been much restoration and there are many good examples of this ancient city's traditional church architecture. The different architectural styles that developed in Kiev, in Vladimir-Suzdal, in Novgorod, and in Pskov were much influenced by the materials used. Kiev continued in the Byzantine tradition of bricks and mortar, Vladimir-Suzdal used the magnificent white stone available locally, and the northern cities used what stone they could find and set it in thick mortar, smoothing out the surface, plastering it over, and painting it. Brick was used for pilasters and cornices, often very effectively. Building in the north however had always been of wood and the forms and decorations of the new stone buildings retained many characteristics of wood structure.

Pskov churches demonstrate a 'coarsening' of the characteristics of Novgorod architecture. The columns supporting the piers inside are very squat, the walls are thicker and the detail more rude. The idea of a church porch originated in Pskov in the 12th century. Ivan III summoned Pskov architects to restore the Annunciation Cathedral in the Kremlin, and they also helped in the construction of the monastery at Zagorsk. Old fashioned ideas were an important aid in emphasising the continuity of the princely line and also of Moscow's supremacy. Besides, the Pskov architects' skill in roofing was well known.

A good way to see Pskov is to leave the *Oktyabrsky Hotel* by turning right and walking along *Oktyabrsky Prospect* until the 16th-century *Church of St. Anastasia the Roman* appears on the opposite side of the street. Cross Oktyabrsky Prospect and walk down *Nekrasova St.*, passing *New Voznesenskaya Church* (1467) on the right, until you come to the local museum on the left, at No. 7, in *Pogankin House*. Buy tickets at the entrance to the Soviet Section; they are valid for the Historical Section now housed inside Pogankin House and for the art exhibition in the small building behind the museum.

Pogankin House consists of a two-storey building with deep cellars, a single-storeyed house with smaller cellars, and a third house without cellars. These are all united into a single massive building reminiscent of a small fortress. The house was built by one of the leading Pskov merchants, Pogankin, who was the manager of the Pskov Mint in the middle of the 17th century. During World War II the place was badly damaged by the Germans, but it has since been reconstructed and adapted to house the local museum. Among the exhibits is Dovmont's Sword (see below, p. 261), weapons, 13th–17th-century jewellery, old manuscripts, and books. In the picture gallery in the same building are paintings of outstanding Russian artists, including Repin and Aivazovsky.

From the museum, walk down to the river

where *St. George-from-Vzvoz* stands to the left, in Libknekhta St. This church was built in 1494 and has well-preserved slit-windows, typical of most of the churches in Pskov, which had to serve as military fortifications. The buildings lying across the river to the left belong to *Mirozhsky Monastery*. The most important of the group, *Spaso-Preobrazhensky Cathedral*, is well worth seeing. The old frescoes have recently been restored. Opposite the Monastery, but a little to the right is the *Church of St. Climenti*. One can follow the embankment along under the old walls of the town right up to the Kremlin.

The stronghold is entered through a series of archways, the first from the river bank into *Sredny Gorod* (middle town) past the *Governor's House* (1693–5) with 19th-century windows, and the second from *Sredny Gorod* into *Dovmont Gorod* where excavations show the foundations of a number of churches. In the 15th–16th century there were 18 of them here but they were destroyed in the 18th–19th centuries. The last archway leads into the inner stronghold of the Kremlin.

We have no historical evidence as to what ancient Pskov looked like. It is known that in the 13th century the Kremlin (called 'detinets') was built of oak. Oaken walls also surrounded the part of the city closest to the Kremlin. In the 14th–15th centuries the oaken walls were replaced by limestone ones which surrounded the whole of Sredny Gorod. The emergency stock of gun-powder, cannon balls, and food was kept in the northern part of the Kremlin. The market place was inside the inner city and there was a rule according to which no foreigner on pain of death could enter the Kremlin of the inner city and see the defences. Foreign merchants had to trade with the inhabitants of Pskov in a specially allotted place.

In the centre of the Kremlin stands *Troitsky (Trinity) Cathedral*. According to legend, the first cathedral in this place was built in the 10th century. The building which has survived is the fourth and was completed in 1699. Built on Trinity Hill, 72 m. high to the top of the cross, the building can be seen at a distance of 30–35 km. from Pskov. It has five domes and is entered by a wide, covered flight of steps. Inside the cathedral is the tomb of the first Prince of Pskov (d. 1138) and the oaken tomb of Prince Dovmont (d. 1299), the most capable and honoured prince in the history of the city. Dovmont's sword, with which later princes were girt at their coronation in the cathedral, used to be kept here; it is now in the local museum (see above). The vaults below the cathedral contain the tombs of the princes of Pskov. The open place in front of the church served as the People's Forum. The belfry was founded in the 17th century and was reconstructed in the 19th century. From the south the Kremlin was protected by a strong wall called Persy with two towers. The name was the old Russian word for 'breasts'. The wall was reconstructed in the 1860s but the original shape was not preserved.

Outside the Kremlin again is a square which was the site of the old market place and which was surrounded with trading arcades until they were destroyed along with most of Pskov's buildings during World War II. Now there is the impressive building of the *Teachers' Training College*, the *Trade Unions' House of Culture* and, in the centre, a *statue of Lenin*. From here Sovietskaya St. runs down to the bridge over the little R. Pskov, leading to the Zapskoviye Region.

Walking along Oktyabrskaya St. one passes, on the left side of the street, two small rows of shops on either side of the belfry-gateway of the *Church of the Archangels Michael and Gabriel*. This was built in 1338 but its appearance was much changed during the reconstructions of 1699 and 1819. Further along, close to the street, on the right, is the 14th-century church of *St. Nikolai-na-Usokhiye*, rebuilt in 1537. Standing further back and in a bad state of preservation is a church formerly dedicated to Ogiditri and founded in 1537; it was rebuilt in 1866 and called *Vvedyenskaya Church*. It stands on the site of the Pechersky Podvorye (Pechersk Monastery compound). On higher ground to the left is *St. Vasili-on-the-Hill* (1413), close to which once stood a tower where Pskov's alarm bell hung.

On *Sovietskaya St.* are two examples of 17th-century houses which once belonged to the *Menshikov* and *Sutotsky* families. Another example of 17th-century civil architecture is the building called *Solodyezhnya*, 'the Malt House', on Gogolya St., and in Kalinina St. the *Church of Joachim and Anna* (15th century) is a fine specimen of the Pskov style of church architecture.

Zavelichye is the part of the town across the R. Velikaya, on its left bank. *Uspeniya-u-Paroma Church* (the Assumption-by-the-Ferry) is the first one you come to after crossing the bridge and is locally known as Paromenskaya Church. It was built in 1521 on the site of an older church but in its present form dates from 17th–18th centuries.

St. Climenti Church down by the river's edge was built in the 16th century and has a 17th-century cross on the roof. It was called after the Roman Catholic Pope and belonged to the Mirozhsky Monastery (so called because its stands by the mouth of the small R. Mirozha). This is the oldest monastery in Pskov, founded in 1156 by Nifont, Archbishop of Novgorod and Pskov, who was trying to make Pskov a stronghold of Christianity. The *St. Stephen Gate-Church* (late 17th century) was called after an archdeacon. The monastery bell-tower is over another gate. *Spaso-Preobrazhensky* (Transfiguration Cathedral) was founded in 1156. Despite later additions, the interior of the cathedral is little changed from its original appearance. Some wonderful 12th-century frescoes can be seen inside the cathedral although a number of them were spoilt in the 19th century by bad restoration. The most interesting are those of the Annunciation, Nativity, Assumption, and the Entombment. The frescoes are closely akin to Byzantine work. Of great interest is the small *Church of Nikolai Kameno-*

gradsky (St. Nicholas by the Stone Wall) built in the 15th century and formerly also belonging to Mirozhsky Monastery. Its arched roof was built without any pillars and it is the only church of this type in Pskov.

Along the river in the other direction from the Paromenskaya Church is the *Ivanovsky Cathedral* (12th century), all that is left of the Ivanovsky Convent first mentioned in the chronicles in 1243. This convent served for centuries as the burial place for the princesses of Pskov. The cathedral was rebuilt several times after the 15th century, burned down during World War II, and restored to its original appearance in 1949–50.

In the Zapskoviye Region, lying across the R. Pskova which flows by the north-eastern walls of the Kremlin, are the following churches: *Cosma and Damian* (1463) on Leon Pozemsky St., the *Church of the Epiphany* (1489) beside the river, an outstanding piece of Pskov architecture with an interesting four-arched belfry, the *Resurrection Church* (1532), and *Varlaamy Khutynsky Church* (1495) which is open for services. Also in the Zapskoviye Region is another example of 17th-century civil architecture, the *house of the merchant Postnikov*, consisting of two buildings with deep cellars and secret vaults, called the Sack because of its shape. In 1482–1525 this part of the city was surrounded by walls with several towers of which the *Varlaamova* and the *Gremyzchaya Towers* remain. They played an important role in the defence of the city from the Poles and later from the Swedes.

Pogankin House Local Museum, Nekrasovskaya St. 7; open 12–6; closed Fri. There are historical and Soviet Departments and a picture gallery on the second floor.

Lenin Museum, Lenin St. 3. Lenin lived here in 1900 and the museum is in the room that he used.

Liberators' Memorial, Martyrs of the Revolution Sq., in the north-eastern part of the city.

Pushkin Drama Theatre, Pushkin St.

Racecourse, Ippodromnaya St.

Trud (labour) Stadium

Pushkin Garden

Oktyabrsky Hotel and Restaurant, Oktyabrsky Prospect 36, TEL. 4254

Tourist Hotel and Restaurant, Krasnoarmeiskaya Naberezhnaya

Telegraph Office, Sovietskaya St. 20

Department Store, Sovietskaya St. 13

Souvenirs, Oktyabrsky Prospect 18

Snetogorsky Monastery is 5 km. from Pskov. It was founded in the 13th century and the *Cathedral of the Nativity of the Virgin* is 14th century.

Mikhailovskoye

Mikhailovskoye, Pushkin's house and estate, is 120 km. from Pskov. It was the estate of the Pushkin family to which the Russian poet, Alexander Pushkin (1799–1837), belonged. It was given to the poet's great-grandfather, Abram Hannibal, by Empress Elizaveta in 1742.

Alexander Pushkin came here frequently and spent two years here (1824–6) when he was exiled

from the capital for his dissident poetry. It proved a prolific period; he wrote over 100 significant works here. The estate was destroyed by the Germans during World War II and recreated after the war. Inside the house everything is as it was during the poet's life. Some of Pushkin's personal belongings as well as those of his close friends or relatives are displayed there.

Near the main house is a small cottage which belonged to Pushkin's nurse, Arina Rodionovna, whom he mentions affectionately in many of his works. The surrounding park has matured beautifully.

There are other places in the vicinity associated with Pushkin's life: the villages of *Petrovskoye* and *Trigorskoye* and *Svyatogorsky Monastery*—all of them 3–4 km. from Mikhailovskoye. The most interesting of these is the monastery which was founded in 1569 upon the order of Ivan the Terrible. Until the end of the 17th century it was officially listed among Russia's 30 principal monasteries. A legend tells how the tsar's order followed reports of miraculous deeds performed by a shepherd boy who lived in these parts and had visions of holy icons with extraordinary healing powers. Historians, more prosaically, point out that the founding of the monastery coincided with a terrible epidemic. The main gates and parts of the wall date back to the 16th century. *Svyatogorsk Cathedral,* inside the monastery, was also built in 1569 but it has two annexes added at the end of the 18th century. The cathedral is 23·5 × 13·5 m. in area and 9 m. high. Its austere style is typical of the old architecture of the Pskov region. The top of the cathedral was badly damaged during the war, and later restored. The belfry, built in 1821, is 37 m. high. There are two exhibits inside the cathedral, one about the building itself including some of the icons, and the other about Pushkin. The poet was fatally wounded at a duel in St. Petersburg on 8 February, 1837. To avoid publicity, his body was brought secretly to Svyatogorsk Monastery and buried here in the family grave.

Izborsk

This is a small village on the way to Pechory Monastery. Below it lies Gorodischenskoye Lake and the R. Smolka. Izborsk was founded in the 8th–9th century and being older than Pskov has many stories about its history.

At one time it was called Slovensk, after the prince who founded a 'great town'. Then his son, Izbor, inherited it and the name was changed to Izborsk. Later it became dependant upon Pskov and being nearer to the border, it bore the brunt of countless attacks, withstood sieges, and was burnt and ruined. In the 18th century, after Russia gained her access to the sea, Izborsk lost its strategical importance and gradually declined until it was only a small town and then no more than a village.

There is now a plaster-of-Paris factory here and the region specialises in growing flax.

The fortress which remains was built on Zheravi Hill in 1330 but has been reconstructed several times in the course of time. There are six towers (early 15th century) which vary in height from 13 to 19 m.

St. Nicholas Church. In the same way that Pskov was considered the home of the Holy Trinity, Izborsk was the home of St. Nicholas.

St. Sergei Radonezhsky Church, 18th century
Goroischenskaya Church, 17th century

Pechory Monastery

Long ago hermits lived in the caves in the hill here. In 1470 some hunters heard their singing and found the caves. They called the place Svetaya (holy) Hill. Only one of the hermits, Mark, is known by name. Possibly they were monks who had fled here from Kiev.

In 1473 a priest, Ioann, settled here with his family, because they had been persecuted by the Germans in their home town of Yuriev (now called Tartu). When his wife, Vasa, died, Ioann buried her in the caves but the legends say that the following day he found that her coffin had leapt out of the ground. Afraid that he had not recited the funeral service properly, he repeated the ceremony and buried her again. A second time the same thing happened, so he left her simple wooden coffin unburied and today it rests in an alcove on the right at the entrance to the caves. Vasa came to be considered the guardian of the caves and the earthly mother of the monastery. It is said that on one occasion intruders tried to force the coffin open but, as the lid was prised up, flames shot out. The monks still show the scorch marks that remain.

After Vasa's death, Ioann became a monk, taking the name of Iona. He excavated the underground church dedicated to the Assumption of the Virgin. When he died, he was buried near the tomb of the hermit, Mark, and that of a monk called Lazar who had died aged 91 after sealing himself into his cell. His food and water had been passed through to him daily and he wore an iron harness and cross weighing 12·5 kg. (28 lb.)

There have always been monks living in this way and there still are today. The temperature of the caves is always 5°C. in both summer and winter. The monks estimate that it takes about twenty years for the body to get so used to the underground climate that it will not decay after death. The passages of the caves stretch for perhaps 300 m. and about 10,000 people are buried here. The Fraternal Sepulchre holds 400 coffins and many individuals have their own memorial plaques on the walls. Some of these belong to nobles who gave money to found a family vault.

The monastery grew gradually. Many of the fortifications date from 1519 and the walls with their towers from 1565. It was robbed several times and damaged, and in the 16th and 17th centuries because of its strategical position it was besieged by the Poles and partly destroyed by the Swedes and the Lithuanians. In 1701 Peter the Great surrounded the monastery by an earth wall and a moat, and two years later the Swedish siege failed.

The entrance to the monastery is through the *Holy Gate* and the first church down the slope is dedicated to *St. Nicholas* (late 16th century). The *Church of the Annunciation* (Blagoveshenskaya) (1556–70) is the red and white one in the centre of the grounds and *St. Lazar's* (18th century) is the yellow church across the courtyard. The *Pokrova Church* (1759) stands high above the caves and that of the *Archangel Michael* (1820) commemorating the liberation of Pskov from Napoleon is up by the wall. It is large and white, with three imposing porticos and a broad green dome. Inside are impressive 19th-century decorations and plaques of honour. The monastery belltower (1521) now has 13 bells instead of the original 18.

In the underground *Assumption Cathedral*, the woodwork of the iconostasis is in a Baroque style called Yelizavetinskoye Baroque after the Empress Elizabeth who preferred her Baroque to have a little more symmetry to it than was customary at the time. The figure on one of the icons, on the left as you enter, bears a strong resemblance to her. Most of the icons in the iconostasis are 17th century. In this cathedral is the *tomb of St. Cornelius* who was head of the monastery for 42 years in the 16th century. He was responsible for reinforcing the surrounding walls. Legend has it that Ivan the Terrible was angered by this show of independence and ordered that Cornelius be beheaded. When the deed was already done, the tsar repented of his hasty demand and he himself carried the body into the cathedral where it now lies. Then in retribution he made rich presents to the monastery including that of a golden cross weighing 8 lb.

Here also is a wonder-working icon, hung around with pale blue satin and embroidery. When it is carried out with all its decorations of silver and silvergilt, it weighs more than a quarter of a ton. The lamp in front of it is decorated with inscriptions of prayers, and words of prayer even form the fringe of letters hanging from it. The icon was painted in 1521 by a monk, Alexei Maly, and it is said that it helped to save Pskov from the army of the Polish king Stephan-Batory in 1581 and from Napoleon in 1812. The Virgin is said to be the guardian of the whole Pskov area. Another underground church is that of the *Resurrection* which was excavated in the 1930s.

Today about 80 monks live in the monastery. Three-quarters of these are over 80 years of age, but their lives are calm and ordered and they live long. They have 10 cows, 50 chickens, and 8 hives of bees and they care for their apple orchards and vegetable garden. Their fish is bought locally.

Just outside the Holy Gates is the long dark blue building of *St. Barbara's Church* (early 17th century) which is used for Russian Orthodox services in the Estonian language. Near it is the white *Church of the Forty Martyrs* and between these two stands the little *Chapel of St. Alexander*

Nevsky, both built in the 19th century.
   Restaurant, Svoboda St.
   Eating House, Oktyabrskaya St.

PUSHKIN

See Leningrad, p. 181

PYATIGORSK

See Mineralniye Vody, p. 189

RIGA

Population—733,000 (1970)
Capital of the Latvian Soviet Socialist Republic.

LATVIA

Area: 64,000 sq. km.
Population—2,364,000 (1970) of which 62% are Latvians and 27% Russians.
Latvia is situated in the west of the U.S.S.R., on the eastern coast of the Baltic Sea. Its capital is Riga.

The Latvians trace their origin from several Baltic tribes, the Latgali, the Zemgali, and the Livi, who were akin to the East Slavonic tribes.

In the 12th century these tribes and the lands they occupied attracted the attention of both German landlords and the Teutonic Knights. After the failure of the crusades, the conquest of the country began under the guise of converting 'pagan tribes' to Christianity.

In 1196 the Pope proclaimed the Northern Crusade against the Livs. In 1201 the Livonian Bishop (Livonia was the name under which these lands were known at that time) founded the fortress of Riga which became the main stronghold of the German invasion. After a bloody struggle which continued until the end of the 13th century the Archbishop of Riga became sovereign of the Baltic provinces. The Order of the Brethren Sword (or the Livonian Order) proved to be the strongest force and by the end of the 14th century all real power in the area belonged to the Grand Master of that order.

In 1558 Ivan the Terrible in his efforts to gain access to the Baltic Sea declared war upon the Livonian Order and, having reached Riga, soon defeated the Knights. Poland, Sweden, and Denmark claimed the area as well and Russia had to withdraw. Western Livonia went to Denmark and the central part with the newly-formed Duchy of Kurland went to Poland. After the 1598–1624 war between Poland and Sweden the whole of northern Livonia with the exception of Kurland was taken by Sweden.

In 1721, after the Russo-Swedish War, the Swedish possessions in Livonia went to Russia, and by the end of the 18th century all Livonia (as well as the other Baltic provinces) was taken over by Russia as a result of the partitions of Poland, and it remained part of the Russian Empire until the 1917 Revolution when it became a Soviet Republic. This however lasted for a very short time and from 1919 until 1934 Latvia was an independent republic. In 1934 the Prime Minister, Ulmanis, set up a dictatorial nationalist régime which existed until 1940 when Soviet troops entered the country. Soon after this Latvia was proclaimed a Soviet Republic and included into the U.S.S.R.

Foreign visitors may go to Riga, the capital of Latvia, and to the seaside resorts that lie along the coast to the south-west of it.

The following national dishes are well worth trying:
   Zamieku Brokastis—'peasant's breakfast', a super-omelette
   Maizes zupa ar putukrejumu—corn soup with whipped cream
   Skabe Putra—sour milk
   Biezpiens ar kartupeliem, krejumi—cottage cheese with potatoes, sour cream, and butter.

The Latvian language is unlike Russian and the Latin alphabet is used. To avoid confusion, please remember that in the public lavatories 'V' stands for 'Gentlemen' and 'S' for 'Ladies'. Here are a few words of Latvian:

hello	sveiki
I am a tourist	es esmu turists
please	lŭdzu
thank you	tálties
yes	ya
no	ne
good	labi
bad	slikti
I don't understand	es nesaprotu
I need an interpreter	mau vajag túltu
goodbye	sveiki (as for "hello")

Riga

Latvia's capital city lies beside the R. Daugave (the Western Dvina) not far from its mouth in Riga Bay. Its name was taken from that of a stream called Ridzene or Rige, meaning 'pure'.

In the 12th century German merchants began to trade with the tribes who lived by the West R. Dvina and Riga was founded in 1201 by Bishop Albert of Bremen who came here with the Teutonic Knights and established a trading station on the right bank of the river, where Old Riga now stands.

In 1223 Riga was given municipal rights. The Baltic coast was at that time inhabited by the Livi, the Kursi, the Zemgali, and other tribes. Bishop Albert set himself the task of bringing Christianity to the area. He established the Order of the Brethren of the Sword. The citizens of Riga, which was quickly becoming an important trading centre, soon joined in serious rivalry with both the Bishop and the Order. Then Riga joined the Hanseatic League in 1282. Sometimes the burghers had an upper hand in their quarrels, but finally in 1330 Riga had to submit to the supremacy of the Order. In 1561 Riga became a merchant city-state.

In 1582 after the Russo-Polish War Riga fell under Polish domination and during the 17th century it frequently changed hands between the Poles and the Swedes. During the Russo-Swedish

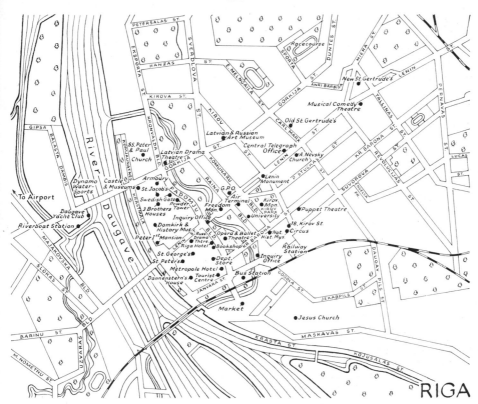

War at the beginning of the 18th century the Russian army siezed Riga (1710) and as a result of the war the Baltic countries, including Riga, became part of the Russian Empire.

After the 1917 Revolution in Russia and the disintegration of the Russian Empire, Riga became the capital of the Latvian Republic (1918–40) and has been the capital of the Latvian S.S.R. since 1940.

Riga is an important industrial centre producing electrical and radio goods, road vehicles, agricultural equipment, and chemicals, and there are woodworking, light, and food industries. The city is also a scientific and cultural centre with the Latvian Academy of Sciences (which has 14 affiliated research institutes), a University (founded in 1861 as the Polytechnical Institute), and a wide assortment of colleges, and technical and trade schools.

Lenin St., formerly Brivibas (Freedom) St., is the principal thoroughfare. In it stands the *Freedom Monument* which was erected in 1935. Zale was the sculptor and Stalbergs the architect, and the inscription 'Tevsemei un Brivibai' means 'Fatherland and Freedom'. Further on, where Kirov St. crosses Lenin St., stands a *statue of Lenin* erected in 1950. The sculptors were Ingal and Bogolubov and the architect was again Stalbergs. The best shops and the most popular cafés are along this street.

The most interesting part of the city is Old Riga,

a small region covering an area of about 35 hectares (87 acres), which lies just around the corner from the 'Riga' Hotel. The oldest section is that lying between L. Kaleju St., Daugavas St., and Lenin St. Old Riga suffered heavily during World War II when several historic buildings including the 14th-century House of the Blackhead and the 13th-century Rathaus were burnt down.

The *city walls* were erected in 1201 and were rebuilt several times. They used to be 11 m. high and as much as 2 m. thick. Remains of the walls can be seen from Troksna, Minsterejas, and Janeseta Sts. Several of the original 24 towers have survived to the present day. One of them is the *Powder Tower* (once called the Sand Tower) on Smilsu St. It took its first name from the sand dunes nearby, but later came to be called the Powder Tower when it was turned into a gunpowder depot. In the 14th and 15th centuries it served as a dungeon and torture chamber. It was badly damaged in 1621 when the Swedes besieged the city, and at the end of the 19th century it was reconstructed although the outward appearance was little damaged. It now forms part of the Museum of the Revolution.

Riga Castle, Pioneriu Sq. 3. The Castle was built in 1330 and was the Livonian Order's stronghold in Riga. In the 15th century the townspeople ruined it during their conflicts with the Order, but subsequently when the Order regained its powerful position the burghers had to rebuild the Castle for the Knights in 1515. From the middle of the 16th century the Castle was the residence of the Governors of Livonia and later that of the President. In the 18th century a new building was added to it and the White Hall was constructed at the beginning of the 19th. The tower with the spire is a 20th-century addition. Now the Castle houses the *Palace of Pioneers* and the *Local Museum*.

Mater Dolorosa Church, Pils St. 5. This church stands next to the Castle. It is a Roman Catholic Church. A little further along the embankment and facing the river stands:

St. Saviour's Church, now closed, which was built as the English Church in Riga.

The *Domkirk and Monastery*, 17 Junija Sq. Formerly the Cathedral of Our Lady, the Domkirk (Doma Baznica) was founded in 1211, a brick building designed as the seat of the Bishop of Riga. Since the second half of the 15th century it has been converted, restored, and reconstructed several times. It bears evidence of the Romanesque, Gothic, Renaissance, and Baroque periods of architecture. The floor and walls are lined with numerous tombstones and memorials with epitaphs. The pulpit dates from 1641 and there is a statue of the Order's Grandmaster, Walter von Plettenberg. The organ is one of the largest in the world. It was made in 1883–4 and has 6768 pipes ranging from 13 mm. to 10 m. in length. It was restored in 1961 and is now used for concerts. Visitors are advised not to miss the opportunity of attending one of these.

The cloisters, with Romanesque columns, Gothic arcades and the tonsorium, now houses the *Historical Museum*. The Domkirk tower and spire rises to a height of 90 m.

The Reformation reached the Baltic countries in the middle of the 16th century and the Cathedral was sold to the Lutherans by the last Archbishop of Riga for 18,000 Riga marks. The Lutheran faith is still dominant in Latvia but the Domkirk is no longer used for services. This is not the first time the building has been put to secular use; in 1681 it was converted into a winestore.

Peter Ist Mansion, Komjaunatnes Embankment, on the way down to the river from the Domkirk. Peter the Great lived in this house in 1711. It had belonged to a rich merchant, but Peter was offered it as a gift from the city and he was glad to accept. He was fond of the house especially the garden terrace on the first floor for which he was said to have ordered trees and flowers from abroad.

The next group of buildings are all to be found in the oldest section of Old Riga, where they stand at no great distance from each other.

Warehouse, formerly *St. George's Church*, 10 Skarnu St. The Church was built by the Order of the Brethren of the Sword at the beginning of the 13th century and served as both their chapel and hall. In 1297 it was damaged during the city uprising against the Order and was subsequently rebuilt. In the second part of the 17th century it was turned into a warehouse. The huge roof of the building is covered with old tiles.

The *Convent of Ekk*, Skarnu St. 22. The building was put up in 1435 out of city funds as a guesthouse for visitors, and at the end of the 16th century it was rebuilt and N. Ekk, then Mayor of Riga, established a 'convent' here which was a home for poor widows. The medieval heating system is preserved; it includes a huge, pyramid-like pipe with room enough in the bottom for a small kitchen.

St. John's Church, Skarnu St. 24. This church which at one time belonged to the Dominicans was built at the beginning of the 13th century and consists of two parts, the higher in Gothic style and the lower in Renaissance style. It was rebuilt in the 16th century and decorated with star-studded vaults. A richly ornamented Baroque altar was added in the 18th century and the existing small pseudo-Gothic tower was built in 1849.

St. Peter's Church, Veerigas Sq. This church was built in the 13th century and rebuilt in the 15th. In the 17th century the steeple collapsed and a new one was built upon a wooden frame. In 1721 however both the steeple and the frame were struck by lightning and badly burnt. They were later restored by special order of Peter the Great who had himself taken part in the fire-fighting. When restored the new steeple was 130 m. high. It was again burnt down in the summer of 1941 during enemy attack on Riga, and is still under restoration.

House of Reitern, Marstalu St. 2/4. This house was built in 1684–5 for a rich merchant named Johann von Reitern. It is elaborately decorated with reliefs and garlands cut in stone.

Reformed Church, Marstalu St. 10. Members of the Reformed Church appeared in Riga in the 16th century, but they were only granted a legal parish there in 1721. This church was built between 1727 and 1733. In 1805 the interior was divided into two floors, the ground being used for storage and the first for religious services. The wooden turret on the façade is about 35 m. high and the church itself is one of the largest in Riga.

The *House of Dannenstern*, Marstalu St. 21. Built in 1696 this house is typical of any rich Riga merchant's.

There are as many as 24 *medieval warehouses* in Old Riga, the most characteristic of them being the ones at 7 and 11 Sakarnas Gvardes St. (behind the Reformed Church) and 10 and 11/17 Vecpilsetas St. The one at 11 Sakarnas Gvardes St. still has the hoisting mechanism intact.

The *Guild Halls*, Amatu St. 3 & 6. The Virgin's Guild Hall at No. 6 was formerly known as the Great Guild Hall. Its present form dates from 1854–9 when the architects Beine and Schel designed it in Anglo-Gothic style to preserve its original appearance. In fact it embraces two much older constructions. The first is the Münster Hut founded in 1330 and used as a meeting hall by the merchants of Riga. It can now be seen as a cross-vaulted, divided room, painted in medieval character with the coats-of-arms of the forty-six member cities of the Hanseatic League. Twelve cross-vaults rest on six octangular columns. The chandeliers date from the 17th and 18th centuries and the oaken musicians' gallery from 1644. In the centre of the hall is a display of gifts presented to Riga Philharmonic Society which now has the use of this hall for concerts.

In the past the main hall was used for wedding parties. It is recorded that the 'floor had to be covered over with hay to protect it from pouring beer'. The Bride's Room (Brantkammer) is the second oldest part of the building. It was built in 1521 and now contains a collection of national instruments. The beautiful sandstone chimneypiece dates from 1633 and the chandelier from 1649.

St. John's Guild Hall (or the Small Guild Hall) stands at No. 3 Amatu St. It was built in 1864–6 by Felsko in Gothic style to match the Great Guild Hall, and was the meeting hall of the town's craftsmen. Appropriately it is now the House of Culture of the Riga Trade Unions. St. John was the patron saint of the guild and his statue can be seen on the outside under the Gothic tower. Of special interest inside is the Hall of the Elders (or the Upper Hall) which is decorated with oak. There are painted views of St. Petersburg, Lübeck, Riga, Moscow, Hamburg, Bremen, and Rostock, although the latter two are now hidden by the stage. The stained glass windows which were put in in 1888 depict the presidents of the guild in medieval costume. Permission to see the hall can easily be obtained from the door-keeper.

St. Jacob's Church, Vestures Sq. This church was built at the beginning of the 13th century and its altar and interior are well preserved. The spire was erected in 1756 and is now the only authentic Gothic one in Riga although all the churches had them in the middle ages.

Three Brothers' Houses, 17, 19, and 21/23 Maza Pils St., beside St. Jacob's Church. No. 17 was built in the 15th century and is the oldest surviving dwelling in Latvia. It is typical of houses of that time. Since 1687 it has been used as a bakery. No. 19 was built in 1646 by a merchant. The ground and first floors were lived in and the upper floor used for storage. Only the outer appearance of No. 21/23 is preserved.

The *Armoury*, Torna St. 1, on the other side of St. Jacob's Church. The Armoury was built in 1828–32, using part of the old city walls and the Maiden Tower. Now it is used as a storehouse.

The *Swedish Gate*, Torna St. 11. This gate was built into the city wall in 1698 during the Swedish occupation. It stood near the semicircular Yurgen Tower, and later on several houses were put up and the whole complex came to be known as the Swedish Gate. It now belongs to the Latvian Architects' Union.

SS. Peter and Paul Church, in the citadel district. The plan of this church forms a cross. It was built in 1776–86 by order of Catherine II to replace the Swedish Citadel Church. The stone towers were built without a trace of wood. Services are held.

Jesus Church, on the crossing of Sevastopol and Odessa Streets. This is one of the few historic buildings outside the bounds of Old Riga. It lies beyond the market and the skyscraper. It was built in 1818–22 on the site of earlier wooden churches, the first of which was founded in 1638, and is the largest wooden structure in Latvia. The building is octangular with a flat wooden cupola resting upon 16 pairs of columns, following the plan of the Roman Pantheon. There are four symmetrical wings to the main body of the building and the tower is 40 ft. high.

Voznesenia Church (Russian Orthodox), Meness St. 2. This church is open for religious services, as are the Synagogue and the churches listed below, with the exception of the Nativity Cathedral and the old St. Gertrude Church.

St. Joseph's Church (Roman Catholic), Embutes St. 12/14

Baptists' Church, Hospitalu St. 32

Cathedral of the Nativity of Christ the Saviour, Lenin St., in the centre of the city. The architect Flug designed the building in new Russian-Byzantine style in 1876–84.

St. Alexander Nevsky Church (Russian Orthodox), Lenin St. 56. Built in 1820–5 following the plan of the Pantheon.

Old St. Gertrude Church, Karl Marx St. 78. Built in Gothic style in 1867 by Felko.

New St. Gertrude Church, Lenin St. 112. Built in 1903–6 with a side tower in new Greek style.

All Saints' Church, Kiycvas St. 10. Founded in 1812 and reconstructed in 1870–83.

Troitsky-Sergievsky Convent, Krasnova Barona St. 126. Forty nuns live here. Their cathedral is the *Trinity Cathedral* which was built in Russian style with five domes in 1892–3. Near the cathedral is the small wooden *St. Sergei's Church* where among other relics are some of St. Andrew the First-Called, and some pieces of Christ's Cross and Sepulchre.

Synagogue, Peitavas St. 6/8

History Museum, Palasta St. 4, in the building of the Domkirk Monastery. The museum has existed since 1764 and has departments of archaeology, history, navigation, and politics. It covers the history of Riga from ancient times to the present day. Included are 16th-century guns and ammunition, parts of the decor from the destroyed House of the Blackheads, and a minor coat-of-arms (stone carving of 1777) from the town gateway. Open 11–5, closed Mon.

Latvian History Museum, Pionieru Sq. 3, in the Castle. The museum was founded at the end of the 19th century and has a large collection of arms starting from the 16th century. Open 11–5, closed Mon.

Fine Art Museum, Pionieru Sq. 3, in the Castle. Founded in 1920, the museum contains a collection of Dutch and German paintings, French engravings, antique sculpture, china and, among other things, an Egyptian mummy. Open 12–5, closed Tues.

Janis Rainis Literary Museum, in the Castle. When it was founded in 1940 the museum was entirely devoted to the Latvian poet, but now there is also material on display on other Latvian authors and a collection illustrating the history of the theatre in Latvia. Open 10–5, closed Mon.

Museum of the Revolution, Smilsu St. 20. Formerly the Military Museum built in 1938, the present lay-out was opened in 1940. Part of it is in the adjoining Powder Tower. Open 11–5 (Sun. 11–6), closed Mon.

Latvian and Russian Art Museum, Gorky St. 10a. Once the Fine Art Museum, the building was designed by Neumann in 1905 in South German Baroque style of the 18th century. The four Ionic columns hold a portico with figures including that of Pallas Athene. The collection of Latvian and Russian paintings dates from 1905. Open 12–5 (Sun. 12–6), closed Mon.

Natural History Museum, Kr. Barona St. 4. Among the different sections are those devoted to zoology, anthropology, geology, and botany. The earliest collections included date from the 18th century. Open 11–5, closed Mon.

P. Stradius Museum of the History of Medicine, Leona Paegles St. 1. The museum, based on Academician Stradius's collection, was opened in 1958.

Open-air Museum of Latvian Peasant Life in 17th–19th Centuries, 12 km. from Riga, beside Lake Yugla. The buildings stand in an area of pinewood covering 90 hectares. The collection was founded in 1924 and the 46 buildings which were brought here from various parts of Latvia vary from 80 to 400 years in age. The wide variety of utensils, tools, and farming and fishing equipment furnishing the buildings number more than 4000 items, and in addition the museum attendants wear national dress. Apart from houses and farm buildings there is the old *Lutheran Church* from Usma which was built in 1704 and a *warehouse* (1697) from the port of Liepaja. The Museum Park is open 9–9 and the interiors of the building 11–5. It is closed Mon. and the days immediately following public holidays. It can be reached by a No. 1 bus.

Johan Gotfrid Herder Monument, near the Domkirk. The bust in memory of the poet and city librarian (1744–1803) was designed by Schaller in 1864.

Peter Stucka Monument, in front of the castle. The sculptor was E. Melderis and it was unveiled in 1962.

Opera and Ballet Theatre, Padomju Boulevard 3. The building was constructed in 1863.

Latvian Drama Theatre, Kronvalda Boulevard 2
Latvian Drama Theatre, Lacplesa St. 25
Russian Drama Theatre, Komunala St. 1
Musical Comedy Theatre, Lenin St. 96
Puppet Theatre, Krasnova Barona St. 16/18
Circus, Merkela St. 4. This is one of the largest circus buildings in the Soviet Union. It was opened in 1872.

Riga Philharmonic Concert Hall, Amatu St. 6, in the Great Guild Hall

Conservatoire Concert Hall, Krasnova Barona St. 1

The large pinewood beside Lake Kiserzers is called *Mezaparks*. It can be reached by tram, trolleybus, or river-bus from the centre of the city. The Riga Park of Culture and Rest is in Mezaparks. There is a *cinema* there, some *restaurants*, and a large *open-air concert platform* where the annual song festivals are held; the tradition of the festivals goes back to 1873. There is room for an audience of 30,000 and for 10,000 singers. An *exhibition* of the national economy has also been opened in the park, and there is a *Children's Railway* with three stations.

Riga Zoo is to the right of the park entrance. It was founded in 1912 and there are about 3000 animals there.

The *Warriors' Cemetery* in Mezaparks was laid out in 1923 and attractively decorated with fountains, sculptured groups, and careful landscaping.

Nearby is *Rainis's Cemetery* where a birch avenue leads to the grave of the Latvian poet. The monument of polished red granite was designed by K. Zemdega. War victims and prominent people from the realms of art, literature, and politics are buried here.

The oldest park in Riga is the *Viestura Garden* at the far end of Ansekla St. It was laid out in 1721 by order of Peter the Great. An elm which he planted still stands there with a memorial stone beside it. Also in the garden is *Alexander's Triumphal Gate*, erected in 1818 by the merchants of Riga to commemorate the victory over Napoleon. Until 1923 the garden was called the Tsar's Garden.

Kirov Park is in the centre of Riga, bounded by Kirov, Merkela, Krasnova Barona, and Petera Stucka Streets. It was founded in 1816–17.

Arkadijas Park in the Pardaugavas district was opened at the end of the 19th century.

The other parks and gardens in Riga include the *University Botanical Garden*, Kaudavas St. 2. It dates from 1922 and has a rich collection of tropical and sub-tropical plants.

Hippodrome Racecourse, Michurina St. 30 and Grostonas St. 6

Yacht Club, Mezaparks, Bernudarza St. 19

Riga Hotel & Restaurant (Intourist), Padomju Boulevard 22, TEL. 22–78–95

Metropole Hotel, Restaurant and Café, Padomju Boulevard 36

Astorija Restaurant, Audeju St. 16, on the top floor of the Department Store

Tallina Restaurant, Gorky St. 27/29
Staburags Restaurant, Suvorov St. 55
Maskava Restaurant, Kirov St. 53
Kaukazs Restaurant, Merkela St. 8, Caucasian cuisine
Lira Restaurant, Dzirnavu St. 45/47
Pribaltika Restaurant, Merkela St. 13

Daugava Restaurant, P. Stuckas St. 7, but the entrance is from Dzirnavu St.

Baltija Restaurant, Melnsila St. 22

Kosmos Restaurant, Vienbas Allee 51, on the other side of R. Dvina

Sports Restaurant, in Mezaparks, Kokneses Prospect 35

Fish Restaurant, Suvorov St. 55

Shashlik Bar, Suvorov St. 46

Astoria Café, Valnu St. 18

Confectioner's and Café, Kirov St. 55

Flora Café, Lenin St. 35

Luna Café, Padomju Boulevard 18

Lira Café, Valnu St. 9

Daugava Café, Lenin St. 25

Nika Café, Lenin St. 70

Vidzeme Café, Lenin St. 83

Sigulda Café, Gorky St. 25

Pancake Kitchen, Blaumana St. 8

Latvian Society for Cultural Relations with Foreign Countries, Leona Paegles St. 2, TEL. 21607

G.P.O., Lenin St. 21

Central Telegraph Office, Lenin Street 33

Bank, Gorky St. 2a

Dzintars (foreign currency) Shop, Lenin St. 4 and Teatra St. 9

Central Market, Negu St. 7

Central Department Store, Audeju St. 16

Souvenirs and Jewellery, Lenin St. 40

National Arts and Crafts, Lenin St. 52

Paintings and Sculptures, Padomju Boulevard 20

Jewellery, Lenin St. 15 & Suvorov St. 11

Photographic Equipment, Suvorov St.

Photo Processing, Kirova St. 69 & 77

Central Bookshop, Teatra St. 11

Foreign Books, Padomju Boulevard 24

Central Second-Hand Bookshop, Lenin St. 46

Taxi Ranks, by the railway station, Kirov Park, Agenskalne Market, and at the crossing of Lenin and Revolution Streets. Phone for a taxi by dialling 00.

Riga has been a famous seaside resort for many years. Sand dunes topped with pinetrees stretch for over 10 miles along the coast of Riga Bay from Lielupe to Kemeri and they are paralleled by a wide, sandy beach. The climate is temperate and the sea averages 18° or 20°C. during the summer. The place has been used for summer holidays since the end of the 18th century but it was only at the end of the 19th century that it acquired its real popularity as a resort.

Since 1959 the area has been administered as a single resort region known as Jurmala, but as in fact it consist of a series of coastal villages they are listed here in turn as they lie westward from Riga. Jurmala can be reached from Riga by electric train, bus, river-bus, or taxi.

Lielupe

15 km. from Riga, at the mouth of the R. Lielupe. Near here is High Dune, the highest point along this part of the coast with a wide view over the sea. The Daugava Yacht Club is on R. Lielupe.

Bulduri (formerly Bilderlingshof)

19 km. from Riga. The new building of the *railway station* is the best in Jurmala. *Bulduri Horticultural College* (founded in 1911) on Viestura St. has many lime-trees on its 207-acre grounds.

Intourist Hotel and Jurmala Restaurant, Bulduru St. 52

Avoti

a small place 20 km. from Riga

Dzintari and Majori

(formerly Majorenhof)

22 km. from Riga. These are Jurmala's cultural and social centres. In the former is a concert hall for 700 with a garden and open-air theatre seating 3000, right beside the shore, Turaidas St. 1.

Juras Perle Restaurant, on the beach front at Jurmala. This is the best restaurant in the region.

Dzintars Restaurant (formerly Lido), Turaidas St. 6/8

The following are items of interest in Majori:

Majori Hotel and Restaurant, Jomas St. 29. This is one of Jurmala's tallest buildings.

J. Rainis's Cottage, Alexandra St. 7. Here is a small museum dedicated to the Latvian poet (1865–1929).

History Museum, Jomas St. 43. This is a branch of the History Museum in Riga.

There is a *statue of Lacplesis* in Majori. Lacplesis the Bear-Slayer is a legendary giant-hero of Latvia. He is reputed to have been able to break a bear's jaws with his fist and even to harness bears to the plough. His great strength was sometimes a hindrance because in spite of his good intentions to be of service to his people and his country he frequently broke the man-made tools he had been given to use. The giant met his match in a terrible duel with a three-headed ogre, as fierce a fight as any described in Beowulf. While the struggle was on, the ogre's mother travelled the Seven Seas to learn from the inhabitants of the Underworld just where Lacplesis's weakness lay. The ogre had already lost two of his heads when he was told to strike off Lacplesis's ears. The writhing pair fell into R. Daugava and were carried out to sea.

Dubulti

(formerly Dubbeln)

28 km. from Riga. This is the oldest settlement near the sea in this area. A 4-km. birch avenue leads to Jaundubulti.

Jaundubulti

Famous for its natural parkland and its pine groves on the dunes.

Pumpuri, Melluzi, Asari (formerly Assern), and Vaivari, quiet, seaside places with an abundance of locally grown fruit and vegetables.

Kemeri

(formerly Kemmern)

40 km. from Riga. This is the largest and best organised unit of the Baltic resort region. The curative qualities of the local mineral water and mud

have been known since the end of the 18th century. Early in the 19th century a forester by the name of Ans Kemer built some wooden huts here with primitive baths. Now the accommodation can take 20,000 patients a year, but still the place bears its founder's name.

Sanatorium No. 1 is called the *White Palace*. It is a building in classical style with Corinthian columns.

In the *Warriors' Cemetery* lie those who fell during both World Wars.

Hotel, Tukuma St. 19
Restaurant, Tukuma St. 23

Sigulda
(German: Segewold)
Population—7,000 (1970). Sigulda is situated 52 km. from Riga on the road to Pskov and Novgorod. Russian soldiers marched along this road on their way home from Paris at the end of the Napoleonic War and the area around Sigulda is renowned for its beautiful scenery which has led it to be known as 'Livonian Switzerland' (Livlandische Schweiz).

Sigulda was founded in 1207 when the area around the town was divided between the Teutonic Order (also known as Livonian Order of Sword Brethren) and the Archbishop of Riga. The land on the left bank of the R. Gauya went to the Archbishop of Riga and that on the right to the Teutonic Order. Stone castles were built on both banks of the river, the remains of which can be seen today.

However, the area around Sigulda passed through many hands, both before and after the foundation of the town. Recent archaeological excavations have revealed weapons and other articles dating from the beginning of the second millenium B.C. when the area was inhabited by Finn and Ugor tribes.

In the 16th century Sigulda was captured in turn by the Russian, Polish, and Swedish armies. After the Northern War (1700–21) Sigulda and the surrounding country came under Russian power. Only a third of the population remained after the war and the ensuing plague, but the town soon grew as people moved here from other parts of Latvia. After the Russian Revolution of 1917 Soviet power was established here until 1920 when Latvia became an independent country.

The ruins of a number of castles remain in Sigulda. At the end of Livkalna St. are the *Satezel Ruins* of the ancient town which stood here long before the foundation of Sigulda. A castle was built here later. Nearby is *Peter's Cave*, so named as a child called Peter was born here during the Northern War.

If one follows the path from here to the top of the hill, known as *Artists' Mountain*, one obtains a good view of Sigulda and the R. Gauya. The path leads on to a cemetery where there is a monument to those killed during the 1905 Revolution.

The steps lead down to the ruins of *Sigulda Castle* which was built by the Teutonic Order in 1207–26. It was destroyed on several occasions and not restored after the Northern War. In the inner courtyard is a platform which is used for song and dance festivals. In the outer courtyard is the 'new' castle which was built in 1878–81 and once belonged to Prince Kropotkin. It is now a sanatorium. In front of the sanatorium is a *monument* to the Latvian linguist Atis Kronvald (1837–75).

At the end of Turaidas St. on the other side of the river is the *Cave of Gutman* (Gutmana Ala). The cave is about 14 m. deep and 9 m. in height and depth. There are some inscriptions on the wall dating from the 16th century. The cave is said to be named after a man named Gutman who lived here and healed sick people with water from a spring inside the cave. Water from the spring is also reputed to bring back lost love. There is a tradition that young girls unsure of their lover's feelings drink the water. According to another legend a girl known as Turaid's Rose because of her remarkable beauty was killed in the cave by a Polish nobleman who wanted to marry her. Turaid's Rose was already engaged to a gardener in the castle. The meeting in the cave was proposed by the nobleman who sent her a letter in the name of her fiancé. When Turaid's Rose saw she had been tricked, she still refused to marry the nobleman and told him that the scarf she was wearing was a magic scarf which would protect her from any attack. She challenged the nobleman to strike her with his sword, and was thus killed. Her grave is at the top of the hill near the cave. 263 steps lead up the hill where an old lime tree stands. A marble plaque on the tree reads: 'Here lies Turaid's Rose .

On the same hill are the remains of *Turaid (Treyden) Castle* which was built in 1214 for the Archbishop of Riga. It later belonged to Baron Stael von Holstein. The castle was destroyed by a fire in 1776 and only the main tower remains. It was restored to its original height of 35 m. and the walls are 3 m. thick. Near the ruins is a *local museum*.

On another hill nearby is an attractive *church* which was built by Latvian craftsmen in 1750. Inside the church are some paintings and carved wood benches. The path down the hill from the church leads to the ruins of the *Castle of Krimuld* which was built in 1255–73 and was used as a residence for foreign dignitaries. It was destroyed at the beginning of the 17th century.

RITSA
See Caucasian Coastal Road, p. 77

ROSTOV-ON-DON
Population—789,000 (1970)
In the 18th century a fortress was built beside the R. Don to withstand the Turks. It was called after St. Dmitiri Rostovsky, and from this fortress the city got its name. When Alexander I approved the town plans in 1811, 'On-Don' (Na Donu) was added to the name to distinguish it from Rostov

Yaroslavsky, an ancient Russian town north-east of Moscow. In Russian the city is often called 'the Gate to the Caucasus'.

Rostov stands at the meeting place of roads running from the Ukraine, the Volga region, Siberia, and the northern Caucasus and Transcaucasia. It is 46 km. from where the R. Don flows into the Sea of Azov, and it spreads for more than 12 km. along the high right bank of the river. Since the completion of the Volga-Don Canal its port has grown in economic importance, for it is now connected with five seas. The canal links the Don with the Volga near Volgograd (formerly Stalingrad) and is 100 km. long. The first attempt to build such a canal was made by the Turks in 1569, and from the time of Peter the Great onwards there were repeated plans to build it; it was finally constructed between 1947 and 1952.

The port was established in 1749 by the order of Empress Elizabeth, and was then known as Tamernik. It was an important place for trading in the Sea of Azov and in the Black and Mediterranean Seas, and was founded as a customs point. The fortress date from 1761. In 1779 Armenians were transferred here from the Crimea and it was they who founded the township of Nakhichevan to the east of the fortress. The name was taken from that of the ancient Armenian capital ruined by the Tatars in the 13th century. The new Nakhichevan was absorbed by growing Rostov in the 1920s.

Important foreign trade began to develop in Rostov, and the settlement, which had become a large economic centre, was declared a town in 1797. The port's freight traffic was the third greatest in Russia. Goods destined for shipment to Turkey, Greece, Italy, and even England sailed down the Don. Foreign merchants encouraged Rostov's growth. Among others Sidney, James & Co., an English company, was established here in 1778. The garrison was transferred in 1835 and the fortress was later demolished. The town then grew rapidly as the region's industrial and agricultural potential began to develop, overtaking the Urals in the output of both coal and metal. The railway link with Moscow was completed in 1871 and that with Ordzhonokidze (then called Vladikavkaz) in 1875. Its standards of hygiene, however, did not rise with its rapid growth and at the turn of the century it took third place, after Calcutta and Shanghai, for the number of its deaths by cholera.

Rostov played its part in Russian revolutionary history: 30,000 workers went out on strike in 1902. During the Civil War it was one of the White Generals' strongholds and the Germans occupied the city for some time in 1918. They also held it twice during the Second World War.

Today Rostov is the administrative and economic centre of a region of 100,000 sq. km. equal to the combined territories of Belgium, Holland, and Denmark, and is one of the granaries of Russia. There are 20 project organisations here, making plans for factories in the Caucasus and other parts of Russia. The University was founded in 1869 in Warsaw and was transferred to Rostov in 1915; it now has 6 faculties. There is a statue of Lomonosov by Aleschenko in the garden in front of the main building. There are besides many institutes, including an institute of agricultural machinery; machinery of this sort has been produced here in Rostov since 1898 and this institute has 10,000 students. Rostov's main industrial development dates from 1846, and it now has tobacco, food, shoemaking, textile, aircraft, and ship-building industries. The wine-making factories offer a selection of table wines. One of the Soviet Union's most famous is a local sparkling red wine. Often called red champagne here, its real name is Tsim-

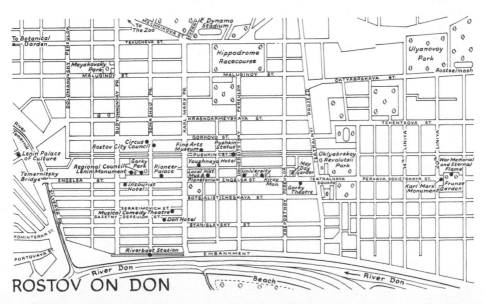

ROSTOV ON DON

lanskoye Igristoye. One of the largest Soviet factories to produce agricultural machinery, the Rostselmash factory, was built in 1930. Rostov now produces 86% of Russia's combine harvesters and 70% of her cultivators and seeding machines, and one of the newest colleges is a factory-institute where students who work at Rostselmash attend lectures. Rostov's 25 libraries contain more than 2,000,000 books.

A number of Soviet writers have lived and worked here, among them Alexandr Fadeyev and Vera Panova. Mikhail Sholokhov, best known for his book 'And Quiet Flows the Don', still lives in the village of Veshenskaya, about 200 km. from the town.

Engels St. (formerly Bolshaya Sadovaya) begins at Temernitsky Bridge, near the railway station. It is the main street and most of the buildings of interest are to be found along its 3 km. length. The 11-storey block of flats at the beginning of the street was completed in 1958. Many of the large pre-revolutionary buildings were also built as flats, not always in the best of taste. One merchant-landlord, Cherikov, argued with his architect about the decoration of a 6-storey block. He wanted two large columns on the façade, but the architect said that they would spoil the proportions of the Renaissance-style house. Cherikov replied, 'Who is paying you, the Renaissance or me?' and the columns were put up.

The crossroads of Engels St. and Budyonnovsky Prospect is known as the architectural entrance to the town because it has one of the most impressive architectural ensembles of Rostov. Nearby is *Gorky Park* behind which can be seen the western façade of the Town Hall (1896–9). Engels St. runs next to Dom Sovetov Sq. The *House of Soviets* was built between 1929 and 1941. It was partly burned down during the war, but now its reconstruction is almost complete. In the square is a fountain with two stone lions by the sculptor Vaide, dating from 1917. Nearby stands the huge building of the *Bank* (1910).

Engels St. ends in Teatralnaya Sq., which was once at the edge of the town and had a sign saying 'Border'. Now it is the biggest square in Rostov and the place where sports parades and public festivals are held. In the 1930s some houses, and also the *Gorky Theatre* (1930–5) built by the architects Schuko and Gelfreich, were still designed in the Constructivist style much in favour immediately after the Revolution, when all forms deriving from the past were cast aside. This style was soon to be officially condemned and these buildings are among the last of their kind. The Gorky Theatre is unusual in that it has two halls in one building; the main auditorium seats 1200 and the smaller concert hall seats 550. The building is situated on a hill and its white 'forehead', which can be seen for miles around, forms part of the silhouette of the city. It was damaged during World War II and reconstructed in 1963.

Further east begins the part of Rostov originally known as Nakhichevan. The continuation

of Engels St. is called Pervaya Sovietskaya St., and ends in Karl Marx Sq., where a *monument* to the philosopher was unveiled in 1935. In Frunze Garden opposite is a *War Memorial* dedicated to all those who perished in World War II, and near this is an *Eternal Flame*. Running parallel to the full length of the north side of Engels St. is Pushkin St. The Promenade on the river embankment was built in 1949 and steps lead down to it from Budyonnovsky Prospect. Attractive woods can be seen across the river and also one of the best river beaches in the south of Russia.

New blocks of flats and whole new residential areas are springing up throughout the town and around it. Among other impressive new buildings is the *Rostelmash Palace of Culture* built in 1961 (Selmashevsky Prospect 3). There is a theatre of opera and ballet here for the use of amateur groups.

Cathedral of the Nativity of the Virgin, Stanislavsky St. 58. The cathedral is open for services.

All Saints' Church, Dolomanovsky Pereulok 70. This church is open for services.

Armenian Cathedral, Nakhichevan. Built in the 19th century by Starov and now used as a young technicians' club.

Synagogue, Gazetnyi Pereulok

Also in Rostov are *churches* of the Old Believers and the Baptists and six other Russian Orthodox churches.

Local History Museum, Engels St. 79. Open 10–6; closed Mon. The stone idols worshipped by nomads in 11th–12th centuries are of interest. The *Rostov Planetarium* is located in the same building.

Fine Arts Museum, Pushkin St. 115. Open 10–6; closed Mon. Here are paintings by Repin and other Russian and Soviet Realists.

Museum of the Revolutionary Past and the Glory of Labour, Gusev St. 2

Lenin Monument, at the entrance to Gorky Park. This statue by Nyeroda was unveiled in 1929.

Lenin Monument, Lenin Prospect. Unveiled in 1963.

Kirov Monument, Kirov Sq. By Vilenski, unveiled in 1939.

Pushkin Statue, Pushkin St., where it is crossed by Karl Marx St. The 4-m. statue by Schultz was unveiled in 1959.

Gorky's Statue, on the embankment. Maxim Gorky worked here as a docker in 1891. The 3·5-m. statue was unveiled in 1961.

Gorky Theatre, Teatralnaya Sq. 1

Youth Theatre, Engels St. 170

Musical Comedy Theatre, Serafimovich St. 88

Open Air Theatre (Zelenyi Teatr), Oktyabrskoy Revolutsii Park. Built in 1962 with 3000 seats.

Circus, Budyonnovski Prospect 45. Completed in 1957, this is the biggest permanent circus building in the Soviet Union.

Gorky Park, Engels St. 45
May Day Garden, Engels St. 129
Zoo, Zoologicheskaya St. 3

Botanical Garden, Zheloznodorozhni Raion

Ulyanovoy Park, Oktyabrskaya St. Here is the Rostov Exhibition of Agricultural and Industrial Achievements. There is also a childrens' railway.

Rostelmash Stadium, Oktyabrskaya St. Room for 33,000 spectators. At the entrance is a monument commemorating the launching of the first Soviet sputnik.

Dynamo Stadium, Tekuchev St.

Hippodrome Racecourse, Maluginoy St. 233

Bathing Beach. From the centre of Rostov the main road to the Caucasus crosses the Don. After the bridge one can turn left to the beach on the river bank.

Intourist Hotel and Restaurant, Engels St. 115, TEL. 5–90–66

Moskovskaya Hotel and Restaurant, Engels St. 62, TEL. 6–53–91

Don Hotel and Restaurant, Gazetny Pereulok 34, TEL. 6–23–40

Youzhnaya (south) Hotel, Karl Marx Prospect 20, TEL. 6–54–38

Tsentralny Restaurant, Engels St. 76

Volgodon Restaurant, Beregovaya St. 31

Teatralny (theatre) Restaurant, Oktyabrskoi Revolutsii Park

G.P.O., Podbelskova St. 24

Telegraph Office, Serafimovich St. 62

Telephones, Semashko St. 34

Bank, Sokolova St. 26

Department Stores, Engels St. 46 and 65

Podarki (gifts). Engels St. 60

Art Salon, Engels St. 128

Market, Oborony St.

Tanais

Tanais was the ancient Greek name for the Don and also for the town at the river mouth. Now there is a museum and an archaeological reservation. Open between 25 April and 10 November 9–5; closed Tues. Tanais is near the village of Nedvigovka, about 30 km. from Rostov on the way to Taganrog.

For more than 600 years (3rd century BC–4th century AD) Tanais was the economical and cultural centre of the area. Excavations to date have revealed the remains of a fortress and towers and a number of streets.

Starocherkasskaya Stanitsa

Founded about 1570, this is the oldest Cossack settlement. Formerly known as Cherkassk, it was called after the Cossack, Avgust Cherkas. Between 1644 and 1805 it was the capital of the Don Cossacks. The town was well fortified with earth walls and wooden towers where 80 guns were mounted.

It is well known in Russian history for its capture in 1670 by the Cossack and peasant leader, Stepan Razin (see below, p. 274), and again in 1708 by Kondrat Bulavin. Peter the Great came here several times and on one occasion he noticed a naked Cossack with a rifle riding on a barrel. It was explained to him that a Cossack can drink

away everything except his rifle and the tsar was so delighted by this that he approved as the design for the Cossack army a naked Cossack on a barrel holding a rifle.

St. Ephraim's Convent in Cherkassk was one of the richest in Russia.

Ataman (Cossack leader) Platov found a better place for the administrative centre and the capital was transferred to Novocherkassk in 1805. Cherkassk lost its importance and was given its present-day name. The prominent Russian artist Surikov came here in 1893, looking for Cossack models for his painting, 'The Conquest of Siberia by Yermak'.

Today one can visit the nine-cupola *Voskresenky (Resurrection) Cathedral* (1706–19), which is now a branch of Novocherkassk museum. Some interesting fortified houses of the 18th century also remain.

The town is often flooded in the spring and the people use small boats to get about in. It still keeps its old name of Cossack Venice. The road to Starocherkasskaya is very bad and visitors are recommended to go there by boat.

Novocherkassk

Population—162,000 (1970)

The town stands on a high hill dominating the R. Tuzlov and R. Uksai. It was founded in 1805 by the Cossacks, and the settlement soon became their centre and a Russian stronghold on the R. Don. It is well known to Russians as the Don Cossacks' capital.

During its early years the town received material help and considerable privileges from the government.

There are buildings which remain from these times including the Cossack headquarters, some 19th-century barracks, and a number of attractive small houses once owned by rich Cossacks.

There are veterinary, hydro-technical, and hydro-chemical institutes in Novocherkassk.

Voznesensky Sobor (Ascension Cathedral), Yermak Sq.

The architects Zlobin and Yashenko designed this cathedral in Byzantine style, and it is one of the best examples of its kind in Russia. It was built between 1891 and 1905 and is 74·5 m. high, 77 m. long, and 62 m. wide while the diameter of the cupola measures over 21 m. It can hold a congregation of 5000 and was formerly the Don Cossack Army's Cathedral. Pictures of life in the army decorate the choir stalls. The cathedral is open for services.

St. Konstantin's Church

St. George's Church

History of the Don Cossacks Museum, Sovietskaya St. 38. Open 10–5; closed Tues. Here is an interesting collection of banners and a two-hundred-guinea English sword presented on 8 June 1814 to Hetman Count Platov for 'consummate skill, brilliant talents and undaunted bravery' in 'securing the liberties, the repose and the happiness of Europe'. Matvei Platov (1751–1818) was a general who was famous for his fights with Napoleon's army. During the retreat of the French, he led the Cossack regiment and recaptured Smolensk, and seized Danzig (1813) and Namur (1814). He went to London where the presentation of the sword was made and where he left his uniform in exchange. The museum also contains the works of a 17th-century English clock which was captured from the Turkish fortress of Azov in 1695. Local excavations of the burial mounds near Novocherkassk in 1864 brought to light the much-prized golden items worked by the Sarmats in the 2nd century B.C. Most of the collection is now in the Hermitage museum in Leningrad, but some originals and a number of copies can be seen in Novocherkassk Museum.

Near the Don Cossacks Museum is the *Gauptwachter*, the Guard House, built in 1853, and also the old wooden building of the *Posting Inn* which was used by Pushkin (1820) and Lermontov (1840).

Ataman Palace (1863), beside Lenin Garden. This now serves as the town hall and the local Party Headquarters.

Grekhov Museum, Grekhov St. 124. Open 11–5; closed Mon., Wed., and Fri. Mitrofan Grekov (1882–1934) was a well-known Soviet artist who painted military pictures and battle scenes. The museum is in his house.

Yermak Monument, Yermak Sq. The monument by Mekeshin and Beklemeshev was unveiled in 1904. The various inscriptions read, 'To the Don Ataman Yermak Timofeyevich, Conqueror of Siberia, in memory of three hundred years of the Don Army from the grateful descendants— 1570–1870'; 'He lost his life beneath the waters of the Irtish on 5 August, 1584'; 'Russia, History, and the Church together accord honour to Yermak's undying memory' (Karamzin, Russian historian); and 'To Yermak from the Don Cossacks, 1904'. The Siberian campaign lasted from 1581–4.

Baklanov's Tombstone, Yermak Sq. Yakov Baklanov (1809–73) was a Cossack general and writer.

The *two triumphal arches* of Novocherkassk were erected in 1817 to mark the triumphal return of Ataman Platov and his Cossacks from Paris after the defeat of Napoleon. There are other personal memorials to Platov and to Cossack Stepan Razin who was the leader of a peasant revolt in 1670 to 1671 and who became a popular hero of Russian folklore.

Drama Theatre, Karl Marx St. 16

A new Theatre is under construction inside the walls of the old Law Court (1909), Sovietskaya St.

Park, Karl Marx St. 7

Trud Stadium, Podtelkov St.

Hotel, Podtelkov St. 90

Yuzhnaya Restaurant, Moskovskaya St. 1

Druzhba (Friendship) Restaurant, near the entrance to the town, approaching it from Moscow

Bank, Moskovskaya St. 9

Telegraph Office, Podtelkov St. 102

ROSTOV VELIKY
(or Rostov Yaroslavsky)
Population—35,000 (1970)

This town was called Rostov the Great to distinguish it from the town of Rostov-on-Don. Founded before the days of Rurik, it is one of the most ancient towns in Russia. It is situated on Lake Nero and was first mentioned in the chronicles in 862. It was called after Prince Rosta. The local merchants traded with Scandinavia in amber and silver coins from the Arabian east, exchanging them for honey, fur, and grain. Christianity was officially accepted in 989, when the local inhabitants were divided into groups of about 10 or 15 and forced to bathe in the lake. Priests from Byzantium sailed around on rafts and boats and gave one Christian name to each group. Paganism, however, did not die out completely for some years.

Rostov was first called the Capital of the North, then in the 12th century it received the title of Great because its territory and population were no less than those of ancient Kiev and Novgorod. As it grew wealthier, the number of its churches increased until it was said:

The devil went to Rostov
But the crosses scared him off!

In 1207 Rostov became the capital of a separate princedom, which, like other parts of Russia, was under Tatar rule in the 13th and 14th centuries. It came into the possession of Moscow under Dmitri Donskoi in 1474. At the end of the 16th century it grew in importance as a town on the trade route between Moscow and the White Sea, and in the 17th century it was invaded by Poles and Lithuanians; it was ruined and sacked by them, and among the rich booty was a golden sepulchre weighing 100 kg., stolen from the Uspensky Sobor and presented to a Polish lady.

The earth wall, the remains of which can still be seen, was built in 1631–3.

The town now has an area of 50 sq. km. and its industry includes the production of chicory coffee, food (especially treacle), linen, and enamel work, which has been manufactured here since the 19th century. The main streets are Proletarskaya, Lenin, and Sverdlov. The Agricultural College has a botanical garden of its own.

The *Kremlin*, until the mid 19th century called Rostov Metropolia, is surrounded by a wall with 10 round towers. Its territory is a rough rectangle covering 2 hectares (5 acres), and it differs from other Russian kremlins and monasteries in that it has no main cathedral dominating the other buildings. Its churches are good examples of Russian 17th-century architecture and were built under the aegis of Metropolitan Ion Sisoyevich between 1667 and 1691. The wall and towers were built not for military defence, but simply to guard the Metropolitan's palace. When the ecclesiastical centre moved to Yaroslavl little more building of interest took place here.

The Kremlin has two gate-churches. The

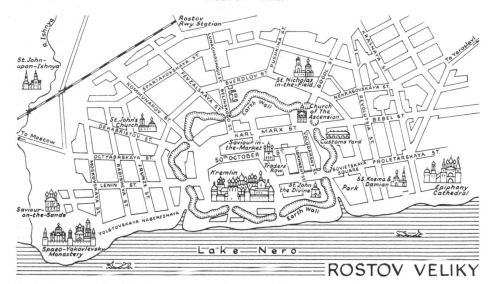

ROSTOV VELIKY

Church of the Resurrection (1670) on the north wall has five domes and gates known as the Holy Gates; the southern door is decorated with allegorical paintings. The *Church of St. John the Divine* is in the west wall. This church has some interesting canopies above the choir stalls. Both gate-churches contain well-preserved wall paintings and old frescoes restored in 1954, and both have holes in the west walls which held empty jars to improve the acoustics.

The *Church of the Smolensk Mother of God,* built in 1693, is painted in brightly coloured triangles.

The *Church of the Redeemer* also has pot-holes in the walls; and its iconostasis has been replaced by a screen with 5 arches.

In the complex of civil buildings is the *Metropolitan's Palace* (1672–80) and a series of halls. The *Byelaya Palata* (White Palace) was built in 1670 to accommodate the tsars. There is now a museum inside it.

The Kremlin was damaged by a hurricane in 1953 but has since been restored.

Uspensky (Assumption) Cathedral, outside the Kremlin. This cathedral was founded in 1214 and consecrated in 1230. It was built on the lines of Moscow's Uspensky Cathedral, but its present appearance dates from the 15th to 16th centuries. To the left of the Holy Door is the wonder-working icon, the Vladimir Virgin, painted in the 11th century by Alimpi. The 4-domed belfry of the cathedral (1620–82) is 32 m. long and 17 m. high. It has four arched openings and the 13 bells play 4 tunes; the heaviest, the Sisoi Bell, weighs 32,000 kg. (about 32 tons).

Church of St. Gregory, near the Kremlin. This church was built in 1670.

The *Saviour-in-the Market-Place Church.* This church was built in 1960 and now houses the town library.

The *Saviour-on-the-Sands Church,* Kirov St., was built at the end of the 17th century.

Church of the Ascension, to the north-east of the Kremlin. Built in 1566, this is a typical Moscow-style church. The people of Rostov usually refer to this as the Church of Isidore the Blessed. It was built in 1566 with 5 domes in typical Moscow style, and there is an interesting stone engraved with the builders' names. The belfry dates from the 19th century.

Epiphany Cathedral, in the eastern suburbs of the town. This cathedral was built in 1554 as part of the Abraham Monastery, which was founded at the beginning of the 11th century, and was the oldest in Russia.

Spaso-Yakovlevsky (Jacob) Monastery, in the western suburbs of the town, on the banks of the lake. This monastery was built during the 17th to 19th centuries and the original wall is still standing. Inside is the *Zachatyevsky (Immaculate Conception) Cathedral* (1686) and *St. Dmitri's Church* (1794–1801), designed in Classical Russian style. Close to the monastery is the *Church of the Transfiguration;* this was built in the 17th century as the cathedral of a now-vanished 13th-century monastery.

Services are now conducted in two churches: in *St. John's Church* (1761), Dekabristov St., where there are 14th–16th-century icons, and in *St. Nicholas-in-the-Field,* Gogol St., which was built in 1830 and has a two-storey belfry behind it. Inside are icons of the 15th and 16th centuries.

Traders' Row was built to serve as small shops in 1830. The architect was Melnikov and his design was then used for the building near Babel St. known as the *Customs Yard.*

Local Museum, in the Kremlin Halls and the former Church School. Open 9–5; closed Wed. This museum was established in 1883 when the Kremlin was first restored. There is an interesting collection of presents made to the monasteries, and of porcelain, icons, and woodcarving of the 16th–20th centuries. There is also a small prison cell called the 'stone sack'.

Hotel and Eating House, Karl Marx St., near the Kremlin

   Beryozka Restaurant

   Park, beside the lake. Boats can be hired here.

There are some more churches and remains of monasteries around the town, among them the *Borisoglebsky Monastery*, 24 km. from Rostov. This was built in the 16th century as a fortress against Uglich and has strong wall towers and two gates. The oldest churches inside are the *Cathedral* of 1524, its outside decorated with remarkable tiles, the *Church of the Annunciation* (1527), and *Sergius-over-the-Gate* (1545). There is also a bell tower.

Just outside Rostov, on the Moscow Road, a bad side road to the right leads to the interesting wooden church of *St. John-upon-Ishnya* in the village of Bogoslov. There are many legends attached to this church. Perhaps the best is that the church was not built by human hands but drifted from the lake along the R. Ishnya until it washed up high and dry upon its present site. It is open 10–5; closed Wed.

SAMARKAND

Population—267,000 (1970)

Samarkand is situated 700 m. above sea level in the fertile valley of the R. Zeravshan which is 11 km. from the centre of the town. The climate is extreme, the temperature sometimes falling below zero in January and rising up to 40°C. in July, but the town is considered more healthy than other Central Asian towns because of a cold wind from the Hissar range of mountains to the south.

Samarkand is known as the city of Timur (1333–1405), the Tatar conqueror who ruled a vast area from Yelets in Russia to Kuch in Sinkiang, and from Izmir to Delhi. In 1369 he conquered Samarkand and made it his capital. Timur, who called himself the 'Scourge of God and Lord of All the Earth', planned to make Samarkand the capital of the world and he gave small villages near Samarkand the names of the greatest cities of the world, such as Baghdad, Damascus, and Cairo with the idea that, compared with Samarkand, these cities were only poor villages. He built many fine palaces and monuments in Samarkand and decorated them with the booty from his plundering raids. During his reign Samarkand became the most important cultural and economic centre of Asia. Timur, who was also known both as Timur the Lame and Tamberlaine, became a legendary figure and is the eponym of Marlowe's play, 'Tamberlaine the Great'.

However the history of Samarkand dates from long before Timur. In the 4th century B.C. it was known as Maracanda and was the capital of Sogdinia. Even then it was renowned for its beauty, and Alexander the Great wrote after his capture of Maracanda in 329 B.C. that 'everything I have heard about the beauty of Maracanda is true, except that it is more beautiful than I could imagine'. Alexander's stay in Maracanda is well recorded as it was here that he murdered his favourite general Clitus during a banquet.

Samarkand began to prosper from the 2nd century A.D. as it was an important town on the Great Silk Route from China and the East to the ports of Syria and thence to Europe. It was overrun many times though, and its periods of prosperity were interspersed with deep depressions. At the beginning of the 8th century the whole of this part of Central Asia was conquered by the Arabs who brought Islam with them. The 'Great Power' of the area though was not so much the Arabs as the Chinese who were petitioned by the local princes for help and by the Arabs who feared Chinese intervention and looked upon Turkestan as a province wrested from the Chinese Emperors. Direct Arab rule only lasted until 750, after which date Samarkand became part of the territory of the Samanid dynasty of Persia. Under the Samanids Samarkand was a famous seat of Arabic civilisation, and Islam was firmly established.

In 1221 Samarkand was seized and pillaged by Genghis Khan. It is said that the soldiers looted the city for three days and nights, after which the population was reduced to a third. The soldiers destroyed the main water-pipe so that the town was without water. Over a thousand of the inhabitants gathered in a mosque which the Mongol invaders burnt. This story seems to have been true as in 1905 a Russian archaeologist, V. Vyatkin, found remains of a mosque and traces of a fire on this spot.

Samarkand remained under Mongol rule until it was captured by Timur in 1369. Timur died in 1405 at the age of 70 but Samarkand continued to flourish under Timur's grandson, Ulug Beg, the famous astronomer who was also known as 'the Great Enlightener'. Ulug Beg continued building splendid monuments and during this time Samarkand was also a famous seat of learning.

In the 16th century rule passed to the Shaibanides, but although Bukhara was their capital some remarkable edifices were also put up in Samarkand at this time.

By the beginning of the 18th century the countries of Western Europe were obtaining their goods from the East by sea. Samarkand, together with other towns on the caravan route, gradually slipped into oblivion. In 1784 it fell under the rule of the Emir of Bukhara and in 1868 it was captured by the Russians under General Kaufmann. A new Russian quarter was built to the west of the old town and Samarkand was slightly helped economically by the opening of the Transcaspian railway in 1896. From 1924–30 it was the capital of the Uzbek Soviet Socialist Republic, but in 1930 Tashkent was made the capital.

Today Samarkand is an important centre for fruit, cotton, wine, and sheepskins. Recent construction includes a new airport and a new railway station.

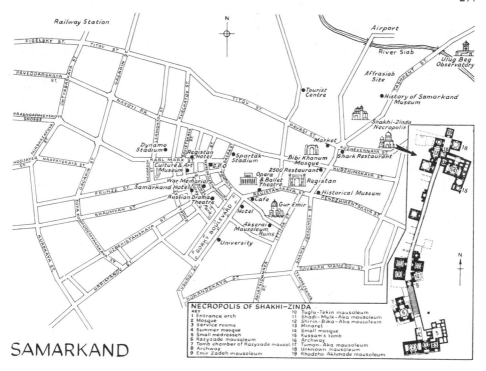

NECROPOLIS OF SHAKHI-ZINDA

KEY
1 Entrance arch
2 Mosque
3 Service rooms
4 Summer mosque
5 Small medresseh
6 Kazyzade mausoleum
7 Tomb chamber of Kazyzade mausol.
8 Archway
9 Emir Zadeh mausoleum
10 Tuglu-Tekin mausoleum
11 Shadi-Mulk-Aka mausoleum
12 Shirin-Bika-Aka mausoleum
13 Minaret
14 Small mosque
15 Kussam's tomb
16 Archway
17 Tuman-Aka mausoleum
18 Unknown mausoleum
19 Khodzho Akhmade mausoleum

SAMARKAND

The *Registan* in Registanskaya St. was the old trading centre of Samarkand. The name Registan means 'sandy place' after a spring which flowed here and washed sand onto the surrounding ground. The square is enclosed on all but the southern side by three medressehs. A medresseh is a Mohammedan college, and the basic plan of all three is similar: a large portal leading onto an enclosed courtyard around which were the rooms of the college and a mosque. All three have been restored and are in good condition.

The *Ulug Beg Medresseh and Mosque* on the west side of the square were built in 1417–20 by Ulug Beg, and are the oldest buildings in the square. The medresseh was exceptional for the 15th century as the syllabus included astronomy and mathematics as well as theology. Ulug Beg, who ruled Samarkand after Timur's death in 1405, was renowned as 'the prince of astronomers' and is said to have taught in the medresseh himself. There is no evidence for this, but it is known that many of the clergy considered astronomy blasphemy and that they plotted together with Ulug Beg's son to assassinate him in 1429. The medresseh was considerably damaged in the 18th century and later the 4 minarets leaned at a dangerous angle. In 1932 the north-east minaret, which was the most precarious of the four, was straightened.

The *Shir-Dar Medresseh and Mosque* on the east side of the square were built between 1619 and 1636 by Yalangyushbee, the military governor of Samarkand under the Astrakhan khanate. The proportions of the medresseh are the same as those of the Ulug Beg medresseh opposite, of which it is clearly a copy. During Ulug Beg's rule a 'khanaka', a religious rest house for travellers, had been built on this site but it fell into ruins by the beginning of the 17th century. The portal of the medresseh is 24 m. high and the tympanum over the main arch is decorated with a colourful design of a lion chasing a doe, from which the building takes its name which means 'lion-bearing' medresseh, although in fact they look more like tigers.

The *Tillah-Kari Medresseh and Mosque* on the north side of the square were also built by Yalang-yushbee in 1618. The name means 'covered with gold' and was probably given because of the elaborate gilding on the inside walls of the mosque. The medresseh was clearly planned to give the square a unified view. The southern façade is much longer than was usual for a building of comparable height, and this gives the square an enclosed appearance.

The *Chorsu*, a few yards to the north-east of the Shir-Dar Medresseh was built at the beginning of the 19th century when Samarkand was under the rule of the Emir of Bukhara. The sextagonal building with a cupola was built as a trading centre with bricks taken from the ruins of the Bibi Khanum mosque.

About a third of a mile north of the Registan along Tashkentskaya St. is the *Bibi Khanum Mosque* which was built from 1399 to 1404. Only the ruins remain today but they are worth seeing.

According to legend it was built by Timur's wife Bibi Khanum, the daughter of the Emperor of China, while Timur was on a campaign in India. There is no historical evidence of Bibi Khanum's existence and it is much more likely that Timur himself built the mosque when he returned from his victorious campaign in India, during which he captured Delhi. The legend says that Bibi Khanum was very beautiful and in order to be remembered by future generations as Timur's favourite wife, she asked the best craftsmen to build a mosque which would surpass all oriental architecture in size and grandeur. The craftsmen doubted their ability, but when they saw the piles of gold which were to cover the cost they began to work. The building rose quickly and was completed except for the portal when the work slowed down. The architect had fallen in love with the beautiful Bibi Khanum and he knew that once the mosque was completed he would never see her again. He laid down the condition that if the mosque were to be completed before Timur's return, she must allow him to kiss her. She tried to persuade him to kiss one of her ladies-in-waiting instead but the architect was adamant. Just as he was about to kiss her she covered her face with her hands, but even so the heat of the kiss burnt her cheek and left a mark. When Timur returned, she was unable to conceal the story behind her burnt cheek and Timur immediately ordered the guards to find the culprit. They were unable to find him and were told by one of his pupils that he had made wings for himself and flown down from the top of one of the minarets.

The remains of the mosque show that it measured 101 m. by 140 m. It was one of the largest in the Moslem world and of all the cathedrals in Europe only the cathedral in Milan was larger. The height of the main mosque was 36 m. and the cupola was 20 m. in diameter. The main portal was 34 m. high. It is said that it was originally slightly lower, but that Timur was dissatisfied with it and ordered it to be rebuilt. The building techniques of the time were not sufficiently advanced for such a building and extra strong mortar had to be used in order to make it sound. Heavy mortar is more susceptible to earthquakes than normal mortar and the mosque began to collapse on the heads of worshippers during services, but as it was a holy building it could not be demolished in any way. It gradually fell into ruins and the earthquake of 1897 damaged it irrevocably. Today nothing remains of the outer walls and only part of one of the four minarets is standing. A fragment of Arabic remaining on the peeling tiles reads: 'Ask Allah His forgiveness before you die.'

Between the main mosque and the entrance arch there were a number of small mosques, two of which partly stand today. In the courtyard there is a grey marble Koran desk which originally stood inside the mosque where it was placed by Ulug Beg. It consists of two huge, wedge-shaped stones lying on a pedestal 2¼ m. long and 2 m. wide. There is a legend that a childless woman who crawls under the desk will bear children.

Opposite the Bibi Khanum mosque is the *Mausoleum of Bibi Khanum*. This is also attributed to Bibi Khanum who is said to be buried here, but historians consider that it was built by Timur in honour of his mother-in-law, Sarai Mulk-Khanum. There was also a medresseh here but it was destroyed in the 17th century. Only the ruins of the mausoleum, an octagonal building with a cross-shaped interior, stand today.

The largest group of monuments in Samarkand is in the *Necropolis of Shakhi-Zinda*. It is situated in the north-east of the town to the left of Kozhevennaya St. and just over a kilometre from the Bibi Khanum Mosque. Mausoleums were first built here in the 10th century but they were almost totally destroyed during the Mongol invasion and the mausoleums which one can see today were all built during the 14th and 15th centuries.

Shakhi-Zinda, which means 'shrine of the living king', takes its name from the grave of Kussam-ibn-Abbas, a Moslem saint and cousin of the prophet Mohammed who is reputed to have brought the Islamic faith to Samarkand in the 7th century. The legend says that during a sermon in Samarkand, Kussam-ibn-Abbas lifted his head off his shoulders and, carrying it under his arm, climbed down a well leading to an underground garden where he continues to live to this day. Other reports say that he died in battle, and, according to some historians, he died not in Samarkand, but in Merv. Nevertheless, *Kussam's tomb* in Samarkand attracted visitors as far back as the 15th century and is considered the most holy place in Samarkand. The mausoleum of Kussam is situated at the far end of Shakhi-Zinda from the main entrance arch and is approached through a beautifully carved walnut door with the date, 1404–5, carved on the bottom. Kussam's tomb is composed of 4 tiers and is covered with elaborate brightly-coloured tiles and much gilt. On the 2 lower tiers is written the quotation from the Koran, 'Those who were killed on the way of Allah are not to be considered dead; indeed, they are alive . . .'. It was perhaps this quotation that gave rise to the legend of the living king. Beside the mausoleum is a *small mosque* which is thought to be the oldest building in Samarkand. It is separated from the mausoleum by a carved wooden fence. The mausoleum is not dated, but it is thought that it was built soon after the mosque, that is in the first half of the 14th century. From the accounts of travellers in the 14th century, it is clear that the mausoleum of Kussam was much more elaborate then than it is now, and it is thought that there was another mausoleum on this site before the present one was built.

The *entrance arch* to Shakhi-Zinda has an inscription on the west wall saying it was built by Ulug Beg in 1434–5. On the left of the arch is a *mosque* which was built at the same time, and to the right there are some *service rooms* leading to a *small medresseh* (1812–13). The arch itself gives onto a passage on both sides of which are buildings of some size in varying states of preservation. In many of the mausolea there are good mosaics and decorated majolica.

The *summer mosque* on the left with a painted wooden porch (aivan) was built in 1911. Further on on the same side is the *mausoleum* with the two highest turquoise-coloured cupolas. It is thought to contain the grave of Kazyzade Rumi, a 15th-century astronomer and Ulug Beg's teacher and friend. The *tomb* is under the smaller cupola, while the larger covers a prayer room. It was all restored in 1950–2.

The 36 brick steps were built in the 18th century over the remains of the town wall. They lead up to a small cupolaed *archway* built in the 18th century which opens onto a very narrow passage, along the beginning of which are a group of colourful mausolea built in the second half of the 14th century when Timur made Samarkand his capital. The first one on the right side is the *Tuglu-Tekin mausoleum*, built in 1376 in honour of the mother of Emir Hussein, who was one of Timur's military commanders. The second one on the right is that of *Shirin-Bika-Aka*, Timur's sister. She died in 1385 and the mausoleum is of the 14th–15th century, built on the remains of the old town wall. The decorations inside show birds, trees, and rivulets. The first mausoleum on the left side after coming through the arch is known as the Emir Zadeh mausoleum. That means 'Emir's son' but the real name of the person buried here is unknown. The inscription over the portal only gives the date of his death, 1386, but the mausoleum was built a little later. The second one on the left is the *mausoleum of Shadi-Mulk-Aka*, daughter of Timur's eldest sister, Kutlug-Turkan-Aka, who was probably also buried here. This mausoleum is in a very good state of preservation and the interior is worth seeing for the majolica work. It was the first mausoleum to be built here during Timur's rule.

Passing other less interesting monuments, towards the end of the passage is a third *archway* leading on the left to the *mausoleum of Tuman-aka*, one of Timur's wives who was responsible for building the lodging house for travellers which stands beside it, and which was where Timur stayed on his return from India. At the end of the passage is a small square on the far side of which stood the *mausoleum of Khodzha Akhmade*, which was built at the beginning of the 14th century, but of which only the portal remains. To the right of the square is an *unknown mausoleum* which was mistakenly attributed to Timur's wife, but which was also built before Timur's rule in 1366. The cupola and interior are covered with coloured terracotta. There is no mosaic in these earlier mausolea as this only appeared during Timur's time.

To the right of the little archway over the passage is a 16th-century mosque with a minaret leading to the revered *shrine of Kussam-ibn-Abbas*, described above.

The *Gur Emir* is in Akhunbabaeva St., which goes south west from the top of Gorky Boulevard where it runs into Registanskaya St. Timur started building this large mausoleum for his grandson Mohammed Sultan who died in Iran on his way to meet Timur. Timur died a year later in 1405 and was buried here himself. The mausoleum was then given the name of Gur Emir which means 'grave of the king'. The tombs of other members of Timur's family were later placed here, including those of his two sons Shakhrukh and Miranshakh and that of Ulug Beg. Timur died before the building was completed but it was finished under Ulug Beg. The building suffered much from earthquakes and a fire, but parts of it have been restored recently and the portal is in a fairly good state of preservation.

The blue dome of the mausoleum is 33·5 m. high, with decorative tiles on the drum. The mausoleum is entered by a large portal which was completed in Timur's lifetime and is the best preserved part of the building. It is decorated with a bright mosaic which stands out against the almost plain walls of the façade. The inner chamber of the mausoleum is 22 m. high. In the centre of the chamber is the tombstone of Timur. It consists of two blocks of dark green nephrite fitted into each other. They are the largest pieces of nephrite known and the tombstone is 2 m. long, 45 cm. wide, and 35 cm. high. The Arabic inscription on the tombstone claims that Timur and Genghis-Khan were descendants of the same ancestor who was the son of a virgin named Alankuva who conceived from light which came through a door. There are 8 other tombstones in the chamber and they are all made of grey marble or alabaster. One is situated in a niche opposite the entrance and the others in the centre of the chamber around Timur's tombstone. Except for the tombstone in the niche, they are all surrounded by marble railings. The lower part of the wall of the chamber is decorated with octagonal blocks of alabaster, above which is a band of jasper on which the genealogy and deeds of Timur are written.

The graves which are in a crypt below were opened in 1941. The skeletons were examined and it was clear that Timur was lame and that Ulug Beg was murdered. The skeletons were replaced in the graves together with an account of the investigations which was sealed in a glass tube and set in marble.

In the courtyard of the mausoleum is the *Kok-Tash-Stone*. This is a dark grey marble stone 3¼ m. long with arabesques on the sides which was the coronation stone of the Emirs of Bukhara.

53 m. south-east of Gur Emir are the ruins of the *Ak-Serai Mausoleum*. Little is known about this mausoleum, but historians consider that it was built in the latter half of the 15th century as the interior decoration is very similar in style to that of another monument of the same period, the Irshat-khana. It is thought probable that it served as a family tomb for the male members of the descendants of the Timurides. Although in ruins, some restoration work has been done, and there is

a very beautiful fresco inside.

A little to the north of Gur Emir is the *Mausoleum of Ruh-Abad*. It contains the grave of Burkhan-eddin Sagardee, a 14th-century mystic, and was therefore given the name Ruh-Abad which means 'the abode of the spirit'. The date of the mausoleum is not known but it is thought to belong to the latter half of the 15th century.

The *Ulug Berg Observatory* is situated about 2 miles from the centre of Samarkand along the road to Tashkent. It was built in 1428 by Ulug Beg, but was destroyed soon after his assassination in the following year and its exact location was not known until it was discovered in 1909 by the Russian archaeologist V. Vyatkin. During excavations in the same year remains of the outer wall were found as well as part of a large sextant which was the astronomer's principal instrument. From later excavations it was ascertained that the observatory was a large circular three-storey building. The observations made by Ulug Beg at the observatory were very advanced for the time and surprisingly accurate, such as his calculation that the stellar year is 365 days, 6 hours, 10 minutes and 8 seconds—only 62 seconds more than the present estimation. In 1914 the sextant was covered by an arched roof and an entrance arch was built. A marble monument to Ulug Beg was erected on the site of the observatory in 1949 and a museum is also open on the site.

Not far from the observatory of Ulug Beg is the *Mausoleum of Chupan-Ata*, which commands a very good view over the town and beyond to the Hissar mountains. It is thought to belong to the period of Ulug Beg and is remarkable for its simplicity and fine proportions. Although a mausoleum in style, no graves or crypts were found here during excavations, and this has given the building an air of mystery.

To the north-east of the present town is *Afrasiab*, the ancient site of Maracanda. There is a legend that the true founders of Maracanda were the Emperors Kaikaous and Afrasiab who lived *c.* 4000 B.C. and that Afrasiab takes its name from the latter, but few believe this legend today. Maracanda was situated on a high plateau above the Zeravshan river 5 km. in circumference. After the Mongol invasion in the 13th century the plateau was deserted except for the extreme northern part which was inhabited until the 15th century. The ancient ramparts and approaches to the town from below are still recognisable. The first excavations here were carried out in 1874 and since then many pieces of Graeco-Bactian coins, plain and enamelled tiles, cooking utensils, tools, frescoes, terracotta figurines, and jewellery have been found. A large collection of these can be seen in the *History of Samarkand Museum*. In 1885 remains of the wall of the ancient town were found. Later the remains of dwellings, other buildings, and also the mound on which the citadel stood, were discovered. Excavations made in 1965 revealed 6th- and 7th-century frescoes, and

probably further work will tell more about ancient Sogdiana.

Below Afrasiab on the left bank of the R. Zeravshan there is a large brick archway which is all that now stands of a large dam and sluice for regulating the river. It is known as the *Bridge of Timur*, but was actually built at the very beginning of the 16th century by Shaibani Khan.

In Tashkent St., in the courtyard of the former Shaibani-Khanum medresseh, is the *Shaibani-Khanum Monument*, which is a block of grey marble 6·5 m. long, 5·5 m. wide, and over 2 m. high. It is covered by 30 tombstones decorated with inscriptions and designs of the Shaibanid rulers of Bukhara of the first half of the 16th century.

Only the ruins of the *Ishrat-Khana Mausoleum* remain. The name means 'house of amusement', which is rather a misnomer as it is in fact a mausoleum and mosque. It was given this name on account of the elaborate interior decorations and architectural design. It was built from 1451 to 1469, apparently at the wish of the wife of Abu-Sanda in memory of their dead daughter.

The *Mausoleum of Abdi-Darun* is situated in an old cemetery in the south-east of Samarkand. It was built in the 15th century on the site of a more elaborate 11th-century mausoleum which fell to ruin. Abdi-Darun was an Arab ruler who died in the 9th century.

The *Mausoleum of Abdi-Birun*, the son of Abdi-Darun, is situated in the south of Samarkand. It was built in 1633 by Nadir-Divanbegi.

There is one mosque open for worship in Charaga St. and another, the Khodzha Akhror, is 4·5 km. from town.

Pokrovsky Cathedral, Vorovskova St., is the Russian Orthodox cathedral.

Synagogue, Khudzhunskaya St.

Culture and Art Museum, Sovietskaya St. 47. The final section of the museum contains many items of interest illustrative of the old life of Samarkand. Open 9–4; closed Fri.

Anti-Religious Museum, at the foot of the hill

Town Hall, Voikova St. This is an interesting building with oriental-style domes.

University, Gorky Boulevard 15. 7000 students study here.

The *Karakul Institute*, Karl Marx St. This institute breeds sheep for research, and has here a good collection of samples of famous skins, including gold, bronze, platinum, and white.

War Memorial, Bortsov Revolutsii Sq., next to Gorky Park. On 6 November, 1962, an Eternal Flame was lit here to burn in memory of the victims of the Civil War.

Khamid Alimdzhan Uzbek Drama Theatre, Gorky Park, TEL. 3–25–13

Opera and Ballet Theatre, near the Registan. This modern building designed by Balayev seats 1000 and was completed in 1964.

Russian Drama Theatre, Lenin St. 51, TEL. 3–27–36

Concert Hall, Lenin St. 58

Son et Lumière, Registan Sq. in the old city. This is the only show of its kind in the Soviet Union. The 45-minute performance covers Samarkand's 2500 years of history. The narration is in Russian and Uzbek, but French, English and Arabic translations are planned.

Summer Concert Hall, Gorky Park

Gorky Park, Sovietskaya St.; there is an amusement ground here and a dance floor.

Spartak Stadium

Dynamo Stadium

Intourist Hotel & Restaurant, Gorky Boulevard

Samarkand Hotel & Restaurant, Sovietskaya St. 55, TEL. 5–08. Service bureau, TEL. 3–36–85. This is also an Intourist hotel. There is a souvenir kiosk in the hotel with pottery and lengths of silk for sale.

Registan Hotel & Restaurant, Karl Marx St., at the corner of Lenin St.

Shark Restaurant, Kozhevannaya St.

Café, Lenin St.

Ice cream parlour, opposite the Registan

G.P.O., Kommunisticheskaya St.

Department Stores, Karl Marx St. and Registan Sq.

Souvenir Shop, Tashkentskaya St. near the Bibi Khanum Mosque. Look for local pottery—dishes, vases, and curious little monster for ornaments.

Taxi Ranks, near the Samarkand Hotel, the railway station and Registan Sq.

SERPUKHOV

See Yasnaya Polyana, road to, p. 342

SEVAN, LAKE

See Erevan, p. 105

SEVASTOPOL

Population—230,000 (1970)

The name 'Sevastopol' means 'town of glory', and it was appropriately made a Hero City after World War II.

The harbour has an average depth of 20 m. and is the best harbour in the Black Sea. The Northern Bay divides the town into the Northern and Southern Sides (Severnaya and Yuzhnaya Storona). On the Southern Side are Gorodskaya Storona (City Side) and Korabelnaya Storona (Ship Side), which are in turn divided by the deep and wide Southern Bay.

In 1774 Prince Potemkin recognised the outstanding shape of Sevastopol Bay for use as a fortress and a port. The port was accordingly laid out in 1784 on the site of the Tatar village of Akhtiar. Stone for the building was taken from the ancient town of Hersones, and the admirals Ushakov and Mackenzie were also instrumental in the founding of the city. In 1804 Sevastopol was proclaimed the main port of the Black Sea Fleet.

Sevastopol was almost wholly destroyed during the siege of 1854–5, after which only 14 buildings remained intact. After the Crimean War Russia was forbidden to possess a Black Sea Fleet or to use Sevastopol as a fortress; this restriction lasted until 1871, after which the city was again fortified. The commercial port was closed in 1890.

During the 1905 revolution 15 ships of the Black Sea Fleet joined in the revolt in Sevastopol. About 6000 seamen were arrested, 40% of the total number of men, and Lieutenant Shmidt, who was leading the revolt, was shot with other seamen. There is a monument over their grave.

The siege of 1941–2 during the Second World War lasted for 250 days and again 97% of the city was laid waste.

Today Sevastopol has the biggest brick and tile factory in the Crimea and also produces other building materials, food products, textiles, and shoes. There are two stadiums, two boating stations, and two yacht clubs in the town.

SS. Peter and Paul Cathedral, Lunacharsky St. 34. This cathedral was built in Doric style in 1843 and rebuilt after the Crimean War. It resembles the Temple of Theseus in Athens and has 44 columns on the façade. It is now used as a House of Culture.

Vladimirsky Cathedral, on the town hill. Half ruined during World War II, this cathedral is the burial place of 4 Russian admirals, Kornilov, Istomin, Nakhimov, and Lazarev, whose names are inscribed on black marble plaques on the outside wall. The cathedral was founded during the 1854 Crimean War; the crypt where the admirals are buried was opened in 1881, and the rest in 1888. The architect, Thon, designed it in Byzantine style, and its interior marble columns were brought from Italy. The cathedral is now to be restored and used as a sepulchre for famous Russian seamen.

The *Tower of Winds* opposite Vladimirsky Cathedral. This is all that remains of the old building of the Marine Library. It is a copy of the marble tower of the same name in Athens and the upper frieze displays bas-reliefs of Greek mythological heroes.

Grafskaya Pristan (Count's Quay). This is a broad stone staircase with a 12-columned portico dating from 1846, called after Admiral Count Voinovich who commanded the Black Sea Fleet in the 1840s.

Black Sea Fleet Museum, Lenin St. 11. Open 10–5; closed Mon. Founded in 1869, this is one of the oldest museums in the country. The building by A. Kochetov was constructed in 1895. The figure '349' on the façade commemorated the duration in days of the siege of 1854–5, and the guns also date from that time.

Sevastopol Panorama, Istorichesky Boulevard; open 9–8; closed Mon. This circular building, completed in 1905, contains a painting by the artist Roubaud of Munich illustrating the storming of Sevastopol by the British and the French on 6 June 1855. The painting is 115 m. in length and 14 m. deep. Roubaud was an Academician of the Petersburg Academy of Fine Art, who, having collected his material, went to Munich to create the Panorama in a specially constructed circular building. His work was badly burnt in 1942 but the building was reconstructed and the painting copied and recreated. This formidable task was carried out under the guidance of Academicians Yakovlev and Sokolov-Skalya, and was completed on 16 October 1954.

Picture Gallery, Nakhimov Prospect 9. Open 12–6; closed Tues. Opened in 1927, this gallery contains Russian classical paintings by Repin, Aivazovsky, Shishkin, and Levitan, among others. The section on Soviet art includes work by Brodsky and Grabar. The Western European section has 14th- to 17th-century Italian, Dutch, and Flemish masters, among them a 'Madonna and Child' by Raphael, and canvasses by Giordano, Ruysdael, Rubens, and Sneyders.

Kovalevsky Biological Station of the Academy of Sciences, Primorsky Boulevard. Aquarium and museum open 10–4; closed Mon.

Kazarsky Monument, Matrosky Boulevard. Captain Kazarsky distinguished himself during the naval war of 1828 against the Turks. His ship was the brig Merkury.

Count Totleben Statue, Istorichesky Boulevard. This statue by Bilderling was unveiled in 1909. The pedestral depicts part of the bastion where soldiers are laying mines.

Nakhimov Monument, Nakhimov Sq. The original statue by Bilderling and Schröder was unveiled in 1898 but was destroyed by the Germans, and the existing one is a copy.

The *Eagle Column*, Primorsky Boulevard. The column stands on an artificial rock close to the shore. Designed by Adamson, it was unveiled in 1904 to commemorate the Russian warships which sank in the harbour mouth on 11 September 1854 in an attempt to block the way. The column, surmounted by a bronze eagle with outstretched wings, is now used as the symbol of the city. At the time of the Crimean War the story was told of one of the ships which would not sink, in spite of being holed and then shot at by her sister ships. At last a sailor boarded her again and returned with her icon and she went down immediately.

Lenin Monument, on the highest point of the town hill. This monument by Bondarenko stands 2·5 m. high.

Gorky Monument, Lunacharsky St., in a small garden opposite the Cathedral of SS. Peter and Paul.

Liberation Monument. This can be seen from Primorsky Boulevard; there are the Constantine and Mikhail Batteries and the monument to the soldiers who fell in the liberation of Sevastopol in 1944.

Lunacharsky Theatre, Nakhimov Prospect 6

Circus, Korabelnaya Storona, near the 'Sevastopol' wide-screen cinema.

Bathing Beach, Primorskii Boulevard

Sevastopol Hotel and Restaurant, Nakhimov Prospect 8, TEL. 25–65

Primorsky (Marine) Restaurant, Lenin St. 8

Volna (Wave) Restaurant, Primorsky Boulevard, by the sea

G.P.O., Bolshaya Morskaya St. 21

Malakhov Kurgan

This ancient burial ground, which is what 'Kurgan' means, is 4 km. from the town centre. The town was called after a Captain Malakhov who spent many days and nights drinking in its inns. The plateau, the highest point in the neighbourhood of Sevastopol, is 350 m. long by 149 m. wide and its seizure in 1855 decided the fate of the rest of the town. The turrets from which the guns were fired have been restored. Three admirals met their deaths on and around the Kurgan; cannonballs fatally wounded Kornilov, and blew off Istomin's head, while Nakhimov was shot in the temple.

Admiral Kornilov Monument. This was designed by Bilderling and Schröder, and erected in 1895. The admiral is depicted at the moment when he was struck by the fatal bullet and uttered his words: 'Defend Sevastopol.' To the right, below, is a figure of the sailor Koshka (see below). The monument is under restoration.

On the Kurgan is a monument to the Soviet airmen who died in 1944, and there is also an eternal flame burning on the grave of the Unknown Sailor.

Koshka Monument, near Malakhov Kurgan. The sailor Pyotr Koshka, whose name appropriately means 'cat', participated in numerous reconaissance sorties, and was famed for going into the enemy trenches and putting their guns out of action. He survived the war, though his grandson, Pavel Kucher, fell here in 1942.

Sapun-Gora

This hill is 6 km. along the road to Simferopol. There is a diorama by the artist Maltsev depicting the storming of the hill in May, 1944.

The *Glory Monument* commemorates those who fell during World War II.

Severnaya Storona

Here, 10 km. from the centre of Sevastopol, is the common *grave* of 127,587 of those who fell in the 1854–5 defence of Sevastopol. *St. Nicholas's Church* was built of white Inkerman stone in 1870; it stands 20 m. high, and is built in the shape of a pyramid and surmounted by a cross. The interior is decorated with mosaics in Byzantine style, and 38 black marble slabs list the regiments and naval divisions involved in the defence of Sevastopol and also the names of the commanding officers. There are 117 different war memorials and monuments in the vicinity.

Hersones

Russian: Korsun.

Hersones lies 3 km. south-west of Sevastopol. Its name means 'peninsula', and it is also appropriately known as 'Russian Pompeii'. On a headland by the sea are the remains of a town which bear the marks of the three main periods of its history,

Ancient Greek, Roman, and medieval Byzantine, and the ruins of 2000-year-old walls whose grandeur was described by Pliny are to be found there. The town was founded in the 5th century B.C. by colonists from Heraclea in Bithnyia; it was an important trading centre and was known in old chronicles as Korsun. Political exiles were often sent here and it was here, in exile, in the 1st century A.D. that Pope Clement died. The Byzantine Emperor Justinian II was banished here at the end of the 7th century. The town was taken in the 10th century by Prince Vladimir of Kiev, who, so it is said, adopted the Christian religion on this spot. Its trade with Russia ceased at the time of the Mongolian invasion. It suffered at the hands of the Lithuanians in 1397, and then became completely desolated under the Turks.

The site has been under excavation since 1772. The stones of Hersones were used for building Sevastopol and Odessa until a stop was put to the entire destruction of the historic place. The excavations are proving very valuable; some of the finds have been sent to the Hermitage Museum in Leningrad, some to the Historical Museum in Moscow, and some remain in the Hersones Local Museum (founded in 1892). Ancient streets, a square, a theatre, and 6th-century mosaic floors in excellent condition have been discovered.

In 1888 a *monastery* planned by Grimm was constructed here, its principal building being a copy of the ancient Church of St. Serge in Istanbul.

The *Hersones Museum.* Open 10–5; closed Mon. This museum contains a rich numismatic collection.

SIBERIA
See Novosibirsk, p. 244

SIGULDA
See Riga, p. 270

SIMFEROPOL
See Crimean Circular Route, p. 82

SMOLENSK
Population—211,000 (1970)
Once known as 'the key and gate of Russia', Smolensk is attractively situated on either side of the R. Dnieper. It was first mentioned in a document of 863 and was the chief town of the large Slav tribe known as the Krivichi. It stood on the ancient north-south trade route, linking the Baltic and the Black Sea. In 882 Prince Oleg conquered Smolensk on his victorious way from Novgorod to Kiev and made it a part of the principality of Kiev, but after 1054 it continually changed hands and was attacked in turn by Tatars, Muscovites, Lithuanians, and Poles.

The town became independent in the early 12th century and flourished under the rule of Prince Rostislav, the grandson of Prince Vladimir Monomakh. A terrible epidemic of plague and cholera was recorded in 1388 as having left no more than 10 survivors. A large Lithuanian army led by Prince Vitovt besieged the town for 2 months in 1404 before it fell, and then it remained in Lithuanian hands for 110 years. In 1653, after the third war with Poland, Smolensk became Russian again.

Napoleon was in the town twice during his Russian campaign of 1812. As he was finally leaving he gave orders that the Kremlin should be blown up, and accordingly gunpowder was placed under all the towers; 8 were destroyed but the rest were saved. At that time only 600 people remained alive in the town, but it quickly recovered and grew into a small industrial centre, becoming especially active when the railways were opened.

The old part of the town is enclosed by a wall 5 km. in length, and lies amid trees on the steeply sloping left bank of the river. The walls date from 1596–1602 when they were built by Boris Godunov from plans by F. S. Kon. They are 5·5 m. thick and 15·2 m high, and originally boasted 38 towers of which today only 16 remain. Once the walls were known as 'the precious necklace of Russia'. Parts of them are to be seen in many places in the centre of the town; some towers are now enclosed by the Park of Culture and the Kutuzov Garden. Also in the town park is part of the great 17th-century earth wall.

Reconstruction work is now taking place in Smolensk, and the old houses in the streets leading to Smirnov Sq. in the centre of the town are interspersed with new buildings. Perhaps the most spectacular street is Oktyabr Revolyutsii, particularly at the point where it is crossed by Dzerzhinsky St. One of the biggest buildings is the post-war House of Soviets, on Karl Marx Sq. The old Kievskoye Chaussée was recently renamed Prospect Yuri Gagarin. In the south-west part of the town are the new Ryadovka and Popovka regions, the latter designed to provide accommodation for 50,000.

Smolensk has four colleges, including those for medicine and teachers' training, and the various local industries include machine building, woodwork, and clothes manufacture.

Cathedral of the Assumption (Uspensky Sobor), Sobornyi Dvor 5, on a hill to the south of the bridge. This huge 5-domed building dominates the whole town. When Napoleon walked into it he was so struck by its splendour that he took off his hat and set a guard to protect the building from his own men. It was founded at the beginning of the 12th century and was destroyed by the Poles in 1611. Reconstruction began in 1677 under Alexei Korolkov of Moscow, the idea being to create a monument to the heroic defence of Smolensk against the Poles in 1609–11, and the plans resembled those of the great Moscow cathedrals. Work on it stopped completely when the east wall collapsed in 1679 but was started again in 1732 under the architect Shedel.

The cathedral is in use today. It stands 69·7 m high and is 42·6 m. in width; the central dome is built of wood and is decorated. The iconostasis of

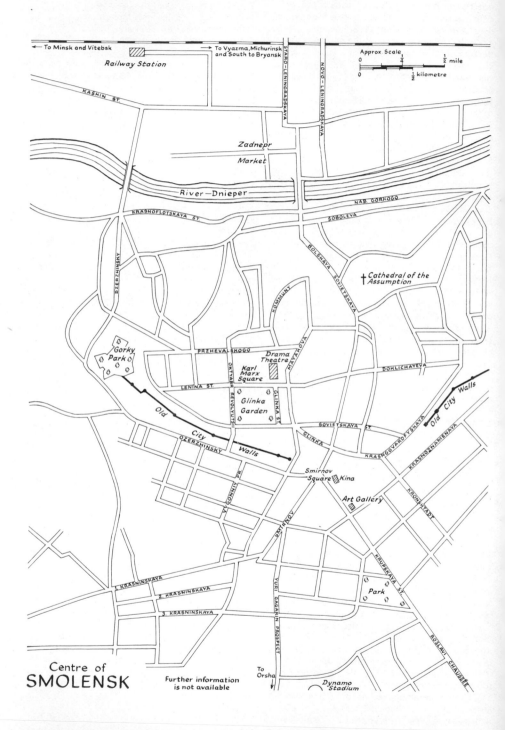

← To Minsk and Vitebsk

→ To Vyazma, Michurinsk and South to Bryansk

Railway Station

Approx Scale

0   ¼   ½ mile
0   ½   1 kilometre

KASHIN ST.

STARO-LENINGRADSKAYA

NOVO - LENINGRADSKAYA

Zadnepr
Market

River—Dnieper

NAB. GORKOGO

KRASNOFLOTSKAYA ST.

SOBOLEVA

DZERZHINSKY

BOLSHAYA SOVIETSKAYA

† Cathedral of the
Assumption

KOMSOMY

MAYOROVA

Gorky
Park

PRZHEVALSKOGO

Drama
Theatre

DOKLICHAVEVA

OKTYABR REVOLYUTSII

Karl
Marx
Square

LENINA ST.

GLINKA ST.

Glinka
Garden

SOVIETSKAYA ST.

Old City Walls

Old   City   Walls

DZERZHINSKY

GLINKA

KRASNOGVARDYSKAYA

KRASNOZNAMENAYA

RUTANAYA

Smirnov
Square Kina

Art Gallery

KRONSHTADT

SMIRNOV

KRUPSKAYA ST.

1. KRASNINSKAYA

2. KRASNINSKAYA

3. KRASNINSKAYA

YURI GAGARIN PROSPECT

Park

ROSLAVL CHAUSSEE

Centre of
SMOLENSK

Further information
is not available

To
Orsha

Dynamo
Stadium

gilded lime-wood stands 10 m. high; ten people worked for twelve years to complete it. The principal treasure is a wonder-working icon of the Virgin, said to have been painted by St. Luke for the ruler of Syria. Afterwards the icon went to Jerusalem and Constantinople, and came to Russia when the Emperor Constantine gave it to his daughter Anna on her marriage to Prince Yaroslav. It was brought to Smolensk in 1103; the original was stolen in 1923 and the present one is a 16th-century copy, equally revered and standing upon a stone platform. Other valuable icons are those of our Lady of Vladimir, brought to Smolensk in 1445, and of Our Lady of Jerusalem, painted probably as early as the 12th century. Also to be seen here is a shroud, dated 1561, embroidered with a picture of the Entombment. This formerly belonged to the Uspensky (Assumption) Cathedral in Moscow's Kremlin, but was stolen by Napoleon in 1812, and recaptured in Smolensk where it then remained.

Church of SS. Peter and Paul or Gorodyanke Church, near the railway station, towards Kashin St. Dating from 1146, this is the oldest church, and indeed the oldest building in Smolensk. It was built in the Kievan style, but was changed and reconstructed until the 18th century.

Church of St. John The Divine (Tserkov Ivana Bogoslova), Krasnoflotskaya St., near the bridge. Built in 1173 and reconstructed in 1770, the church is in the Kievan style and is similar to the Church of SS. Peter and Paul.

Svirskaya Church, Malaya Krasnoflotskaya St., near the R. Smyadinka. Also known as St. Michael's Church, this was built in 1191–4 as a court cathedral by Prince David Rostislavich, whose tomb is inside. It was heavily damaged in World War II.

Local History Museum, Lenin St. 9. The most interesting exhibits here come from the ancient barows of which there are 3000 at Gnezdovo, near Smolensk. The barows mostly date from the 10th century and scientific excavation began in 1868.

Local Natural History Museum, Sobornyi Dvor 7

Art Gallery, Krupskaya St. 7. This collection is housed in a building specially designed in 1905 for a Museum of Ancient Russia. The Gallery is open 10–7 and closed Fri.

1812 Monument, at the entrance to the Park of Culture. This huge monument commemorating the defenders of Smolensk against the French was designed by Antoni Adamini, cast in St. Petersburg, and unveiled in 1912, the centenary of the victory.

Sophia Regiment Monument, on the earth wall in the Park of Culture. The Sophia Regiment was one of those engaged in the defence of Smolensk in 1812; this monument to it was unveiled 100 years later.

Monument with Eagles, Kutuzov Garden. This is an interesting symbolic monument. One eagle prevents a man dressed as an Ancient Gaul from attacking the nest with his sword, and the other guards the nest while preparing to attack the marauder from behind: the great rock symbolises Russia, and the two eagles are the 1st and 2nd Russian armies.

Kutuzov Monuments. In the central walk of the Kutuzov Garden there is a bust of Field Marshal Kutuzov, unveiled in 1912; the other Kutuzov monument, this time in a standing position, is on Bolshaya Sovietskaya St. By Motorilov, it was unveiled in 1954. Both commemorate the liberation of the town from Napoleon.

Glinka Monument, in the Glinka Garden, locally known as 'Blonye'. This bronze statue of the composer Mikhail Glinka (1804–57) was unveiled in 1885. Phrases of the composer's music are included in the iron fence around the statue. Glinka was born in the province of Smolensk.

Drama Theatre, Karl Marx St. 4

Puppet Theatre, Lenin St. 5a

Philharmonia Concert Hall, Bolshaya Sovietskaya St. 18

Spartak Stadium, Dzerzhinsky St. This stadium can seat 12,000.

Park, Lenin St.

Smolensk Hotel and Restaurant, Glinka St. 9/30, TEL. 3–18–25. This hotel has an attended car park.

Rossia Hotel and Restaurant, Karl Marx St. 2/1, TEL. 3–17–42, 3–36–04. Intourist office TEL. 3–16–53

G.P.O., Oktyabr Revolutsi St.

Department Store, Yuri Gagarin Prospect 1

Beryozka Souvenir Shop, Kommunisticheskaya St. 22

Souvenirs of Smolensk, Lenin St. 11/1

Talashinko

13 km. off the main road, along the Roslav Chaussée. Please notify Intourist before making this trip. Here, on the former estate of Princess Maria Tenisheva, stands Teremok, a wooden house built in 1901–3 in Russian fairy-tale style after a design by Malyutin. Teremok is now a museum containing 2000 different items of folk art; the wood carvings are of especial interest. Beside Teremok is a small family chapel built in 1902. Over the entrance is a large mosaic of Christ. The artist Rerikh helped design and decorate the chapel, and many other prominent Russian artists including Vasnetsov, Vrubel, Polenov, and Serov lived and worked here to revive Russian folk art. The museum is open from May till November 9–6; closed Mon.

SOCHI

See Caucasian Coastal Road, p. 72

SPASSKOYE-LUTOVINOVO

See Orel, p. 251

STAVROPOL

Known as Voroshilovsk from 1935–43
Population—198,000 (1970)

The Stavropol region lies in the steppeland to the north of the Caucasus Mountains. In the past it was crossed by hordes of nomads migrating to the west with their herds. The city of Stavropol occupies a higher part of the Stavropol Plateau in the north-west of the region.

It was founded in 1777 as one of the fortresses on the Azov–Mozdok defence line and was at first simply known as Fortification 8. Its present name, derived from the Greek for Cross-town, was given later. According to legend a cross was found when the foundations for the fortress were being laid at the place where the park of Komsomolskaya Gorka is today.

The site for the fortress was selected by General Suvorov and at first it was occupied by the army, but in 1780 the first civilian settlers moved in from the central part of Russia. Then in 1808–10 about 50 Armenian merchants and their families arrived and the town gained considerably in economic importance. In 1842 the seat of the Bishop of the Caucasus was transferred to Stavropol and it was also declared the provincial centre, which further increased its importance. The construction of the Vladikavkas Railway at the end of the 19th century detracted from Stavropol and with the loss of its advantageous position, its economic importance dropped.

The city was occupied by the Germans during World War II but now has well-developed food and light industries and an important gas pipeline. Its higher educational establishments include colleges for agriculture, medicine, and foreign languages.

The town is well planned with a rectangular pattern of streets and high buildings in the centre although most of the buildings are only one or two storeys high. The town's main street links the centre with the railway station.

St. Andrew's Cathedral (19th century), Dzerzhinksova St. 155. Open for services.

Uspenskaya (Assumption) Church (19th century), Yarmarochnaya St. Open for services.

Mosque (19th century), Morozova St. 12. Now used to house archives.

Local Museum, Dzerzhinkova St. 135. Open 10–5; closed Sat. This museum was founded in 1904 and named after the founder's wife, Maria Prave. Now it has a collection of 55,000 items with pride of place given to the sepulchre of a chieftain of the Alan Tribe, and to a mammoth's skeleton. There is also a picture gallery here.

Fine Arts Museum, Dzerzhinskova St. 115. Open 10–5; closed Sat.

Lenin Monument, Lenin Sq.

Bust of Ossetian writer, Kosta Khetagurov, Marx Prospect

Drama Theatre, Marx Prospect 45

Concert Hall, Dzerzhinskova St. 115

Lenkomsomol Park, Oktyabrskoy Revolutsii Prospect 22

Botanical Garden, in south-east suburbs of Stavropol

Stavropol Hotel and Restaurant, Karl Marx Prospect 34, TEL. 3–76–14

Hotel Elbrus, Gorkovo St. 43

Gorka Restaurant, Suvorova St. 1

Kolos Restaurant, Dzerzhinskova St. 100

Elbrus Restaurant, Marx St. 56

Otdykh (rest) Café, Oktyabrskoy Revolutsii Prospect 25

G.P.O., Oktyabrskoy Revolutsii Prospect 12

Bank, Lenin St. 286

Department Store & Souvenirs, Karl Marx Prospect 44

Bookshop, Karl Marx Prospect 70

Market, Gorkovo St. 44

SUKHUMI
Population—102,000 (1970)

ABKHAZIA

Sukhumi is the capital of the Abkhazian Autonomous Republic, which has a population of 490,000 (1970) and covers an area of 6000 sq. km. The people of the republic are Georgians, Abkhazians, and Russian.

The coastal climate is sub-tropical, and tobacco, tea, and citrus fruits are grown, and coal and honey produced. There are also some good health resorts in the region.

Along the sea coast, on the border between the strip of coastal lowland and the inland mountainous part of the country, many stalactite caves in the limestone strata are to be found. A famous cave is *Abrskilova Peschera*, about 45 km. from Sukhumi on the Ochemchire road. Its galleries have a total length of 2 km. and some of the halls are up to 30–40 m. in length with stalactites in the form of curtains and palm tree crowns. Its name derives from a local legend similar to the legend of Prometheus. The *Gumistinskiye Caves* also deserve a visit, the most interesting being Jackal Cave which is divided into three parts by its stalactites.

Abkhazia belonged in turn to Colchis, Pontus, Rome, and Byzantine before gaining its independence in 756. Christianity had begun to spread here in the 5th century. In 985 Abkhazia became a part of Georgia, but later regained its independence until taken by Turkey in 1578. Russia ruled it from 1810 and following local uprisings many Abkhazians emigrated to Turkey, especially after 1864.

Sukhumi Bay lies between the R. Gumista and the R. Kelasuri while the town itself is crossed by the R. Besleti. Behind the town Sukhumi Hill stands 201 m. high. There is no other place on the Black Sea coast with so much sun and warmth as Sukhumi; from April until November there are sea breezes during the day and a light wind from the mountains at night. Citrus, banana, palm, and eucalyptus decorate the parks and streets of the town. 'The Sukhumi Valley is a corner of Spain or Sicily dropped at the foot of Old Man Caucasus,' wrote Russian travellers in the 19th century. In fact it lies on the same latitude as Nice and has an annual average temperature of 15°C. (50°F.), and approximately 270 sunny days during the year. It is at its best in autumn, winter, and spring.

When the Argonauts sailed to faraway Colchis to claim the Golden Fleece, among the travellers who went with Jason were the Dioscuri brothers, the twins Castor and Pollux. Their name comes from 'Dios Kouros' (sons of Zeus). Legend has it that the brothers founded a rich and flourishing town in Colchis, which was called Dioscuria after them. A little way out to sea, and buried beneath 5·5 m of mud and fine silt, the ruins of this town have lain hidden for 1500 years. It is supposed to have been robbed and ruined by Pompey's Roman legions in A.D. 65, but an acropolis, a contemporary of the Parthenon, still stands under the water. The site is under investigation and exhibits, including an ancient marble tombstone, have begun to come to the local museum.

The Romans built Sukhumi in the 2nd century B.C. on the order of Emperor Adrian, and they knew it as Sevastopolis, while the Georgians spoke of it as Tukhomi. In 1455 it became Turkish and was called Su-Khum-Kale (water-sand-fortress). It was annexed to Russia in 1810, but it was held by the Turks again in both 1855 and 1877. It had previously been one of the chief slave markets on the Black Sea.

Local industry now deals with tobacco, sweets, and food products. There is a pedagogical institute in the town.

Sukhumi Fortress, by the sea. Possibly this fortress was founded at the time of Colchis. In 1578 the Turks built a new fortress on the remains of the old one and there was a slave market outside the walls. In the 19th and 20th centuries it was used as a prison.

King Bagrat Fortress, Chelyuskintsev St., in the south-eastern part of Sukhumi. The fortress was founded in the 10th or 11th century either by the Georgian King Bagrat III (965–1014) or by Bagrat IV (1027–72). Only the ruins remain now and the entrance gateway shows traces of underground tunnels.

Besledski Most (The Venetian Bridge), 6 km. to the north-east of Sukhumi along the Besledski Chaussée. The bridge was built in the 10th–12th century and was from that time on of certain military importance, as the ruins of a defence tower nearby show. 300 m. from the bridge on the left bank of the R. Besleti are the ruins of an old church. The bridge itself is 13 m. long and varies in width from 5–7 m.; it has not yet been established whether it is of Venetian or local construction.

Blagoveschensky (Annunciation) Cathedral, Leselidze St. 59. The cathedral was built at the end of the 19th century and was formerly a Greek church.

Monkey Colony, Baratashvili St. Founded in 1927, this research enterprise under the auspices of the U.S.S.R. Academy of Sciences is situated on the slopes of Mount Trapetsaya. By 1962 there were over 1000 monkeys in this colony, 75% of which were born there, and they had reached the 8th generation. The inmates are mostly baboons and macaque monkeys. They thrive out of doors in this southern climate and eat locally grown fruit for which they each have a daily spending allowance of 70–80 kopeks. They are there for medical experiments. In 1948 after nine years of experiments on cancer, artificial sarcoma was induced. The fifty scientists at the colony work in 7 laboratories.

Local Museum, Lenin St. 20. Open 9–5.

Scientific Museum

Lenin Monument, in front of the House of the Government. By Asatiani and Georgadze and unveiled in 1959.

Shota Rustaveli Monument, in Rustaveli Park. Merabishvili made this monument to the Georgian poet which was unveiled in 1939.

Dmitri Gulia Monument, Lenin St. 18. Gulia (1874–1960) was an Abkhazian poet. Rukhadze made this monument which was unveiled in 1962.

Akaki Tsereteli Monument, in Tsereteli Garden. By Razmadze and unveiled in 1954.

Ordzhonikidze Monument, in Ordzhonikidze Park. By Eshaba and unveiled in 1961.

S. Chanba Monument, Pushkin St. 1. Chanba was a local writer. Gogoberidze was responsible for this monument, unveiled in 1959.

Drama Theatre, Pushkin St. 1. Built in 1952 in Georgian style, decorated with stone carving, a waterfall in a grotto and griffin fountains. On the façade are busts of Georgian representatives of the arts.

Summer Theatre, Kirov St., in the park

Dynamo Stadium, Ordzhonikidze St. 33

Botanical Garden, Chavchavadze St. 18. The gardens were founded in 1840, devastated by the Turks in 1878, and restored in 1894. There are four ponds for water plants, and many of them, including the Blue Water Lily, the Water Poppy, and the giant Victoria Regia with leaves 2·5 m in diameter, are subtropical. The Indian Lotus is also grown, and the greenhouses contain many rare tropical plants and cacti.

Park, near Frunze St.

Ordzhonikidze Park, Kirov St.

Shota Rustaveli Park, Teatralnaya St. There is a monument to Shota Rustaveli, and the many palm trees include Blue Palms.

Park on Sukhumi Hill. A road leads up to the car park at the top. The *Amza (Moon) Restaurant*, which has a good view, is reached by a wide flight of steps.

The best bathing beaches are 1 km. from town and reached by either car or motor boat. The Intourist beach has sand and shingle.

Abkhazia Hotel and Restaurant, Frunze St. 2. Built in 1937, this is now an Intourist hotel. TEL. 33–11 and 33–91.

Tbilisi Hotel, Djguburia St.

Ritsa Hotel, Rustaveli Prospect 34

Tkvarcheli Hotel, Lenin St. 1

Aragvi Restaurant, Mir Prospect 67

Ritsa Restaurant, Lenin St. 2

Kavkaz Restaurant, Frunze St. 2

Psou Restaurant, Tbilisskoye Chaussée 15

Amza (Moon) Restaurant, on the top of Suk-humi Hill

Amra (Sun) Restaurant, Rustaveli Prospect, by the sea

Shashlik Bar, in the open air, about 10 km. along the Sukhumi Military Road

G.P.O., Mir Prospect 92

Bank, Lenin St. 14

Department Store, Mir Prospect 52

Market, Tarkhnishvili St. 7

Filling Stations, beside the road, both on the way into town and on the way out

Sinop Motel, 1 km. from Sukhumi along the Tbilisskoye Chausseé; near the road, among tropical and subtropical trees. Eating house, carwash, and service station. 100 m from the exit gate is the:

Medicinal Beach with car park, a café, and a shop.

SUZDAL
See Vladimir, p. 330

TAJIKISTAN
See Dushanbe, p. 94

TALLINN
Formerly German Reval: Russian Revel
Population—365,000 (1971).
Capital of the Estonian Soviet Socialist Republic

ESTONIA
Estonian: Eesti
Area: 47,559 sq. km. of which 4167 sq. km. is made up of the 818 islands and 2328 sq. km. of the country's 1512 lakes. Estonia is larger than Denmark, Holland, or Switzerland.

Population—1,360,000 (1971) of which 73% are Estonians and 22% Russian.

Estonia is in the extreme north-west of the U.S.S.R., on the coast of the Baltic Sea. It is bounded in the east by Lake Peipsi and by Russia, and in the south by Latvia. Its principal cities are Tallinn (the capital), Narva, and Tartu.

In the early days of its history this land was inhabited by Finnish-speaking tribes who established close economic ties with the neighbouring territories. From the end of the 12th century the Teutonic Knights and Scandinavian nobles tried to conquer this area, under the pretext of converting the local tribes to Christianity. After a long and bloody struggle the Teutonic Knights seized southern and central Estonia while Denmark took the northern part of the country.

In the second half of the 16th century Estonia became the field of contest between Russia, Poland, and Sweden who were fighting for the Baltic provinces. The result was that Poland gained southern Estonia and Sweden took northern Estonia. During the next 50 years Poland and Sweden fought for possession of the whole country. In 1721, after the Russo-Swedish War, the whole of Estonia was included in the Russian Empire.

During the First World War, Estonia was occupied by German troops, but it was freed in 1919 and remained a parliamentary republic until 1934 when a dictatorship was established by President Päts. He was turned out of office in 1940 and Estonia was proclaimed a Soviet Republic and joined the U.S.S.R.

Estonians use the Latin alphabet. Here are a few words of the language:

Hello!	Tervist!
I am a tourist	Olen turist
Please	Palun
Thank you	Tanun
Yes	Ja
No	Ei
Good	Hea
Bad	Halb
I don't understand	Ma ei saa aru
I need an interpreter	Ma vajan tolki
Goodbye	Hääd aega *or* Nägemiseni

The following are among the favourite Estonian dishes:

Hapukapsa supp—sauerkraut soup

Seaspraad—pork with sauerkraut

Milgikapsad sealihaga—mulgi cabbage with pork

Seajalad—pig's trotters

Mannakreem piimaga—Estonian semolina pudding

Tallinn
The name of the city comes from 'taani linn' meaning 'Danish Castle', but Tallinn is only one of the city's three names. The Revele were a local tribe and for many years it was known as Revel, although some believe the town's name to have come from the Danish word 'revel' which means 'reeds' and would have signified the treacherous nature of the submerged rocks in the bay. However in 1154 Revel appeared on a map by the Arabian geographer Idris as Koluvan. Koluvan was taken from the name of Kalev, an Estonian folk hero, reputed to be the guardian of the stronghold.

The first settlement of all was made on Toompea (called Vyshgorod in Russian), the 49-m. limestone hill in the centre of the present city. Legend has it that the hill was made by Linda, the mother of Kalev, as a burial mound over the grave of her son. Tonismagi Hill is 30 m. high.

The average temperature in July is 20.7°C. (69°F.) and in January —9.9°C. (14°F.). The bathing season lasts from mid-June until the end of August.

It was in the first centuries A.D. that the Estonians, a people of Finno-Ugric stock, moved into

---

PLATE OPPOSITE

Tchaikovsky's study in his house at Klin, now a museum to his memory, where the composer wrote the music for 'The Sleeping Beauty', 'The Nutcracker' and the *Symphonie Pathétique*.

TALLINN

KEY:
1 Narva Hotel
2 Horse-Mill (14th-18thcent.)
3 Tourist Centre: Three Sisters House (15thcent.)
4 Marine Museum
5 Two 15th century houses
6 Swimming Pool
7 Seaport
8 Civil War Memorial

9   Former Almshouses (14th-17thcent.)
10 Old Pharmacy
11 Viru Gate
12 Toome Hotel
13 Pikk Yalg Gate tower
14 Façade of private house (1798)
15 Foreign Currency Shop
16 Department Store

17 Telephone Office
18 Summer Theatre
19 Revolutionaries' Monument
20 Assaube Tower
21 War Memorial
22 Russian Drama Theatre
23 Kungla Hotel
24 Sports Centre

this area. Their central stronghold was called Lindanissa. Early in the 13th century they were united under one chieftain but were attacked by the Danes and the German knights.

King Waldemar II of Denmark founded Revel 'in the country of the Revelers' in 1219 on the site of the ancient fortress and after a battle on 15 June of that year. It is recorded that at a critical point in the encounter his weary soldiers were inspired by the appearance of a red flag with a white cross which floated down from the heavens and which has ever since been the national flag of Denmark. The Danish castle was founded on Toompea in the autumn of 1219, but Revel was besieged by the Estonians between 1221 and 1223 and came under the Order of the Teutonic Knights in 1227. They occupied the fortress on Toompea and added to it until Revel again fell to the Danes in 1238. In 1248 Revel attained 'Lübeck Law' and it remained in

force until the 19th century; it meant that in spite of different conquerors and masters, Estonian law suits could always be taken to the Lübeck court for final jurisdiction.

From 1284 when Revel became a member of the Hanseatic League, the town's trading importance grew rapidly. It even controlled the trade of the great inland centre of Novgorod. The Estonians again besieged the city in 1343. They were led by the Estonian Knights of St. George, but were entirely vanquished at the Battle of Revel. Three years later the Danish King Waldemar IV sold Revel with the rest of his share of Estonia to the Teutonic Knights, who held it until the area fell to Sweden in 1561. There were Russian attacks on Revel in 1560, 1570, and 1577, but it remained in Swedish hands until the Great Northern War at the beginning of the 18th century and finally fell to Peter the Great in 1710.

PLATE OPPOSITE
Tree roots in the Siberian 'taiga', about which Chekhov said: 'Its strength and magic lie not in the size of its giant trees nor in the depth of its deathly silence, but rather in the fact that perhaps it is the migrant birds alone of all living creatures that know its limits . . .'

The city suffered the usual run of triumph and tragedy throughout its medieval history. There are records of the terrible fire of 1433, of Revel rising to the foremost place in the Hanseatic League in 1496, and of the plagues of 1591 and 1657. The Russian constitution was in force from 1786, and the port's economic importance led it into trouble in the 19th century. Nelson was in Revel in 1801, the harbour was blockaded by the British Fleet in 1809 and again, this time jointly with the French Fleet and under Admiral Napier, during the Crimean War.

Estonian independence was proclaimed on 24 February 1918, but it lasted a single day. On the 25th the Germans moved in and were in occupation for eight months. It seemed likely that the Red Army would take over, but they were prevented from doing so by the Estonians themselves with help from Britain, Finland, and Scandinavia. Parliament met in April 1919, and the following year the country was at peace with Russia. Tallinn remained the capital of independent Estonia until 1940.

In Tallinn is an *Art Institute and Conservatoire*, founded in 1919, the *Vilde Pedagogical Institute*, the *Polytechnical Institute* (1936), and the *Academy of Sciences* (1946). Local industries include shipbuilding and the manufacture of textiles, electrical and mechanical equipment, and food products.

About two-thirds of the original length of the old town walls remain, as do 18 of the original 25 towers, and the ruins of 6 more can be seen. The north-west side of the wall is particularly well preserved and starting from Mooruse St., the first 3 towers are open to the public; their names are *Köstritorn, Saunatorn (Bath House Tower)*, and *Kuldjalatorn (Golden Leg Tower)*. The average height of the wall is 15 m. and its thickness varies between 2·25 and 3 m. The towers are extremely varied and many bear attractive names which suit their particular character. *Kiek in de kök (peep-into-the-kitchen)* (46 m. high) was built in 1475 on the slopes of Harju Hill. It is 5 storeys high and has 2 vaulted cellars. Once it afforded an excellent view over the most thickly populated part of the town; it is said that one could even look down the wide chimneys, hence its strange name. *Stout Margaret* together with another thinner tower guards *Rannavärava*, the ancient Sea Gate, founded in 1510; the coat of arms above the arch bears the date 1529 which is when the construction was finished. *Viru Gate* (15th century) stands at the end of Viru St.; the main gate is no longer there, and these two towers stood on either side of the outer archway. *Bremer Tower* stands in Vene St. The two gates on the *Short-* and *Long-Toompea* were put up about 1380; the former has a thick oaken door. In places parts of the old *Maiden's Wall* remain. This used to divide the 'toom' from the lower part of the town. Its name recalls the legend that it was a warrior-maiden who brought the stones for the construction of the wall, coming secretly, under cover of night. Perhaps the story

springs from the same source as that of Kalev's mother, Linda, bringing stones in her apron to form Toompea.

The Dom has always lived a life a little apart from that of the bustling streets below. It had its own administration which it even retained after 1346 when the city passed to the German knights.

Dom Castle and the *Long Herman watchtower* were already standing in 1227, but now only the western part remains. The last rebuilding dates from 1780. Long Herman is the only remaining one of the four corner towers. It is 47 m. high and there are another 30 m. of stonework underground. Its height is emphasised by the 30-m. deep ravine which falls away below. The Castle housed, in succession, the Danish Governor, the Commander of the Order of Knighthood, Swedish and Russian Governors-General, Russian commissioners, and German generals. Finally it was used as Estonian government offices. Some of the old rooms were once used as a prison but they were burned down in 1917.

Domkirk, Kiriku St., Toompea. This church was built in 1232 but it suffered many fires and much reconstruction. It was finally rebuilt after the fire of 1684. One of the bells of the church bears an inscription in German which points to the building's fiery past. 'The heat of the fire melted me as the whole of Toompea burnt down. One year later I was cast in this shape and called Maria's Bell.' There are several interesting tombstones to be seen. One of marble near the altar marks the grave of the Swedish General Pontius de la Gardie, who was of French origin, and his wife, daughter of King Johann III of Sweden and sister of King Gustav Vasa. The tombstone of Admiral Samuel Greig (1736–88) was designed by Giacomo Quarenghi. Greig came to Russia from Scotland in 1764 and served gallantly in the Russian Navy, notably against the Turks (1770) and the Swedes (1788). Another great seaman buried here is Admiral Johann von Krusenstern (1770–1846) who was the first Russian to sail around the world (1803–6). From the end of the 18th century it was forbidden for burials to take place in the Domkirk, but von Krusenstern was laid to rest here by special order of Nicholas I. The altarpiece of the Domkirk is by Ed. von Gebhardt. The church is now used by the Lutherans and is open for services.

The *Nobility House* stands in the centre of Toompea. The oldest part, in Kohtu St., was rebuilt after the fire of 1684 and the main part, opposite the Domkirk, was built in 1840. The assembly hall is decorated with noble coats-of-arms and with portraits and busts of Russian tsars.

Also commanding a fine position on Toompea is the *St. Alexander Nevsky Russian Orthodox Cathedral*. It was constructed during the reign of Alexander III, between 1894–1900. It measures 43 m. long and 26 m. wide and the steps leading up on three sides are of Finnish granite. The domes were once gilded and of the eleven bells the largest weighs about 17·5 tons. The mosaics inside are the only ones of their kind in Estonia. The cathedral is open for religious services. In 1934 it is recorded that by far the greatest proportion of the population was Lutheran but that more than 10% were Russian Orthodox; there were besides a very small number of Jews and even fewer Roman Catholics. Today the Domkirk and St. Alexander Nevsky Cathedral are among 17 churches and meeting houses open for worship.

Kalinin's statue is one of the later additions to Toompea; it is by Kaasik and was unveiled in 1950.

The best view of the city is from the top of *Patkuli Trepp*.

A walk from the town hall down Pikk St. to the Sea Gate takes one past a good selection of the sights of the old town. The *town hall* (1371–4) stands in the centre of the large market square, laid out in 1288 and used as a market place until 1896. In style the town hall is a solid and gloomy Gothic building with a Renaissance tower resembling a minaret added in 1629 and surmounted by a special weathervane known as 'Old Thomas'. This depicts an ancient warrior of the town and is a copy made in 1952 of a vane of 1530 now in the town hall museum. The citizens of Tallinn are very fond of Old Thomas, and from being their guardian he has come to be regarded almost as a mascot.

Inside the town hall there are vaulted ceilings in the rooms of all three storeys.

The tapestries were made in the Netherlands in 1547 and are marked with the arms of Tallinn. In the museum are paintings, friezes, and instruments of torture, as well as some fine examples of carved furniture of the 15th and 16th centuries including a bench depicting Tristan and Isolde (15th century) and a beautiful carved frieze with hunting scenes (17th century) in the main hall by a local master, Elert Thiele, and presented to the city in 1697 by Charles XI of Sweden. This is the only medieval Gothic-style town hall surviving in the Baltic countries. It was restored in 1959–60.

Also in the market square is the old *Weighing House*. Its steeply gabled roof is tiled and the side walls are decorated with busts of German rulers.

On the southern side of the market square is the *Old Pharmacy*. The house itself was built in 1461 but the pharmacy business was founded earlier, in 1422.

The first building of especial interest in Pikk St. (Pikk Tan) is the *Great Guild* (1405–10) in Gothic style. It stands on the left as one prepares to walk down the street. Once it was used for weddings, trials, religious services, plays, concerts, etc. The central pillars are decorated with inscriptions and with the figures of animals.

On the right is the *Church of the Holy Spirit*, at Püha Vaimu St. 4; 'Vaimu' means 'spirit'. The church, built at the end of the 14th century, is one of the oldest in the town. It was built in Gothic style but the Baroque spire is 17th century. On the corner of the church facing Pikk St. is the oldest clock in Tallinn, with carvings of 1684, and in the

tower is Estonia's oldest bell (1433) with the inscription, 'I chime just as accurately for all, for maid and servant, for mistress and master, and for that I am beyond reproach.' The church is now used for worship by the Lutherans. Its original altar has been transferred to *St. Nicholas's Church* which serves as a museum.

A little further down on the right side is *St. Kanuti-Guild*, a large building in Roman style. The zinc statues represent King Canute and Martin Luther, and the medallions on the façade bear the coats-of-arms of the old city. Inside, the lofty hall on the ground floor is decorated with paintings, as are some of the other rooms.

St. Olai-Guild is further down on the same side. It was built in the 14th century and has a Gothic-style hall.

Next door to St. Olai-Guild is the *Blackheads' Club*. The Blackheads were a corporation of bachelor merchants, founded in the 14th century with St. Mauritius as their patron saint. His head, represented by that of a Moor, was part of their coat-of-arms and it was from this that they derived their strange name. The Blackheads were the oldest of a number of similar corporations in the Baltic states. The façade of the club was rebuilt in 1591 and is decorated with limestone bas-reliefs. Over the door are the coats-of-arms of Bruges, Novgorod, London, and Bergen, the four most important cities of the Hanseatic League. Higher up on the façade are two 'blackheads' and, above them, figures of Jesus Christ, Justice, and Peace. Inside the building is a museum where paintings, arms, and plate are on display.

Further down Pikk St., but this time on the left, stands *St. Olaf's Church*, in Lai St. Officially it was called after King Olaf II of Norway who died in the Battle of Trondheim Fjord (1033), fighting against King Canute. However, in spite of the official dedication, popular belief is that when the citizens of Tallinn decided to build a new and marvellous church to beautify their city, they found an architect called Olaf to help them. When the edifice was almost completed he fell to his death from the roof, and as he lay on the ground a toad and a serpent crept out of his mouth. He was buried where he fell, and a stone plaque illustrates the story. A wooden church was first mentioned as being on this site in 1288, restored in 1329 and the spire was struck by lightning six times during the 17th and 18th centuries. In 1625 the fire that resulted from the lightning was so severe that the bells melted with the heat. It was again restored in 1628 and the spire was built in 1651. In 1820 after being burnt to the ground it was rebuilt in Gothic style and now it is 58 m. long, 28 m. wide, and 28 m. high. The steeple rises to 140 m. and was again struck by lightning in 1931. Beside the church stands the *Bremen Chapel of St. Mary* built between 1502–14 by Hans Pavels. The work was financed by a donation from the merchant, Poulsen. A memorial to him dated 1513 decorates the wall facing the street. There is also a curious memorial depicting a skeleton with a toad on its chest and a serpent round the skull, perhaps linked to the legend of the architect. The church is used by the Baptist and Methodist communities of Tallinn.

Pikk St. ends with the Sea Gate, guarded on the right side by the formidable figure of *Stout Margaret*, 24 m. in diameter and the largest of all the towers in the town wall, constructed between 1510 and 1529 during the reign of Queen Margaret of Denmark, mother of Erik VI. The walls are 4 m. thick at the base and the tower itself is 4 storeys high. It was used as barracks at the end of the 19th century and after 1905 it served as a prison until 1917. It was restored in 1937.

St. Nicholas Church, Nicholas St. is also a museum. The church was built between 1316 and 1350 and dedicated to the saint among whose other responsibilities are the seamen of the world, which explains his popularity in this ancient port. In the early 16th century it was saved from the ravages of the iconoclasts by a quick-thinking warden who poured molten lead into the locks. After 1524 it belonged to the Lutherans. The building measures 48 m. long and 28 m. wide. Its steeple was rebuilt in 1898, but was badly damaged during the Second World War. The oldest dated memorial slab on the stone floor is from 1330. The St. Anthony Chapel now houses the altarpiece from the Church of the Holy Spirit (see above, p. 291) which was made in Lübeck in 1483 by Berent Notken, a professional woodcarver and painter. Also from Lübeck is the 15th-century painting, 'Danse Macabre'; a copy which used to be in St. Mary's, Lübeck was destroyed during the war, and for some time it was believed that the original had perished and that the painting in Tallinn was the copy, instead of the other way about. There is a second large altarpiece, by Herman Rode of Lübeck, which was commissioned by the Blackheads. It is 6 m. long and 3.5 m. high and when the inner covers are closed there appear 16 scenes from the lives of St. Nicholas and St. Victor, the last scene of all showing the earliest known picture of Lübeck. Another altarpiece with scenes of the Passion was made in Bruges in the late 15th century. The chandelier in front of the main altar was made in north Germany in 1519. On the wall is a memorial to a Tallinn merchant called Bugislaus von Rosen who died in 1651 and whose loans largely financed Sweden's part in the Thirty Years' War. It was he who donated the 17th-century carved wooden pulpit to the church; on its door are his coat-of-arms and those of his two wives. There are also some interesting carved wooden pews in the church. St. Nicholas's was also famous for a number of years for a more gruesome sight, the mummified body of Duke Charles de Croix. This Belgian nobleman sought adventure and joined the Russian army where he rose to be given the rank of field-marshal by Peter the Great. He was in command at the outbreak of the Great Northern War, but was taken prisoner by the Swedes in 1700 and confined to Tallinn. His gambling and heavy drinking led him into such debts

that when he was released he had to leave the town to avoid his creditors. He died suddenly in 1702, but his creditors still pursued him, saying that he should not receive proper burial until his debts were paid. Meanwhile his body was laid in the crypt of St. Nicholas's, and there it remained until, at the beginning of the 19th century, it was discovered that it had turned into a mummy, probably because of the sandy nature of the ground there, but many suspected it was because of the vast quantities of alcohol he had consumed in the last years of his life. The mummy was on view to the public for several years and it was only given due burial under the floor of the Klodt Chapel, beside St. Nicholas's, 117 years after the Duke's death.

In Vene St. 12–18, not far from the town hall, are the remains of the *Dominican Monastery*. Its principal church was St. Catherine's and part of its cloisters were converted into the Roman Catholic church of SS. Peter and Paul in 1840.

Further along Vene St., just before it runs into Pikk St., is the Russian Orthodox *St. Nicholas's Church*. Its existence is first mentioned in documents of 1422. It was rebuilt, again in Novgorod style, in 1825. The chandelier was received as a gift from Boris Godunov in 1599.

Kazansky Church, Kazan St. Founded in 1749 and still used for Russian Orthodox services.

Rootsi-Mikhkli Church, Rüütli (knights) St. 9. This church with no steeple used to be the alms house chapel and a part of the city hospital. It was given to the Swedes in 1733 but it is now disused. There is a round Roman Catholic font with statues of the apostles and also a memorial slab mentioning the plague of 1602.

Issanda-Muutmise Church, S. Kloostri St. 14

Preobrazhensky (Transfiguration) Cathedral, at the Süstern Gates, Noorusti St. This Russian Orthodox church, still open for religious services, stands on the site of the ancient Convent of St. Michael which belonged to the Cistercian Order. The original cathedral was turned into a Lutheran church for the local Swedish garrison, but in 1716 Prince Menshikov ordered that it be handed over to the Russian Orthodox Church. It was soon after this that the spectacular iconostasis of carved woodwork was presented by Peter the Great. It was specially made by Zarudny, the master who was also responsible for the iconostasis in the Cathedral of SS. Peter and Paul in St. Petersburg. This cathedral was rebuilt in 1828 using money donated by Nicholas I.

Siimeoni Church, Siimeoni St. 5

Kopli Church, Kopli, Vene-Balti Tehas 73

St. John's Church, Vabaduce (Liberty) Sq. This bears a strong resemblance to St. Nicholas's Church except that the steeple is not so tall. It was constructed in limestone in 1867 and is now used by the Lutherans.

St. Charles' Church, Kaarli Avenue. This church with two steeples was built in Roman style without pillars and with large windows in 1870. It was named after King Charles XI of Sweden.

Inside is a fresco of Christ by the Estonian professor, Koehler. The acoustics are good and there is an excellent organ.

The *Boys' High School*, Kloostri St. This school was founded in 1630 by Gustavus Adolphus.

Linda Statue, on the slope of Toompea known as Linda's Hill; the site was chosen by the sculptor, August Weizenburg. Linda, who is said to have turned to stone, was the mother of Kalev, Estonia's national hero. This statue was unveiled in 1920 having been cast from the original marble made in 1880.

The *monument* to those who fell during the Russian Revolution of 1905 was made by Palutedre and unveiled in 1959.

Kingissep Monument, on the slopes of Harju Hill, sculpted by Roos and unveiled in 1951. Victor Kingissep (1888–1922) was a leading Estonian communist. He lived illegally in Estonia between 1918 and 1922, but was betrayed and executed.

Lenin Monument, Lenin Boulevard. Sculpted by Tomsky and unveiled in 1950.

City Museum, Pikk St. 70. Open 11–6 (Sat. 11–5); closed Tues.

Historical Museum, Pikk St. 17. This museum was founded in 1864 and now belongs to the Estonian Academy of Sciences. Open 12–6; closed Wed.

Art Museum, in Kadriorg Palace, Kadriorg Park (see below). Open 12–7; closed Tues. Here are examples of Estonian art from the 19th century to the present day.

Theatrical and Musical Museum, Müürivahe St. 12. Open 12–6; closed Tues.

House of Arts, Voidu (Victory) Sq. 8. Temporary exhibitions are held here. Open 12–7; closed Tues.

Peter the Great's House, Kadriorg Park. Peter the Great lived here during the construction of the harbour and Kadriorg Palace. Open 11–5 from May till October; closed Tues.

Vilde Museum, Koidula St. 34 Kadriorg. Edward Vilde (1865–1933) was a well-known Estonian writer; he spent his last years in this house.

Natural History Museum, Lai St. 29, in a 15th-century house.

Open-air Folk Museum, Rocca-al-Mares, Vabaohumuuseumitee Road 12. Established in 1960.

Estonian State Opera House, Estonia Boulevard 4

Kingissep Drama Theatre, Parnu Chaussée 5

Puppet Theatre, Lai St. This theatre was founded in 1952.

Philharmonic Society, Estonia Boulevard 4

Circus, Lenin Boulevard 6. The circus operates during the summer only.

Komsomol Stadium, Staadioni St. 3

Dynamo Stadium, Roheline Aas 20

Kalev Tennis Stadium, Herne St. 28

Kalev Ice Hockey Stadium, Suvorov Boulevard 2

Hippodrome Racecourse, Paldis Chaussée 50

Zoo, Mazkalda St. 45 (Kadriorg) Open in summer 10–8, winter 10–5.

Viru Hotel & Restaurant, Viru Sq.

Palace Hotel & Restaurant, Voidu Sq. 3, TEL. 4–82–16

Evropa Hotel & Restaurant, Viru St. 24, TEL. 440–49

Kopli Hotel & Restaurant, Kalinin St. 2A, TEL. 427–61

Tallinn Hotel, Gagarin St. 2, TEL. 436–88

Balti Hotel, Vaksali Lane 3, TEL. 440–47

In the restaurants in Tallinn, music and dancing begin at 8.0 pm and the establishments are open until midnight.

Kevad Restaurant, Lomonosov St. 2

Gloria Restaurant, Müürivahe St. 2

G.P.O., Suur-Karja St. 20

Telegraph office, Vene St. 9

The building of the *Estonian bank* was designed by Saarinen.

Souvenir Shops, Voidu Sq. 8, Viru St. 19, and Pikk St. 27

Art Salon, Voidu Sq. 6

Folk Art, Kullaseppa St.

Taxi Ranks, Balti Railway Station, Town Hall Sq. (Raekoja Platsil), Voidu Sq., and Central Market

Kadriorg (Catherine Dale) lies on the eastern side of Tallinn. The palace and park were laid out by Peter the Great for his consort. The Baroque-style building contains some beautiful painted ceilings and interesting fireplaces. The architect was an Italian by the name of Michetti. Once there were fountains and statues to beautify the park but the Empress Anna had them transferred to Petrodvorets (see Leningrad).

Kreutzwald Monument, in Kadriorg, near the Swan Pond. Friedrich Reihold Kreutzwald (1803–82) was the most popular Estonian poet, regarded as the founder of the nation's literature. He collected folk songs and proverbs but was especially famous for rewriting the ancient epic, 'Kalevipoeg', which was performed in modern dress in 1861. The sculpture by Saks and Taniloo was unveiled in 1958.

Peter the Great's House (see above) is where Peter I lived while the palace was under construction. Nearby is a Dutch-style *bath house*.

Choir Festival Platform. The Estonians are famous for their choirs. Up to 30,000 people participate here, and the auditorium can take 100,000. The tradition of a song festival originated in Tartu in 1869. This open-air platform was completed in 1960.

Rusalka Monument, by the edge of the sea at Kadriorg. The monument, a figure of an angel holding a cross, by the Estonian artist, Adamson, was put up to commemorate the sailors of the 'Rusalka' (mermaid), a Russian battleship which sank in the Gulf of Finland in 1893. The bronze statue stands 16 m. high on a pediment of Finnish granite. It was unveiled in 1902.

Nikonov Monument, by the seashore. Yevgeni Nikonov was a seaman who was captured by the

Germans in 1941, tied to a tree, and burned alive. He was declared a Hero of the Soviet Union. The monument that marks his grave is by Haggi and was unveiled in 1960. The ash-tree, against which he died, has been transplanted to his grave.

Another monument here beside the sea is an *obelisk* (architect: Port, sculptor: Tolli) which was unveiled in 1960. It commemorates the 1918 ice-crossing when most of the Russian Baltic Fleet made the dangerous midwinter journey of 300 km. through the ice from Tallinn to Kronstadt to escape capture by the German army.

Marienburg Castle, behind Kadriorg, by the seashore. The gate pillars are surmounted by cast iron eagles and inside is an attractive tower. Steps lead down to the sea from the stone pavilion by the gates.

Kose Forest, further on to the north-east. Here, near the mouth of Pirita Brook, are the ruins of *St. Bridget's Abbey*. In the 14th century a Swedish woman by the name of Birgitta (Pirita in Estonian) was widowed, took the veil, and founded a new religious order with its centre at Vadstenas in Southern Sweden. Birgitta was the author of some mystical 'Revelations'. She died in 1373 and was canonised in 1391 by Pope Boniface XI. The order spread until there were more than 70 abbeys in different parts of Europe. This one was of the duplica or mixta type which served both monks and nuns of the order. It was built in 1407–36 and the monks lived on the ground floor and the nuns above. It was ruined in 1577 during the Russo-Livonian War. The cathedral church was 56 m. long and 24 m. in width, but now only part of it remains. In the south-west corner is an old staircase which used to belong to the belfry and there is an excellent view from the top of the wall.

The village of *Pirita* is a seaside resort and thousands of people come here to watch the motor-cycle racing. There are yacht clubs. Boats can be hired and the sandy beaches stretch for 2 km. There are other good beaches at the nearby resorts of Vaana-Joesuus, Rannamoisas, Keila-Joal, and Kloogal.

Agricultural Exhibition, Pirita Tee 12 & 24; open 12–7.

Pirita Restaurant, by the sea.

Nomme, on the opposite side of Tallinn, 7 km. to the south.

Mustamäe, further on in the same direction. There is an excellent view from the highest point of the castle here.

Viljandi

German: Fellin

Long ago there was an Est settlement here and in the 13th century it was invaded by the Teutonic Knights. They built the *castle*, the ruins of which remain. The town which grew up around the castle joined the Hanseatic League in the Middle Ages. The local horses were much sought after.

Later Viljandi changed hands between the Russians, the Poles, and the Swedes.

Parts of the town are located upon three hills, Well Hill, Cherry Hill, and Kissing Hill, from all three of which there are good views upon Lake Viljandi.

To the south of the castle ruins stands a *monument* to the victims of the 1905 Revolution and to the 30,000 people who died in the local concentration camp during World War II.

Food products, matches, and furniture are made here today.

Local Museum

TARTU

Population—88,000 (1971)

(Tarpatu; Yuriev; Dorpat)

The town was founded in 1030 by Prince Yaroslav the Wise (Yuri) of Kiev, called Yuriev after him. It grew up beside the R. Emajogi on the site of an old Estonian settlement, Tarpatu, which dated back perhaps as far as the 5th century B.C. The name Tarpatu may be linked with the word 'tarvas', wild ox, or perhaps with Taara, a god of Estonian mythology. The present name of Tartu derives from that of Tarpatu. Yuriev was ruled by the Kievan princes until 1212 when the Teutons took it over and later it became the seat of the Livonian bishops.

Situated strategically between warring Russia, Sweden, and Poland, Tartu was seldom left in peace. It is on record that the town was destroyed by the Germans in 1212 but was soon rebuilt. It was captured by them again in 1215 and all the inhabitants were then baptised. Christian Tartu took SS. Peter and Paul as its patrons and its coat-of-arms still bears their crossed key and sword motif. Advancing and retreating armies continually burnt and ravaged the town until in 1710 Russia, under Peter the Great, finally established control over the region. From 1918 Estonian rule lasted until 1940, then from 1941–4 the town was under German occupation.

Wars apart, Tartu also suffered badly from fires, and after the Great Fire of 1775 only two houses remained standing, Voimala St. 12 and Ulikooli St. 40. The latter is where Peter I stayed in 1704, after taking Tartu from the Swedes. Tradition has it that he attended a wedding party there. Trees were planted following the lines of the old fortifications after the Great Fire.

Tartu once served as an important economic centre. It was a member of the Hanseatic League and even now ranks as Estonia's second city, but its chief claim to fame has long been its university. Founded in 1632 by the Swedish king, Gustav II, the university was transferred to the town of Pärnu. It reopened in Tartu in 1802 and grew and prospered until, in the 19th century, it ranked among the very best European centres of learning. During World War II Tartu University was evacuated to the city of Voronezh and was influential in the foundation of Voronezh University. Today there are seven faculties and a student population of 4000. Ulikooli, the name of the main street, means 'university'. The university is justly proud of its laboratories, museums, and particularly of its library of two million books, where there is a copy of Thomas More's 'Utopia' printed in 1516. Most of the library is housed in the *Cathedral of SS. Peter and Paul* on Toome Hill. The cathedral was in ruins and was reconstructed when the University was reopened in 1802. Part of the cathedral dates from the 13th century and so it is probably the oldest building in Tartu.

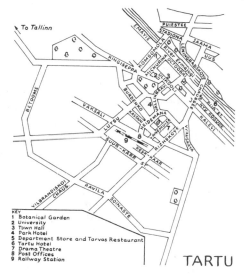

KEY
1 Botanical Garden
2 University
3 Town Hall
4 Park Hotel
5 Department Store and Tarvas Restaurant
6 Tartu Hotel
7 Drama Theatre
8 Post Offices
9 Railway Station

TARTU

There is a legend attached to the cathedral. When it was founded, the building made no progress because the stones that the masons laid during the day were pulled down again during the night. Someone suggested that the only way to combat the problem was to immure a beautiful virgin in the walls of the cathedral. The girl who was chosen was only told that she would be the keeper of the keys and when she realised what the job entailed, she pleaded and cried to no avail. It is said that the unfortunate maiden is allowed out once a year, some say on New Year's Eve and some say on midsummer night, to look for another woman around whose neck she can hang the cord upon which the keys are threaded.

Other stories about the cathedral tell of hidden treasure and underground passages and a hall where ravens meet once in a hundred years; whoever overhears their talk will become immensely wise.

Among the other notable buildings on Toome Hill, most of them used by the medical or scientific members of the university community, are the *observatory* and the *Old Anatomical Theatre*. The observatory was built in 1807 and in 1824 the largest refracting telescope in the world at the time was presented by Alexander I and installed there. The observatory was in use until 1963. The central part of the Old Anatomical Theatre, the rotunda, was completed in 1805 but in 1825 and 1856 the wings and then the annexes were added.

The *Powder Cellar* was built into the slope of Toome Hill at the end of the 18th century in such a way that it has only one external wall. The main room is about 30 m. × 11 m. and is surrounded by a corridor. The ceiling is vaulted and there is an efficient ventilating system. The cellar served as a gunpowder store until 1809 and then as a store for beer. At the end of the 19th century the university installed a pendulum here to record earth tremors but after World War I the building was neglected and reverted to a storehouse.

Also on Toome Hill are the busts of a number of scientists associated with the University, and at the foot of the hill is a *monument* to 'persons of several nationalities. . .', marking the new resting place of those who had been buried in an ancient graveyard which was discovered on the site chosen for the university. The *park* on the hill was laid out in 1802 on the initiative of the first university rector, Goerg Parrot. It was considered to be English in style and one of the decorative bridges is still known as *Angel's Bridge*, the name supposedly being a corruption of 'English Bridge'. However there is also a *Devil's Bridge* not far away, and a tradition for students to sing from the bridges is still observed.

Historically, Toome Hill has probably seen more of interest than any other part of Tartu. It is thought to have been the site of heathen temples and sacrificial altars. Certainly early Christian churches were almost always founded in places which had been held sacred by the ancient Estonians and May Day celebrations took place here until 1874. The hill was also a natural site for a fortress, although nothing now remains of the castle that stood where the observatory building is today.

There are other buildings of interest to be seen on Ulikooli Street. Nos. 13 and 15 are 18th-century houses, No. 16 was formerly a medical clinic and No. 18 is the main building of the university. Nearby is *St. John's Church*, founded in 1330. Partially ruined since 1944, there still remain lavish decorations of rare terracotta sculpture. Notable are the 15 figures of the Judgement Day over the main entrance. It is planned to restore the church completely.

The *Town Hall* (1782–9), Sovietskaya Sq. The architect of this structure was master-builder J. Walter from Germany who took 17th-century Dutch buildings for his models. Of interest are the two clocks; the student body was of such importance that the university asked for one to be installed so that it would be visible to the students from Toome Hill. Sovietskaya Square was built up by rich merchants at the end of the 18th and the beginning of the 19th centuries and today only the southern side is new.

Uspensky Church (1776–83), city centre. This church stands on the site of a Jacobite Monastery. There was a wooden church here before the Great Fire.

St. Peter's Church (1882–4), Leningrad Chaussée

Local Museum, Oru St. 2

Ethnological Museum, Burdenko St. 22

Art Museum, Vallikraavi St. 2

Botanical Garden, Michurina St. 38–40 (open May to September)

Barclay de Tolly Monument, in a small square not far from the town hall. The Russian Commander-in-Chief (1761–1818) lived in Tartu on Soviet Square, and owned an estate at Jogeveste not far from Tartu where all that remains is his mausoleum. The monument by Demut-Malinovsky and Schedrin was unveiled in 1849.

Kreutzwald Monument, on the right bank of R. Emajogi. Friedrich Kreutzwald (1803–82) was a physician who is now better known for his literary work. He compiled Estonian folklore and did much to form the Estonian literary language. Saks and Hirv were the designers of this monument which was unveiled in 1952, the year of the university jubilee.

Pirogov Monument, on the slope of Toome Hill, behind the town hall. Nikolai Pirogov (1810–81), a surgeon of international repute, was a graduate of the university here. He pioneered the use of ether anaesthesia in field conditions and was among the first to employ women as professional nurses. Raudsepp and Mölder designed the monument, also unveiled in 1952.

Lenin Monument, in front of the Agricultural Academy

World War II Memorial, Raadi Park. The figure of a soldier, erected in 1945, marks a mass grave.

Victims of Fascism Monument, 2 km. along the Riia Highway, marking the site of an anti-tank trench where 12,000 people were massacred.

Drama Theatre (the Little House), Vanemuise St. 45. The theatre company was founded in 1870 but this building was completed in 1967.

Concert Hall (the Big House of Vanemuise Theatre)—Vanemuise Street 6

Eduard Vilde People's Theatre

Park Hotel, Vallikravi St.

Tartu Hotel, Riia St.

Kaunas Restaurant, on the bank of the river

Volga Restaurant, Kingissep St. 10

Tarvas Restaurant, Riia St. 2

Kaseke Restaurant, Tähe St. 19

G.P.O., 21st June St. 19

Department Store, Riia St. 2

Bookshops, Ulikooli St. 1 & 11; Soviet Sq. 16

Souvenirs, Soviet Sq. 4

Art Shop, Soviet Sq. 8

Taxis, Soviet Sq., at the crossing of Pargi and Tähe Streets, and by the railway station

TASHKENT

Capital of the Uzbek Soviet Socialist Republic
Population—1,385,000 (1970)

UZBEKISTAN

Area: About 500,000 sq. km.

Population—12,000,000; people of more than 100 different nationalities live here, but the majority (over 65%) are Uzbeks, of Turkic stock.

Uzbekistan is the largest republic in Soviet Central Asia and it is also economically the most advanced. Its capital is Tashkent. Uzbekistan lies in the south-east part of the country, between the two great rivers, the Amu-Darya and the Syr-Darya, and borders with Afghanistan and Pakistan. Also adjoining it are the Soviet republics of Kazakhstan, Kirghizia, Tajikistan, and Turkmenia.

Archeologists have found traces of the very earliest civilisations here. There is a camp of primitive man in the Samarkand region dating back over 100,000 years. The skull and bones of a Neanderthal man were discovered in the south of Uzbekistan together with remarkable rock drawings. Once the fire-worshipping Sogdians and Baktrians lived near present-day Tashkent and Khorezm, and as long ago as the third millenium B.C., the inhabitants of the lower reaches of the Amu-Darya made pottery and built houses large enough for more than a hundred people each.

For centuries the country suffered countless wars and conquests. In the 6th century B.C. Cyrus the Great, founder of the Persian Empire, conquered Central Asia, but the Persian Empire fell to Alexander the Great in 330 B.C. In the 6th century A.D. the whole of Central Asia was held by the Turks, but they were driven out by the Arabs in the 7th–8th centuries only to return in the 10th century.

It was then that the territories of Central Asia became known as Turkestan and the name remained in use until the 1920s. The region flourished under Timur who created a huge empire with Samarkand as its capital. The time of his rule was a golden age of architecture, science, and the arts. The emergence of the Uzbek nation is attributed to the 16th century.

In 1868 the Kokand and Bukhara Khanates recognised their dependency on the Russian Empire and submitted to Russian authority. Soviet power arrived in November 1917, but was immediately followed by a period of civil war. The Uzbek Soviet Republic was finally set up in October 1924.

Uzbekistan is now the Soviet Union's primary cotton producer. In world cotton production the republic stands next to the United States and China. It also holds leading places in manufacturing silk and cotton fabrics, different machinery and mineral fertilisers, and its natural gas reserves are immense. Although three-fifths of the country is desert, extensive irrigation has made it an important region for commercial fruit- and vine-growing. The markets of Tashkent, Samarkand, Fergana, and other Uzbek towns display mountains of grapes, melons, and other fruit. Over a thousand varieties of melon alone are grown. The famous Astrakhan pelts also come from Uzbekistan and are now produced in a wide range of shades and colours.

TASHKENT

Further information is not available.
See the text for additional facts
concerning locations

The climate here is continental with extreme variations between summer and winter temperatures. The sky is clear and sunny for more than 250 days a year and in summer the temperature is often 42°C. (108°F.). Thermez, a town in the south of the republic, sometimes records more than 50°C. (122°F.) which is the maximum for the Soviet Union. In winter the temperature occasionally drops to 25°C. (−13°F.).

The Uzbeks value their national traditions and although many people wear European dress, the old costumes are often to be seen. Both men and women wear long, tunic-like shirts and broad trousers, with colourful robes as outer garments. They both wear skull-caps, but the men sometimes put on turbans. The women do their thick, black hair in 2 plaits, while young girls may have as many as 40 thin braids.

The Uzbeks are famous for their public spirit and for their respect for the elderly. Children are brought up to be quiet and polite and they would never raise their voices when speaking to an adult. A typical Uzbek would automatically remove a stone from the path so that others would not stumble over it.

An old and very popular tradition is a competition of wit and quick thinking. Such an occasion may draw crowds numbering thousands. They assemble around a platform on which two men, the competitors, stand facing each other. One of them begins with a witty remark about the other and it must be immediately parried by his opponent. The two go on to the delight of the onlookers until one of them fails to answer promptly or cleverly enough, when the crown announces him the loser. At present the most popular form of this 'battle of wits' is called 'payr'; the opponents have to keep to one particular topic, chosen beforehand.

The sights of Central Asia, and of the cities of Uzbekistan in particular, include a wide variety of examples of Moslem architecture. There are mosques and minarets and Moslem seminaries called 'medressehs' built around a square or rectangular courtyard. Other architectural terms that are most frequently encountered include 'pishtak'—large portal, 'chortak'—small gateway, 'gur-khona'—mausoleum containing a sepulchre, and 'ziaret-khona'—a prayer room, often to be found adjoining the gur-khona.

The written language of the Uzbeks is very poetic but it has changed alphabets three times in its history. Arabic letters were used from the 8th century until 1929 when Latin letters were introduced, and in 1940 the Russian alphabet was adopted.

Here are a few more words of the Uzbek language:

Hello	salaam aleikhem
I am a tourist	men saiarkhatchiman
please	markhamat
thank you	rakhmat
yes	shundei
no	yok
good	yasha
bad	yomon
I don't understand	men tushumaiman
please fetch me an	Iltemoss, tardzhim
interpreter	on-ne chakharin
good-bye	haiyere
how do you do?	akhwallar halei

Uzbek dishes are highly seasoned. Many of them are of rice, mutton, and vegetables. Their favourite is 'plov' (pilaff) of which there are countless variations. The making of plov when guests have been invited is considered the host's job. Plov is always followed by green tea. Other dishes that can be recommended are 'shashlik' (small pieces of spit-roasted mutton), 'shurpa' (mutton soup), 'manty' (meat-filled dumplings), 'samsa' (meat-and-onion pies), and 'logman' (meat-and-noodle soup).

Tashkent

The city which is the capital of Uzbekistan was originally called Chach-Kent which means 'stone town' or 'fortress' in the Tajik language.

Tashkent stands in the valley of the R. Chirchik, whose old name, Parak (rushing), indicates its behaviour, as its waters pour down from the Chatkalski Mountains. The climate is very warm, especially between April and October. The average July temperature is 43°C. (109°F.) and the surface temperature of the ground may rise as high as 74°C. (166°F.). In spite of the heat, Tashkent ranks as one of the Soviet Union's greenest cities.

The city covers an area of 160 sq. km., the third largest city in the Soviet Union after Moscow and Leningrad. Its inhabitants are mostly either Uzbek or Russian, and visitors are often surprised at the way Europe and Asia mingle here. In many places modern buildings are still surrounded by mud houses. Tashkent is however more interesting as a new city than as an old one, and for those who have the opportunity of going on to Bukhara and Samarkand, the few ancient monuments here are of comparatively little importance.

Tashkent's earliest historical reference is in a Chinese chronicle of 2nd–1st century B.C.; it then formed part of ancient Khorezm. From the 7th–11th century A.D. Tashkent was ruled by the Arabs, from then until 1363 by the Khorezmians, until 1500 by the Mongols, until 1814 by the Uzbeks and the Kirgiz-Kaisaks, and between 1814 and 1840 and then between 1846 and 1863 by the Kokandians. In 1865 Tashkent was taken from the Bukharians by the Russians.

Like most of the cities of Central Asia, Tashkent is divided into the old and the new towns. Beginning from 1865 (following the union of Turkestan with Russia) the left bank of the Ankhor Canal was used for building houses for Russian administrative offices. They were single-storey like the Uzbek houses, but nevertheless the Ankhor and the Bozsu Canals became the geographical boundary and the social border of the city.

The new town grew rapidly, planned by Russian architects who made no attempt to change the older part. In 1866 the Tashkent slave market was closed and slaves were granted their freedom. The following year the town became the administrative centre of Turkestan Region and was the seat of the Governor-General. The Russians mainly consisted of ex-servicemen and their families, but Governor-General von Kaufman encouraged newcomers to move in on a three-year contract before deciding to settle permanently.

Tashkent soon became the principal centre for Russian trade with Central Asia and the construction of the railway in 1898 stimulated the development of local industry. It was the railway workers who led the strikes and demonstrations of 1905–7. The 1916 revolt was instigated by the Bolsheviks and the Moslem nationalists. After the 1917 revolution Tashkent was the capital of the Turkestan Republic until 1924, and in 1930 the capital of Uzbekistan was transferred from Samarkand to Tashkent.

The city is now a stop-over for flights between Europe and the Far East.

Local industry is mainly concerned with the production of textiles, agricultural machinery, and food products. American cotton was planted here experimentally in 1878 and it has become one of Uzbekistan's principal forms of agriculture. Under construction is one of the largest power stations fuelled by natural gas; the gas is piped from Bukhara.

The Uzbek Academy of Sciences, formed in 1943, is centred here and there are 28 research institutes carrying out important work in physics, cybernetics, heliotechnique, and other branches of science. Lenin University, founded in 1919, has 11 faculties with over 4000 students and is the largest of the city's 16 higher educational establishments.

Tashkent is located in a seismic area and earthquakes have been recorded in its history. That of 26 April 1966 was the worst ever suffered. Over 1000 tremors were recorded in a period of several months. 35% of the homes were destroyed and 78,000 families made homeless. In addition, 2100 public buildings that housed offices, shops, and schools were either destroyed or badly damaged. Rebuilding began almost immediately after the disaster. Help and construction material came from all parts of the Soviet Union and as a result Tashkent quickly changed its appearance and whole new regions sprang up.

A tour of the city may be conveniently started from *Teatralnaya (theatre) Sq.* It used to be the noisiest market place and was known as the Drunken Bazaar. Its importance as a shopping centre was revived after the earthquake for that was where the main department store was built.

The *Opera and Ballet Theatre* after which the square was renamed in 1947 by Shusev and can seat almost 1500. The six foyers are interesting, for each is decorated in the traditional style of one of the six cities whose names they bear— Tashkent, Bukhara, Samarkand, Khiva, Ferghana, and Termez. Opposite the theatre is the *Tashkent Hotel* and on the north side of the square is a big publishing house where about 40 newspapers and magazines are printed. 'Moscow Pravda' and 'Izvestia' are received by photo-telegraph and appear on the streets earlier than they do in Moscow because of the time difference. Nearby is the Central Trade Union Club, called the *Palace of Labour*.

Pravdi Vostoka St. leads from the square to another hotel, the *Shark* (east), which bears a memorial plaque saying that during the civil war it housed the headquarters of the Turkestan military front. Mikhail Frunze, the Red Army organiser, was in command here. A little distance from the hotel is the *Sverdlov Concert Hall*. At the crossing of Pravdi Vostoka and Proletarskaya Sts. is the *city council building* and opposite, on Proletarskaya St., is *Gorky Children's Park*. Nearby stands the *clocktower* built by Mukhamedshin in 1947 to commemorate the victory in World War II. Further down the street, in the *Kafanova Garden*, is the common grave of 14 Turkestan commissars, the first Soviet ministers in Tashkent, who were killed during a counter-revolutionary uprising in 1919. An obelisk stands on the grave. Close by are buried the first Uzbek president, Yuldash Akhunbabaev, the first Uzbek general, Sabir Rakhimov, and the poet, Khamid Alimdjan, one of the founders of Tashkent University. The garden and the street leading to the railway station are called after Kafanov, a leading Uzbek communist, who is also buried here. In Voksalnaya (railway station) Sq. there is another monument to the 14 commissars. Sculptured in Ukrainian granite, it stands 12 m. high with an eternal flame burning near it. It was unveiled in 1962.

Revolutsii Sq. and Garden is at the end of Proletarskaya St. and links 5 other streets, Karl Marx, Engels, Pushkin, Leningradskaya, and Kuibishev. The *Karl Marx Monument* was unveiled in 1968 to mark the 150th anniversary of his birth. The bronze head was made in Moscow and the granite foundation was brought from the Ukraine.

Karl Marx St. is one of Tashkent's main thoroughfares and, with the new department store and

other shops, is also one of the busiest. It runs from Revolution Garden to cross Kirova and Lenin Sts. Where it crosses Lenin St. there is an old garden with a palace, now the *House of Pioneers*, which used to belong to Grand-Prince Nikolai Konstantinovich. The Prince was born in 1850, a cousin of Nicholas II, and he came to Tashkent in 1881. It was then that this palace was built for him, following a plan by Geintselman based on the outline of the double-headed eagle (also used for the former Russian Embassy in Tokyo). In spite of his background, the Prince was an unexpectedly progressive person; he even took part in the demonstrations in 1917. When he died that same year (of natural causes), he bequeathed everything he possessed to Tashkent University. Many of his belongings and some of the furniture from the palace are in the museum. Opposite the palace is *St. George's Church* which was built at the same time. Opposite the House of Pioneers is the *Puppet Theatre*.

Marx St. ends in Lenin Sq. (formerly known as Cathedral Sq.) where stands the building of the Uzbek Supreme Soviet (the local parliament), built in 1940 by Polupanov. The square is used for parades, and the pedestal of the *Lenin monument* here which is decorated with red granite and black labradorite is used as a tribune by members of the government and important visitors during festivities. The Council of Ministers and the Uzbek Komsomol buildings are at the end of the square. The *Alisher Navoi Library* which stands nearby was founded in 1870 and has over 2,000,000 books and is the largest library in Central Asia. Navoi Prospect is the main street of the old town. It is lined by the dignified buildings of the *Central Telegraph Office*, the *Ministry of Culture* and other administrative organisations and by some of the University buildings. The *Vatan (motherland) Cinema* is an interesting structure which was built in 1939 by Timofeyev. Its 6 columns resemble the decorations of mosques in Khiva and Bukhara, but the carving is upon concrete instead of wood. Another unusual building on Navoi Prospect is the *Palace of Arts*. It has the city's largest hall for stage performances and films. It is also used for all gala meetings on important occasions. A broad avenue leads from the Palace to the *Pakhtakor (Cottonworker) Stadium* which, after reconstruction, seats 100,000. The largest building in the street is the *Press House*. Here are the headquarters of the Ministry of Culture, the Press and Cinematography Committees, and the editorial offices of a number of newspapers. The local television studios and tower are nearby. Further on, the *Khamza Drama Theatre* is considered to be one of the most attractive new buildings in the street.

Running from Navoi Prospect to Uzbekistan St. is a wide space called *Alleya Paradov* (Parades Avenue). It was inaugurated with the first parade on 7 November 1967 to mark the 50th anniversary of the Soviet state. Alleya Paradov at its Navoi Prospect end comes almost right up to *Ankhor Canal* which, before the reconstruction of the city, used to divide the old and the new parts of Tashkent.

The central street of the new Chilanzar region is called after astronaut Gagarin as is a new *garden* there. The blocks of flats here are designed to accommodate 100,000 people.

Minguryuk, Proletarskayà St. Here are the remains of an ancient town. The 7th–8th century fortress of Tashkent which used to stand on Ak-Tepe Hill, Unus-Abad St., has been completely demolished to make room for new buildings.

Kukeldash Medresseh, Chorsu-Navoi St., near the market. This disused Moslem theological college was built in the 16th century and has been reconstructed several times. It is now a museum. The square used to be an execution place and it is said that unfaithful wives were sewn into sacks and then thrown down from the top of the building.

The *Khast-Imam Ensemble,* at the end of Khamza St., about 1·5 km. to the north of Kukeldash Medresseh. Here is the Masar Qaffal Shashi, a domed brick mausoleum to Abubakr-Ismail-Qaffal, one of the first local Islamic prophets, who died in 976. The mausoleum was built in 1541 by the architect, Gulyam Husein, in an old cemetery. There is a disused mosque standing near the mausoleum.

Barak-Khan Medresseh, Khamza St. 103. Barak-Khan, a relative of Timur, ruled in the 16th century and built this medresseh in the centre of the old city of Tashkent in 1531. It is the best architectural monument of its time still remaining in the city. Here is the mausoleum of the Tashkent Sheibanid dynasty (16th–17th centuries). The medresseh's excellent present state is due to reconstruction in 1904–5. It is now the residence of the Mufti of Central Asia and Kazakhstan and can be visited if one asks permission at the time.

The *mosque* across the road from the medresseh was built in the 1880s and is open for religious services. In the courtyard of the mosque is the Mufti's library containing 2000 unique books, some very old and some relatively new. Of especial interest is the 800-year-old Koran which has had marginal notes added by each reader. Permission may be granted to visit the library, but remember that shoes should be removed at the entrance just as they should on entering a mosque.

Sheikh An-Takhur Cemetery, Navoi St. One of the ways into this area, which is now enclosed by new houses, is opposite the Estrada Theatre and the television tower. Walk up the steps and through a small garden where Shashliks (charcoal grilled skewers of meat) and tea are on sale. The place was used as a cemetery for over six centuries and, together with others which were engulfed by the growing city, was closed at the end of the last century. In 1924 the territory was replanned and built up with new houses, but some of the ancient buildings were preserved. Most impressive of all is the *Mausoleum of Unus-Khan* who once ruled Tashkent; it has interesting stone carved columns inside. It was built at the end of the 15th century as

was the medresseh which stands near it.

The *Mausoleum of Sheikh An-Takhur*, whose name the cemetery bears, stands to the right of the Mechanics Institute. It was built in accordance with a 16th-century design. The 15th-century *Kaldirgach-Bia Mausoleum* with a pyramid-shaped roof was reconstructed in 1911–12.

The *Zengi-Ata Mausoleum and Mosque* were built by order of Timur. They have been reconstructed several times, but the carved wooden doors of the 15th century are of interest.

Sheikh Zein-ad-Din Mausoleum and Mosque, Viloyat St., in an old park which was formerly a cemetery. These date from the 16th century. There is an underground crypt (hor-hana) where people went to pray; many people gathered here especially on religious holidays.

Uspensky (Assumption) Cathedral, Kafanova St. 91. This was a hospital church in the 1890s, but was rebuilt in 1957, and is open for services.

St. George's Church, opposite the palace. This church was built in the 1880s.

All Saints' Baptist Chapel

Roman Catholic Church, Zhukovsky St.

Lutheran Church, down Karl Marx St. and across the bridge. This was built at the end of the 19th century.

Synagogue, Chempiona St. 101

'Rakat' (new) Mosque, Pryadilnaya St. This mosque is practically new, having been built at the end of the 1950s, and is one of the city's 17 mosques still in use, including the Barak-Khan (see above).

Art Museum, Gogol St. 101. The building was constructed as a stock exchange at the beginning of the century and was so used until 1915 when it was turned into the Winter Theatre. The collection displayed here now was founded in 1918 on the basis of the collection of the imperial Romanov family which was confiscated locally. The twenty halls contain carpets, embroidery, woodcarving, and Western, Oriental, Russian, and Soviet art (mostly in reproduction) including the works of local artists. Open 10–6, closed Tues.

History Museum, Kuibisheva St. 6. Here there are over 3000 examples of local applied art. Open 10–5, closed Mon.

Natural History Museum, Sagban St. 16

Lenin Monument, Lenin Sq. Unveiled in 1935.

Navoi Monument, Navoi St. Nizamaddin Alisher Navoi (1441–1501) was the poet who is now celebrated as the founder of Uzbek literature. The *Literature Museum* nearby was opened in 1967. It has some rare manuscripts.

Akhunbabaev Monument, Akhunbabaev Sq. Yuldash Akhunbabaev (1885–1943) was the first Uzbek president.

Kalinin Statue, in a garden near Khamsa St. Mikhail Kalinin (1875–1946) was president of the U.S.S.R. for 8 years.

Gogol Statue, near Pushkina St. Nikolai Gogol (1809–52) was the author of, among other works, 'The Government Inspector'.

Frunze Monument, Frunze Sq. Mikhail Frunze

(1885–1925) was a leading Bolshevik, and the Red Army commander who did most to establish Soviet power in Central Asia.

Bust of Kuibishev, near Pushkina St. Valerian Kuibishev (1888–1935) was a leading Bolshevik who helped to establish Soviet power in Central Asia.

Russian Drama Theatre, Karl Marx St. 28

Mukimi Musical Theatre, Almazar St. 189

Sverdlov Concert Hall, Pravdi Vostoka St. 10

Conservatoire, Pushkina St. 31

Puppet Theatre, Karl Marx St. 6

Circus, Lenin St. 46

The Molodaya Gvardia Cinema building used to be the Court Theatre. It was built in 1910 and decorated with sabres.

Zoo, Alimdzhana St. 23

Botanical Garden, Karamurtskaya St.

Hippodrome Racecourse, Ak-Ui St. 30

Pakhtakor Stadium, Sotsializma St. 23

Komsomol Lake Park, Almazar St. 188. In this park boats can be hired. The bathing beach is the most popular in the city.

Pobeda (victory) Forest Park, Shevli St. 6. There is also a bathing beach here.

Tashkent has 16 other parks and 27 smaller public gardens. They all seem to illustrate the Uzbek saying: 'Before chopping down one tree, plant three or four young ones.'

Tashkent Hotel and Restaurant (Intourist), Lenin St. 50, TEL. 3–23–28. Service Bureau, TEL. 3–35–83. When ringing a number in the town, hotel residents should dial 9 before the number they wish to engage.

Rossia Hotel & Restaurant, Rustaveli St. Built in 1967.

Shark (eastern) Hotel & Restaurant, Pravdi Vostoka St. 16

Zeravshan Hotel & Restaurant, Akhunbabaeva St. 15a

Uzbekistan Hotel, Dzerzhinskova St. 17

Pushkinskaya Hotel, Pushkin St. 18

Bakhor (spring) Restaurant, Kuibishev St. 15

Gulistan Restaurant, at the crossing of Kalinin Sq. and Khamza St., seats 800.

Anchor Tea Room, Tukaeva St. 33

G.P.O., Krilova St. 4

Bank, Kirov St. The Renaissance-style building dates from 1915.

Central Telegraph Office, Navoi St.

Local Society for Cultural Relations with Foreign Countries, Akhunbabaeva St. 1, TEL. 2–69–63

Interesting purchases which can be made locally include small, embroidered skull-caps called 'Tubeteiki', a 'khalat', a quilted men's coat with a silk scarf for a belt that could be used as a dressing gown or housecoat for men or women, and lengths of gaudy zig-zag-striped silk material.

Department store where there is a *souvenir department*, Karl Marx St. 35

Souvenir Kiosk, in the Tashkent Hotel

Bookshop, Karl Marx St. 31

Antique and secondhand goods, Karl Marx St. 25

Children's World, children's department store, Rustaveli St. 43

Embroidery, carpets, etc., Marx St. 20

Jeweller's, Kirova St. 29 & Navoi St. 1a

Florist's, Revolutsii Garden 1

Tobacconist's, Karl Marx St. 26

Gramophone Records, Pravdi Vostoka St. 24

Paintings, Karl Marx St. 25

Wine, Karl Marx St. 26

Alaiski Market, Engels St.

Oktyabrsky Market, at the end of Navoi St. in the old town

Taxi Ranks, in the square near the Tashkent Hotel, in Pushkina Sq. and in Engels St., near the market

With special permission from Intourist, trips can be made to a number of small townships near Tashkent.

Chirchik

30 km. north-east of Tashkent; founded just before World War II and now boasting a population of over 60,000. Here can be found an electrochemical works and the hydropower station on R. Chirchik. There are collective farms nearby. Agricultural machinery and building materials are produced, as well as foods.

Yangi-Ul

35 km. south-west of Tashkent. This is the centre of the local cotton-growing area with a cotton refinery.

Angren

115 km. from Tashkent; founded during World War II, population is over 60,000. This is the centre of a coal-mining area. There are also a hydropower station, building materials, and food industries.

Almalyk

Founded in 1949, population over 50,000. There are large deposits of copper ore here and the town, which has copper, lead, and zinc refineries, is growing fast.

Begovat

Also founded during the Second World War and now with a population of over 40,000. Here is a hydropower station, and food and building materials are produced. Here also is the only metallurgical plant in Uzbekistan.

Bostandyk, Mojikent, Brichmolla, Chimgan, Aktash, and Khumson

All located in the resort area which supplies Tashkent, Chirchik, and Angren with agricultural produce. Until 1956, this region was part of Kazakhstan.

Fergana

Population—130,000 (1971)

Formerly Novyi Margilan; 1907, renamed Skobelev; 1919, renamed Fergana.

The fertile Fergana valley is one of the main cotton, silk, and fruit-growing districts in the Soviet Union. Although it is usually thought to be in Uzbekistan, parts of Tajikistan and Kirghizia also run into it. It is an almond-shaped valley about 300 km. long and a maximum of 140 km. wide with mountains on all sides except for a pass in the west. The Tien-shan Mountains lie to the east and the Pamir-Alayas to the south. Within the valley are reserves of oil, gas, and coal.

According to Chinese travellers who called the valley Davan, it was inhabited in the 4th–2nd centuries B.C. Ruins of Ersh, the early capital, lie near the village of Markhamat; it stood on one of the main caravan routes from China and the east. In the 17th century there were already trade relations with Moscow, but when in the 18th century the Kokand Khanate was formed, the ensuing wars with Bukhara tended to isolate the valley again. Fergana was founded in 1876, the year after the Russians took the area.

Fergana stands 580 m. above sea level with a good view to the south of the snow-covered Alaya Mountains. It is on the edge of an oasis and is watered by the Margelan-sai, a branch of the R. Shakhimadan which has its source in the nearby mountains.

It was founded as the centre of the region and its site included the territory of 2 villages, Yar-Mazar and Chim, and as it was only about 10 km. from the ancient town of Margelan, it was called Novyi (new) Margelan. In 1907 it was renamed in honour of General Mikhail Skobelev (1843–82) who made his name campaigning in Central Asia and later in Turkey. The city was given its present name after the Revolution.

The original town plan followed the same lines as the new parts of Tashkent and Samarkand. The first building was the *fortress*, which still stands behind the impressive modern building of the Party Committee. There were barracks nearby. From the fortress three long streets radiated to the north-west and the west. The first settlers were encouraged to plant shade trees and orchards, and the tradition had continued. By the turn of the century there were about 4000 inhabitants, but then with the construction of the railway in 1899 the town began to grow more rapidly. It is now the industrial and the cultural centre of the valley. Textiles and food production are the most important, but there are also an oil refinery and chemical factories. There is a teachers' training college here.

In the central square is a multi-tiered fountain. The main thoroughfare is Karl Marx St. which leads towards Margelan and then runs on further as the road to Kokand. Along Karl Marx St. (formerly Abramovsky Prospect) and Lenin St. (Gubernatorskaya St.) a number of old houses can still be seen.

Mosque, Pamirskaya St.

St. Sergius's Church, Krupskaya St. 8

Local Museum, 1st May St. 18; opened in 1896.

War Memorial and Eternal Flame, Marx St.

Gorky Russian Drama Theatre, Marx St. 36; the

building dates from the 1880s and was formerly the Governor's House.

Park, Lenin St. 29

Intourist Hotel & Restaurant, Kommunarov St.

Hotel, Lenin St. 22

Fergana Restaurant, Lenin St. 42

Café, Lenin St. 37

G.P.O., Marx St. 5

Department Store, Lenin St. 54

Khamzaabad

52 km. to the south of Fergana. Formerly known as Shakhimardan, this is a pleasant health resort up in the mountains, 1550 m. above sea level, and reached by driving up the river valley. There is a tea-house here and 6 km. away is another picturesque spot known as the *Blue Lake*.

Khamza's Tomb can be reached by driving up a steep and winding road from the resort, or by climbing the flight of stone steps. Khamza Khakim-zade Niyazi (1889–1929) is regarded as the founder of modern Uzbek literature. He began to write at the age of 16, poems, revolutionary songs, and also plays which were the first in the Uzbek tongue. He was murdered here, in Shakhimardan (which was later renamed after him), and on the mausoleum overlooking the town were inscribed these lines of his as an epitaph:

> The happiness of bright, new life
> Soon across the world will bloom,
> Will be our joy for evermore:
> Just grief lies hidden in the tomb.

Equally as prominent, at the top of the stone steps, is a *monument* to those who fell in the Civil War, dated 1921, an *eternal flame*, and a *statue*.

Margilan

Formerly known as Marginan

Population—100,000 (1971)

Margilan lies 12 km. north of Fergana and 475 m. above sea level. The maximum temperature is 28·9°C. (84°F.) and the minimum is −2·9°C. (27°F.). The town is crossed by R. Margilan-sai and the South Fergana Canal. It is planned to unite Margilan and Fergana to make the third largest urban complex in Uzbekistan.

The exact date of Margilan's foundation is not known, but it is certainly one of the oldest towns in Central Asia, probably dating from the 1st or even the 2nd century B.C. It stood on or near one of the great caravan routes and between the 10th and the 12th centuries was an important trading centre. In the 13th century it was overrun by the Mongols but under Babyr in the 16th century it was again a very important town in the Fergana Valley. Ruins of the medieval *fortress of Urda-Tagi* remain and also some narrow streets with mud houses, and an ancient stone mosque. In the 18th century Margilan formed part of the Kokand Khanate and a high gated wall was built around it in the 1840s as a defence against the attacks of the Emirs of Bukhara. In 1875, when it was taken over by the Russians, there were more than 250 mosques here.

The centre of Margilan is at the point where Karl Marx and Kirov Sts. cross, on the site of the old fortress. Here also is the town's main bazaar and there is a legend that the grave of Alexander the Great is somewhere in the vicinity. Karl Marx St. is the main thoroughfare with the most important modern buildings on it. It runs into the centre from the railway station, 3 km. outside.

The town has been famous for its silk for hundreds of years, as well as for the pomegranates and apricots that grow there. The Institute of the Uzbek Silk Industry is here and also the largest silk factory in the country.

Mosque, Shevchenko St. 12

Yuldash Akhunbabaev Museum, on the right of the central square. Yuldash Akhunbabaev was the first president of Uzbekistan and came from Margilan. This was opened as a memorial museum.

Nurkhon Yuldasheva Monument, at the crossing of Kirov and Karl Marx Sts. Miss Yuldasheva was a local actress.

Park, Krasina St.

Hotel, Karl Marx St. 152

Shark Restaurant, Karl Marx St. 139

Café, Karl Marx St. 150

G.P.O., Kirov St. 115

Department Store, Karl Marx St. 115

TBILISI
Old Russian: Tiflis
Population—890,000 (1971)
Capital of the Georgian Soviet Socialist Republic

GEORGIA
Russian: Gruzia; Georgian: Sakartvelo
Area: 72,000 sq. km.
Population—4,690,000 (1970), 45% of which lives in the towns. The people are mostly Georgians (63%), but other nationalities include Armenians (11%), Russians (11%), Azerbaijanis (4%), Ossetians (3·5%), and Abkhazians (2%). The Georgian people are far from being homogeneous, although they speak more or less the same language; some of the various groups of people still preserve definite features peculiar to them in their speech and habits, and some of them, such as the Mingrelians, still use their historical names.

Georgia is one of the oldest countries in the U.S.S.R. A Georgian kingdom of Iberia was known to exist as early as the 3rd century B.C. Christianity came in 318, and since 337 it has been the official religion of the country. The natural wealth of the area and its strategic position drew the attention of various invaders: it suffered conquest and domination by Romans, Byzantines, Persians, Arabs, Mongols, Seljouk Turks, the Ottoman Empire, and finally the Persians again. There were times when the country was united and when it included, together with vassal territories, the whole of Transcaucasia and neighbouring areas. At the end of the 18th century Western Georgia was under Turkish domination and Eastern Georgia under Persian rule. The King of Eastern Georgia sought Russian protection, and then in 1800 his successor ceded his country to Russia, being helpless against the Persian threat.

In 1921 a Soviet Republic was established in Georgia, but from 1922 to 1936 it was a part of the Transcaucasian Soviet Federal Republic and only after that did it come to be called the Georgian Soviet Socialist Republic.

The present Republic consists of Georgia proper, the Ajar Autonomous Republic (the population of which is mainly Moslem), the Abkhazian Autonomous Republic, and the South Ossetian Autonomous Region.

Climatically the country can be divided into two zones:

(1) Western Georgia (the Abkhazian and Ajar Autonomous Republics, Imeretia, and Mingrelia) has a Mediterranean climate with subtropical vegetation.

(2) Eastern Georgia (South Ossetian Autonomous Region and Kakhetia) has a dry, continental climate.

Georgia has the best manganese in the world, and its other mineral resources are coal, iron ore, oil, natural gas, and stone. The country's industry includes engineering, metallurgy, oil extraction and refining, manganese- and coal-mining, and light food industries. Agriculture is mainly concerned with tobacco, tea, maize, wheat, citrus and other fruit, vines, silk, sheep-, pig-, and poultry-breeding.

Georgia's principal towns are Tbilisi (capital), Batumi, Sukhumi, Kutaisi, and Poti.

A NOTE ON GEORGIAN CHURCHES. The acceptance of Christianity from Byzantium led to the Georgian Orthodox Church's adoption of Byzantine forms of church architecture. By the 10th–12th centuries a more complex type of church, with three to five elongated aisles and a decorated façade, had evolved. Later still the characteristic Georgian tower developed, drum-shaped and crowned by a many-faceted conical dome. The height of the cone sometimes equalled the width of the drum, but the more recently constructed churches tend to have taller cones.

The interior of the churches have very simple frescoes in imitation of Byzantine style, and there is usually little statuary, although there may be some very attractive decorative stone work (patterned reliefs and borders).

The head of the Georgian Orthodox Church is the Katolikos Patriarch.

Useful expressions in Georgian:

Hello	gamardzhobut
how do you do	rogor brdzandebit
I am a tourist	me tooristivar
please	getakhvat
thank you	madlobt
yes	ki
no	ara

good	kargyet
I don't understand	ar mesmis kartuli
good-bye	nakhvamdis

Georgian dishes, popular far beyond the national boundaries, are shashlik and chicken tabaka. Others you may enjoy are:
suluguni—mild, flat cheese
khachapuri—cheese-filled bread
lobio—beans in walnut sauce
chicken satsivi—chicken in walnut sauce
chakhokhbili—chicken stewed with tomatoes
Tsinandali—good white wine
Mukuzani—good red wine

Tbilisi

The capital of Georgia is located in the eastern part of the country and in the central part of the Caucasian isthmus. It is 350 km. by rail from the Black Sea and 550 km. from the Caspian. The highest part of the town rises 91 m. above the rest of Tbilisi, and altogether it covers over 6000 hectares (15,000 acres), twice as much territory as in 1921. On the west side of the town is Mtatsminda Mountain (Holy Mountain or Mount David) (727 m.), to the east lies the Makhat Range (650 m.), and to the south the Sololax (488 m.).

R. Kura, the longest river in the Caucasus, rises in Turkey and flows through Tbilisi to the Caspian Sea. From ancient times the site of Tbilisi has been a trading point between Europe and India.

The climate is continental with an average annual temperature of 12·7°C. (55°F.). The summer is long, dry, and hot with an average temperature of 24·5°C. (76°F.), but it may rise to more than 40°C. (104°F.). The winter is mild with little snow; the average winter temperature is 1·3°C. (34°F.) but if there is a north wind it may sink to −15°C. (5°F.). Autumn is considered to be the best season of the year, and in general the climate must be a healthy one, for in Georgia there are over 20,000 people who are more than 90 years old and over 600 of them live in Tbilisi.

The name Tbilisi came from the Georgian word 'tbili' meaning 'warm' and now it is understood to mean 'the town of warm springs'. The Georgians however have long called it simply Kalaki meaning 'town' because it is the biggest built-up area in Georgia. A legend chronicled by Leonti Mraveli says that long ago the Georgian King Vakhtang Gorgazali (452–502) was hunting in the place where Tbilisi now stands, and he wounded a deer. While it was bleeding to death, the beast fell into a

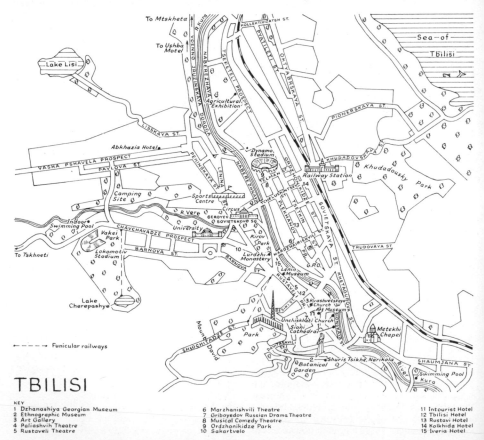

TBILISI

KEY
1 Dzhanashiya Georgian Museum
2 Ethnographic Museum
3 Art Gallery
4 Paliashvih Theatre
5 Rustaveli Theatre
6 Marzhanishvili Theatre
7 Griboyedov Russian Drama Theatre
8 Musical Comedy Theatre
9 Ordzhonikidze Park
10 Sakartvelo
11 Intourist Hotel
12 Tbilisi Hotel
13 Rustavi Hotel
14 Kolkhida Hotel
15 Iveria Hotel

warm sulphur spring where its wound was washed. It was cured and rushed from the spring and ran off into the forest. The King examined the spring, found its waters warm and curative, and ordered that a settlement be made on that spot. There is a monument to the king here, in Tbilisi, commemorating his discovery.

The first written mention of Tbilisi as a town dates from the 4th century, and in the 5th century, under King Vakhtang Gorgazali (Vakhtang VI), it became the capital of Georgia instead of Mtskheta. During its history it has been pillaged by enemies 40 times, and during the space of 1400 years was entirely devastated 29 times. Especially severe were the attacks by the Mongols at the end of the 13th century and those made at the end of the 18th century by the Persian Shah Aga-Mohammed. Khazars, Huns, Persians, Byzantines, Arabs, Mongols, Turks, and numerous tribes from the mountains have all forced their way inside its walls. Each time it was rebuilt Tbilisi showed the influence of its new masters, and that of the Persians was especially strong.

Georgia has had contact with Russia since the 15th century. As the Georgians held the Orthodox faith in common with the Russians it was to them that they appealed for help in moments of crisis. Ivan the Terrible sent his Cossacks as reinforcements in the 16th century, and Russo-Georgian relations were even closer in the 17th and 18th centuries when Peter the Great and King Vakhtang established a military alliance. In 1736 Georgia was divided between Turkey and Persia, the Turks dominating West Georgia and the Persians East Georgia and Tbilisi. Since that time the Georgian kings were appointed by the Persian shahs, but the Georgians frequently revolted and sought the protection of the Russian tsars. In the second half of the 18th century the Georgian King Erekle II came to power and in 1783, to save his country from military disaster from Persia and Turkey, signed an agreement passing supreme power to Russia. The last king, Georgi XII, passed practically all power to Russia after the massacres and seizure of Tbilisi by the Persians under Shah Aga-Mohammed in 1795. This warlike leader was a eunuch and was renowned for his ferocity; his men would take babies from their mothers and try to cut them in half at a single blow to test the sharpness of their swords. After this attack on Tbilisi nothing remained of the town except two caravanserais and a few houses.

In the second quarter of the 19th century many new houses appeared in Tbilisi, especially in the central part of the town. The architecture shows elements of Russian Classicism combined with the old Georgian style; for instance, on the traditional flat roofs appeared a second floor with balconies and carved columns. With its ancient culture and natural beauty Georgia attracted Russian intellectuals as visitors. These included the dramatist Alexander Griboyedov, Pushkin, Lermontov, and Tolstoy. In 1851 Tolstoy wrote 'Tiflis is a very civilised town, closely imitating Petersburg and doing it rather well. The high society is select and fairly large and there is Russian theatre and Italian opera.' Tchaikovsky, Chaliapin, Chekhov, Rubinstein, and Gorky all visited it with pleasure.

The first *funicular railway*, 501 m. in length, was built on Mount David in 1905. It ends with a three-storey house, the top floor of which is used as a *restaurant*. Tbilisi's largest *park* is at the top of Mount David. The old Asian quarters of Tbilisi are not very extensive but their narrow streets and lanes form a labyrinth fascinating to tourists. The section known as *Maiden* may be reached by walking from Lenin Sq. along Leselidze St. One of the old *caravanserai buildings*, now used as a depot, stands at the end of Sionskaya St., to the southeast of the Sioni Cathedral. There are other similar buildings still in existence in Tbilisi. The *palace* at Rustaveli Prospect 6 was built in 1807 and reconstructed in 1865. Before the Revolution it was the residence of the governor of the Caucasus, and until 1941 when the new government building was put up nearby it was the seat of the Georgian government. Now it is a Palace of Pioneers, the Soviet equivalent of the Boy Scouts' and the Girl Guides' Associations. Ilyi Chavchavadze St. 33 is the building of the former seminary, and was erected in 1905; now it is used by the Agricultural Institute. The new Government building, Rustaveli Prospect 8, was built between 1938 and 1953 by architects Kokorin and Lazhava; it is 5 storeys high and contains an unusual covered courtyard. The *Georgian State Museum* was designed by Severov and built between the establishment of Soviet rule in 1921 and the outbreak of the Second World War. A university and 12 institutes are among Tbilisi's educational establishments. An underground railway is being built to improve its communications and new housing is going up on all sides. Saburtalo on the city's northern outskirts is probably the best looking of the new residential areas. The main road to Ktskheta runs through it.

30 km. from Tbilisi is the newly-built industrial town of Rustavi, which was founded in 1944 and now has a population of 60,000. It has a large metallurgical factory and chemical works.

The reservoir known as the *Sea of Tbilisi* was completed in 1951. There is a *bathing beach* there, and a regular bus route connects it with the city.

The town's greatest wealth has always been in its warm sulphur springs, but for many centuries only the Moslems used them. Most are to be found in the Maiden sector on the banks of the R. Kura. Those on the right bank are similar to the springs of Bataglia and those on the left resemble the waters of Ems and Baden. The waters come from Mtabori Hill and emerge from thermal cracks in the bituminous layers. Their temperatures fluctuate from 47.5°C. (117.5°F.) to 24°C. (75°F.). The old bath-houses, similar to the caravanserai in architecture, are mostly to be found in the old town in the Legvis Hevi Ravine. The oldest is the *Erekle Bath*, on the corner of Bannaya and Akhundova Sts. It was long a bone of contention between the kings and the clergy until King David gave it to Sioni Cathedral in 1549. Opposite the bath-house is another dating from the 17th century, known as the *Sumbatovskaya Bath*, and another of similar date is *Bebutovskaya Bath* on the southern side of Akhundov St. Further on from this is *Kazonnaya Bath* which in the 18th century belonged to Tamara, daughter of King Georgi XII. The *Seidabadskaya Bath* in Mesnikov St. was built in 1840. There are several others, but these are the best and the most interesting. They are certainly worth a visit; there are Turkish baths with traditional massage and separate baths for men and women.

Sioni or Assumption Cathedral, Sionskaya St. 4. The original cathedral was built between 575 and 639. After the death of Queen Tamara it fell into decay. According to legend, Sultan Gelal-Eddin tore down the dome in 1226. The local Metropolitan Bishop, Saginashvili, rebuilt the dome and redecorated the whole church. It was afterwards repeatedly restored, and in 1853–4 the cathedral was newly painted by the Russian artist Gagarin as a result of which the old frescoes were lost. At the same time the stone iconostasis was built. In 1882 the paintings in the dome were restored. The belfry stands nearby; it was built in 1425 and restored in 1939. To the west of the cathedral is another belfry in Russian Empire style, built between 1805 and 1812. St. Nina's Cross, interwoven with vines and her own hair, was brought to the Sioni Cathedral from Mtskheta and can be seen here. Among the cathedral's other treasures are two cherished icons, 'St. Nina' and 'Our Lady of Sioni'.

Unchiskhati Church, Shavteli St. 5/7. This church standing beside the R. Kura is called after the 11th-century icon which was brought here in the 17th century from the village of Unchi in south-western Georgia. Now the icon hangs in the Art Museum. The church was founded in the 6th century, and reconstructed several times, extensively in 1675 when new gateways and a belltower over them were added upon the orders of Catholicos Domenti. The external form of the basilica was spoiled by the 19th-century reconstruction of the dome in Russian style.

St. David's Church, Mtatsminda Mountain. This church was founded in 1542, restored several times, and completely rebuilt, including the dome, at the end of the last century. Since 1929 it has been known as the Pantheon of prominent Georgian public figures and writers, including Nikoloz Baratashvili, Akaki Tsereteli, Vazha Pshavela, and Ilya Chavchavadze. St. David was one of the missionaries who came from Syria in the 6th century to preach Christianity, and he lived on Mount Mtatsminda where the church now stands. On the summit there used to be an observatory, built by the Arabs under whom Tbilisi rose to be the third most important town in the Caucasus. There is a second Pantheon of public figures and writers at Brdzola St. 40, in the Didubei region of Tbilisi. It was founded in 1939.

Kvashvetskaya Church, Geordzhadze St. 2, just off Rustaveli St. Kva means 'stone' and shva means 'to give birth'; the church is so called, so the story runs, because long ago the daughter of a Tbilisi noble was expecting a child and she accused St. David of being the father. He was summoned to court and touching her with his staff asked, 'Who is the father of this child?' From within her a voice proclaimed the name of the real father, and thereupon the girl began to labour. She brought forth a stone which was used as the foundation of a new church. The present building was erected between 1904 and 1910.

Dzhvaris Mama Church, Leselidze St. The name means Holy Cross; the church was built in the 15th century and reconstructed in the first half of the 18th century.

Metekhi Chapel, crowning the cliff above a bend in the R. Kura. This chapel is a good example of the efforts of an architect to harmonise a building with the landscape. It is designed with regard to its silhouette and placed so that it can be seen from many points in the town. Founded in 1278–83 and reconstructed several times, it was for some while the chapel of the Georgian Catholics. A new dome was built at the beginning of the 18th century; then in the 1820s the chapel was turned into a prison; the three buildings near it also formed part of the prison—the rest of it was demolished in 1937.

Didubi-Pantheon, Tsereteli Prospect 38. Open 12–7, closed Mon. Georgian writers, artists, actors, and scientists are buried in this cemetery. In the Church of Our Lady of Didubi is a miracle-working icon of the Virgin.

Lurdzhi Monastery, near Kirov Park. The name means 'blue', referring to the blue glazed tiles which decorate it. The basilica dates from the 12th century although the dome is of more recent date.

Synagogue, Leselidze St. 37

Mosque, Botanicheskaya St.

St. John the Baptist's Church, Vasha-Pshavela Prospect 21. This Russian Orthodox church was built in 1901 and is open for services.

SS. Peter and Paul Roman Catholic Church, Kalinin St. 55. This church, built in the 1860s, is open for services.

Shuris Tsikhe, Komsomolskaya Alleya, Narikala. The ruins of the 'rival fortress', also known as Sololaksky Citadel, can be seen above the old part of the town on Sololaksky Hill. The oldest fortress in the town, it is supposed to have been founded by the Persians in 368 to counter-balance the power of nearby Mtskheta. It was reconstructed several times during its history, and was newly rebuilt in the 17th century; in the earthquake of 1827 it was severely damaged but some parts were again restored in 1909.

Sachino (Noble) Palace, Avlabari. Formerly the castle of Queen Darya, wife of King Erekle II, the palace was built in 1776 and partly rebuilt in the 19th century. The chapel also survives. Nearby in Avlabari, at Metekhskaya St. 18, stands a typical example of an *old Tbilisi house*.

The *Academy of Art*. This was built in 1857–8, and was at that time the most beautiful building in Tbilisi. Balls and banquets were held here and the parquet floors, marbles, and carved decorations are still well preserved.

Town Hall, Lenin Sq. The Town Hall was erected in the 1880s in Moorish style.

Lenin Museum, Rustaveli Prospect 29. The museum is located in the large building of the Marxism-Leninism Institute, designed by Academician Shusev in 1938.

Ethnographic Museum, Komsomolskaya Alleya 11. This collection was founded on that of the old Municipal Museum.

Georgian Literary Museum, Georgiashvili St. 8

Georgian Art Gallery, Rustaveli Prospect 13. Open 11–9. The building was originally that of the Khram Slavi (temple of glory), built in the 1880s to commemorate the victories of the Russian Army in the Caucasus.

Georgian Art Museum, Ketskhoveli St. 1. Open 11–9, closed Tues. There is an excellent collection of icons, frescoes, and china and among the Georgian paintings worthy of note are those by the primitivist Niko Pirosmanashvili (Pirosmani, 1862–1918).

Dating from the 1830s, this building once housed the Tbilisi Ecclesiastical Seminary and on the outside wall by the entrance is a plaque saying that J. Stalin lived and studied here from 1 September 1894–29 May 1899.

Dzhanashiya Georgian Museum, Rustaveli Prospect 3. Open 10–4, closed Mon. Originally the Caucasian Museum founded in 1852, this museum was renamed after the Georgian Academician S. Dzhanashiya. It contains much of interest, especially in the ethnographical section.

Chavchavadze's House, Ordzhonikidze St. 22. Open 10–6, closed Mon. Alexander Chavchavadze (1786–1846) was an outstanding Georgian romantic poet who translated both Russian and French poetry.

Museum of Children's Toys, Rustaveli St. 6

Marx Library, Ketskhoveli St. 5. The library was founded in 1846. On the façade of the building, only completed in 1913, ancient Georgian architectural motifs were used in decoration. The carving was executed by the famous Georgian stonemason brothers, Agladze.

New Funicular Railway, entrance from Rustaveli St. up a spiral staircase. This overhead railway is 906 m. long and rises to a height of 287 m. It can take 30 people at a time.

Obelisk, Vakhtang Gorgazali St. This commemorates the 300 warriors who lost their lives on 11 September 1795 as they covered the retreat of the Georgian army from the Persians.

Pushkin Monument, Pushkin Sq. This monument was designed by Hodorovich in 1892.

Lenin Monument, Lenin Sq. By sculptor Topuridze, the 18·5-m. monument was unveiled in 1956.

General Leselidze Bust, Leselidze St. Leselidze was a hero of World War II, and this monument to his memory was unveiled in 1945.

Kamo Monument. This monument was erected in 1957 in memory of the revolutionary, Ter-Petrosyan, who used Kamo as his nickname. It was designed by Okropiridze.

Shota Rustaveli Monument, Rustaveli Sq. Designed by Merabishvili and unveiled in 1942 to commemorate the 750th anniversary of the appearance of Rustaveli's poem 'The Knight in the Tiger's Skin'.

Griboyedov's Grave, on St. David's Mount, by the church. This Russian writer was killed in 1829 while serving as Ambassador to Persia. His tomb is of black marble with a bronze crucifix and a mourning female figure on it. To the left is a monument to his wife, Nina, who was left a widow at the age of 16 and who never remarried although she lived on until 1857. A statue of Griboyedov by Merabishvili (1961) stands beside the R. Kura.

Symbol of Georgia Statue, Komsomolskaya Alleya. The 16-m. figure of a woman holding out a sword for her enemies and a bowl to her friends was designed by Amashukeli and unveiled in 1958.

Paliashvili Opera House, Rustaveli Prospect 25. The company was founded in 1851 and the building was completed at the end of the 19th century, in Moorish style. Zahari Paliashvili was a composer of Georgian national music. His grave is in the theatre garden.

Mardzhanishvili Theatre, Mardzhanishvili St. 8. The theatre bears the name of the well-known Georgian producer, Kote Mardzhanishvili, whose grave is in the garden of the Paliashvili Opera House.

Rustaveli Theatre. The company was established in 1920 on the basis of the old Georgian Theatre. The Rustaveli Georgian Theatre Institute is to be found in the same building.

Griboyedov Russian Drama Theatre, Rustaveli Prospect 2. The building dates from the 1850s and was originally constructed as a caravanserai.

Shaumyan Armenian Drama Theatre, Shaumyan St. 8. This theatre was opened in 1936.

Georgian Youth Theatre, Rustaveli Prospect 37. The Georgian Puppet Theatre is at the same address.

Georgian State Philharmonic Concert Hall, Plekhanov Prospect 123. This is the house of the State Symphony Orchestra, the Capella Choir, the national dance ensemble (which has earned high praise during its tours abroad, and is well worth seeing), and a string quartet.

Vano Saradzhishvili Tbilisi Conservatoire, Griboyedov St. 8. The conservatoire is named after the 'nightingale of Georgia' who now lies buried in the garden of the Paliashvili Opera House.

Concert Hall, Melikishvili St.

Musical Comedy Theatre, Plekhanov Prospect 182

Circus, Geroyev Sovietskovo Soyuza Sq. The building was completed in 1940.

Funicular Park, Mount Mtatsminda. The park lies 362 m. above the town and is reached by two funicular railways. It was opened in 1935.

Ordzhonikidze Park, Plekhanov Prospect 180/182. The park was laid out on the base of the old Mushtaid Garden, named after the one-time head of the Persian clergy in Tbilisi. There is a children's railway here.

Khudadovsky Park, Khudadovskaya St. The park was planted in 1893.

Kirov Park, Lenin St. 37. The park was opened in 1933 and there is a monument to Kirov in it.

Kommunarov Garden, Rustaveli Prospect 13. This was formerly the Alexandrov Garden, founded in 1859. There is a Gogol Monument designed by Hodorovich in 1903 and other monuments to Georgian revolutionaries.

Vakei Park, Chavchavadze Prospect. The park covers 120 hectares (300 acres) and contains the Burevestnik Stadium which can hold 35,000 people. 'Burevestnik' is the Russian name for the stormy petrel or Mother Carey's chickens.

Park of Physical Culture and Sport, Patrisa Lumumby Naberezhnaya 1. There is an open-air swimming pool in the park.

Dynamo Stadium, Brdzola St. 2. Completed in 1935, the stadium can seat 40,000. It also has a swimming pool.

Palace of Sport, Ordzhonikidze Sq. 1. There are seats for 10,000 people.

Heated Swimming Pool, Chavchavadze Prospect

Zoo, Geroyev Sovietskovo Soyuza Sq. Opened in 1927, the grounds cover 20 hectares (50 acres).

Botanical Gardens, Botanicheskaya St. These gardens were founded in 1845 and based on the old garden of Tbilisi fortress.

Iveria Hotel and Restaurant, Inashvili St. 6, TEL. 99–70–89

Intourist Hotel and Restaurant, Rustaveli Prospect 7. This was formerly the Orient Hotel, built in the 1880s.

Tbilisi Hotel and Restaurant, Rustaveli Prospect 13. This hotel was built in 1915.

Abkhazia Hotel and Restaurant, Vasha Pshavela Prospect 25

Georgia Hotel and Restaurant, Melikishvili St. 12

Sakartvelo Hotel and Restaurant, Melikishvili St. 113

Rustavi Hotel, Plekhanov Prospect 103

Aragvi Restaurant, Pushkin St. 29

Daryal Restaurant, Rustaveli Prospect 22

Dynamo Restaurant, Dynamo Stadium, Brdzola St. 2

Isani Restaurant, Meshkishvili St. 3

Samgori Restaurant, Nekrasov St. 10

Funicular Restaurant, in the Park, Mount David

Nad Kuroy Restaurant, Ordzhonikidze Park, Plekhanov Prospect

Kazbek Restaurant, Elbazvidze Spusk 1

Sulkhino Restaurant, Sherozia St. 2

Gemo (taste) Restaurant, Lenin St.

Tsiskari (twilight) Café, Chavchavadze St. 52

Gazabkuli (spring) Café, Melikishvili St.

G.P.O., Plekhanov Prospect 44

Central Telephone and Telegraph Office, Rustaveli Prospect 12

Bank, Kirov St. 3/5

Tsitsinatella (Foreign Currency) Shop, Rustaveli St. 23, open 9–6

Art Salon, Rustaveli St. 19, next to the Tbilisi Hotel. Handicrafts are on sale here.

Georgian Tea Shop, Rustaveli St. 20

Souvenir Shop, Lenin Sq.

Department Store, Mardzhanishvili St. 5

Filling Station, on the right embankment of R. Kura

Repair Stations, Saburtalinskaya St. and Plekhanov Prospect

Camping Site, at the entrance to the town by the 196/11 km. milestone. A little further on is a motel and a filling and service station.

TERNOPOL

Population—105,000 (1973)

Ternopol is a regional centre of the Western Ukraine. It stands on the R. Seret and people have been known to live here since the 10th century. At the time of the Tatar invasions of the 13th and 14th centuries the village was entirely devastated and the ruins were soon hidden by a thick growth of blackthorn. 'Ternovoye Polye' means a field of blackthorn and this is the origin of the name of the town.

The Polish baron, Jan Tarnavsky, was ordered by his king, Sigizmund I, to build a fortress by the river. In 1540 a strong castle was accordingly constructed with walls 4·5 m. thick and with formidably deep moats and dungeons. Part of the castle remains to this day. It is on Svobody Sq., near the Ternopol Hotel, but it is now known as the Palace of Sports.

During the 16th, 17th and 18th centuries Ternopol remained an undistinguished town of merchants and craftsmen which failed to reach any great degree of prosperity. In 1772 it was incorporated, together with the surrounding region, into Austria but by the end of the 18th century it was in Russian hands again. Growing unemployment and poverty led many people to emigrate; between 1900 and 1914 thousands left the area, many of them to North America.

After the Russian revolution and the years of civil war Ternopol returned to Poland and so remained until 1939 when it was incorporated into the Soviet Ukraine.

The Germans occupied the town in 1941, at the outbreak of war with the Soviet Union, and held it until 1944. During this period about 23,000 of the inhabitants were shot and a further 42,000 deported to Germany. When the Soviet army regained the area in 1944, they had to fight for the town literally building by building. The fighting went on for forty days and little of old Ternopol survived. 85 per cent of the town was levelled to the ground and for a number of years the townspeople that remained dug themselves into the ground for shelter while branches of the local administration had its headquarters in neighbouring towns.

Present day Ternopol was rebuilt according to the original town plan. Noteworthy among the new buildings are the Ternopol Hotel, the post office, the Music and Drama Theatre and the Regional Council Building. Of old Ternopol there remains the castle, some Roman Catholic churches, and several small residential houses on Karl Marx Boulevard which have been carefully restored and are now used as town offices. On Lenin St. there are a number of pleasant two-storey houses which date from the end of the last century.

Ternopol has an electrical equipment factory, a machine-building plant, a polytechnical school, a medical institute with 2,300 students and pedagogical and financial institutes.

16th century castle, Surorov St., near Ternopol Hotel

Rozhdestva Church, Lenin St. Built in 1602, this is the town's oldest church and is open for services. In 1653 a meeting of townspeople held here decided against union with Turkey.

SS. Peter and Paul Dominican Church, near the monastery. This was built in 1749 in late Baroque style. It was reconstructed in 1959 to house the local museum.

Nadstavnaya Church, the church above the lake

Local Museum, Muzeinaya St. 17

Music and Drama Theatre, Karl Marx St. 6

Philharmonia Concert Hall, Ostrovsky St. 9. The Ukrainian poet and writer, Ivan Franko, read his works there in 1911.

Pushkin Monument, Teatralnaya Sq.

Taras Shevchenko monument, Shevchenko Park. The famous Ukrainian author and artist visited Ternopol in 1846.

Lenin monument, Svobody Sq.; unveiled in 1967.

Karl Marx bust, Karl Marx Sq.

Obelisk to the victims of World War II, Lenin St. The obelisk is 20 m. high.

Tank monument, Peremogi (victory) Sq.; erected in 1969 on the 25th anniversary of the liberation of Ternopol from the Germans.

The *grave of the Unknown Soldier*, Slavy (glory) Park, which was formerly called the Old Garden. The grave and the eternal flame also date from 1969, marking the 25th anniversary of the town's liberation.

Fighter plane monument, eastern residential district

Ukraina Hotel, Karl Marx St. 27, TEL. 246–47

Ternopol Hotel (Intourist), Svobody Sq., TEL. 799–31. Intourist office—TEL. 225–37

Khutor (village) Restaurant, Shevchenko Park

Bank, Shevchenko St. 6

G.P.O., Krasnoarmeiskaya St. 3

Kashtan foreign currency store, Suvorov St. 9

Beriozka gift shop, Lenin St. 32

Kobzar Bookshop, Karl Marx St. 37

Market, Myaskovsky St. 4

The *lake of Komsomolskoye Ozero*, also known as the Ternopol Sea, covers 400 hectares (1,000 acres) just outside the town.

TIFLIS
See Tbilisi, p. 303

TRAKAI
See Vilnius, p. 324

TRANSCARPATHIA
See Uzhgorod, p. 317

TSARITSYNO
See Moscow, p. 231

TSKHALTUBO
See Kutaisi, p. 157

TSIKHIS-DZIRI
See Batumi, p. 63

TULA
See Yasnaya Polyana, road to, p. 343

TURKMENISTAN
See Ashkhabad, p. 50

UGLICH
Population—30,000
Pronounced 'ooglich'

Uglich is one of the oldest Russian cities. According to legend it was founded in 937, but the first written records date from 1149. The name Uglich is believed to be derived from the word 'ugol' (angle) because of the sharp turn made by the R. Volga where the town stands.

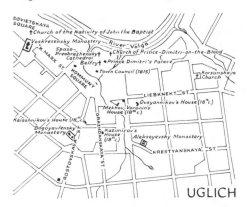

In 1207 chronicles recorded Uglich as being part of the Rostov Princedom, but in 1218 it became the centre of an autonomous princedom. It was razed to the ground in 1237 and again in 1284 by the invading Tatars, but in 1375 Ivan Kalita purchased it back from the Tatars and brought it into the domain of the Grand Princes of Moscow.

In the middle of the 15th century Dimitri Shamyaka of Uglich challenged the rights of his cousin,

Vasili II, Grand Prince of Moscow. Vasili was captured, blinded, and banished to Uglich while Dimitri took his place in Moscow. Dmitri was soon betrayed however and his cousin ruled again as Vasili Tyomni (the blind).

Ivan the Terrible presented Uglich to his new-born son, also called Dimitri, and in 1584, after Ivan's death, it was to Uglich that two-year-old Dimitri and his mother, Maria, were banished by Tsar Fyodor, his step-brother. Seven years later Dimitri was found dead in the palace courtyard with his throat cut and the news was tolled out on the big bell of Spassky Church. The event gave rise to serious unrest, and it was believed that the Prince's death had been arranged by Boris Godunov, Fyodor's right-hand-man. In fact the tragedy may have been a pure accident as all little boys like playing with knives and this particular little boy was an epileptic. At the time however anti-Moscow feelings ran so high that much blood was shed and many citizens of Uglich were exiled before Godunov felt there was no longer a threat of disturbance. Later, a number of pretenders to the throne took the name of Dimitri, denying that the young prince had ever been killed.

Uglich was much fought over during the Time of Troubles, and changed hands between the Russians and the Poles several times until the Polish defeat in 1612. In 1619 Tsar Mikhail Romanov hoped to revive the town by bringing in several thousand new inhabitants from other places but by the middle of the century fewer than 3000 lived there. Uglich nevertheless became a dis-trict centre, under the jurisdiction of St. Peters-burg, until 1727 when the district was included in the Province of Moscow.

In 1784 it is recorded that the town was replanned with straight streets; this planning has survived but up till the beginning of this century the town was of little economic, cultural, or polit-ical significance. In 1911 the population was about 10,000, only a quarter of what it had been before Godunov's massacres, nearly 300 years before. It has tripled now and its most important industries are metal-working and machine-building. There is also a watch factory. The local dairy farming is also reflected in the town's Insti-tute of Butter- and Cheese-making and Uglich is one of the country's major cheese-producing centres.

Nothing remains of the ancient wooden Krem-lin which stood in the centre of Uglich, but on its territory stands the Palace of the Princes of Uglich, originally built in 1480 by Andrei Bolshoi, the brother of Ivan III. It is usually known as *Prince Dimitri's Palace*, after its last occupant. The three-storey structure is square and built of large red bricks. The ground floor consists of two rooms, and was probably used for domestic pur-poses. It appears to be sunken as the level of the ground around the palace has already risen by some 1·5 m. An outside staircase leads to the next floor which has three rooms. The top floor has a single spacious room, probably used as a throne room and for ceremonial receptions and gather-ings.

In 1892 *Uglich Museum* was opened in the palace. Now the museum has a collection of about 16,000 exhibits of the 16th–19th centuries. Among them are manufacturing and agricultural tools, badges of the artisan's guilds, and armaments. Of special interest is the bell which rang from the belfry of Spaso-Preobrazhensky (Transfigura-tion) Cathedral on the day of Prince Dimitri's death, causing unrest in the town. After an investi-gation was carried out, the bell, upon the orders of Boris Godunov, was pulled down, whipped and exiled to Siberia after its 'tongue' had been re-moved. When it reached its destination, it was registered as 'the first inanimate exile from Uglich'. It was only in 1892, 300 years later and after numerous requests by the people of Uglich, that a special commission was sent to Tobolsk to bring the bell back.

Close to the Palace, on the spot where Prince Dimitri had been found dead, a wooden chapel was built at the beginning of the 17th century. In 1630 a wooden church was built here and, in 1692, a stone one. This church came to be known as the *Church of Prince-Dimitri-on-the-Blood*. It is small in size and is characteristic of the decorative archi-tecture of the second half of the 17th century. The decorative style is emphasised by the coloured tiles on the façades. Some late-18th-century fres-coes may be seen inside the church; those on the western wall give a full account of the happenings connected with the death of Prince Dimitri in 1591. The frescoes in the refectory are mainly bib-lical, illustrating the story of the creation. The rea-listic treatment of Adam and Eve is rare for Russian Orthodox paintings of the period.

Spaso-Preobrazhensky (Transfiguration) Ca-thedral is the largest building on the Kremlin terri-tory. It was built at the beginning of the 18th century to replace a church pulled down by the order of Peter the Great. It occupies a dominant position with its five domes visible from every part of the town. The span of the central vault is 14 m. The decorations were painted at the beginning of the 19th century. In front of the eastern wall is a huge iconostasis; the two lower rows contain the oldest, though not the best preserved, icons. The cathedral, together with the Palace and the Church of Prince-Dimitri-on-the-Blood, is part of Uglich Museum.

The *belfry* to the south of the cathedral and close to the Palace was built in 1730. Its high bulky structure has an unexpectedly light and elegant spire.

Kazansky Church on Kommuny Sq. was built in 1778 in place of an old wooden church. It played an important part as a focal point at the end of one of the main streets. Only the lower part has been preserved.

Voskresensky (Resurrection) Monastery and the *Church of the Nativity of John the Baptist* (1689) are picturesquely situated on Sovietskaya Sq. by the Volga. They are fine examples of 17th-century

Russian church architecture. The monastery was built in 1674–7 by the order of and under the supervision of Iona, Metropolitan of Rostov Veliki. The monastery buildings have much in common with similar buildings in Rostov. Here, for the first time in Uglich, green tiles were used with pictures of battles and daily life, animals, and emblems. The largest building here is the *Voskresensky Cathedral* with five cupolas. Even the rich decor cannot detract from the pure lines of this building. The other buildings are the *belfry*, the *Church of Odeghitria*, and the *refectory*. The small fragments of frescoes preserved in the Church of Odeghitria and in the cathedral give an impression of the quality of the original decoration of the monastery. In 1764 the monastery was closed and the churches turned into parish churches. Though some restoration has been done recently, the structures are still much in need of attention.

The *Church of the Nativity of John the Baptist* was built before the monastery. It attracts attention by the contrast between the light, well-proportioned belfry and the squat, heavy porch with massive columns.

Alekseyevsky Monastery at Krestyanskaya St. 27 was founded in 1371 by Aleksei, Metropolitan of All Russia, upon the orders of Dimitri Donskoy, Grand Prince of Moscow. It was planned to guard Uglich from the Yaroslavl side. In 1609 Polish troops approaching Uglich besieged the monastery where about 500 citizens had taken refuge. Infuriated by their staunch defence, the Poles burnt down the wooden structure, killing everybody inside and burying some people alive.

The monastery was rebuilt after the Time of Troubles, and in 1628 the *Uspenskaya Divnaya Church* (Wonderful Church of the Assumption) was erected. It is a masterpiece of old Russian architecture. A characteristic feature is its three octagonal spires topped with onion-shaped cupolas. The ground plan is quite simple. The refectory adjoins a small church hall on the first floor. At various times the vaults of the crypt served as a prison. Uspenskaya Church is one of the best examples of the old Russian architecture of the 16th and early 17th century.

When *Bogoyavlensky (Epiphany) Monastery* at Rostovskaya St. 22 was originally founded, it was housed in the north-western part of the Kremlin, but in 1661 it was transferred to new buildings by the road leading to Rostov. The earliest stone structures date from the end of the 17th century. In 1853 the huge *Bogoyavlensky Cathedral* was built. Its most interesting feature is the cost of construction—60,000 silver roubles—an enormous sum for that time. *Smolenskaya Church* (1700) and *Fyodorovskaya Church* (1818) are also in Bogoyavlensky Monastery.

Other churches, less interesting from the architectural and historical point of view include:

Pyatnitskaya Church (1764), Sovietskaya Sq.

SS. Frol and Lavr Church, Ostrovskovo St. 1a. This church, built in 1762, stands on the site of the mews of the Princes of Uglich.

Korsunskaya Church (1730), Narimanova St. 7.

A number of old houses also remain in the town. There is *Mekhov-Voronin's House* at Kamenskaya St. 4, which some experts think dates from the 17th century. It follows the usual plan with the ground floor occupied by household implements and storage rooms, while the living quarters and accommodation for guests occupy the upper floor. Of interest are the carved wooden banisters and the decorative tiled stove. *Kalashnikov's House* at Pervomaiskaya St. 13/10 is an 18th-century stone house and *Kasatkin House* at Nekrasova St. 13, decorated with elaborate wood carving, was built at the beginning of the last century.

Museum, in the Kremlin. Open 10–5, closed Wed.

Trud (labour) Stadium, Liebknecht St. 54
Hotel, Liebknecht St. 16
Uglich Restaurant, Rostovskaya St. 2
Volga Café, Liebknecht St. 54
Bank, Liebknecht St. 23
G.P.O., Liebknecht St. 18

UKRAINE
See Kiev, p. 139

ULYANOVSK
Population—351,000 (1970)
Known as Simbirsk until 1924. Ulyanovsk stands on a high hill on the Volga–Sviyaga watershed, on the right bank of the R. Volga with the R. Sviyaga flowing through the town. Its old Chuvash name of Simbirsk meant 'hill of the winds', but some contend that the name has another source; a Bulgar tsar once ruled here and his name was Sinbir. Lenin was born here in 1870, and lived here for 17 years; after his death in 1924 the town was renamed after his family name, Ulyanov. It is the centre of the Ulyanovsk Region.

When the town was founded in 1648 it was first called Sinbirsk after the ancient settlement of Sinbir 30 km. further down the Volga. It served as the first fortress on the Russian line of defence against the Nogai Tatars. To the south-west of it a continuous earthwall was built, fortified with a stockade and occasional wooden towers. The wall was intended as a barrier against 'the thieving people' and also to facilitate the collection of taxes on goods being carried in and out of Russia.

Some 20 years after its foundation, Simbirsk was the centre of one of the bloodiest peasant uprisings in Russian history, that of the Cossack leader, Stepan Razin, when Simbirsk held out against the rebels for a month until the arrival of government troops. By the end of the 17th century Simbirsk had lost its military importance and become a peaceful country town. After the Pugachev uprising of 1773, Catherine the Great awarded Simbirsk the coat-of-arms of a coronet on a pole because unlike most of the towns along the Volga it had remained loyal to the throne. The name 'venets' (coronet) belongs to the hilly part of

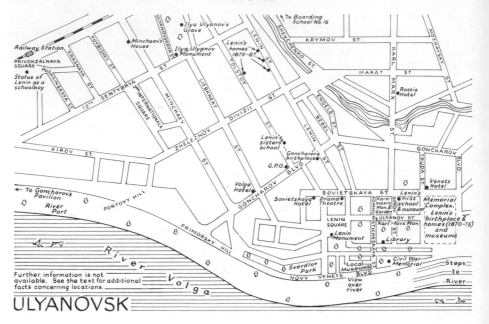

the town which stands 140–170 m. above the
Volga.

In 1796 Simbirsk was made the capital of a
province of the same name. At the beginning of
the 19th century the exiles sent there included the
Georgian princess, Tamara, who spent 10 years in
Simbirsk after a plot to regain Georgian independence had failed. In 1864 a fire broke out and continued for 10 days, destroying three-quarters of
the town.

Simbirsk was often referred to as the birth-place
of poets. The names of many prominent Russian
writers, scientists, and statesmen have been connected with the town, including Karamazin, the
18th-century historian, and Goncharov, author of
'Oblomov', after whom the main street is named.

Among the town's more impressive old buildings is the *Palace of Books* on Karl Marx St. This
was formerly the House of Nobles, built in 1847,
but now it is a library which was formed by merg-
ing the Karamazin and the Goncharov Memorial
Libraries. The first collection was founded in 1848
and contains 2100 expensive volumes which the
historian Karamazin himself presented to the
town, and the second collection dates from 1891.
Lenin Sq. is where the *House of Councils* stands,
the home of the local municipal offices. Ulyanovsk has grown in importance. It boasts 3 institutes, and its position as both a railway junction
and a river port have encouraged the development
of industry. There is a large automobile factory,
machine tools are made here, and there are
leather, food, and timber industries.

Its chief claim to fame however are its associations with Lenin, whose real name was Vladimir
(Volodya) Ilich Ulyanov and who was born here
in 1870 soon after his parents and elder brother

and sister moved here from Nizhny-Novgorod
(now Gorky). His father, Ilya Nikolayevich
Ulyanov, had been appointed inspector of public
schools in Simbirsk Province. Their first home,
where Volodya was born, was in Streletskaya St.
(now Ulyanov St.) but they moved house several
times before they finally settled at 48 Lenin St.
where the museum now is. From 1876–8 they lived
at 28 Tolstoy St. When he was old enough
Volodya followed his brother Alexander (Sasha)
to the local grammar school, the headmaster of
which was Fedor Kerensky. It was Kerensky's
son, Alexander, born in 1881, who grew up to
head the Provisional Government which was
overthrown by Lenin's October Revolution of
1917.

The *Lenin Memorial Complex* was opened in
April 1970, to commemorate the 100th anniversary of Lenin's birth. The chief architect was Boris
Mezantsev from Moscow. The complex includes
the top of Venets Hill and the semicircular area
formed by the Goncharov Boulevard and the
Volga Embankment, and incorporates Lenin Sq.,
Lenin St., Sovietskaya St., and Ulyanov St., all
places connected with Lenin's youth. In addition
there are some impressive buildings which were
specially erected.

The *Memorial Centre* is a huge quadrangle with
sides 100 m. long. The building stands upon 8-m.
columns and so one is able to see into the quadrangle from outside. Within it stands the house
where the Ulyanov family lived from 1869 to 1875,
and where Lenin was born.

The Centre houses a branch of the *Lenin Museum* on the first floor with a large gallery of paintings of him. There is also a *House of Political
Education* with study rooms and a lecture hall and

a combined cinema and concert hall which seats 1400. Also in the Centre is the white marble *October Hall* with a 6-m. statue of Lenin.

From the Centre a wide flight of steps leads down to the Volga, and nearby stands the *Venets Hotel*, the study block of the *Pedagogical Institute*, and in Sovietskaya St. overlooking Karamazin Garden, *Lenin School No. 1*, formerly Simbirsk Grammar School. It was founded at the beginning of the 19th century and the outside has been altered but it was here that Lenin studied from 1879 till 1887. It is still run as a regular school, but next to the assembly hall is the classroom where Lenin worked when he was in the 7th form (1885–6). This is kept as a memorial room to him and his desk stands in its place near the window. In April 1970, 100 young trees were planted to mark the centenary; one more is added each year.

48 Lenin St. is also quite nearby. Here is the *Lenin Museum* in the house where the Ulyanov family lived from 1878–87. It contains a portrait room, a drawing room with a piano, the inspector's study, his wife's room with her knitting basket and her library of books in French, English, and German as well as Russian, and the dining room which was the largest room in the house. The children's rooms were in the attic. Sasha, who was 4 years Volodya's senior, had a strong influence upon his brother. His chemical equipment is in place in his room as a tribute to his love of the subject. He left school with a gold medal and was awarded another at St. Petersburg University for his scientific research work. Gradually he became involved in student revolutionary activities which led to his execution in May 1887, when he was 21, for the attempted assassination of Alexander III. Volodya's room, above the staircase, is the smallest in the house. It contains an iron bedstead, a table, two chairs, a bookshelf, a large map, and the boy's school-leaving certificate. On the table are the books Lenin received at school as annual prizes. There is a croquet lawn outside the house. Open 10–6.

Close to the river at the beginning of Goncharov Boulevard is a new *Pioneer Palace* with workshops, studios, and gymnasia to cater for 2000 children at a time. There is also a hotel for young visitors. An old wooden house has been left just as it was when a group of Simbirsk revolutionaries used to gather there at the time of the first Russian Revolution in 1905. They had contact with Lenin through his younger brother Dmitri.

St. Nicholas's Church (20th century), Verkhniya Polevaya St.

Goncharov Local Museum, Novy Venets Boulevard 3/4, facing the river. Donations came from all over Russia to commemorate the centenary of the birth of Ivan Goncharov (1814–91), the Russian novelist and editor. The museum bearing his name houses all sorts of exhibits including those of the Provincial Ethnographic Museum and the pictures of the local art gallery and some icons, but there is a special room devoted to Goncharov himself, showing family portraits and a

number of watercolours he painted in Japan. Open 11–6, closed Tues.

Karamazin Monument, in Karamazin Garden. Nikolai Karamazin (1766–1826) was a historian who wrote 'The History of the Russian State', the first comprehensive work on the subject. The inscription on the monument reads: 'To N. P. Karamazin, an historian of the Russian State. By order of Emperor Nicholas I, 1844.' Local nobles were responsible for following out the imperial order. The bronze figure of Clio, muse of history, lays Karamazin's book upon an altar. The statue, by Galdberg, was cast by Klodt. The pedestal is decorated by two brass bas-reliefs showing episodes from Karamazin's life and in a niche in the front wall of the pedestal is a bust of Karamazin by Ramazanov and Klimchenko.

Bust of Goncharov, in a garden near the Palace of Books, on Karl Marx St. This bust of the novelist by Vetrov was unveiled in 1948.

Goncharov's Birthplace, Goncharov Blvd. 16. The house is marked by a black marble plaque and a bas-relief by Mikeshin, unveiled in 1907.

Ilya Ulyanov Monument, in a garden on 12th-Sentybrya St. The bust of Lenin's father was sculpted in pink granite by Manizer in 1957. Below him, at the corner of the pedestal, stands the bronze figure of a peasant boy with a staff in one hand and an open book in the other, symbolising Ulyanov's work as an educationalist. Ilya Ulyanov's grave is nearby, in a cemetery on Liebknecht St.

Civil War Memorial, Novy Venets Boulevard, near the Volga. The white obelisk marks the grave of soldiers killed in Simbirsk in 1918. The architect was Voltsev and the unveiling took place in 1927.

Karl Marx Monument, at the crossing of Kommunisticheskaya and Ulyanov Sts. The 2-m. figure in black granite stands on a pedestal of grey granite, 1·8 m. high. It was designed and executed by Schuko, Merkurov, and Antonov and unveiled in 1921.

Lenin Monument, Lenin Sq. The statue in granite by Manizer stands 14·5 m. high and was unveiled in 1940.

Lenin as a Schoolboy, in front of the railway station. This statue by Tsigal was unveiled in 1954.

Drama Theatre, Sovietskaya St. 8. Built in 1879 and reconstructed in 1970.

Sverdlov Park, Plekhanov St. 12

Regional Economic Exhibition, Narimanov Road, in a forested park

Venets Hotel, Sovietskaya St. 13, TEL. 9–48–16

Volga Hotel & Restaurant, Goncharov Blvd. 3, TEL. 145–77

Rossia Hotel & Restaurant, Karl Marx St. 23, TEL. 1–78–62

Sovietskaya Hotel & Moskva Restaurant, Sovietskaya St. 6

Bank, Goncharov St. 42/1

G.P.O., Goncharov St. 9/58

Department Store, Goncharov St.

Art Salon, Goncharov St.

Vinnovskaya Grove, a little way out of town, to the south along the Volga. This was formerly known as Kindyakovskaya Grove and is a popular recreation spot. Goncharov described it in his novel 'Obryv' ('The Precipice') and to commemorate the centenary of his birth a rotunda was built here with an obelisk and a bas-relief of the writer.

Bathing beach, on Paltsensky Island 30 km. up the Volga. One can get to this very pleasant beach by boat from Ulyanovsk.

Lenin Hydropower Station, 150 km. down river, reached by hydrofoil.

URGENCH

Population—76,000 (1970).
Urgench airport also serves Khiva which is 32 km. to the south-west. Local flights from Tashkent to Urgench take about 5 hours and one can get to Khiva either by bus or taxi.

Urgench is situated 10 km. from the left bank of the R. Amu-Darya and the Shavat Canal runs through the town.

The place was first settled in the middle of the 17th century when the inhabitants of Old Urgench moved here because their water supply had failed. A fortress was built, but the town did not really grow until the last half of the 19th century. The first cotton mill was built here in 1889, but before the Revolution only 200 of the town's population of 5000 worked in industry.

It is now an important trading and industrial centre, the main local product being cotton. The area of the town is now 13 times what it was in 1917 and there is a pedagogical institute with 4 faculties.

Lenin Monuments, Red Sq., Revolution Sq. and Mir St.

Music and Drama Theatre, Mir St.

The *Stadium* is in Bazarnaya St. and Central Park covers 33 hectares (82 acres).

Urgench (Intourist) Hotel and Restaurant, Kommunisticheskaya 27, TEL. 37–61

Khorezm Hotel, Turgenev St. 37/68

Restaurant, Gorky St.

G.P.O., Uzbekistanskaya St. 13

Department Store, Mir St. 43

Khiva

Population—37,000 (1970).
Khiva is situated in the Khorezm Oasis on the Palvan Canal and the left bank of the R. Amu-Darya. To the south stretches the Karakum Desert and to the north-east, the Kysylkum Desert. The average temperature in January is −5°C. (23°F.) and in July 28·5°C. (83°F.). The irrigated area surrounding the city produces fruit, cotton, maize, and rice.

The history of Khiva begins with the legend of how Shem, son of Noah, lay asleep on a hill of sand and dreamed of a future city in that very place. He dug a well which he named Kheivak and which is to be seen in the north-west part of Ichan-Kala (the old city) today. Khiva is supposed to derive its name from that of the well.

Certainly Khiva was known in the 4th century B.C. as part of the state of Khorezm, when the Amu-Darya still flowed into the Caspian Sea and not into the Aral Sea as it does today. In A.D. 712, along with the rest of Khorezm, Khiva fell under Arab domination. It was at this time that Abu Mohammed ibn Musa al Khwarizmi (d. 850?) wrote some of the first treatises on mathematics. The word 'algebra' comes from his own 'al-jabr'. 'Algorism', which means the Arabic system of numerals (1–9 with 0), is really a corruption of his own name. However it was only in the 10th century that the first written account of the place itself was made, by two Arabian travellers, Istakhri and Makdisi. At that time it began to become an important port on the trade routes from China, India, and Iran to Bulgaria and to Ryzan, Pskov, and Novgorod on the way to the Baltic countries and the rest of Europe.

Khiva suffered severely in 1220 from Ghengis-Khan's Mongol invasion and little of the city was left standing. By the 16th century however it had recovered sufficiently to become the capital of the Khanate which was formed by Khan Ara-Muhammed in 1511. It grew to be the centre of Islam in Central Asia and had one of the most important slave markets in that part of the world. Its growing prosperity attracted the attention of both Iran and Bukhara and there followed a long period when its possession was under hot dispute. It was for some time held as a province of Iran, but the Persians were driven out in 1741. It is on record that Khiva was ruled by 33 different khans during the course of the 18th century, finally being taken over by the Uzbek 'Inaqs' (nobles). Inaq Iltuzer declared himself khan in 1804 and his family maintained possession of Khiva until 1920.

The Khivan khans kept themselves cut off from the infidel western world and found the position of the newly-crowned Queen Victoria almost impossible to comprehend, even with the careful explanation provided by Captain Abbott in 1839–40. The interview with Khan Hazurut went as follows:

'Is your king really a woman?' he asked.
'She is.'

The khan smiled, and all his satellites, as in duty bound, giggled.

'How', he inquired, 'can she rule, being "rooposh" (concealed)?'

'Our females, like those of the Turcumuns, are not concealed. The Queen of England has ministers who transact business for her.'

'Are they women?'

'No, they are men. They receive their general instructions from the Queen and act accordingly.'

The khan continued, 'Do you always choose women as your kings?'

'No, we give preference to heirs male, but when there is a female and no male, rather than disturb the country by introducing a new family of claimants to the crown, we crown this female. One of the greatest of our kings was a woman.'

'Is your king married?'
'No, she is very young.'
'But will she marry?'
'Inshallah.'
'And if she marry, does her husband become king?'
'By no means. He has no authority in the state.'
Here there was some more smiling.*

Eventually it was a Russian force that brought this eastern city nearer the west, but it was much earlier than 1917 when the main Russian expeditions first came here. In 1717 Peter the Great sent a military force under the leadership of Bokovich-Cherkassy to search for gold in the sands of the Oxus; few lived to tell the tale of how the Russians were trapped and slaughtered. Another expedition under Perovsky set out in the winter of 1839, especially to avoid the summer heat, but instead of meeting with success it became stuck in the snow in the desert. In 1873 Khiva was taken by the Russian Army under Kaufman, and was subsequently crippled by the indemnity that was imposed. In 1920 Khiva was made the capital of Khorezm and remained so until the state was incorporated into Uzbekistan in 1924.

Khiva long retained its eastern character. There was a large bazaar and besides the 94 mosques, there were 63 medressehs in the city. Today the architectural ensembles are much better preserved than those of the more ancient cities of Bukhara and Samarkand, and have a further advantage over them in that they were properly planned and completed. Although many of the buildings in Khiva were built comparatively recently, the architects made use of the best traditional designs of Central Asian architecture while they developed a new style in town planning. Much restoration was carried out before 1967, but it was only then that the oldest part of the city was declared a 'town-reserve' (like Suzdal, near Moscow) and restoration work began to be carried out scientifically, following the original plans. Today the projects include the laying of telephone and power lines underground and then repaving of the streets with square bricks, just as they used to be. The organisation in charge of the restoration work is buying up private houses to complete the complex of the city, but often people are unwilling to leave for the new apartments set up outside the ancient walls.

All the monuments of greatest historical interest are located in *Ichan-Kala* (the inner city) which was surrounded by walls, of which some parts still remain. The walls are thought to have been built in the 5th–6th centuries. Where they are still intact they are over 2 km. in circumference, stand 7–8 m. high and their thickness at the bottom is 5–6 m.

Ichan-Kala covers 26 hectares (65 acres) and is crossed by two main streets; from north to south runs Bukhara St., and Marx St. crosses it from

* From 'Narrative of a Journey from Heraut to Khiva, Moscow and St. Petersburg', 2 vols. by Capt. James Abbot; W. H. Allen & Co. Ltd., London, 1884.

east to west. At each end of the streets is one of Ichan-Kala's 4 gates.

The buildings of greatest interest are close together, and it doesn't matter in which order they are visited, but if one starts at the site of the western gate (which was removed in 1924), where Marx St. enters Ichan-Kala, the first complex on the left is that of *Kunya-Ark*, the ancient citadel, founded in the 12th century. Its name means 'old palace fortress' and indeed it used to be the palace of the khans. Most of the remaining buildings date from the 17th century when the palace stretched right along the western wall of Ichan-Kala. The Kurnysh-Khana (reception hall) has been restored since the Revolution. Its ceiling is decorated with paint made from mineral glue. In one of the walls is the niche where the khan's throne used to stand; it is now in the armoury in the Moscow Kremlin. The harem has been restored to its original appearance. There is also a *summer mosque*, built in 1838 and notable for its decorative tiles, particularly the majolica work in the prayer niche in the southern wall. The khan's mint functioned in Kunya-Ark in 1806–25 and the building has been fully restored.

Besides these buildings put up by the khans of the last century, inside Kunya-Ark, on a small hill, are the ruins of the oldest part of the town, Ashik-Baba. Perhaps called after a certain Ak-shikh (white sheik), the clay tower that used to stand here was the place where the khans took refuge from their rebellious vassals. Certainly it is true that Shirghazi-Khan (1715–28) so feared for his life that he used to lock himself in the tower and kept it always ready for withstanding a siege.

On the right side of the street opposite the citadel is the *Muhammed-Amin Khan Medresseh* and the colossal base of the unfinished *Kalta-Minar minaret*, nearly 53 m. high, built in 1851–5 and decorated with blue tiles. 'Kalta' means 'short' and there are different stories attached to it. It is said that construction work on the minaret ceased in 1855 either because the khan was killed in battle or because there was a disagreement between him and the architect responsible. The base of the minaret is 14·2 m. in diameter, much larger than most minarets, and suggests that the finished structure was meant to be exceptionally tall. There is a story that the architect had agreed to build a similar minaret for the emir of Bukhara when this one was completed, but when the jealous Muhammed-Amin Khan learned of this, he ordered that the architect be thrown from the tower to his death. Another version says that the architect was to be imprisoned inside the minaret until it was finished, but he managed to escape and so the work was abandoned.

Close to the Kalta-Minar is the *Matiyez Divan-begi Medresseh* (1871) and the *Mausoleum of Seid Alauddin* (1310) which is the only monument in Khiva to have survived from the time of Mongol domination. Built by Emir Kullal, the mausoleum is of burnt brick and the tomb covered with elaborately decorated tiles.

Next are the *Kazi-Kalyan Medresseh* (1905) and the *Dzhuma Mosque* which was first mentioned in the 10th century but was rebuilt in 1788. It is 55 m. long and 46 m. wide, the wooden ceiling inside being supported by 212 carved wooden columns standing 3·5 m. apart. Today only 15 of the original pillars remain; the newer ones are plain. It is said that the old pillars were brought here from a mosque in Kyata, the capital of Khorezm in the 10th century.

On the left side of the street after the citadel are the high walls of the *Muhammed Rakhim-Khan Medresseh* (1871). Close to it is the *Arab-Khan Medresseh* (1616).

At the crossing of Marx St. with Bukhara St., to the right (the southern side), is the *Mausoleum of Pakhlavan- (or Palvan-) Mahmud*, now part of the *Khorezm Historical and Revolutionary Museum*. Pakhlavan-Mahmud was the son of a furrier whose workshop stood on the site of the mausoleum. Pakhlavan means 'mighty one', because he was very strong and generally respected and even had considerable influence over the khan. He was also a poet. When he died he was buried here and he was later declared a saint; the mausoleum was built over his grave in the 14th century. Palvan-Ata was considered the guardian of the Khivan Khanate and his mausoleum was revered as a sacred shrine. It was rebuilt in 1910 by Muhammad Rakhim-Khan after it had been used as the family mausoleum of the Kungrad Khans. The tomb is now decorated with blue tiles and the doors are of carved ivory.

Just south of the mausoleum is the *Shirghazi-Khan Medresseh* (1718–19), built after a campaign by Shirgazi-Khan against the Persian city of Meshed during which he took 5000 prisoners. The prisoners were enslaved and brought back to Khiva and put to work to build this medresseh on the understanding that they would be freed when the building was complete. However the khan delayed the completion and employed them for other construction work, whereupon they lost patience and murdered him there, in the medresseh. Later the medresseh became one of the most important in the whole of Khorezm and earned the name of Maskanfazylan, the House of the Learned.

To the east of the Shirghazi-Khan Medresseh is the *Islam-Khodja Medresseh* with a minaret (1908), at 44·6 m. high, the tallest in Khiva; its base is 9·5 m. in diameter. Islam Khodja, who built it, was the khan's minister. The *Bogbouli Mosque* (19th century) is nearby.

In the opposite direction, to the north of Marx St., along Bukhara St., are the *Muhamed-Amin-Inaq Medresseh* (1765), the *Dos-Alim Medresseh* (1882), the *Yusup-Yaszhaulibashi Medresseh* (1906), the *Musa-Turya Medresseh* (1841), and the *Emir-Turya Medresseh* (1870). Bukhara St. ends with the northern gate, *Bogcha-Darvaza*, which is in the form of a covered passage 10 m. long and 5 m. wide. It is roofed with two cupolas and at each side there is a semicircular tower, 10 m. high, and

joined together by a gallery.

Following Marx St. further along towards the eastern gates of Ichan-Kala, on the right side are the *Abdula-Khan Medresseh* (1855), the *Ak-Mosque* (1857) and the *Anusha-Khan Bath-house* (1657); Anusha-Khan, son of Abul-gari-Khan, was presented with these baths by his father after having fought particularly valiantly in battle. The building is now deep in the ground. Also on the same side of Marx St. is the *Seid-bai Medresseh and Mosque* (1842).

To the left of Marx St., and along Lermontov St. which runs northwards from it parallel with Bukhara St., is the *Kutlug-Murad-inaq Medresseh* (1804–12). Kutlug-Murad-naq had said that he wished to be buried in the medresseh he had built, but he chanced to die while he was in the outer city, Dishan-Kala, and it was forbidden to carry dead bodies into Ichan-Kala. The problem was solved by pulling down part of the wall of Ichan-Kala near the eastern gate (the Pavlan-Darvaza Gate) so that the medresseh appeared to stand in Dishan-Kala.

The *Khodzhamberdibiya (or Khurdzhum) Medresseh* (1683) is also in Lermontov St. and adjoining it is the *Uch-avlya Mausoleum* (16th century). Its name means Three Saints' Mausoleum and there is a legend that once three brothers feared that drought would ruin their crops so they diverted some water from the irrigation channels in the khan's fields to their own smallholding. They were sentenced to death but at night they went out into the fields to pray to Allah—and immediately a heavy downpour of rain began, a rare occurrence in Khorezm. The khan's crops were spoiled because his fields had only just been watered, but the rain was just what was needed by the three brothers' fields and they later yielded a good crop.

At the end of Marx St., but still within the walls of Ichan-Kala and near the east gates, the *Local Museum* is located in the *Palace of Allukuli-Khan (or Tash-Khauli)* and in the former *Allakuli-Khan Medresseh* (1835). It has been fully restored and its main façade is most interesting architecturally and uses decorative majolica. Thousands of slaves were employed to build the palace. There were 163 rooms arranged around 3 large courtyards and 5 smaller ones, and the whole complex was surrounded by a high stone wall. Most of the inside walls are of burnt brick. The 3 ceremonial courts and some of the rooms are decorated with blue, white, and turquoise tiles and with carved wooden columns rising from carved marble bases; many of the doors are intricately carved. The 3 large courts are the blue-tiled Harem Court, Ishrart-Hauly (the reception court), and Arz-Hauly (the court of justice). The latter has 2 gates, the main one and a second through which prisoners were led to trial.

Adjoining the palace is the *Allukuli-Khan Cara-vanserai*, built in 1832 and fully restored. It has 105 rooms and was an inn for travelling merchants. Next to the caravanserai, built at the same time, are the buildings of the *bazaar*, mainly a long, covered passage roofed with 14 cupolas, the central one rising high above the others.

The southern side of the Allakuli-Khan complex joins the *Palvan-Darvaza gate*, rebuilt in 1806. This gate leading into Ichan-Kala is a passageway 60 m. long, roofed by 6 cupolas. The small recesses in the walls were used as prison cells in the 17th and 18th centuries and later as trading stalls. There used to be a slave market to the right of the gate and it is on record that runaway slaves were nailed to the gate by their ears. It was by this gate that the khan's edicts were read out to the people.

Outside the walls of Ichan-Kala lies what was the poorer region of the city, known as Dishan-Kala. This was enclosed in the middle of the 19th century by walls with watch towers and ten gates.

Local Museum, Allakuli-Khan Medresseh, Marx St. Here is an exhibition of objects found during excavations of the territory of ancient Khorezm.

Local History and Revolutionary Museum, Gagarin St.; open 8–5. This museum is located in the former official residence of the late Seid Asphendiar Bogadur Khan. The palace, Khiva's first European-type building, was constructed in 1902 for the khan by his father, Muhammed Rahim Khan II. It was here that ambassadors were received. The impressive chandeliers in the reception hall were a present from the last Russian tsar, Nicholas II. The palace's small generator fed the building with electricity and it was in fact the only place that was lit in the whole country. Among the exhibits is silk money which was used for some time here in the 1920s.

Close to the museum is the former *harem*, now a boarding school, and the *pavilion* where Asphediar Khan was killed in 1918. Opposite the local savings bank office, the khan used to receive complaints and petitions from his subjects.

G.P.O., Pochtovaya St., in the building formerly known as the Khan's Post Office; standing opposite is the *Khan's Hospital*.

Hotel and Café, Gagarin St. 13

Taxi: at the time of writing it is recommended to keep the taxi from Urgench to make the return journey.

UZBEKISTAN
See Tashkent, p. 296

UZHGOROD
Population—65,000 (1970)
Ukrainian: Uzhorod; Czech: Užhorod; Hungarian: Ungvár
The town is situated in the foothills of the Carpathian Mountains, on either side of the R. Uzh (meaning 'grass snake', so Uzhgorod is 'grass snake town'). The surrounding area is a wine-growing region and the ancient coat-of-arms of the town bears a vine with two bunches of golden grapes. Uzhgorod is the largest town in Transcarpathia.

TRANSCARPATHIA
Russian: Zakarpatiye

The name of this region means 'beyond the Carpathians', but it is also called the Ukrainian Caucasus.

Nearly a million people live here: 80% of them are Ukrainians but there are also Russians, Hungarians, Jews, Rumanians, and Slovaks. Their occupations are timber and wood-working, wine-making and horticulture, and only 28% of them live in the towns.

For nearly 1000 years, from the time when, at the beginning of the 11th century, the Hungarians took it from the state of Kiev Rus, Transcarpathia was outside Russia. In the 16th century it was attacked by the Turks and then the region was divided into two parts: Uzhgorod, which was under the rule of the Hapsburgs, and Mukachevo, which belonged to Transylvania. Early in the 18th century the whole Carpathian country, together with Hungary, was under Austrian rule. Count Schönborn was the most influential landlord in the area. The Hungarian revolution of 1848–9 also affected Transcarpathia, and in the mid-19th century Austria stimulated the building of factories there. After the fall of the Austro-Hungarian Empire, Transcarpathia passed to Czechoslovakia.

When the Germans attacked Czechoslovakia in March, 1939, Hungary again took this territory. After World War II, in June, 1945, the Soviet Union and Czechoslovakia signed an agreement by which this region passed to the Soviet Union, and in the following year it was united with the Ukrainian Republic.

Since the early 1960s Soviet oil from the Volga–Caspian area has flowed through the Druzhba pipeline to refineries in Eastern Europe.

Uzhgorod
Uzhgorod, known in the chronicles since the 9th century, it is one of the oldest Slavonic towns, and today its industries include the manufacture of veneered furniture, bricks, tiles, and food products.

There are mineral springs of the carbonic acid type in front of the main university building in Gorky Park, and in Podgradskii and Protskii Streets.

Castle, Kremlovskaya St. 27. The castle dates from the end of the 9th century, and the Slav Prince Laborets lived here until he was executed in 903 by the invading Hungarians. In 1312 Uzhgorod, with its castle, was given by the Hungarian King Karl Robert to the Italian Count Drugget, and the Drugget family held it until 1692, during which period '1598' was engraved over the entrance gate. After this, the castle was sold to Count Berceni. In the 17th century it was seized several times during local disturbances.

In 1649, in the Roman Catholic chapel in the park, the local Orthodox Church signed a union with Rome which marked the foundation of the Uniate, or Greek Catholic, Church. The present castle has a 16th-century façade; it was reconstructed in 1598 and in 1653 to suit the require-

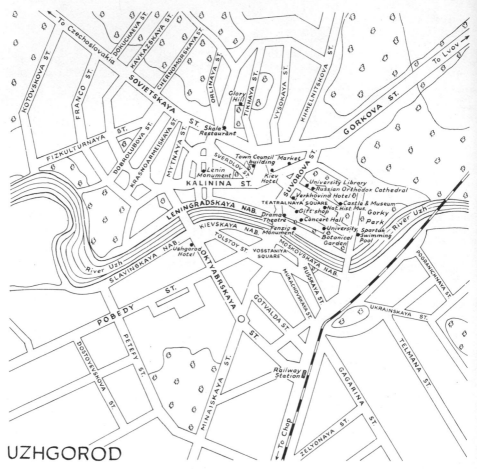

UZHGOROD

ments of new military techniques. In 1703 it was captured by rebellious peasants led by Ivan Betzei. Later in the 18th century the castle lost its military importance, and when the upper storey of the main castle building was burned down in 1728, it was not rebuilt. In 1775 it was presented to the Bishop of Mukachevo. Soon after that a seminary was opened in the castle and was only closed in 1944.

There are extensive dungeons and cellars in the castle, and from the top of the eastern tower there is a good view of the valley of the R. Uzh; in fine weather the ruins of Nevitzkoye Castle can be seen. In the castle garden stands a bronze statue of the mythological Hungarian bird known as the 'Turul'. Originally the castle had a moat on three sides of it, the fourth being naturally protected by a steep hill.

Russian Orthodox Cathedral, on the way to the castle. This was built in 1646, originally as a Roman Catholic Cathedral.

Greek Catholic Church, Oktyabrskaya St.

St. Paul's Church (Russian Orthodox), Moskovskaya Naberezhnaya. This church was built in 1932 to commemorate the Russian soldiers who

fell in the Carpathians in World War I.

Calvinists' Church, Sovietskaya St.

Main Building of the University, Gorky Sq. The university, founded in 1946, now has more than 4000 students attending its seven faculties. Its other buildings are in Lenin Sq. and Oktyabrskaya St.

University Library. This building was originally founded in 1644 as the residence of the Uniate Bishops of Transcarpathia; it was reconstructed in 1848 in Baroque style, and encloses an interesting old sundial.

Local Executive Building, Lenin Sq. This huge building was put up between 1934 and 1936.

Town Council Building. This was built in 1809 in Baroque style and is now used for newspaper offices.

Local Museum, Kremlyovskaya St. 27, inside the castle. Open 11–7, closed Wed. There are sections of natural history and local handicrafts in the museum.

Picture Gallery, Kremlovskaya St. 27, inside the castle. Open 11–7, closed Mon. Opened in 1948, this gallery now contains the works of Russian and Ukrainian artists.

The *Pyramid Memorial,* Karl Marx Sq. and the *Monument,* Leningradskaya Naberezhnaya. These two memorials were built in memory of those who fell in World War I.

Fenzig Monument. This monument is in memory of a local poet. The iron statue of Hercules in the park near the castle was cast in Uzhgorod.

Heroes' Cemetery, Geroyev St. There are a number of beautiful memorials here.

Ukrainian Drama Theatre, Teatralnaya Sq. This theatre dates from 1907.

Philharmonia Concert Hall, Teatralnaya Sq. This hall was formerly a synagogue; the Transcarpathian Folk Choir sings here.

Spartak Swimming Pool, Roshcha Gogolya St. in Gorky Park

Uzhgorod's Avangard Stadium. The stadium can seat 10,000.

Gorky Park, on the right bank of the R. Uzh, on the north side of Castle Hill. The park contains playgrounds, an open-air stage, sports pavilions, a library, a dance floor, a pets' corner, and a children's railway, the 'Small Carpathian Railway', opened in 1947 and running for 1200 m. along the river bank.

Botanical Garden. Here there are more than 3000 plants including many that are only to be seen in this region. Tropical and subtropical plants can be seen in the hothouses.

Verkovina Hotel and Restaurant, Teatralnaya Sq. 5, TEL. 37–46

Kiev Hotel and Restaurant, Koryatovicha St. 1, TEL. 34–24. Part of the restaurant is in the open air.

Gift Shop, Suvorov St. 10

Uzhgorod is near to Chop, an important railway junction on the Soviet border with Czechoslovakia and Hungary. In Chop the *Hotel Ukraina* is at Privokzalnaya St. 4, TEL. 230.

Also near Uzhgorod is Mukachevo, the second largest town in this region.

Mukachevo

Hungarian: Munkács; Czech: Mukacevo; Population—56,000 (1972)

Mukachevo is now the second largest town in Soviet Transcarpathia but archaeological finds date the earliest settlements on the site right back to the Stone Age. In the 'Gesta Hungarorum', Hungarian chronicles of the 12th century, it is mentioned that the town was known in the 9th century. In the 10th and 11th centuries it was part of Russia under the rule of Kiev, then it became Hungarian. During the Tatar invasion of 1241–2 Mukachevo was burned to the ground.

Prince Fedor Koryatovich of Podolia owned the town between 1396 and 1414. He is credited with encouraging the development of local arts and crafts and with fostering trade; he also built a castle there. After his death Mukachevo was a jealously guarded prize of both the Transylvanian princely family of the Rakoczis and the Hapsburgs of Austria and it continued to change hands

between them until the 20th century.

In 1919, under the Treaty of St. Germain, Mukachevo was incorporated into Czechoslovakia. Then, in 1938, after the Munich treaty, it was occupied by German and Hungarian forces until 1944 when the Soviet army moved in. It has since been part of the Soviet Ukraine.

The town's population is multinational for Ukrainians, Russians, Jews, Hungarians, Czechs and Bulgarians have all made their homes here. Among Mukachevo's modern enterprises are a machine-tool plant, and furniture and ski factories which produce goods for export.

Palanok Castle, on a lofty hill to the south of the town. This ancient stronghold was built at the crossroads of important trade and military routes. Archaeological excavations on the site have yielded rich trophies dating from the Stone, Bronze and Iron Ages. The main buildings were constructed at the end of the 14th and the beginning of the 15th centuries under Prince Fedor Koryatovich, as mentioned above; King Sigizmund of Hungary had given him Mukachevo as a present. Three round towers date from that time but subsequent owners further enlarged and reinforced the castle. The Middle and Lower Castles were built in the 17th century.

The slopes of the rocky hill upon which the castle stands were once covered with fertile soil, and many fierce battles were fought for possession of Palanok. Princess Ilona Zrini of Hungary was besieged here for two and a half years, 1685–8, before the castle was finally taken by Austrian troops. In 1703–11 it was her son, Fernz Rakoczi II, who led the Hungarian uprising and then made the castle his headquarters. Peter the Great of Russia sent his ambassadors here and the coat-of-arms of the Rakoczi family still remains above the Old Fortress gates.

The Austrians later turned the castle into a prison with an awesome torture-chamber and after 1897 there were military barracks here. The castle was restored after World War II and it now houses both an agricultural school and the local museum. The museum is in the building of the 1624 armoury in the Middle Castle.

St. Martin's Chapel, Mira St. 51. Built in Gothic style in the 14th century, this is the oldest example of stone architecture in Transcarpathia. From the 16th century it served as the altar end of a Roman Catholic church, but the latter fell to ruin at the beginning of the 20th century, and the chapel stands in the yard of a church built in 1904. There are interesting stone carvings around the windows of the chapel and the stained-glass windows are very fine; it was restored in 1969.

Convent on Chernechya Gora (monks' hill). In the 11th century Anastasia, daughter of Prince Yaroslav the Wise of Kiev, came here to be married to King Andrei I of Hungary accompanied by a number of monks who were the first to inhabit this site. In the second part of the 16th century both a monastery and a convent were built here, but both were destroyed in the ensuing wars. The present Baroque structure dates from 1766–72. It is used by the Russian Orthodox and services are held in the church. The convent library has a collection of valuable books.

White Palace, Mira St. 28. This was built in the second half of the 17th century as the town residence of the Rakoczi family. When the town changed hands in 1711 the Palace became the property of the Austrian Emperor. Then, in 1728, when Mukachevo was presented to Count Schönborn of Germany, the Palace became his residence. In 1748 it was enlarged by the architect, Johann Neimann, and now it houses a school.

Lenin monument, Mira Sq. There is also a *War Memorial* on this square and the building of the City Council which was once the town hall.

Liberation monument (1970), in the town park

Mukachevo Civil Guards' monument, in the park, on the bank of R. Latoritsa. This was built in 1901 in honour of the Guards who took part in the Hungarian Revolution of 1848–9.

Munkacsy House, Mira St. 15. Mihaly Lib (1844–1900) was a famous Hungarian painter who was born in a house which stood on this site. He was made an honorary citizen of Mukachevo in 1880 and took the name of Munkacsy. The original house was burnt down in 1925 and this one was built in 1941. The memorial plaque was put up in 1969.

Zirka Hotel, Mira St. 20, TEL. 24–37

Svezda Restaurant, Mira St. 22, TEL. 14–57

Latoritsa Restaurant, Mira St. 2, TEL. 21–00

Krasnaya Gorka Restaurant, TEL. 23–26

G.P.O., Lenin St. 9

Aeroflot agency, Fedorova St. 4, TEL. 30–73

Souvenir shop, Mira St. 24, TEL. 15–00

Taxis, TEL. 14–92

VILJANDI

See Tallinn, p. 294

VILNIUS

Population—372,000 (1970)

Capital of the Lithuanian Soviet Socialist Republic

LITHUANIA

(Lithuanian: Lietuva)

Area: 65,000 sq. km.

Population—3,129,000 (1970) of which 79% are Lithuanians, 8·5% Russians, and 8·5% Poles.

Lithuania lies on the coast of the Baltic Sea in the north-west of the U.S.S.R. It is the most southerly of the three Baltic republics. Its principal cities are Vilnius (the capital), Klaipeda, and Kaunas.

The Lithuanians are one of the most ancient peoples of Europe. Their language is the only living one that is closely allied to Sanskrit.

The Lithuanian state dates from the beginning of the 13th century. From its foundation this state had to fight for its independence against the Teutonic Knights but at the same time it expanded to the east and south at the expense of declining

Kievan Russia. By the middle of the 15th century the Grand Duchy of Lithuania stretched from the Black Sea in the south almost to Moscow in the east. At that time the majority of its population were Orthodox Russians. One of the most outstanding Dukes of this period was Gediminas (1316–41) who conquered many Russian principalities to the south-east and established his capital in Vilnius.

In 1385 the Grand-Duke Jagaila (in Polish, Jagello) married the Polish Queen Jadviga and was himself elected King of Poland, thus uniting the two countries. In 1569 Lithuania and Poland were united in the Polish Commonwealth.

In 1795, after the third partition of Poland, most of Lithuania was included into the Russian Empire. During World War I Lithuania was occupied by the Germans and after the 1917 Revolution it seceded from Russia and became, in 1919, a parliamentary republic which in 1926 was turned into a dictatorship under President Smetona.

In 1940 the newly elected parliament proclaimed Lithuania a Soviet Republic which joined the U.S.S.R. two months later.

Here are a few words of Lithuanian:

hello	lobas (pr. lábas)
I am a tourist	aš turistas (ush tooristas)
please	prašau (prashaoo)
thank you	dëkoju (dekoyoo)
yes	taip (to rhyme with "ape")
no	ne
good	gerai
bad	blógai
I don't understand	aš nesuprantu (ush nesooprantoo)
I need an interpreter	man reikalingas vertejas (mun . . . verteyas)
goodbye	viso gero (visa gýaro)

Vilnius

This town stands at the confluence of the little R. Vilneles (Vilnios) and the Neries (Vilijos) and is surrounded by attractive hilly country.

Archaeologists have found that there have been settlements here since the 5th or 8th century A.D. There are some documents belonging to the Order of Teutonic Knights in existence which mention that in the time of Duke Mindaugas (in the middle of the 13th century) Vilnius was already the centre of the Lithuanian State, but the majority of the chronicles state that the city was founded by Gediminas, Grand-Duke of Lithuania (1316–41).

Legend has it that Gediminas spent a day hunting in the hills here. While resting he dreamed of a gigantic iron wolf standing on the hill where he lay, howling 'like a hundred wolves'. The High Priest (Christianity did not reach Lithuania until nearly the end of the 14th century) explained the dream as an omen sent by the gods which meant that Gediminas should build his capital city on the

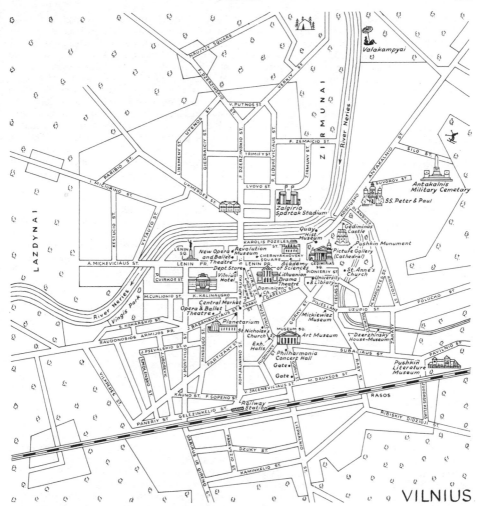

VILNIUS

place where he rested. Accordingly two castles were built, one in the valley and another on the hill.

A more practical reason for establishing the fortified city in this place was the necessity of blocking the way to the country of the Teutonic Knights and also of establishing a secure and efficient trading route both eastwards and westwards.

Old Vilnius consisted of two parts, the Grand-Duke's court and the castles belonging to his courtiers, and the city proper. In 1387 the city was granted the Magdeburg city rights, but the importance of Vilnius as a political centre considerably decreased after 1569 when Poland and Lithuania merged into one state, Pzecz Pospolita, according to the Liublin Union. The Grand-Dukes of Lithuania, who were at the same time Kings of Poland, ceased to reside in Vilnius, and spent most of their time in Warsaw. The 'golden freedom' of the nobility which characterised the Polish state took the place of law and order and no

one was safe from the persecutions and insults of his superiors.

Vilnius suffered a great deal during the 17th-century Russo-Polish wars over the Ukraine and Byelorussia. During the Northern War between Russia and Sweden at the beginning of the 18th century Vilnius fell to Sweden on several occasions but after the last partition of Poland it became part of the Russian Empire. In 1812 it was seized by Napoleon.

In 1831 and 1863 anti-Russian rebellions in Poland and Lithuania both had their effects on the life of Vilnius. In 1863 an underground committee directed the uprising in Lithuania from Vilnius. The leaders of the uprising, Zigmont Sierakauskas and Kastus Kalinauskas, were hanged in Lukiskiai (now Lenin) Sq.

After the Revolution of 1917 Soviet power was established in Lithuania, but only for a very short period (8 December 1918–2 April 1919). In 1919 Vilnius was captured by the Poles but was soon recaptured by the Red Army and freed in 1920. The same year the new Lithuanian Republic was annexed by Poland. In 1939 Vilnius once more became the capital of Lithuania which became part of the U.S.S.R. as a Soviet republic in 1940.

Vilnius Castle, more usually known as *Gediminas Castle*, stands on Gediminas Hill, overlooking the city. The name of Gediminas was given to the castle although in his time the fortress was only made of wood. There is a story about the castle's foundation:

Gediminas asked the pagan priestesses what should be done in order that the castle should never be taken by enemies. They advised him to find a mother willing to sacrifice her son. As it happened a number of mothers volunteered, but one succeeded in bringing her 18-year-old son to the construction site before the others, and ordered him into the pit where a huge rock was to be thrown as the castle's foundation stone. The young man did not resist; he just begged the Grand-Duke to allow him to put three questions to the priestesses before he died. The questions were: What is the lightest thing on earth, what is the sweetest thing on earth, and what is the hardest thing on earth? The priestesses replied, 'The lightest thing is a feather, the sweetest thing is honey, and the hardest is iron.' 'No,' said the youth, 'you're wrong. The lightest thing on earth is a child in its mother's arms, the sweetest is mother's milk, and the hardest is the heart of a mother who, without a single tear, sends her only son to his death.' The Grand-Duke was pleased with these words and spared the youth his life.

A stone castle was built here in 1420 by Grand-Duke Vytautus, but it was badly damaged in the Russo-Polish War of 1654–61 and was never rebuilt. Best preserved is the octangular Western Tower. The castle was last used for military purposes in 1705–8 when Peter the Great stored food and munitions here. The flag-staff rising from the centre of the flat roof of the tower carries the Lithuanian standard.

Of the Lower Castle which stood at the foot of the hill, on the southern side, nothing remains but the tower which was converted into the cathedral belfry. The *Cathedral* itself was founded in 1387 as the Church of St. Stanislav by Grand-Duke Jagaila after his marriage to Polish Queen Jadviga and after the subsequent introduction of Christianity to Lithuania. The site had previously been used for a pagan shrine where sacrifices were brought to the god Perkunas (whose name is still used for swearing in Lithuanian). From the tower the Chief Priest announced the will of the gods to the people and in the cellar grass-snakes were kept because they were considered holy by the Lithuanians.

The Cathedral has been restored and reconstructed several times. Between 1777 and 1801 it was fully reconstructed by the prominent Lithuanian architect, Laurinas Stuoka-Gucevicius. He managed to preserve several Baroque parts of the old Cathedral, such as the St.

Casimir Chapel with Italian frescoes by Palloni, although his building is in Renaissance style. Six sculptures by the Italian artist, Riggi, stand at the main façade, representing Abraham, Moses, and the four Evangelists. The sculptor's autograph is carved at the foot of the Moses statue. Also on the façade is a sculptured group showing Noah and his family sacrificing a lamb after the flood. The sculptures on the southern side are of the Grand-Dukes of Lithuania and on the northern side of some of the apostles and some Jesuits. The two sculptures by the altar are also by Riggi. There are interesting tombstones and memorial tablets on which the biographies of those they commemorate are carved.

The *Picture Gallery* is at present housed inside the Cathedral. It includes 16 paintings by the Italian, Viliani, and other paintings of the Italian schools of the late- and post-Renaissance periods, Flemish, German, and Dutch paintings of the 16th–18th centuries which are of no special significance, and works by Lithuanian artists from the 16th to the beginning of the 20th centuries.

Ruins of the City Wall and Tower, at the end of Boksto St. Very little remains of the city wall which was erected at the beginning of the 16th century. The area encircled by the wall totalled 120 hectares (300 acres), and the wall was 2·9 km. long, 12 m. high, and up to 3 m. thick.

Medininsky Gate (or Ausras Gate), at the end of Gorky St., one of the oldest streets in Vilnius and where about a third of the architectural monuments of the Old City are to be found. This gate is the only one remaining. It is called the Pointed Gate in all the Slav languages and in Polish, Osztra Vrata, probably because of the Gothic features in its earlier appearance. When approaching the gate from the outside, one can see a bas-relief of the coat-of-arms of the Grand Duchy of Lithuania held by two griffins. Above the gate is a *small chapel* founded by the Carmelites in the 17th century. The icon of the Virgin in the chapel is believed to be part of the loot taken by the Grand-Duke Olgherd during a raid on Khersones (Crimea) in 1363. It is considered to be miracle-working and a constant stream of people come there to pray. An inscription on the chapel wall reads, 'Mater misericordiae! Sub tuum praesidium confugimus!' The icon is about 2 m. high and 1·5 m. wide. The way to the chapel is through a side door and up the stairs.

The *Church of St. Theresa* is behind the Gate, on the right side of Gorky St. It was built in 1635–50 of imported materials such as Swedish granite and white marble. The adjoining chapel was built in the 18th century. The Rococo decoration is 18th century too. The building is 106 m. long and 15 m. wide.

The *Church of the Holy Spirit* (Russian Orthodox) was first built of wood by Orthodox monks in 1593–7, but was rebuilt in stone in 1633. In the crypt are relics of the Holy Martyrs of Vilno, Anthony, Ioann, and Eustaphy. They were three courtiers of a Grand-Duke, who secretly practised

Christianity while the country was still pagan. One of them had his legs broken up to the knees and was scalped, after which they were all hanged.

One of the priors of the monastery was Melety Smotritsky, author of the first Russian grammar book. The church was rebuilt in 1873 and was roofed with eastern-style cupolas.

The *Gate of the Basilian Monastery* is on the other side of the street. It was built in 1761 in Rococo style and the wrought-iron railing in the upper part of the gate is the work of local craftsmen. Through the gate are the Church of the Trinity and another 18th-century building that used to belong to the monastery.

Pyatnitsa (Pentecost) Church (Russian Orthodox), at the crossing of Gorky St. and Boksto St. This was 'the first stone chapel of the true God to be erected in the Lithuanian capital and land'. It was built in 1345 in place of a pagan temple by the orders of Maria, the Russian-born wife of Grand-Duke Olgherd. It was reconstructed several times because of fires; the most recent reconstruction took place in 1865. It was in this church that Peter the Great had an African Negro called Hannibal baptized in 1705. Hannibal took the name of Abraham, rose to become a full general in the Russian army, and is chiefly remembered for being the great-grandfather of Alexander Pushkin, the Russian poet.

There are some 15th–17th-century houses in Gorky Street. No. 12 and No. 14 have interesting Gothic decoration and No. 4 and No. 6 have typical 16th–17th-century attic storeys.

St. Nicholas's (Mikalojaus) Church, at the crossing of Kretingos and Lydos Streets. This is probably the oldest structure in the city. It was built in the early 15th century in Gothic style with some elements which are characteristic of Lithuanian national architecture.

The *Dominican Church*, at the crossing of Garelias and Giedris Streets. Originally founded in the 15th century, this church was rebuilt in the late Baroque style in the 18th century. The interior is richly decorated with reliefs, sculptures, frescoes, and other ornaments of both wood and metal. The main cupola is also painted with frescoes. The organ was built in 1776 by Casparini. The church has huge underground vaults, constructed on two floors. Here many parts of human bodies were mummified naturally due to the dryness of the place. The entrance to the vaults was sealed in 1849. The church was converted to serve as a prison in the first half of the 19th century.

St. Anne's Church, Tiesas St. This is one of the most interesting Gothic-style buildings in Lithuania. According to a chronicle, the church was built in 1500–1, but in 1563 the vaults collapsed and the church was finally reconstructed in 1581, the most important date in its history. Neither the name of its architect nor of its builders are known.

The yellow bricks, painted red, of which it is constructed are of 33 different shapes and the building is 22 m. long and 10 m. wide. The façade has three towers separated by pinnacles. Its decorations form rectangles and arcs and on a sunny day there is an interesting play of light and shade on its surface.

The belfry to the right of the church was designed by the architect, Chagin, who tried unsuccessfully to imitate the Gothic style of the church itself.

The Bernardines' Church, near St. Anne's. This church, founded in 1469, was rebuilt in 1550 and 1677 (having suffered from the fighting of 1655) and although Gothic in style it is at the same time a fine example of the 15th–16th-century religious architecture of the fortress type. The Baroque features were added after the reconstruction of 1677.

St. Michael's (Mikolas) Church, opposite St. Anne's and the Bernardines' Churches. This is the only Renaissance-style church in Vilnius. It was built in 1594 and of especial interest are the vaults decorated with geometric figures and stone rosettes. The tomb of coloured marble belonging to Chancellor Leon Sapieha, the church's founder, was placed in position in 1632. The building is at present used to house a display on architecture and construction methods. Its exterior is best observed from the side facing Svietimo Street.

SS. Peter and Paul's Church, at the end of Kosciusko and the beginning of Antakalnio Streets, in the Antakalnis (on the hill) region of Vilnius. Standing on the site of a pagan temple to Milda, the Goddess of Love, this is the most famed of the Baroque structures in Vilnius. It was built in 1668–74 and the decoration continued until 1684, but was never completed. At various times different Italian architects took part in the construction and decoration of the church, including Di Luca and Giovanni Maria Galli from Rome and Pietro Peretti from Milan. The exterior is quite simple. It is a Baroque-style building surrounded by a stone wall intended for defence purposes. There is an astonishing contrast between the exterior and the interior of the church. Inside every corner of the walls and ceiling are decorated with sculpture, bas-relief figures, and elaborate ornaments. There are well over 2000 sculptured and bas-relief figures, most of which were created by 200 craftsmen working under Peretti and Galli, but they were unable to complete their project fully and 120 years later another group of artists undertook the completion of the decoration. The Italians Beretti and Piano supervised the work until they realised that they could not equal Peretti and Galli's standards and so gave up the task.

By the entrance door stands the figure of Death, scythe in hand, trampling royal and papal crowns and bishops' mitres. The whole interior of the church is divided into small chapels, each with specific decorations. Most of the sculptures depict mythological, historical, or biblical scenes. Some of them tell the history of Vilnius and Lithuania and the themes of others were taken from the city life of the period when they were made. One of the most beautiful figures in the church is the statue of Mary Magdalene in the St. Ursula Chapel.

The frescoes on the vaults were painted by Martino de Alto Monte. The big crystal chandelier in the shape of a ship was hung before the altar in 1803. Recent research has shown that the strong but easily worked material from which the statues were made is composed of egg white, lime, and marble dust. The two big copper drums standing by the entrance door are Turkish war drums, captured in 1673.

The *Governor-General's Palace,* Kutuzov Sq., not far from Gorky St. In the 14th century this was the site of the Episcopal Palace. It suffered several fires and was rebuilt. At the end of the 18th century and the beginning of the 19th, the palace was among the finest buildings in the city. Napoleon stayed here after the French entered Vilnius in 1812 and at the end of the Russo-French War of 1812–13 it was used as Field Marshal Kutuzov's residence (hence the name of the square where it stands).

In 1820–32 the palace was wholly rebuilt in Empire style following a project by Stasov and other architects.

University, Kutuzov Sq. The University was founded in 1579 as Academia et Universitas Vilnensis, and by 1586 it had already 700 students enrolled in its two faculties of philosophy and theology. The law faculty was opened in 1644 and the medical faculty in 1781. The central building of the university is a complex structure which has existed since the 16th century but which was rebuilt and reconstructed several times since then. The *University library* which occupies the middle part of the building has a good collection of old manuscripts and books. In the buildings on the south side are the *Hall of Columns* (built in 1817) and the *Graduation Hall.* The *Observatory* (1782) is also interesting. In 1944, when the Germans were leaving the city, they set fire to the University buildings but these were saved by the efforts of people living nearby.

Synagogue, Komjaunimo St. 41

Local Museum, Traku St. 2; open 1–7, closed Tues. Material shows the history of Vilnius. Gediminas Castle is also open to the public under the same administration.

Historical Museum, Karolis Pozelos St. 32/1. Items on display start from the second half of the 19th century.

Picture Gallery, in the Cathedral, Gediminas Sq.

Exhibition Halls, Museyaus St., near the *Art Museum.* This building of glass and concrete was completed in 1967. There is an art salon on the ground floor and a shop selling artists' materials; on the first floor are three exhibition halls, the largest of which is 1000 sq. m. There is also an open-air sculpture exhibition here.

Art Museum, Gorky St. 55

Mickiewiez Museum, Pilies Lane 11. Adam Mickiewiez was a Polish poet of the 19th century.

Planetarium, Basanaviciaus St. 15, on the corner of Komjaunimo St.

Opera and Ballet Theatre, Basanaviciaus St. 13; TEL. 2–18–87

Lithuanian Drama Theatre, Lenin Prospect 4

Russian Drama Theatre, Kapsukas St. 4

Philharmonia Concert Hall, Gorky St. 69, TEL. 2–03–78. Here on 15–16 December, 1918, Soviet Power for Lithuania was proclaimed.

Central Park, Pioneriu St. 8

Zoo, Zverinas St.

Zalgirio Spartak Stadium, Eidukeviciaus St. 3

Jaunimo Stadium, Lentipiuvie St. 19

Darbo Reserve Stadium, Vingis Park

Vilnius Hotel & Restaurant, Lenin Prospect 20, TEL. 2–36–65. This is an Intourist Hotel and also the home of the main Intourist office in Vilnius (TEL. 2–41–57).

Neringa Hotel & Restaurant, Lenin Prospect 23, TEL. 2–05–16. This is another Intourist hotel.

Astoria Hotel, Gorky St. 59/2

Narutis Hotel, Gorky St. 24, TEL. 2–38–80

Zvaigzde Hotel, Komjaunimo St. 63, TEL. 2–09–26

Palanga Restaurant, L. Gira St. 1/16

Sesupe Restaurant, Lenin Prospect 22; national dishes served here. There are also good restaurants at the airport and at the railway station.

Neringa Café, Lenin Prospect 23

Literaty Svetain (Authors' Club) Café, Lenin Prospect 1

Ruta Café, Lenin Prospect 22

Snaige (snowflake) Icecream Parlour, L. Gira St. 9/2

Lokys Café, Antolsky St. 8. A very popular café in a restored 15th century cellar. Many other old buildings in the neighbourhood are also being restored.

Kregzdute Café, Antakalinio St. 51

Saulute Café, Kestucio St. 35

Tauras Café, P. Cvirkos Street 30/8

Bank, Lenin Prospect 6

G.P.O., Lenin Prospect 9

Department Store, Lenin Prospect 18

Books, Lenin Prospect 13; foreign publications, Lenin Prospect 4; books on art, Lenin Prospect 62

Souvenirs, Lenin Prospect 31

Art Salon, at the crossing of Kapsukas and Girka St.

Folk Art, Lenin Prospect 1

Central Market, at the crossing of Basanaviciaus and Komjaunimo St.

Collective Farm Market, Eidukeviciaus St.

Taxi Ranks, railway station, Gediminas Sq., Gogol St. 2, Gorky St., and Kosciusko St. 34

Trakai

Trakai is a small town lying 28 km. west of Vilnius. It can be reached by rail and by a good road. It is situated in an area which has inspired many Lithuanian poets and which is now one of the most popular recreation areas near the Lithuanian capital.

The town is located on a long, narrow peninsula which separates the lakes Galvé. Totoriskés, and Bernadinai and there are about 30 other smaller lakes in the vicinity. Trakai was founded in the 14th century by Duke Gediminas and was his capital for some time. Then it was the seat of one of his seven sons, Kestutis, who later built a new castle by Lake Galvé in New Trakai, abandoning his father's less strongly fortified castle in Old Trakai. Prince Vitautas, son of Kestutis, built in his turn a new castle on an island in Lake Galvé. It was completed at the beginning of the 15th century. In the 16th century the town lost its importance and the castles were turned into prisons.

The *ruins of the first castle* are still there and the *castle of Vitautas* has largely been restored, partly in 1929 but mostly in the 1960s. The reception hall (21 m. long by 9 m. wide) can be visited as can a number of rooms and towers. There are very few medieval castles on Soviet territory and Trakai attracts tourists from far away.

The *palace* beside the lake which is now used as a sanatorium was built in the 19th century and belonged to the Counts of Tyszkiewicz.

As one enters Trakai by the road from Vilnius, the *ruins of a 17th-century Bernardine Monastery* can be seen on a hill to the right. In the town itself is the Roman Catholic *Church of Vitautas* and by the gates of the town park are the *ruins of a Dominican monastery and a church.*

Karaim Church (Karaimu kinesé), Meluikaité St. The Karaites were Jews from the Crimea who settled in Trakai in the 15th century and whose descendants still live here. The church was built in the 19th century.

Local Museum, open 11–6, closed Tues.

Restaurant

Boats can be hired.

VINNITSA

Population—215,000 (1971)

The town probably derives its name from the old Slavic word, 'vyeno', meaning 'transferred property'. It was founded in the 14th century and stands on the R. Youzhny (South) Bug. First it was Lithuanian but in 1569 it became Polish and, commanded by Bogdan Khmelnitsky, it played an important role in the 1648–54 war against the Poles. In 1793 it passed to Russia.

The town's first castle, built to protect Vinnitsa from the Turks and the Tatars, stood on the high left bank of the river, opposite the old town bridge. At the beginning of the 17th century the first stone houses, a Catholic church, and a school were built in the centre of the town and surrounded by a stone wall, 'muri', remains of which can be seen near Lenin Street 15, where the town archives are now kept.

During World War II 40% of the town was destroyed. The occupation lasted for 970 days and during this time many citizens suffered torture and a total of 42,000 lost their lives. Little is now left of the old buildings in the town centre. Kozitsky Street is interesting because one can see there houses showing the changing architectural

styles of this century; no. 18 is in the Constructivist style of the 1930s and there are others in Empire style. No. 16 is an old water tower which is kept as a historical monument.

The main thoroughfare is Lenin Street and the central department store and the Youzhny Bug Hotel are on Gagarin Square. Among the more impressive of the new buildings is the Lyalya Ratushnaya Pioneer Palace, built in 1969 with facilities, including a swimming pool, for 3000 children. During the war Lyalya Ratushnaya left her studies at Moscow University to serve with the resistance for four years; she was killed on the eve of the liberation of Vinnitsa from the enemy.

The Pirogov Regional Hospital was opened in 1914 and now has beds for 600 patients, and the Pirogov Medical Institute for 2500 students was built in 1931. There is also a pedagogical institute in Vinnitsa. The town is noted for its food processing and its light industry; it has electro-technical and fertiliser factories, and in the surrounding region sugar-beet is both grown and refined.

Vinnitsa celebrated its 600th anniversary in 1962.

Dominican Monastery, Lenin St. This monastery was built in 1634, but was converted into a Russian Orthodox church in 1774. It is now used as a sports club.

Muri Jesuit Monastery was built in the 17th–18th centuries. It originally consisted of a fortified monastery-house but now only the ruins remain.

Capuchin Monastery, Lenin St. This monastery was founded in 1760 and one building now serves as a lecture hall.

St. George's Church, Starye Khutora. This wooden church was built in 1726.

St. Nicholas's Church, in the old part of the city; one turns down from the main road just past the Lenin monument and the church is across the bridge, on the other side of the river. It was built, without nails, in 1746.

Local Museum, Lenin St. 11a. Open 10–6; closed Mon. The museum is in a new building, next to the Dominican Monastery building. There is a kremlin made entirely of sugar on display.

Kotsubinsky's House, Deputatskaya St. 13. This is where the Ukrainian writer, Kotsubinsky, was born and lived as a child.

Lenin monument, Lenin St., in front of the large, new building housing the town's administrative offices.

In *Kozitsky Children's Park* there is an obelisk commemorating World War II, an Eternal Flame, and a monument to those who fell during the 1917–19 Civil War. Another *monument* of granite on the left bank of the river commemorates the victory of the Cossack Colonel Ivan Bogun over the Poles in 1651. It was unveiled in 1954.

Space Exploration monument, in front of the entrance to Gorky Park, in the centre of the town. This monument is in the form of an arch and a rocket.

War Memorial, along the Kiev highway

Air Force Pilots' monument, on the Khmelnitsky road. This monument is of an aeroplane on a pedestal.

Sadovsky Musical and Drama Theatre, Dzerzhinsky St. 13

Philharmonia Concert Hall

Gorky Park, Liebknecht St. 1

Yuzhny Bug Hotel (Intourist) and Restaurant, Gagarin Sq., TEL. 246–56, 238–76

Zhovtnyevaya (October) Hotel (Intourist), Pirogova St. 2; Intourist TEL. 246–56

Ukraina Hotel and Restaurant, Lenin St.

G.P.O., Kozitsky St., where it crosses Lenin St.

Pirogovo

Formerly Vyshenky. This is on the outskirts of the town. 1 km. from the main road is the *Pirogov Museum*, in the house occupied by the Russian surgeon from 1866 until his death in 1881. Open 10–7, closed Wed. Nikolai Pirogov (1810–81) was accepted as a medical student at Moscow University when he was only 14 and he qualified at 18. From there he went on to Tartu University where, at 22, he took his Ph.D. and where, four years later, he became professor of surgery. He acquired world fame when in 1841, and upon the basis of 15 years' work, his 'Surgical Anatomy' with an accompanying surgical atlas was published in St. Petersburg. In 1847, during the Caucasian War, he became the first doctor in the world to use ether as an anaesthetic during operations in the field.

1 km. from the house is *Pokrovsky Church* which was built in 1882 over Pirogov's glass tomb; this is now in the crypt. The surgeon's body was embalmed by a pupil of his, Dr. Vyvodtsev, and was then dressed for burial in the uniform of an army doctor. Pirogov's son, also called Nikolai, was buried in the same crypt and there is a gravestone set in the floor to mark the spot.

Tolchin

In the years 1796–7 this town served as the headquarters of Alexander Suvorov. The *palace* of the Ukrainian hetman Pototsky is also in Tolchin.

Timonovka

There is a *Suvorov Museum* in this village, in the house where the great general wrote his book, 'The Art of Victory'.

Voronovitsa

In this village, 18 km. from Vinnitsa, is the 17th-century *house* where Alexander Mozhaisky (1825–90) lived from 1869–76. He was the Russian inventor who in 1881 was credited with having constructed the first full-size aeroplane. It was tested in 1882–5 and there are indications that once it even left the ground. It possessed all the essential parts of modern planes—body, wings, motor, and undercarriage. There is now a school in the house.

VLADIMIR and SUZDAL

The ancient towns of Vladimir and Suzdal are within easy reach of Moscow, but require at least a two-day visit to do them justice. All the churches are remarkable for their finish and sophistication. They were mostly built between about 1150 and 1240, at which date the Tatars gained control of this part of Russia.

Frequent trains leave Moscow from the Kursk railway station and one can stay at the Vladimir Hotel and use it as a base from which to go by road to Suzdal, Bogolyubovo, and the Pokrovskaya Church on the Nerl.

The Moscow – Vladimir Road

Leave Moscow by Entusiastov Prospect which runs into Kazansky Chaussée.

(The numbers refer to km. from Moscow.)

22: BALASHIKA; ZHELEZNODOROZHNY

To the south of the road is a circular *church* with two bell-towers standing near an old, columned mansion which now houses a scientific research institute.

52: BOGORODSK

Turning to Noginsk which lies 8 km. north of the main road. There, in Rabochaya Ul., is a large *church* in a bad state of repair.

63: KLYAZMA

On R. Klyazma. *Church* with a cemetery to the south of the road.

68: PAVLOVSKIYE POSAD

Church on the south side and *eating house* on the north side of the road.

95: KIRZHACHSK

On R. Kirzhachsk. There is a *restaurant* and a *filling station* in this village.

101: POKROV

Pokrovskaya Church (18th century, enlarged in 1853), on the south side of the main road, was reopened for services during World War II. On the north side of the road are *Druzhba Restaurant* and *Vstrecha Café*. *Troitskaya Church* (1836) is closed.

117: THE CHURCH OF JOHN THE BAPTIST, open for services, stands on the south side of the road.

120: PETUSHKI

Red brick *Uspenskaya Church* (1910) stands to the north of the road. It is open for services and over the door is the inscription: 'Faith without work is dead.'

150: LAKINSK

This small town was formerly called Undola, but was renamed in memory of a revolutionary killed near the textile factory in 1905. On the side of the road is *St. Sergius' Church* which has been closed and which has a cemetery behind it. *Kolokshenka eating house* and a *beer hall*.

161: VORSHA

Alexander Nevsky Church, built of brick with five cupolas, stands on the north side of the road.

164: *Lukovskovo House Museum*

168: KOLOKSHA

Near here is the village of Zherekovo where in 1647 lived a princess of the Vsevolozhsky family. She was so beautiful that she was chosen from 200 fair maidens by Tsar Alexei Mikhailovich as his bride. When she learned of her good fortune, she fainted with joy, but this was understood to be a sign of epilepsy and she was exiled to Siberia with her parents until 1653.

174: BOGOLYUBOVO (See below, p. 329)

184: VLADIMIR

Service station on the right on the way into the city.

Vladimir

Population—234,000 (1970)

This ancient city stands on the left bank of R. Klyasma.

According to the chronicles, Prince Vladimir Monomakh who later became Grand-Prince of Kiev founded this city bearing his name in 1108. It was then designed to serve as a frontier fortress guarding the north-east of his domain. The original fortress was built of earth and wood and had a wall 2·5 km in circumference.

Vladimir's heir, Yuri Dolgoruki, founder of Moscow, turned his attentions to these lands only during the last years of his reign when he understood that the Kievan State was losing its economic and political influence. Vladimir owed its rise and subsequent period of glory to Dolgoruki's son, Andrei Bogolubsky (god-fearing). He realised that in order to unite all the lands of Russia, the Grand-Princes would have to centralize and consolidate their power, but to achieve this the seat of power should be transferred from Kiev further up, to the north-east. Dolgoruki opposed his son's decision to go north, fearing that without him he would be unable to defend his throne. Nevertheless in 1158 Andrei Bogolubsky, with his family and household, left the south secretly at dead of night under the protection and guidance of a holy icon which was said to have been brought from Constantinople and to have been painted by St. Luke himself. Later, under the name of Our Lady of Vladimir it became the most revered object in northern Russia.

Having chosen Vladimir for his capital and settled there, Andrei strengthened its defences and welcomed architects, icon-painters, jewellers, and other craftsmen to beautify it. Dolgoruki died in 1157 and Andrei became Grand-Prince of Kiev. He wished to remain in Vladimir, but in order to hold his title he marched against his opponents in Kiev in 1169, defeated them, and appointed a governor of his own. He himself was killed by the nobles in 1174 because they could no longer tolerate his autocratic government. He was succeeded by his brother, Vsevolod III, who managed to suppress the nobles with the citizens' help. During his rule (1176–1212) the Rostov-Suzdal princedom with Vladimir as its capital reached the peak of its political power.

In 1237 the Tatars under Baty-Khan (Ghengis-Khan's grandson) invaded Russia. Vladimir, like dozens of other Russian cities before and afterwards, suffered heavy damage, and she never regained her status as a major city because the Princes of Moscow received the title of Grand-Prince from the Tatars, and Moscow accordingly became the political centre of the lands of Russia. In spite of this for the next 200 years the nominal seniority among Russian cities belonged to Vladimir. It had as its coat-of-arms a crowned lion rampant on a red field and it was here, in the Uspensky (Assumption) Cathedral, that the grand-princes were crowned, and it was here that the Russian princes held council.

Between the 15th and the 17th centuries Vladimir's importance was mainly due to her position as a centre of trade and transport. It has now taken a new, industrial appearance and produces tractors, electrical machinery, and chemicals. There are also food and light industries.

IIIrd International Street, the city's main thoroughfare, follows the route of the pre-revolutionary Vladimirka Road along which exiles and prisoners were sent to Siberia, usually on foot.

Zolotiye Vorota (the Golden Gate) (1158–64) stands in the centre of the city today. It is a unique masterpiece of ancient Russian defence architecture and was built to serve as a powerful tower guarding the western part of Vladimir. It was also used as the ceremonial entrance gate to the city. While building his capital, Prince Andrei Bogolubsky tried to copy the architecture of the southern capital of Kiev as much as possible. The Golden Gate of Vladimir was built to resemble the Golden Gate of Kiev of which only the ruins remain.

It is said that when the tower was finished, crowds of people came to wonder at the beauty of its construction. However the mortar was still damp and the gate fell, trapping twelve people. Prince Andrei prayed to the Virgin, accusing himself of the death of innocent souls, and the general surprise was great when the gates were lifted to reveal all twelve safe and sound.

During the Tatar invasion of 1238 the gate was badly damaged, but it was reconstructed in the 15th century. It was the custom that on the principal religious holidays processions would wend their way from the Archbishop's Palace to the Uspensky Cathedral and from there to the Golden Gate, and costly embroideries were hung on cords along the route. The originals which perished in the great fire of 1183 were of cloth-of-gold and pearl. There are now no traces of the other four gates of ancient Vladimir.

In the 18th century, in the course of general reconstruction, the church surmounting the gate was rebuilt, and the side walls had to be reinforced when the adjoining town walls were pulled down. The gate itself is a gigantic cube pierced by a high arch. There is a second, lower, arch inside where, on the east side, can be seen the upper pair of the huge iron loops upon which the gates hung; the lower ones are below ground level now. The gates themselves were plated with sheets of gilded copper, hence the name.

The building now forms part of the *Local Museum* and houses the section dealing with military

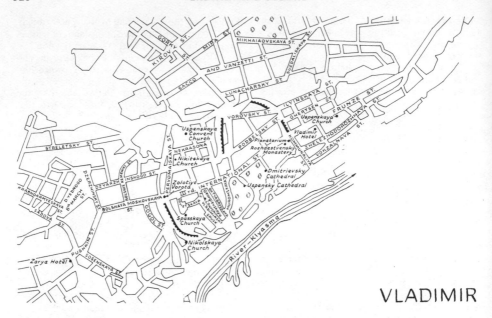

VLADIMIR

history. Open 11–5.30; closed Thurs.

The *Uspensky (Assumption) Cathedral* (1160), IIIrd International Street 56, was the most important building in Prince Andrei's new capital and the one upon which he chose to bestow 'a tithe of the income from trade'. It was so richly decorated that it was compared with the Temple of Solomon and for centuries it served as Russia's principal cathedral. The original outer walls were frescoed and had gilded half-columns. It was here that all the princes of Vladimir and of Moscow were crowned until the time of Ivan III (1440). In the first quarter of the 14th century the cathedral was the seat of the Metropolitan Bishop of All Russia.

Exquisite proportions, faultless masonry, and beautifully finished architectural details made the cathedral a masterpiece of ancient Russian architecture. The best architects of Russia and Europe were summoned by Prince Andrei to Vladimir to contribute to the work and there is some evidence that Frederick Barbarossa may have sent builders to work on the project. When at the end of the 15th century the Italian architect, Aristotle Fioravente, was building the Uspensky Cathedral in Moscow's Kremlin for Ivan III, he chose the cathedral at Vladimir as a model.

In 1185–9, after the terrible fire, Prince Andrei's brother, Vsevolod III, erected a two-storey gallery around three sides of the structure as the old limestone walls had been irreparably calcined. At the same time, the east end of the cathedral was enlarged. Thus the original building was encased and the old walls were pierced with arches so large that what was left simply formed pillars inside the body of the new structure. The cathedral was given four additional cupolas and had room for a congregation of 4000. In 1238 it suffered at the

hands of the Tatars who set it on fire together with the people who were seeking sanctuary within its walls. With time the frescoes gradually became dilapidated and in 1408 Andrei Rublyev and Daniel Chornei came from Moscow to replace the earlier decorations and to paint the iconostasis. In 1411 the Tatars again attacked, ransacked the cathedral, and again set fire to it. They carried off the original flooring of copper plates framed with ceramic tiles.

Reconstruction began in the 18th century, the Baroque iconostasis was installed in 1774, and work continued until the end of the 19th century. Since the 1917 Revolution the building has been constantly in the hands of artists and architects. The 12th- and 13th-century frescoes, including fragments of the 12th-century 'Last Judgement' on the western wall, have recently been restored. In the centre, under the choir gallery, are the unique 'Last Judgement' frescoes of Andrei Rublyev (c. 1360–1430). Particularly noteworthy is his depiction of heaven and the saints being summoned by St. Peter. There are other frescoes by this great master on the altar pillars. The Uspensky Cathedral was the burial place of the princes of Vladimir, including Andrei Bogolubsky and Vsevolod III. The tomb of Alexander Nevsky is also here, on the right as one faces the Holy Gates. The tomb on the left is that of Prince Georgi, grandson of Vladimir Monomakh.

Beside the Uspensky Cathedral stands a three-storeyed *belfry* with a pointed golden spire. It was built in 1810 to replace a 16th-century belfry which had been destroyed by lightning. The building linking it to the cathedral dates from 1862.

The *Dmitrievsky Cathedral* (1194–7) stands close to the Uspensky. It was once enclosed by the courtyard of Vsevolod III's palace and was used for his private services. The tsar built it in honour of his patron saint and his new-born son, Dmitri, and when it was finished he enriched it with relics of St. Dmitri specially brought here from Saloni-ka. It is one of the best finished structures of ancient Vladimir and almost two-thirds of the total wall area is richly decorated with bas-reliefs of fantastic creatures, trees, and human figures including King David, a series depicting the labours of Hercules, and one figure that is thought to be Vsevolod himself holding his little son. Inside the church are some 12th-century frescoes by Byzantine and Russian painters. The monument and grave to the right of the door inside the cathedral belong to Count Roman Vorontsov (1717–83), the first governor of Vladimir.

In 1834 Nicholas I ordered that the church be restored to its 'original appearance' and although literal adherence to his command meant the loss of some valuable frescoes, the cathedral's purity of line is now unspoiled. It is the most beautiful building in Vladimir and indeed among the loveliest in the country. Certainly it is the best example of ancient white-stone construction where carved decorations play an important role. Now the cathedral is part of the Local Museum where materials on the architecture of Vladimir are exhibited. In winter the key may be obtained from the Local Museum.

The white battlemented walls of *Rozhdestvensky (Nativity) Monastery* (1191–6) stand to the east of Dmitrievsky Cathedral. Until the middle of the 16th century it was Russia's most important monastery. Many future bishops served here in their early years and it was here that the oldest existing Russian chronicle, the Lavrentyevskaya, was kept. Prince Alexander Nevsky (1220–63) who defeated the Swedes and the Germans in 1240 and 1242 was buried here and his remains were transferred to St. Petersburg in 1724 at the instigation of Peter the Great. In 1744 the monastery was closed and in 1864 the main church was dismantled stone by stone and a full-sized replica of it was later made by local architects.

Nikolskaya Church, just outside the monastery wall, was built in the 18th century and now serves as a *planetarium.*

In Vladimirsky Spusk, to the north-west of Vladimir, stands the *Uspenskaya (Assumption) Convent Church* (1200–2), built of small bricks instead of the usual limestone as the cathedral church of the Convent of the Assumption (and now the only building of it remaining), founded by Maria Shvarnovo, wife of Vsevolod III. It was later called Knyagynin, meaning 'princess's', and ever afterwards the convent was used as the burial place of the princesses of Vladimir. The whole building and the frescoes too were restored after World War II. On the south-west side are paintings of the princesses, depicted as saints. The church is now used as the headquarters of the organisation in charge of the restoration of ancient buildings in and around Vladimir.

The Baroque church with the attractive belfry standing nearby is *Nikitskaya Church.* It was built between 1762 and 1765, added to in the 19th century, and was restored in 1970.

The *Uspenskaya (Assumption) Church* (1644–9), Frunze St. This church has five cupolas and a belfry and is surrounded by other, smaller buildings. It was built with the donations of rich merchants and is notable for its interesting brickwork.

Spasskaya (or Spasopreobrazhenskaya) Church, Sovietskaya St., up the hill, not far from the Golden Gate. Spasskaya Church was built in 1778 on the site of a church of 1164. In the same street is *Georgievskaya Church* which was built in 1784 on the site of a limestone cathedral of 1129 which Yuri Dologoruki dedicated to St. Yuri the Russian name for St. George). It now houses a radio club.

The red brick church by the Golden Gate was built at the beginning of this century and was used by the Old Believers, a large sect which separated itself from the Russian Orthodox Church in the 17th century.

Local Museum, IIIrd International St. 64. Open 10–4.40; closed Thurs. Among the exhibits is the white sepulchre of Alexander Nevsky whose remains were transferred from Vladimir to St. Petersburg in 1724. Also here are the Gospel and a piece of a winter coat which belonged to Prince Pozharsky who drove the Poles out of Moscow and who was buried in Suzdal. There is a rich collection of old manuscripts and books, rare old Russian paintings, and weapons.

Planetarium, IIIrd International St., in the 18th century Nikolskaya Church near the corner of Rozhdestvensky Monastery.

Exhibition of Economic Achievements, Mira St. Open from May until October.

In front of the Baroque Nikitskaya Church is a garden where there is a *bust of the writer, Gogol,* painted blue. Near the Golden Gate is a *bust of P. I. Lebedyev-Polyansky* (1881–1948), literary critic.

Lunacharsky Drama Theatre, Lenin St. 3

Music House, Pushkin Sq.

Vladimir Hotel & Restaurant, IIIrd International St. 74, TEL. 26–14 or 30–42

Klyasma Hotel & Restaurant, Lenin St. 2, TEL. 22–72

Dieticheskaya Restaurant, Frunze St. 88

Café, IIIrd International St. 6

G.P.O., Podbyelskovo St. 2

Long-distance Telephone calls office, IIIrd International St. 24

Central Bookshop, IIIrd International St. 34

Bogolyubovo

This village lies 10 km. from Vladimir and is best reached by road.

Its history goes back to 1158 when Prince Andrei Bogolubsky secretly left Kiev and went north. According to the legend, his horses stopped where Bogolyubovo is now and would go no further. Later the Virgin appeared to Prince Andrei in a dream and asked him to build a church here. Accordingly he founded the *Rozhdestven-*

skaya (Nativity of the Virgin) Church and subsequently built his new 'city of stone' which he called Bogolyuovo, his own surname, although whether he was called after the city or the city after him is not clear. Apart from the legend, the reason for building the city was Andrei Bogolubsky's desire to create a stronghold of autocratic power against the rebellious nobles. Certainly it was worthy of being a royal residence. Of the decoration of the church alone the chronicler wrote, 'It was hard to look at all the gold.'

The chronicle says that Prince Andrei 'hath built himself that city of stone' but until recently scientists thought that the chronicler had exaggerated and that the actual city was built of wood with only the towers of stone. After the prince's assassination the city of Bogolyubovo lost its status of royal residence and gradually fell into oblivion. The Tatar invasion and numerous fires left little standing. It was only in 1954 that the words of the chronicler were proved to be true. Excavations revealed the foundations of 12th-century white-stone walls.

Rozhdestvenskaya Church survived the earlier period of destruction but it suffered in the 17th century when an ignorant priest ordered that the windows be made wider; as a result in 1722 the building collapsed. Architects think that the church which was restored in the 18th century on the old foundations closely resembles the original structure. It stands well to the left of the big cathedral which now dominates the territory.

Beside the Rozhdestvenskaya Church and adjoining it is an entrance gate and a staircase tower which are all that remain of Andrei Bogolubsky's *12th-century palace*; these are interesting as they are unique examples of early Russian secular architecture. On the inside walls the story of Prince Andrei's death had been painted. Legend has it that the assassins of the prince, who was later canonized by the Russian Orthodox Church, were put into tarred coffins. These are still supposed to be floating in the swamps near Bogolyubovo and it is said that the weeping and wailing of the evil-doers can still be heard at night. These buildings are open as a museum, 10–4, closed Mon.

The *Uspensky (Assumption) Cathedral* (1866) is the largest construction on the territory. The belfry at the gate was built between 1820 and 1840. On the opposite side of the big cathedral is a *16th–17th-century refectory*, now used as a bank. The holy well dates from the foundation of Bogolyubovo, but the existing stonework is 18th century.

The *Pokrovskaya (Intercesssion) Church* on the R. Nerl is less than a mile south-east of Bogolyubovo. To get there, turn right from the main road about 200 yds. before reaching the churches. The path leads under a railway bridge and across the fields, making a pleasant walk in summer, although in winter the snow is likely to be deep. The little white church is the loveliest of all that have survived from the days of Vladimir's great-

ness, and stands in the meadows, reflected in the slow moving waters of the Nerl. The perfectly proportioned, faultlessly finished structure was built in 1165 in memory of Prince Andrei's son, Izyaslav, who was killed in a victorious campaign against the Kama Bulgars.

The site of the church is usually flooded in the spring, so the builders put the limestone foundation into a 2 m. trench and on this erected walls 4 m. high which they filled and covered with earth, forming a hill. The hill was then paved with limestone in which special drainage holes were made. On this 6 m. foundation they proceeded to erect the church walls. It is interesting that the foundations of the 150 m. Leningradskaya Hotel in Moscow are not so deep as those of this 20 m. church.

The church is well preserved with the exception of the frescoes, the last traces of which disappeared 100 years ago. At the end of the 18th century the Bishop of Vladimir gave his permission for the peasants of the village of Novoye to pull down the church and use the stone to build a church in their own village. When the first worker climbed the cupola to take down the cross, particles of gold paint from the cross got into his eyes and he cried out that he had been blinded. When he was helped to the ground, he regained his sight and what appeared to be a miracle saved the church from destruction.

SUZDAL

Suzdal is situated on R. Kamenka, just 35 km. north of Vladimir. Vladimir was once its younger rival but now is superior in most things except the wealth of ancient architecture Suzdal still possesses. There are more than 50 examples of church and secular architecture dating from the middle of the 12th to the middle of the 18th century. The town's coat-of-arms, a falcon in a prince's crown, bears witness to the grandeur of its past; only the red part of the background shows its connection with Vladimir, while all the other townships in the region repeat the crowned lion of Vladimir above their own particular symbol.

The town was first mentioned in chronicles of 1024 and there are several theories concerning the origin of its name. It was once 'Suzhdal', indicating that perhaps it was here that the princes meted judgement. Until the middle of the 11th century it was, however, nothing more than a small settlement. Several of the streets even today have names derived from the names of the old Slavic gods—Yarunova St. and Kupala St. among them.

As early as 990 Prince Vladimir of Kiev came to Suzdal and established a missionary bishop there who later built a church. From 1096 onwards Suzdal is always mentioned in the chronicles as being a town. Its heart was the Kremlin, fortified with earthen walls of which traces still remain. At the very end of the 11th century builders from Kiev constructed Suzdal's first stone church there.

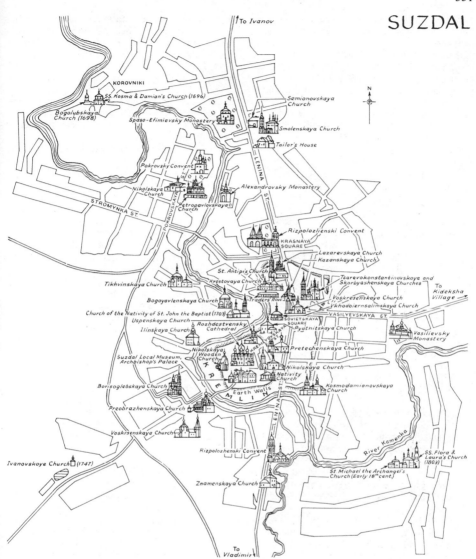

To Ivanov

KOROVNIKI

SS. Kosma & Damian's Church (1696)

Bogolubskaya
Church (1698)

Semionovskaya
Church

Spaso-Efimievsky Monastery

Smolenskaya Church

Tailor's House

Pokrovsky Convent

LENINA ST.

Nikolskaya
Church

STROMYNKA ST.

POKROVSKAYA

Petropavlovskaya
Church

Alexandrovsky Monastery

Rizpolozhienski Convent

KRASNAYA
SQUARE

Lazarevskaya Church

Kazanskaya Church

Tikhvinskaya Church

St. Antip's Church

Krestovaya Church

Tsarevokonstantinovskaya and
Skorbyashenskaya Churches

To
Kideksha
Village

Bogoyavlenskaya Church

Traders' Row

Voskresenskaya Church

Vkhodoiernsalimskaya Church

VASILYEVSKAYA ST.

Church of the Nativity of St. John the Baptist (1703)
Uspenskaya Church

Ilinskaya Church

Rozhdestvensky
Cathedral

SOVIETSKAYA
SQUARE

Pyatnitskaya Church

Vasilievsky
Monastery

Suzdal Local Museum,
Archbishop's Palace

Nikolskaya
Wooden
Church

Pretechenskaya Church

Nikolskaya Church

Borisoglebskaya Church

Nativity
Church

Kosmodamianovskaya
Church

K R E M L I N

Earth Walls

Preobrazhenskaya Church

LENINA ST.

Voskrsenskaya Church

River Kamenko

SS. Flora &
Laura's Church
(1803)

Ivanovskoye Church (1747)

Rizpolozhenski Convent

St Michael the Archangel's
Church (Early 18th cent.)

Znamenskaya Church

To
Vladimir

Prince Yuri Dolgoruki (who later founded Moscow) decided in 1125 to make Suzdal his capital, but after his death, his son Andrei Bogolubsky moved to Vladimir in the vain hope of escaping the hostility of the nobles. This was the beginning of the rivalry between the two neighbouring towns, which gradually led to Vladimir's superiority.

In 1238 Suzdal was seized and burnt by the Tatars, but it was soon rebuilt and in 1328, when the seat of the grand-princes was transferred to Moscow, Suzdal became the centre of the political struggle against Moscow's domination. It held this position until Grand-Prince Vasili annexed it to Moscow at the end of the 14th century. Although it lost its former political and economic importance, the town was still one of the major religious centres of northern Russia. At the end of the 16th century local builders restored and added to the existing buildings, especially the Kremlin, the town walls, and the monasteries, but their work was damaged by the invading Poles and then again by the Tatars, and also by recurrent fires, notably that of 1644. At the end of the 17th century more building work was undertaken including the Archbishop's Palace.

From that time Suzdal's religious importance dwindled little by little and now the town is nothing more than the centre of a small food-producing district of little importance. Architectural restoration is progressing on a large scale, but one needs to remember that between 1238 until the beginning of the 16th century no stone buildings were constructed in Suzdal so no architecture of that time remains.

It is suggested that visitors to Suzdal turn right from the main road coming in from Vladimir before they get into the centre of the town. 5 km. further on is the little village of Kidekshu, standing on the high bank of the R. Nerl. Inside a walled enclosure stands the *Church of Boris and Gleb*, built in 1152 for Prince Yuri Dolgoruki who had a small palace here too. This was the first of all the white stone edifices to be constructed in this region. It should not prove hard to find the villager in charge of the key to the church, and inside are the remains of some frescoes as well as plans and pictures illustrating the history of the place. Yuri Dolgoruki's son, Boris, and his daughter-in-law, Maria, were buried here. The whitestone church was somewhat spoiled by reconstruction in the 16th and 17th centuries. Beside it stands *St. Stephen's Church and belfry* (1870), the design of which is typical of a stone church following the characteristics of wooden architecture.

The *Vasilievsky Monastery* stands a little to the south of the Kidekshu Road. It was founded at the beginning of the 13th century and was run as a monastery until 1899. The cathedral was built in 1668 and the other stone buildings including the smaller, two-storey Sretenskaya (Purification of the Virgin) Church, a belfry and the white walls surrounding them all date from the 17th and 18th centuries.

Znamenskaya Church (1749) stands beside the road leading into Suzdal from Vladimir and the south, and the elegant white church to the right of the same road on a hill is *Kosmodamianovskaya Church* (1725).

The best view of the town is obtained from the west side. The main street is still lined with small houses typical of a Russian provincial town of the last century.

The *Kremlin* lies beside R. Kamenka, to the south-west of the central square, surrounded by well preserved 11th-century earth walls. Once they were 10 m. high and 1400 m. in length; on top of the earth walls are wooden walls and towers. The Kremlin was surrounded on three sides by the waters of the river and along the fourth, the eastern side, ran a moat 8·5 m. deep and 35 m. wide.

Inside the Kremlin walls the blue-domed *Rozhdestvensky (Nativity of the Virgin) Cathedral* commands immediate attention, but it is wisest to keep to the rule of visiting the local museum before setting off on a sightsee:ng tour, and the *Suzdal Local Museum* is housed in the obtuse-angled building of the Archbishop's Palace, built in the 16th–17th century in the western part of the Kremlin.

In the museum is a portrait of Solomonia and the tomb and little shirt of her son, all of which items illustrate the legend of the Pokrovsky Convent (see below, p. 333). The museum contains much of interest concerning the history of Suzdal and its ancient architecture. There is an exhibit

showing the type of decorations to be found on the Church of Boris and Gleb (Kideskshi, 1152), the Pokrovsky Church on the Nerl (Bogolyubovo, 1165), the Dmitrievsky Cathedral (Vladimir, 1194–7), and the Rozhdestvensky Cathedral (here, in Suzdal, 1222–5), and demonstrating how in the course of 75 years the ornamental stonework gradually changed from a simple frieze to an intricate tapestry of stone. The evolution was brought to a sudden halt by the Tatar invasions which began in 1240.

The Art Section of the museum is reached by passing through the gateway on the left of the Archbishop's Palace and going on to where a porch and stairway lead up to the floor above. Here are some of the best examples of 'basma': thin sheets of gold or silver were beaten onto moulds and then cut out for use as icon frames or buttons. There are also embroideries here, items of metalwork, icons, silver and gold lace, pottery, and decorative tiles. The modern crafts section of the museum is also interesting.

A guide from the museum will open the doors of the *Cathedral* and point out the items of greatest interest. This is the oldest church in Suzdal, built in 1222–5 on the site of a brick church which Vladimir Monomakh had built. It was added to in the 16th century. Here princes and eminent clergy were buried and the tomb of Fyodor (1023) and Ioann (1372), the first and sixth Bishops of Suzdal, are here. Generally speaking, the lower part is 13th and the upper part 16th century; the building was restored in 1964. Some small fragments of frescoes painted in 1230 remain but there are more of the 17th century. The south and west doors of the cathedral are especially interesting. The west doors, known as the Korunskiye Gates, have scenes from the New Testament depicted in gold on copper which has darkened with age. This type of decoration, called damascene work, was much used in Byzantium. Some of the icons inside the cathedral date from the 17th century and standing on the floor is the 17th-century King of the Lanterns which used to be filled with lighted candles and carried in religious processions.

The octagonal belfry to the south of the cathedral was built in 1635. Besides the numbers on the old clockface there are also Slavonic letters to tell the time, A for 1, B for 2, etc.

Other churches on the territory of the Kremlin are the 17th-century *Uspenskaya (Assumption) Church*, the *Nikolskaya Church* (1720–39) with its bell-tower and, close beside it, a *church* for use in summer only and dedicated to the same saint. Also here is the *Nikolskaya wooden church*, built in 1766 and brought here in 1960 from the village of Glotovo, near Yuriev-Polsky.

Voskresenskaya Church (1732) stands in the centre of Sovietskaya Sq. (formerly Trade Sq.). It is a white-washed brick cube with a single dome, typical of the local church architecture of the 18th century. The belfry has attractive tiles.

Kazanskaya Church (1739) is another on the square and at present is the only one among so many that is open for services.

Between Voskresenskaya Church and the R. Kamenka is the 18th-century *Traders' Row*. This is a good example of the arcades of small shops which used to be rented out to merchants for the storage and sale of their wares. On the bank of the river, standing side by side, are two very small churches, the *Vkhodoierusalimskaya* (1686) and the *Pyatnitskaya* (1772). South of the square is *Pretechenskaya Church* (1720) and nearby, *Krestovaya Church* (1765). On the north-east side of the square, standing together, are the *Skorbyashenskaya Church* (1750), which was used in winter, and the *Tsarevokonstantinovskaya Church* (1707), a summer church, the small classical rotunda of which was added at a later date. Going north up the main road, Lenina St., is *Lazarevskaya Church* (1667).

Further on up Lenina St., on the left in the highest part of the town, stands *Rizpolozhenski Convent*. It was founded in 1207, before the Tatar invasion, and there is a story told about its early years. The 15-year-old daughter of Prince Mikhail of Chernigov, himself later murdered by the Tatars, entered this convent under the name of Evfrosiniya when her fiancé died on the eve of their wedding. In 1238 during the tenth year of her sojourn in the convent, the Tatars who had already invaded Russia came right up to its walls. By some miracle they left it standing and it was popularly believed that her prayers were responsible. She was canonised at the end of the 14th century.

The wooden walls were replaced by stone ones in the 17th century and the *Holy Gates* were constructed in 1688. The 60 m. belfry which dominates the town was built into the eastern part of the wall in 1813–19 to commemorate the victory over Napoleon.

The *Alexandrovsky Monastery* stands a little back from the main road, again on the left-hand side of it, but nearer the river, on its high left bank. It was founded in 1240 by Alexander Nevsky and was once known as the Great Monastery. Now only a small section of its white walls remains. Inside is Voznesenskaya (Ascension) Church and its red belfry, both built in 1695. The gates which were built at the beginning of the 18th century were restored in 1947. The monks left the monastery in 1764 but the church remained open to the public.

Instead of continuing up Lenina St., it is possible to go down to the river past the Alexandrovsky Monastery walls and across it to the *Pokrovsky Convent*. The latter, however, is a pleasant place to rest when one has finished the walk through Suzdal and so perhaps it is advisable to go straight on to the little town's largest monastery complex.

The *Spaso-Efimievsky Monastery* stands right above the high bank of R. Kamenka and dominates the surrounding territory. It was founded in 1352 and the high stone walls over 1 km. long and the twelve mighty towers make it look like a fortress,

and indeed it served as such for centuries. In 1445 the Russians who were defending the monastery from the Tatars were all killed in a bloody battle and the Tatars captured Grand-Prince Vasili Tyomni ('the blind').

The present-day brick walls replaced the wooden ones in the 17th century. They are 6 m. thick and on the north, east, and south sides they stand 8·5 m. and on the west side, 7·5 m. Of the greatest interest is the massive entrance tower protecting the Holy Gates on the southern side. Its height of 23 m. made it a good watchtower. The stone carving gives an impression of lacework. Near the entrance is the *Blagoveschenskaya (Annunciation) Gate Church* (17th century).

The most important building in the ensemble is the *Spaso-Preobrazheniya (Transfiguration) Cathedral* (1594) which was founded on the site of an older church. It has five main domes and the outside decoration of half-columns echoes Vladimir-Suzdal architecture of the 12th–13th centuries. The southern and western outside walls were decorated with frescoes which is unusual in Russian church architecture. It is on record that they were painted in 1689 by Nikitin and Savin from Kostroma, and the frescoes on the inside walls were painted by artists from Vologda at the same time. The bell-tower was probably finished in the 1530s but arches were added in 1599 and 1691. Beside the eastern wall of the cathedral, facing the bell-tower, is the tomb of Prince Pozharsky who drove the Poles from Moscow in 1612; his mausoleum has been removed, but there is a monument to his memory by Z. I. Azgur outside the main entrance gate saying 'Dmitri Mikhailovich 1578–1642'.

The prison was built in 1764 and a second one was constructed inside the *Uspenskaya (Assumption) Refectory Church* (1525) by the order of Catherine II in 1766. Most of the prisoners were those who had committed crimes against the Church. More recently the German Field Marshal von Paulus was held here for some time after his capture in Stalingrad in 1943. Adjoining the Uspenskaya Church is the *Archimandrate's Palace* (17th century). The two-storey residential block in the north-east part of the territory is 18th–19th century and *Nikolskaya Church* was built in 1669.

Outside the monastery, near the entrance, is *Smolenskaya Church* (1707) with an elegant belfry. Beside it is the 17th-century stone-built *Tailor's House*, a unique structure because such houses were invariably built of wood.

The whitewashed *Pokrovsky (Intercession) Convent* (1364) stands across the R. Kamenka on the low right bank, opposite the Spaso-Efimievsky Monastery. The present-day walls and towers were built in the 18th century, except for the two 17th-century towers which remain in the north wall.

The convent is known in Russian history as the place of exile of many Russian ladies of noble blood, including the wives of Vasili III and Ivan the Terrible and Peter the Great's first wife, Evdokia. The following story is among those connected with the convent's past:

Vasili III divorced his wife, Solomonia, in violation of Church law, having accused her of barrenness. Surviving chronicles however describe Solomonia as an energetic woman in the prime of life and accuse Vasili of sterility. Nevertheless with the consent of the Moscow Metropolitan Danil, a shrewd and unscrupulous politician, Vasili obtained his divorce. He sent Solomonia to the Pokrovsky Convent in Suzdal and married a noble girl of Polish origin named Elena Glinskaya. Later news reached Moscow that Solomonia had given birth to a son whom she had named Georgi. An inquiry was ordered and as the child was in obvious danger, Solomonia put him into the hands of people she could trust, spread rumours of his death, and staged a fake burial.

Historians regard all this as a folk legend, but in 1934 in the crypt under the Pokrovsky Cathedral a small 16th-century white-stone tomb was discovered beside the tomb of Solomonia who died in 1542. There was however no skeleton, nor any bones at all under the stone, only a bundle of rags stuffed into a tiny expensive silk shirt embroidered with pearls. It is hardly surprising that the son born to Vasili III by Elena, no less a person than Ivan the Terrible, saw to it that evidence of the findings of the inquiry should disappear. The small shirt and the little white-stone tomb are to be seen in the local museum.

Inside the convent walls is the three-domed *Pokrovsky Cathedral* which was built in 1518 on the site of a wooden church and restored in 1963. It is surrounded by an arcade on three sides. The lower part of the octagonal belfry was built in 1515, but the upper part was reconstructed in the 17th century. The refectory building dates from 1518 too, as do the three-domed *Blagoveschenskaya (Annunciation) Gate Church* in the south wall and the *Zachatievskaya (Immaculate Conception) Church*, both of which were built by Vasili III. The Blagoveschenskaya Church is interesting for the way in which church and fortress architecture are smoothly blended. Inside the main gates, by the wall on the left, is a single-storey 17th-century building which served as the monastery's administrative offices; in its cellars were punishment cells.

The *Tikhvinskaya Church* was built in the late 17th century and it is unusual in that it is without apses. It is now used as a bakery. Also nearby are the *Petropavlovskaya Church* (1694) and *Nikolskaya Church* (1712). The many other churches on this side, the low bank of the river, include the *Bogoyavlenskaya (Epiphany) Church* (1755), the *Illinskaya Church* (1788), the 17th-century *Borisoglebskaya Church,* and the *Spassky Church* with its dome in a state of dilapidation.

Further along on this side of the river and overlooked by the Kremlin, is the *Museum of Wooden Architecture* with a collection of buildings which have been moved here recently. The *Preobrazhenskaya (Transfiguration) Church* (1756) was brought here from Kozlyatyevo in 1967 and

Voskresenskaya (Resurrection) Church (1766) was brought from Potakino. There is also a *house* with outbuildings and two *windmills.*

Suzdal Hotel & Restaurant, Lenina St., on the central square.

Trapeznaya Restaurant, Kremlin, on the ground floor of the Archbishop's Palace. Closed Mon.

Pogrebok Restaurant, Kremlyovskaya St. (that leading from the Kremlin to Torgoviye Ryad). Open 11–7; closed Mon.

Sokol Restaurant, Lenina St.

Tea Room, Lenina St.

Souvenir Shop, Kommuny St. 3, very near the Kremlin and easily identified by its Swiss-style window shutters. Open 9–5.

There is a *bus station* and a *taxi rank* near the hotel, in Lenin St., and a *filling station* on the left side of the road from Vladimir just before entering Suzdal.

VOLGOGRAD

Population—818,000 (1970)

Known as Tsarytsin until 1925, then as Stalingrad until 1961

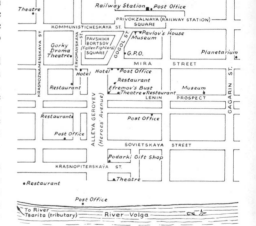

VOLGOGRAD

Further information is not available

The city stretches along the right bank of the R. Volga for more than 70 km. and its width varies from 2 to 10 km. The architects describe it as a ribbon-city because of the way it has grown. The Volga bank is cut by deep ravines which divide the city into sections. It was originally the lack of rain combined with the strong, dry winds blowing from the nearby steppes in the heat of summer that forced people to settle close to the water.

The old Tsarytsin coat-of-arms, a design with two fish, can be seen on the façade of the two-storey, red brick building of the Trud Sports Club (formerly the fire station) at Kommunisticheskaya St. 5. The new coat-of-arms, adopted in 1968, has red battlements and the golden star medal awarded to heroes on the upper half; the lower part, which has a blue background, bears a golden cogwheel and a sheaf of wheat symbolising the powerful industry of the city and the fruitful soil upon which it stands.

Tsarytsin was founded in 1589 as a fortress on Russia's southern boundary, guarding the country against the Tatar nomads which were the survivors of the Golden Horde. Its name was derived from the Tatar words 'sary-chin' which mean 'yellow sand'. Its fortifications were increased and its importance grew during the reign of Peter the Great (1682–1725) and later it was the centre of several popular uprisings. There was the Stepan Razin uprising in 1670, the Cossack uprising under Bulavin in 1708, and in 1774 the peasant revolt led by Yemelyan Pugachev who designated himself Emperor Peter III and who was subsequently quartered.

By the mid-19th century Tsarytsin was of considerable commercial importance, particularly as far as the transport of oil from Baku was concerned. During the Civil War (1918–20) it saw much fierce fighting because all the food supplies for Moscow and Petrograd from the south passed through it. The 'defence of Tsarytsin' against the Whites was an important step towards the establishment of Soviet power.

The biggest tractor plant in Russia was built here in the 1930s and by 1941 the city had a population of 445,000 and was one of the Volga Basin's biggest industrial centres. Then during World War II the city once again became the scene of fighting and it was at the Battle of Stalingrad that the Germans suffered one of their most significant defeats.

When the Germans turned their attention to Stalingrad in the summer of 1942, they intended to cut off the Red Army's supply of Caucasian oil and to reach Moscow from the south-east. This was after they had attacked from the west in December 1941 and failed. Hitler declared in November 1942 that Stalingrad was 'of decisive importance' to him, just before the turning point in the battle, which lasted from July 1942 to February 1943. The course of the battle can be roughly divided into four periods:

1) The German advance followed by fierce street fighting, 17 July–19 November.

2) The pincer-like Soviet advance from the north-east and the south which split the German forces in two, 19 November–30 November.

3) German attempts to relieve their encircled troops were rebuffed, December 1942.

4) The encircled German troops were defeated and destroyed, 10 January–2 February 1943.

During the street fighting in November neither side was willing to give up a single house, staircase, or even a room. The defence of Pavlov House for two months by a handful of soldiers under Sergeant Pavlov has become a legend. Among the prominent Soviet military leaders who distinguished themselves in the Battle of Stalingrad were Marshals Voronov, Rokossovsky, and Chuikov. Mr. Khruschev was a member of

the Military Council of the Stalingrad Front during the battle.

As a result of the fourth period of the battle (as described above) a German grouping of twenty-two divisions (330,000 men) under Field Marshal von Paulus was taken with 6000 guns, 1312 mortars, and 744 aircraft.

In the course of the battle the city of Stalingrad was utterly destroyed. There had been 48,190 houses in the city, most of them built of wood. During the German attack the enemy dropped nearly a million bombs on Stalingrad, not counting land bombardment. By comparison, about 50,000 were dropped on London during the blitz. Out of the 48,190 houses, 41,685 were burned or otherwise destroyed. But housing was only one of the many problems the city authorities had to solve. According to official statistics they had to bury, between February and April 1943, 147,200 German dead and 46,700 Russians. People aged between 18 and 60 were all mobilised to collect and bury the corpses.

There was a suggestion that a new city be founded nearby and the ruins left as they were as a gigantic war memorial, but it was more sensibly decided to reconstruct the city where it stood. Immediately after the Germans were defeated the work of reconstruction was decreed a matter of prime importance to the state and so the stupendous task was undertaken. Even the clearing of the site was no easy matter when it is realised that it took 8000 railway trucks of rubble and dust to clear the territory of the tractor plant alone. Bricks from the ruins were used again, scattered doors and window frames collected, and iron hammered into shape.

Today Volgograd is the administrative and economic centre of the Lower Volga Region and is also the major transport centre of this area. It has over 150 industrial enterprises, including one of the country's biggest tractor plants, a metallurgical plant, and machine-building factories. Volgograd region now ranks sixth in the Soviet Union's oil producing areas. The city also has five research institutes.

Down by the Volga, Central Quay now serves as a promenade and a river-bus station. The *monument* on the embankment is to Victor Kholzunov (1905–39), a test pilot and hero of the Soviet Union who was killed in 1939. The embankment with 100 steps of grey granite and a monumental colonnade was built in 1952 on the completion of the Volga–Don Canal (properly known as the Lenin Canal). It makes an impressive entrance to the city from the river. On the lower terrace of the embankment there is a *children's railway*, and on the upper terrace is the 7 m. *Victory Fountain*.

The heart of Volgograd is *Pavshikh Bortsov* (Fallen Fighters Sq.) Before the Revolution it was called Alexander Sq. and was the trading centre of the city. Now it is the venue of demonstrations, parades, and meetings and is also revered as a shrine. Where the boulevard leads out of the square towards the river, a common grave is situated. A *monument* has been erected to those who fought against the White Guards in 1919 and against the Nazis in 1942–3. Here too is the grave of Ruben Ibarruri, son of the Secretary General of the Spanish Communist Party, who died during the Battle of Stalingrad while serving in the Soviet Army.

The building of the *Gorky Drama Theatre*, on one side of the square, housed the City Soviet in 1917–18. On the northern side of the square a new department store stands on the site of the old store which von Paulus used as his headquarters before his capture.

The *railway station* nearby was built in 1954 in place of the one destroyed during the war.

A 9 m. *monument to Lenin* stands on a red granite pedestal in the square bearing his name; it was designed by Vuchetich with a semicircular colonnade by Zakharov and was unveiled in 1960. Nearby is *Pavlov House* (see above, p. 335) which is reached by going through the colonnade. The ruins of the flour mill not far from Pavlov House are preserved as a *war memorial*. Between the two a new *museum* is being built to commemorate the defence of Stalingrad. There will be a panorama of the Battle of Stalingrad. The foundations were laid in 1968 on the occasion of the 25th anniversary of the battle, and the building will be circular with sixteen stone slabs bearing the names of all the divisions which took part.

To the north of the central part of the city stands *Mamaev Kurgan*, dominating the whole area and being the place where the fighting was most fierce (see below) A flight of triumphal steps lead up to it from Lenin Prospect, the city's main street. In many places near Lenin Prospect one can see the gun turrets of T-34 tanks mounted on small pedestals marking the line of defence of the 62nd Army. The prospect is one of the longest in the world; it runs for nearly 70 km. and was built on the sight of the most terrible ruins. Among the very few old houses that survived here is No. 2, a red brick mansion now the *House of Architects*. Along the street are government, party, and trade union buildings as well as apartment houses. The part between Krasnoznamenskaya and Lenin Squares has been planted as an avenue which makes it most attractive.

Mamaev Kurgan was called, according to legend, after the Tatar Khan Mamai who once made his camp on the hill. It stands 102 m. high. During the Battle of Stalingrad the fight for the possession of this vantage point lasted more than four months. The surface was left absolutely riddled with bullets and shells. Pieces of shrapnel can still be found here, which is hardly surprising when it is estimated that there were 500–1250 shells and bullets in every square metre. In the spring of 1943 no grass grew at all on the hill.

The memorial complex which has been built here and which starts with the flight of steps up from Lenin Prospect, was designed by the sculptor Evgeni Vuchetich and the architect Belopolski, but of course there were many others assisting in

the work. The sculptural groups on the steps depict various scenes of the battle, and halfway up is a platform with a circular pool. A stone plaque on one side is engraved with the words: 'A steely wind hit them in the face, but still they went forward, and again a feeling of superstitious fear seized the enemy—were these really people going into attack? Were they mortals?' Here, in the Hall of Military Glory, a round building, burns an eternal flame. Thirty-two mosaic plaques carry the names of the fallen. The 12 m. statue of a soldier with a machine gun and a hand grenade is called 'Stand to the Last Man'. The ruined walls symbolise the ruined city and here and there are inscription such as 'Not a Step Back', and 'Beyond the Volga is No Place for Us'; these slogans were to be seen in many parts of the city during the fighting. The main sculpture on the top of the hill, that of a woman with an uplifted sword, can be seen from all parts of the city. She symbolises the Motherland calling upon her sons to rise to her defence. The statue is 51 m. high and, with the pedestal, 72 m.

Kazansky Cathedral, Lipetskaya St. 10. Built in 1903 and restored in 1948.

Local Museum, Lenin Prospect 38; entrance from the courtyard. The museum has five halls and the exhibits include items excavated in Serai-Berka, a 13th–14th-century settlement 80 km. from Volgograd. Here there are also a cap and a stick which belonged to Peter the Great and some documents dating from the time of the Revolution and others pertaining to World War II. Open 11–6; closed Tues.

The Defence of the City Museum, Gogol St. 8. The building served as the headquarters during the defence of the city in 1917–18, but the exhibits belong to the 1942–3 defence as well. There is a printing block left behind by the Germans; it has been prepared to print leaflets announcing 'The Fall of Stalingrad'. There are German flags, medals, and a model of the ruined city. Also displayed are gifts presented to the city, including a sword sent by King George VI in 1944 which bears the inscription: 'To the steel-hearted citizens of Stalingrad—the gift of King George VI in token of the homage of the British people.' There is also a shield which was presented by Emperor Haile Selassie of Ethiopia, a copy of a scroll sent by F. D. Roosevelt, a tea-set from Iran, a chess-table from Luxembourg, and a tablecloth from Coventry with 830 embroidered signatures. Open 11–6; closed Tues.

Art Museum, Lenin Prospect 21. The antique section of the museum is represented by copies. The pride of the West European section are two small sculptures by Rodin, 'Jealousy' and 'The Kiss', which were presented in 1947 by Lady Westmacott. The Russian section includes a portrait of Catherine II by Antropov and in the Soviet section is Dostoevsky sculpted by Konenkov. The museum has over 3000 works. Open 12–7; closed Wed.

Planetarium, Yuri Gagarin St. This planetarium was a gift from the German Democratic Republic and the main auditorium seats over 500. Open 9–9.

Dzerzhinsky Monument, Dzerzhinsky Sq., in front of the tractor factory. This was unveiled in 1935.

Chekist's Monument, in the garden on the right bank of R. Tsaritsa, near Astrakhan Bridge. This statue of a soldier with a sword raised is dedicated to the members of the security forces who fell between August 1942 and February 1943, defending the city. The 5 m. sculpture is mounted on a 17 m. pedestal. The project was by Kaimshidi and was unveiled in 1952.

Efremov's Bust, at the corner of Lenin Prospect and Alleya Geroyev (Heroes Avenue). Airforce Captain and Pilot Vasili Efremov was twice made a Hero of the Soviet Union.

A 24 m. granite *obelisk* dedicated to those who fell in 1919 stands in front of a fraternal grave decorated with a 4 m. bronze wreath. It was designed by Shalaev in 1958.

Gorky Drama Theatre, Pavshikh Bortsov (Fallen Fighters Sq.)

Musical Comedy Theatre, Central Quay. Before the 1917 Revolution the building was a club and in 1918 it was occupied by the Communist Party committee. It was badly damaged during World War II and was reconstructed and then rebuilt in 1960.

Puppet Theatre, Lenin Prospect 15

Circus, Volodarsky St.

The *Volga Stadium* can seat 40,000.

City Garden, Kommunisticheskaya St.

Bathing Beach, on Golodny (hungry) Island, in the middle of the Volga, facing the city. It is reached by boat.

Volgograd Hotel & Restaurant, Pavshikh Bortsov Sq., TEL. 33–17–72

Intourist Hotel & Restaurant, Pavshikh Bortsov Sq., TEL. 33–45–53

Leto (summer) Restaurant, in the City Garden

Mayak (lighthouse) Restaurant, on the Volga embankment. There is an excellent view from this restaurant and it is easily identified by its spire surmounted by a sailing ship.

Molodyozhnoye (youth) Café, Lenin Prospect 10

G.P.O., Pavshikh Bortsov Sq.

Bank, Lenin Prospect 18

Department Store, Ostrovskovo St. 2. Souvenirs can be purchased here.

Art Salon, Sovietskaya St. 8

Podarki Gift Shop, Alleya Geroyev, where it crosses Krasnopiterskaya St.

Market, Sovietskaya St.

There are boats which go for excursions along the river to the hydropower station and along the Volga–Don Canal as far as the second lock.

The Volga Hydropower station is one of the largest in the world. It started working in 1959 and since 1961 has been operating at its full strength of 2,575,000 kilowatts. Not far from it is the largest aluminium plant in Europe.

The Canal connects the Volga and the Don Rivers and so makes Volgograd a port of five seas, the Caspian, the Black, the Azov, the Baltic, and the White. It is 101 km. long and was opened in 1952. The main source of water for the canal is the Tsimlyansky Sea, an inland stretch of water 360 km. long, 38 km. wide, and 30 m. deep. It holds 24,000,000,000 cu. m.

First attempts to build the canal were made by Peter the Great at the end of the 17th century. Now it is finished it has 15 locks and is decorated with sculptural groups commemorating the events of the Civil and Second World Wars. At the opening from the Volgograd end stands a *lighthouse* with rostral columns in honour of the sailors of the Volga flotilla who fought here in 1918–19 and in 1942–3. Between the 9th and 10th locks is a *monument* to the Heroes of the Civil War with busts of several of them. By the 13th lock is a *monument* devoted to the encirclement of the German forces by Soviet troops during the Battle of Stalingrad. On the towers of the 15th lock stand *equestrian statues* of Cossacks.

VOLZHSKII

Population—142,000 (1970)

Volzhskii lies 30 km. from the centre of Volgograd, on the left bank of R. Volga, 2 km. from the hydropower station. R. Akhtuba forms its western boundary.

The site was first settled in 1951 and to start with most of the population were those who were working at the hydropower station. It received town status in 1954.

Volzhskii was planned as one architectural ensemble and it was built by a single construction organisation which enabled them to put up parts of the town in large, completed sections. Most of the houses are heated from a central plant.

The main streets were planned to run from north-west to south-east to protect the houses from the frequent winds. Many 15-year-old trees were transplanted to form boulevards and a park.

Lenin Prospect is the main thoroughfare. It is 40 m. wide and leads to the central square which is surrounded by impressive buildings with columns, the *Palace of Culture*, which seats 830 people, a hotel, shops, and administrative buildings.

The growing industry of the town includes ball-bearing and synthetic rubber factories, and one of the country's largest chemical plants is under construction.

At the *Sport complex*, on the high and low terraces by R. Akhtuba, there is a stadium for 10,000 and an indoor swimming pool.

Volga Restaurant, Lenin Prospect 15

VORONEZH

Population—660,000 (1970).

Voronezh is situated on the bank of R. Voronezh, 12 km. from the point where it joins the Don. Its name comes from *voron* (raven) and its ancient coat-of-arms shows a raven perched upon a gun.

Archaeologists have found that Slav tribes have inhabited this region for the past 1000 years and the area is mentioned in chronicles of 1177. In 1586 a fortress was built here as a link in the chain of defences called the Belgorod Line, across the Don Steppes, which was designed to stop Tatar raids.

Your town stood as Russia's shield
'Gainst the nomadic Eastern horde.
Konstantin Gusyev.

The fortress guarding the south-eastern border of the Moscow state stood on the high right bank of the river, and beyond it stretched 'the wild field', the limitless steppe.

Voronezh was important as the point where prisoners of war were exchanged, as the place where foreign ambassadors were greeted as they travelled up the R. Don, and also where they took their leave when their missions were accomplished. Its situation beside the waterway leading to the Black Sea and the Sea of Azov led to the town's rapid growth and by the 17th century it had become the centre for trade with the south. Bishop Mitrophan, who died in 1703 and was later canonised, was influential in its development and so was Peter the Great who first visited Voronezh in 1694 and was struck by its strategic location. The following year, when he had failed to take the Turkish fortress of Azov, Peter proclaimed, 'Any potentate who has infantry only is one-handed; he who has also a fleet has two hands', and Voronezh accordingly became a shipyard. Shipbuilders came from far and near to construct sea-going vessels. Peter himself travelled to Holland and to England to study the profession and invited shipwrights to Voronezh from both countries. The new fleet was built in record time and in 1696 Peter, as captain of the 'Principium', led his fleet to capture Azov.

Voronezh lies in the black earth region which has long been Russia's breadbasket. Consequently most of the town's trade was at first in grain, but later the exports of wool and fat increased considerably. Voronezh was also celebrated for its cattle and particularly for its horses; Russian Trotters originated here.

Foreigners who settled in the town brought their own architectural styles with them. There were wide-roofed Swiss houses with balconies, narrow-windowed English cottages, and the Dutch houses with their pointed roofs, although built of wood, were painted over to resemble brick. Open fireplaces caused a great sensation and indeed a local historian described the new buildings as 'a real miracle'. Voronezh was one of the first Russian towns to conform to Peter's innovations and reforms during his campaign to modernise his country, including such recommendations as that those of noble birth discard traditional dress and adopt French fashions. Most of the buildings put up in Peter's time were destroyed in a great fire in 1748, including a palace

and the houses which belonged to foreigners.

At the end of the 19th century the town's industry began to catch up with its flourishing trade. New factories were built on the left bank of the river, including a synthetic rubber plant. During the 1905 Revolution, local workers rebelled and in the civil war which followed the 1917 Revolution the town changed hands several times. The local Jews suffered much from the pogroms.

Voronezh was a front-line town during the Second World War. The German army occupied the right bank of the river but were unable to cross it, so for several months the place was the site of continuous fighting. Only Stalingrad and Sevastopol were riddled with more mines than Voronezh. 92% of the houses (a total of 18,000 buildings) were burned down and after the liberation the place was like one enormous minefield. A further 58,000 unexploded mines were detected among the rubble.

After the war many old buildings were reconstructed to preserve the town's original appearance. The main street is Revolutsii Prospect, formerly Great Nobles' St., which ran for more than 2 km. parallel to the river. No. 22 in this street is the building of the Governor's House which was built in 1725. Nearby is Petrovsky Garden with a statue of Peter the Great by Gavrilov; it was put up in 1956 in the place of another statue of Peter which had been erected in 1860 but which was destroyed during the war. There is a pleasant fountain behind the statue.

During the early 1930s a number of buildings in Constructivist style were put up along this street: the House of Books, Communications House, and the offices of the South-eastern Railway. They too were badly damaged but have been restored. At the southern end of the street is the House of Trade, built in 1934 by Popov-Shaman and popularly known as the Smoothing Iron because of its shape.

Lenin Sq. is in the centre of the town. The monument to Lenin here is by Tomsky and was restored in 1950. The big House of Soviets (1959) was designed by Mironov. Parades and demonstrations take place in this square.

Voronezh has ten higher educational establishments, including the university which was opened in 1918 when Dorpat University and the Agricultural Institute (founded in 1913) were both evacuated here from Tartu in Estonia.

In an island in the river stands Peter the Great's Arsenal, having survived all the disasters that have befallen the town. On the left bank is the newer part of Voronezh, founded in 1928. It is an industrial area, now stretching along the river for over 16 km. One of its main thoroughfares is Heroes-of-the-Stratosphere St.

Local industry produces equipment for agriculture and the food industry, construction machinery such as excavators, chemical products (especially synthetic rubber), and food products. An atomic power station stands just outside the town.

Pokrovsky Cathedral (1792), Bekhtereva St. Open for services.

St. Nicholas's Church (1712–49), Taranchenko St. This church was built in the style of Moscow churches; it is also open for services.

Alexeev Church, Osvobozhdeniya Truda St. Although this church was built in the 19th century, its belfry, belonging to the Alexeev Monastery, was built in 1674 and is the oldest architectural monument in the town, although it was badly damaged during the war.

Vvedenskaya Church, Osvobozhdeniya Truda St.

Local Museum, Plekhanovskaya St. 35. Founded in 1894.

Nikitin Museum, Nikitinskaya St. 23. Ivan Nikitin (1824–61) was a very popular poet. The museum was founded in 1924 and the stone building in which it is housed is a replica built in 1955 of the wooden house in which the poet lived and died. There is a monument to his memory in Koltsov Garden, just off Lenin Sq; it was designed by Shuklin and was unveiled in 1911.

Fine Arts Museum, Revolutsii Prospect 18, in the building of the Coaching Palace (1770). Ground floor: ancient Egypt, Greece and Rome; 1st floor: Russian art from the 15th century to the present day (including icons and the works of the 19th–20th century artists Shishkin, Levitan, and Repin); 2nd floor: west European art, including a Van Dyck self-portrait and some of Rembrandt's etchings. Open 10–5; closed Tues.

War Memorial to those who fell in World War II, 20th October St.

Koltsov Drama Theatre, Revolutsii Sq. 67. The company was founded in 1802 and the building was put up in 1886, but it has been reconstructed several times.

Music Theatre, Lenin Sq. Performances of opera, ballet, and musical comedy take place here; it can hold 1200.

Circus, Pervomaisky Garden, Revolutsii Prospect

Puppet Theatre, Komisarzhevskoi St. 5

Philharmonia, Lenin Sq. Voronezh is famous for its choir which gives concerts all over the country and also abroad.

Detsky Sad (Children's Garden), Universitetskaya St.

Town Park, Lenin St. Open-air theatre.

Botanical Garden, by the Agricultural Institute

Hippodrome Racecourse, Begovaya St. 2

Dynamo Stadium, Lenin St. 12

Trud Stadium, Studencheskaya St. 17. This stadium can seat 20,000.

Lisaya Gora, a hill in the suburbs, is a popular recreation place from which there is a good view of the town. The Gorky Sanatorium is here.

Uzmansky Forest (40 km. from town) has a nature reserve for beavers and deer which was established in 1922. There is a museum of the local flora and fauna which is open 10–5, 1 May–10 November; closed Mon.

Voronezh Hotel & Restaurant, Plekhanovskaya St. 22

Don Hotel & Restaurant, Plekhanovskaya St. 10

Rossia Hotel & Restaurant, Teatralnaya St. 23, TEL. 6–00–98

Molodyozhnoye Café, Pushkinskaya St. 4

G.P.O., Revolutsii Prospect 23

Telegraph Office, Revolutsii Prospect 35

Bank, Teatralnaya St. 18

Department Stores; Dom Torgovli (House of Trade), Nikitinskaya St, Revolutsii Prospect and Plekhanovskaya St. 125.

Bookshop, Revolutsii Prospect 33

YALTA
See Crimean Circular Route, p. 85

YAROSLAVL
Population—520,000 (1970)

Yaroslavl stands on either side of the R. Volga, at the point where the R. Kotorosl flows into it, and where the Volga is nearly 1 km. wide. The town covers an area of 170 sq. km., stretches along the river for about 26 km., and reaches inland on either side for about 9 km.

Yaroslavl is the oldest town on the Volga, first mentioned in writing in 1071 and said to have been founded by Yaroslav the Wise (978–1054) in about 1024. The town emblem is a bear rampant with a halberd on his shoulder. According to the legend, when Yaroslav the Wise first came to the place where he later founded the town, the local inhabitants let a bear out of its cage to chase him away, and Yaroslav killed it with his halberd. Now lorries made in the town have a bear on the bonnet.

Early in the 13th century Yaroslav established the first school in northern Russia. In 1238 the town was sacked and burnt by the Tatars, and in 1463 the principality of Yaroslavl was united with Moscow, when Prince Alexander Brukhatyi, 'the Paunch', exchanged his ancestral princedom with Tsar Ivan III for some land near Moscow.

During the reign of Ivan the Terrible trade relations were established with western Europe through the White Sea. Yaroslavl then became prominent as an important British trading station for commerce with the near east and the Volga, and it began to attract foreign investments. During the Time of Troubles it was the temporary capital of the country. It was badly damaged by the Poles and the Cossacks and then, in the middle of the 17th century, was rebuilt and grew in commercial and industrial importance. An 18th-century poet wrote:

Athens in ancient time boasted of its sciences;
Other towns were proud of the art of their hands
—But you have all these in one.

Under Catherine II, in 1777, the town was made a provincial capital. Eventually the Baltic ports took much of its trade, but until the opening of the Moscow–Volga Canal in 1937 Yaroslavl continued to be Moscow's Volga port.

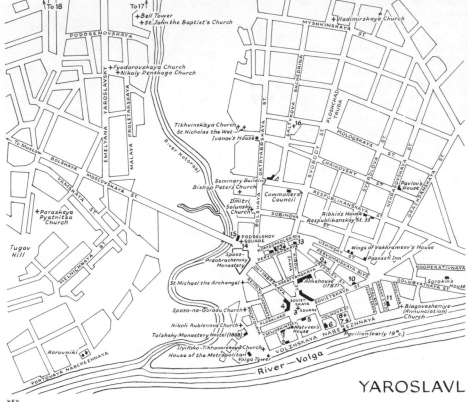

To 18
To 17
+Bell Tower
+St.John the Baptist's Church
VLADIMIRSKAYA Church
MYSHKINSKAYA ST.
PODOSENOVSKAYA
+Fyodorovskaya Church
+Nikoly Penskogo Church
Tikhvinskaya Church
St.Nicholas the Wet
Ivanov's House
16
PLOSHCHAD TRUDA
MOLOGSKAYA ST.
Seminary Building
Bishop Peter's Church
Dmitri Solunsky Church
Commoners' Council
Pavlov's House
RESPUBLIKANSKAYA
Ribkin's House
Respublikanskoy St. 33
+Paraskeva Pyatnitsa Church
Tugov Hill
PODBELSKOV SQUARE
15
14
Spaso-Preobrazhensky Monastery
13
Wings of Vakhrameev's House
Passazh Inn
KOMSOMOLSKAYA
St Michael the Archangel +
Almshouse (1787)
10
Sorokin's House
11
Spasa-na-Gorodu Church
4
Blagovesheniye (Annunciation) Church
Nikoli Rublenova Church +
Tolzhsky Monastery Hostel (1808)
5
Matveev's House
6
Pavilion (early 19ᵗʰc.)
Ilyinsko-Tikhonovskaya Church
House of the Metropolitan
Korovniki
Volga Tower
PORTOVAYA NABEREZHNAYA
River Kotorosl
River — Volga
To Moscow
BOLSHAYA
MOSCOVSKAYA ST.
YAMSKAYA ST.
EMELYANA
YAROSLAVSKY
MALAVA PROLETARSKAYA
MELNICHNAYA
OKTYABRSKAYA
SVOBODY ST.
CHAIKOVSKY ST.
SOBINOVA ST.
SALTYKOVA
SHCHEDRINA
ST.
PERVOMAISKAYA BLVD
USHINSKY ST.
TREFOLEV ST.
KIROVSKAYA
REVOLUTS KRESTYANSKAYA
SOVIETSKAYA
VOLZHSKAYA NABEREZHNAYA

YAROSLAVL

KEY
1 Vakhrameev's House (1780)
2 Doctors' Club (c.1700)
3 Church of Elijah the Prophet
4 Office building (1781-84)
5 Sorokin's House (1816)
6 Dedulin's House (c.1800)

7 Nikoly Nadeina Church
8 Rozhdestva Kristova (Nativity) Church
9 Kazan Monastery Cathedral
10 Lopatin's House (1780's)
11 Kudasov's House (late 18ᵗʰc.)
12 Traders' Row (1814-18)

13 Apparition of the Virgin Tower (1662)
14 Bogoyarleniye (Epiphany) Church
15 Ecclesiastical court (1815)
16 St.Nikita the Martyr's Belfry
17 Nikoly-Melinsky Church
18 Peter and Paul Church

Today Yaroslavl is a big industrial town; apart from making cotton and linen fabric in one of the oldest factories in Russia, it also produces synthetic rubber, motor tyres, lorries, diesel engines, electro-machines, chemicals, and leather, and processes tobacco and oil. There are three institutes, pedagogical, medical, and technological, in the town.

The oldest part of the town is the Strelka (arrow), where the R. Kotorosl flows into the Volga. This is where the Kremlin once stood, and where one of the oldest civil buildings, the *House of the Metropolitan*, built in 1690, still survives.

The centre of Yaroslavl is Sovietskaya Sq. (formerly Illinskaya Sq.) with the *Church of Elijah the Prophet* in the centre. The houses around the square were built as regional government buildings in 1781–4. From this square run two streets, Kirovskaya and Bolshaya Oktyabrskaya, which end in two towers, *Znamenskaya*, dating from 1660, and *Uglichskaya* (1646) both built as lookout towers on the town's old earthen wall. The Pervomaiskaya (formerly Kazansky) Boulevard, in the centre, is a favourite place for the local inhabitants to take the air. Yaroslavl is probably the

best place for visitors who wish to see old Russian churches because it was not damaged at all d' 'ng World War II. In the centre of the town there are many typical Russian mansion houses which add to the special charm of the place.

The churches include several from the 16th and 17th centuries which are of considerable interest. In particular the Yaroslavl frescoes are unique for the colossal area they cover; Moscow churches are smaller and consequently have less interior wall space. Most of the churches in the town were built by merchants. Yaroslavl is also noted for having the best wood-carvings in Russia.

Spaso-Preobrazhensky (Transfiguration of our Saviour) Monastery, Podbelsky Sq. 25. This monastery was founded at the end of the 12th century, and in 1787 it was converted into an archbishop's palace. The wall was built in the first half of the 17th century to replace the original wall. It is 2·8– 3 m. thick and 188 m. in circumference. The Holy Gates at the entrance were built in 1616, and the frescoes inside the archway illustrating St. John's apocalyptic vision were painted in 1664. Within the walls is the *Transfiguration Cathedral*, built in 1516 by Moscow architects. It was one of the most revered and rich cathedrals in Yaroslavl and through the years has been altered several times. The frescoes were painted in 1563-4 by three Moscow and two local artists; the whole of the western wall depicts the Last Judgement. Some frescoes were added in 1782. It was in this monastery in 1795 that the manuscipt 'The Lay of Igor's Host' was discovered, a medieval epic which provided the subject for the opera 'Prince Igor'.

Besides the cathedral, the monastery also comprises the *Church of Yaroslavl Miracle-Workers* (1831), now used as a cinema and lecture hall, the 16th-century *refectory*, the 16th century *belltower* (reconstructed in the 19th century), and the *monk's cells* of the 16th and 17th centuries. Restoration began in 1958 and is still in progress. Parts of the *Local Museum and the Art Museum* are now located in the monastery.

Nikoly Nadeina Church, Narodnyi Pereulok 2a. This church was built in 1620-2 but has suffered much alteration; some of the frescoes inside, dating from 1640, are reminiscent of miniatures stuck to the wall. The 18th-century iconostasis is said to have been constructed following a sketch by Fedor Volkhov, the founder of the Russian National Theatre in 1750. (His company was the first to stage 'Hamlet' in Russia.)

Rozhdestva Khristova (Nativity) Church, Malaya Fevralskaya St. 1. This church was built in 1644 and reconstructed in the 19th century. The frescoes were painted by local artists in 1683. There is a 17th–18th-century iconostasis and the mid-17th-century bell-tower is one of the loveliest examples of its kind in Yaroslavl.

The *Church of Elijah The Prophet*, Sovietskaya Sq. in the centre of town. This church is very well preserved. Its frescoes were completed in 6 or 7 months in 1680-1; they are divided into five horizontal strips, the first showing Christ arisen, the second the Gospel story of Christ's life on earth, the third the lives of the Apostles, the fourth the life of Elijah (to whom the church is dedicated), and the bottom one the life of Elijah and his disciple Elisha. The iconostasis dates from the 18th century, and the tsar's and patriarchs' pews were brought here from another church in 1930. This is the most impressive church in Yaroslavl and certainly the one in the best condition. It is now a museum; if it is closed tourists should apply to the museum authorities in the Spaso-Preobrazhensky Monastery to have it opened.

Group of churches in *Korovniki*, Portovaya Naberezhnaya 2. The church of *Ioan Zlatoust* (John the Golden Tongued) was built in 1649 and is one of the most picturesque churches in Yaroslavl. It has a 17th-century iconostasis and frescoes painted in 1732-3 by local artists. The outside of the altar window is decorated with coloured tiles. The smaller church is *Vladimirskaya Church* (1669), and between the two churches stands a 17th-century octagonal *bell-tower*; it is 37 m. high and is known as the 'candle of Yaroslavl'.

Church of Saint Michael the Archangel, Pervo-maiskaya St. 67. This church was built in 1657-80 and has a bell-tower. Its frescoes were painted by local artists in 1731; they are divided into nine strips and give the impression of brightly coloured tapestry.

Church of St. Nicholas The Wet, Chaikovsky St. 1. The church was built in 1665-72, copying the Church of Ioan Zlatoust, and the outside of the altar window is framed with coloured tiles in the same way. The frescoes were completed in 1673; on the left side of the fresco of the Last Judgement on the west wall, among a group of sinners, are depicted foreigners in 17th-century European dress and Persians in turbans. At the same address is *Tikhvinskaya Church* (1686).

Dmitri Solunsky Church, Bolshaya Oktyabrskaya St. 41. This church was built in 1671 and altered in the 18th and 19th centuries. The frescoes were painted by local artists in 1686.

Spasa-Na-Gorodo Church, Pochtovaya St. 3. The church was built in 1672 and decorated with frescoes by local artists in 1693; of these the most interesting are the two lower strips which show processions, and battles between the larger towns.

Nikola-Melinky Church, Stachek St. 60. The church was built in 1672 and the frescoes were completed by Yaroslavl artists in 1707. On the northern wall is shown the invasion by Timur and the carrying of the holy icon from Vladimir to Moscow. Even in the dirty fresco one can see in the background Saint Basil's Cathedral and the Ivan Veliky Bell-tower in Moscow.

Vladimirskaya Church, Rybinskaya St. 44. This church was built in 1670-8.

Ioana Predtechi-V-Tolchikovye (St. John the Baptist) Church, Kotoroslnaya Naberezhnaya 69. The whole population of the region around about contributed either physically or financially to the building of this church in 1671-87. With its 15 domes it is very grand, and is the best church of 17th-century Yaroslavl. The bricks imitate woodcarvings and the impression is that they are made of wood. There are also many coloured tiles in its decoration. The frescoes painted in 1694-5 took only 5 months to complete and they are among the best of their time. Instead of the usual Last Judgement on the west wall there are six illustrations of the Song of Songs. There is an 18th-century iconostasis, and the *bell-tower* was built in about 1700.

Fyodorovskaya Church, Yaroslavsky St. 74. This church was built in 1687 and contains frescoes painted by local artists in 1715; they are like illustrations to fairy tales, showing the details of secular life in Peter the Great's time. Battles, architecture, ships, etc. are depicted.

Nikoly Penskogo Church, Malaya Proletarskaya St. 59. The church, together with its bell-tower, was built in 1691.

Bogoyavleniye (Epiphany) Church, Podbelsky Sq. Built 1684-93, the façade of the church is decorated with tiles. The frescoes by local artists date from 1693, and there is a 17th-century iconostasis of beautifully carved wood with icons of the same date.

Nikoli Rublenova Church, on the site of the Kremlin. The church was built in 1695; it contains no frescoes.

Blagovesheniye (Annunciation) Church, Volzhskaya Naberezhnaya 51. The church was built in 1688–1702. The 18th-century domes resemble flower buds; the frescoes were painted by local artists in 1709.

Peter-and-Paul Church, Peter-and-Paul Park. Built in 1736 in honour of Peter the Great by the owner of a Yaroslavl textile factory of which the tsar was the patron, the church is in the St. Petersburg Baroque style of the 18th century and resembles the Peter-and-Paul Fortress in Leningrad. The bell-tower stands 57 m. high. The church is now used as a club.

Iliinsko-Tikhonovskaya Church, Volzhskaya Naberezhnaya 5. This church was built in 1825–31 and is now in a bad state of repair.

Kazan Monastery Cathedral, Pervomaiskaya St. 19a. Built in 1845, this cathedral used to house the regional archives.

Historical and Local Museum, Sovietskaya Sq. 19/1. Open 10–5; closed on Sat.

Art Museum, Chelyuskintsev Sq. 2. Open 10–5; closed Tues.

Planetarium, Trefolev St. 20. Open 11–7; closed Tues.

Nekrasov Monument, on the embankment. The famous poet Nekrasov spent most of his life in this region. His home at Karabykha, 16 km. south of Yaroslavl, is now a museum. This monument was unveiled in 1958.

Lenin Statue, Krasnaya Sq.

Obelisk, in the garden opposite St. Elijah's Church. This obelisk commemorating Civil War heroes was unveiled in 1958.

Volkhov Drama Theatre, Volkhov Sq. The theatre was built in 1911.

Puppet Theatre, Komitetskaya St. 8

Concert Hall, Komitetskaya St. 11

Butusov Town Park, Chaikovsky St.

Volga Hotel and Restaurant, Kirov St. 10. The local Intourist office is in Rooms 201 and 202, TEL. 2–12–58.

Tsentralnaya Hotel, Volkhov Sq.

Yaroslavl Hotel and Medved (bear) Restaurant, Ushinsky St. 40/2, TEL. 2–12–75

Moskva Restaurant, Komsomolskaya St. 1

G.P.O., Podbelsky Sq. 22/28

Yaroslavl Department Store, Svobody St.

Gift Shop, Svobody St. 16

Taxi Rank, Krasnaya Sq. TEL. 2–51–23

Just south of Yaroslavl, beside the main road is *Krestovskaya Church*. During an epidemic of cholera a cross was erected here, and after the spread of the disease stopped short of the town the church was built in thanksgiving.

Road to YASNAYA POLYANA

It is possible to drive south to Tolstoy's Home, Yasnaya Polyana, which is 201 km. from Moscow and back in one day, but many people prefer to spend a night in Tula on the way.

Podolsk

Population—169,000 (1970)

Podolsk stands on the R. Pakhra, near which there are large marble and limestone quarries.

In 1781 it became a town and was given a coat-of-arms with crossed pickaxes, symbolising the inhabitants' work in the quarries. At the end of the last century a Singer sewing machine factory was built; this was later enlarged and is still working today. Podolsk itself has grown into an industrial centre with factories producing concrete and machinery.

The *Troitsky Sobor (Trinity Cathedral)*. This cathedral dates from the 18th century.

Lenin Museum, Moskovskaya St. This is in a house where Lenin's family lived for some time during the 1890s.

Molodi

This village is some distance south of Podolsk, on the main road to the south and contains a picturesque church dedicated to St. Peter and St. Paul.

Chekhov

This town was formerly known as Lopasnya, and stands beside the river of that name. It has been known historically since the 12th century, and it was near here that the Russians defeated the Crimean Tatars in a battle in 1572. It was renamed after the writer, Anton Chekhov, in 1954. The town has a woodworking factory, and under construction is the biggest printing works in Europe.

Church of the Immaculate Conception. This dates from the 19th century.

Eating House, Melikhovo:

Melikhovo

13 km. from Chekhov. It was here that Anton Chekhov (1860–1904) lived on his own estate between 1892 and 1898. He was responsible for building the local school, and during the cholera epidemic he resumed his work as a doctor. There is now a museum on the estate, and among other exhibits is the wooden platter upon which the peasants presented him with bread and salt (an old Russian custom) upon the occasion of the opening of the school.

The *Chekhov Monument* was erected on the Melikhovo Estate in 1951. Chekhov wrote 'The Seagull' while living here.

Serpukhov

Population—124,000 (1970)

The town stands on the R. Nara, which is a small tributary of the R. Oka, and it dates from 1328. Down the R. Nara, on either side, stood two fortresses; these were the Vladichny Convent, founded by Metropolitan Alexei in 1362, and the Vysotsky Bogoroditsy Monastery, founded by St. Sergius of Rodonezh in 1373. The fate of Serpukhov was linked with that of Moscow, but the princes of Serpukhov still had their own independence to a certain extent in the 14th and 15th centuries and minted their own money. Like so many other Russian towns, Serpukhov was destroyed several times by the Tatars and later by the Lithuanians.

In 1556 by the order of Ivan the Terrible it was built up into a powerful fortress with a stone wall and towers replacing the original fortifications of earth and oak. Its situation made it one of the strategic points on the Oka thoroughfare, protecting the road to Moscow from the encroachments of the Tatars. At the end of the 18th century Tsar Paul I ordered the defences to be dismantled; this was duly done, and now only remains of the earth wall and some parts of the Kremlin walls can be seen.

Today Serpukhov is an important centre of the chemical and machinery-building industries and has several large textile mills.

The local churches, all of different styles, can be seen from the top of the Kremlin Hill.

Troitsky (Trinity) Cathedral. This cathedral was built in 1380 by Prince Vladimir Andreyevich. It was reconstructed in 1714 and is still open for religious services.

Church of St. Nicholas the White, Kaluzhskaya St. 26. This church was built in 1649 and reconstructed in 1835.

Church of the Prophet Elijah, Volodarsky St. This church was founded in 1748 and is open for services.

Uspensky (Assumption) Church. This church was built in 1851.

Vladichnyi Convent. The walls with four towers remain; these were built in the 16th century and reconstructed in the 18th century.

Vysotsky Bogoroditsy Monastery. The 15th-century cathedral, reconstructed in the 17th century, still stands and the remains of the walls with towers of 1664 can be seen.

Lenin Monument, on the central square

History and Art Museum, Chekhov St. 87. This is located in a house built in the 1870s. The museum was founded in 1920, to house the local nobility's collections of icons and western European works of art, which had passed to the museum after the revolution.

Drama Theatre, Chekhov St. 58/27

Moskva Hotel and Restaurant, Lenin Sq.

Tula

Population—462,000 (1970)

Tula is an industrial town lying on either side of the R. Upa, a tributary of the R. Oka. It lies 180 km. south of Moscow and covers an area of over 10,000 hectares (25,000 acres) measuring 9 km. from north to south. Like most old Russian towns it is built on a plan of concentric circles centering on the Kremlin. The present-day layout of the town was planned in the middle of the 19th-century, and now there are as many as 570 streets.

The first records of Tula date from 1146, and the town developed at the same time as Moscow, which it protected from the Crimean Tatars. Tula itself suffered much from their invasions.

Iron deposits were discovered in the vicinity in the 16th century, and the first gun factory was established in 1632 by a Dutchman named Vienius. The town's period of prosperity dates from 1712 when Peter the Great founded the Imperial Small Arms Factory here. This was built under the superintendence of an Englishman, Trewheller, and is situated near the Kremlin. It supplied Russia with her arms for many years, and is still in operation. Napoleon planned to capture Tula and so to disarm Russia; in World War II the Germans had a similar plan, but although they managed to seize part of the town they failed to capture it all.

Tula iron-workers have long been famous for their craftsmanship, and a favourite story by the 19th-century Russian writer Leskov tells how at the beginning of the 18th century a present of a life-size metal flea was sent to the tsar from England to show the skill of British metal-workers. The tsar sent it to Tula to a certain Master Levsha (left-handed) who, to prove that his skill was greater than that of the British, made for the flea a set of 'horseshoes' which could only be seen through a magnifying glass.

Besides the local iron ore, coal has been mined from valuable deposits nearby and has also added to the town's prosperity.

Tula is famous as the home of sweet biscuits called Tulskie Pryaniki, but more important are the 'Tula ware' objects made of brass, such as samovars, and of nickel-plate, iron, and steel, especially knives. The so-called 'Tula work' consist of black enamel inlaid with silver, and is often imitated elsewhere.

The main streets of the town are all near the Kremlin, including the principal Lenin Prospect. On Mendeleyev St. is the *Lenin Library,* built in Classical style with massive columns. Tula's main square is Chelyuskintsev to the south-west of the Kremlin; on this square stands a huge *Palace of Pioneers,* reconstructed from the original town hall, which contains a planetarium and a concert hall for 500. Close to the Kremlin wall on the other side of the square is a technical school, and in the centre is a *statue* of a Soviet soldier with a rifle. Nearby in Revolutsyii St. is one of the biggest maternity hospitals in Russia with 280 beds, and not far away in Dennisovsky Pereulok are the remains of the palace which belonged to the factory-owners, the Levintsevs; its magnificence can now only be judged by the Baroque gates, built in the middle of the 18th century, which are still standing. The *Luginin Palace,* now housing the Pedagogical Institute, stands near the crossing of Mendeleyev St. and Lenin Prospect. Mendeleyev St. leads to the horseshoe-shaped Sovietskaya St. which is the town's second most important thoroughfare and which was built to follow the line of the old earth wall in the 18th century. This street runs through Vosstania Sq. where stands a huge bronze monument to Lenin and where parades and demonstrations take place. Nearby is Pioneer Garden Sq., where a church used to stand. The busiest spot in Tula is at the cross-road of Sovietskaya St. and Lenin Prospect. Lenin Prospect is 4 km. long and passes to other garden squares, Ploschad' Gogolya and Ploschad' Pushkina where Pushkin's bust was unveiled in 1889.

In Lenin Prospect 44 is the *House of Officers,* formerly the House of Nobles, which contains a Hall of Columns with room for 800 people—a replica of the famous Hall of Columns in Moscow. Opposite this building is another garden square with the graves of soldiers who fell during the Civil War of 1918. Nearby Gogol St. was the street of Tula's nobility; it has been partly reconstructed but many original houses remain. A number of Russian writers have lived in this street.

Not far from *Komsomol Park* is the beginning of Oktyabrskaya St. where, beside Chugunnyi Most (Pig-iron Bridge), stands the 18th-century *Nikolo Zaredskaya Church.*

The south-east of the town, the Novotulsky Region, is the newest part, built to house the metal factory workers. Although it belongs to Tula, there are 4 km. of allotments between these two parts of the town.

Tula's industrial station for the underground gasification of coal is one of the biggest in the world; the coal is burnt below ground, and the gas supplies many Tula factories.

The *Kremlin* stands on Vosstaniye Sq. in the centre of the town. It is rectangular with a perimeter of over 1 km. enclosing an area of 6 hectares (15 acres). It is about 320 m. long and 200 m. wide. Its architecture is characteristically Russian; it was built between 1514 and 1521, and in spite of restorations in 1784 and in 1824 it has changed little during the past 400 years. The walls are 3 m. thick and about 13 m. high, built of limestone with battlements of brick. There are 4 corner towers with 5 square towers between them.

Within the walls stands the *Uspensky Sobor* (Cathedral of the Assumption), founded in the 16th century, but reconstructed in Russian Baroque style between 1742 and 1744. It is famous for its frescoes which were painted by artists from Yaroslavl, and which repeat the motifs of the ancient churches of Yaroslavl, Vladimir, and Moscow. The technique used is quite outstanding, and they are considered to be the finest examples of old Russian fresco work. Some of the frescoes illustrate the Song of Solomon.

Another church within the Kremlin walls is the *Bogoyavleniya (Epiphany) Church,* built in the middle of the 19th century.

Outside the Kremlin, but close to the western wall, is the *Church of the Annunciation,* built in 1692, and typical of the older Russian churches.

Church of the Uspensky Monastery, at the crossing of Mendeleyev St. and Lenin Prospect. This church was built in the 19th century.

Local Museum, Sovietskaya St. 68

Art Museum, Lenin Prospect 44

Museum of the History of Arms, Lenin Prospect, on the main Moscow–Yalta road just opposite the Kremlin. Open 11–3; closed Mon. This museum, established in 1724, contains collections of Russian arms of all ages and includes many mini-

atures. There are also some foreign arms on display, and the museum is well worth a visit.

Vsevolod Rudnev Monument, at the entrance to Tula from Moscow. Rudnev (1855–1913) was commander of the man-of-war 'Varyag', famous for its lone stand against the Japanese fleet in January 1904 when the Japanese War began. The monument to commemorate the 50th anniversary was unveiled in 1956.

Gorky Drama Theatre, Lenin Prospect 51

Youth Theatre, Kominterna St. 10

Puppet Theatre, Sovietskaya St. 78

Zenith Stadium, in the eastern half of the Kremlin territory

Komsomol Park. This park was laid out in 1895 on an area of 45 hectares (111 acres). It has many oak and lime trees and in the centre of the park is the so-called Pushkin Oak. There is also a summer café, a dance floor, a musical variety stage, and a monument which commemorates the Soviet soldiers who died in 1941.

Sezhensky Forest. This is another favourite playground for the people of Tula.

Central Hotel and Restaurant Moskva, Sovietskaya St. 29

Filling Station, on the main road leading out of the town to the south, by the bus station. Round-the-clock service.

Yasnaya Polyana

Yasnaya Polyana (sunlit meadows) was the birthplace and beloved home of Count Leo Tolstoy (1828–1910). Of it he wrote, 'Without Yasnaya Polyana I can hardly think of Russia or of my attitude to her.'

The estate lies 1·5 km. from the main road, the turning being marked by a bust of the writer.

Tolstoy would probably have died in Yasnaya Polyana as well as spending most of his life here if, ten days before his death, he had not left home and caught pneumonia so that he died at a small railway station not far away. His grave surrounded by nine oaks is in the park, on Staryi Zakas Hill.

Preserved in the house are portraits of the writer by Repin and Kramskoy (the latter painted in 1873 while Tolstoy was working on 'Anna Karenina'), a library of 22,000 books in more than 20 languages of which Tolstoy himself spoke 13, a phonograph presented by Edison, an English-made Grandfather clock, and a portrait of the real Anna Karenina. The desk at which Tolstoy's wife transcribed 'War and Peace' many times is in her bedroom. The other simple furnishings remain much as they were during Tolstoy's lifetime.

There is now a literary museum in the building where Tolstoy organised a school for the peasants, and one of the curators was his last secretary, Valentin Bulgakov.

The museum ticket office is by the main gates of the estate. The museum is open 9–5; closed Wed.

Restaurant and Café, just outside the gates of the estate

YEREVAN
See Erevan, p. 98

YESSENTUKI
See Essentuki, Mineralniye Vody, p. 191

ZAGORSK
Population—90,000 (1970)
This town, situated on the R. Koshura and the R. Glimitza, received town status in 1917. Until 1930 it was called Sergiev, and was then renamed after Vladimir M. Zagorsky (1883–1919), a revolutionary well known for his political work who was killed by an anarchist's bomb.

Zagorsk is a centre of the handmade toy industry and is particularly renowned for its carved woodwork. Its other factories produce agricultural machinery, furniture, and textiles.

It can be visited from Moscow, but arrangements are best made well in advance with Intourist.

The *Troitskio-Sergievskaya Lavra* (Trinity Monastery of St. Sergius). This monastery is one of the most important architectural and historical monuments of medieval Russia, and is also the centre of Russian Orthodoxy today. Founded in

1340, it soon rose to be the religious capital of northern Russia. Its founder, St. Sergius (1319?–92), came from the small town of Rodonezh, which was in 1610 completely ruined by the Poles. St. Sergius also founded other monasteries around Moscow and elsewhere, and monks from Zagorsk continued his work; they were responsible for the founding of the Solovyetsky Monastery on a island in the White Sea. The history of Russia in medieval times is closely connected with that of Zagorsk monastery, for Sergius was influential and played an important role in Grand-Prince Dmitri's rousing of the Russian people against the Tatars; the Russian princes and soldiers were blessed by Abbot Sergius before the battle of Kulikovskaya against the Tatars in 1380.

In 1408 the whole region, including the monastery, was again devastated by the Tatars, and afterwards the Abbot Nikon found Sergius' body uninjured among the smoking ruins of the monastery, a sure sign of his sanctity. Abbot Nikon managed to rebuild the monastery by using much of the treasure he had been able to save.

The monastery grew very rich and became the second most important educational centre in Russia after Kiev. Its reserve of fighting men num-

ZAGORSK : Trinity Monastery of St.Sergius

KEY
1 Troitsky (Trinity) Cathedral
2 Church of the Descent of the Holy Spirit
3 Uspensky (Assumption) Cathedral
4 Refectory
5 Belfry
6 Monastery Walls
7 Pyatnitskaya Tower (1640)

8 Krasnaya Gate Tower (16th–19th c.)
9 Assumption Gate (mid–17th c.)
10 Gateway Church
11 Drying Tower (16th–17th c.)
12 Duck Tower (17th c.)
13 Ringing Tower (16th–17th c.)
14 Stable Tower & gates (1758–78)
15 Smolensky Church

16 Carpenters' Tower (17th c.)
17 Cellarer's Tower (1642–1849) & Beer Tower with ice-house (16th–17th c.)
18 Water Tower (17th c.)
19 Water Gate (16th–17th c.)
20 Bow Tower (16th–17th c.)
21 Chapel
22 Hospital Buildings, Church & Museum

bered 20,000 and in 1513 the strong fortress wall was built, 1 km. in circumference, 15 m. thick, and with nine towers. In 1608–10, during the Time of Troubles, the monastery was besieged for 16 months by 30,000 Poles, but although there were only 1500 men to defend it, it never surrendered. The fate of the whole of Russia was dependent upon the outcome of the siege.

In 1612 an army headed by Minin and Pozharsky halted at Zagorsk for rest and blessing before they set off southwards to liberate Moscow from the Poles, and in 1682 and 1689, during the mutinies of the royal Streltsy guards, the boytsars Peter and Ivan were sheltered here. Zagorsk remained an important fortress defending Moscow until the end of the 17th century.

Troitsky (Trinity) Cathedral. This cathedral was built between 1422 and 1427, with a single dome in the Suzdal-Vladimir style. Its frescoes date from the 16th century and there are many icons of value and interest among those in the second, third, and fourth rows of the iconostasis. The icon of the Holy Trinity is a copy of the one painted by Andrei Rublyev especially for this cathedral; the original is now in Moscow's Tretyakov Gallery. The cathedral was erected on the site of the wooden Church of St. Sergius which Abbot Nikon had built over the founder's grave; the body of St. Sergius, which is still visited by pilgrims, lies inside the cathedral in a dull silver sarcophagus presented by Ivan the Terrible. The silver canopy over it weighs 409 kg. (8 cwt.) and was a gift from the Empress Anna. The porch was added to the southern wall of the cathedral in the 18th century.

Church of the Descent of the Holy Spirit. This church, built in 1476–7 by architects from Pskov, stands to the east of Trinity Cathedral. The top of the single dome was once used as a watchtower.

Church of St. Nikon. This church, adjoining the southern wall of Trinity Cathedral, was built in 1548 and reconstructed in 1623.

Uspensky (Assumption) Cathedral. This cathedral reminds one, by its size and its shape, of the Uspensky Cathedral in the Moscow Kremlin. It was built in the reign of Ivan the Terrible to commemorate the capture of Kazan and Astrakhan from the Tatars, and was consecrated in 1585. The frescoes were painted in 1684 by local and Yaroslavl artists. Near the west door of the cathedral, outside, is the tomb of Boris Godunov, his wife, and two of his children. The five domes of the cathedral are painted blue and are decorated with golden stars.

The *Gateway Church.* This church, which is decorated with frescoes, was built 1693–9.

Smolensky Church. This church is called after its principal icon, Our Lady of Smolensk. With its wide entrance, the church resembles a decorative rotunda. It was designed in 1746–8 by Prince Ukhtomsky.

Belfry. This stands near Smolensky Church and, although founded in 1741, was the last of the whole ensemble to be completed, being finished

only in 1769. It was designed in Baroque style by Rastrelli and Prince Ukhtomsky; it stands 98 m. high and has five tiers. At one time it boasted forty bells.

Refectory. This refectory stands by the monastery's southern wall. It was built in 1686–92 in Baroque style, is 73 m. long and gaily painted.

St. Sergius' Well. Just outside the Uspensky Cathedral stands a small chapel, built at the end of the 17th century to cover the well. Many of the pilgrims who still visit the monastery bring bottles to fill with holy water.

The *Hospital Buildings,* with the Church of SS. Zosim and Savvati, built in 1635–7, are the oldest of the secular structures in the complex.

Chertogi. Built at the end of the 17th century and gaily decorated with paintwork and coloured tiles, this building was once the tsar's Palace. The interiors date from the 1740s and one of the halls has a painted ceiling depicting the victories of Peter the Great. The building, which lies near the northern wall of the monastery, now houses the Theological College (founded 1749) and an Ecclesiastical Academy.

The Metropolitan's House. This is an 18th-century building which was reconstructed from the 17th-century cells of the archimandrites. Stoves decorated with 17th-century coloured tiles can be seen inside.

The vestry and adjoining monastery buildings now house an interesting museum. The collection is displayed in the order in which it was presented to the monastery, and includes gifts from Russian nobles and the tsars Ivan the Terrible and Boris Godunov. The museum contains one of the richest collections of Russian ecclesiastical art with some icons by Simon Ushakov (1626–86). Besides 18th- and 19th-century portraits, there are collections of 17th- to 19th-century furniture, pottery, china, and glass. The fabrics are French and Italian of the 14th and 15th centuries, and there are Persian, Syrian, and Turkish tissues of the 17th century. The Russian handicrafts displayed include carving, fabrics, costumes, embroidery, metalwork, and toys. There is a small souvenir stall where local wood work may be purchased. The museum is closed Fri. and on the 30th of each month.

Toy Museum, Krasnoi Armiyi Prospect 136. This is the only museum of its kind in the Soviet Union. It was founded in 1918 and has a rich collection of toys dating from the Bronze Age to the present time, many of them of local production. There is a laboratory in the town where scientific research on toys is carried out.

ZAPOROZHYE
Population—658,000 (1970)
(formerly Alexandrovsk)
In the 15th and 16th centuries the Ukrainian Cossacks settled in Zaporozhye Sech on the island of Khortitsa in the Dnieper. The island is 12 km. long and 2·5 km. wide and can be reached today from the old town. There are sanatoria and child-

ren's camps there now. The 600-year-old oak which legend maintains is the one under which the Zaporozhye Cossacks wrote their challenging and insulting letter to the Turkish Sultan can be seen 5 km. outside the town at Verkhnyaya Khortitsa, Gogol St. It is certainly the oldest tree in the Ukraine and the girth of its trunk measures 6·32 m. It is also said that in 1648 Bogdan Khmelnitsky addressed his warriors here with an appeal that in battle against the Poles they should be as firm and strong as this oak tree.

In 1770 a fortress was founded here as part of the defences against the Turks. In the 1806 the settlement that had grown up alongside was called Alexandrovsk. Later, when the border with Turkey was at the edge of the Black Sea, this fortress lost its importance and the demobilised soldiers settled in the town. The records say that before 1917 there was only one three-storey house in the town and nine with two storeys. No more than 120 were brick built. The old name of Zaporozhye ('Beyond the Rapids') was given to the town for the first time in 1921.

Zaporozhye saw much fighting in 1918–19 and 70% of the town was ruined during the occupation from 1941–3, but it finally recovered by 1949. With the development of industry, a new town grew up, 10 km. from the old one. Its first streets were laid out in the 1930s and it grew up as a model socialist town with multi-storey houses and wide avenues—Metallurgov Prospect is over 30 m. from side to side. Among other factories here is Zaporozhstal, a huge steel mill. Apart from metal, the town produces 'Zaporzhets' baby cars, and a variety of food products.

The main thoroughfare of the town proper is Lenin Prospect which runs from Yuzhny Vokzal, through Svoboda Sq. Sovietskaya Sq., Oktyabrskaya Sq., and Mayakovskaya Sq. for a distance of over 15 km. The old and the new parts of the town are linked by a 1 km. long causeway, 30 m. wide and 33 m. high. The local population is 68% Ukrainian and 25·5% Russian, the rest belonging to any of thirty different nationalities, including Tatars, Jews, Greeks, Bulgarians, Georgians, and Poles. Navigation on the Dnieper used to be impossible because of the rapids. The first attempt to avoid them was made in the 18th century, and in the 19th century some by-passing channels were built. The river was finally made navigable along the whole of its course by the construction of the Dnieper Hydro-electric Station (known as Dne-

proges). This was the first big hydropower station to be built in Russia. The plans were begun in 1905 and the construction in 1927. Many foreign firms were consulted before its completion in 1932, and the General Electric Company supplied most of the equipment to build up its 558,000 kilowatt capacity. Alexandrov was the Russian engineer hydrologist and Vesnin headed the team of architects. The dam is 760 m. long and 62 m. high. There are 47 sluices. Three-quarters of the whole construction was destroyed during the war and it took three years after the war before it began producing current again. It had regained its former capacity by 1950. The second power house on the left bank of the river doubles the power output of Dneproges.

Local Museum, Lenin Prospect 59

Tank Monument, Soviet Sq. This is the first tank that entered the town when it was liberated.

Lenin Monument, at the end of Lenin Prospect

Glinka Monument, Lenin Prospect 183, outside the concert hall; designed by Strakhov.

Steel Smelter's Statue, near the Palace of Culture. This statue by the local sculptor, Vlasenko, stands 4·5 m. high. It was unveiled in 1959 as a symbol of the city's industrial might.

Revolutionaries' Monument, in the garden in Svoboda Sq.

Schors Drama Theatre, Lenin Prospect 41.

Glinka Concert Hall, Lenin Prospect 57. Built in 1952 with seats for 860.

Circus, in Metallurgov Park

Bathing Beaches, at Zhdanov Prospect. Metallurg Park has a stadium for 23,000 spectators.

Zaporozhye Hotel and Restaurant (Intourist), Lenin Prospect 135, TEL. 33–05–54

Dniepro Hotel and Restaurant, Lenin Prospect 202

Teatralnaya Hotel and Restaurant, Chekista St. 23

Bank, Lenin Prospect 49

G.P.O., Sverdlov St. 21

Bookshop, Lenin Prospect 232

Ukraina Department Store, Lenin Prospect 147

Gift Shop, Lenin Prospect 192

Taxi Rank, Lenin Prospect 151

ZELYONI MYS
see Batumi, p. 62

ZHELEZNOVODSK
see Mineralniye Vody, p. 188

PART III

Railway Journeys

INTRODUCTION

The towns of the Soviet Union have mostly grown up following a similar pattern. For hundreds of years, from medieval times, they lived their isolated, sleepy lives, sometimes disturbed by wars, or rumours of wars, sometimes ravaged by fire and plague, but changing little with the passing of time.

Then, towards the end of the 19th century, the railways pushed out in all directions from the big cities west of the Urals. As the lines spread, each provincial town that was connected to the network was infused with new life.

It is an important chapter in the country's history and certainly the most exciting part of the railway story is that concerning the construction of the Trans-Siberian railway. This runs almost 10,000 km., from Moscow to Vladivostok on the Sea of Japan. It crosses seven time zones and passes through various geographical regions—through rich farming land, across the low, wooded Ural mountains which divide Europe and Asia, across the wheatlands of Western Siberia, through steppelands, taiga, and through the mountainous area south of Lake Baikal. It passes through important industrial centres including the coal centre of Cheremkhovsky and the oil belt between the Volga and Urals.

The journey on the world's longest railway line has attracted many travellers since it was completed in 1916. Before the railway was built, the only way to cross Siberia was by sledge, coach, or cart along the extremely rough Great Siberian Tract. The Tract was laid in the middle of the 18th century, on a line almost parallel to the present railway, and was an important outlet for Chinese silk, cotton, spices, and tea. The journey took weeks or months and was very much an endurance test with numerous rivers to cross, poor posting houses, and endless waits for horses and drivers. Known abroad as the Great Siberian Post Road, the Tract was no more than a narrow track, covered with thick dust in summer and often impassable snow in winter. At the beginning of the 1890s it was still quicker to reach the Pacific from St. Petersburg by taking a train to Germany, boarding a boat to New York, travelling across America by train and sailing across the Pacific to the east coast of the Russian Empire!

Siberia remained a largely undeveloped source of natural wealth and was mostly known for the thousands of exiles and convicts who were sent there on foot. From 1823, when official records on the number of deportees were opened, and 1888, nearly 773,000 exiles and voluntary followers made the long journey. In spite of the common belief that convicts were sent to work in the salt mines, these were a small minority and far more were allocated to the gold and silver mines which were owned by the imperial family. Some convict labour was used on the Trans-Siberian railway, especially on the eastern section from Khabarovsk to Vladivostok where appalling conditions made labour particularly hard to find, but this was halted when many of the convicts escaped and brought the local crime rate to astronomical figures.

Siberia was first opened up in the 16th century following the expansion of Russia to the south. Ivan the Terrible had conquered the Tatar strongholds of Kazan and Astrakhan in 1552 and 1555 respectively and in 1574 he gave the Stroganov brothers the right to extend their mining and mercantile interests beyond the Ural mountains, then known as the Stone. They hired a Cossack band under Yermak Timofeevich who set out in 1581 with a force of about 800 men. Travelling mostly along the rivers, they reached the R. Ob in Central Siberia where they fought against the bands of Khan Kuchum who claimed the title of Tsar of Sibir. After initial victories, the Russians were driven back from Siberia but it was no longer an unknown land and Russian forces continued to advance into Siberia against the Tatars during the reign of Boris Godunov. By 1633 Russian garrisons had been installed as far east as the R. Lena, north of Lake Baikal, and in 1639 a Cossack band reached the Sea of Okhotsk. Adventurers and merchants were attracted to Siberia by the wealth of valuable furs and the tales of rich deposits of silver and gold.

In 1649 a rich fur merchant, Yerofei Khabarov, set out with an expedition to explore the area around the R. Amur. Finding a land abundant with furs, grain, and fish, Khabarov determined to conquer it, and committed atrocities against the indigenous population whom he tortured and burned. News of this shocked many Russians in the capital, but the tsar sent Russian troops to support Khabarov. Instead of obeying the tsar's command to treat the natives justly, the troops followed Khabarov's precedent with the result that the land was devastated and some of the richest agricultural lands lost. Russian troops then extended their newly acquired lands into Manchuria, the home of the ruling Chinese dynasty, and fought battles with the Chinese over the R. Amur. In 1689 China made its first treaty with a Western power, the Treaty of Nerchinsk, by which the Eastern part of the Russian-Chinese border was fixed at a point roughly 200 miles north of the R. Amur.

In spite of this setback in the east, Russian power was consolidated in central Siberia and military garrisons set up in Kurgan, Tomsk, Krasnoyarsk, and Omsk.

In the reign of Nicholas I expeditions were again sent into China, and Vladivostok was captured. This gain was of immense importance as it gave Russia a sheltered harbour which was ice-free for longer than any other eastern port. Russian expansion came shortly after French and British expansion in the area and was partly determined by fears that these powers were gaining control. At the end of the Opium War with China,

Britain had been granted considerable trading rights with China as well as the annexation of Hong Kong. By the Treaty of Aigun in 1858 China conceded to Russia the area north of the Amur and by the Treaty of Peking in 1860 the area of Manchuria eastwards from the Assuri to the coast and south to the Korean border, including, of course, Vladivostok which had been captured earlier.

The first proposal for a railway to link the east coast of the Russian Empire with the capital was put forward in 1857 by Lieutenant-General Muravyev, given the title Count Muravyev-Amurski after his victories in the Amur area. Various proposals for railways and tramways were put forward during the next two decades by Russian, American, and British groups but, like the first proposal, they were all turned down by the Russian government for the sake of economy. The idea of a direct rail link with the east coast was finally approved in 1887 and in 1891 Tsarevich Nicholas, later Nicholas II, tipped a wheelbarrow of soil onto the future embankment of the Trans-Siberian railway at Vladivostok in a ceremony to inaugurate work on the line. Work on the western part of the line eastwards from Chelyabinsk, already linked by rail to Moscow and St. Petersburg, was begun in the following year and by 1899 a through route to Vladivostok had been opened. This date does not mark the opening of the Trans-Siberian railway, however, as the eastern part of the line ran along the Chinese Eastern railway through Manchuria. The route through Manchuria was much shorter than the later route north of the R. Amur and was decided upon because of the considerable saving. It was built by the Chinese Eastern Railway Company which was totally controlled by Russia. A Chinese diplomat was nominally chairman of the board of management, in order to give a semblance of Chinese ownership, but all the directors were Russian and the imperial treasury owned almost all the shares. Construction began in 1897 but during the Boxer Rebellion of 1900 it was almost totally destroyed. In the same year Russia, together with Japan and the Western powers including the United States, captured Peking briefly in order to quell the revolt, and then took control of Manchuria. The Chinese Eastern railway was completed in the following year.

The Trans-Siberian was now complete except for the line around the southern shore of Lake Baikal, but it was still not the easy journey one imagines today. Owing to insufficient ballast, deficient materials, and bad workmanship, many parts of the railway were extremely unsafe and the number of accidents was high. The speed was slow, however, and many derailed passengers emerged from their upturned carriage unhurt, only to wait days for a relief train. Many of the wooden bridges visibly sank beneath the weight of the train and the icon of St. Nicholas the Miracle Worker on every bridge, before which passengers crossed themselves and prayed for a safe passage,

was not so out of place as it may seem.

Before the bridges were built, mostly by Italian masons, the crossing of rivers was even more dangerous. In summer ferries were used, but these were often very feeble against the swift currents of the Siberian rivers, and passengers might have to wait for days for a train on the other side before continuing their journey. Two ferries large enough to carry the train and its passengers were ordered from a British company for Lake Baikal. The ferries were sent in parts to Russia where they were assembled on the spot. Large and ungainly in appearance, they were regarded as wonders by the local inhabitants and travelling Russians but they proved useless, unable to break through the ice in winter and often port-bound in autumn and spring through the fog for which Lake Baikal is famous.

The most terrifying method of all for crossing the rivers and lakes, however, must have been when the trains were driven across the ice. The rails were frozen to the ice and kept in place by additional water which was poured onto them and immediately froze. The passengers usually walked across or were driven by sledge, no doubt the safest course as, according to the accounts of early travellers, one could hear the ice 'crack and quiver as the train moved over it'. After the outbreak of the war with Japan in 1904, the same method was used on Lake Baikal to accelerate the supply of troops and arms to the battlefield. Tracks were laid across the lake at a temperature of below –40°C. The first engine to test the rails disappeared through the ice, leaving a hole 1·4 m. wide and 20 km. long and causing all the tracks to twist and break. The ice was believed to be 1·6 m. thick and it was only after this accident that it was learnt that there are warm springs in the lake which cause the ice to be very thin in places. The trains then had to be dismantled before being towed cautiously across the ice and reassembled on the other side. Nevertheless, in the course of five weeks thousands of troops, gun batteries, 65 locomotives, and 22 laden railway carriages crossed the lake.

In spite of the hazards of travel on the Trans-Siberian railway, it attracted travellers from all over the world. Throughout its construction the foreign press had been extremely disparaging about its worth and termed it Russia's white elephant. The Russian government advertised it endlessly and had plans for making it the most luxurious and economical train journey in the world. According to the brochures it was to have compartments equal in comfort to those reserved for royalty in the West, a library with Russian and foreign books, a church car with a priest and church-bells on the roof, a bathroom with shower, a gymnasium, a darkroom for photography, a barber, multi-lingual waiters, medical service free of charge, and almost everything any traveller could possibly wish for. Needless to say, the trains did not differ much from those in Western Europe and there was neither gymnasium nor photography room. The reports of the many foreigners who made the journey differ tremendously, some praising the service and food, others decrying it. This probably reflects the varying services to be found on the trains as much as the varying temperaments of the travellers. The journey then took ten days, only two and a half days more than it does now.

The opening of the Trans-Siberian railway also benefited the economy of the country. The famine of 1891 had illustrated the need to transport grain across the empire and Siberia was gaining importance as a centre of livestock farming, eggs, and poultry as well as wheat. Since 1889 the government had favoured emigration to Siberia (earlier it was discouraged and the necessary permission hard to obtain) and at the end of the century 200,000 people were emigrating every year. In Siberia they were given slight financial aid and allotted land. Emigration was facilitated by the railway and the increased harvests which resulted from more workers were transported by rail to Central Russia and abroad.

In the period between the two world wars a second track was built and the railway is now almost totally electrified. Many new branch lines have been built and, in spite of aeroplanes which make the journey in ten hours, it is still an important link between Vladivostok and Moscow.

THE TRANS-SIBERIAN RAILWAY, FROM MOSCOW TO NAKHODKA

The first stretch of line, from Moscow to Yaroslavl, is one of the oldest in the country; it was completed in 1868. In 1929 it was the first section to be electrified.

The towns and villages along the line just after leaving Moscow have a long and eventful history. The region is mentioned in ancient legends and is often called the heart of Russia and the cradle of the Russian nation. The surrounding landscape deserves to be called 'typically Russian' and its beautiful forests and quiet rivers have inspired both artists and writers.

Taininskaya is the third station outside Moscow. The village was first mentioned in the 14th century. It belonged to the Russian court and Ivan the Terrible (1533–84) used to come here frequently.

Mytischchi was known as a customs post since the 16th century, and now it has grown into an important industrial centre with a population of over 100,000. One large machine-building plant actually adjoins the railway tracks; it produces dumper trucks and underground railway carriages.

A little further on is **Tarasovka**, with a long tradition of manufacturing high-quality fabrics. The silks and brocades were sold as far afield as Mongolia and Tibet.

30 km. from Moscow is **Pushkino**, which probably took its name from the 'pushkari' (cannon

makers) who worked here in a village known since the 16th century. Pushkino now supplies Moscow's drinking water. From a reservoir of 150,000,000 cu. m. capacity fed by the Volga, a canal runs to a filtering station and then the water goes to Moscow.

About 60 km. from the capital, the railway leaves the area which is used by the city dwellers during the summer months, some maintaining their own cottages and others renting accommodation from the villagers. Now the countryside is less densely populated, although the people here are still closely connected with Moscow.

The ancient town of **Zagorsk** (q.v.) has a population approaching 100,000. It is known as the centre of the hand-made toy industry, but has also between 20 and 30 other industrial enterprises. The famous *Troitsko-Sergievskaya Lavra* (Trinity Monastery of St. Sergius) lies to the left of the train. Built in the 14th–18th century, the monastery played a considerable part in Russian history and is besides one of the country's most important medieval architectural complexes.

Soon after Zagorsk the train passes from the Moscow Region to the Vladimir Region. The landscape changes too, with woodland giving way to vast fields, and the villages are now the homes of farmers rather than craftsmen. Grain is the most important product of this area as it has been for hundreds of years and some of the oldest Russian towns are to be found here.

Strunino on the R. Chornaya (black) is immediately recognisable as a textile centre. On the right of the track and quite close to it stands the big, old, brownstone building which was known before the revolution as *Asaf Baranov's Sokolov Factory*. At the beginning of the century it already employed several thousand workers.

The first stop on the journey after leaving Moscow is at **Alexandrov**. It serves as a boundary town because it marks the limit of direct Moscow influence. The places beyond Alexandrov are more closely bound to their own regional centres than they are to the capital. Written historical references to Alexandrov go back as far as the 13th century. Ivan the Terrible lived here for a while after he had quarrelled with the Moscow nobles and left the city. Alexandrov was then the *de facto* capital of the country, and it was here that Ivan laid his plans for future conquests to enlarge his domain. It was here at the same time that one of Russia's first printing presses was set up and the Orthodox Prayer Book was printed. Alexandrov was also famous for its gunsmiths and its cannon and bell founders. Part of the *tsar's residence*, a *cathedral*, and a *belfry* from that time remain. Now the town has a population of 50,000 and runs a radio plant, a textile mill, and a distillery.

Soon after **Berendeyevo** the track begins running down into the Volga basin. Berendeyevo is a small village inhabited by peat diggers. The peat is used by the chemical industry as well as for fuel, and it is taken from a peat bog of considerable size. The bog, like the village, has the name of

Berendeyevo and there is a legend that it was the secret home of the forest-king, Berendei. This legend was used by the 19th-century playwright, Alexandr Ostrovsky, for 'The Snow Maiden', and later Rimsky-Korsakov wrote an opera on the same theme.

Among the next few small stations **Itlar** is worthy of mention for it was the favourite summer haunt of the singer, Fyodor Chaliapin, and he used to be visited there by Maxim Gorky. Konstantin Korovin, the artist, also lived in Itlar.

As the track runs gradually downhill there are glimpses of water between the trees until Lake Nero comes into view. The water varies in depth from 1·5–6·5 m. and when Peter the Great found it too shallow for his shipbuilding experiments he gave it together with its rivers and the nearby village as a present to Count Musin-Pushkin. The village on the opposite side of the lake from the railway is Ugodichi, known since the 10th century.

Rostov Yaroslavsky (q.v.) is nearly 300 years older than Moscow and many buildings of both historical and architectural interest have survived.

Yaroslavl (q.v.) is only a little distance farther on. The rail approach is from the south-east, through a new industrial district. There is a good view of the city from the point where the railway crosses R. Kotorosl. The part on the right bank is called Tugovaya Hill and it is said that it was there that the people of Yaroslavl mourned for their dead who had fallen fighting the Tatars. The domes in the distance belong to *Ioan Zlatoust Church*, and on the left are the white walls and the belfry of the *Kremlin*. There is another good view of the city when the train crosses the bridge over the Volga.

Beyond the Volga the track runs northwards and then swings round to the north-west where it is joined at Bouy by the line from Leningrad. From that point as far as the Urals it runs eastwards in an almost straight line.

30 km. from Yaroslavl is the small station of **Utkino** and nearby, to the left of the railway line, is the village of *Fatianovo*. Excavations of the local barrows at the end of the 19th century revealed a number of interesting items including stone axes, pottery jugs, and objects of bronze estimated to be 4000 years old and now described as belonging to the Fatianov culture.

At the beginning of another vast wooded area is **Danilov** junction. Timber is dispatched from Danilov to many different towns in the Yaroslavl Region to be worked. One local speciality is the summer hats made of thin wood shavings.

After Danilov begins a stretch of track which was built in 1918 and which straightened the route considerably. It runs as far as Bony. It passes 2 km. south of Lubim which was, until the construction of the railway, a forgotten place, more dead than alive and symbolising utter backwardness. Here the landscape is already unmistakenly northern and indeed the same thick coniferous forests run right up to the shores of the

White Sea. The population density is only 8 per sq. km. and most of these are engaged in the timber industry. Some timber from here is exported but the local demands are also high. Almost all the buildings are of wood and in many places the very roads are paved with logs. There is also good hunting to be had in the forests. Mink, marten, fox, and squirrel are among the pelts most highly valued and bears and wolves are also to be seen.

Bouy on the left bank of R. Kostroma is a busy railway junction. The population numbers 30,000 and the local produce includes cheese, mineral fertilisers, and flax fibre.

The railway now runs along beside R. Veksi which, with a maximum width of 10 km., is a continuation of Lake Galich, also clearly visible from the train.

In **Galich**, built at the beginning of the 13th century, are the remains of an old *fortress* destroyed by the Tatar leader, Khan Batuy, in 1238. Today there is a population of 20,000 and it is planned to make a resort of the lake shore.

R. Viatka is the tenth longest river in the European part of Russia, running for 1367 km. It follows a very winding course and the train crosses it several times. When the train first reaches the Viatka River basin, there is a notable change in the landscape; there are more open fields and more villages too.

The railway junction of **Kotelnich** stands on the high right bank of the Viatka. It is very similar to Bouy. Kotelnich was known as a fortress from 1459, but in 1926 it was almost completely burned down. The new town has a population of 30,000.

Orichi, **Strizhi**, and **Liangasova** are fast-growing industrial satellites of the city of Kirov. Just south of the railway line near Strizhi is a large silicate plant and to the north is a peat-processing factory.

Kirov, formerly known as Viatka, is 957 km. from Moscow. It is an old city which is now undergoing rapid industrial expansion. It is said that the first settlement appeared here in the 12th century, but there is no written evidence of its existence before 1374. For a long time it was almost completely independent and virtually inaccessible, a Russian colony in an area inhabited by other indigenous peoples. In the second half of the 15th century it took three military expeditions before the rulers of Moscow could assert their authority over Viatka. It was renamed Kirov in 1934 after the Soviet leader and revolutionary who had been assassinated in Leningrad. Now there is a population of 320,000 and a variety of industries. Kirov craftsmen are famous for their wooden toys and about half the country's teaching aids come from here, as do also the Dimkov toys.

Beyond Kirov the railway line runs for some distance parallel to the main road to Kazan and then at Novoviatsk the track crosses it. Novoviatsk only received town status in 1955, but already its population is 30,000. 20% of the Soviet Union's skis are produced at one of the timber plants here.

After Novoviatsk the railway follows R. Cheptsi, a tributary of the Viatka. Among other small stations passed by the train, **Kordiaga** and **Kosino** are interesting for their very old paper mills. That in Kosino was founded in 1785. At **Falenki** is one of the first agricultural research centres to be opened in Russia; it dates from 1895.

The industrial region of the Urals has such immense natural resources that it is often called the stronghold of the country. There are about 1000 different minerals in over 12,000 known deposits. Metallic ores, fuel, raw materials for the chemical industry, and precious stones are all found here. The Ural region has been the country's armoury since Peter the Great's time (1689–1725).

Nearing the Urals the railway goes through Udmurtia, one of the 16 autonomous republics of the Russian Federation. The Udmurt language is spoken in **Yar** where there is a small metallurgical plant over 200 years old. As the train passes the stations of the northern part of the republic, timber-loading is much in evidence. **Glazov**, with a population of 75,000, is the largest city in the area. Beyond the station buildings is an old sector dating back to 1780. Glazov was once a home for political exiles and was called an 'unreal city'. Now it has a sizeable industry supplying local requirements.

20 km. from Glazov, at **Balezino**, is a railway junction where all trains bound for Vladivostok stop to change engines. The new engine is a fast electric one made in Czechoslovakia, and from here the rails are new too, specially constructed to take the high-speed trains which have a cruising speed of over 100 kph. One metre of the new rail weighs about 65 kg.

At **Kez**, 53 km. farther on, passengers who want to travel 36 km. to the source of the R. Kama leave the train. The Kama is a branch of the Volga.

The small station of **Kuzma** marks the point where clocks must be advanced two hours. Udmurtia has been left behind and the track now passes through the Perm Region. This is where, many centuries ago, the Russians began their conquest of the Urals and Siberia. This part of the Urals has not so much iron ore as the others, but it is rich in the raw materials required by the chemical industry and this is developing here very fast.

Vereschagino is perhaps not very easy to pronounce, but its name is worth remembering. The town has grown up around the railway station which was built in 1898 and called after the artist, Vasili Vereschagin, who made a stop here on his way to the front during the Russo-Japanese War of 1904–5.

27 km. further on is **Mendeleyevo**, also named after a famous Russian, this time the chemist, Dmitri Mendeleyev, who often visited this place when he was inspecting metallurgical plants.

Tchaikovskaya is another station with its name taken from the Russian 'Who's Who'. The composer Pyotr Tchaikovsky was born in Votkinsk, a town not far distant.

This stretch of the line is so full of curves and bends that the engine or the end of the train often come into view. Laying the track in any other way would have entailed much expensive excavation. The rivers, streams, hills, and valleys here posed plenty of problems for the engineers and they found the easiest solution was to build along the ridges wherever possible.

Shortly after Tchaikovskaya billowing smoke from factory chimneys marks the city of **Krasnokamsk**, built on the bare banks of the R. Kama in 1930. Krasnokamsk is known industrially for its cellulose- and paper-producing complex and for the country's only wirenetting factory. The city is also renowned for its springs and medicinal mud.

Approaching the city of **Perm**, the Kama widens out and carries a busy traffic of tugs and barges. Perm, formerly called Molotov, has a population of 900,000 and is one of the largest cities on the line. It is 1438 km. from Moscow. It stretches for 80 km. along the banks of the Kama, as is evident from the view from the long bridge built in 1899. In this part of the country the winters are really cold and the rivers are frozen for several months. However, thanks to the power plant here, the Kama is free of ice for the whole distance it runs through the city. The trains stop here long enough for passengers to take a look at the square in front of the station. Perm dates from 1723 when a copper foundry was built and over the centuries it has grown into a large industrial centre. The region is rich in oil, over 50 deposits having been discovered, and so there are a number of refineries in Perm itself. The city also boasts a unique cultural heritage. Its university was the first to open its doors in the Urals and later it was joined by 6 other institutions of higher education. The local opera house was founded in 1871 and so ranks as one of Russia's oldest. Alexander Popov, who invented the wireless before Marconi and was awarded a gold medal for its discovery at the Paris World Fair of 1900, studied here at the local theological seminary. As it leaves Perm, the train crosses a small bridge over a busy thoroughfare; this is the road to Siberia, tramped in the past by political prisoners sent into exile. Among them were a group of Russian aristocrats who plotted in 1825 to overthrow the tsarist rule; they were arrested and condemned to death by Nicholas I, but were later reprieved and exiled for life.

Soon after Perm the landscape changes abruptly, the forest giving way to pleasant meadows and fields, and about 100 km. further on and on the left of the track is the old Urals town of **Kungur**. The population is now about 80,000 and the town is an important industrial centre of the western part of the Urals. The city was built in 1648 as a stronghold to reinforce Russia's subsequent eastern conquests. A number of old single- and two-storey buildings which were the mansions of the local merchants can be seen from the train. Interesting souvenirs can be bought at the station here; they are made from the local minerals and include stone sculptures of people and animals.

Soon after leaving Kungur one can see the steep banks of R. Sylva. The local population call them mountains, and indeed they are most precipitous. In the one known as Ice Mountain are the Kungur Caves, where one cave has a below-freezing temperature all the year round. The caves are visited by about 25,000 tourists annually and the total length of the caves so far explored is over 5 km.

By now it is not only the landscape that has changed, but also the railway station architecture. The buildings are now decorated with turrets and other traditional Russian ornaments in defiance of the custom for stations to be designed like military quarters.

The next river encountered by the railway is one of the Ural's most beautiful, the R. Chusavya. The line follows the course of the river for some 30 km. and one can see how it has cut its way through the rocks, polishing them and staining them with a variety of colours.

Pervouralsk dates from 1732 when a metallurgical plant was founded. The population is now 130,000 and the city produces metal pipelines and many different kinds of complicated and up-to-date machinery for use in all parts of the country. Just a few minutes after leaving Pervouralsk, on the right-hand side of the train, stands a rectangular column topped by a globe with spaceships orbiting around it. On one side of the column is inscribed the word 'Europe' and on the other 'Asia', because this is the border between the two continents.

The city of **Sverdlovsk** is often called the capital of the Urals. It was founded in 1821 as a Russian military stronghold and trading centre and called Yekaterinburg in honour of Empress Catherine the Great. After the 1917 Revolution it was renamed after Yakov Sverdlov, one of the country's leading revolutionaries and its first president. It is an important railway junction with 7 lines radiating from it and its airport is linked with 55 major Soviet cities; the volume of air freight handled in Sverdlovsk is second only to that passing through Moscow. There are about 200 industrial complexes in the city and 11 higher educational establishments connected with the Urals branch of the U.S.S.R. Academy of Sciences. One of Sverdlovsk's many museums is quite unique; this is the *Museum of Minerology* where some 20,000 minerals, including precious stones, are on display, all mined in the Urals. The only building on the station square is that of the mill. The *monument* in the square is in honour of the Urals Voluntary Tank Corps which fought in the Second World War. A quick walk up the main street brings one to Komsomolskaya Sq. Here is the *Ascension Cathedral* (18th century) which can also be seen from the train and which now houses a museum. Another building on the square, architecturally the city's most important, is the *mansion* constructed at the beginning of the 19th century by two local goldmine owners. Across Liebknecht

St. is a small stone house which was where the deposed Nicholas II was shot in 1918.

56 km. beyond Sverdlovsk is **Bazhenovo** station where one of the Soviet Union's atomic power plants is. The scientist Igor Kurchatov is known as 'father of the Russian atom bomb' and the Igor Kurchatov Boloyarskaya Power Station began to operate in 1964 with its first turbine of 100,000 kilowatt power. The second turbine is twice as powerful and it is claimed that the plant is completely free of nuclear fall-out.

The small town of **Kamishlov** 143 km. past Sverdlovsk dates from 1666 and is one of the oldest Russian settlements in this region. It is the last place of any size in the Ural Region and the railway next runs into Western Siberia. A smooth and level plain stretches ahead for 1500 km. without a hill in sight on either side of the track. This is the Western Siberian Lowland, one of the largest flat areas in the world. It is bounded in the north by the Arctic Ocean and it goes southwards as far as the Caspian Sea. It is now developing into one of the country's most valuable oil-producing regions. Eighty huge deposits have already been located and it is estimated that there are still more to be discovered.

The first city in Siberia to be reached by the railway is **Tumen**, 2143 km. from Moscow. It is also Siberia's oldest city. It was founded in 1586 on the site of a Tatar settlement called Chinghi-Tura which had been captured by the Cossack leader, Yermak, in 1581. Now it has a population of 300,000 and a rapidly expanding oil-refining industry. It is also an important railway junction linking the lines that serve the Arctic regions of the country. The city lies on either side of the R. Tura with the part on the right bank being the more developed.

Yavlutorovsk, 74 km. farther on from Tumen, is another old town. It was established in 1639 when the former Yavlu-Tur was won from the Tatars. Immediately after it the railway crosses the R. Tobol and from this point as far as R. Irtish the country is well developed and, by Siberian standards, densely populated for there are 17 people per sq. km. On either side of the track there are a number of small lakes to be seen, most of them salt.

With a population of almost a million, **Omsk** (q.v.) is Siberia's second largest city (after Novosibirsk). It stands beside R. Irtish which at the point the railway crosses it is about a kilometre wide. Omsk is also proud to be known as the greenest city in Siberia. Its boulevards and its 80 gardens cover a total of 2500 hectares (6250 acres). The Russian novelist, Feodor Dostoyevsky, lived here in exile between 1849 and 1853 and set down his experiences in 'Memoirs from the House of the Dead'.

Past Omsk the railway runs through Barabinskaya Steppe for 600 km. The number of lakes here and the groves of trees make this an excellent hunting ground; at least 5,000,000 ducks and geese are shot here each season. Beneath the steppe lies an enormous underground reservoir of hot water. It lies between 900 and 3000 m. deep and the temperature varies between 70° and 100°C. (158°F. and boiling point). It is under great pressure and there are plans to use it instead of coal or oil for heating whole towns.

Approaching the great R. Ob the train slows down a little. There is a bridge to cross before reaching **Novosibirsk** (q.v.), and indeed the city owes its very existence to the position of the bridge. Now, with its population numbering over a million, Novosibirsk is by far the most important economic and cultural centre of Siberia and one of the largest cities in the country.

The other side of Novosibirsk the line runs through farmland where besides vast fields of corn and flax there are places where medicinal herbs are grown. After about 150 km. it enters the Kuzbas (Kuznetsk Basin) and a branch line leads down to the southern part of this region which is economically one of the most important in the country. The industrial centres are all to the south and the train only passes near the Andger coal-mines, incidentally the oldest here for they were opened up in 1897 when this part of the railway was built.

For 100 km. the tracks run beside R. Tchulim, a tributary of the Ob, and make a big loop around the Arga Mountains. These are not very high, 528 m. at the highest point, but in good weather they can be seen to the right beyond the river.

After finally crossing the river, the train stops at **Achinsk**, an old town and as yet little developed. It was founded in 1641 by the Cossacks to help them collect taxes from the local tribes. Now it has a population of about 70,000 and links the Trans-Siberian Railway to the southern part of Siberia. Since deposits of nephelin were discovered in the vicinity, Achinsk appears to have a promising future as part of a large aluminium-producing complex.

Krasnoyarsk, 4107 km. from Moscow, is a fast-growing Siberian city. Its population of 700,000 is rapidly increasing. In the late 17th century the town was little more than a fortress built to ward off the attacks of the local tribesmen. The high hill where the watchtower used to be can still be seen from all over the city. The chapel which now stands there was built in the middle of the 19th century. Krasnoyarsk has grown up on both banks of the R. Yenisei. It is a gigantic waterway flowing from the mountains of Central Asia to the Karskoye Sea in the Arctic over a distance of about 400 km. It is the Soviet Union's second longest river, after the Lena, but even so its volume of water is greater than that of the R. Lena. Krasnoyarsk stands at the point where the railway crosses the river and its position was partly responsible for the part the city played in the history of the Russian Revolution. One of the very first Soviets was proclaimed here by the railway workers at the time of the 1905 Revolution. Eight hundred men barricaded themselves inside the repair shop and held off 10,000 tsarist troops

for a week before they capitulated. Another landmark in Krasnoyarsk's history is commemorated at the port where a plaque tells how Lenin made a short stop here on his way to exile in the village of Shushenskoye in 1897. The Yenisei is now crossed by a 2100-m. bridge which carries all kinds of traffic. Along the banks of the river near Krasnoyarsk attractive stone pillars can be found. Not far from the city one of the world's largest power stations is under construction; it is to have a capacity of 6,000,000 kilowatts but the total capacity of the river is over 20,000,000 kilowatts and there are plans for other power stations too. After leaving Krasnoyarsk station the line runs for at least half an hour before it is out of the industrial part of the city which lies on the right bank.

After crossing Yenisei passengers travelling eastward usually expect to find themselves in dense 'taiga' straight away, but there is still some distance to go. After Krasnoyarsk there is an area of steppe which is this region's most important agricultural land.

Soon after crossing the R. Rybnaya the railway reaches **Zaozerniy**, a small town which was founded in 1932 to process the mica which is to be found in the river basin. This is still the principal occupation here. Just beyond the eastern limits of the town are huge deposits of coal which are worked by opencast methods; this coal is cheaper than oil and a serious competitor to natural gas.

Kansk is another of Siberia's oldest towns, established in 1628 by the Cossacks as a small fortress. The original site of the fortress was farther upriver but in 1640 it was moved to its present place where it guarded the crossroads which led to the territory inhabited by the Buryats. It received town status in 1822 but its present thriving industry really dates from the Second World War when a number of plants and factories were evacuated here from the western part of the country. The population is now over 100,000.

The real Siberian 'taiga' only begins after Kansk. It was about this region that Anton Chekhov wrote after his journey here in 1890: 'Its strength and its magic lie not in the size of its giant trees nor in the depth of its deathly silence, but rather in the fact that perhaps it is the migrant birds alone of all living creatures that know its limits . . .'

The small station of **Kliuchi**, 370 km. beyond Krasnoyarsk, marks the beginning of the Irkutsk Region. Its territory is equal to that of France and Great Britain combined, but its population is only slightly more than 2,000,000. Its natural resources are the richest in the country but only recently has it become the Soviet Union's fastest developing area. The railway gradually swings round to the south-east and timber-processing plants are much in evidence for there are useful rivers flowing down from the Sayan Mountains which bring the logs right to the railway.

The town of **Taishet**, 4525 km. from Moscow, which was established in 1897 at the time the railway was being built, is now an important junction.

From here a track branches off which runs for over 700 km. through forests and mountains to link up with the R. Lena. Before this line was completed the most usual form of transport was horse-drawn vehicles. Taishet has recently taken on new importance with the construction of a gigantic metallurgical plant.

From Taishet onwards as far as Irkutsk the railway crosses numerous rivers flowing in deep ravines and the train is constantly climbing and descending.

Nizhneudinsk, founded in 1648, was another Cossack settlement, and it was only the construction of the railway that brought it to life. A little way past the town the 'taiga' yields to steppeland which is the main agricultural area for the entire region.

Cheremkhovo is a city with a population of about 150,000 and a growing coal mining industry. The first mine can be seen 20 km. before the station is reached. Some of the mines are of considerable age because coal was discovered here soon after the appearance of the town in the 1840s. The coal is of very high quality and possesses such valuable chemical properties that it is unpractical to use it for fuel; it is planned to convert the mines to opencast and to use the coal entirely for the chemical industry.

The next station is called **Polovina** (meaning 'half') because when the railway ran through Manchuria this was exactly half way between Moscow and Vladivostok. Since the route was altered and shortened however, its position has changed; although it is 5090 km. from Moscow, it is now only 4212 km. from here to Vladivostok.

After crossing the R. Belaya (white), the railway reaches a station unexpectedly called **Malta** and a half an hour later it runs into **Usolje-Sibirskoye**. This town was founded in the 1660s by a Cossack called Anisim Mikhalev who was allocated a plot of land here and began to extract the salt he found. The town is picturesquely situated on the high left bank of the R. Angara and the salt works down by the river are easy to pick out. In general the salt deposits in the Irkutsk Region are among the largest in the Soviet Union. The prosperity of the local works is guaranteed because they are the main suppliers of salt to the fishing regions of the Far East. Although the population has risen to almost 100,000, the central part of the town looks much as it has always done, even the old salt works are unchanged. The new buildings are all going up on the outskirts. Usolje-Sibirskoye is also known for its match factory, founded over a hundred years ago.

10 km. farther on, at **Telma**, the first Siberian textile mill was opened in 1731. The same building now houses a ready-to-wear clothing factory.

Angarsk, founded in 1949, is one of Siberia's youngest towns. It stands in thick pine forest and is known for its excellent layout and planning which has preserved as many trees as possible. It has a population of 200,000 and one of the highest birthrates in the country.

By far the most important industrial and cultural centre of this part of the country is **Irkutsk** (q.v.). It is often called the capital of Eastern Siberia.

After leaving Irkutsk the train follows the R. Irkut for a while. It can be seen on the right, sometimes just beside the railway and sometimes falling away again. Next the track enters the Primorski Mountains, and takes a considerable time to pass through them. The track twists and turns to such an extent that one loses all sense of direction. This stretch is considered, from a construction point of view, as the most complicated in the whole country. Quite suddenly wide expanses of water come into view, the 'glorious sea', Lake Baikal (see Irkutsk). Baikal is the deepest lake in the world and, after the Caspian Sea, the second largest inland volume of water. If the sources that feed it were to dry up completely, it would take the mighty R. Angara, which is the only river flowing out of the lake, 500 years to empty it.

The first large city to the east of Lake Baikal is **Ulan-Ude**, capital of the Buryat Autonomous Republic. The Buryat language and customs are akin to those of the Mongolians. The city was founded in 1666 as a winter base by Russian explorers. Its favourable position on the established trade routes ensured a fairly rapid development and today the population numbers over 250,000. Among the city's varied industries is a meat-processing plant, one of the largest in the country, which mostly handles meat from Mongolia.

Petrovsky Zavod, 160 km. from Ulan-Ude, is already outside the bounds of the Buryat Republic and in the Chita Region. The station's name refers to the metallurgical plant opened here in 1789 and which was for a long time the only one of its kind in the trans-Baikal area. In 1830 Petrovsky Zavod was the place of exile of many officers and noblemen who had participated five years previously in the St. Petersburg rebellion against the tsar. There are bas-reliefs of some of those who served their sentences here on the wall of the station building.

The engineers who built the railway followed the route that was easiest to construct and soon after Petrovsky Zavod the tracks make a sharp turn to the east and run beside the R. Khilok. Russians founded the first settlements here when they appeared in these parts in 1653 and in the 18th century whole families of Old Believers who were moved here forcibly began to farm the land.

Khilok is the largest town on this stretch of the railway. The station was built in 1896 and the town's population is now 20,000. The granite monument topped by a star which stands near the station commemorates the eleven young communists who were slain here during the Civil War.

The train soon begins its climb up the Yablonovy Mountains to a height of 1500 m. above sea level. The eastern slope is even steeper than the western and heavy trains travelling westwards may require two extra engines to make the grade. Once over the mountains the track passes Lake

Kenon, 16 sq. km. in area but only 6 m. deep. The lake seems to have appeared because of some thawing of the permafrost, and now a large power station is being constructed here.

Chita, 6208 km. from Moscow, was established by the Cossacks in 1653. Many nobles were exiled here in 1827 after the abortive rebellion against the tsar in December 1825. The church that they used remains in the city centre. Chita's development was encouraged by the construction of the railway and now the population exceeds 200,000.

On leaving Chita, the train follows the rivers Ingoda and Shilka for some hours. This region is rich in gold and valuable minerals. The small station of **Ayachi** is the first in the Far Eastern Economic Region of the U.S.S.R. and now until almost the end of the run the railway follows the course of the R. Amur and R. Ussuri, the latter forming the border between the Soviet Union and China. This region covers an area of 6,200,000 sq. km.—a quarter of all the Soviet Union's territory. It has abundant natural resources, a wide range of climatic conditions, and very varied flora and fauna. The western parts are the harshest. The train follows the line of the 54th parallel for a while, passing through the earth's pole of cold. The railway builders had a hard time here. The rivers freeze solid in winter here and there was no water for either the humans working here or for the engines they were trying to run. The ground had to be thawed out with gigantic bonfires before the track could be laid. Since that time the situation has eased slightly for underground rivers have been discovered with wells down to them.

The first station in this region where the train stops is **Erofei Pavlovich**, 7123 km. from Moscow. It was so called in memory of Erofei Pavlovich Khabarov, the Siberian pioneer and explorer who led Russian settlers to these parts in 1649. Alexei Gorky, the writer, said of those firstcomers that 'they opened up new lands and new waterways at their own expense and at their own risk'.

Although the track still makes frequent ascents, it more often now runs downhill, for the Pacific Ocean lies ahead. **Skovorodino**, the first real town in the Far Eastern Region, is already 128 m. lower in altitude than was Erofei Pavlovich. It is at a distance of 7316 km. from Moscow and has a population of 15,000. There is a permafrost research station here where new principles of construction have been evolved which have helped to establish industries farther north than before.

Soon after Skovorodino the tracks turn southeast again and a climatic change is obvious. The larches grow much taller here, reaching 35 m., and birches are in evidence again.

At the station of **Ushumun**, 7613 km. from Moscow, the train leaves the southernmost border of the permafrost country and oak trees are occasionally to be seen. They are, however, different from the European oaks in that they do not lose their leaves in winter, but hold them, stiff and brown, to rustle in the cold winter winds.·

Svobodny is a town of 70,000 in the estuary of the R. Bolshaya Pera. It is 7818 km. from Moscow and serves as a supply base for the local gold mines. It has two railway stations.

Beyond the town the line crosses R. Zeya, the Amur's largest tributary on Soviet territory. In the rainy seasons of spring and autumn the water level may rise as fast as 30 cm. an hour, and severe floods have been recorded of 10 m. of flood water. Beyond the river stretches the farmlands which are the main granary of the far eastern region. Especially in good weather the landscape is very similar to that of the Ukraine and the likeness is strengthened by the Ukrainian speech frequently heard at the stations; over half the population here are of Ukrainian descent, but it took several generations of farmers to get used to the climate here. The humidity is very high and the variation between the summer temperature and the winter is as much as 85°C.

As the train approaches **Byelogorsk**, one can see the 80-m. tower of the grain elevator which also serves as a television tower. The town has a population of 60,000 and is 7877 km. from Moscow. The station here is as busy as those in the western part of the country. A branch line runs from Byelogorsk for 110 km. to Blagoveschensk on the Chinese border.

The town of **Bureya**, 8041 km. from Moscow, is closely linked to the coal mining industry. It produces mining tools and machinery and serves as a transit point for coal mined in the vicinity.

The name of **Obluchje** station is written up in both Russian and Hebrew for it is already within the Jewish Autonomous Province. Many Jewish settlers moved here in the 1920s and the Province's autonomous status was proclaimed in 1934. The total population is now over 200,000.

All the way to **Birobidjan**, capital of the province, the railway runs beside R. Bira, a distance of over 100 km. The hills passed on the way contain billions of cubic metres of raw cement. The name of the capital city is derived from those of two rivers, the Bira, already mentioned, and the Bidjan. The first Jewish settlers appeared here in 1928 and town status was granted to Birobidjan three years later. There is now a population of over 50,000. The wooden buildings near the station are the first that were built. Notable among the town's industries is the plant that produces combine harvesters for rice.

The area on the other side of Birobidjan is remembered for the fierce fighting that took place there during the Civil War. On Ijun-Koran Hill which stands alone in the plain to the left of the railway there is a memorial museum and a monument to the Red Army Soldiers who were buried in a common grave there. The memorial was completed in 1928.

Now there are many small stations which the train passes through, each busier than the last as the next big city comes onto the map. First, however, the line crosses R. Amur, one of the largest waterways of the Far Eastern Region, almost 5500 km. long. For many hundreds of kilometres it marks the border between the Soviet Union and China. It is known by the Chinese as Heilung chiang (R. Black Dragon).

Next the train draws in to **Khabarovsk** (q.v.) station. The city is already 8533 km. from Moscow. After leaving Khabarovsk, the track makes a sharp turn to the south and on both sides rise the Khekhtsir Mountains with their highest peak 950 m. above sea level. In the mountains on the right-hand side there is a large game reserve, and the flora here is particularly rich. Before the settlers came in from the west, the area was inhabited by the Udeghe, also known as the Forest People. There are now only 1500 of them left but their birthrate has shown a slight increase in recent years. They live mostly by fishing and hunting. They tell an ancient legend of how two birds were sent by the fairies of the north and of the south to sow the seeds of trees over the empty spaces of land. It was at this point that the two birds collided. This accounts for the trees of both hot and cold climates growing here side by side. The red cedars are especially fine.

The railway now enters the Soviet Maritime Province which lies on the same latitude as the Black Sea coast. The climate here is influenced by the cold waters of the Sea of Japan. The spring is cold and long-lasting but the warm summer rains create a hothouse atmosphere and grass and plants of all kinds reach enormous dimensions.

The town of **Ussuriisk** is already very near the Pacific coast. Its population is 150,000 and by local standards it is a significant industrial centre. Nearby is an Academy of Sciences' research station with a large nature reserve where there are tigers and leopards.

Vladivostok is only 100 km. ahead and there are two branch lines from the main track, one to the Korean border and the other to the seaport of **Nakhodka** (q.v.).

MOSCOW TO BREST, ON THE POLISH BORDER

Byelorussky (White Russian) Railway Station is Moscow's gate to the west. The distance from Moscow to Brest is 1100 km. The first part of the track, from Moscow to Smolensk, was opened in 1870 and the rest was completed the following year. It was known as the Moscow–Brest Railway until 1912 when it was re-named the Alexandrovsky Railway but now it is called the Moskovsko–Byelorusskaya Railway.

Within the Russian Federation the line runs through the Moscow and the Smolensk Regions, and in the Byelorussian S.S.R. it crosses the Vitebsk, the Minsk, and the Brest Regions.

Long distance trains do not stop at the first few suburban stations they reach. It was in **Fili** in 1812, after the Battle of Borodino, that Field-Marshal Kutuzov held the military council which decided that Moscow should be abandoned. **Kuntsevo** has records dating from the mid-17th century

when Tsar Alexei Mikhailovich presented it to his father-in-law, Kyril Naryshkin.

Nemchinovka

Bakovka

Odintsovo

Pionerskaya

Perkhushkovo

Zhavoronki

Golytsino village, quite near the station of the same name, used to belong to Boris Godunov, who reigned from 1598 to 1605. In 1694 Peter the Great gave the estate to his assistant and ex-tutor, Prince Boris Golytsin, and the place took on his name.

Polushkino

Both **Tuchkovo** and **Dorokhovo** are called after Russian generals who distinguished themselves in 1812.

Shalikovo

Mozhaisk is an ancient Russian town which was known at the beginning of the 13th century. Until the middle of the 15th century it was the centre of an autonomous princedom, and it has always played the role of a fortress guarding the western approaches to Moscow. It played a particularly important part at the beginning of the 17th century when the Poles occupied Moscow, and in 1812 it was the hub of military actions against the French. Again in December 1941, during the Second World War, the vicinity of Mozhaisk was the scene of a number of engagements during the Battle of Moscow.

Borodino, next along the line after Mozhaisk, was the site of the Battle of Borodino (1812) against the French.

After **Uvarovka** begins the Smolensk Region.

Gzhatsk, Gagarin, formerly founded by Peter the Great in 1715, was a river port on the grain supply route to the newly built St. Petersburg. At first it was difficult to get people to settle in the new town, and so Peter the Great had some rich merchants imprisoned and they were only freed after they had promised to move there. The town, on the R. Gzhat, was renamed Gagarin after Yuri Gagarin, the world's first spaceman, who was born here.

Tumanovo

Vyazma is another very old Russian town, first mentioned in the 11th century. It stands on R. Vyazma, a tributary of the Dnieper. It was regarded as being of great military and economic importance and during the Time of Troubles at the beginning of the 17th century it frequently changed hands between the Poles, the Lithuanians, and the Russians. It was completely burnt down during Napoleon's retreat from Russia in 1812. The town's best-known products are the jam-filled biscuits called 'Vyazemsiye Pryaniki'.

Semlyovo

Izdeshkovo

Durovo

The history of **Dorogobuzh** goes back to 1150. It stood on an important trade route and also served as a frontier post. During the campaign of 1812 it was the centre of military action.

Near **Milokhovo** there are fine pine forests to be seen.

Yartsevo is an old textile town.

Kardymovo

Kolodnya is the last station before Smolensk and is in fact one of its suburbs.

Smolensk (q.v.) is one of the most ancient of all Russian cities and celebrated the 1100th anniversary of its foundation in 1963. It stands astride the R. Dnieper and has had a long and eventful history as can be imagined from its old name of 'the Key and Gate of Russia'.

Krasny Bor (Red Forest) was called Chorny Bor (Black Forest) before the 1917 Revolution.

It was in the vicinity of **Gnyezdovo** that the world's largest ancient burial ground was discovered. There are about 2500 mounds here, some of them as much as 10 m. high and visible from the train windows.

Gusino

Krasnoye stands near the site of a fierce battle between the Russian army and retreating French in 1812 during which about 26,000 French prisoners were taken. After Krasnoye the railway runs on into Byelorussia.

Osinovka

The ancient town of **Orsha** was first mentioned in chronicles of 1067. As it stood on an important trade route which was at the same time of strategic military value, it changed hands several times between the Russians, the Lithuanians, and the Poles until it was finally ceded to Russia in 1772. In 1781 Orsha was given its own coat-of-arms, five arrows on a blue field because, as the edict read, 'the said town was founded by the ancient Scythians who were highly skilled in the use of the aforesaid weapons'.

Kokhanovo

Tolochin was known as far back as 1433 and in the 17th century it belonged to the Sapiegas, an aristocratic family from Poland.

Slavnoye

Bobr is the centre of the local timber industry, the name appropriately meaning 'beaver' and reflecting the presence of these animals in this part of the country.

Krupki

Borisov on the R. Berezina was probably founded in about 1102 by Boris, Prince of Polotsk, from whom it took its name. It had a fortress and from the 14th century until 1795 it belonged to Lithuania and then to Poland. It was granted town status in 1563. There is a beaver reserve a little farther along the river and 13 km. upstream at Studyonka is one of the places where, in November 1812, the survivors of Napoleon's retreating army spent three days attempting to cross the Berezina and where 30,000 French soldiers lost their lives.

Zhodino

Smolyevichi

Minsk (q.v.), the capital of Byelorussia, although now largely rebuilt and modern-

looking, was known in 1067.

The name of **Koydanovo** station derives from that of a Tatar leader whose army was defeated here in 1249. It is only the station that is now so called as the town of Koydanovo was renamed Dzerzhinsk after Felix Dzerzhinsky (1877–1926) who was born in the district into a gentle family of Polish origin. His father was a mathematician and he himself became a well-known communist and founded the secret police force, known variously as the Cheka or OGPU.

Negoreloye was until 1939 the last Soviet station on the way to the Polish border.

Gorodeya

Baranovichi was founded as a railway station in 1870 and with its six lines it is still an important junction. Before the Second World War as much as half the town's population was Jewish.

Ivatsevichi

The name of **Beryoza-Kartuska** means 'birch-tree'. 5 km. from the station are the remains of a *Catholic Monastery* which served as a large prison both when the town was held by the Poles and when the Germans occupied it during the World War II. The latter also organised a concentration camp here.

Zhabinka

Brest (q.v.) is the town on the Polish border, and stands on the right bank of R. Mukhovets at the point where it flows into the Bug. The history of Brest goes back to 1017.

MOSCOW TO CHOP, ON THE HUNGARIAN AND CZECHOSLOVAKIAN BORDER

The train leaves Moscow from Kiev station. The building was erected in 1913–17 by I. I. Rerberh (who also designed the city's Central Telegraph Office in Gorky St.). The station was originally known as Bryansky (from the city of Bryansk, down the line on the way to Chop), but in 1934 when Kiev became the Ukrainian capital instead of Kharkov the station was renamed.

18 km. from Moscow is **Peredelkino** where many of the most prominent writers live. It was here that Nobel Prizewinner Boris Pasternak spent the last years of his life.

Not far from **Vnukovo** is the airport of the same name, one of Moscow's largest, which handles internal flights and also V.I.P. arrivals and departures.

The forest country which surrounds Moscow is very beautiful, especially in the autumn. **Krekshino, Selyatino, Rassudovo,** and **Bekasovo** all lie within this forest region.

Naro-Fominsk is a textile centre on R. Nara, a tributary of the Oka. Its history dates back to the 13th century and in October 1941 it was the site of strong resistance to the advancing Germans.

Vorsino and **Balabanovo** are the first stations in the territory of the Kaluga region.

Obninsk is a new town which has grown up since 1954 when the construction of the atomic power station began.

Shemyakino

Maloyaroslavets (121 km. from Moscow) is among the oldest of all Russian towns. It was founded in the 14th century by Prince Vladimir the Brave of Serpukhov, famed for the active part he played in the Battle of Kulikovo against the Tatars in 1380. From 1485 it was part of the Grand Princedom of Moscow, and in the 15th and 16th centuries it served as a fortress protecting Moscow from the raids of both the Crimean Tatars and the Lithuanians. In October 1812 a battle was fought in the valley below the town between the Russian army and the retreating French who suffered a heavy defeat. Maloyaroslavets saw military action again in 1941, but today it is a sleepy town of little importance.

Tikhonov Pustyn is an important railway junction from which a branch line runs to **Kaluga** about 40 km. away.

Near **Vorotynsk** station the railway crosses R. Ugra at the point where it flows into R. Oka. It was here that in 1480 the Russian and the Tatar armies stood defying each other on opposite sides of the Ugra. This Great Stand, as it came to be called, marked the end of the 250 years of Tatar domination.

The first stop within the Bryansk Region is its centre, **Bryansk**, on R. Desna. One of the most ancient Russian cities, with records dating back to 1146, Bryansk grew among the thick forests and was first of all known as Dyebryansk (from 'dyebry' meaning thick, impenetrable forest). It stood in an important geographic and strategic position on the trade route between Moscow and the Ukraine and served as a stronghold defending the borders of the Moscow State, so frequently assaulted by Tatars, Poles, and Lithuanians. Its industrial importance began in the middle of the 18th century. Today it has a population of 340,000 (1971) and produces railway engines and rolling stock among other items, along with various light industrial goods.

Navlya

Suzemka

Khutor Mikhailovsky is the first station in the Ukraine. Together with the following stations—**Yanpol, Makovo,** and **Tereshenskaya**—it is situated in sugar-beet country.

Shostka

Pirotchino

Brytelovetsky

Krolevets

Altynovka

Myelna

Vyrevka

Konotop, now an important railway junction, was founded in 1640 as a fortress by the Poles. The population is 70,000 (1971) and local industry is primarily metal working and engineering. The country around is noted for bee-keeping.

Bakhmach is another railway junction town. Its industries are mainly concerned with food production.

Logachevo, Plisky and **Kruty** are in another

sugar-beet region.

Nezhin, an old Ukrainian city, is the centre of the surrounding region. The Russian humorist, Nikolai Gogol (1809–52), attended the local grammar school. He would no doubt have appreciated the fact that today it is better known for the special brand of gherkins grown here.

Nosovko, Kobyzhchi, Borovitsky, and **Markovtsy** stations all handle shipments of sugar and other products of the sugar refineries which are numerous in this part of the country.

Brovary is a satellite town and **Darnitsa** one of the swiftly growing suburbs of **Kiev** (q.v.). Beyond the Ukrainian capital, **Post Volynsky, Zhulyani,** and **Boyarka** are other suburban stations.

Vasilkov station is some distance from the town of the same name which was founded at the end of the 10th century by Prince Vladimir. It was Prince Vladimir who was responsible for the adoption of Christianity as the Russian religion.

Motovilovka

Fastov is one of the oldest Ukrainian towns and is now an important railway junction.

Zhitomir lies off the main railway line, but in the area around quarries of red, pink, and white granite and labradorite can be seen. This stone was used to decorate the Lenin Mausoleum in Moscow and also some of the stations of the Moscow Metro.

Kazatin is another important railway junction.

Kordyshevka, Golyendry, and **Gulevtsy** are more towns which are chiefly dependent upon sugar-beet growing and the sugar industry.

Kalinovka is an important crossing point with a 500-km. narrow-gauge railway.

Vinnitsa (q.v.) was founded in the 14th century and is now a regional centre and an important railway junction.

Gnivan

Brailov

Zhmerinka is another important junction. Its station building was destroyed during the war, but the local inhabitants are justly proud of the new one.

Komarovtsy and **Derazhnya** are concerned with the transport of agricultural produce.

Khmelnitsky was originally called Proskurov, but was renamed in 1954 to commemorate the 300th anniversary of the union of Russia and the Ukraine in which the Ukrainian leader Bogdan Khmelnitsky was instrumental.

Grechany

Chorny Ostrov

Narkevichi

Voitovtsy

Volochisk stands on R. Zbrouch and until 1939 it was a frontier post on the Polish border.

Ternopol's (q.v.) history starts in 1524 when it was razed by the Tatars. In 1540 a new castle was built and formed the nucleus of another town. For 15 years the population was not subject to taxation and the economic growth was considerable. However, frequent enemy raids seriously hampered the town's development, particularly a devastating Turkish attack in 1675. This area was part of Austria until 1918 and then until 1939 it belonged to Poland. Now it is an important railway junction, the regional economic and cultural centre with a population of 85,000 (1971) and an important centre of the sugar-beet industry.

Zborov stands near the battlefield where the Cossacks under Khmelnitsky and the Poles under King Jan Kazimierz fought in 1649.

Zolochev is important for its food industries.

Krasne is a transit railway junction.

Lvov (q.v.), with 700 years of history and a population of 560,000 (1971), is a regional centre. The section of the railway from Lvov to Chop has been electrified.

Stree's records go back to 1396 and today it is important for its engineering and production of food, also as a railway junction. From Dashava (just 12 km. from here) a natural gas pipeline goes to Kiev.

Sinovudzko-Vizhnya

Tukhlya

Lavoche

Beskid is the first station in the Transcarpathian region. (See Uzhgorod.)

Volovyets

Svalyava is famous for its mineral water springs and has existed since the 13th century. There are timber and furniture industries.

Chinadeyevo

Mukachevo (see Uzhgorod) dates from 903.

Chop is the railway junction at the meeting place of the Soviet, Hungarian, and Czechoslovak borders.

INDEX